Contemporary Environmental Law and Policy

The Contemporary Environmental Law and Policy series is a comprehensive scholarly platform dedicated to advancing research and discourse in the field of environmental law, presented through monographs, edited volumes, textbooks, and research handbooks. This series is designed to explore the dynamic and ever-evolving landscape of environmental law within a global context. Each peer-reviewed volume in the series focuses on pressing issues at the forefront of the field, serving as a critical resource for legal scholars, policymakers, scientists, industry experts, and practitioners.

The series encompasses a broad range of topics and disciplines, providing a platform for researchers addressing law and policy issues related to the environment, sustainability, climate change, energy and natural resources, marine environment, land use planning, and heritage protection. By tackling emerging challenges and proposing innovative solutions, the series aims to inspire action and contribute to the advancement of environmental protection and sustainability for future generations.

Key areas covered by this highly topical book series include Climate Law and Policy, Biodiversity Conservation, Environmental Justice, Environmental Pollution and Control, Transnational Environmental Law, Indigenous Environmental Law, Technological Innovation and Environmental Governance, as well as the Sustainability and Resilience of Urban Environments.

This book series adopts a multidisciplinary perspective and encourages diverse research methodologies. By showcasing a variety of approaches and providing enhanced depth and breadth in environmental legal scholarship, readers can gain a comprehensive understanding of environmental law in a global context. The series offers fresh insights into contemporary environmental challenges and innovative legal solutions, making it suitable pedagogical tools for both students and practitioners. If you are interested in contributing a monograph, edited volume, textbook or handbook to the series, please contact the Publisher: Mamun Mishra (mamun.mishra@springernature.com).

Alessandro Pelizzon

Ecological Jurisprudence

The Law of Nature and the Nature of Law

Springer

Alessandro Pelizzon
School of Law and Society
University of the Sunshine Coast
Sippy Downs, QLD, Australia

ISSN 3059-3409 ISSN 3059-3417 (electronic)
Contemporary Environmental Law and Policy
ISBN 978-981-96-0172-1 ISBN 978-981-96-0173-8 (eBook)
https://doi.org/10.1007/978-981-96-0173-8

This work was supported by Alessandro Pelizzon.

This Springer imprint is published by the registered company Springer Nature Singapore Pte Ltd.
The registered company address is: 152 Beach Road, #21-01/04 Gateway East, Singapore 189721, Singapore

To Yvette

Foreword

It is difficult to overstate the significance of the present time and of the decisions humans will make during the next few decades. Their consequences will be apparent in the fossil record millions of years hence. Perhaps as deep layers of fossilized bones (mainly of humans and the animals we ate), ash, flood sediment, plastic and other enduring traces of the 6th period of mass extinction. Perhaps as a shallower layer overlain by fossils indicating a resurgence of the profusion of life that characterized the Cenozoic era.

The key determinant will be how humans govern themselves in the twenty-first century. Will the ecologically destructive modes of civilization that now dominate global society transform their cultures and legal, economic and political systems so that they are directed toward ensuring that people seek fulfilment by contributing to the health of Earth, instead of at its expense? However difficult that may be, it must be done if humanity (and many other species) are to have a future. Any population that progressively degrades its habitat is unviable in the long term. But how might such a transformation be achieved?

This is why this book is so important. It presents a comprehensive, scholarly and insightful exposition of the philosophical underpinning of the legal systems of thought and practice that legitimize and facilitate human exploitation of Earth. More importantly, it explains how these problems can be, and are being, addressed, and of the implications and significance applying an ecological approach to law.

Thomas Berry wrote and spoke about the 'Great Work' of human civilizations at this time being to become a benign presence within the Earth community and he called for people 'to assist in establishing a mutually enhancing human presence upon the Earth'. His insight that the dominant legal philosophies that were too narrow to encompass more-than-human beings were unrealistic and, ultimately, unviable, inspired me to write *Wild Law* (first published in 2002). In that book, I sketched the outlines of what I termed 'Earth Jurisprudence' based on ten principles that Thomas had articulated to inform the development of a new jurisprudence. I presented, in general terms, a vision of how jurisprudences (particularly those heavily informed by Western-European thought) could, and should, be reconceptualized to enable people to govern themselves in accordance with the reality that we are part of, not superior to, or separate from, Earth.

Ecological Jurisprudence is a major contribution to the Great Work identified by Thomas Berry. Ecologically viable civilizations cannot be founded on legal systems and governance structures that were designed to enable humans to exploit the community of life, instead of guiding them to live harmoniously within it. Law can be seen as analogous to the DNA of a society in that it determines the internal organization of the society and how it changes and reproduces itself. Consequently, the necessary transformative change cannot occur without changing the philosophies of law and governance that shape the legal system. *Ecological Jurisprudence* adds great clarity, new perspectives and academic gravitas to this crucial endeavour.

Alessandro Pelizzon's diligent scholarship is evident throughout this work. A scholarship based on his own classical education, but hugely expanded by his sensitivity to, and understanding of, diverse cultures and legal systems, and his experiences within the global rights of Nature movement. He has done us all a great service by carefully locating ecological jurisprudential thought within the extensive landscape of legal thought—situating it in relation to the philosophical traditions of many cultures, including Western European, Chinese, Indian, Aboriginal, and other traditions. He exposes the flaws in the philosophies, jurisprudence and legal reasoning that have contributed to development of ecologically destructive societies, and discusses how these can, and are being addressed (although still to a very limited degree).

Ecological Jurisprudence is the most comprehensive, well-researched and insightful exposition of this new jurisprudence that I have encountered. I feel sure that in time it will be recognized as one of the finest scholarly contributions to the transformation of law and society, and on that basis alone it will come to be recognized as a 'great work'. However, it goes further. It makes a persuasive argument that the 'grand narrative' of an ecological understanding of law that is presented in this book, is inextricably implicated in the greater, existential journey which those of us currently entranced by the distractions of the modern world, must undertake. A journey to rediscover that the universe is our true home and that the fulfilment that we seek is to be found in celebrating our participation in this gorgeous, living community we call 'Earth' and in contributing to its flourishing.

In my view, very few legal scholars alive today have the breadth of vision, the depth of understanding of how Indigenous Peoples translate their understandings of ecological principles and constraints into ethics and law to guide people to live more wisely, to have done justice to this subject. Alex has done so and I am grateful that he had the courage and determination to write and publish this fine book.

Cape Town, South Africa
September 2024

Cormac Cullinan

Preface

I would like to begin this book by acknowledging the Countries upon which it was conceived and it was written, as well as the Countries upon which the reader sits at the moment of reading it, wherever the reader may be. In so doing, I want to recognize the legal and political implications of such an acknowledgement. At the very least, I would like to suggest that such an acknowledgement raises important questions for any otherwise hegemonic claim to Country, particularly (although not exclusively) in a colonial and post-colonial setting. Perhaps even more importantly, however, I want to remind myself (and maybe the reader) that the very concept of Country is a multifaceted and culturally layered one. For the Aboriginal peoples of Australia, to whose culture I am deeply indebted for my own learning, Country is more than a somewhat abstract geopolitical entity. Rather, it constitutes a powerful statement about the continuity and enduring power of a distinct and ancient worldview, and it is the expression of an unending and uninterrupted cosmology with roots firmly placed in the dreaming. In the words of Deborah Bird Rose, Country is 'the nexus of shared being'. Country can also be described as 'the matrix of interconnectedness, identity and relationship'. Country is comprised of all beings, processes, events and phenomena that surround each one of us at this particular moment of time. Moreover, Country is the totality of the relationships with and among all those beings, events and phenomena. And even further, Country is embodied in the stories within which such relationships are contained and construed. With this in mind, therefore, I also want to pay respect to the owners and custodians of such stories, the elders—those who were, those who are and those who are yet to be. And finally, since I am always reminded that Country is not only inscribed in place, but also in time, I wish to pay respect to the reader for the time they share in engaging with this book.

Another small disclaimer before I begin, if I may. While throughout the book I attempt to endeavour absolute care in the choice of language, I need to note that much of the language is still inevitably positioned, and it is likely to become even more so in the future. I hope the reader will engage with the text cognisant of the context and time it is written in.

In late 2009, I had the great privilege of attending the first Australian Conference on Wild Law and Earth Jurisprudence, organized by Peter Burdon in the Adelaide hills. The idea of Wild Law and Earth Jurisprudence was entirely novel, at the time. Upon encountering it, my interest as a burgeoning legal theorist trained in legal anthropology and comparative law (and who was in the process of completing a thesis on legal pluralism and Native Title in the Illawarra region of New South Wales, in Australia) was immediately piqued. The conference organizers, under Peter's inclusive guidance, made sure that the event was radically distinct from most academic conferences. Participants were immersed in all the events throughout a long series of experiential activities, which acted as a powerful counterpart to the deep and stimulating conversations that were had throughout the days. The evenings, unlike most academic events, were filled not with formal (and somewhat impersonal) dinners at expensive restaurants. Rather, these evenings were filled with music and with house-made dinners, with deep exchanges in informal circles and with great aspirations for things to come. The setting acted as the perfectly fertile terrain for the germinating power of the novel idea of Wild Law and Earth Jurisprudence, an idea that captured my legal imagination then, and has not abandoned me ever since.

For well over a decade, I had been training as a legal anthropologist and a comparative lawyer, with a deep interest in the intersections among distinct legal orders. In particular, I had always been interested in interrogating the intersections, conflicts and (it has always been my hope) the cooperative possibilities offered by those legal orders that have been more profoundly impacted by the process of colonization, and that have been unjustly marginalized by the homogenizing project of modernity. The plurality of worldviews of the majority of the world's legal orders (most of which are often those of the thousands of Indigenous cultures that inhabit the planet) has always been a source of inspiration and fascination for me. Knowing that there are many ways of seeing—and being in—the world always told me that there are *other* ways of thinking, of acting, of feeling, and that none of us is bound to *be* in any particularly rigid and inflexible way. The plurality of the world's legal orders, for me, has always been the most powerful reminder of the inner freedom we all ultimately possess. When I encountered the ideas of Wild Law and Earth Jurisprudence for the first time, my horizon of possibilities expanded even further. Exponentially. Beyond anything I had ever imagined, in fact. What if, the theory asked, we were to expand the boundaries of the normative worlds we inhabit beyond the human? What if all of the cosmos, all its beings, all its phenomena, all those things that are seen and those that are not, what if *all* is to be an active part of the ongoing dialogue about how we *ought* to be in the world? The possibilities of being in the universe suddenly expanded beyond anything I had previously conceived. I became enamoured with the theoretical, intercultural and inter-normative possibilities this novel path of legal theory entailed. I thought that Wild Law (and now, I believe 'ecological jurisprudence') is to the discipline of law what quantum physics has been to the discipline of physics. It represents the horizon of theoretical pursuits that asks questions previously thought impossible. And it allows a space to explore the answers to those questions.

I offered to organize a second conference on the topic a year later. This time, I wanted to create a space to show the many ways of seeing (and being within) 'Nature' that already exists. I wanted to privilege the often-dispossessed voices of those Indigenous cultures whose normative and legal relationship with the nonhuman world presents, to this day, a far more nuanced example of a more sustainable (and more deeply rewarding) cultural way of being. As a result, the conference, held in 2010, was structured as a participatory dialogue between the University of Wollongong and the (then) Sandon Point Aboriginal Tent Embassy. I made sure that cultural events and protocols of interaction with Country took centre stage, and that the intellectual and rarefied world of academic events could align with the lived experience of being immersed and enmeshed in a particular place at a particular time, and that those knowledge-holders who knew the relationships of that time and place, the local elders (under the guidance of Aunty Barbara Nicholson) were the guides and guardians of the entire event. To organize the event, I had established a small temporary organization, called Earth Laws, which was soon made more permanent and, together with Peter Burdon, Michelle Maloney and other original founders, took the name of Australian Wild Law Alliance (AWLA). The name of the organization was changed but a few years later to Australian Earth Laws Alliance, and the organization, under the leadership of Michelle Maloney, is still one of the most prominent organizations in the field in Australia to this day.

Two months after the conference concluded, I was invited to attend a gathering just outside Quito, in Ecuador, at the feet of the Tungurahua volcano, who stood guard for three days while the many gathered there reached an agreement. That agreement was the establishment of the Global Alliance for the Rights of Nature (GARN), the leading organization worldwide for the promotion, advocacy and investigation of the emerging Rights of Nature (RoN) movement. After serving on GARN's Executive Committee for a few years, I returned to it a decade after its original foundation, and became the director of its Academic Hub, with which, among other things, we launched the Eco-Jurisprudence Monitor, a comprehensive overview of all recorded eco-jurisprudential initiatives around the globe.

In the decade and a half since my original engagement with Wild Law and Earth Jurisprudence, I dedicated my career to interrogate further the ideas that had captured my legal imagination in the serene setting of the Adelaide hills. A particular interest of mine has always been the intersection of the world's legal orders (particularly, although not exclusively, the Indigenous ones) with the many norms and agentic powers that populate the perceptual worlds, the *ümwelts*, we all individually live in. This book is thus the sum of the reflections, interactions, researches, interviews and dialogues I have actively had, conducted, dedicated myself to since my inception into the world of what I now call an 'ecological jurisprudence'.

This book was consciously started on the 50th anniversary of Christopher Stone's ground-breaking article *Should Trees Have Standing?* written in 1972, and on the 20th anniversary of the publication of Cormac Cullinan's *Wild Law*, written in 2002. It was also written on the 50th anniversary of the Stockholm Declaration of 1972, and the 40th anniversary of the Rio Summit in 1982. I would have liked for it to coincide with a decennial anniversary of the Ecuadorian constitution of 2008, but mathematics made it simply impossible. The number of anniversaries, although ultimately rather coincidental, and relatively insignificant in the grand scheme of things, is nonetheless important for me. It marks a symbolic milestone to reflect on my own involvement with the theories and movements that this book explores. When I gathered in Quito with the co-founders of GARN, there were but a handful of legal initiatives that considered Nature as a legal subject within the world of human legal relations, and the scholarly literature on the matter in English could be counted on the fingers of one hand (maybe two). There were more documents in Spanish, of course (given the centrality of the discourse to the Ecuadorian Constitution of 2008), but not many more. At the time the first manuscript of this book was completed (at the end of 2022), there were more than 430 eco-jurisprudential initiatives across 42 countries plus the international level. A little over a year later, in early 2024, the number had increased by more than 20%, reaching well over 500 initiatives. The scholarly artefacts on the topic (books, articles, documentaries, et cetera), which were easily covered in full by any dedicated reader just over a decade ago, are now too many to count. A simple Google Scholar search for 'rights of Nature' alone in 2023 would have yielded over 18,000 results. The number increased to over 20,000 in mid-2024. The movement has clearly progressed at a speed that outpaces any other legal movement I am aware of.

The theoretical appraisal of the movement, which had initially been more fragmentary and protean, is displaying an equally profound growth, with great monographs, such as Margaret Davies's *EcoLaw*, being produced. However, the many theoretical strands are still operating somewhat separately, and their process of co-becoming is still unfolding. My hope, with this book, is to draw together the many different ideas, thoughts and theoretical perspectives that have emerged, and present them as a cohesive (albeit internally differentiated) whole. It is my hope that casting the light onto the overall theoretical emergence of what I describe and define throughout the book as an 'ecological jurisprudence' will enrich any future interactions, intersections and creative exchanges in the field.

Moreover, I write this book not only with the aim to clarify the field that I have observed growing since its birth, but also with a sense of urgency in relation to the need for alternative pathways our current environmental predicament demands. In the allegorical tale of the teaching gorilla Ishmael and his human pupil, Daniel Quinn—in his book *Ishmael*—paints the story of two different cultural attitudes, that of the 'Takers' and that of the 'Leavers'. The former represents what appears to be (currently, at least) a highly destructive culture, one whose own survival is now at risk. The parallels with modern (primarily, although not exclusively) Western civilization are for all to see. The latter, on the other hand, represent the worldview of those many dispossessed cultures that have been able to live in relative homeostasis with the environments they inhabited for millennia, without having to suddenly alter their internal structures in a distressing and destructive manner. In 2007, while I was discussing the state of uncontrolled bushfires in the Northern Territory of Australia with a local fire fighter, I was reminded of this story. I asked the fire fighter if (and if not, why not) people were engaging with local Indigenous knowledge-holders to continue the practice of land fire management known as 'fire-stick farming' (a traditional practice of controlled burning based on an intimate knowledge of the land, the seasons and the atmospheric conditions—and deeply steeped in ritual and ceremonial knowledge—that had prevented the uncontrolled burning of the land over millennia). My interlocutor firstly acknowledged that a legacy of colonization still prevented the recognition of the ecological wisdom of Indigenous science (and such is still the case, albeit thankfully less so, today). Moreover, though, he noted that the land itself had been altered by the process of colonization. Prior to colonization, the grasses burned relatively quickly, allowing the fires to 'wash over' the land in rapid manner, leaving the buried roots and trunks of the trees intact. However, the introduction of grazing cattle during colonial times had been accompanied by the introduction of larger grasses. As a result, the fires now burned more slowly and more intensely, in turn burning trees that were not evolutionarily adapted to the new ecological conditions.

The effect of the ecological alterations to the landscape at a pace that has not been matched by evolutionary forces has become ever more visible worldwide in the almost two decades since. What the story told me, in the light of Quinn's idea of the 'Takers' and the 'Leavers' and of my own exposure to the many worldviews that make up the world's 'ethnospheres', was that there exist, effectively, two ways of being in the world at present. One, the traditional one, develops slowly and carefully. It conservatively adopts a strong precautionary principle, and its ways and language evolve and adapt in line with the evolution and adaptation of the environment in which it exists. This way changes slowly, but it changes sustainably over long periods of time. The other way changes rapidly, and it can rapidly adapt to any need it perceives or it creates for itself. Its capacity for specialized attention to minute, individual and separate details is unprecedented, and the technological effects of this degree of hyper-specialization are nothing short of marvel. Is it cold? Turn on the heater. Is it hot? With the press of a button, an air conditioner begins buzzing. What this way of being in the world does *not* do, however, is to consider the long-term impact of pressing that button, and thus its own long-term sustainability is always, inherently and inevitably, in question. While this way can alter the geophysical fate of the planet as a whole (an idea that *could* be used positively, for example, to prevent the effect of another major Ice Age), it does not do so in a way that is sustainable or even self-aware.

It thus became clear to me that humanity is presently at a crossroad. Its ways of being threaten its own (collective) survival in the form it exists in today, and thus a more sustainable way of being must be once again embraced. The 'Leavers'' way must, once again, lead the way. However, the speed and intensity of the current environmental changes are such that the scientific attention to hyper-specialized details and the rapidity of adaptation it entails are necessary to meaningfully respond to the current predicament. The Leavers' and the Takers' ways must work together if humanity (as a whole) wishes to adapt to the coming changes with the least amount of disruption and devastation.

While all that had become clear to me before joining my first Wild Law conference in 2009, the emergence of Wild Law and Earth Jurisprudence told me that the cooperative boundaries I had intuited above needed to be expanded even further. If humanity were to live in harmony with (and within) the planet it inhabits, then it needed a regulatory system that could incorporate an ongoing reflection on its way of being in the world, it needed a legal theory that was aligned with the ecological understanding of its own practices, it needed an 'ecological jurisprudence'.

In this book, I thus chart, articulate, and somewhat advocate for the emergence of such an ecological jurisprudence, as embodied in many of the initiatives I have alluded to above, as well as a full spectrum of theoretical, ontological, axiological and jurisprudential perspectives that underpin these initiatives. Overall, I will use three texts/legal documents as the milestones of my overall argument. Firstly, Christopher Stone's 1972 essay titled 'Should Trees Have Standing?', which fully introduced within the Western legal discourse the prospect of Nature (both as a whole and in its component parts) as a potential legal subject. Secondly, I will select Cormac Cullinan's *Wild Law*, published in 2002, as the symbolic moment in time when Stone's proposal was given a theoretical underpinning (while I am aware that Cullinan was not the first author to articulate a 'theory' behind the proposal of Nature's legal subjectivity, his text has acquired a symbolic power within the movement that allows it to be marked as a significant symbolic threshold). Finally, I will identify the Ecuadorian Constitution of 2008 as the moment that Stone's proposal and Cullinan's theory were given *actual* recognition within a particular legal initiative (once again, although the Ecuadorian Constitution was not the first historical instance of a legal initiative that extended legal subjectivity beyond the human, its constitutional character and its international import make it the symbolic threshold that complements the former two).

Without further ado, then, I invite the reader to join me in the journey of discovery of the emergence of an 'ecological jurisprudence'. May such journey be as inspiring for you as it has been transformational for me.

Sippy Downs, Australia Alessandro Pelizzon

Acknowledgments

While I am deeply thankful for the great fortune of being able to dedicate time to writing this book, all that it contains—its ideas, its questions, its very essence—would not have been possible without the invaluable contributions of the many people who guided, accompanied or simply witnessed me along my journey.

First of all, I would like to thank those who have supported me along the long process of thinking through, developing, and ultimately channelling the ideas I present in this book: my mother, Ida Aurora, who has always supported my pursuits with unmatched and astounding generosity, and even *physically* supported my journey to the point of feeding not only me, but also all the participants to many of the events I have organized along the way; Yvette Holt, who stayed close to me for the entirety of the time I have dedicated to imagining, and then realizing, this book, and whose patience, curiosity and playfulness have always been a beacon to steer the way; my father, Sergio, who has always been there for me notwithstanding the physical distance that has separated us for years, and my sister, Alice, who brought me food in the long days I was glued to the keyboard, staring at a screen for hours; Barbara Ruozzi, who inspired me to become a writer over two decades ago and who has never stopped believing in my capacity to do so; Shelly Rowell, whose presence and reflections guided me into the world of ecological jurisprudence to begin with; Cristina Casale, who was there before the journey had even begun and whose creativity has always inspired my own; Vana Karkasi, whose capacity to see magic in the world has shaped the gaze with which I look at everything; my uncle Miguel, whose teachings and endless support have shaped, for my entire life, the journey to become who I am today; Chris Adams and Bruna Cazzaro, whose curiosity for the journey I have been on has always been refreshingly inspiring.

I also want to thank those who have allowed the ideas to emerge, to germinate, to take shape and ultimately to crystallize into the form they are presented in: Monica Gagliano, whose endless depth, inspiration and integrity have made this book possible. I am convinced that without her guidance, this book would simply not exist. Peter Burdon, who introduced me (and so many others) to the world of Wild Law and Earth Jurisprudence a decade and a half ago, and without whom this journey would never have happened. Cormac Cullinan, whose trailblazing work made it possible for me to follow, and whose reflections have always allowed me to see where I was going. William MacNeil, who inspired me, supported me and guided me in transforming my ideas into this book. It is to Bill that I owe the very possibility of the book I am now offering to the world.

I want to thank the elders and knowledge-holders who have shared their wisdom and insights with me over the years, and who have gently guided me through life: Aunty Barbara Nicholson, who showed me another way to see the world, and who has been there for me for over two decades. Uncle Geoff Ross, whose laughter and capacity to 'listen to the bones' accompanies me forever. Uncle Charles Moran, with his inspiring quiet happiness, and whose suggestion to always 'speak softly and listen well' I consistently return to. Jade Kennedy, Johnnie Aseron and Ramsay Taum, for all the many conversations we have had, and continue to have, that guide me in my journey of becoming a more complete human being. Betty McGregor, for never stopping being connected.

I also want to acknowledge all colleagues—many of whom are also dear friends—within the Global Alliance for the Rights of Nature, the Harmony with Nature programme and the many other organizations I have been involved in, whose ideas made it possible for me to make sense of my own: Katarina Hovden, Nati Greene, Linda Sheehan, Katy Gwiazdon, Herman Greene, Maria Mercedes Sanchez, Pamela Martin, Craig Kauffman, Léa Serrano-Corbière, Shannon Biggs, Osprey Orielle Lake, Casey Camp Horinek, Nnimmo Bassey, Tom Goldtooth, Enrique Viale, Rafaela Iturralde, Galo Chiriboga, Francesco Martone, Ashley Cline, Josefina Mosle, Samantha Novella, Michelle Bender, Juan Sebastián Acosta and Somabha Bandodhay. While I cannot thank each one individually for their help, I certainly would love to. I also want to thank those with whom, over two years ago now, we established GARN's Academic Hub: in addition to many of the people I have already mentioned above, I want to thank Lauren Tarr, Caitlyn Sutherlin, Kelsey Leonard, Mariana Ribeiro, Shrishtee Bajpai and Michael Lane. I want to thank the many interviewees who kindly accepted to discuss many of the book's ideas with me, as it is their insights that prompted the book in the first place: Hana Begovic, Bill Twist, Klaus Bosselmann, Pella Thiel, Margaret Stewart, Valerie Cabanes, Ngozi Stewart, Justice Jorge Iván Palacio, Doris Rigletti, Mario Melo and Gabriela Eslava.

I want to acknowledge and thank the friends and colleagues with whom I started the journey of mapping the emergence of an ecological jurisprudence in Australia, whose work continues to inspire and support me: Nicole Rogers, Michelle Maloney, Nicole Graham, Maria Zotti, Ben Mylius and all those who attended the various conferences organized over the past decade and a half. I also want to thank the friends and colleagues with whom I have had the pleasure of working with along the journey, and in particular my dear friends Afshin Akhtar-Khavari, Cristy Clark, John Page, Nia Emmanouil, Erin O'Donnell, Anne Poelina, Katie O'Bryan, Elizabeth Macpherson, Sarah Laborde and Margaret Davies.

I want to acknowledge the colleagues and friends whose pursuits have paralleled, and overlapped with, mine over the years. Emanuela Borgnino, with whom I started this journey long before I even knew it, well over two decades and a half ago, and to whom I am forever grateful. Roberta Aluffi, who supported me to become a thinker to begin with. Alessandro Michelucci, whose tireless work has accompanied mine for more than two decades. John Seed, Frank Forencich, Anthony James, Jean Renouf, Richard Hil, and Ivan Vargas Rocancio, whose paths constantly inspire me to continue on my own. I also want to thank all the colleagues who have supported me in my academic career. Among them, in particular, Rick Mohr, Bruce Duthu, Luke McNamara, Warick Fisher, Tim Peters and Jay Sanderson. I want to acknowledge my students, who over the years have shared their own exploration with me. In particular, I want to thank Keelan Parker for his endless curiosity.

I want to thank my friends, who have been patiently listening to me working through my ideas for years and who stayed close when I was particularly 'enthused': Samuel Stutz and Asako Suzuki, Yuping Zhou, Yoshiko Takakura, John Kim, Jess Schultz, Wanda De-Verelle Hill, Rohini Drury and Kim O'Sullivan, Carla Versitano and Leon King, Joshua Williams, John Williams, Matt Wood, Renaud Joannes-Boyau, Liz Deschaseux, Mirko Casagrande and Gianluca Morini, as well as all my friends who have witnessed the journey from afar: Marco Vercellino, Dario Marchis, Andrea Tolli, Paolo Chiariglione, Fabrizio Cardaci, Andrea Dragone, Francesca Ferracin, Elena Laguzzi, Enrico Tenaglia, Anna Spennati, Filippo Tenaglia, and all those who I cannot list for the list would be too long but who are always in my thoughts. Last, but perhaps first in order of time, I want to acknowledge all my relatives, my many uncles, aunties and cousins, without whom I would not be who I am.

And finally, I want to acknowledge your time, the reader, for the time you are dedicating on coming along this journey with me.

Contents

1 Introduction 1
1.1 Legally Invisible Environmental Damages and the Rise of an Ecological Jurisprudence 1
1.2 Worldviews, Paradigms, Discourses and Myths 4
1.3 Worldviews and Legal Formants 9
References 12

2 Climate Disruptions and the Coming Dark Age 15
2.1 The Environmental Predicament 17
2.1.1 Weather, Climate Observations and Human Attribution 17
2.1.2 Scientific Consensus and Discrediting Campaigns 20
2.1.3 Climate Disruptions and Human Flourishing 23
2.1.4 Ecological Limits and the Metabolic Rift 27
2.2 Problems, Predicaments, Solutions and Responses 30
2.2.1 Environmental Predicaments and Technological Solutions 30
2.2.2 Planned Obsolescence and the Mirage of Endless Consumption 34
2.2.3 Collapse: The Coming Dark Age 39
2.3 Environmental Apocalypse and the State of Exception 45
2.3.1 Toward an Ecological Götterdämmerung? 45
2.3.2 The State of Environmental Exception 48
2.4 Ontological and Epistemological Interconnectedness 51
Reference 52

3 Anthropocentrism Redefined 61
3.1 Anthropocentrism: A Textual Genealogy 63
3.1.1 'Replenish the Earth, and Subdue It' 64
3.1.2 The Birth of Metaphysics 67
3.1.3 To Transcend the World 73
3.1.4 The Rise of Science 78
3.1.5 Romanticism and Modernity 84

3.1.6 The Human Condition 89
3.2 Anthropocentrism: A Primer 92
3.3 Law, Nature and Property 98
3.3.1 The Nature of Property 100
References 104

4 Deus Sive Natura 109
4.1 Imagined Nature 110
4.1.1 The Invention of the Wilderness 111
4.2 Counternarratives of Interdependence 117
4.2.1 Physis and Kosmos 118
4.2.2 'Fratello Sole, Sorella Luna' 121
4.2.3 Natura Naturans and Natura Naturata 123
4.2.4 A 'New Science' 126
4.2.5 Sturm Und Drang 129
4.2.6 The Twentieth Century 133
4.3 The Tao that You Can Speak of 136
References 140

5 Wild Law 145
5.1 Welcome to the Revolution: Enter the Environment 146
5.1.1 Animal Suffering, the Reverence for Life and the Omega Point 148
5.1.2 Transcendentalism and Conservationism 150
5.1.3 Vitalism, Organicism and Ecology 153
5.2 Land Ethics and Modern Environmentalism 158
5.2.1 A Silent Spring 160
5.2.2 Deep Ecology 161
5.2.3 A Pluralist Environmental Landscape 162
5.2.4 Beyond Anthropocentrism 167
5.3 Ecology and Legal Theory 169
5.3.1 The Extension of Rights 171
5.3.2 Earth Jurisprudence 176
5.3.3 Ecological Law 182
5.3.4 Ecological Jurisprudence 187
References 191

6 Rights of Nature 199
6.1 The Rise of Environmental Law 200
6.1.1 Modern Environmental Law 200
6.1.2 Environmental Litigation 204
6.2 International Law and the Environment 205
6.2.1 International Environmental Legal Principles 211

6.3 The Rights of Nature ... 213
6.3.1 Animal Rights and the Rights of Species ... 214
6.3.2 Rights of Nature and Legal Personhood for Nature ... 216
6.4 Ecocide and Ecocrimes ... 240
6.5 The Ecological Civilization ... 242
6.6 Soft Law and Eco-Jurisprudential Organizations ... 245
6.6.1 Organizations ... 248
6.6.2 Activism ... 250
6.7 Reflections ... 252
References ... 257

7 Relationality, Reciprocity and Responsibility ... 265
7.1 Environmental Law v Earth Law ... 266
7.1.1 The Rights of Nature: A Critical Appraisal ... 267
7.2 The Onto-Axiological Spectrum ... 273
7.2.1 From Human Instrumentalism to the Intrinsic Value of Nature ... 274
7.2.2 Ethical Justifications ... 276
7.3 Rights and Duties ... 282
7.3.1 Rights 'of' Nature or Rights 'to' Nature? ... 284
7.4 Personhood, Representation and Agency ... 292
7.4.1 Nature's Personhood: Critiques ... 293
7.4.2 The Legal Persona ... 294
7.4.3 Nature as a Persona ... 297
7.4.4 Representation and Agency ... 301
7.5 Nature or Natures? ... 304
7.6 Relationality, Reciprocity and Responsibility: Evaluating Nature's Legality ... 308
7.6.1 Ecological Jurisprudence as the Homeostatic Horizon of Law ... 309
7.6.2 Evaluative Matrices ... 311
7.6.3 Deep Transformations ... 314
References ... 315

8 Neither Natural nor Posited ... 321
8.1 The Death of Nature? ... 322
8.1.1 Beyond Materiality ... 324
8.1.2 The Multicultural and the Multinatural ... 327
8.1.3 The Law of the Land ... 332
8.2 Neither Natural nor Posited ... 333
8.2.1 Is Ecological Jurisprudence a New Form of Natural Law Theory? ... 334
8.2.2 The Laws of Nature ... 336
8.2.3 Neither Natural nor Posited ... 341

8.2.4 Is Nature Normative? 346
8.2.5 Toward an Ecological Jurisprudence 352
8.3 The Land Is the Source of the Law 355
8.3.1 Indigenous Strategies 356
8.3.2 Laws, Knowledge and Ancestral Persons 361
8.3.3 Environmental Colonialism 368
8.3.4 The Common Ground We Always Seek 371
References 372

9 Conclusion 379
References 392

Appendix A: World Charter for Nature 395

Appendix B: The Earth Charter 399

Appendix C: Universal Declaration on the Rights of Mother Earth 407

Appendix D: The Hague Principles for a Universal Declaration on Responsibilities for Human Rights and Earth Trusteeship 411

Appendix E: Oslo Manifesto 415

Appendix F: Chief Seattle 1854 Oration–Ver. 3 419

Appendix G: A Bill of Rights for the Planet Earth 423

About the Author

Dr. Alessandro Pelizzon was born, raised and schooled in Turin, Italy. He completed his LLB/LLM at the University of Turin (Italy), specializing in comparative law and legal anthropology, and concluded his degree with a field research project on pre-Colombian family legal protocols in the Andes, conducting his research primarily in Peru.

During his university years, together with fellow students, he established a small NGO, 'Gruppo Indipendente di Ricerca' (G.I.R.), with the aim to support the drafting of, and inform the public about, the United Nations Declaration on the Rights of Indigenous Peoples.

Upon moving to Australia in 2005, his Doctoral research, conducted at the University of Wollongong (Australia), focused on native title and legal pluralism in the Illawarra region.

In 2009, he discovered the emerging discourse on rights of Nature, Wild Law and Earth Jurisprudence and was particularly fascinated by the intersection between this emerging discourse and different legal ontologies. A year later, he organized the second Australian conference on Wild Law and Earth Jurisprudence, intended as a dialogue between the University of Wollongong and the Sandon Point Tent Embassy around the idea of a shared more-than-human world.

In the same year, he led the transformation of the Earth Laws Alliance, the entity he had established to coordinate the previous event, into the Australian Wild Law Alliance, which then morphed, a few years later, into the Australian Earth Laws Alliance.

In 2010, he was one of the co-founders, in Ecuador, of the Global Alliance for the Rights of Nature, on whose Executive Committee he is currently serving. In 2020, he became the inaugural Director of the Global Alliance for the Rights of Nature Academic Hub, the main output of which has been the creation of the Eco-Jurisprudence Monitor.

Alessandro has been working as an academic at the University of Wollongong, at Southern Cross University, and currently at the University of the Sunshine Coast. In his decades-long academic career, he has written and presented extensively on his area of research in a number of fora around the world.

Alessandro's main areas of research interests are ecological jurisprudence, legal anthropology, legal theory, comparative law, constitutional law, sovereignty and Indigenous rights.

Abbreviations

AAAS	American Association for the Advancement of Science
AELA	Australian Earth Laws Alliance
AFADA	Argentinian Association of Professional Lawyers for Animal Rights
CELDF	Community and Environment Legal Defense Fund
CITES	Conventions on International Trade in Endangered Species of Wild Flora and Fauna
CMA	Meetings of the Parties to the Paris Agreement
CMP	Meetings of the Parties to the Kyoto Protocol
CONAIE	Confederation of Indigenous Nationalities of Ecuador
COP	United Nations Conference of the Parties
ECOSOC	Economic and Social Council
ELGA	Ecological Law and Governance Association
ETI	Earth Trusteeship Initiatives
FAO	Food and Agriculture Organization
GARN	Global Alliance for the Rights of Nature
GEMS	Global Environmental Monitoring System
GESAMP	Joint Group of Experts on the Scientific Aspects of Marine Environmental Protection
IAEA	International Atomic Energy Agency
IBRD	International Bank for Reconstruction and Development
ICA	International Civil Aviation Organization
IDA	International Development Association
IFC	International Finance Corporation
ILO	International Labour Organization
IMF	International Monetary Fund
IMO	International Maritime Organization
INFOTERRA	International Referral System
IPCC	Intergovernmental Panel on Climate Change
IUCN	International Union for the Conservation of Nature and Natural Resources

LEBOR	Lake Erie Bill of Rights
NASA	National Aeronautics and Space Administration
NOAA	National Oceanic and Atmospheric Administration
OECD	Organization for Economic Co-operation and Development
PETA	People for the Ethical Treatment of Animals
PETM	Paleocene-Eocene thermal maximum
RoN	Rights of Nature
RSPCA	Royal Society for the Prevention of Cruelty to Animals
UKELA	UK Environmental Law Association
UN	United Nations
UNCED	United Nations Conference on Environment and Development
UNCLOS	United Nations Convention on the Law of the Sea
UNDP	United Nations Development Programme
UNDRIP	United Nations Declaration on the Rights of Indigenous Peoples
UNEP	United Nations Environment Programme
UNESCO	United Nations Educational, Scientific and Cultural Organization
UNFCCC	United Nations Framework Convention on Climate Change
UNIDO	United Nations Industrial Development Organization
USA	United States of America
WECAN	Women's Earth and Climate Action Network
WHO	World Health Organization
WMO	World Meteorological Organization
WTO	World Trade Organization
WWF	World Wide Fund for Nature

Chapter 1
Introduction

The fundamental thesis of this book is that all the initiatives it explores, and all the theories that underpin them, constitute a single, (perhaps unintentionally) cohesive and novel way for legal theory to imagine itself. Not only, they also represent a single overall attempt to harmonize legal theory with an ecological view of the world and of humanity's role within it. Just as ecology has entered the vernacular of most disciplines, it has done so within law and legal theory as well. The fundamental thesis of this book, therefore, is that the Western legal world (and the legal world in general) is in the midst of the emergence of a veritable *ecological jurisprudence.*

1.1 *Legally Invisible* Environmental Damages and the Rise of an Ecological Jurisprudence

In 1972, Professor Christopher Stone of the University of Southern California, concluded a property law class with what was then (and arguably, still is) a very provocative question: 'should *trees* have standing?'. 'My thoughts were not even on the environment' (xi), Stone recalls decades later. His question was instead concerned with the way a legal order can shape the society from which it emerges.

> Throughout history, there have been shifts in a cluster of related property variables, such as: what things, at various times were recognized as ownable (land, movables, ideas, other persons [slaves]); who was deemed capable of ownership (individuals, married women); the powers and privileges ownership conveyed (the right to destroy, the immunity from a warrantless search); and so on. It was easy to see how each change shifted the locus and quality of power. … "So", I wondered aloud, reading their glazing scepticism, "what would a radically different law-driven consciousness look like" … One in which Nature had rights," I supplied my own answer. "Yes, rivers, lakes, …" (warming to the idea) "trees … animals …" (I may have ventured "rocks"; I am not certain.) "How would such a posture *in law* affect a community's view *of itself*?" This little thought experiment was greeted, quite sincerely, with uproar.' (xi-xii)

A. Pelizzon, *Ecological Jurisprudence*, Contemporary Environmental Law and Policy,
https://doi.org/10.1007/978-981-96-0173-8_1

Undeterred, Stone soon found a case that would allow him to explore the issue of what the criteria were for any entity having their own rights, since, he realized, the law 'lends its mantle to protect all sorts of things, but not in a manner that would lead us to say that these things have rights' (xii). The case, *Sierra Club v Hickel*, concerned a permit granted by the US Forest Service to Walt Disney Enterprises, Inc. for the construction of a 35 million US$ ski-resort and related complex of motels, restaurants and facilities in the Mineral King Valley, a wilderness area in California southern Sierra Nevada mountains. The Sierra Club, long term self-appointed protector of the area, brought suit for an injunction, arguing that the project would damage the area's ecological balance (primarily, though not exclusively, via the destruction of the valley's old growth forest), as well as negatively affecting the area's aesthetic and recreational value. However, the Ninth Circuit initially argued (ignoring the question as to whether the permit had been rightly or wrongly issued) that the Sierra Club had no 'standing' to bring the question to the courts, since it did not 'allege that it [was] "aggrieved" or that it [was] "adversely affected" within the meaning of the rules of standing … The right to sue does not inure to one who does not possess it simply because there is no one else willing and able to assert it' (at 32). The appeal was then reviewed by the US Supreme Court in 1972 under the name of *Sierra Club v Morton* (the name of the new Secretary of the Interior), and the Supreme Court, with a four Justice majority (albeit with a powerful dissenting opinion from Justice Douglas), upheld the Ninth Circuit's decision, affirming 'that the injury in fact test require[d] more than an injury to a cognizable interest. It require[d] that the party seeking review be himself among the injured' (Stone, 2010, xiv).

However, Stone argued, although the Sierra Club was not directly injured by the proposed development and therefore had no standing—standing, broadly speaking, being 'the authority of someone to initiate an action' (Stone, 2010, 35)—something definitely *was* being injured (in fact, destroyed): the valley's old growth forest. Therefore, if standing was the necessary precondition to prevent such damage to occur, maybe standing ought to be granted to the old growth forest, to the trees, themselves.

> Perhaps the injury to the Sierra Club was tenuous, but the injury to Mineral King – the park itself – wasn't. If the courts could be persuaded to think about the park itself as a jural person – the way corporations are "persons" – the notion of Nature having rights would were make a significant operational difference – the difference between the case being hear and … being thrown out of court. In other words, if standing were the barrier, why not designate Mineral King, the wilderness area, as the plaintiff "adversely affected", let the Sierra Club be characterized as the attorney or guardian for the area, and get on with the merits? (Stone, 2010, xiii)

Stone could scarcely have predicted how his suggestion would have affected the dominant legal paradigm in decades to come. In the author's words, '[this suggestion] has since assumed a modest but apparently enduring place in contemporary environmental law and ethics, quite out of proportion to its actual impact on the courts'. The most challenging (for the dominant legal system) implication of Stone's question is the question as to why those very evident environmental damages (the complete destruction of an old growth forest) can be legally *invisible*. In other words, why was *the law* unable to see those as 'damages'. Or, even if it *did* see them as damages, even if they were not invisible, why were they *irrelevant* (i.e. *legally* irrelevant)?

The above question—why are environmental damages *legally invisible*, or at least *irrelevant*—will guide the unfolding of this book. In the next chapter, I will first explore the question as to whether, indeed, environmental damages exist in the first instance. Is the alteration of the planet to be construed as 'damage'? And if so, to what extent? I will then propose, in the following chapters, that the reason that makes any environmental damage invisible or irrelevant is to be found in a particular worldview, a particular *weltanschauung* that shapes the way one not only 'sees' the world but also acts in and upon it. I will dedicate a chapter to identify and define the worldview that underpinned both the US Supreme Court's decision and the colonial mindset of what can be provisionally called 'the West', a worldview that is heuristically called 'anthropocentrism' (in an enlarged sense). Then, in the following chapter, I will explore a host of existing perspectives that have attempted to counter that anthropocentric worldview as it was developing, as well as the explicit emergence of an environmental and ecological consciousness and ethics over the past one and a half-century. I will then provide an overview of the legal theories that have emerged, within Western jurisprudence, in parallel with the emergence of that environmental and ecological consciousness, and then, in the following chapter, I will provide an overview of the legal initiatives that have emerged as a result. These initiatives range from the most basic environmental law principles (often informed by a slightly more enlightened form of anthropocentrism) to far more ecocentric provisions, such as Rights of Nature and the proposed crime of Ecocide. Then, I will critically analyse these initiatives and provide an evaluative matrix to consider them in the light of the theoretical and philosophical perspectives introduced in the previous chapters. Finally, I will explore the multidisciplinary, jurisprudential and inter-normative implications of the emergence of this ecological jurisprudence, to investigate the most creative and promising possibilities it entails. Firstly, an ecological jurisprudence that is cognisant of both the *idea* of ecology and of its own philosophic positioning is inherently multidisciplinary, and thus I will gesture toward the rich parallel development of a host of related theoretical pursuits in relation to the idea of 'Nature'. Secondly, the emergence of an ecological jurisprudence also represents a novel attempt to develop a 'grand narrative' of law that transcends the boundaries of the classical dichotomy between legal positivism and natural law theory and rather attempts to create a novel terrain to interrogate both the meaning and the boundaries of normativity itself. Finally, the emergence of an ecological jurisprudence, perhaps for the first time, represents the theoretical possibility for distinct legal systems that have operated within asymmetrical relationships of power to find a common term of reference, a common 'ground', to enter into a dialogue on the relationship they have with the nonhuman *other*.

The book is intended to communicate with a large audience, marked by a great range of interdisciplinary backgrounds. As a result, much of the information contained in the book, by necessity, will appear introductory to some and yet novel to others. Similarly, the book will have to be, at the same time, deep and protean, in order to reach the diverse readerships for which it is intended. As a result, I hope the reader will forgive me for taking the time to present the many theoretical contexts within which the book's main argument is located, and yet, at the same time, for being unable to engage in more depth with each of these contexts. Equally, it is my hope that the reader will engage with the overall narrative at a pace that is relevant to their own disciplinary expertise and thus use the book as they see fit. Those who are already familiar with some of the introductory sections are welcome to skip them and rather focus their attention to the relevant arguments that are developed toward the final part of the book. Practitioners interested in evaluating the practical implications of the many eco-jurisprudential initiatives introduced in the chapter titled 'Rights of Nature' may want to focus their attention on the subsequent chapter, titled 'Relationality, Reciprocity and Responsibility'. Legal theorists intrigued by the emergence of an ecological jurisprudence may dedicate their attention to the final chapter, titled 'Neither Natural Nor Posited', while those who are new to the emergence of an ecological jurisprudence may be interested in reading its historical emergence in the chapters titled 'Wild Law' and 'Rights of Nature'. Others still, I hope, will enjoy the overall journey that this book entails, the overall argument that inscribes the emergence of an ecological jurisprudence within a clear ecological and theoretical space and time, and the way in which, it is my hope, the book will guide the reader along that journey.

1.2 Worldviews, Paradigms, Discourses and Myths

The shift toward an ecological jurisprudence, this book will argue, has occurred at multiple levels and to multiple degrees, from a relatively minor movement toward more enlightened anthropocentrism to far more radical ecocentric proposals that invite legal scholars to reimagine normativity beyond the boundaries of humanity. To explore the emergence of an ecological jurisprudence, however, I believe it is necessary to pursue a question that follows Stone's proposal: what is within Western legal theory that makes the destruction of an old growth forest—and of the environment more in general—legally invisible or at least legally irrelevant?

If science appears to be uncontroversial in pointing to an environmental predicament that is both real and urgent (as will be established more fully in the next chapter), and if this predicament—as well as any response to it—is ultimately and fundamentally influenced—in fact, even shaped—by legal structures and considerations, the question remains as to what it is that makes this predicament *legally* invisible, or, at least, *legally* irrelevant. The next chapter will show that environmental damages are undoubtedly scientifically visible, and the effects of these damages engender a high degree of scientific consensus. Furthermore, the scientific community agrees that environmental damages are caused by human activities, and that they are also immediately relevant to our very survival as a species. Yet, the paradox contained in Stone's argument remains: while these damages are both *scientifically* visible and relevant, *legally*, that is not the case. Therefore, we ought to rightfully ask, where is this disjuncture between scientific knowledge and the legal discourse to be located?

'What is it about our modern consciousness that enables us to avoid seeing the disastrous results of our way of life?', evolutionary cosmologist Brian Swimme and historian of religion Mary Evelyn Tucker (2011, 103) ask. Clearly, while the authors invite their readers to populate their rhetorical 'us' with the totality of humanity, it is important to remain fully aware that different cultural paradigms provide very different responses to their questions. With such a caveat in mind, the authors' inquiry implies that the disjuncture between that which science observes and that which law recognizes is to be found in the lens through which the world is socially construed. What makes the current environmental predicament *legally* invisible or irrelevant is thus to be located in a particular view of the cosmos that shapes the world's dominant normative and legal systems. Central to the articulation of this book, therefore, is the engagement with the worldview (or better, the worldviews—plural) that underpin the shift the book investigates.

To identify such a worldview, however, is not a merely descriptive exercise, nor is it an attempt to locate a single 'culprit' for the predicament the world is currently mired in. Indeed, Gwynne Dyer writes that

> [n]obody is to blame for the crisis that looms over us. Not my mother, who had five children and contributed to a population explosion that saw the world's population triple from 2.6 billion to 6.7 billion between the end of the Second World War and now [8.2 billions as of 2024, 14 years after Dyer's book was written]. Not William Levitt, who invented the modern suburb in the late 1940s, or Henry Ford, who applied mass-production techniques to the manufacture of automobiles in 1913, or Thomas Newcomen, who devised the first practical steam engine in 1710. And certainly not the first woman who planted seeds with a digging stick ten or twelve thousand years ago and began the agricultural revolution that set us on the path to mass civilization ... None of them could imagine that we might actually change the way the world works to our own disadvantage. (2010, 42)

Dyer's words propose that the ultimate responsibility for the current predicament—and, consequently, for any response to it—cannot be cast as individual and agentic, but rather is best conceived of as collective and diffuse. While individual choices certainly accrue to determine the current trajectory of our global human society, the current state of affairs cannot be attributed to a single individual, a single event, or a single idea. That notwithstanding, it is useful to investigate some key instances, both within history and within the history of ideas, that point to the collective forces currently conspiring to enact a caesura between contemporary and dominant scientific and legal discourses. Individual choices can be described as part of a greater trend, one in which abstract—almost archetypal—ways of seeing the world can be more easily identified among the apparent plethora of ever-shifting individual perspectives. Such was, indeed, the insight of Alexander von Humboldt's idea of a *weltansicht* (Naugle, 2002), the comprehensive understanding of reality shared among a particular language community.[1] Immanuel Kant followed suit, by coining the term *weltanschauung*,[2] not long thereafter translated in English as 'worldview',

[1] Notably, von Humboldt also originated the idea that language and thought are inextricably intertwined.

[2] The term is first attested in Immanuel Kant's 1790 *Kritik der Urteilskraft (Critique of Judgment)* (Naugle 2002).

'a largely unconscious but generally coherent set of presuppositions and beliefs that every person has which shape how we make sense of the world and everything in it',which, 'in turn, influences such things as how we see ourselves as individuals, how we interpret our role in society, how we deal with social issues and what we regard as truth' (Oxford Reference, 2022).

The work of Wilhelm Dilthey was instrumental in defining the idea of the 'world-view' as a hermeneutic and cognitive tool with which to interrogate reality (Rickman, 1961). While natural sciences can only observe and explain (*erklären*) external events, Dilthey argued, human beings can move beyond the constraints of mere observation and can understand (*verstehen*) these events and their own interactions with them in terms of their own thoughts, goals and value judgments. Furthermore, each individual interpretation of, and interactions with, the world, is inevitably placed within a larger understanding of the world itself (a *weltanschauung*, or worldview) that is historically determined and is commonly shared among a cultural—and generally linguistic—group. For Dilthey, all *weltanschauungen* are thus partial views of the world, relative to specific cultural, historical and geographical positions.

The inevitable variability of individual perspectives can thus be approached by reference to some historically and contextually determined collective markers, which can provide a degree of hermeneutic objectivity. American missiologist Hiebert (2008) described these markers as the 'fundamental cognitive, affective and evaluative presuppositions a group of people make about the nature of things and which they use to order their lives'. Furthermore, Lester Milbraith attributes a somewhat autopoietic quality to worldviews by describing them as 'epistemological structures for interpreting reality that ground their picture of "reality" in their own construction' (1994, 117).

Far from even attempting to meaningfully and systematically engage with the vast, complex (and utterly fascinating) field covered by the philosophy of cognition, the brief reference to the concept of a worldview is rather offered as foundational to engaging with the dichotomic opposition between the scientific and legal perspectives discussed above. Since both are located within a particular worldview, an exploration of such a worldview requires the necessary engagement with a number of branches of philosophical inquiry, such as epistemology (the branch of philosophy concerned with the theory of knowledge, its methods, its validity and the distinction between justified belief and opinion), metaphysics (the branch of philosophy concerned with the most fundamental principles of reality, such as the nature of being, identity, time and space), ontology (the philosophical study of being), cosmology (the philosophical and scientific study of the universe and its evolution), teleology (the study of nature in relation to its intrinsic end, goal or purpose) and axiology (the philosophical study of value), to cite the most important. While the engagement with every branch of philosophy would warrant a dedicated treatise for each, for the purpose of the present text, it is sufficient to gesture to their necessary involvement.

An initial question may assist to navigate the theoretical breadth that these various branches of philosophy entail: if a particular way to observe the world, rather than the mere observation of objective (some would say scientific) facts, underpins axiological, normative and ultimately behavioural considerations, how, then, is a worldview best approached? In 1962, American philosopher of science Thomas Kuhn introduced the idea of the 'paradigm' as a set of 'universally recognized scientific achievements that for a time provide model problem solutions to a community of practitioners' (xiii). This idea, later echoed by what Australian legal theorist Margaret Davies names the 'theory dependence of observation' (2008, 131), suggests that '[f]acts do not speak for themselves', but are rather defined by the lens through which they are observed and by which they are ultimately constituted. Knowledge, Khun states, is not just a process of accretion, but rather results from the interplay of a given theoretical perspective and social and environmental circumstances. Echoing the definition of a 'worldview' explored above, Kuhn argues that 'paradigms provide scientists not only with a map but also with some of the directions essential for map-making' (109). The shift toward an ecological jurisprudence, as this book will show, constitutes a veritable paradigmatic shift in the above sense.

Readers will immediately identify the connection between Kuhn's radical challenge to the scientific theoretical artifices of modernity and the postmodern edifice built upon the rejection of objective universal theories, what Lyotard (1984) called 'grand narratives'. Moreover, as Joseph Rouse further points out, paradigms are not just ways of seeing the worlds, but also ways of doing things in the world: 'normal science involves shared practices, not shared beliefs' (1978, 31). This idea of a 'paradigm' as a way of both knowing and doing is akin to the classical definition of an *episteme*, a term that 'could mean both knowledge and skill, both knowing that and knowing how … The word *episteme*, "knowledge" (in Plato opposed to the world of *doxa*, or "opinion") was thus very close in meaning to the word *tekhne*, "skill"' (Hintikka, 1991).

Furthermore, the assertion that science (and, by extension, knowledge about the world) is not cumulative, but rather proceeds through a series of paradigmatic shifts, is best encapsulated in French philosopher's Michel Foucault's overall work. Foucault's writing was concerned with a particular focus on history, not in the traditional sense of a collection of reconstructed events, but rather as a 'genealogy' of knowledge production evinced from an 'archaeological' observation of the discontinuities between what he defined, departing from the classical definition presented above, as 'epistemes' (1973). Various authors, such as Swiss psychologist Piaget (1971, 132), have often equated Foucault's concept of the *épistéme* with Khun's notion of the *paradigm*. Rather than being limited to science, however, Foucault's *épistéme* applies to all knowledge systems, each informing thinking at a particular time and defining a particular epistemological age. In *The Order of Things,* Foucault asserted that '[i]n any given culture and at any given moment, there is always only one *episteme* that defines the conditions of possibility of all knowledge, whether expressed in a theory or silently invested in a practice' (1973, 183).

Foucault's idea of the *épistéme*, akin to Kuhn's *paradigm* and Dilthey's *weltanschauung*, thus represents the 'knowledge subconscious' of an era, the total sum of the invisible parameters of knowledge that define what is, and is not, permissible to think. 'I would define the episteme retrospectively as the strategic apparatus which permits of separating out from among all the statements which are possible those that will be acceptable', Foucault writes, 'and which it is possible to say are true or false. The episteme is the "apparatus" which makes possible the separation, not of the true from the false, but of what may from what may not be characterized as scientific' (1973, 197). As the necessary a priori that delimits historical knowledge and truth, *epistemes* are often virtually invisible to those—individuals and institutions alike—who operate within them. As a result, purportedly universal and objective truths about the cosmos are, in reality, contingent expressions of particular ethical and political orientations of a given society.

Importantly, *epistemes* are embodied and practically articulated within specific *discourses*. Jorge Ruiz, in noting how most definitions of the term are derived from Foucault's original work, defines a *discourse* as 'any practice (found in a wide range of forms) by which individuals imbue reality with meaning' (2009, 26). A *discourse* is thus both a way of thinking about the world that is expressed through language and the theoretical milieu that defines which statements can be legitimately said about any particular topic. In this sense, a *discourse* is not limited to linguistic elements, but rather refers to institutionalized patterns of knowledge that are made possible by a particular set of epistemological parameters. For Foucault, a 'discourse' is a way of socially ordering knowledge, a collection of 'practices that systematically form the objects of which they speak' (1972, 49). Accordingly, 'discursive fields', such as 'the law' or 'science', are part of Foucault's 'attempt to understand the relationship between language, social institutions, subjectivity and power' and 'contain a number of competing and contradictory discourses with varying degrees of power to give meaning to and organize social institutions and processes' (Weedon, 1987, 35).

Discourses, Foucault further argues, are intrinsically related to the operation of power, through the recursive application of rules of exclusion, which determine what can, or cannot, be spoken of, with the result, as Iara Lessa points out, that they act as 'systems of thoughts composed of ideas, attitudes, courses of action, beliefs and practices that systematically construct the subjects and the worlds of which they speak' (2006, 283). In identifying the power-knowledge nexus, Foucault asserts that truths are construed and maintained by a series of rules and categories that define the criteria to legitimate knowledge within a particular discourse. Power, in this context, is conceived of as 'a dynamic of control and lack of control between discourses and the subjects, constituted by discourses, who are their agents' (Weedon, 1987, 113). Knowledge and power are, therefore, indissolubly interrelated and combine to establish what Foucault describes as distinct 'regimes of truth'. In this sense, a discourse is a medium through which power relations produce different truths and specific knowing subjects.[3] Power, therefore, is not merely repressive, but actively productive[4]: it does not repress and control a pre-existing original truth, but rather participates in its creation. Truth, therefore,

[3] Foucault adds that any discourse is always controlled by a series of objects (what can be spoken of), rituals (where and how anyone may speak), and privileged subjects (who may speak).

[4] Similarly, Khun wrote that '[i]f authority alone, and particularly if non-professional authority, were the arbiter of paradigm debates, the outcome of those debates might still be revolution, but it

is a thing of this world: it is produced only by virtue of multiple forms of constraint. And it induces regular effects of power. Each society has its regime of truth, its "general politics" of truth: that is, the types of discourse which it accepts and makes function as true; the mechanisms and instances which enable one to distinguish true and false statements, the means by which each is sanctioned; the techniques and procedures accorded value in the acquisition of truth; the status of those who are charged with saying what counts as true (Foucault, 1980, 109)

Foucault's articulation of distinct 'regimes of truth' is echoed by Barthes's (1972) notion of the 'myth'. For Barthes, a 'myth has the task of giving an historical intention a natural justification and making contingency appear eternal'. Myth, to him, is a form of 'depoliticized speech', a form of language-robbery that hijacks a primary meaning to turn it into a naturalized statement about something else. 'Myth does not deny things … it purifies them, it makes them innocent, it gives them a natural and eternal justification, it gives them a clarity which is not that of an explanation, but that of a statement of fact' (142–3). The fundamental insight of Barthes is that, as Edward Said had already noted, 'words and objects have in common the organized capacity to say something: at the same time, since they are signs, words and objects have the bad faith always to appear natural to their consumer, as if what they say is eternal, true, necessary, instead of arbitrary, made, contingent' (Barthes, 1972).

1.3 Worldviews and Legal Formants

The very brief paradigmatic and methodological overview hereby offered is seen as particularly useful in highlighting the existing discontinuities between the scientific and the legal discourses with which this chapter began, thus already gesturing toward a potential answer to the question raised by Stone's argument: why is the current environmental predicament legally invisible or irrelevant. While multiple worldviews coexist, intersect and often conflict within any given discourse, a dominant worldview regularly emerges from within the power-knowledge nexus, leading to different sets of values, a set of aspirations and goals related to things that are seen as worthy or desirable. In this sense, values are not relevant in a normative sense per se, but only insofar as they lead a particular group of people to prioritize very different things and to endorse very different actions. This book is thus overall interested in engaging in a 'genealogical' reconstruction of the dominant discourse underpinning contemporary legal axiology (the legal system of values) in relation to the environment.

Less concerned with power relations and more focused on the ontological justifications of existing legal structures—thus wishing to cast its gaze primarily upon discursive formations that underpin and support historically contingent legal structures for which environmental damages emerge as legally invisible or irrelevant—the book adopts the ideas of *paradigm* (from Kuhn), *episteme* (from Foucault) and *myth* (from Barthes) as its broad units of investigation. However, since a comprehensive

---

would not be *scientific* revolution. The very existence of science depends upon vesting the power to choose between paradigms in the members of a special kind of community' (1962, 166–167).

and detailed catalogue of all relevant concepts would require a dedicated monograph for each one of them, the book aims to limit its inquiry to uncovering some key 'epistemological obstacles', some of the fundamental thought structures that, French philosopher Gaston Bachelard suggested (1986), are immanent principles within the realm of any given knowledge system (such as, for example, the Cartesian mind/body dualism).[5] The process is aligned with what sociologists Berger and Luckmann (1966) described as 'social construction', the idea that individuals and social groups within any social system collectively generate a series of concepts that form the basis for shared assumptions about the cosmos.

Such shared concepts and beliefs are captured by the idea of the *meme*, a metaphor introduced by evolutionary biologist Dawkins (1976) to identify a self-replicating unit of transmission of a particular idea or behaviour that successfully spreads within a linguistic, social or cultural group, carrying within itself 'mythical' properties in a Barthian sense.[6] The first four chapters of the book thus identify particular *memes* that act in a mythical fashion and are enshrined in clearly defined philosophical (ontological, epistemological, metaphysical, axiological) concepts. Moreover, such a Foucauldian genealogical analysis aims to show that the particular system of thoughts that underpin the current dominant legal system is the result of the contingent flow of history, rather than the inevitable outcome of linear progress.

Before proceeding further, however, a final note must be made as to the relationships between these paradigmatic/epistemic/mythical *memes* to be uncovered and the practice and theory of law. In other words, how can the relationship between law and worldviews best be characterized? Finnish legal theorist Kaarlo Tuori introduces the idea of a 'multilayered' nature of law, distinguishing between a 'surface level', whereby 'the legal order assumes the form of linguistically expressed norms' (2002, 193), and a 'deep structure of the law', one informed by both general doctrines (the preconceptions, or *vorverständnis*, upon which judges rely in deciding particular cases, the 'conceptual element of the legal culture') and general legal principles (the 'normative elements of the legal culture'). The idea of law being multilayered had already been introduced, centuries prior, by Aquinas's fourfold division (with the *lex aeterna,* the *lex divina,* and the *lex naturalis moralis* underpinning any human law) and was further advanced by Carl von Savigny and Georg Friedrich Puchta's idea of the *volksgeist*, the people's legal convictions representing a more fundamental layer than legislation and 'formal' law (Wilhelm, 1958). More recently, Robert Cover noted that

> [a] legal tradition is ... part and parcel of a complex normative world. The tradition includes not only corpus juris, but also a language and a mythos - narratives in which the corpus juris is located by those whose wills act upon it. These myths establish a repertoire of moves - a lexicon of normative action - that may be combined into meaningful patterns culled from

---

[5] Bachelard argued, preceding Kuhn's description of the process of scientific revolutions through the succession of discontinuous paradigms, that the history of science is defined by a cycle of establishment of these epistemological obstacles and the subsequent 'epistemological rupture' of such obstacles.

[6] Therefore, 'memetic', Philippe Descola suggests, becomes the study of 'memes', the 'elements of information which constitute culture' (2013, 3).

> the meaningful patterns of the past. The normative meaning that has inhered in the patterns of the past will be found in the history of ordinary legal doctrine at work in mundane affairs; in utopian and messianic yearnings, imaginary shapes given to a less resistant reality; in apologies for power, and privilege and in the critiques that may be levelled at the justificatory enterprises of law. (1983, 9)

Cover's insight is inscribed in a rich comparative legal tradition that has developed a number of theoretical heuristics to identify the underpinning narratives Cover refers to. Mark Van Hoecke speaks of 'deep level comparative law' (2004, 165), while the great figure of Italian comparative law, Rodolfo Sacco (1991), developed the idea of 'legal formants' that underly any legal formulation (be it in statutory or judicial form). Sacco focused his attention on 'declaratory statements', statements that may not be 'strictly legal', but are rather 'propositions about philosophy, politics, ideology or religion', yet contribute heavily to the development of legal norms. Presenting at the first Australian conference on Wild Law and Earth Jurisprudence in Adelaide in 2009, Liz Rivers proposed the metaphor of a multilayered pyramid to represent law's relationship with the worldview within which it is inscribed. Building upon Rivers's metaphor, and categorizing Sacco's idea of 'legal formants', such a pyramid (see, Fig. 1.1) can be conceived as one where law (as conceived of in common parlance) sits at the top, underpinned by a set of jurisprudential (or theoretical) principles, further underpinned by a series of political assumptions, a host of ethical premises, and, ultimately, a fundamental layer comprising the particular worldview by which law, its norms and its institutions are informed.

Just as one of the progressively disappearing icebergs floating in the frozen northern or southern oceans, 'law' is thus just the operative tip of a far more complex and nuanced host of *norms, memes* and *ideas* strictly intertwined to form a complex and relatively closed (although not always necessarily coherent) worldview. Robert Cover captured this idea aptly, when he stated that '[t]he rules and principles of justice, the formal institutions of the law, and the conventions of a social order are, indeed, important' However, he continues, 'they are … but a small part of the normative universe that ought to claim our attention. No set of legal institutions or

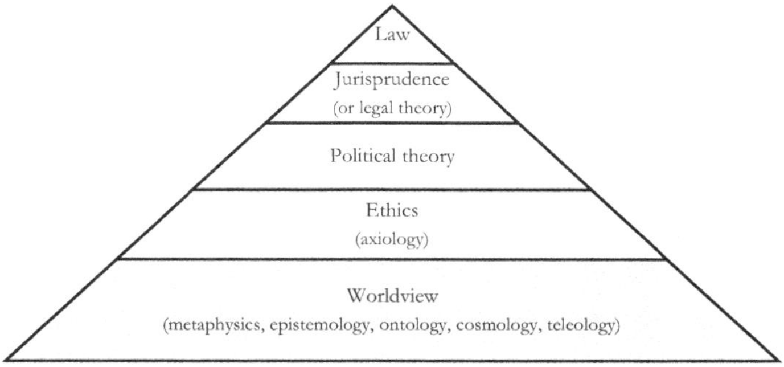

Fig. 1.1 The legal formants pyramid

prescriptions exists apart from the narratives that locate it and give it meaning. For every constitution there is an epic, for each decalogue a scripture' (1983, 4).

Furthermore, law operates not only as the pinnacle of this metaphorical pyramid, but also—because of its pervasive power but also because of its special position between theory and praxis, straddling the divide between ideas and actions—as the crucial axis around which worldviews revolve. The relationship between truth and power that is entailed in the daily operation of law, therefore, implies that law can *enable* particular worldviews. In other words, while it is intuitively easy to see how the underpinning layers shape and determine the form, the nature and the operation of the ones above them, such an influence is not merely unidirectional. In reflecting upon positing his question, Stone recalled wondering aloud,

> reading their glazing scepticism, "what would a radically different law-driven consciousness look like" ... One in which Nature had rights," I supplied my own answer. "Yes, rivers, lakes, ..." (warming to the idea) "trees ... animals ..." (I may have ventured "rocks"; I am not certain.) "How would such a posture *in law* affect a community's view *of itself*?" (2010, xi-xii)

References

Bachelard, G. (1986). *The formation of the scientific mind: A contribution to a psychoanalysis of objective knowledge*. Beacon Press (First published in French 1938).

Barthes, R. (1972). *Mythologies*. Farrar, Strauss and Giroux (First published in French 1957).

Berger, P. L., & Luckmann, T. (1966). *The social construction of reality: A treatise in the sociology of knowledge*. Anchor Books.

Cover, R. (1983). Nomos and narrative. *Harvard Law Review, 97*, 4–68.

Davies. M. (2008). *Asking the law question* (3rd edn). Thomson Lawbook Co.

Dawkins, R. (1976). *The selfish gene*. Oxford University Press.

Descola, P. (2013). *The ecology of others* (G. Geneviève Godbout, & B. P. Luley Trans.). Prickly Paradigm Press.

Dyer, G. (2010). *Climate wars. The fight for survival as the world overheats*. Oneworld Publications.

Foucault, M. (1972). *The archaeology of knowledge* (A. Sheridan, Trans.). Harper and Row (First published 1969 as L'archéologie du savoir).

Foucault, M. (1973). *The order of things* (A. Sheridan, Trans.). Vintage (First published 1966 as Les mots et les choses).

Foucault, M. (1980). *Power/knowledge*. Knopf US.

Hiebert P G (2008) *Transforming worldviews: An anthropological understanding of how people change*. Baker Academics.

Hintikka, J. (1991). *Knowledge and the known: Historical perspectives in epistemology*. Kluwer.

Kuhn, T. (1962). *The structure of scientific revolution*. University of Chicago Press.

Lessa, I. (2006). Discursive struggles within social welfare: Restaging teen motherhood. *The British Journal of Social Work, 36*(2), 283–298.

Lyotard, J. F. (1984). *The postmodern condition: A report on knowledge* (G. Bennington, & B. Massumi, Trans.). University of Minnesota Press (First published 1979).

Milbraith, L. (1994). Stumbling blocks to a sustainable society. In D. McKenzie-Mohr, & M. Marien (Eds.). (1994). *Futures* (special issue: Visions of Sustainability) *26*(2), 117–124.

Naugle, D. (2002). *Worldview: The history of a concept*. Eerdmans.

Oxford Reference. (2022). https://www.oxfordreference.com. Accessed August 17, 2022.

Piaget, J. (1971). *Structuralism*. Harper Colophon Books (First published in French 1968).
Rickman, H. P. (Ed.). (1961). *Meaning in history: W. Dilthey's thoughts on history and society*. Allen & Unwin.
Rouse, J. (1978). *Knowledge and power. Toward a political philosophy of science*. Cornell University Press.
Ruiz, J. R. (2009). Sociological discourse analysis: Method and logic. *Forum: Qualitative Research, 10*(2).
Sacco, R. (1991). Legal formants: A dynamic approach to comparative law. *The American Journal of Comparative Law, 39*(1), 1–34.
Sierra Club v Hickel 433 F.2d 24 (9th Cir. 1970).
Sierra Club v Morton 405 U.S. 727 (1972).
Stone, C. (2010). *Should trees have standing? Law, morality, and the environment* (3rd ed.). Oxford University Press.
Swimme, B. T., & Tucker, M. E. (2011). *Journey of the universe*. Yale University Press.
Tuoori, K. (2002). *Critical legal positivism*. Ashgate.
Van Hoecke, M. (2004). Deep level comparative law. In M. Van Hoecke, (Ed.), *Epistemology and methodology of comparative law*. Bloomsbury Academic.
Weedon, C. (1987). *Feminist practice and poststructuralist theory*. Blackwell.
Wilhelm, W. (1958). *Zur juristischen Methodenlehre im 19. Jahrhundert*. Vittorio Klostermann.

Chapter 2
Climate Disruptions and the Coming Dark Age

Soylent Green is People!
(Robert Thorn, Soylent Green, 1973)

In his opening remarks at the United Nations Climate Change Conference of the Parties (COP25), held in Madrid at the beginning of December 2019, UN Secretary General António Guterres stated in no uncertain terms that 'we [i.e. the entirety of humankind] are knowingly destroying the very support systems keeping us alive'. To validate such a radical assertion, Guterres cited the most recent scientific information on the state of the world's environment (the IPPC Reports), leading him to the realization that a possible path—certainly the darkest—ahead of humanity is one 'of surrender, [one] where we have sleepwalked past the point of no return, jeopardizing the health and safety of everyone on this planet ... If we don't urgently change our way of life' Guterres concluded, 'we jeopardize life itself'. The sense of urgency conveyed by the UN Secretary General's words is far from a single, isolated cry to attention. On the contrary, the idea of a veritable climate *apocalypse* pervades the current global discourse, within scientific and political circles as much as within popular culture.

This is likely to be unsurprising to the reader. After all, the European Union's Copernicus Climate Change Service (C3S), in its 2023 State of the Climate Report, confirmed that 2023 was the hottest year ever recorded—perhaps the hottest year in well over 100,000 years—after 12 months during which climate records were consistently broken and exceeded. On Friday 17 November 2023, the Earth's temperature had exceeded 2 °C above pre-industrial levels for the first time in recorded history. At the latest I could check before sending this book to printing, the C3S declared Monday 22 July 2024 to be the hottest day on record. Only three years prior, a combined report, from the US National Aeronautics and Space Administration (NASA) and the National Oceanic and Atmospheric Administration (NOAA) had indicated that 2016 and 2019 had been the two hottest years on record, with the decade 2010–2019 being the hottest decade in recorded human history: the data, confirmed by (among numerous others) the World Meteorological Organization revealed that six out of the ten hottest years on record were to be found in the last decade. At the same time, according to the Global Carbon Project's 18th annual report card, global emissions

A. Pelizzon, *Ecological Jurisprudence*, Contemporary Environmental Law and Policy,
https://doi.org/10.1007/978-981-96-0173-8_2

of fossil carbon dioxide (CO_2) hit the record of 36.8 billion tonnes in a single year in 2023. These numbers, which lead Guterres to state, in 2023, that '[t]he era of global warming has ended [and] the era of global boiling has arrived' (UN, 2023), are likely to have increased further since the time of writing this book.

These records are not isolated outliers, but rather form part of a consistent global trend toward a significantly warmer planet, one where global average levels of carbon dioxide (CO_2) in the atmosphere have now passed the previously unthinkable threshold of 400 ppm. Science tells us that the last time there was a comparable concentration of CO_2 in the atmosphere was between 3 and 5 million years ago, when the temperature was between 2 and 3 degree Celsius[1] warmer than now and sea levels were 10–20 metres higher than today. Most likely as a direct consequence of the changes mentioned above, extreme weather events, from hurricanes to droughts to floods to wildfires, are also regularly increasing, both in intensity and frequency. Hansen et al. noted how, 'under the present geopolitical approach to GHG emissions, global warming will exceed 1.5 °C in the 2020s and 2 °C before 2050'. The resulting '[i]mpacts on people and nature will accelerate as global warming increases hydrologic (weather) extremes. The enormity of consequences', they concluded 'demands a return to Holocene-level global temperature' (2023, 1). Similarly, the Intergovernmental Panel on Climate Change (IPCC) Sixth Assessment Report had already alerted us all that such events are merely the beginning of increasingly frequent weather-related devastations. Sadly, such events consistently lead to 'widespread adverse impacts on food and water security, human health and on economies and society and related losses and damages to nature and people … [with v]ulnerable communities who have historically contributed the least to current climate change [being] disproportionately affected' (2023, 42). Undoubtedly, the most recent scientific information on the state of the world's environment makes for a sobering reading.

It is difficult to engage with such statistics without reflecting upon Stone's question, as foreshadowed and discussed in the Introduction. What is it, we may once again ask, that makes such staggering data legally *invisible*, or at least legally *irrelevant*? Before we can explore an answer to this question more in depth, however, two precursory questions must be investigated. Firstly, why are these numbers important (and also, are they accurate—although the answer to this corollary question, I can already anticipate, is unquestioningly in the affirmative)? And secondly, is the best description of the current predicament one that defines it as a *crisis*, an *emergency*, or, indeed, an *apocalypse*?

[1] While the measurement of temperature in Kelvin degrees is related to the 'absolute 0' (the point at which all molecular activity ceases—with 0 K degree being equal to the absolute 0), the Celsius scale is generally more pragmatically useful because its main numbers are closer to the range that humans experience on a regular basis.

2.1 The Environmental Predicament

Ross Garnaut (2019), the economist appointed in 2007 by then Australian Prime Minister Kevin Rudd to examine the impact of climate change on the Australian economy, once noted that climate change science is 'genuinely complex'. This rather understated remark underscores the vast, complex and profoundly interdisciplinary field of study that engages with climate science, politics and economic policies. This complexity notwithstanding, it is useful to identify some of the key parameters that underpin the field, in anticipation of the ontological discussions that will take centre stage in following chapters.

2.1.1 *Weather, Climate Observations and Human Attribution*

While the *weather* is what happens in the atmosphere at any one particular time, the *climate*, instead, represents a long-term look at the weather over a period of time and is 'a synthesis of meteorological variables such as average monthly rainfall and maximum and minimum daily temperatures … [m]ore than averaging, such syntheses also take into account extremes and frequencies of occurrence' (Burroughs et al., 2008, 16). Unsurprisingly, due to the immediate relevance they have for any agricultural enterprise, climate observations are found among the oldest written documents of humankind (Edwards, 2011). Tablets attributed to the Assyrian king Ashurbanipal, dated around 650 BCE, exist alongside the architectural backdrop of megalithic structures such as Stonehenge in England or the Nazca lines in southern Peru, with such structures likely acting as both calendars and weather observatories. A Chinese calendar dividing the year in 24 distinct festivals, each with precisely associated weather, is dated around 300 BCE, thus being roughly contemporaneous with Aristotle's *Meteorologica* and Theophrastus's *Meteorological Phenomena*, and only shortly predating Pliny the Elder's *Historia Naturalis*. Greek geographers such as Erathostenes and Ptolemy had not only deduced the Earth's spherical shape, but also the connection between the climate and the inclination of the sun.

Since the offset of the scientific revolution, efforts were made to quantify and record the weather, with the first meteorological network formed in northern Italy in 1653 and weather reports published in the earliest scientific journals. Official climate recording, however, only began in the nineteenth century, at the Radcliffe Observatory in Oxford in 1814. Synoptic forecasting, which involves the 'rapid collection and analysis of weather observations from as wide an area as possible' (Burroughs et al., 2008, 72), was developed, shortly thereafter, by Heinrich Brandes at the University of Breslau in Poland, between 1816 and 1820. The International Meteorological Organization, created in 1873, morphed into the World Meteorological Organization (WMO) in 1950. As a United Nations agency, the WMO launched the World Weather Watch in 1963 and ran the Global Atmospheric Research Programme in 1978–1979.

Since the beginning of these official records, climate observations have been accompanied by the increasing awareness of human influence on the world's weather (Brolin, 2007). In 1822, Joseph Fourier's calculations, aimed at understanding all factors contributing to Earth's temperature, indicated that the planet ought to have been far cooler than in fact was and attributed this discrepancy to the role of the atmosphere as an absorbing layer with crucial influence on the Earth's surface temperature. Not long after, Swiss naturalist Louis Agassiz proposed that natural features, such as misplaced boulders and polished rocks, suggested previous extensive glaciations of most of Europe in the geological past, naming these periods 'ice ages'. The existence of ice ages suggested a climatic fluctuation in Earth's past of previously unexpected magnitude. In 1861, Irish physicist John Tyndall demonstrated that gases such as CO_2 and methane could heat the atmosphere by absorbing incoming infrared radiation. Swedish Nobel Prize recipient Svante Arrhenius calculated, at the end of the nineteenth century, the mathematical relationship between the quantity of CO_2 in the atmosphere and the Earth's temperature. While Arrhenius remarked that the human emission of carbon in the atmosphere would eventually lead to warming, he estimated, in line with the quantity of CO_2 emitted at the time, that the process would take place over thousands of years, ultimately resulting in beneficial effects for humanity. The metaphor of a 'greenhouse', introduced in 1901 by one of Arrhenius's countrymen and colleagues, meteorologist Nils Gustaf Ekholm, led to the adoption of the term 'greenhouse effect' in 1909 by English physicist John Henry Poynting to describe the warming effect of carbon on the Earth's atmosphere.

Although a warmer planet was a welcome prospect at the beginning of the twentieth century, as often remarked by those very scientists mentioned above, the potentially negative impact of rapid temperature changes soon started to become more apparent. At the same time that Serbian astronomer Milutin Milankovitch demonstrated that long-term climate changes are caused by the relative position of the Earth to the Sun—what are now known as the 'Milankovitch cycles' (Edwards, 2011)—British steam engineer Callendar (1938) meticulously collected temperature records from all over the world and calculated (without the aid of a computer) the temperature of the planet, producing the first evidence that the Earth's surface was indeed warming. In 1957, Roger Revelle and Hans Suess realized that the ocean surface had a limited ability to absorb CO_2, while geochemist Charles Keeling, working for the Scripps Institution of Oceanography at the Mauna Loa Observatory in Hawai'i, established a method to record CO_2 levels in the atmosphere, leading, a few years later, to the development of the 'Keeling Curve', a graph showing the exponential accumulation of CO_2 in the atmosphere based on measurements continuously taken at the Observatory from 1952 until present. In 1955, Norman Phillips developed the first computerized 'General Circulation Model' of the atmosphere at the Princeton Institute for Advanced Study, thus shuttering the complacency with which the amount of CO_2 in the atmosphere produced by human activities had been viewed until then and paving the way for the modern generation of theoretical meteorologists. In 1960, NASA launched the first meteorological satellite, TIROS-1, and US researchers pioneered, in the 1960s and 1970s, the analysis of climate change as a potential threat to humankind, particularly through the work conducted at the Geophysical

Fluid Dynamics Laboratory at Princeton (Brolin, 2007). In 1967, taking advantage of the technological advances offered by digital computing, Syukuro Manabe and Richard Wetherald released what is still considered today the most influential climate change article ever to be published, in which they provided the first detailed calculation of the greenhouse effect by incorporating both the Sun radiation and the greenhouse effect, as well as the conduction of heat from the Earth's surface to the atmosphere and the evaporation of surface water, in an algorithm defined as 'convective adjustment'. Their computer model, soon followed by countless others, presented an unavoidable correlation between an increase of CO_2 in the atmosphere and an increase in temperature, with a doubling of atmospheric CO_2. The scientific evidence for anthropogenic climate change was inexorably mounting, with over 95% of the climate change scientific literature since 1834 being published after 1951 and accelerating exponentially over recent decades (Le Treut et al., 2007).

The scientific implications of carbon-induced climate change began to enter the world of national politics in 1965, via a report by the US President's Science Advisory Committee to US President Lyndon Johnson titled *Restoring the Quality of Our Environment*. Climate sensitivity,[2] then, notably exited the halls of academia in 1980, when US President Jimmy Carter commissioned the *Global 2000 Report* and requested the US National Academy of Sciences 'to prepare a report about [among a number of forecasted risks] the potential climate threat posed by increasing atmospheric carbon dioxide' (Hansen, 2009, 40).[3] After publishing, with a number of colleagues, the first paper to explicitly suggest that coal and other fossil fuels ought to be left underground (Hansen et al., 1981), atmospheric physicist James Hansen testified, in 1988, to a US Senate committee, stating that '[h]uman made climate change is, indeed the greatest threat civilization faces' (2009, 70). The reason for such a harrowing assertion, Hansen noted twenty years later in his book *Storms of My Grandchildren*, was that '[g]lobal warming does increase the intensity of droughts and heat waves, and thus the area of forest fires'. Moreover, 'because a warmer atmosphere holds more water vapour, global warming must also increase the intensity of other extremes of the hydrogeological cycle—meaning heavier rains, including thunderstorms, tornadoes and tropical storms' (2009, xv). The scene for the identification of human-caused climate change[4] was thus set.

[2] How much climate responds to a specific 'forcing'—that is, how much temperature will change—is called 'climate sensitivity (Hansen 2009).

[3] The US National Academy of Sciences had been established by President Abraham Lincoln in 1863 'to advise the nation on important matters that required the best scientific expertise'.

[4] A more technical descriptor is that of 'climate forcings', the changes to Earth's radiative equilibrium—the difference between absorbed sunlight and energy radiated back into space—that cause temperatures to rise and fall over time.

2.1.2 Scientific Consensus and Discrediting Campaigns

In 1988, over 46 countries, together with the WMO and a number of other scientific institutions, gathered in Toronto for the first International Conference on the Changing Atmosphere, to 'address the effect of industrial fuel use on atmospheric change' (Shiva, 2002, 41). As a result of the conference, the WMO and the United Nations Environment Programme (UNEP) launched the Intergovernmental Panel on Climate Change (IPCC), a UN body tasked with providing 'regular assessments of the scientific basis of climate change, its impacts and future risks and options for adaptation and mitigation'. Comprised of over 195 UN and WMO member States, the IPCC harnesses contributions by scientists from all countries, who assess 'the thousands of scientific papers published each year to provide a comprehensive summary' of the current science of climate change. The review process, which has been described as 'one of the most rigorous in the history of science … [as i]t is hard to conceive of a more comprehensive and transparent process than that used by the IPCC' (Feldman, 2010),[5] leads to the release of comprehensive Assessment Reports (AR, which culminate in a Synthesis Report), as well as Special Reports and Methodology Reports. The fifth AR Synthesis Report, released in 2014, asserted in uncertain terms, in its Headline Statement, that '[h]uman influence on the climate is clear, and recent anthropogenic emissions of greenhouse gases are the highest in history'. Moreover, in case the connection had not been clear to any casual observer, '[r]ecent climate changes have had widespread impacts on human and natural systems'.

Anyone would be understandably justified, given such a global effort, in considering the scientific consensus settled, particularly since the IPCC statement has been regularly confirmed by a growing body of literature[6] as well as numerous scientific

---

[5] Each of the three IPCC Working Groups and the IPCC Task Force are comprised of experts in their fields nominated by governments and other relevant bodies with the view to produce geographical and gender balance. Then, groups of 10–20 experts prepare individual chapters covering their area of expertise, leading to a Zero Order Draft, which is then distributed to a small number of reviewers providing comments on the structure and proposed content. The feedback is then incorporated into a First Order Draft, which is distributed for expert review. At this stage, anyone can self-nominate as an 'expert' if they can justify their credentials and expertise. The comments are then individually addressed, and are incorporated into a Second Order Draft, which also includes a Summary for Policymakers that summarises the most important conclusions, and which is then distributed to the experts and to governmental panel members for another review and series of comments. These comments are then included in a Final Draft, which is then passed to government members for a final review. The Working Group Plenary finally discusses the revised draft, approving the Summary for Policymakers line-by-line (and, if necessary, word-by-word). The final Report is then released with as clear and formal a language as possible. It is indeed hard to deny that such a process constitutes the most nuanced peer review process any scientific document (or any document, for that matter) has ever had to undergo, and thus to disagree with Nicholls's assertion that '[it's impossible to] see how a fairer, more comprehensive, or more credible alternative could be designed'. The IPPC Reports inform the yearly international Conferences of the Parties (COP), where States that are parties to the United Nations Framework Convention on Climate Change (UNFCCC) gather to collectively address climate change and develop responses to the threat it causes (Nicholls 2013).

[6] In 2004, geologist and science historian Naomi Oreskes undertook a comprehensive review of over 928 papers from refereed scientific journals over the decade 1993–2203 and concluded that

institutions, such as, for example, the American Association for the Advancement of Science (AAAS) and the leaders of 18 highly respected scientific organizations' *Scientific Consensus Statement* (2007), which confirmed unequivocally that 'climate change caused by human activities is now underway, and it is a growing threat to society'. Equally convincing is NASA's identical position, as well as the position of well over 200 scientific organizations and tens of thousands of scientists, all asserting that climate change is not only occurring, but is also caused by human action. Since the release, in 2007, of a revised statement by the American Association of Petroleum Geologists (Brigham-Grette et al.), no scientific body denies the existence of human-induced climate change. However, while it appears that the scientific community has reached agreement on the nature, impact and implications of anthropogenic climate change for decades, the same level of understanding appears to have been missing from the broader discourse.

Scepticism and denial have abounded for decades both in media reports and among popular commentators. Approaches range from climate change and, or, global warming scepticism—the often-unsubstantiated doubt or dismissal of the current scientific consensus—and environmental scepticism—the belief that environmental claims are either false or largely exaggerated—through outright denial, to active anti-environmentalism—the direct opposition of any actions that plans to stop or mitigate the effects of climate change and, or, global warming. In some cases, the dissenting voices are represented by solitary authors, often without any relevant disciplinary expertise, such as Danish political scientist Bjørn Lomborg and British writer Matt Ridley. Lomborg asserted, in a popular book published in 1998, that climate change's 'total impact will not pose a devastating problem for our future' (4).[7] Ridley, in his book *The Rational Optimist* (2010), argues that increasing specialization and division of labour combined with the increased use of fossil fuels[8] place humanity on a trajectory of endless progress, one that will inevitably avoid any consequences of climate change, which he defines as mere exaggerations. While both authors display

scientific consensus on climate change was already undeniable. After dividing the papers into six categories (explicit endorsement of the consensus position, evaluation of impacts, mitigation proposals, methods, paleoclimate analysis, and rejection of the consensus position), she found that, even as far back as 2003, 75% of all papers explicitly or implicitly accepted the consensus view, while the remaining 25% dealt with methods or paleoclimate, without taking a particular position on anthropogenic climate change (Oreskes 2004).

[7] Since then, Lomborg has notably changed his position, more recently suggesting a far greater sense of urgency, although his current response to what he now explicitly acknowledges as a significant problem comes in the form of an over-reliance on yet hypothetical large-scale geo-engineering technology.

[8] Ridley's main argument suggests that fossil fuels are going to fuel growth endlessly because history has shown that, notwithstanding their predicted scarcity, they have not yet exhausted, whereas renewable resources upon which past civilisations were based did. Such an argument is, of course, a clear logical fallacy, since it assumes that the points being considered—those of resource depletion—are identical. On the contrary, the same argument about endless availability of existing resources could have been advanced by any society in the midst of a depleting resource base that had, nonetheless, *not yet* been depleted, and there is no guarantee that the *current* availability of fossil fuels is an inevitable guarantee of *future* availability.

a rather fideistic belief in linear progress and underplay the relevance of science (and it may be worth noting that neither is a disciplinary expert in the scientific fields they critique), their work has, nonetheless, often been included in a much more calculated campaign of misinformation and disinformation.

The nature, evolution and effects of this campaign, often explicitly aimed at sowing doubt about existing science in order to remain safe from litigation and regulation for as long as possible, have been documented by historians of science Naomi Oreskes and Erik Conway. In their book (and later documentary) *Merchants of Doubt* (2010), the authors reveal how corporate interests have attempted to manipulate scientific consensus on climate change for more than two decades, through a 'so-called balance campaign [that] involved aggressive dissemination and promotion to editors and publishers of "information" that supported the industry's position' (16), by manipulating and overinflating data to create an overall atmosphere of uncertainty. After all, the inherent falsifiability of the scientific discourse lends itself to the creation of a fabricated opposition between falsely divergent scientific positions, which did not—and do not—reflect the actual scientific consensus. Such an explicit strategy of misinformation has been made possible by the active participation in the process of many media outlets (Bowen, 2008),[9] as well as many individuals previously involved in parallel misinformation campaigns (such as that of the tobacco industry a few decades prior), who 'joined forces with think tanks and private corporations to challenge scientific evidence on a host of contemporary issues' (Oreskes & Conway, 2010, 6).

In the face of the overwhelming scientific consensus represented by the IPCC reports, as well as the many documents mentioned above, this campaign of misinformation appears, at present, to have lost some momentum. While it is still hard to avoid the ghost of Orwellian 'Newspeak' in the mediatic portrayal of a somewhat manufactured climate change 'debate', it appears that the staggering numbers, data, statistics and assertions with which this chapter began are, indeed, accurate when cast against the overwhelming consensus expressed by the scientific community, notwithstanding direct and strategic attempts to construct a falsely opposing narrative to the contrary. The first corollary question posited at the onset of this discussion—that is, are the number that introduced this chapter accurate—thus appears to have been answered overwhelmingly in the affirmative. However, while the importance of the data mentioned above will surely be inferred by readers, it is worth paying more attention to its implications, in order to answer that very first question in full: why are this numbers important?

---

[9] Examples abound. Jay Rosen, for example, describes very clearly some of the discrediting strategies adopted by News Corp, whereby there exist a direct attempt to discredit the sciences by both overreporting dissenting voices (which are, moreover, often manufactured) and by actively discrediting scientists (Rosen 2011). Similarly, in 2011, Australian scientist and former Chief Commissioner of the Australian Climate Commission Tim Flannery, reported how a local Australian radio, 2 GB, manufactured an interview to actively discredit his ethical credibility and thereby diminish any possible credibility in its scientific arguments, by casting them as politically motivated (Flannery 2011).

2.1.3 Climate Disruptions and Human Flourishing

While IPCC reports are virtually unanimous in confirming the primary influence of human activities on contemporary climate change, changes in the Earth's climate occur, naturally, in the absence of human intervention, and they display significant fluctuation throughout the history of the planet: the Precambrian period, for example, reached temperatures of 9 °C higher than today, while five known major glaciations have occurred over the entirety of Earth's climate history (Stager, 2011). Non-anthropogenic climate forcings are due both to astronomical forces—such as the amount of radiation coming from the Sun and cyclical variations of Earth's orbit (the above-mentioned Milankovitch cycles)—and geological forces—such as tectonic activity and continental shift, volcanic activity and the creation and gradual disappearance of mountain ranges. Such forces, however, operate along a timescale that American palaeontologist Jay Gould (1987) defines as 'deep time', and human activities (at least thus far) are unable to change either the overall amount of incoming solar radiation, or its geographical distribution.

However, much more rapid changes are due to the influence that ice sheets, cloud formations and forest coverage exert on the Earth's albedo (a measure of the reflection of solar radiation). More importantly, they are due to the quantity of so-called greenhouse gases present in the atmosphere, which trap the radiation emitted by the Earth back into the cosmos and thus tend to warm the atmosphere.[10] While astronomical and geological forces alone have been unable to explain the rapid changes in global surface temperature observed over the past two centuries, computer-based climate models have justified the observed warming by including greenhouse gas emissions in the calculations. Ongoing climate observations, combined with both computer-based climate models and paleoclimate studies, have thus unequivocally confirmed that recent changes in global surface temperature are both unusual and are caused by a sudden change of the concentration of greenhouse gases in the atmosphere.[11]

The amount of CO_2 in the atmosphere is, therefore, a good indicator of the current state of the Earth's climate. Hansen indicates that the ideal upward CO_2 limit is 350 parts per million (ppm—a figure revised down from an initial 450), a number later popularized by American environmentalist Bill McKibben's initiative *350.org*.

---

[10] While the most common gases comprising the atmosphere—oxygen and nitrogen (as well as argon)—do not have any major effect on temperature, a number of gases absorb and emit infrared radiation in the same wavelength as that of the Earth, and thus have a clear 'greenhouse' effect. The most notable of these gases are water vapor (H_2O), carbon dioxide (CO_2) and methane, with others (nitrous oxide, ozone, chlorofluorocarbons and hydrofluorocarbons) playing a minor role (Tudge 1991).

[11] The Earth's climate is thus influenced by three fundamental forcings: the amount of incoming solar radiation (which is determined by the Sun itself as well as the Earth's orbit and axial tilt), the Earth's albedo (determined by a host of factors, such as the position of the continents, the extent of ice sheets, the overall cloud cover and the amount of forest surface), and the amount of longwave radiation that is reflected back into space (which is affected by the amount of greenhouse gases in the atmosphere). Furthermore, there are many feedback mechanisms within the climate system that can amplify (positive feedback) or diminish (negative feedback) the effects of any climate forcing.

The most current observations (2024) from the Mauna Loa observatory in Hawaii, however, mark atmospheric CO_2 at over 426 ppm. While the increase is certainly troubling, the rate of the increase is even more staggering: CO_2 atmospheric concentration increased from 280 ppm in 1750 (where they had likely hovered since the end of the last ice age) to 387 ppm in 2009, with an increase of 100 ppm over 250 years, and a further increase of another 40 ppm over the last fifteen years alone. If any doubts were left as to the magnitude of anthropogenic influence on the quantity of greenhouse gases in the atmosphere, the forced changes in production, transportation and consumption patterns caused by the 2020 COVID-19 global pandemic showed an overall decrease of more than 17% of daily CO_2 emissions during the period of forced confinement in the first half of the year (LeQuéré et al., 2020). Current changes in global temperature are thus unequivocally caused by emissions of greenhouse gases in the atmosphere due to human activities, such as burning of fossil fuels and extensive deforestation. Curt Stager suggests that, depending on the amount of carbon ultimately released in the atmosphere, a return to its pre-industrial amounts may take between 400,000 and 500,000 years (2011, 42).[12]

It may be worth considering, at this point, what these numbers mean for humanity. Earth's surface temperature makes the existence of life possible. However, life in general and human life in particular—and even more so the lifestyle of the most widespread human cultures of today—depend on very specific 'goldilocks' conditions.[13] Too cold or too hot a surface temperature and major extinction events occur, and no life appears to exist under the hothouse conditions of Venus (above 700 °C) or in the gelid coldness of space. Life, as it is defined by science and as far as current science can determine, only exists within a relatively narrow range of habitable temperatures. This range is narrower for the existence of human life, and it is even more narrow for the continued existence of civilization in its current from. Anthropologist Stanley Ambrose (1998) suggests that the sudden cooling caused by the Mount Toba explosion of 70,000 years ago nearly drove human populations to extinction.[14] Moreover, archaeologist Brian Fagan (2008) documents how agricultural civilization

---

[12] As a comparison, the amount of CO_2 in the atmosphere was around 180 ppm during the last ice age, whereas concentrations similar to the present and forecasted ones existed during the Paleocene-Eocene thermal maximum (PETM), circa 55 million years ago, when at least 2000 Gtons of carbon (and possibly up to 5000 Gtons—the magnitude of the current worst-case emissions scenario) flooded the atmosphere (at present, human activities have vaporized about 300 Gtons of fossil carbon in the atmosphere). Carbon isotopes indicate a sudden acidification of the oceans during the PETM, with a gradual return to normal carbonate deposition over 50,000–200,000 years, a rate consistent with a dramatic CO_2 rise followed by a long and slow drawdown. Current IPCC scenarios suggest a potential anthropogenic release of between 1000 and 5000 Gtons of CO_2, with a recovery time that may vary between 1000 and 500,000 years, and the very real possibility of causing, as a result, a mass extinction.

[13] The term, which refers to the conditions that are 'just right' for the existence of a particular quality or entity, has been used extensively in the sciences. For example, Hawking (2010) uses it to refer to a planet's habitable zone around a star.

[14] Genetic data appears to confirm that human populations were reduced to between 1000 and 10,000 individuals in what seems to be the greatest 'bottleneck' event experienced by *homo sapiens* (Oppenheimer 2003).

is the result of a temporarily mild and stable interglacial climate, while Hansen (2009, 39) notes how the unusual stability of sea levels over the past 7000 years contributed to the development of complex agricultural societies, whereby food yields provided by stable seaside settlements could sustain large numbers of non-food producing social roles.[15] On the other hand, the medieval climatic optimum, which allowed the establishment of Viking settlements in Iceland and Greenland, was followed, from mid-fifteenth century until mid-nineteenth century, by a 'little ice age', a cooler period marked by harsh winters, cold and wet summers, and a surge in alpine glaciers, as well as significant social disruptions.[16]

Paleoclimatologist William Ruddiman (2003) argues that anthropogenic greenhouse gas emissions, beginning with the establishment of agriculture some thousands of years ago and accelerating exponentially over the last century or two, have disrupted the cycles that led to the ice ages that have marked the Quaternary period (the current geological period).[17] Hansen agrees, noting that 'human-made climate forcings added in just the past several decades already dwarf the natural forcings associated with the Little Ice Age' (2011, 9) and 'a single chlorofluorocarbon factory would be more than sufficient to overcome any natural tendency toward an ice age' (37). Without sufficient policies to mitigate climate change, current projections suggest an overall increase in global mean temperature by 2100 of 3.7–4.8 °C relative to pre-industrial levels.

Will Steffen et al. (2015) have called the present situation the Great Acceleration, 'the steep, exponential rise in global greenhouse gas emissions and indeed the overall human imprint on the Earth system which has distinguished the second half of the twentieth century and beyond' (Rogers, 2020a, 2020b, 95), also speculating as to whether such an acceleration will culminate in a Great Collapse. This rate of change, measured in decades (rather than tens of thousands of years) and occurring

[15] Warningly, Hansen further notes that 'Earth in recent millennia was warm enough to prevent an ice sheet from forming in Canada but cool enough to keep the Greenland and Antarctic ice sheets stable. Also, the tendency for continued ice sheet mass loss after the demise of the large Laurentide (North American) ice sheet was opposed by the slight global cooling trend since peak early Holocene temperatures (6000–10,000 years ago) … If ice sheets begin to disintegrate, there will not be a new stable sea level on any foreseeable time scale' (84–5).

[16] James Hansen also writes that 'in 1780, for example, soldiers in the American Revolution could drag cannons across the frozen New York harbor from Manhattan to Staten Island. The River Thames frequently froze over in the 1700s, and people held ice fairs on it. The twentieth century was too warm for such events to be possible' (2009, 8).

[17] The Quaternary period has been marked by glacial epochs, interspersed with interglacial ones. Curt Stager writes that '[g]eologists designated the last two epochs largely on the basis of their climatic conditions; the Pleistocene was dominated by numerous glacial coolings, and the Holocene was the latest of several shorter interglacial warm spells, the one during which the first complex human civilizations were born' (2011, 7). The peak of the last ice age occurred around 18,000 years ago, with an inter-glacial epoch known as the Holocene starting roughly 10–12,000 years ago. Although the epoch's trajectory was heading toward a global cooling of the planet, since 1900 there has been a clear and rapid increase in temperature concentrated in two periods (1920–1940 and then since the mid 1970s), coupled with a decline of 80% of formation of cold, deep ocean water in the Greenland sea, an increase in acidic rains, a rapid increase in ozone depletion and a significant drop in biodiversity.

at an unprecedented speed that no natural process can explain, led ecologist Eugene Stoermer to coin—and atmospheric chemist Paul Crutzen to popularize—the term *Anthropocene* to define a geological epoch in which humanity itself has become a veritable geological force (Trischler, 2016).[18]

Far from being cause for celebration, human activities run the significant risk of generating a cascade of positive feedback loops, causing the crossing of irreversible tipping points beyond which the stability of the Earth's temperature cannot be further controlled. One such tipping point is the sudden release of methane (a more potent greenhouse gas than CO_2) in the atmosphere, largely as a result of the release of large methane clathrate deposits currently locked in permafrost, oceanic muds and peatlands.[19] To an almost unanimous scientific community, the patterns are clear: a release of greenhouse gases in the atmosphere capable of increasing the temperature by about 6 °C (something which humans are capable of doing faster than the PETM event, over a mere few centuries) is likely to trigger a cascade effect of releasing methane locked in ice, increasing the temperature of another 6 °C and potentially leading to a mass extinction. This is known as the 'clathrate gun scenario', a hypothesis suggesting that runaway climate change may occur much faster and much more irrevocably than currently predicted (Hartmann, 2013, 30). Other tipping points, identified, for example, by Tim Flannery (2006), are the collapse of the Gulf Stream, capable of causing rapid and dramatic cooling in large parts of Europe and North America, and the destruction of the Amazon rainforests.

Most of these events are likely to occur both suddenly and rapidly, 'with speed and violence' in the words of climate journalist Fred Pearce (2007). James Hansen captured the predicament in dismal, albeit somewhat poetic, terms:

> Humanity treads today on a slippery slope. As we continue to pump greenhouse gases into the air, we move onto a steeper, even more slippery incline. We seem oblivious to the danger – unaware how close we may be to a situation in which a catastrophic slip becomes practically unavoidable, a slip where we suddenly lose all control and are pulled into a torrential stream that hurls us over a precipice to our demise (2009, 70)

Over the history of life on Earth, there have been five major extinctions (i.e. events marked by the reduction of over 65% of existing species, with a recovery rate measurable in millions of years), all due to significant and relatively sudden changes in the

---

[18] The term echoes the word 'Anthropozoic', introduced by geologist and priest Antonio Stoppani and then later adopted by George Perkins Marsh, where he defined humanity as a 'new telluric force that for its strength and universality does not pale in the face of the greatest forces of the globe' (Biello, 2016, 54–5) the concept of the 'Psychozoic' introduced by Joseph LeConte and then adopted by Polish futurist and sci-fi author Stanislaw Lem, and A P Pavlov's 'Anthropogene' as a replacement for the Quartenary (the fourth period of the Cenozoic, covering the last 2.5 million years).

[19] Following a pattern similar to that of the PETM, the rapid increase in global temperature can cause melting of permafrost and warming of the seas, which in turn would rapidly release vast quantities of methane in the atmosphere, which, in turn, would warm it even further (Hartmann, 2013). The consequences of temperatures similar to those presently forecasted caused a major extinction event, and the effects lingered for 170,000 years.

Earth's temperature (Sepkoski & Raup, 1982).[20] One of the risks of climate change, therefore, is what some scientists have termed the 'sixth extinction', a major decrease of life's overall biodiversity (Leakey & Levin, 1996). It is important to note that the collapse of biodiversity is likely to cause a cascading collapse of a multiplicity of lifeforms, including humans; as a result, the maintenance of biodiversity is necessary for humanity's own survival, and thus, the threat of a potential mass extinction is a threat to humanity itself.

2.1.4 Ecological Limits and the Metabolic Rift

Although climate change studies constitute the bulk of current scientific discourse surrounding the emergence of the Anthropocene, they are not its only focus. Since Aldo Leopold's holistic land ethics (1949) pointed to the role played by predators in maintaining the health of an entire ecosystem, and Rachel Carson's *Silent Spring* (1962) decried the detrimental environmental and health effects caused by the use of pesticides, many studies have emerged to indicate the existence of a number of *ecological limits*. The intertwined ideas of humanity's *ecological footprint* and of the Earth's overall *carrying capacity* were developed, in the early 2000s, by Mathias Wackernagel and colleagues,[21] who defined the ecological footprint as 'the land area that would be required to provide the resources (grain, feed, wood, fish and urban land) and absorb the emissions (carbon dioxide) of global society'. Moreover, 'when compared with the available land … human resource[22] use is currently some 20 per cent above the global carrying capacity' (Meadows et al., 2014, xiv). This means that humanity has *already* overshot its limits (the last time it was within its limits was in the 1980s), and, according to the Global Footprint Network, its present modes of consumption require more than 1.75 Earths to be sustained.

The fragility of the Earth's climate thus reveals a host of limits, many of which are not necessarily restricted to climate or temperature alone. The capacity of humanity to alter the planet beyond its pre-existing, 'natural', functioning, to 'end nature' in the words of McKibben (1989), extends to extensive deforestation, active reduction of biodiversity and emission of pollutants on land, in the atmosphere and in the ocean

[20] The theory was first proposed in 1982 by palaeontologists Jack Sepkoski and David Raup, who noted that the relatively rapid disappearance of most of world's species was connected to relatively rapid periods of climatic change, and each of these extinction events heralded the end of a major geological period.

[21] Wackernagel's term and mathematical approach was later adopted by the World Wide Fund for Nature (WWF) in its semi-annual *Living Planet Report*, which maps the ecological footprint of more than 150 nations.

[22] A *resource* 'is a concept related to the total quantity of a material in the crust of the earth; *reserve* is a concept related to the amount of the material that has been discovered or inferred to exist and that can be used, given reasonable assumptions about technology and price. Resources go inexorably down with use, but reserve figures may go up, as discovery proceeds, prices rise and technology improves' (Meadows, 2004, 89).

and water cycles, all contributing to overall biodiversity loss, soil nutrient depletion,[23] and depletion (through usage and pollution) of water sources. If climate change acts as the proverbial canary in the mine, these issues are all profoundly interconnected: anthropogenic climate change, ecological footprint and environmental limits and environmental degradation and biodiversity loss. In theory, addressing each one is a separate task, and it may indeed be theoretically possible to address and contain climate change without necessarily affecting our ecological footprint or solving the problem of environmental degradation. In reality, however, the three are interdependent: rapid climate change is likely to increase the rate of biodiversity loss, which, in turn, is likely to affect soil composition and agricultural yields, thus having a direct impact on overall ecological limits. Hence, the issue of human relationship with the environment, although multifaceted, can be treated as a single cohesive whole.

The concept of ecological limits engages the intertwined elements of population numbers, available resources and technological capacity. A growing population requires an increased number of resources, the rate of usage of which is determined by the technology available at any given time. There undoubtedly exists a direct relationship between increased abundance (due to the appearance of novel resources, novel technologies, or a combination of the two), increased population, increased consumption and pressure on existing resources. Thomas Malthus had already noted a direct relationship between food abundance and population growth, speculating, in 1798, that infinite population growth is impossible within a finite space; in fact, Malthus predicted that when abundance increases, populations increase accordingly, rather than stabilizing and increasing overall prosperity. Therefore, Malthus concluded that upon reaching a certain threshold, a population is destined to collapse, often as a result of widespread famine and disease. The argument was further articulated by American biologist Paul Ehrlich in 1968, who expanded the relationship between population and available food sources to include all other available resources that contribute to food production. While Ehrlich's prediction about a nearing population collapse proved incorrect, the argument of finite resources cast against infinite growth of resource consumption was then explored by the Club of Rome, a group comprised of heads of state, UN bureaucrats, politicians, government officials, diplomats, scientists, economists and business leaders, who commissioned the System Dynamics Group within the Sloan School of Management at the Massachusetts Institute of Technology to thoroughly examine the issue of overall limits to growth. The project, which used 'system dynamics theory and computer modelling to analyse the long-term causes and consequences of growth in the world's population and material economy' (Meadows, 2014, xiv), led to the publication, in 1972, of *The Limits to Growth.* The research used advanced computing capabilities to create distinct scenarios, via a computer model named 'World3', to map the interaction between population growth and resource consumption, concluding that 'global ecological constraints (related to resources use and emissions) would have significant influence on global developments in the twenty-first century' (Meadows, 2014).

[23] Worldwide, soil is becoming progressively thinner, although regenerative agriculture provides hope (*Biggest Little Farm,* Neon, 2019).

The idea that resources are ultimately scarce, which has been explored by a number of authors (Leggett, 2005) and is best exemplified by the 'peak oil theory' initiated by American geologist Marion King Hubbert (1959), has been often countered by the argument that technological advances can use existing resources more efficiently, and thus, effectively, endlessly defer any predicted scarcity. The argument, famously advanced by economist Julian Simon (1981),[24] has been applied to suggest that all above-mentioned predicaments will be resolved through a natural process whereby scarcity and price fluctuation will always inevitably engender sufficient incentives to develop either more efficient technologies or alternative resources. Such an optimistic statement however has been countered by significant scholarly research on the collapse of past societies (Diamond, 2005; Tainter, 1988). Moreover, historically, the increase of technological advancement has always been accompanied by an increase in resource usage, not the opposite. This counterintuitive fact, known as the *Jevons paradox*, was formulated in 1866 by British economist William Stanley Jevons. In his exploration of British reliance on coal, while at the same time observing the expansion of usage of coal with ever-growing technological prowess, Jevons noted that when the efficiency of resource consumption increases, the amount (or rate) of consumption of the same resource increases accordingly, due to a decrease in its costs and a related increase in demand: since decreased costs make the resource more easily available to more users, and since more uses can be developed for a more easily accessible resource, its consumption is inevitably bound to go up, if the regulation is entirely left to the market.[25]

The consensus about the fact that humanity appears to be living in a manner that transcends a host of ecological limits, in turn causing general ecosystem depletion and leading to potential ecosystemic collapse, seems uncontroversial. American sociologist John Bellamy Foster notes that Marx had already gestured toward a *metabolic rift*, a 'rift in the metabolic exchange between humanity and nature' (2010, 45). Indeed, Marx's insight seems to have been scientifically vindicated by the majority of contemporary authors. Michael Klare (2012) convincingly shows how energy is increasingly produced by accessing more unconventional sources—such as, for example, tar sands, deepwater drilling and shale oil—with the world's total fuel output supplied by these unconventional sources tripling over the course of the next few decades. At the same time, modern industrial agriculture is marvellously cost-effective, but also remarkably brittle (Shiva, 2000), while fisheries are experiencing rapid depletion (Edgar et al., 2024; Myers & Worms, 2003), and water—which is primarily used in food production, with a rate of usage 500 times greater than individual consumption (2000 L to 4 individual ones)—is becoming progressively scarcer (Brown, 2003). The world, according to futurist Chris Martenson, is currently experiencing a 'food bubble ... in the sense that the harvests are now running at a rate higher than the aquifers can sustain' (2011, 209). Klare notes that the belief in future

---

[24] Julian Simon became famous as a result of a scientific wager between himself and Paul Ehrlich, where they bet on the prediction of resource scarcity by the year 1990, a bet that Ehrlich lost.

[25] Famously, Jevons said that '[i]t is wholly a confusion of ideas to suppose that the economical use of fuel is equivalent to a diminished consumption. The very contrary is the truth'.

scarcity is not limited to scientific predictions: in February 2005, David O'Reilly, the chairman and CEO of Chevron, 'startled participants at an annual oil-industry conference in Houston by declaring that their business was at an epochal turning point … "Oil is no longer in plentiful supply. The time when we could count on cheap oil and even cheaper natural gas is clearly ending"' (2012, 210). Thomas Berry had already noted that 'petroleum will never again [within any meaningful span of human time] be made in any volume. The geobiological conditions by which petroleum came into being will never exist again' (1999, 156). According to the Global Footprint Network, the yearly *overshoot* day (the day in any given solar year when the amount of yearly resources has been depleted) has steadily been moving earlier in the year, from the 19th of December in 1987 until the 1st of August in 2024. The Stockholm Resilience Centre indicates that six of the nine *planetary boundaries*—the 'safe operating space for humanity with respect to the functioning of the Earth System' (Rockström et al., 2009)—have already been passed.[26] The UN-commissioned Millennium Ecosystem Assessment indicates that 16 of the 25 *ecosystem services*—the benefits humans obtain from ecosystems—are used unsustainably.

2.2 Problems, Predicaments, Solutions and Responses

In *The Long Descent* (2008), John Michael Greer distinguishes between *problems* and *predicaments*. The former are relatively temporary situations to which there can be *solutions*, which allow a return to a pre-existing status quo. The latter, instead, are situations in which no return to a pre-existing condition is possible, and thus they only elicit *outcomes* and *responses*, but no 'solutions'. Ageing is an apt example of a predicament, whereby no solution, however ingenious, will ever be able to restore youth. The current environmental reality within which humanity is located is thus best described as a *predicament*. As a result, it is also useful to note the tension between proposed *solutions* and *responses* to such a predicament, to determine the underlying construction of the conditions for which these solutions and responses are proposed.

2.2.1 Environmental Predicaments and Technological Solutions

As discussed extensively above, the current environmental predicament is marked by three separate and yet intertwined issues: the direct alteration and degradation of the environment, with human-induced events such as anthropogenic climate change and the release of high quantities of toxic pollutants; the existence of a human 'ecological footprint', with the related idea of ecological limits, resource scarcity and limits to

[26] In 2009, 'only' three of those limits had been passed, and 'only' four had been passed in 2015.

growth; and the high rate of biodiversity loss currently experienced by the world's biota, often as a direct consequence of the former. The first issue is routinely construed as a 'technical' issue, as a problem to which a wide range of solutions are possible. The second issue, on the other hand, represents a contested terrain in which political and economic arguments are hotly debated, often with a greater emphasis on teleological, rather than ontological, justifications. The third issue is more deeply inscribed within a discursive space in which ethics, science, and politics are inseparable. The climate change discourse, as well as the broader environmental one, is thus one where multiple disciplines interact and coalesce, often without a precise awareness of each other's overall paradigmatic positions and terminological directions. Similarly, the current predicament is marked by a number of possible outcomes, from the continuation of the status quo in relatively stable terms, through societal collapse (of different magnitudes), through a veritable social and, or, environmental catastrophe, to an extinction scenario (either of humanity or of life on Earth itself).

At one end of the spectrum are those who believe that the current technological trajectory of humanity will prevent any predicted collapse or catastrophe. The more extreme examples are post-scarcity economists often known as 'cornucopians' (Oreskes, 2004, 256) or 'prometheans' (Giddens, 1981), who argue that the rate of technological progress will always be able to outpace resource depletion, by substituting current sources of energy with alternative ones yet to be discovered or imagined. Post-scarcity economists, such as Julian Simon, regularly dismiss Malthusian arguments on the basis that their dire predictions have consistently proven to be incorrect. Indeed, the famous 'Ehrlich-Simon wager' seemed to vindicate, in the 1990s, the belief in the collective and compound power of humanity's imagination and technological innovation.[27] However, the argument is neither logically rigorous (as the inductive belief in past occurrences is not, in this case, an inevitable predictor of future certainty), nor is it 'borne out by the historical evidence' (Oreskes & Conway, 2010, 260–1). Numerous studies of past societal collapses demonstrate that the interplay between technology and resource availability has led to far more uncertain societal outcomes, with many examples of relatively rapid (albeit retrospectively identified) collapse throughout history (Diamond, 2005). This has led some authors to describe the absolute belief in technology as 'technofideism' (Oreskes & Conway, 2010, 261).

[27] In 1980 Paul Ehrlich predicted, in *The End of Affluence*, global decline and possible collapse by the end of the 1980s. Simon publicly challenged the prediction and a famous wager was made, using the prices of five selected commodities at the end of 1990 as the agreed marker. At the turn of the decade, the prices of all five commodities had consistently increased, thus leading to Simon's victory.

A more moderate form of optimism,[28] however, is shared more widely by scientists and environmental advocates alike. David Boyd, current United Nations Special Rapporteur on Human Rights and the Environment, writes that

> [t]ens of thousands of new parks and ecological reserves have been established across the globe …[d]eforestation is declining, and in many countries forests are rebounding from historical lows. Human ingenuity inadvertedly threatened the vital ozone layer, … but when scientists discovered and described the magnitude of the threat, people and politicians responded swiftly and effectively, phasing out the use of CFCs and other chemicals that caused the problem. Clean, renewable energy harnessing wind, water, and most importantly the sun is growing at an exponential rate. … We've made remarkable progress in reducing air and water pollution … leaded gasoline … has been passed out in almost every country. … Over the past 50 years, we've also witnessed an extraordinary transformation of legal systems and the rules that govern our societies … A new human right – to live in a healthy environment, has emerged and is now endorsed by 90 percent of the world's countries. (Boyd, 2015, xxiii–xxv)[29]

Technology also features prominently within the responses proposed by numerous scientists, both to avoid the bottlenecks of food and resource scarcity, as well as to reverse anthropogenic environmental damages (Charlton, 2011; Martenson, 2011). These 'technocures', as they were once defined by Isaac Asimov and Frederick Pohl, are predicated on the assumption that 'greener' technologies will be able to satisfy all food and energy requirements of an even larger human population while at the same time limiting, and possibly reversing, the environmental destructive effects of the current global society, including climate change. Already in 1976, Amory Lovins had advocated for a 'soft path', marked by a 'serious commitment to efficient use of energy, rapid development of renewable energy sources matched in scale and in energy quality to end-use needs, and special transitional fossil-fuel technologies'. Lovins's invitation now features prominently within the current environmental discourse, and even scientists known for sounding many of the initial alarm bells of anthropogenic climate change, such as Australian environmentalist Tim Flannery (2015), write of an 'atmosphere of hope' based on current technological solutions. Perhaps the most extensive overview of these solutions is offered by Project Drawdown, a comprehensive list of the most effective solutions to reverse global warming gathered by a thorough engagement with large numbers of scientists and policy makers (Hawken, 2017). Scientific and technological tools, such as renewable and more efficient energy technologies, biological tools (some of which, such as increased plant growth, happen automatically because of increased CO_2) such as reforestation and seaweed farming, and even geo-engineering, are all measured in terms of their costs, savings and capacity to actively reduce the amount of carbon present in the atmosphere. A combination of energy efficiency, carbon capture and storage (which,

[28] David Boyd notes that 'human beings are hard-wired for optimism—neuroscientists believe it was selected for success through the trials and tribulations of evolution … We need to be optimistic to have children, making tremendous investments of time, energy, and money in the belief that their lives will be as good as, or better than, our own … Thus, optimism is more than [a] sunny disposition that makes a person a pleasant company. Optimism is a powerful causal factor in shaping outcomes and futures' (Boyd, 2015, xvii-xviii).

[29] It is worth noting that, at present, over 15 per cent of the world's land is now protected.

although theoretically possible while continuing to use coal, appears to be far too costly), renewable energy and transitional solutions such as nuclear power, enables a narrative that promises a 'green' world devoid of the negative consequences of environmental degradation predicted by the authors mentioned above. It is useful to remind that, within such a technofideistic approach, the risk of 'greenwashing' is always present (Clegg, 2009).

A more extreme version of these 'technofixers'—as opposed to what Ernest Callenbach (1977) called the 'pastoralists'—are the advocates of extreme geo-engineering solutions, some of which appear to be more at home in sci-fi literature than in real proposals, such as the installation of sun-shields or mirrors into space to reduce the amount of solar radiation or injecting sun-blocking particles into the atmosphere. While there is no doubt that humanity has already been geo-engineering the planet for millennia (intensive agriculture being the most prominent example of this), many of these more extreme solutions are regarded with great suspicions by the scientific community, as their consequences are deemed far too unpredictable.

Overall, the current enthusiasm for technological solutions is best described as '*a race to adapt*: a contest to become among the first to adopt new materials, methods and devices that will free the world from its dependence on finite resource supplies' (Klare, 2012, 227–228). Although some of these solutions have, thus far, proven to be less successful (both technologically and economically) than originally predicted (Romm, 2005), the overwhelming scientific consensus nonetheless points to the need of some degree of technological adaptation in order to reverse, arrest, or at least mitigate the direst effects of the current environmental predicament. However, while alternative sources of energy are undoubtedly promising, they are still somewhat controversial in their ability to deliver the same energy output. The question thus remains as to whether energy availability sits not on a linear progress but rather on a bell curve, since the availability of abundant energy sources is far from being a certain historical *constant*. Moreover, while human ingenuity has always existed, to believe it operates on a linear trajectory, capable of always finding and, or, inventing new sources of abundant energy is a hopeful assumption rather than a historical observation. Therefore, while human ingenuity is certainly a historical fact, it is not *inevitably* associated with the current level of prosperity, which, on the other hand, is *uncontrovertibly* linked to the condensed energy sources humanity has been able to exploit over the past two centuries. Furthermore, technological solutions (as well as many economic and fiscal ones, such as carbon pricings) engage aptly with the first of the three intertwined issues that constitute the current environmental predicament—the direct anthropogenic alteration and degradation of the environment, including climate change—but remain inscribed in a current worldview in which political, ethical and ultimately ontological considerations are generally obscured. Even the political suggestions advocated by those who firmly believe in the power of technology to provide a solution are often purely technical and fail to engage with the broader social discourse.

2.2.2 *Planned Obsolescence and the Mirage of Endless Consumption*

What some of the most fervent advocates of the technological solutions seem to be ignoring is the profound interplay between worldviews that enable, and are in turn shaped by, particular economic and regulatory regimes. The symbolic power of the human collective, which, according to historian Yuval Noah Harari, is the defining feature of humanity as a species, is construed within particular worldviews, and the very idea of technology is, in itself, a social construct prone to multiple uses, as George Lueddeke (2020) suggests. The call for solutions focused on deeper societal changes is thus unsurprising. Prefigured by Charles Reich's *The Greening of America* (1970), a classic of the 1970s counterculture, this call has been fully realized in Lester Brown's *Plan B* (2003), Thomas Friedman's call for a 'Green New Deal' (2008), and Donella Meadows's (1999) twelve leverage points—those 'places within a complex system ... where a small shift in one thing can produce big changes in everything'.

Jim Bendell argues that 'climate change is not just a pollution problem, but an indicator of how our human psyche and culture became divorced from our natural habitat' (2019, 18). Such a disjuncture, according to Australian environmentalist Paul Gilding (2011), is located at the intersection of resource depletion and consumerist economics. The link between resource depletion, environmental degradation and planned consumerism[30] has been explored in details by authors such as Annie Leonard (2010) and Fred Pearce (2008). In *The Story of Stuff*, Leonard articulates an ecological critique of a contemporary capitalist system that is predicated on endless growth guaranteed by debt, which requires an ever-increased amount of consumption to be maintained. The intentional design of a consumer class, the author argues, can be traced back to the beginning of the twentieth century, in particular thanks to the workplace changes enacted by Henry Ford,[31] and even more clearly to the period after the end of World War II. Retailing analyst Victor Lebow is quoted to say that

> [o]ur enormously productive economy ... demands that we make consumption our way of life, that we convert the buying and use of goods into rituals, that we seek our spiritual satisfaction, our ego satisfaction, in consumption ... we need things consumed, burned up, replaced and discarded at an ever-accelerating rate. (Leonard, 2010, 205)

Lebow's enthusiastic language, which wouldn't be amiss among any of Aldous Huxley's prophetic *Brave New World* characters, highlights the emergence of what Leonard defines as planned and perceived obsolescence: that is, the planned and

[30] Annie Leonard distinguishes between consumption, consumerism and overconsumption: 'consumption means acquiring and using goods and services to meet one's needs, consumerism is the particular relationship to consumption in which we seek to meet our emotional and social needs through shopping, and we define and demonstrate our self-worth through the Stuff we own. And overconsumption is when we take far more resources than we need and that the planet can sustain' (2010, 185).

[31] In addition to the introduction of the modern assembly line, in 1914 Henry Ford doubled workers' salary while reducing the length of their workday, thus vastly increasing the customer base that could purchase the industrial goods being produced.

timed decay or devaluing of the vast majority of objects currently consumed. That a mass shift from a thriftier and often frugal lifestyle to one of often meaningless consumption has occurred is hardly disputable. The impact of this shift on the current environmental predicament becomes even more apparent in the detailed reconstruction, in both Lenoard's and Pearce's books, of the material origin, as well as the ecological cost from extraction to disposal, of a host of everyday objects. The authors clearly show how the entire planet is deeply enmeshed within a complex network of extraction, production, distribution, consumption and disposal, whereby the treatment of even minimal waste currently requires a large amount of energy. In fact, Pearce writes,

> the average household in Europe and North America has so many devices and such a variety of food and clothing that to produce the same lifestyle in Roman times would have required 6000 slaves – cooks, maids, minstrels, ice-house keepers, wood-cutters, nubile women with fans, and many more ... we now rely on machines and cheap energy to do the things that servants would once have done for an elite. (2008, 3)

The magnitude of this consumerist carousel creates a social, as well as an ecological, footprint, the tendrils of which are often too distant or too hidden to be readily apparent. When properly accounted for, the resources required to produce even a single average cotton T-shirt are astounding: '80 g of fertilizer, 3 g of active ingredient in pesticides, and between 2000 and 7000 L of water' (Pearce, 2008, 125). Equally staggering statistics appear in relation to food production and consumption, as documented by Michael Pollan in *The Omnivore's Dilemma* (2006). Unsurprisingly, then, a possible response to the consumerist mandate is the approach, taken by many, to reduce—or, at least, rationalize—individual consumptions.[32]

Apart from the statistical incongruences of a global consumerist lifestyle, Leonard notes, the 'real problem is the underlying set of values and assumptions and beliefs—the paradigm—on which these institutions [underpinning the current consumerist society] are based'. In fact, '[m]ost of the people running these hugely influential institutions actually believe that their prescriptions work and will ultimately improve life for everyone' (2010, 174–5). An almost fideistic belief in economic growth as the necessary panacea with which to treat any of the world's ailments dominates the cultural landscape. Any news outlets will generally include a daily section in which the health of an economy is measured by how much growth it displays. However, economic growth—often measured in monetary terms—is a rather crude measure of well-being. Futurist Chris Martenson notes that '[f]or a long time ... economic growth has been synonymous with increasing prosperity, [by which] I mean a higher standard of living defined by more of everything, easier access to all of the conveniences, luxuries, products and services that define modern life, and varied jobs and opportunities', and concludes by warning that 'unless we are careful, we might

---

[32] This, however, may be far more complex than it may appears: travel, for example, consistently depends on a host of variables (such as how full the train, plane, or overall mode of carriage is, which may make its choice more or less effective due to energy source and relative consumption), while, at times organic seasonal vegetables grown locally may require more intensive energy due to them being 'alien' to the area in which they are grown.

accidentally pursue growth when what we really are seeking is prosperity' (2011, 37). The decoupling of growth, prosperity and wealth,[33] *pace* Malthus,[34] shows that the Industrial Revolution brought an increase in both growth *and* prosperity as a direct consequence of, and depending from, the energy surplus provided by the rapid exploitation of fossil fuels. However, while, generally, in the presence of an energy surplus, the surplus can be directed toward an increase of either further growth or prosperity (rarely of both, as has been the case since the Industrial Revolution), when energy reserves drop or demand increases above its available offer, then collapse is ultimately inevitable (Tainter, 1988). Indeed, World Bank Chief Economist Carmen Reinhart and Harvard economist Kenneth Regoff (2011) looked at over 800 years of economic data, including debt and banking crises, inflation, currency crashes and debasements, and found that governments have found themselves, consistently throughout the ages, into too much debt, resulting in regular and repeated economic collapse, often only countered (or further deferred) by an ever-growing colonial expansionist agenda.[35] The idea of endless growth as a historical constant was thus put to rest, even within the discipline of economics, by this historical overview.

Nonetheless, in 1987, faced with the prospect of resource scarcity cast against economic growth, the World Commission on Environment and Development (often referred to as the 'Brundtland Commission' after its chairman) defined 'sustainable development' as 'development that meets the needs of the present without compromising the ability of future generations to meet their own needs'. This, in theory, entails a rather linear mathematical calculus: population numbers, needs, desires and related consumptions cast against available resources required to fulfil such needs and desires and technological capabilities to efficiently use such resources. When looking at resource availability alone, human populations live on a finite planet, and thus, consequently, the planet's wealth (or its 'resources', to continue with the usage of the economic descriptor) is inherently finite. Therefore, although limits may not be immediately visible, it is a logical necessity to assume that they do exist. Indeed, some resources can be replenished at a rate higher than their consumption, but that's not always the case. Moreover, it is certainly theoretically possible that the rate of technological development will outpace the depletion of resources, but, as discussed

---

[33] Primary wealth is comprised of the natural resource base. Secondary wealth is what we make of primary wealth (and what Adam Smith focused on, as the first was relatively abundant in his time). Tertiary wealth is comprised of all paper abstractions layered upon the first two sources (as such, it is only relative wealth, and only recently decoupled from the first two). Wealth, for most people today, is not related to the primary (or even secondary) source of wealth, but rather it is only a *claim* to wealth. Moreover, money can be a *store* for wealth, a convenient way to measure and transfer ownership of true wealth from one entity to another, but it is equally inherently just a *claim* to wealth. It has value only because we collectively attribute relative value to it. Original wealth was the soil, from which the expressions 'dirt poor' and 'dirt(y) rich' are derived.

[34] Malthus had introduced the idea that, in a place with finite resources, growth and prosperity are, in fact, in conflict with each other.

[35] The authors demonstrate that tertiary economy leads to 'bubbles' when asset prices rise above what income can sustain (for example, house mortgages costing more than income). An example is the Tulip bubble of the 1630 s, which spectacularly crashed in a single day in 1637.

above, that is more likely a statement of faith, rather than an inevitable historical fact: there is, indeed, no historical *guarantee* that this will always be the case.

Since nothing that consumes finite resources to fuel its growth can grow infinitely, since there is no historical guarantee that either the available resources or the modes of production will ensure an endless availability of resources, and since exponential consumption occurs where growth is exponential,[36] it is unsurprising that an alternative economic model has emerged over the past few decades. Prefigured by John Stuart Mill's quest for an economically stationary state (1848), the movement was first introduced by Romanian economist Nicholas Georgescu-Roegen (1971), who argued that the law of entropy applies to the economic process as to all physical process, with the result that natural resources irreversibly degrade upon entering any economic process. German economist Ernst Schumacher (1973) further argued that natural resources, particularly non-renewable ones, are incorrectly treated as expendable income, rather than being more correctly treated as capital. Herman Daly, one of Georgescu-Roegen's pupils, in *Steady-State Economics* (1991) persuasively paved the way for a conception of human economy deeply embedded within, and dependent from, a finite environment comprised of limited resources and fragile ecosystems. Environmental *externalities*, *post-growth* economic models, already encountered concepts such as *carrying capacity* and *ecological footprint*, have all since become part of an emerging branch of economics known as *ecological economics*, and the relationship between human economic systems and their ecological impact has become ever-more apparent. Counter to an economic narrative that engenders individual selfishness, rational self-utility maximization and ontological separateness, a new wave of economists is currently challenging previously accepted economic dogma. Mariana Mazzucato (2018), for example, questions what constitutes 'value', suggesting that its definition is a result of cultural pressure rather than a reflection of any inherent and objective quality, and that, moreover, modern capitalism rewards actors who *extract* value from the overall economy, rather than *adding* to it. Perez and Murray Leach (2018) argue for the urgent need for a dematerialization of growth, while Kate Raworth (2017) further challenges the global economic obsession with growth and what she argues is now the outdated concept of a Gross Domestic Product (GDP). Following along the tradition initiated by Polish economic historian Karl Polanyi (1944), and his articulation of the emergence of a market-based (and dominated) economy as historically contingent, this new wave of economic scholars points toward an interrogation and eventual redefinition of the very idea of prosperity, one that is aware of the complex relationships between economic growth, environmental pressures and social recession, and that is directed toward a form of more appropriate 'ecological macro-economics' (Jackson, 2009, 209).[37]

---

[36] And risk is, furthermore, exponential.

[37] The 'degrowth' movement, prefigured by the work of authors such as Georgescu-Roegen (1971), Goldsmith and Allen (1972), Schumacher (1973) and Illich (1973), is a good example of these responses, aptly captured in Ernest Callenbach's classic *Ecotopia* (1977) or John Michael Greer's hypothetical description of an inevitable transition to an 'ecotechnic' future. In these instances, the partial or progressive collapse of the current political-economical system is seen as leading toward a more desirable post-consumerist society.

Finally, there exists an undeniable connection between prosperity, poverty and environmental concerns, since patterns of consumption and environmental exploitation are not equally distributed around the globe. As a result, any attempt to achieve a significant reduction in consumptions must be balanced against third world demands for technological progress to achieve the same level of prosperity of the world's richer countries. 'Two global challenges—poverty and the environment—are the twin imperatives of the twenty-first century', Andrew Charlton points out. 'One ravages billions of people alive today; the other threatens billions yet unborn' (2011, 7). Although environmental degradation and poverty are two interrelated problems, the relative importance placed upon each varies:

> [t]hose who are focused mainly on the environmental challenge are usually based in rich countries. In these countries the "green" agenda is to reduce energy consumption, raise the price of fossil fuels, reduce the impact of mining, scale back our land use, practice sustainability, cover fields with wind and solar power generators, return to organic farming and preserve ancient forests. But green groups miss the point that many of these solutions don't work for the poor. The developing countries want more economic growth, more food for their hungry people, more light in their dark villages and more vehicles shipping goods from farms to markets. (Charlton, 2011, 7)

And, as Nicholas Stern pointed out,

> [i]f we try to manage climate change by putting obstacles or appearing to be putting obstacles in the way of rising standard[s] of living in the developing world … we will not succeed in putting together the coalition which is vital on a global scale to manage climate change. If of course on the other hand we fail to manage climate change, then the environment will become so hostile over the course of this century and into the next that we will … set back the whole story of development (Charlton, 2011, 65)

The awareness of the intertwined nature of environmental and social issues, of poverty and environmental degradation, of environmental sustainability and social justice, is not lost. Indeed, Oreskes and Conway (2010) note that casting action against climate change as alternative to action against world poverty is a false dichotomy, since the lack of response to either issue is likely to amplify the effects of the other, and among the most important 'technical' solutions proposed by Project Drawdown are, indeed, the provision of universal health and education, as well as the pursuit of women's rights. Women's education and family planning are ranked, respectively, 6th and 7th in the project's list as two of the most efficient and effective ways to reduce carbon emissions by 2050.

To conclude, economic responses propose to resolve the first of the three key environmental issues presented above—anthropogenic climate change and the release of high quantities of toxic pollutants—by addressing the second—the existence of ecological limits, resource scarcity and ultimate limits to growth. In this sense, they appear to be more nuanced propositions than merely 'technical' ones, capable of addressing climate change as a political narrative inasmuch as a scientific model. However, economic responses are more teleological than ontological, and the world they envision and observe still operates within a very familiar ontological landscape. But, as Gosh writes, '[t]he climate crisis is also a crisis of culture, and thus of the imagination' (2016, 9).

2.2.3 Collapse: The Coming Dark Age

If technological and economic responses to the current predicament constitute one end of the spectrum, at the other end of the spectrum are those who argue that the runaway effects of climate change, with the rapid release of methane in the atmosphere, could potentially cause a human-induced mass 'sixth extinction'. Biologist E O Wilson (2006), indeed, describes the twenty-first century as a 'bottleneck' for most species. This hypothesis, the most extreme (and, hopefully, the most unlikely) is closely followed by the predicted risk of the extinction of human life, if not necessarily of *all* life on Earth. Greer (2008), however, counterargues that, given the extent to which humans have colonized the entirety of the globe, combined with the ongoing, albeit progressively dwindling, availability of technological artefacts, it is unlikely that humanity will completely disappear.

Barring such dire predictions, are those who believe in the inevitability of near- or medium-term social collapse due to climate change and, or, other environmental causes. Aside from quaint 'doomsday preppers', a somewhat typical contemporary version of nineteenth century Millerites fully enmeshed within an apocalyptic discourse and whose very *raison d'être* is predicated on the occurrence of the predicted collapse, the more serious permutation of this group includes numerous scientists and military experts alike. Naturally, the prediction of future scenarios and relative consequences constitutes an inherently speculative exercise. Nonetheless, many successful attempts have been made, and a trend has emerged over time.

The study of historical decline, collapse and regeneration has interested scholars for centuries, since Ibn Khaldun's fourteenth century work the *Muqaddimah* (Schwartz, 2006), and thus, it is no surprise that the interrelated issues of anthropogenic climate change, population numbers, resource availability, soil depletion and overall soil, atmosphere and water pollution have led various authors to imagine a number of potential future scenarios over the short, medium and long term. The study of societal collapse as a result of the connection between environmental conditions, available resources and social structures featured prominently in the work of American anthropologist Marvin Harris, founder of the anthropological theory known as cultural materialism. Harris noted the historical relationship between social symbols—particularly, although not exclusively, religious ones—and changing environmental conditions, suggesting that there exists a 'population size at which nutritional deficiencies and degradation begin to occur … the upper limit of what ecologists call the habitat "carrying capacity"' (1984, 66). Harris further proposed that such ecological pressure historically gave rise to many religiously sanctioned food practices as adaptive socio-ecological strategies inscribed within powerful symbolic social motivators.

The full study of societal collapse was the focus of American anthropologist Tainter's (1988) *The Collapse of Complex Societies*. In this seminal text, Tainter defined complex societies as 'problem-solving organizations, in which more parts, different kinds of parts, more social differentiation, more inequality, and more kinds of centralization and control emerge as circumstances require' (37). Furthermore, *complexity*

> is generally understood to refer to such things as the size of a society, the number and distinctiveness of its parts, the variety of specialized roles that it incorporates, the number of distinct social personalities present, and the variety of mechanisms for organizing these into a coherent, functioning whole. Augmenting any of these dimensions increases the complexity of a society (23).

It is important to note that, for Tainter, the identification of social complexity is a mathematical measure, not a normative statement: complex societies are not necessarily more 'advanced' or in any way 'superior' to less complex ones. Indeed, '[c]omplex societies … are not a discrete stage in cultural evolution. Each society represents a point along a continuum from least to most complex' (193).

Tainter argues that the maintenance of any socio-political system is dependent not only on generic energy flow, but also, and more importantly, on a sufficient amount of energy according to the level of complexity of the system itself, with more complex systems being significantly more energy demanding. Ultimately, '[c]ontinued investment in socio-political complexity reaches a point where the benefits for such investment begin to decline, at first gradually, then with accelerating force' (92). The diminishing returns of resource investments in the increase and, or, maintenance of social complexity have often, throughout history, reached a point of *collapse*: that is, 'a sudden, pronounced loss of an established level of socio-political complexity' (193). Tainter further notes that

> [a] complex society that has collapsed is suddenly smaller, simpler, less stratified, and less socially differentiated. Specialisation decreases and there is less centralized control. The flow of information drops, people trade and interact less, and there is overall lower coordination among individuals and groups. Economic activity drops to a commensurate level, while the arts and literature experience such a quantitative decline that a dark age often ensues. Population levels tend to drop, and for those who are left the known world shrinks. (193)

While complex societies 'routinely withstand catastrophes without collapsing' (50), when marginal returns on investments on complexity are reached, and sudden additional demands—such as unexpected environmental ones—are placed on available resources, collapse becomes a very present possibility, and has, indeed, been an historical reality in a number of cases, such as, among others, Rapa Nui, the Western Roman Empire and the Wari empire in the Andes (Schwartz & Nichols, 2006).

Many of these examples have been further analysed by Jared Diamond, whose book *Collapse* (2005) focused more extensively on the relationship between environmental pressures and societal responses, symbolically adopting the case of Rapa Nui as emblematic of a maladaptive societal strategy in the face of increasingly more stringent ecological limits, which led to relatively sudden (in this case deforestation-triggered) collapse.[38] Additionally, Diamond highlights even further the high cost in human suffering borne by collapse events, one that Tainter had already suggested as

[38] Diamond also presents more positive examples of successful social adaptive strategies, such as, for example, Tikopia and Tokugawan Japan.

leading to a popular image of a 'Hobbesian war-of-all-against-all ... [where] the weak are victimized, robbed and killed [and b]ands of pitiful, maimed survivors scavenge among the ruins of grandeur' (1988, 19). While many of these images are often more effective entertainment tropes than accurate historical depictions, it is nonetheless certain that historically observed conditions appeared far different between pre- and post-collapse societies. Renowned British archaeologist Stanley Casson, for example noted that, while from 'A.D 100–400 all Britain except in the north was as pleasant and peaceful a countryside as it is to-day ... by 500 A.D it had all vanished and the country had reverted to a condition which it had, perhaps, never seen before'. Moreover, '[t]here was no longer a trace of public safety, no houses of size, dwindling townships and the villas and most of the Roman cities burnt, abandoned, looted and left the habitation of ghosts' (1937, 164).

However, most of the above scholars also note that collapse is only perceived and, or, construed as such retrospectively. That is, radical social changes, even dramatic ones, are rarely (if ever) construed as a cultural caesura. Even when they explicitly are—such as, for example, after the French revolution of the eighteenth century, and the Russian and Chinese revolutions of the twentieth century—the rupture with the past is far less complete than its symbolical representation may suggest. Shmuel Eisenstadt asserts that '[a]ncient states and civilizations do not collapse at all, if by *collapse* is meant the complete end of those political systems and their accompanying civilizational frameworks' (1988, 242) As a result, collapse is often the result of a series of cascading (and, at times, violent) events, the sum of which leads to radically changed social landscapes, often in the form of less complex social realities that faintly remember their more complex, often mythicized past.

Whether this may be once again the case in the face of possibly unprecedented climatic and environmental changes is, certainly, purely speculative. Nonetheless, some authors have engaged with such a possibility and have attempted to depict the trajectory of environmentally induced social collapse by extrapolating from all available past examples. A common hypothesis predicts the relatively sudden collapse of contemporary human societies as a result of the many issues discussed above, with a steep population decline and a significant decrease in overall prosperity, what Italian mathematician Roberto Vacca defined, in 1973, a 'coming dark age'. The World3 computer programme used by the Club of Rome to determine the limits to growth looked at four ways in which a growing society can approach carrying capacity,[39] and indicated that, given the current trajectory, collapse (as defined above) is the most likely outcome given the current trajectory. John Michael Greer, who had previously focused on the relationship among 'resources, capital, waste and production [to]

[39] Such are, the following: firstly, a society can grow without interruption as long as limits are distant or the limits grow faster than combined growth of population and consumption; secondly, a society levels off smoothly below the carrying capacity (this is known as a *sigmoid* behaviour); thirdly, a society goes into overshoot without massive and, or, permanent damage: the ecological footprint oscillates around the limits before levelling off; fourthly, a society overshoots its ecological limits with severe and permanent damage to the resources base, with the result that population and, or, at least the economy is forced to decline rapidly in order to achieve a new balance with a recently reduced carrying capacity (what is commonly known as collapse).

form the basis for an ecological model of collapse in which production fails to meet maintenance requirements of existing capital' (2005, 1), in *The Ecotechnic Future* (2005), argues that the energy-yield of fossil fuels is unprecedented in history, and, most importantly, that there is no necessary guarantee that alternative sources of energy will be found before existing resources will be depleted. The result must be, in the eyes of the author, a slow transition through a scarcity world, and a later salvage society, which will inevitably lead to what he calls an 'ecotechnic future'. Importantly, to undertake such a transition consciously, Greer argues, would reduce the amount of inevitable suffering that inevitable collapse will likely cause.[40]

In a self-published and highly downloaded 2018 paper, sustainability expert Jem Bendell suggests that societal collapse due to a delayed response to climate change is not only inevitable but will also happen within a relatively rapid and short timeframe. The paper argues that current scientific information indicates a path of 'inevitable collapse, probable catastrophe and possible extinction', pointing to a 'climate tragedy', a reality that has already long passed the possibility of prevention, mitigation or reduction, noting that since '[d]isruptive impacts from climate change are now inevitable', the only possible solution is acceptance and adaptation to a radically distinct state of the world. The author ultimately suggests that current political and technological responses are too slow and are occurring within too small a window of opportunity, which is either closing faster than we can adapt or has, in fact, already closed. This leads to the 'end of the idea that we can either solve or cope with climate change', and to the consequent development of a 'deep adaptation agenda', a research trajectory focused on the fundamental acceptance of the inevitable and rapid demise of the existing status quo. The Extinction Rebellion movement, an 'international movement that uses non-violent civil disobedience in an attempt to halt mass extinction and minimize the risk of social collapse', clearly operates within the parameters of a deep adaptation paradigm.

All studies of collapse of past societies suggest that what is at a later time defined as 'collapse' is far more gradual than cultural narratives depict, but is also nonetheless accompanied by many clearly identifiable instances of social upheaval, often marked by profound suffering. While the possibility of environmentally induced global social collapse is purely speculative, defence expert Michael Klare notes that, 'of course, the desire to control natural resources has fuelled international strife throughout human history. Ancient dynasties fought wars to secure more agricultural territory', and, he continues, 'European colonial empires battled one another over their resource-rich outposts overseas. To a considerable extent, therefore, the race for what's left can be interpreted as just a continuation of this age-old struggle' (2012, 218). Therefore, while the application of collapse studies to the future of humanity in the face of unequivocal environmental degradation and related pressure is a long-term speculative prediction, specific instances of environmentally induced social disruption are far more measurable.

---

[40] This echoes Isaac Asimov's idea of a fictional 'Foundation' to counter the collapse of the galactic civilization he envisioned in his novels.

Many governmental and military reports have been produced, dealing with the possible societal implications of relatively rapid environmental degradation, as explored by Canadian journalist Gwynne Dyer (2010). Most of these reports are produced by both military agencies and independent analysts and deal with different climate change-induced scenarios in an '[a]ttempt to describe the political, demographic and strategic impacts of the changes' they foresee (3). Among these reports are the 2006 *DCDC Global Strategic Programme 2007–2036*, produced by the Development, Concepts and Doctrine Centre within the British Ministry of Defence, the 2007 *National Security and the Threat of Climate Change* report produced by the CNA Corporation, and the 2007 *The Age of Consequences: The Foreign Policy and National Security Implications of Global Climate Change*, co-published by the Center for Strategic and International Studies (CSIS) and the Center for a New American Security (CNAS). The language adopted in such reports is certainly alarming: '[i]f the environment deteriorates beyond some critical point, natural systems that are adapted to it will break down. This applies also to social organization. Beyond a certain level climate change becomes a profound challenge to the foundation of the global industrial civilization that is the mark of our species' (Dyer, 2010, 16–7). These reports present scenarios that range from 'moderate' (an increase of 1.3 °C by the end of the century) to 'severe' (an increase, by 2040, of 2.6 °C above 1990 levels, with higher temperatures over land and much higher temperatures in high latitudes). Even with moderate scenarios, all reports suggest that agriculture becomes essentially unviable in large parts of the world, leading to massive waves of climate refugees. Such mass migrations are also connected to rise of authoritarian, militarized regimes, as well as internal and international wars. Ultimately, all reports conclude that '[r]unaway climate change threatens to sweep away our stable, familiar world and replace it with a terrifying chaos of famine, mass migration and war that could cut the population to a fraction of its present numbers by the end of this century' (Dyer, 2010, 42). For this reason, the US Pentagon calls climate change a 'threat multiplier' (Parenti, 2011, 9).

Scholars have already begun to point out that recent conflicts, such as, for example, the devastating and recent Syrian civil war of ten years past, have been directly caused by rapidly deteriorating weather conditions and water scarcity (Gleick, 2014). In fact, there are '46 countries—home to 2.7 billion people—in which the effects of climate change interacting with economic, social and political problems will create a high risk of violent conflict' (Smith & Vivekananda, 2008, 7). Furthermore, Indian environmentalist Vandana Shiva notes that 'ethnic and water wars are intimately intertwined' (2002, 72) since droughts—often the cause of many conflicts to control the remaining water sources—are exacerbated by climate change (a phenomenon known as a 'meteorological drought') and soil moisture reduction.[41] Further revealing the connection between the current environmental predicament and international social unrest, American investigative journalist Christian Parenti explores the interplay between environmental degradation, global economic models and colonial forces,

[41] A protean example is represented by the late 1890s Los Angeles, when all local water supplies had been exhausted, and city officials were secretly purchasing land and water rights in the neighbourhood.

which lead to a 'belt of economically and politically battered post-colonial states girding the planet's mid-latitudes [where] climate change is beginning to hit hard' (2011, 9). The author shows that it is impossible to separate the possible devastating impacts of rapid environmental degradation from the colonial process of the past few centuries. Ross Garnaut further asserts that '[m]any of the people who are harmed will be in other countries, and in the future, and in any case we cannot be sure who will be affected by our actions' (2019, 22–3), and ecologists Barnosky and Hadly (2015) provide a comprehensive breakdown of the specific threats that environmental degradation poses in terms of individual issues, such as food and, or, water scarcity, disease, armed conflicts and authoritarian regimes.

A final hypothesis about the future impact of climate change and environmental degradation does not predict a particularly increased risk of social disruption when cast against present and historical trends, but considers the economic implications of climate change and overall environmental disruption. The most notable of such studies is, undoubtedly, the British-commissioned *Stern Review on the Economics of Climate Change* (Stern, 2007), which indicates that inaction on climate change mitigation and adaptation is likely to cause a decrease between 5 and 20% of global Gross Domestic Product (GDP) in perpetuity, whereas rapid action could contain such decrease within 1%. A number of similar reports have focused on processes of climate change adaptation, arguing that, rather than continuing with business-as-usual practices, adaptation is likely to be more cost-effective over time, with increased economic savings the earlier the adaptation occurs. Ross Garnaut's analysis, following the one adopted by American economist William Nordhaus,[42] 'favours stronger mitigation objectives largely for their value as insurance against low-probability but catastrophic outcomes' (Garnaut, 2019, 48). As Garnaut notes, 'even the most committed devotees of unrestrained market exchange—[such as] Friedrich Hayek and Milton Friedman—for example, [see] taxing an environmental externality as dealing with a compelling problem in a way that minimizes distortion of the market economy' (49).[43] Stern had initially opted for 3 °C as the optimal temperature limit, whereas Nordhaus had opted for a higher target since 'costs exceeded benefits at 3 °C' (Garnaut, 2019, 35), the target is far lower today as a result of prior inaction. In fact, Garnaut asserts, the framework initially used by his research in 2008, which then allowed for a 2 °C target, today would not justify a 1.5 °C objective. According to many economists, the time to reduce the economic impact of environmental degradation is thus shortening, while the risk of costly consequences for inaction, both economically and ethically, is proportionally increasing. It may be almost redundant to point out that the economic impacts of climate change and rapid environmental degradation are

[42] Nordhaus demonstrates, in relation to climate change mitigation strategies, that pricing carbon is a more efficient form of taxation, whereas regulatory and fiscal intervention sector by sector would be more costly.

[43] Since the most important goal is the global phase out of carbon dioxide emissions, a rising price of carbon must be applied at the source, such that it affects all activities that use fossil fuel, both directly and indirectly. It's important to note that coal *emissions* must be stopped, not necessarily coal *usage*. However, carbon sequestration makes coal usage far more costly and less efficient.

unevenly distributed, affecting poorer areas of the planet far more greatly (Hallegatte et al., 2015). Garnaut finally warns that '[t]here is a chasm between a world that quickly breaks the link between modern economic growth and carbon emissions, and a world that fails to do so. The side of the chasm that we are now on is a dangerous place. It would be reckless beyond the normal human irrationality for us to stay where we are' (2019, 165).

2.3 Environmental Apocalypse and the State of Exception

The scientific literature almost unanimously presents an incontrovertible picture, one that is dominated by anthropogenic climate change, human-induced pollution of both the atmosphere and the entire water cycle, rapid biodiversity loss, ocean acidification and soil nutrient depletion. When combined with rapid and exponential population growth, increased consumption patterns and the real possibility of resource scarcity, many of the medium and long-term scenarios developed by scientist and military experts alike are, indeed, disturbingly possible, leading Indian writer Amitav Gosh (2016) to state that 'this era, which so congratulates itself on its self-awareness, will come to be known as the time of the Great Derangement'. However, is the current predicament best described, as it often commonly is, as a *crisis*, an *emergency,* or, indeed, an *apocalypse*?

2.3.1 *Toward an Ecological* Götterdämmerung*?*

James Lovelock writes that 'we may be unable to prevent a global decline into a chaotic world ruled by brutal warlords on a devastated Earth' (2007, 198), while, even more grimly, Thom Hartmann chooses the title *Last Hours of Humanity* (2013) for a book describing the details of the previous five 'great extinctions' and their clear connection to a significantly warmer planet. In January 2020, the *Doomsday Clock,* a tool created by a consortium of a number of scientists including 13 Nobel laureates, and that uses the imagery of 'apocalypse (midnight) and the contemporary idiom of nuclear explosion (countdown to zero) to convey threats to humanity and the planet' (the two most important ones being nuclear war and global warming), moved its 'countdown' to 100 s from midnight, the closest it has ever been. It is, therefore, understandable that Tom Griffiths calls climate change 'the colossal story of our time' (2013, 255).

The roots of this story, however, may indeed reach deep into human history. The myth of the Deluge in the book of Genesis, once euhemerised, casts Noah as one of the first weather forecasters. The myth of an environmental catastrophe in the form of a great flood, moreover, has numerous parallels in a number of mythologies, such as, for example, the *Epic of Gilgamesh,* the earliest written work of world literature. Equally, the final book of the New Testament, the Book of Revelation (or, in the Greek translation of 'revelation', the *Apocalypse*) is replete with images of environmental devastation. The Norse mythological event known as *Ragnarök*, described in the thirteenth century *Poetic Edda* and *Prose Edda* and popularized by Richard Wagner's *Götterdämmerung* (the 'Twilight of the Gods'), also accounts for an eschatological narrative in which an inevitable environmental cataclysm underpins the cyclical nature of history. The doomsday prediction, in 1185, by Johannes of Toledo (the so-called *Toledo letter*), where the author predicted that the alignment of all planets would bring storms, famine and disasters, represents what some define as 'astrometorology' (Burroughs et al., 2008), while the *Theologus Autodidacticus*, one of the earliest examples of Arabic literature, concludes its theological reflections with a catastrophic environmental event.

The idea of an environmental 'apocalypse'—as a hypothetical scenario whereby the collapse of human civilization (or even human extinction) is caused by environmental degradation—however, became significantly more prevalent in more recent times, at the onset of the Industrial Revolution. As a result, 'the challenges that climate change poses', Amitav Gosh writes, 'derive ultimately from the grid of literary forms and conventions that came to shape the narrative imagination in precisely that period when the accumulation of carbon in the atmosphere was rewriting the destiny of the Earth' (2016, 7). Climate narratives have spawned an entire genre, known as climate fiction or cli-fi, often a subgenre of apocalyptic fiction. To describe the time scrutinized by this genre, Nicole Rogers proposes the notion of 'wild time', describing 'a future in which the world has been radically transfigured by climate change: the chaotic period in which the logic, institutions, modes of interacting and artefacts of civilization are abruptly or gradually undone as a consequence of climatic and other disruptions' (2020a, 2020b, 4). Such a time is marked by a particular narrative turn and is dominated by a series of clearly identifiable tropes. In this sense, '[c]limate fiction is, almost exclusively, the narrative domain in which the potential dimensions of wild time are fully explored and portrayed' (128).

Historical examples abound. The 1805 novel *Le Dernier Homme* by Jean-Baptiste Cousin de Grainville is the first modern novel to depict this wild time at the end of the world, soon followed by Lord Byron's poem *Darkness*, heavily inspired by the explosion, in 1815, of Mount Tambora (the most violent volcanic explosion in recorded human history).[44] Mary Shelley's 1826 novel *The Last Man* completes a trilogy of novels which, at the onset of the Romantic period, 'in [their] refusal to place humanity at the centre of the universe, [and their] questioning of our privileged position in relation to nature … constitute a profound and prophetic challenge to Western humanism' (Lokke, 2003, 116). Many of the early science-fiction authors of the nineteenth century engaged with the issue of environmental apocalypse, from much of Jules Verne's work to Herbert George Wells's *The Time Machine*, with its depiction of a profoundly altered planet in which humanity itself is split among the

[44] The same climatic conditions, according to Amitav Gosh, were at the root of the emergence of new genres of literature (in the form of the horror and science fiction novels), with the momentous encounter at Geneva between Shelley, Mary Woolstonecraft, Lord Byron and his physician James Polidori, from which both *The Vampyre* and *Frankenstein*, respectively the first modern horror and science-fiction novels, emerged.

socially decaying Eloi and the light-fearing Morlock who prey among them. Matthew Phipps Shiel's *The Purple Cloud* aptly marks the beginning of the twentieth century with a story of environmentally induced grandiose societal collapse.

John Christopher's *The Death of Grass*, on the other hand, emphasizes the fragile relationship between human population, agricultural yield and environmental conditions. The sudden death of all the world's grasses due to a global viral infection plunges humanity into a spiral of rapidly accelerating collapse and tribal violence, reinforcing a trope of individual survivalism in the face of dwindling resources and sudden cataclysmic events. James Ballard's *The Drowned World* is possibly the most famous of the author's series of novels that deal with apocalyptic natural disasters. In it, Ballard explores the psychological implications of an increasingly warmer planet, one in which the reptilian brain is awakened in fascinatingly unexpected ways that transcend the boundaries of the human. Daphne du Maurier's 1952 short story *The Birds*, later adapted for cinema by Alfred Hitchcock in the 1963 homonymous movie, symbolically highlights the growing alienation of humanity from a world that is seen as ultimately hostile to human survival. John Brunner's *Stand on Zanzibar* engages with the growing perceived threat of overpopulation precisely at a time when Ehrlich's *The Population Bomb* was being written, and the last words uttered by Charlton Heston's character Frank Thorn in *Soylent Green* (1972), 'Soylent Green is people!', still resonate as a powerful warning against the risk of (in the movie, unintended) cannibalism connected to an overpopulated Earth. The same trope, of being forced to resort to cannibalism to survive, is explored in countless examples of contemporary popular narrative, such as the movie *Delicatessen* or the novel (then movie) *Cloud Atlas*. One of the most striking features of the cannibalistic trope is that it reveals a sense of narrative normalization, an implicit acceptance of the inevitability (if not necessarily the desirability) of such a solution.

This sense of normalization of the unthinkable is masterfully explored by Margaret Attwood, both in her *MaddAddam* trilogy and *The Handmaid's Tale*. Atwood presents a world where social inequality, genetic technology and catastrophic climate change have finally culminated in some apocalyptic event. One of the most disturbing experiences for the reader is certainly the sense of impotence against a society in which social inequality and previously unspeakable social arrangements have become not only common but are fully embraced by the majority (if not the totality) of the social milieu. Echoes of an unthinkable social shift toward authoritarianism in the early twentieth century obviously abound, reminding the reader that what happened once may happen again. Among the most disturbing moments in the already profoundly disturbing novel (and excellent televised rendition) *The Handmaid's Tale* is one where the main character, the Handmaid Offred, tells the Mexican ambassador about the abuse and physical and psychological torture the Handmaidens are routinely subjected to, to which the ambassador responds in a chillingly utilitarian fashion, implying that, while she empathizes with the Handmaid, ultimately the suffering of the few may very well be justified by the survival of the many. Such a normalized sense of alienation, one where the fictional polity is actively embracing what the reader would consider a dystopian reality, already masterfully depicted by Aldous Huxley in

Brave New World, is scarcely as powerfully portrayed as by *Silent Running*'s protagonist, Freeman Lowell, whose cries for a natural world that has become irrelevant to anyone but himself are consistently derided and tragically ignored.

The depictions of climatic and, or, environmental events that suddenly and dramatically alter the fabric of society in ways that are not only unrecognisable but also profoundly disturbing are far too many to explore comprehensively here, and thus I refer to many excellent texts that have done so elsewhere (Rogers, 2020a, 2020b). Suffice it to say that these depictions range from the mundane, as in Barbara Kingsolver's *Flight Behaviour*, to the catastrophic, as in movies such as the *Mad Max* franchise (dealing with the effects of resources scarcity), *The Day After Tomorrow* (which, in order to harness the power of visually impressive special effects, deals with veritable disaster narrative), the movie *Waterworld*, the videogame series *Fallout* or the comic (and then TV) series *The Walking Dead* (all dealing with a post-apocalyptic world). Equally, the themes can be explored explicitly, or they can implicitly appear as an often-disturbing background, as in Kazuo Ishiguro's *Never Let Me Go*, the book (then TV) series *The Expanse*, or the comic series *Judge Dredd*. Finally, such an exploration needs not to be purely fictional and has also been the focus of science-based or speculative works, such as Oreskes and Conway's *The Collapse of Western Civilization* or Ernest Callenbach's classic *Ecotopia*.

2.3.2 The State of Environmental Exception

What all the above depictions have in common, not only within the genre but also by reference to the popular discourse surrounding the current environmental predicament, is the constant reference to end-of-times tropes. However, far from being accurate depictions of social collapse, the entire genre rather constitutes a complex and deeply interwoven thought experiment akin to Hobbes or Locke's *gedanken* of a mythical 'state of nature', often revealing far more of the author's point of view than any reality being speculatively described. Therefore, the trajectory that the genre as a whole appears to prefigure is not necessarily a guarantee of its inevitability, something that may not be readily apparent from the language generally adopted. While the choice of such language is certainly powerful in alerting the audience to the radical dangers that an environmentally degraded planet would pose to life itself, its fear-inducing tone conjures a more ancient idea, one that John Michael Greer (2009b) has called the 'apocalypse meme'.

The idea of the 'apocalypse' has historically acted as a powerful political justification for the imposition of power. To reconstruct how this has been the case throughout history, Greer applies Richard Dawkins' idea of the 'meme', a 'unit of cultural transmission' (1976, 192)—whereby the replicating entity operates within cultural transmission in a form that is analogous to genetic transmission—to the historical evolution of the idea of the 'apocalypse'. This idea appears to have originated with the birth of Zoroastrianism (Cohn, 1993), when the mythical depiction of solar and stellar cycles was reconstructed as a moral eschatology, one that forfeits time's cyclical nature for a linear time instead, one in which the struggle between good and evil entities leads to an inevitable final defeat of the evil forces of Ahriman and a new eternity of peace. The missionary zeal that this dualistic monotheism engendered has accompanied the expansions of many civilizations since Zarathustra's preaching, and the apocalypse meme, further forged through the crucible of the history of Israel and the Book of Daniel as a justificatory narrative for armed resistance against foreign invaders construed as veritable divine enemies, coalesced in the baroque imagery of the Book of Revelation. Since then, and with the spread of Christianity, the apocalypse meme has come to infiltrate and dominate the entirety of the Western social discourse, and examples of end-of-times predictions abound throughout the past two millennia.

Notably, in the twelfth century, Joachim of Fiore 'immanentized the eschaton' (Greer, 2009b, 90), by shifting the disastrous but relatively brief transition from an age of strife to an age of eternal bliss from 'the otherworldly status that Christian theology had always assigned to it, and revisioned it as a state that could be attained here on Earth' (90). Prefigured by the Peasants' Revolt of 1381, and fully embraced by the age of the enlightenment, the ingress of the apocalypse meme within the world of radical ideology was fully completed with the revolutionary movements of the late eighteenth century, their visions for a new society governed by reason that could break with its primitivist, barbaric and oppressive past, and Condorcet's conceptualization of history as *progress*. Hegel's progressive manifestation of the Absolute through a historically dialectical process, and Marx's inscription of the process of history within a purely economic-political dimension complete the journey of the apocalypse meme toward its present from, with minor apportions from nineteenth and twentieth century millenarist movements (which introduced, for example, the idea of the 'rapture', the sudden salvation vested upon true believers).

Since the apocalypse meme constitutes a powerful thread within the fabric of the current global discourse, it becomes apparent that the scientific analysis of the current environmental predicament is thus not written exclusively in the purportedly objective language of science, but rather, it is inscribed in a broader social discourse informed by eschatological narratives and political rhetoric. Apocalyptic narratives provide immediate psychological relief and fantasy fulfilment: 'to the idealist, the arrival of a world more perfect than human arrangements have ever been able to provide; to the frustrated, the resentful and the angry, a settling of scores on a superhumanly grandiose scale' (Greer, 2009b, 197). Moreover, apocalypse tales are *redemptive* tales: there always exists a light at the end of the tunnel, a promise of salvation irrespective of the dire situations occurring around those who are to be saved. As Nicole Rogers note, 'legal and activist narratives intend to prevent runaway climate change … they offer redemption, the promise that humanity can yet avoid the multiple challenges and devastation of wild time in Hothouse Earth', even though, '[i]n much climate fiction, the reader or viewer is plunged into the post-midnight zone, into a world irreparably damaged by climate change' (2020a, 2020b, 128).

While the possibility of societal collapse is certainly real, the social discourse of climate change and environmental degradation, and of their impact on present societies, is far more complex than any prediction, however accurate, could ever be. The articulation of the apocalypse meme in general—and of the environmental apocalypse one in particular—is always more than a simple prediction about bad (or good) things happening in the future. Indeed, many of the predictions about the state of the environment made by scientists may be more or less accurate, and many of the scenarios described above may come to pass. However, as previously discussed, collapse is rarely construed as such at the time of its occurrence. Rather, collapse is generally defined as such *retrospectively*, often many years hence. Therefore, environmentally driven social collapse may or may not occur, and if (or when) it does, it may occur over such large timescales that it may be unlikely to be construed as collapse at the time of its occurrence and thus may be experienced in far more subtle and incremental ways than cli-fi narratives suggest. Roy Scranton notes that climate change is 'a gradual process happening year by year, punctuated not by one global event, but by an unpredictable series of increasingly damaging local disasters' (2018, 329). Alternatively, it may also happen that, given the unprecedented speed of change, disastrous catastrophic events may unfold at a historically unprecedented speed. What is certain, however, is that, whatever the case, any future event, however bleak, is never going to be an 'apocalypse' in the sense described above, nor can it ever be.

Therefore, a cautionary tales emerges, as the adoption of the language of *crisis*, *emergency* and the *apocalypse* paves the way for a sinister state of environmental exception, with a consequent suspension of democratic protocols and a high degree of hostility toward a collective effort to engage with such a crisis (Sparrow, 2019). The prevention of collapse, when presented as the fight against a pending apocalypse, may certainly engender radical and forceful responses, some that may verge into absolutist political, economic and military behaviour under the banner of environmental justification. After all, fear campaigns are often strategically used to manipulate public opinion, as George Monbiot asserts: '[t]errify the living daylights out of people, and they will protect themselves at the expense of others and the living world' (in Boyd, 2015, xix). The creation of a state of fear establishes the conditions for a suspension of equitable collective regulation, reinforcing an individualist rhetoric typical of the Western dominant tradition. The state of exception, Carl Schmitt already explained, is the liminal space in which sovereign power is fully revealed by the ability to suspend the rule of law. Giorgio Agamben (2005) identifies the state of exception as a political milieu within a declared state of emergency where constitutional provisions can be indefinitely suspended. As a powerful, and often abused, political tool, the state of exception, Agamben asserts, has become 'the dominant paradigm of government in contemporary politics' (2005, 4).

Indeed, Parenti notes, '[t]he idea of emergency, or the state of exception, is crucial in the political theory of authoritarian states. Carl Schmitt famously theorized the legal basis of dictatorship in Nazi Germany by resort to this notion. … emergencies are the means by which democracies smuggle in authoritarian, or absolutist, politics and law enforcement' (2011, 209). Naomi Klein warns that, 'even as we insist on naming an emergency as an emergency, we need to constantly guard against this state of emergency becoming a state of exception, in which powerful interests exploit public fear and panic to roll back hard-won rights and steamroll profitable false solutions' (2009, 40). Conversely, Greer also reminds us that '[t]he realm of apocalypse as a door to Utopia has also encouraged the unproductive habit, very common in today's activist circles, of identifying any available crisis as the final blow that will bring about the sudden unravelling of the existing order and its replacement by a better world' (2009a, 2009b, 84). Moreover, what Lisa Grow Sun calls 'disaster mythology' (2018, 133) may constitute a set of 'narratives that prevent prompt and effective responses to disaster situations' (Rogers, 2020a, 2020b, 154). Timothy Morton also suggests that '[b]y postponing doom into some hypothetical future … [these narratives] inoculate us against the very real object that has intruded into ecological, social and psychic space' (2013, 103–4). Furthermore, the depiction of climate collapse as a pending—but ultimately deferred—apocalypse also obscures the less grandiose but far more pervasive reality of current climate change-induced violence in many of the world regions.

On the other hand, in her investigation on the growing invocation of the defence of necessity in cases of climate-driven civil disobedience, Rogers (2020a, 2020b) distinguishes between two distinct articulations of a state of emergency. The classic articulation discussed above, of a top-down imposition of a government-sanctioned state of exception, is cast against a bottom-up declaration of a state of emergency, one where no other reasonable option is left to the general population but to engage with civil disobedience 'when confronted with the climate emergency and the recalcitrance of our public authorities in coordinating an effective response to this emergency' (223). The latter presents itself as an intriguing and somewhat novel articulation of the 'state of exception', one where the legitimacy of the rule of law is not only suspended by a portion of the citizenry, but also the state of emergency upon which such suspension is predicated is judicially endorsed, rather than executively sanctioned. Whether such a form of globally advocated state of emergency escapes the hidden implications of the apocalypse meme remains speculative, but it is useful to note it offers a differing response to any projected environmental disaster.

Environmental 'facts' are undoubtedly dire. However, their characterization as an 'apocalypse' is a story, a social device inscribed in complex relations of power. As a result, narratives of collapse and apocalyptic tropes justify *reactive* responses that may lead to an environmentally justified state of exception. It is therefore imperative to remain alert against the possibility of environmental cataclysms allowing the application of a permanent state of exception justified by environmental concerns. Within any sudden reactive response, the seeds of the apocalypse meme, and the state of exception that this meme justifies, are indeed ever present.

2.4 Ontological and Epistemological Interconnectedness

This chapter has hopefully brought together three distinct threads: firstly, the scientific consensus on the current environmental predicament; secondly, the implications of such a predicament for current societies (and perhaps humanity overall); thirdly, the narrative and discoursive milieu within which both the predicament and a host of collective responses to it are located. Undoubtedly, climate change remains (and the environmental predicament overall) remains, in the words of American psychologist Richard Lazarus, a 'super wicked' problem (2009), or, in Timothy Morton's description, a 'hyperobject': that is, an event so 'massively distributed in time and space relative to humans' (2013, 8–9) as to become cognitively overwhelming. That notwithstanding, this chapter should further contextualise the question with which it began. What is it, following Stone's query, that makes the environmental predicament *legally invisible* (or, at least, *legally irrelevant*)?

The particular cultural inability to even 'see' the current predicament, to construe a meaningful 'mythology' (in a Barthian sense) around both the current environmental predicament and the natural world as a whole, suggests that climate change is as much a social narrative as it is a scientific issue. The implications of this narrative as a tapestry of interwoven tropes oscillate, within the current urban and ecologically estranged world, between *Gaia* and *Grendel*, as Jules Pretty suggests (2012), between a romantic view of a pristine Eden and a chaotic landscape of incommensurable grief. It is not uncommon to hear the suggestion, even among many environmentalists, that 'Mother Earth' could continue living without humans, as it (or, to maintain the metaphor, she) does not need them. However, against what she defines as an inherently nihilistic approach, Yimardoowarra scholar Anne Poelina asserts (in private conversation with me) that, 'while Mother Earth could indeed go on and recover from the present damages, she would be lonely without the vibrations of human beings walking and dancing upon her skin'. Poelina's insight highlights the fact that human survival and planetary health are a false dichotomy, and that the inaccurate articulation of 'economic' needs in opposition to 'environmental' ones leads to the realization that both an anti-environmental position and a nihilistic one are, ultimately, equally myopic.

What makes the current environmental predicament—the magnitude of which, this chapter has hopefully amply shown, is incontrovertible—*legally invisible* or *irrelevant* is, therefore, to be found in a particular worldview, the development of which can be traced over the past two or three millennia. Such a worldview can be heuristically called *anthropocentrism*.

Reference

350.org. (2020). Home. https://350.org. Accessed June 10, 2020.

Agamben, G. (2005). *State of exception*. University of Chicago Press.

Ambrose, S. (1998). Late Pleistocene human population bottlenecks, volcanic winter, and differentiation of modern humans. *Journal of Human Evolution, 34*(6), 623–651.

American Association for the Advancement of Science. (2007). AAAS board statement on climate change. https://www.aaas.org/sites/default/files/aaas_climate_statement2.pdf. Accessed February 18, 2022.

Asimov, I., & Pohl, F. (1991). *Our angry earth.* Tor.
Ballard, J. G. (1962). *The drowned world.* Berkley Books.
Barnosky, A. D., Hadly, E. A. (2015). *End game. Tipping point for planet Earth?* William Collins.
Bellamy Foster, J., Clark, B., & York, R. (2010). *The ecological rift. Capitalism war on the Earth.* Monthly Review Press.
Bendell, J. (2019). Deep adaptation: A map for navigating climate tragedy. https://jembendell.com/2019/05/15/deep-adaptation-versions/
Berry, T. (1999). *The great work.* Three Rivers Press.
Biello, D. (2016). *The unnatural world. The race to remake civilization in earth's newest age.* Scribner.
Bowen, M. (2008). *Censoring science. Dr James Hansen and the truth of global warming.* Plume.
Boyd, D. R. (2015). *The optimistic environmentalist. Progressing towards a greener future.* ECW Press.
Brolin, B. (2007). *A history of the science and politics of climate change: The role of the intergovernmental panel on climate change.* Cambridge University Press.
Brown, L. R. (2003). *Plan B: Rescuing a planet under stress and a civilization in trouble.* Norton.
Brunner, J. (1962). *Stand on Zanzibar.* Doubleday.
Bulletin of the Atomic Scientists. (2020). Closer than ever: It is 100 seconds to midnight. https://thebulletin.org/doomsday-clock/current-time/. Accessed July 18, 2022.
Burroughs, W. J., Crowder, B., Robertson, T., Vallier-Talbot, E., & Whitaker, R. (2008). *Weather.* The Five Mile Press.
California Governor's Office of Planning and Research. (2020). List of worldwide scientific organizations. In *California Governor's Office Of Planning And Research.* http://www.opr.ca.gov/facts/list-of-scientific-organizations.html. Accessed May 26, 2020.
Callenbach, E. (1977). *Ecotopia.* Bantam.
Callendar, G. S. (1938). The artificial production of carbon dioxide and its influence on temperature. *Quarterly Journal of the Royal Meteorological Society, 64*, 223–240.
Callendar, G. S. (1961). Temperature fluctuations and trends over the Earth. *Quarterly Journal of the Royal Meteorological Society, 86*, 1–12.
Campbell, K. M., Gulledge, J., McNeill, J. R., Podesta, J., Ogden, P., Fuerth, L., Woolsey, R. J., Lennon, A. T. J., Smith, J., Weitz, R., & Mix, D. (2007). *The age of consequences: The foreign policy and national security implications of global climate change.* Center for a New American Security.
Casson, S. (1937). *Progress and catastrophe: An anatomy of human adventure.* Harper and Brothers.
Carson, R. (1962). *Silent spring.* Houghton Mifflin.
Charlton, A. (2011). Man-made World. Choosing between progress and planet. *Quarterly Essay, 44*, 1–72.
Cheng, L., et al. (2020). Record-setting ocean warmth continued in 2019. *Advances in Atmospheric Sciences, 37*, 137–142.
Clegg, B. (2009). *Ecologic: The truth and lies of green economics.* Eden Project Books.
CNA Corporation. (2007). *National security and the threat of climate change.* CAN.
Cohn, N. (1993). *Chaos, cosmos and the world to come. The ancient roots of apocalyptic faith.* Yale University Press.
Copernicus Climate Change Service. (2023). European State of the Climate 2023. https://climate.copernicus.eu/esotc/2023. Accessed August 10, 2024.
Daly, H. (1991). *Steady-state economics* (2nd ed.). Island Press (First published 1977).
Dawkins, R. (1976). *The selfish gene.* Oxford University Press.
Diamond, J. (2005). *Collapse. How societies choose to fail or succeed.* Penguin.
Dyer, G. (2010). *Climate wars. The fight for survival as the world overheats.* Oneworld Publications.

Earth CO_2. (2024). Earth Co_2 Homepage. https://www.co2.earth. Accessed August 2, 2024.
Edgar, G. J., Bates, A. E., Krueck, N. C., Baker, S. C., Stuart-Smith, R. D., & Brwon, C. J. (2024). Stock assessment models overstate sustainability of world's fisheries. *Science, 385*(6711), 860–865.
Edwards, P. N. (2011). History of climate modelling. *Wires Climate Change, 2*, 128–139.
Ehrlich, P. (1968). *The population bomb.* Sierra Club.
Eisenstadt, S. (1988). Beyond collapse. In N. Yoffee, & G. Cowgill (Eds.), *The collapse of ancient states and civilizations.* University of Arizona Press.
Extinction Rebellion. (2020). About us. https://rebellion.earth/the-truth/about-us/. Accessed June 29, 2020.
Fagan, B. (2001). *The little ice age: How climate made history 1300–1850.* Basic Books.
Fagan, B. (2004). *The long summer: How climate changed civilization.* Basic Books.
Fagan, B. (2008). *The great warming: Climate change and the rise and fall of civilizations.* Bloomsbury.
Feldman, S. (2010). Climate scientists defend IPCC peer review as most rigorous in history. In *Inside climate news.* https://insideclimatenews.org/news/20100226/climate-scientists-defend-ipcc-peer-review-most-rigorous-history. Accessed May 15, 2019.
Flannery, T. (2006). *We are the weather makers. The story of global warming.* The Text Publishing Company.
Flannery, T. (2011). Correspondence. *Quarterly Essay, 44*, 108–110.
Flannery, T. (2015). *Atmosphere of hope. Searching for solutions to the climate crisis.* The Text Publishing Company.
Friedman, T. L. (2008). *Hot, flat and crowded: Why we need a green revolution and how it can renew America.* Farrar, Straus and Giroux.
Garnaut, R. (2019). *Super-power. Australia's low-carbon opportunity.* LaTrobe University Press.
Georgescu-Roegen, N. (1971). *The entropy law and the economic process.* Harvard University Press.
Giddens, A. (1981). *A contemporary critique of historical materialism.* University of California Press.
Gilding, P. (2011). *The great disruption: Why the climate crisis will bring on the end of shopping and the birth of a new world.* Bloomsbury.
Gleick, P. H. (2014). Water, drought, climate change and conflict in Syria. *Weather, Climate and Society, 6*(3), 331–340.
Global Footprint Network. (2020). World Footprint. https://www.footprintnetwork.org/our-work/ecological-footprint/. Accessed June 21, 2024.
Goldsmith, E., & Allen, R. (1972). *A blueprint for survival.* Penguin.
Gosh, A. (2016). *The great derangement: Climate change and the unthinkable.* University of Chicago Press.
Greer, J. M. (2005). *How civilizations fall: A theory of catabolic collapse.*
Greer, J. M. (2008). *The long descent: A user's guide to the end of the industrial age.* New Society Publishers.
Greer, J. M. (2009a). *The ecotechnic future. Envisioning a post-peak World.* New Society Publishers.
Greer, J. M. (2009b). *Apocalypse. A history at the end of time.* Quercus.
Griffiths, T. (2013). *Weather and Mind Games: Why Can't We Talk about Climate Change' Griffith Review, 41*, 246–256.
Grow Sun, L. (2018). Disaster law and order. In R. Lyster, & R. R. M. Verchik (Eds.), *Research handbook on climate disaster law.* Edward Elgar.
Guterres, A. (2019). Secretary general's remarks at opening ceremony of UN climate change conference COP25 [as delivered]. In UN https://www.un.org/sg/en/content/sg/statement/2019-12-02/secretary-generals-remarks-opening-ceremony-of-un-climate-change-conference-cop25-delivered. Accessed January 10, 2020.

Hallegatte, S., Bangalore, M., Bonzanigo, L., Fay, M., Kane, T., Narloch, U., Rozenberg, J., Treguer, D., & Vogt-Schilb, A. (Eds.). (2015). *Shock waves: Managing the impacts of climate change on poverty*. World Bank OKR.

Hansen, J., Johnson, D., Lacis, A., Lebedeff, S., Lee, P., Rind, D., & Russell, G. (1981). Climate impact of increasing atmospheric carbon dioxide. *Science, 213*, 957–966.

Hansen, J. E., Sato, M., Simon, L., Nazarenko, L., Sangha, I., Kharecha, P., Zachos, J. C., Von Schuckmann, K., Loeb, N. G., Osman, M. B., Jin, Q., Tselioudis, G., Jeong, E., Lacis, A., Ruedy, R., Russell, G., Cao, J., & Li, J. (2023). Global warming in the pipeline. *Oxford Open Climate Change, 3*(1), 1–33. https://doi.org/10.1093/oxfclm/kgad008

Hansen, J. (2009). *Storms of my grandchildren. The truth about the coming climate catastrophe and our last chance to save humanity*. Bloomsbury.

Harari, Y. N. (2014). *Sapiens*. Random House.

Harris, M. (1984). *Cows, pigs, wars and witches. The riddle of culture* (2nd ed.). Vintage, New York (First published 1974).

Harris, M. (1991). *Cannibals and kings: Origins of culture* (2nd ed.). Vintage (First published 1977).

Hartmann, T. (2013). *Last hours of humanity. Warming the World to extinction*. Waterfront Digital Press.

Hawken, P. (Ed.). (2017). *Drawdown. The most comprehensive plan ever proposed to reverse global warming*. Penguin Books.

Illich, I. (1973). *Tools for conviviality*. Harper & Row.

IPCC. (2015). AR5 synthesis report: Climate change 2014. https://www.ipcc.ch/report/ar5/syr/. Accessed May 26, 2020.

IPCC. (2020). About. https://www.ipcc.ch/about/. Accessed June 9, 2024.

IPCC. (2023). AR6 Synthesis Report. https://report.ipcc.ch/ar6syr/pdf/IPCC_AR6_SYR_Longer Report.pdf

Jackson, T. (2009). *Prosperity without growth. Economics for a finite planet*. Earthscan.

Jay Gould, S. J. (1987). *Time's arrow, time's cycle. Myth and metaphor in the discovery of geological time*. Harvard University Press.

Jevons. W. S. (1865). *The coal question; An inquiry concerning the progress of the nation, and the probable exhaustion of our coal-mines. online library of liberty*. https://oll.libertyfund.org/titles/jevons-the-coal-question. Accessed August 8, 2022 (First published 1865).

King Hubbert, M. (1959). Techniques of prediction with application to the petroleum industry. *American Association of Petroleum Geologists, 43*(7), 1767–1768.

Klare, T. (2012). *The race for what's left. The global scramble for the world's last resources*. Henry Holt and Company.

Klein, N. (2009). *On fire. The burning case for a green new deal*. Penguin.

Kolbert, E. (2014). *The sixth extinction: An unnatural history*. Henry Holt and Company.

Lazarus, R. J. (2009). Super wicked problems and climate change: Restraining the present to liberate the future. *Cornell Law Review, 94*, 1153–1234.

Le Treut, H., Somerville, R., Cubash, U., Ding, Y., Mauritzen, C., Mokssit, A., Peterson, T., & Prather, M. (2007). Historical overview of climate change science. In S. Solomon, D. Qin, M. Manning, Z. Chen, M. Marquis, K. B. Averyt, M. Tignor, & H. L. Miller (Eds.), Climate change 2007: The physical science basis. contribution of working group I to the fourth assessment report of the intergovernmental panel on climate change. Cambridge University Press.

Le Quéré, C., Jackson, R., Jones, M. W., Smith, A. J. P., Abernethy, S., Andrew, R. M., De-Gol, A. J., Willis, D. R., Shan, Y., Canadell, J. G., Friedlingstein, P., Creutzig, F., & Peters, G. P. (2020). Temporary reduction in daily global CO2 emissions during the COVID-19 forced confinement. *Nature Climate Change* (online) https://www.nature.com/articles/s41558-020-0797-x

Leakey, R., & Levin, R. (1996). *The sixth extinction. Patterns of life and the future of humankind*. Anchor Books.
Leggett, J. (2005). *Half gone. Oil, gas, hot air and the global energy crisis*. Portobello Books.
Leonard, A. (2010). The story of stuff. How our obsession with stuff is thrashing the planet, our communities, and our health—and a vision for change. Constable.
Leopold, A. (1949). *A sand county almanac*. Oxford University Press.
Lokke, K. (2003). The last man. In E. Schor (Ed.), *The cambridge companion to Mary Shelley*. Cambridge University Press.
Lomborg, B. (1998). *The skeptical environmentalist*. Cambridge University Press.
Lovelock, J. (2007). *The revenge of Gaia. Why the Earth if fighting back—and how we can still save humanity*. Penguin Books.
Lovins, A. (1976). Energy strategy: The road not taken. *Foreign Affairs* 65–96.
Lueddeke, G. (2020). *Survival: One health, one planet, one future*. Routledge.
Malthus, T. (1798). *An essay on the principle of population*. Johnson.
Manabe, S., & Wetherald, R. (1967). Thermal equilibrium of the atmosphere with a given distribution of relative humidity. *Journal of the Atmospheric Sciences, 24*(3), 241–259.
Martenson, C. (2011). *The crash course. The unsustainable future of our economy, energy and the environment*. John Wiley and Sons.
Mazzucato, M. (2018). *The value of everything: Makin and taking in the global economy*. PublicAffairs.
McKibben, B. (1989). *The end of nature*. Random House.
Meadows, D. (1999). *Leverage points: Places to intervene in a system*. The Sustainability Institute.
Meadows, D., Randers, J., & Meadows, D. (2014). *Limits to growth. The 30-year update*. Chelsea Green.
Millennium Ecosystem Assessment. (2005). *Ecosystems and human well-being: Synthesis*. Island Press.
Morton, T. (2013). *Hyperobjects. Philosophy and ecology after the end of the World*. University of Minnesota Press.
Myers, R., & Worms, B. (2003). Rapid worldwide depletion of predatory fish communities. *Nature, 423*, 280–283.
NASA. (2020). Scientific consensus: Earth's climate is warming. In *NASA global climate change*. https://climate.nasa.gov/scientific-consensus/. Accessed May 26, 2020.
Nicholls, N. (2013). Explainer: What is the IPCC anyway, and how does it work?' In *The Conversation*. https://theconversation.com/explainer-what-is-the-ipcc-anyway-and-how-does-it-work-18164. Accessed March 23, 2022.
OECD. (2015). *The economic consequences of climate change*. OECD Publishing
Oppenheimer, S. (2003). *Out of eden, the peopling of the world*. Constable and Robinson.
Oreskes, N. (2004). Beyond the ivory tower: The scientific consensus on climate change. *Science, 306*(5702), 1686.
Oreskes, N., & Conway, E. M. (2010). Merchants of doubt: How a handful of scientists obscured the truth on issues from tobacco smoke to global warming. Bloomsbury.
Oreskes, N., & Conway, E. M. (2014). *The collapse of western civilization*. Columbia University Press.
Orwell, G. (1949). *Nineteen eighty-four*. Secker & Warburg.
Packard, V. (1960). *The waste makers*. David McKay.
Parenti, C. (2011). *Tropic of chaos. Climate change and the new geography of violence*. Nation Books.
Pearce, F. (2007). *With speed and violence: Why scientists fear tipping points in climate change*. Beacon Press.

Pearce, F. (2008). *Confessions of an eco sinner*. Eden Project Books.
Perez, C., & Murray Leach, T. (2018). Smart & green. A new "European way of life" as the path for growth, jobs and well-being. In Council for Research and Technology Development (Ed.), *Re-thinking Europe: Positions on shaping an idea*. Holzhausen.
Polanyi, K. (1944). *The great transformation. The political and economic origins of our time*. Farrar and Rinehart.
Pollan, M. (2006). *The omnivore's dilemma*. Bloomsbury.
President's Science Advisory Committee. (1965). *Restoring the quality of our environment. Report of the environmental pollution panel*. The White House.
Pretty, J. (2012). *The earth only endures: On reconnecting with nature and our place in it*. Earthscan.
Raworth, K. (2017). *Donought economics: Seven ways to think like a 21st-century economist*. Chelsea Green Publishing.
Reich, C. (1970). *The greening of America*. Random House.
Reinhart, C. M., & Rogoff, K. S. (2011). *This time is different: Eight centuries of financial folly*. Princeton University Press.
Revelle, R., & Suess, H. S. (1957). Carbon dioxide exchange between atmosphere and ocean and the question of an increase of atmospheric CO2 during the past decades. *Tellus, 9*(1), 18–27.
Ridley, M. (2010). *The rational optimist: How prosperity evolves*. HarperCollins.
Rockström, J., Steffen, W., et al. (2009). Planetary boundaries: Exploring the safe operating space for humanity. *Ecology and Society, 14*(2), 32–63.
Rogers, N. (2020a). *Law, fiction and activism in a time of climate change*. Routledge.
Rogers, N. (2020b). Climate activism and the extraordinary emergency defence. *Alternative Law Journal, 94*, 217–229.
Romm, J. J. (2005). *The hype about hydrogen. Fact and fiction in the race to save the climate*. Island Press.
Rosen, J. (2011). Correspondence. *Quarterly Essay, 44*, 103–107.
Ruddiman, W. F. (2003). The anthropogenic greenhouse era began thousands of years ago. *Climate Change, 61*(3), 261–293.
Schmidt, G. A., & Arndt, D. (2020). NOAA/NASA—Annual global analysis for 2019. https://www.ncdc.noaa.gov/sotc/briefings/20200115.pdf. Accessed March 15, 2020.
Schmitt, C. (1985). *Political theology. Four chapters on the concept of sovereignty* (G. Schwab Trans.). University of Chicago Press (First published in German 1922).
Schumacher, E. F. (1973). *Small is beautiful. Economics as if people mattered*. Blond & Briggs.
Schwartz, G. M., & Nichols, J. J. (Eds.) (2006). *After collapse. The regeneration of complex societies*. University of Arizona Press.
Schwartz, G. M. (2006). From collapse to regeneration. In G. M. Schwartz, & J. J. Nichols (Eds.), *After collapse. The regeneration of complex societies*. University of Arizona Press.
Scranton, R. (2018). *We're doomed. Now what?* Soho Press.
Sepkoski, J. J., & Raup, D. (1982). Mass extinctions in the marine fossil record. *Science, 215*(4539), 1501–1503.
Sepkoski, J. J., & Raup, D. (1984). Periodicity of extinctions in the geological past. *Proceedings of the National Academy of Sciences of the United States of America, 81*(3), 801–805.
Shiva, V. (2000). *Tomorrow's biodiversity*. Thames and Hudson.
Shiva, V. (2002). *Water wars. Privatization, pollution and profit*. India Research Press.
Simon, J. (1981). *The ultimate resource*. Princeton University Press.
Smith, D., & Vivekananda, J. (2008). *A climate of conflict: The links between climate change, peace and war*. Swedish International Development Cooperation Agency.
Sparrow, J. (2019). Climate emergency endangers democracy. *Eureka Street, 29*(12) https://www.eurekastreet.com.au/article/-climate-emergency--endangers-democracy
Stager, S. (2011). *Deep future. The next 100000 years of life on Earth*. Scribe.

Steffen, W., et al. (2015). The trajectory of the anthropocene: The great acceleration. *The Anthropocene Review, 2*, 81–99.
Stern, N. (2007). *The economics of climate change: The stern review*. Cambridge University Press.
Stockholm Resilience Centre. (2023). Stockholm University, Planetary Boundaries. https://www.stockholmresilience.org/research/planetary-boundaries.html. Accessed August 12, 2024.
Stuart Mill, J. (1848). *Principles of political economy*. John W Parker.
Svante Arrhenius, S. (1896). On the influence of carbonic acid in the air upon the temperature of the ground. *The London, Edinburgh, and Dublin Philosophical Magazine and Journal of Science, 41*, 237–276.
Tainter, J. (1988). *The collapse of complex societies*. Cambridge University Press.
Trischler, H. (2016). The anthropocene. A challenge for the history of science, technology and the environment'. *NTM Zeitschrift Für Geschichte der Wissenschaften, Technik Un Medizin, 24*, 309–335.
Tudge, C. (1991). *Global ecology*. Oxford University Press.
Tyndall, J. (1861). On the absorption and radiation of heat by gases and vapours, and on the physical connexion of radiation, absorption, conduction—the bakerian lecture. *The London, Edinburgh, and Dublin Philosophical Magazine and Journal of Science, 22*(4), 169–194, 273–285. http://tyndall1861.geologist-1011.mobi
UK Ministry of Defence Development, Concepts and Doctrine Centre. (2007). *DCDC global strategic programme 2007–2036*. UK Ministry of Defence.
UN. (2023). Hottest July ever signals 'era of global boiling has arrived' says UN chief. https://news.un.org/en/story/2023/07/1139162. Accessed July 27, 2023.
UNFCC. (2019). Statement by the UN Secretary-General António Guterres on the Outcome of COP25. https://unfccc.int/news/statement-by-the-un-secretary-general-antonio-guterres-on-the-outcome-of-cop25. Accessed January 15, 2020.
United Nations Framework Convention on Climate Change. 1771 UNTS 107 FCCC/INFORMAL/84 GE.05-62220 (E) 200705. Opened for signature 4 June 1992, entered into force 21 March 1994.
Vacca, R. (1973). *The coming dark age. What will happen when modern technology breaks down?* Doubleday (First published in Italian 1971).
Wackernagel, M., et al. (2002). Tracking the ecological overshoot of the human economy. *Proceedings of the Academy of Science, 99*(14), 9266–9271.
Wilson, E. O. (2006). *Half-Earth. Our planet's fight for life*. Liveright Publishing.
World Commission on Environment and Development. (1987). *Our common future*. Oxford University Press.
World Meteorological Organization. (2020). WMO confirms 2019 as second hottest year on record. https://public.wmo.int/en/media/press-release/wmo-confirms-2019-second-hottest-year-record. Accessed January 15, 2020.
World Wide Fund for Nature. (2020). Living Planet Report 2018. https://www.worldwildlife.org/pages/living-planet-report-2018. Accessed June 13, 2020.

Chapter 3
Anthropocentrism Redefined

Tyger Tyger, burning bright,
In the forests of the night;
What immortal hand or eye,
Could frame thy fearful symmetry?
(Blake, 1794)

What underpins the worldview that sees the environmental damages outlined in the previous chapter as *legally invisible* or at least *legally irrelevant*? Swimme and Tucker point out that, in relatively recent times,

> dynamized by their technology and their dreams of material progress, modern humans transformed the planet into a bundle of resources. They produced food in quantities never seen in history, and consequently populations exploded. [As a result,] feeding and housing this many humans … led to the depletion of the oceans, the degradation of the forests, and the loss of topsoil … The paradox of unintended consequences is now becoming evident. The oceans, the rivers, the atmosphere, and the soil have all been severely degraded by our actions. (2011, 49)

Furthermore, 'we' (the reader should substitute the universalizing 'we' with a historically situated and culturally contingent one) 'have crossed over into an Earth whose very atmosphere and biosphere are being shaped by human decisions … We live on a … planet now, where not biology but symbolic consciousness is the determining factor for evolution. Cultural selection has overwhelmed natural selection. That is,' the authors conclude, 'the survival of species and entire ecosystems now depends primarily on human activities. We are faced with a challenge no previous human has ever contemplated: How are we to make decisions that will benefit an entire planet for the next several millennia?' (49).

Perhaps, the 'unintended consequences' the authors speak of are due to a particularly destructive worldview, one often referred to as 'deterministic materialism.' Such a 'philosophical paradigm', Kuhn notes, 'initiated by Descartes and developed at the same time as Newtonian dynamics … has served both science and philosophy well. Its exploitation, like that of dynamics itself, has been fruitful of a fundamental understanding that perhaps could not have been achieved in another way' (1962, 121). However, 'research in parts of philosophy, psychology, linguistics and even art history, all converge to suggest that the traditional paradigm is somehow askew'

A. Pelizzon, *Ecological Jurisprudence*, Contemporary Environmental Law and Policy,
https://doi.org/10.1007/978-981-96-0173-8_3

(121). Indeed, Swimme and Tucker continue, 'perhaps the destruction [the world currently experiences] comes, at least in part, from an inadequate understanding of matter itself ... for centuries scientists have attempted to explain the universe by means of physical laws expressed in mathematical equations. The universe was thought to consist of mechanisms within mechanisms' (2011, 49). Deterministic materialism emerged in the late sixteenth century and seventeenth century 'amidst intense debates over natural philosophy', as Swimme and Tucker point out, and '[i]t had three tenets: that all things in the universe were composed of tiny particles of matter; that these particles were purely material, without any degree of subjectivity; and that these particles moved according to fixed, mathematical laws' (49). While, this chapter will show, deterministic materialism is certainly one of the main components of the anthropocentric worldview hereby discussed, it did not emerge out of a vacuum. Instead, it is deeply inscribed within a concatenation of ideas that, while not necessarily akin to linear 'progress', nonetheless makes the current environmental predicament legally invisible or irrelevant.

If a host of *memes* (in the sense introduced by Dawkins) and *myths* (in a Barthian sense) are the fundamental units underpinning the worldview the above authors point to, which of those memes and myths are to be privileged? After all, as Thomas Berry points out, 'we' (again, a collective pronoun generically used as a placeholder for all of humanity today)

> are acting on a geological and biological order of magnitude. We are changing the chemistry of the planet. We are altering the great hydrological cycles. We are weakening the ozone layer that shields us from cosmic rays. We are saturating the air, the water, and the soil with toxic substances so that we can never bring them back to their original purity. We are upsetting the entire earth system that has, over some billions of years and through an endless sequence of experiments, produced such a magnificent array of living forms, forms capable of seasonal self-renewal over an indefinite period of time. (1988, 206)

Of course, as the previous two chapters have abundantly demonstrated, this comment is correct in terms of the effects we, as a collective species, are having on the planet as a whole. However, it is not equally correct to assume a degree of inevitable homogeneity across all human cultures in this regard. Clearly, not all human groups throughout history have caused (or are causing) such an upheaval. While the notion of the Anthropocene evokes the idea of a novel era dominated by the role of humanity as a geological force, as Daniel Matthews points out, '[m]any commentators see inherent flaws in the Anthropocene terminology, particularly the implication that a unified *anthropos* is responsible for the present climate emergency' (2021, 33). Murray Bookchin had already asserted that '[t]he notion that man is destined to dominate nature is by no means a universal feature of human culture' (1991, 43).[1] Of course, the narratives of dominance that underpin the current dominant legal systems are neither universal nor necessary, but are rather contingent and historically situated and determined.

---

[1] For Bookchin, 'the concept emerged very gradually from a broader social development: the increasing domination of human by human.'

However, given the power that such narratives clearly display in shaping the current trajectory of the Earth, they need to be investigated in light of their relative uniqueness. Therefore, this chapter will focus on what can be heuristically defined as a 'Western' worldview, in full awareness that such worldview may be politically and economically dominant, but it is, by no means, universal—notwithstanding its modernist belief in its own neutrality, objectivity and scientificity (and the following chapters will engage more in depth with a host of non-dominant worldviews). Furthermore, the chapter will develop a series of interlinked ideas to display a relatively coherent picture of an anthropocentric worldview, but in full awareness that such a picture is, once again, a heuristic device, and that no such a single monolith is ever possible. Finally, the chapter will identify this worldview as an 'anthropocentric' worldview, a term against which, the rest of the book will highlight, an ecological jurisprudence has increasingly cast itself over the past few decades.

3.1 Anthropocentrism: A Textual Genealogy

It could be both apt and appropriate to attempt a paleoanthropological and anthropological reconstruction of humanity's interaction with the planet. Thomas Berry writes that '[w]hen the agricultural civilizations began some ten thousand years ago, the human disturbance of the natural world was begun in a serious way. It may be said in general that these early Neolithic and the later classical civlizations had some deleterious effects on the regions they occupied' (1988, 7). Swimme and Tucker also note that

> [a] pivotal change – ultimately important not only for humanity but also for the rest of life – was the new conceptions of the environment formed in the minds of the fledgling farmers and villagers. Natural habitats were no longer wild places in which to hunt and gather food, and occasionally burn over with ground fires. The habitats instead became land to be cleared for agriculture. This particular conception, that wildland is something to be replaced, has been a mental fixation of most of the world's population to this day. (2011, 102)

Keith Thomas suggest than some anthropologists believe that 'it was the management of herds of domestic animals which first gave rise to an interventionist and manipulative conception of political life' (1984, 46), and indeed the focus on the relationship between changing production patterns, novel political structures and related worldviews has been the purview of a number of authors over the past two centuries, from (among many others) Karl Marx to Marvin Harris (1977), Jared Diamond (1997), Colin Tudge (1998), Spencer Wells (2010) and Yuval Noah Harari (2011). Undoubtedly, the fact that the human population multiplied from around 1 million until the early Neolithic (9000 BCE), to five to ten million by the third millennium BCE, to three hundred million by the first century CE, to five hundred million by the year 1500, to more than eight billion today, must have had an effect on the way not only human cultures interact with the planet they inhabit, but also on the way they view it.

However, rather than relying on anthropological and historical reconstructions, this chapter will instead focus on specific historical (and, in particular, philosophical) *documents*. By focusing on specifically instantiated ideas, the 'genealogical' journey leading to today's anthropocentric dominant worldview will be less *speculative* and more *hermeneutical*. Its main focus will be the history of (Western) philosophy—with particular attention paid to metaphysics and ethics—because, as Friedrich Schleiermacher pointed out, metaphysics and ethics have 'the same subject matter as religion, namely the universe and man's relation to it' (Braun & Bauer, 1911–3, vol IV, 240).

Finally, it is important to be reminded that the term 'anthropocentrism' only emerged at the end of the 1970s. Klaus Bosselmann note that '[u]p until then philosophical dictionaries either didn't list the term at all or included it in its restricted meaning in use since the mid-nineteenth century, [when] it distinguished Christianity's theocentric view of the world from the Ancient Greek way of thinking,' (1995, 4) which did not articulate humanity's position at the centre of the universe. With this final caveat in mind, it is time to embark in the diachronic journey of uncovering the origins of modern anthropocentrism.

3.1.1 'Replenish the Earth, and Subdue It'

In a famous essay published in 1967, titled 'The Historical Roots of Our Ecological Crisis', historian Lynn White Jr suggested that the roots of the current ecological crisis are to be found in the Judeo-Christian tradition, which posited a dichotomy between people and nature, with people being cast as 'masters' and not 'members' of the natural world. 'Created in the likeness of God, unique in their possession of a soul and the expectation of salvation, humans clearly stood above other forms of life', Roderick Nash writes (1989, 88), and Christians traditionally believed, White Jr further argued, that the rest of creation existed solely for human benefit. White Jr concluded by stating that 'Christianity is the most anthropocentric religion the world has seen' (1967, 1205). He was, of course, referring to the Christian tradition, not necessarily to particular Christians at the time of his writing in the 1960s, whose commitment to environmental ethics may very well have been (and still continues to be) rather different.

Human dominion over nature, White Jr argued, was entailed by the idea that human beings were scripturally positioned above everything else in nature. Genesis 1:28–30 is generally adduced as the basis for this claim: 'God blessed them, and God said unto them, be fruitful, and multiply, and replenish the earth, and subdue it: and have dominion over the fish of the sea, and over the fowl of the air, and over every living thing that moveth upon the earth.' The two key words in this passage are *kabash* (שַׁבְּכ translated as 'subdue') and *radah* (הָדָר translated as 'have dominion over', 'rule'). Not everyone agrees with such an interpretation, of course, and Jason John points out that this is, most likely, 'the passage most co-opted by people in Judeo-Christian societies who were going to plunder the environment anyway' (2011, 117). Michael Northcott asserts that '[a]t the heart of Judaism is a God who is encountered through Nature and events rather than words or texts. Christianity, by contrast, and then Islam, is a form of religion that is less implicated in the weather, climate and political power and more invested in words and texts' (Gosh, 2016, 65), suggesting that this interpretation of the Old Testament may be subsequent (and contrary) to its original formulation. Nonetheless, W Lee Humphreys notes that this common interpretation of Genesis 1:28–30 creates an image of 'a conqueror placing his foot on the neck of a defeated enemy, exerting absolute domination' (1971, 67), thus playing a significant role in promoting an instrumental attitude toward Nature.

The passage is further reinforced by Genesis 1:29–30, as well as Genesis 9:2, in the covenant the God makes with Noah and his sons:

> And God said, Behold, I have given you every herb bearing seed, which is upon the face of all the earth, and every tree, in the which is the fruit of a tree yielding seed; to you it shall be for meat.
>
> And to every beast of the earth, and to every fowl of the air, and to every thing that creepeth upon the earth, wherein there is life, I have given every green herb for meat: and it was so.
>
> And the fear of you and the dread of you shall be upon every beast of the earth, and upon every fowl of the air, upon all that moveth upon the earth, and upon all the fishes of the sea; into your hand are they delivered.

A slightly less domineering perspective is found throughout Genesis 2, where the words *abad* (דבע translated as 'to till' and 'to serve') and *shamar* (רַמָש translated as 'to keep', 'to guard') are more commonly used and are later adopted to justify an attitude of stewardship toward the natural world. However, notwithstanding the more benevolent attitude these words entail, the passages still assert humanity's superiority over the rest of creation.

Another Biblical interpretation adduced as a root justification of an intensely anthropocentric worldview is the fact that, Alexander Gillespie argues, 'starting from the Fall, God declares that the Earth and all upon it are corrupt' (1997, 71). As a result of the Fall, the natural world became a wilderness, a cursed land, the antipode of paradise: '[t]he earth was no mother but a kind of halfway house of trial and testing from which one was released at death' (Nash, 1989, 91). J Baird Callicott offers an interesting interpretation of the myth of the Fall. He argues that as a result of the consumption of the forbidden fruit, humanity 'could decide what is good and what evil, in relation to themselves. And this is where they went astray. For the right to decide, and to declare, what is good and what is evil is properly God's alone ... In this interpretation ... of the oldest biblical creation myth, anthropocentrism itself is man's original sin and is responsible for the famous Fall' (1994, 21).

Furthermore, the Bible condemns the worship of anything but the biblical God, and certainly not the natural world.[2] This, Gillespie suggests, inevitably led to 'a view of

[2] J Baird Callicott notes that this exclusion is predicated on a questionable assumption: that monotheism is 'more advanced and sophisticated than polytheism and polyspiritualism (or "fetishism", as the latter practice was often called in an African context). This assumption originated in the Enlightenment, first advanced, in 1760, by the French scholar Charles de Brosses, who argued that fetishism was typical of a primitive human religious consciousness. In the nineteenth century, the French sociologist Auguste Comte and the British anthropologist E B Taylor historicized and

repugnance of the natural world' (1997, 72). Such repugnance is likely contrary to the animistic beliefs that existed among neighbouring (and possibly preceding) peoples, for whom nothing was merely an 'it' waiting for human consumption and domination, but rather was comprised of a collection of beings and entities with whom a personal relationship was always possible. White Jr argued that 'by destroying pagan animism, Christianity made it possible to exploit nature in a mood of indifference to the feelings of natural objects' (1967, 1205). As a result, as White Jr also points out, while the concept of ethical obligations toward animals, plants and even rocks was not foreign to many faiths, 'to the traditional Christian perspective, the question "Do people have ethical obligations toward rocks?" makes no sense at all' (1973, 63). Nash further notes that 'early Christian evangelists felled the sacred groves of northern Europe where pagans worshipped a multiplicity of deities. The contemporary custom of cutting Christmas trees may have vague ties to that ancient ritual' (1989, 91). The progressive shift toward a rejection of the world, Bruno Latour concludes, made Christians 'increasingly indifferent to the fate of the cosmos. Believing themselves to be attached to the Spirit, they have lost the Earth' (2017, 210).

While the Bible naturally occupies a special place (together with Greek philosophy and the Roman political-legal legacy) within the Western tradition, it is not the only religious text of antiquity. Among others, the *Epic of Gilgamesh* stands out. The oldest recorded piece of literature, this Mesopotamian epic poem focuses on the struggle between Gilgamesh, king of Uruk (one of the earliest urban centres in the world), and Enkidu, a wild man sent by the gods to prevent Gilgamesh from oppressing his people. The myth quite explicitly euhemerizes the struggle between the nascent urban hierarchy and the primeval forces of nature represented by Enkidu. The second part of the story depicts Gilgamesh and Enkidu, now friends, journeying to the Cedar Forest in order to cut down the sacred Cedar, as well as the battle between Enkidu and the Bull of Heaven (sent by the goddess Ishtar—perhaps, in this instance, the personification of a primeval natural world—to punish Gilgamesh for rejecting her). The triumph of humanity over nature, albeit far less explicit than in the Biblical Genesis, is here also quite apparent. Much has been written about early religious perspectives on humanity and the environment (an example among many being Baird Callicott's (1994) *Earth's Insights*) but suffices to say that many of the tenets of modern anthropocentrism can already be found in some of the oldest recorded texts we possess.

Darwinized de Brosses' theory, speculating that human religion first took the form of an animistic nature worship, from which there evolved polytheism, followed by monotheism—the end point of progress in religion, as "civilization", preceded in turn by "savagery" and "barbarism", was the end point of social evolution.... [but] Why should monotheism be regarded as less primitive than animism? It apparently arose, at least in its familiar Judeo-Christian-Islamic form, largely because a single group of people insisted that their particular tribal divinity was superior to the ones of their neighbours' (1994, 162–3).

3.1.2 The Birth of Metaphysics

It is impossible to begin any overview of a Western worldview, however construed, without beginning with the oldest philosophical texts on record, those of the Greek philosophers of antiquity. For the pre-Socratic philosophers whose fragments and works have been transmitted through the first book of Aristotle's *Metaphysics*, the world was full of natural symbolism. Early philosophy, historians of philosophy Frederick Copleston (2003) and Anthony Kenny (2010) point out, was concerned with the nature of 'matter'. What is the world made of, they asked? What is the *urstoff*, the primitive element of all things, the unifying principle of reality, what Aristotle defined as the *material* cause of the universe? 'It is often said', Copleston asserts, 'that Greek philosophy centres round the problem of the One and the Many' (2003 ed, vol I, 76). Thales of Miletus, the first to conceive the notion of unity among difference, considers all things as varying forms of one primary and ultimate element. For Anaximander, all things come from a single primal substance that is both infinite and eternal, encompassing all worlds (he thought our world to be just one of many). Importantly, Bertrand Russell suggests (1972), his approach is already defined by a rationalistic and 'scientific' tone rather than a mystical one. Anaximenes expanded upon this theory by making the differences between substances quantitative, rather than qualitative, depending on the degree of condensation of 'air' as the essential substance. Anaximenes's primal element, or *arché* (ἀρχή)—which is (and must be) undetermined, boundless or undefined (ἄπειρον, *apeiron*)—is often rendered as the Infinite. However, '[t]he antithesis between spirit and matter had not yet been grasped; so that, although they [these early pre-Socratic philosophers] were de facto materialists—in that they assigned a form of matter as the principle of unity and primitive stuff to all things—they can be scarcely be termed materialists in our sense of the word' (Copleston, 2003 ed, vol I, 20).

Pythagoras—to whom is attributed the invention of the term 'philosopher' as a 'lover of wisdom', rather than mere 'sophos', or 'sage'—looms large in the history of ancient philosophy. Mathematics, 'in the sense of demonstrative deductive argument, begins with him' (Russell, 1972, 29): 'all things are numbers', Pythagoras is often quoted to have said. The first to introduce the idea of earth as spherical, he is also the first to describe the world as comprised of patterns, mathematical patterns in fact, that can be observed and measured, and from which certain knowledge can be derived. As Russell notes, '[m]athematical knowledge appears to be certain, exact and applicable to the real world; moreover, it was obtained by mere thinking, without the need of observation.' Consequently, 'it was thought to supply an ideal, from which everyday empirical knowledge fell short. It was supposed, on the basis of mathematics, that thought is superior to sense, intuition or observation. If the world of sense does not fit mathematics, so much worse for the world of sense' (1972, 34–5). Pythagoras's teachings thus begin a tradition of rationality and formal logic rather than experiential, intuitive and ecstatic knowledge. Indeed, the very idea of 'theory' changes with Pythagoras: from the original Orphic meaning of 'passionate sympathetic contemplation', a ritual mystical experience whereby the spectator identifies with the divine, for Pythagoras it became an intellectual pursuit issued in mathematical knowledge. The combination of rationality, mathematics and the deductive reasoning it entails led to the emergence of an intellectualized understanding of the world far different from the Orphic mystical tradition in which Pythagoras's theology was deeply steeped. For Russell, 'mathematics is the chief source of the belief in eternal and exact truth, as well as in a super-sensible intelligible world' (1972, 29).

Heraclitus introduced the idea of perpetual change. 'Everything flows, and nothing stays' (τὰ πάντα ῥεῖ καὶ οὐδὲν μένει), Heraclitus asserted. Connected to the idea of perennial change is the belief in strife as an essential, inevitable and ultimately creative force.[3] Hobbes and Nietzsche's later emphasis on conflict and individualism are likely to find their roots in Heraclitus's view. Finally, Heraclitus introduces the idea of *logos* (λόγος), often translated as 'reason', referring both to the reasoning power of humans and the more exalted cosmic principle of order (the Stoics will later pick up on this version of 'reason'). Parmenides, who has been said to have invented the study of metaphysics based on logic, attempted to respond to Heraclitus's idea of impermanence by introducing the idea of eternity. If for Heraclitus everything changes, for Parmenides nothing changes. He believed in a single unified 'One', a cohesive and infinite whole that is material (i.e. not transcendent), extended and ultimately indestructible (an idea articulated by one of his disciples, Melissus). Furthermore, Parmenides introduced the idea of *substance* as the persistent subject of various predicates. With him, matter became an ultimately unchanging substance, a philosophical axiom that has since dominated science until the physics of the twentieth century, which rather sees matter as a 'way of grouping events' (Russell, 1972, 70). Burnet writes that 'all materialism depends on [Parmenides's] view of reality' (1920, 182). Moreover, Parmenides introduces a famous propositional logical requirement about the concept of 'being': 'what is *must* be and cannot *not* be.'[4] Importantly, two categories thus emerge: being and its opposite, 'not being'. For Parmenides, it is worth noting, there can be no 'not being' (he denies the possibility of the void's existence, since, if it exists, it cannot be 'void'), but he introduces it as a categorical *possibility*. As Sartre pointed out in *Being and Nothingness* (1943), Parmenides introduces the objectification of *nothing*. The idea of the *nothing*, the *void*, has significant moral implications, since no moral duties are owed toward that which is not. And, once the category of the 'nothing' extends (much later) to encompass all matter that is deprived of a soul or a mind, then the lack of moral responsibility toward an inanimate world—a world devoid of a soul or mind—is entirely predicated on the conceptual category made possible by Parmenides's proposition. After all, the 'void' is an absence, a privation of reality. Over time, as theological rules of behaviour became increasingly supplanted by a rationalist ethics, a lack of moral responsibility emerged toward the 'not being', the 'void'. After all, it is impossible to be morally reproachable for actions conducted against *nothing*. As a result, what began with

[3] An important corollary of this idea of perennial change dictated by strife is the doctrine of universal conflagration, the basis of the future idea of a cyclical big bang.

[4] Importantly, while this is a *propositional* statement, it forms the basis of the development of all subsequent philosophical inquiry into *ontology*.

Parmenides as a linguistic/propositional category has morphed over the centuries into an ontological one and has then, in turn, morphed into a moral one, leading to the moral neutrality toward vast tracts of the cosmos that underpins the current environmental predicament.

In describing matter, Empedocles[5] introduced the idea of four 'substances' combined by Love and separated by Strife (two other primitive substances/forces, later equated with the fundamental forces of attraction and repulsion that have dominated physical theory for centuries). Empedocles called them 'roots', and Plato later referred to them as *stoicheia* (στοιχεῖα, a word that identifies the syllables of a word), with the Latin translation *elementa* becoming the common term to refer to them (*elementum* literally refers to the letters of a word). Anaxagoras introduced the idea of the mind, *nous* (νοῦς) as an independent substance.[6] It is, however, with the atomists Leucippus and Democritus that the modern idea of matter emerges. Building upon Pyhtagoras and Zeno, the atomists believed that all that exists 'is comprised of atoms, which are physically, but not geometrically, indivisible; that between the atoms there is empty space; that atoms are indestructible; that they always have been, and always will be, in motion; that there are an infinite number of atoms, and even of kinds of atoms, the difference being as regard shape and size' (Russell, 1972, 65). Moreover, *contra* Parmenides,[7] they introduced the idea of an infinite void within which atoms move and collide. Their collisions are explained mechanically (rather than being caused by the mind, as Anaxagoras had suggested), and these collisions happen in accordance with strict natural laws. Democritus, Russell writes, was 'a thorough-going materialist. ... for him ... [t]here was no purpose in the universe; there were only atoms governed by mechanical laws' (1972, 72). Copleston concurs, stating that 'in the atomism of Leucippus and Democritus we may see an anticipation of later materialistic and mechanistic philosophies which would endeavour to explain all quality by quantity and to reduce everything in the universe to matter and its products' (2003 ed, vol I, 77). Democritus's statement that nothing happens by chance (a non-religious interpretation of the idea of Fate or Necessity) is likely one of the clearest points of origin of modern determinism. Furthermore, Russell notes that the atomists looked at the explanation of matter, the 'why', in a 'mechanistic' sense. 'When we ask "Why? Concerning an event", Russell explains "we may mean either of two things". We may mean "What purpose did this event serve?" or we may mean "What earlier circumstances caused this event?" The answer to the former is a teleological explanation, or an explanation by final causes; the answer to the latter question is a mechanistic explanation' (1972, 67). In this sense, the atomists' philosophy represents the birth of science in the modern sense: indeed, while the

[5] Empedocles anticipates much of later scientific theories: he believed that light takes time to travel, that the moon reflects light, in introduced the idea of evolution by survival of the fittest, and the centrifugal theory.

[6] Anaxagoras also argued that the sun and stars are fiery stones, and he was prosecuted for stating that planetary bodies were not alive.

[7] Albeit, as noted before, without Parmenides's categorical *possibility* of the void as 'not being', the atomists' void could not have been conceived.

teleological question was privileged after the Greeks and until the Renaissance, the atomists' mechanistic approach re-emerged with the birth of modern science.

After the atomists, the attention of Greek philosophy shifts from the ontological sphere to the ethical realm. If 'earlier Greek philosophers had been chiefly interested in the Object, trying to determine the ultimate principle of all things ... a swing-over to the Subject as point of consideration' (Copleston, 2003 ed, vol I, 81) occurred from this point forward.

> From this point onwards ... is an undue emphasis on man as compared with the universe. First comes scepticism, with the Sophists, leading to the study of *how* we know rather than the attempt to acquire fresh knowledge. Then comes, with Socrates, the emphasis on ethics; with Plato, the rejection of the world of sense in favour of the self-created world of pure thought; with Aristotle, the belief in purpose as the fundamental concept in science. (Russell, 1972, 73)

Socrates's ethical focus is preceded by a growing focus on the human. Protagoras (as quoted in Plato's *Theaetetus*) famously asserts that 'man is the measure of all things' (πάντων χρημάτων μέτρον ἔστὶν ἄνθρωπος, τῶν δὲ μὲν οντῶν ὡς ἔστιν, τῶν δὲ οὐκ ὄντων ὡς οὐκ ἔστι, 'man is the measure of all things: things which are, that they are, and things which are not, that they are not'—meaning each individual, not just humanity as a whole).[8] Xenophon also suggests that the creative powers of the universe have clearly favoured humans above all animals, by endowing them with particular biological features (such as erect posture, multipurpose hands and articulate language). Other sophists introduced many arguments now familiar to an anthropocentric individualistic worldview: Callicles introduced the idea that might is right, while Thrasymachus defined justice (as Marxist theorists would two millennia later) as the self-interest of those in power. This extreme focus on the human at the expenses of the rest of the universe is fully captured by Socrates, who, in Plato's *Apology*, states, 'I have nothing to do with physical speculation', his concerns being entirely about (purely human) ethics.

Plato, one of the greatest figures in the history of Western philosophy, combined Parmenides's idea of an eternal (and ultimately unchanging) being with Heraclitus's idea that nothing permanent exists in the sensible world, reaching the conclusion that knowledge can never be derived from the senses but can only be achieved by the intellect. A renewed version of Pythagoreanism (i.e. the conception of an eternal world revealed to the intellect but not to the senses), Plato's theory of ideas introduces the distinction between *knowledge* (of an immutable Parmenidean world) and *opinion* (δόξα, *doxa*—of the sensible world). Apart from establishing the path for all future epistemological reflections, this solidifies the rationalistic approach to knowledge, which establishes a degree of self-referentiality of human knowledge. Plato's approach—perhaps paradoxically, some may argue given Plato's aspirations—fully enshrines a rationalistic and intellectual appraisal of the world, a purely *propositional* form of knowledge at the expenses of an *experiential* one. Moreover, the introduction in *Phaedo* of the idea of the soul introduces a novel dualism that diminishes any

[8] Gorgias, the ultimate sceptic, had maintained that nothing exists, and that, if it exists, it is ultimately unknowable, and, if it exists and it is knowable, it can never be communicated to others.

ethical responsibility toward the illusory world of the senses alone. As Russell says, '[t]he distinction between mind and matter ... which has become a commonplace in philosophy and science and popular thought, has a religious origin, and began as a distinction of soul and body' (1972, 134). Furthermore, according to Plato, *ideas* (the ultimate truths to be appraised by the knowing intellect) *pre-exist* knowledge (rather than being contingent and somewhat arbitrary). Plato thus introduces the idea of a transcendent reality, so much so that Nietzsche accused him of 'being an enemy to this world, of setting up a transcendental world ... of contrasting a "There" with a "Here" out of dislike of the world of experience' (Copleston, 2003 ed, vol I, 205). Socrates's ethical legacy is also very visible in Plato, as evinced by the *Republic's* exclusive concerns with the affairs of humanity. Finally, in the *Timaeus*, Plato distinguishes between intelligent causes, endowed with a mind, and other causes that are moved by others and are then compelled to move others (but by chance alone), thus introducing the idea that not all things possess a mind or soul and thus are less worthy of respect. Arthur Lovejoy traces the origin of the idea of 'the great chain of being' in Plato, a *scala naturae* composed 'of an infinite number of links ranging in hierarchical order from the meagerest kind of existence, which barely escaped non-existence, through "every possible" grade up to the *ens perfectissimus* ... every one of them differing from that immediately above and that immediately below it by the "least possible" degree of difference' (1961, 51).

Aristotle attempts to deal with the problem of universals posited by Plato's theory of ideas through a strong biological interest expressed in the categorization of things. However, Aristotelian categories, Copleston notes, are not 'simply modes of mental representation, moulds of concepts: they represent the actual modes of being in the extramental world' (2003 ed, vol I, 279). These categories are deeply connected to the term used by Aristotle to designate 'nature': *physis* (φύσις). Philippe Descola clarifies it as 'the principle that produces the development of a being that contains within itself the source of its movement and its rest. This is the principle that causes it to realize itself in accordance with a particular type' (2013, 65). The 'nature' of a thing, in Aristotle's *hylomorphism*, is teleological, purposively aimed toward 'an end and even a final state in which its immanent nature is fully realized' (Davies, 2022, 43). Hence, some things exist by 'nature' (i.e. they have an internal principle of growth) and the phrase 'according to nature' applies to such things. Russell points out that '[i]t was through this point of view that "unnatural" came to express blame' (1972, 205). Furthermore, Aristotelian categories came to be regarded as inherent and necessary, they were normalized into a self-evident existence. This, in turn, led to a normalization of the *scala naturae*, which sees animals as inferior to humans and plants as inferior to animals. Furthermore, Aristotle defines space as a receptacle, a void within which matter exists (Newton will later agree with this view, Descartes will refuse it, and Leibniz will see space a system of relations—something further articulated by Einstein). Due to the impact of Aristotle's work, his assertion that the earth is at the centre of the universe is of particular import. Finally, Aristotle's distinction between *potentiality* and *actuality* entails the idea that the universe is consistently developing toward a 'better' (more advanced) *form*; in other words, it entails the idea of *progress*.

With the collapse of Greek city-states, Greek philosophy diminished in importance and became diffused throughout the Roman world. In this period, Euclid's *Elements* solidify the idea of deductive logic and the rationality of the world. The Sceptics assert that all things are ultimately *indifferent* toward humanity. Epicurus and Lucretius were materialists and mechanicists, but not determinists. They believed the world to be comprised of material atoms, but not that these atoms are always completely controlled by natural laws. Lucretius 'tells of bodies falling in a void, bodies that are not lifeless stuff but matter on the go, entering and leaving assemblages, swerving into each other' (Bennett, 2010, 18). The idea of the soul is thus preserved, albeit in a material form. The Stoics exalt reason, but move from the materialism of the founder Zeno to a very different doctrine with Marcus Aurelius. Zeno believed in strict determinism, asserting that there is no such thing as chance, that the course of nature is determined by natural laws. For him, the General Law, which is Right Reason, pervades everything, and Nature or God/Zeus are synonyms for it. 'The Stoics were therefore Empiricists', Copleston writes, 'even "Sensualists"; but they also maintained a Rationalism which was scarcely consistent with a thoroughly empiricist and nominalist position' (2003 ed, vol I, 387). The cosmopolitanism of Epictetus and Marcus Aurelius, on the other hand, when combined with the development of the legal *persona* in Roman legal thought and the Antonine Constitution (which extended Roman citizenship to all free men across the Empire), gave birth to the idea of a common 'humanity', a previously unheard-of idea.

With the collapse of the city-states in Greece, Russell writes, 'the outlook of those who thought and felt seriously becomes increasingly subjective and individualistic, until, at last, Christianity evolved a gospel of individual salvation which inspired missionary zeal and created the Church' (1972, 230). The focus on virtue that had begun with Socrates increasingly became a focus on *individual* virtue. At the same time, Neoplatonism rejected the materialism of the atomists and introduced a fully transcendental conception of the world of ideas. The Platonic perfect world of ideas became fully transcendent in Plotinus's conception of a perfect Other World. If, for Philo of Alexandria, the One was still identified with the Parmenidean all-encompassing Being, for Plotinus the One was utterly beyond the world. In fact, the material world is conceived as emanating *from* this transcendent One, even though 'it [the material world] forms the lowest stage of the universe and is the antithesis to the One' (Copleston, 2003 ed, vol I, 469). Iamblichus took the idea a step further, asserting multiple principles of creation: an unintelligible, fully transcendent, One, and a One from whom the material world eventually emanates (the Demiurge, for Numenius). Furthermore, for the corporeal world to emanate from the singular and perfect One, there must be a principle that permits the multiplicity of the corporeal world: such a principle is matter, which, for Plotinus, is a privation of the perfect goodness of the One. The shift to a perception of matter as not only 'lesser' but as actually the principle of 'evil' is fully realized with Gnosticism. Finally, knowledge, in order to be knowledge of the One, must be mystical and transcendental and requires a degree of abandonment of the world of the senses. The Orphic-Pythagorean-Platonic idea of 'otherworldliness' thus became fully realized in Plotinus, while the focus on ethics (Socrates, Plato, the Stoics and Epicureans and ultimately Plotinus) led to a growth of subjectivism and individualism. By the time of Christianity, '[s]cience was no longer cultivated, and only virtue was thought important' (Russell, 1972, 297). As a result, the conception of Nature as matter, combined with the idea of a transcendental perfection that is not of the natural world, and joined together with determinism and a faith in Reason, have been normalized as a unifying ontological substratum ever since.

3.1.3 To Transcend the World

Since at least the fourth century CE, Christianity has displayed a tendency to synthesize its doctrines through the establishment of a central power (the Catholic papacy) which often extinguished dissent (sometimes in the form of crusades against its own disciples, such as against the Cathars and other 'heresies'). Moreover, the Judaic tradition had already introduced an exclusionary form of religiosity (although the commandment 'thou shalt have none other gods but me' suggests the existence of a plurality of gods, only one of which must be worshipped—that is, it did not entail metaphysical monism, but rather worship monotheism). As a result of the influence of Christianity, which extended over two millennia firstly across Europe and then in the rest of the forcibly colonized world, it is no surprise that all subsequent philosophy has everywhere been deeply influenced by its doctrines. According to Russell, Christianity is marked by a number of key features:

1. Certain philosophical beliefs derived mainly from Plato and Neoplatonism (but also the Stoics).
2. Certain theories related to salvation partly traceable to Orphism and Eastern cults.
3. A conception of a sacred history inherited from the Old Testament and the Judaic tradition.
4. The existence of a privileged few (in the case of Christianity, those who have received the word of God and are thus tasked with proselytizing it).
5. A concept of exclusive and universal 'righteousness', and an emphasis on punishment of the 'sinners' inherited from the pre-diaspora Judaic tradition. However, rather than thinking of *others* as sinners, Christians thought of *themselves* as such.
6. A salvific idea via the belief in a messiah.
7. The idea of other-worldliness (with the kingdom of heaven cast not merely in a metaphysically separate space, but into the future, with a curious blend of Heraclitean and Stoic belief in cyclical history and conflagration, and Platonic and Neo-platonic metaphysical transcendence).

Throughout the Christian era, the common interpretation of the Bible is one whereby the Mosaic Creator infuses an inert world with life. The impersonal One of Parmenides and Plato becomes personified (and masculinized) in Christianity. Moreover, the idea of this masculine God is ultimately transcendent (an idea inherited from Neoplatonism), as discussed early on by Origen of Alexandria. God is undifferentiated and superior to substance (matter), of which it does not participate. From the relative simplicity of the three synoptic gospels (Matthew, Mark and Luke), it is possible to see the identification of Christ with the Platonic-Stoic Logos in John (thus incorporating Greek philosophy—particularly Platonic and Neo-platonic—into Christianity very early on). Furthermore, Manicheism (an early Christian sect that influenced Augustine of Hippo) established two warring principles, a positive one (spirit) and a negative or evil one (embodied in matter), leading to an inevitable rejection of the world of matter. For the Gnostics, Plato's reconstructed world of ideas led to the inevitable conclusion that the world of the senses is an illusory one created by a Demiurge and is not the *real* world. Ethical responsibilities toward this real world are thus further diminished, since the sensible world is seen as somewhat evil, or at least imperfect. The Gnostics overtly hated matter (bust such hate was only made possible because of the particular conception of matter previously traced), believing the world to have been created by an inferior being (the Demiurge), *Ialdabaoth*, the rebellious son of *Sophia* (heavenly wisdom).

The standard of early Christian (Catholic) orthodoxy was established at the Council of Nicaea in 325 CE, convened by Constantine to resolve once and for all the Catholic/Arian controversy with the view of constructing a single cohesive and coherent perspective, which established the Nicaean Creed. Not long after, the emperor Theodosius gave full support to Catholicism, in 379 CE. Christianity, marked as a theoretical (derived from Greek and Jewish philosophies, as well as a number of other eastern influences) and political (based on both Jewish exclusivity and Roman universality) synchesis, soon crystallized into a high degree of intolerance and inflexibility. Its zealous and uncompromising religiosity, combined with a deeply proselytizing nature (partly due to the Judaic tradition and partly to the attempt by the late Roman empire in the third and fourth centuries to establish a unifying religious doctrine), led to a host of persecutions of any dissenting voice. Yet, at the same time, Origen introduced the idea of rejecting worldly politics, rather suggesting to focus exclusively on God's government (the Church), while Ambrose established the doctrine of the Emperor 'owing military service to God', meaning that there were matters in which the State must yield to the Church, and thus establishing the growing political power of a politically separate Church.

The anthropocentric tendency of early Christianity is aptly captured by the writings of Hugh of Saint Victor, who argued that God created humanity as His servant, and, in turn, the material world to serve humanity. These ideas were reasserted as recently as 1995, in Pope John Paul II's encyclical *Evangelium Vitae*, which, according to Bennett (2010, 86–7), contains the following claims: that life is radically different from matter; that human life is qualitatively different from all other life; that human uniqueness is an expression of divine intervention; and that the world is a divinely created order in the shape of a fixed hierarchy. Very early on, Christian authors (such as Augustine) developed a complex psychology of sin, turning the gaze that sees evil in matter toward themselves.[9] Christianity's approach to the metaphysically transcendent reality of God is marked by rationality and faith, but such faith is not mystical and experiential, it is rather rational in its intrinsic formulation, as captured by Anselm of Canterbury's motto *Credo ut intelligam* ('I believe in order to understand'), built upon Augustine's *Crede ut intelligas* ('believe so that you may understand'). This rationality is, at the same time, accompanied by a deep rejection of philosophical pursuits, as exemplified by Tertullian's argument that philosophy is the root of all heresies, only slightly amended by Clement of Alexandria's assertion that philosophy is the handmaid to theology. Only Christian revelation is seen as a truly legitimate source of knowledge. The highly zealotic pogroms—for example the one conducted by Cyril of Alexandria against the Hellenised Jewish community in Alexandria (which stopped the philosophical pursuits of many in their tracks) or the killing of Hypatia, or the pogroms that occurred during the crusades, primarily against jews, but also against Christian 'heretics' like the neo-manicheists, the gnostics, the bogomiles, which were a fusion of manicheists and paulicians, and the cathars—culminated in the founding of the Inquisition in 1233 by Pope Gregory IX, with the explicit attempt to ferret out any heresy that would threaten the fideistic integrity of the Church.

The moral nature of Christianity is virtually formed with Augustine and the early Fathers of the Church. An ultimately repressive morality, in line with the rejection of both the material natural world and the corrupted nature of the self, its emphasis is on punishment and purification, leading to the *apocatastasis* (the doctrine of the final restoration of all sinful beings to God and to the state of blessedness) described by Gregory of Nissa. This is, indeed, a far cry from Aristotle's quest for *eudaimonia* (ευδαιμονία, the 'happiness' that emerges from the moderation of the extremes). It is a morality marked by dualism—that is, the contrast between the kingdom of God and the kingdoms of this world, between spirit and matter, between spirit and flesh—as introduced by Augustine's *The City of God.* Augustine also reasserted a strong belief in human exceptionalism, by noting how animals had been created as a single whole, whereas humanity was created in a single individual, Adam. He defined man (definitely in the masculine in his work) as the peak of the material creation. In *De Quantitate Animae,* he distinguished the souls of beasts, which possess the power of sensation but not of reasoning and knowing, from those of humans, asserting that only the latter are immortal. Augustine, however, stopped short of believing (as Origen did) that souls are given bodies out of punishment. He further equated the pagan gods (which he firmly believed to exist) with devils, and in further anthropomorphizing them, he deprived them of any deeper symbolic significance. Augustine also strongly asserted a linear conception of time (against the cyclical nature assigned to it by Heraclitus or the Stoics), with a resurrection of both the soul (a clear adherence to the Platonic idea of immortality) and of the flesh at the end of times. Jewish eschatology is hereby embraced by the universalizing nature of the Catholic Church, inherited from both the Romans and the Stoics.

---

[9] In fact, Augustine's own issue with carnal lust, inherited from Origen and an ascetic tradition, soon became a doctrinal issue within the nascent Catholic Church.

While ascetic and monastic practices continued (along the tradition of Pythagorean and Orphic cults, as well as many other ascetic monastic sects in the east), the practice became monopolized by the Church with Anastasius of Persia, who established that monks had to be priest or ecclesiastical figures (many of them also soon became skilled agriculturalists and keepers of knowledge). This practice of incorporating and replacing pre-existing religious and spiritual practices and beliefs is well exemplified by the replacement of the temple of Apollo in Monte Cassino with the first Benedictine monastery. Such is a paradigmatic example of the physical continuity of places of worship (which still maintained some degree of ecological acknowledgment) with the more abstract and de-physicalized religiosity of Christianity (whose interest lies entirely away from the world of matter). In the ninth century, the creation of the Holy Roman Empire established the absolute power of the Papacy as an arbiter of political power among distinct kings and sovereigns, paving the way for the modern conception of international law in a modern sense and founding the 'unity of Christendom', a melange of the political secular power of the Holy Roman Emperor and the spiritual political power of the Papacy, which, together, combine to establish a singular doctrinal worldview at the same time exclusionary and universal. Both the secular and the spiritual history of the Catholic Church and its accompanying secular kingdoms is a history of very rigid hierarchies. The power of those above is absolute, both in practice and thought. While not unique to Christianity or the history of Europe, the idea of vertical hierarchies occupies a special place within the anthropocentric view that is here being reconstructed.

While human exceptionalism continued well into the second millennium, with Maimonides distinguishing between providence, which looks after humans, and chance, which regulates the fate of all other creatures, and John the Scot's argument that humans share reason and intellect with celestial beings and bodies with inferior animals, reason once again obtained a place of prominence above faith. By placing reason above faith, John the Scot brouht back the Greek idea of rationality. At the same time, his assertion that it was only as a result of sin that human beings were divided into female and male, with women embodying man's fallen and sensuous nature, solidified the patriarchal zeal of medieval Christianity. In reading Aristotle, Averroes suggested that, while there exists a multiplicity of bodies, they all possess a single identical intellect, thus affirming the universality of reason. The idea of Nature as a manifestation of God continued, with slightly less negative connotations, in Bonaventure's doctrine of the material world as the *vestigium* or *umbra Dei*.

The synthesis of Christian theology and Greek rationalism is fully realized with Thomas of Aquinas, whose system had such an impact on later theologians that Pope Leo XIII in 1879 mandated it as the only right system to be taught. Aquinas fully brought rationality, or 'natural reason', to the core of philosophical thinking, reconciling it with revelation in a way that no other scholastic scholar had done before—or did ever after. Aquinas reasserted Aristotle's *scala naturae*, from the baser form of inorganic substances, to the vegetative forms, to the irrational sensitive forms of animals, to the rational soul of humanity (the summit of the corporeal world), to created spiritual beings (angels) to the perfection of the uncreated creator, God. Life, but not knowledge, Aquinas stated, is the essence of a plant, and knowledge, but not intellect, is the essence of an animal. The first is like God only in being alive, the second in having knowledge, but no intellect. Anything else, of course, is not even connected to the divine. Furthermore, the same *scala naturae* is extended to Aquinas's conception of a 'normative ladder', with a 'lower' normativity emanating from the higher one in a Neo-platonic sense. Aquinas introduces the idea of 'natural' (moral) law (*lex naturalis moralis*) in the modern, rationalistic sense, as the expression of a self-evident reality (at least self-evident, according to Aquinas, to a universal 'rationality').

Not long after Aquinas's theological-philosophical synthesis, Thomas Cajetan introduced the idea of a state of 'pure nature,' a state of humanity *in puris naturalibus*. However, where for Aquinas such a state was connected to the supernatural end or goal of humanity (the beatitude in God), this introduction of a non-teleological 'state of nature' (which precedes the social contractarians of a few centuries later) is already inscribed with a great host of assumptions as to what 'nature' is.

Aquinas's *oeuvre* paves the way for a renewed focus on rational inquiry, and, not long after, the rise of science in its modern conception. William of Ockham, in particular, paved the way for the empiricist, rationalist and logical rise of science that followed. Ockham ascribed 'freedom' as a primary characteristic of any *rational* creature—that is, a rational *human*—implying that non-rational creatures do not possess such a characteristic. Furthermore, Ockham also argued that man (gendered in his writing) possesses a natural right to property: God gave man the power to dispose of the goods of the earth in a manner that is dictated by right reason, and, since the Fall, right reason shows that the personal appropriation of temporal goods is necessary for individual survival. The right to private property is thus a natural right willed by God. The Franciscan Peter John Olivi prefigured Descartes' dualism by focusing on the relationship of the soul to the body. Among the three constitutive parts of the human soul (vegetative, sensitive and intellectual), Olivi argued, the higher forms influence and move the lower forms. But while the vegetative and sensitive parts inform the body, the intellectual is not influenced by the body, but only moves the other parts 'as instruments and subjects' (Copleston, 2003 ed, vol II, 452). Giles of Rome introduced a further separation between and soul (or form), with the body maintaining a degree of identity even in the absence of the soul, a theory this that prefigures the mechanistic idea of the body that will arise centuries later. As Russell notes, '[t]he thirteenth century had brought to completion a great synthesis, philosophical, theological, political and social, which had been slowly built up by the combination of many elements' (1972, 467–7). It is from this synthesis that humanism and science (as it is conceived of today within a Western worldview) emerged.

3.1.4 The Rise of Science

The humanistic ideal is one of developing human personality and potentiality to the full. 'This, however,' writes Copleston, 'was the humanistic ideal at its best. In practice the Italian Renaissance became associated to a certain extent with a growth of moral or amoral individualism and the pursuit of fame' (2003 ed, vol III, 208). The humanist idea of self-development and self-culture (more sober and aesthetically less significant in Northern Europe) represents an inherently individualistic movement and forms the basis of the extreme individualism that fully developed with the later rise of liberalism. Humanism thus enshrined human exceptionalism even further. The Neo-Platonic writings of Marsilius Ficinus, for example, emphasized the 'place of man as the bond between the spiritual and the material' (Copleston, 2003 ed, vol III, 212). Heinrich Cornelius Agrippa von Nettesheim suggested that man unites in himself the terrestrial world of the elements, the world of the heavenly bodies and the spiritual world, unique in his ability to know all three worlds.

The rise of science that follows is marked by a few political events:

- The waning power of a centralized Church as a result of the Reformation.
- The loss of belief in a singular worldview: the many translations and languages of the scriptures, which inevitably led to many interpretations, were now constitutive of a number of different perspectives encoded within the rise of Protestantism.
- The continued quest for a singular truth, now replaced by the emerging scientism.
- The rise of centralized and absolutist States.

In parallel with the consolidation of an individualized form of human exceptionalism, empiricism emerged from the discussion of universals and the diatribe between nominalists and realists that had continued throughout the Middle Ages. Ockham's distinction between a *scientia realis* (concerned with real things) and a *scientia rationalis* (concerned with terms that do not stand immediately for real things) also provided the basis for the new interest in empirical science. Thinkers such as Albertus Magnus, Peter of Maricourt, Robert Grosseteste, Roger Bacon and Pietro Pomponazzi all emphasized the importance of observation or 'experience' in scientific studies. This emerging scientific empiricism was, however, a mix of immediate sensory perceptions, Aristotelian/Thomistic logic and a suite of metaphysical assumptions about the nature of the universe. It is important to be reminded of the fact that there is nothing universally 'objective' nor unprecedented about the Renaissance's enthrallment with empiricism. That notwithstanding, the Renaissance heralded the emergence of *empirical* science as the *only* possible type of knowledge. Theofrastus Bombast von Hohenheim (generally known as Paracelsus) drew a sharp distinction between theology and philosophy, the latter being, according to him, entirely devoted to the study of Nature, not of God (he also divided the universe into a terrestrial world, a sidereal world and a heavenly world). The novel appeals to science were entirely rational, even rationalistic and wholly independent of political relations (and thus governments) and of fideistic beliefs (and thus of different Christian Churches). This further enshrined the 'cult of reason', the privileged place that reason had developed for itself over the centuries and that came to occupy with the rise of modern science.

Among Renaissance thinkers arose the idea of nature as a 'self-sufficient unity, as a system unified by all-pervading forces of sympathy and attraction and animated by a world-soul' (Copleston, 2003 ed, vol III, 248). New philosophers of nature during the Renaissance began to introduce 'objective' empirical descriptors of what 'nature' is, rather than principles logically deduced from metaphysical premises. Nicholas of Cusa, Giordano Bruno and Girolamo Cardano, for example, introduced (albeit indirectly) the idea of natural 'laws' and of nature as a unified, law-governed, system. Pierre Gassendi gave a mechanistic account of Nature, with the help of atoms, space and motion. The increase of empirical observations led to a number of challenges to the Aristotelian depiction of a universe with earth at its centre. Nicholas of Cusa's almost Heraclitean idea of unity as the harmonious synthesis of differences, the *coincidentia oppositorum*, depicted nature as an infinite system in which earth occupies no privileged position. Copernicus's heliocentric theory[10] had the effect of 'dethron[ing] ... earth from its geometrical pre-eminence. In the long run, this made it difficult to give to man the cosmic importance assigned to him in the Christian theology' (Russell, 1972, 526). However, it also created a space for a more nihilistic and a negative look toward the world, rather than the humble joyfulness of being in the cosmos that the Greeks and the pre-Christian ancients had displayed, and that many Indigenous peoples displayed at the time of the burgeoning *conquista*, according to the accounts of initial contacts in the Americas, Australia and the Pacific.

Copernican theory (then taken up and popularized by Kepler and Galileo) traditionally marks the birth of modern science (Russell, 1972, 492). Not long after, Galileo's view of nature, which was profoundly indebted to Pythagoreanism, articulated a novel approach to being in the cosmos. In *Il Saggiatore,* Galileo wrote that the 'book of the universe ... cannot be read until we have learnt the language and understand the characters in which it is written. It is written in mathematical language, and its characters are triangles, circles and other geometrical figures'. Newton called 'forces' what were previously known as 'sympathies' and 'antipathies' between bodies. Importantly, Newton conceived of space and time as comprised of distinct points and instants, thus enshrining in modern science Democritean atomism and normalizing it as 'objective'.

Galileo's emphasis on quantitative measurements, when combined with Newton's renewed focus on atomism, led to a mechanistic view of the world. It was, indeed, such an atomist view of the world that led Robert Boyle to propose the idea that tiny clusters of particles combine to form what Amedeo Avogadro then called 'molecules'. Furthermore, induction replaced deduction in the way of knowing the world, and 'the development of astronomy and of mechanics at the time of the Renaissance promoted the growth of a mechanical view of the world' (Copleston, 2003 ed, vol III, 290). Mechanics was defined by Francis Bacon as the application of physics in practice. In drawing a clear and sharp distinction between theology and philosophy, Bacon

[10] Copernicus seemed unaware of Aristarchus of Samo's equal theory from antiquity.

'accorded full liberty to a materialistic and mechanistic interpretation of Nature' (Copleston, 2003 ed, vol III, 300).

Furthermore, the rise of 'objective' technology (what Russell calls *practical* science, as opposed to *theoretical* science) is another hallmark of modernity. 'The power conferred by technique … [u]nlike religion, is ethically neutral: it assures men that they can perform wonders, but does not tell them what wonders to perform' (Russell, 1972, 494). While this was likely always true, it became even more so since technological modernity. While technology, in its fundamental need for a human collective to produce it, is inherently anti-individualistic, it is nonetheless hyper-anthropocentric. Furthermore, the perceived ethical neutrality of technology reinforces a mechanistic view of the world. 'The philosophies that have been inspired by scientific *technique* are power philosophies,' Russell writes, 'and tend to regard everything nonhuman as mere raw material. Ends are no longer considered' (1972, 494).

If Copernicus, Tycho Brahe, Kepler, Galileo and ultimately Newton represent the empirical rise of science, it is first Francis Bacon and then René Descartes that solidified it philosophically. Francis Bacon's 'basis of his philosophy was practical: to give mankind mastery over the forces of nature by means of scientific discoveries and inventions' (Russell, 1972, 542). The idea that 'knowledge is power' is ascribed to him (while not necessarily the first to say it, he was certainly the first to emphasize it). Bacon's anthropocentrism and human exceptionalism are notoriously explicit: in emphasizing the need for humanity to 'subdue' nature, seen as an ultimate enemy, he called men (gendered in his work) to 'unite forces against the Nature of Things. To storm and occupy her castles and strongholds, and extend the bounds of the human empire.' Bacon's scientific version of a gnostic refusal of the world was but the first of many to follow. 'Beginning in the seventeenth century,' Andrew Charlton writes, 'Enlightenment thinkers broke away from the Aristotelian conception of a steady natural order linking the physical and spiritual world. They criticized classical naturalism for holding back the progress of man.' For example, '[i]n his *Free Inquiry into the Vulgarly Received Notion of Nature*, Robert Boyle, one of the fathers of modern chemistry, protested that "the veneration were with men are imbued for what they call 'nature', has been a discouraging impediment to the empire of man over the inferior creatures of God"'. Charlton concludes that, '[w]hereas classical scholars sought to live within the natural order, Enlightenment scientists aspired to conquer nature. Francis Bacon believed that technology could "establish and extend the power and dominion of the human race itself over the universe". Science, he hoped, could recreate the utopia lost when Adam was expelled from Eden' (2011, 60).

The rise of mechanistic science led to 'the removal of all traces of animism from the laws of physics' (Russell, 1972, 537). Most ancient Greek philosophers (with the exclusions of Anaxagoras, Democritus and then the Epicureans) had considered the power of movement as a sign of life and ascribed it not necessarily to the entirety of the cosmos, but certainly to animals and the celestial bodies. All this 'was changed by the first law of motion. Lifeless matter, once set moving, will continue to move for ever unless stopped by some external cause … There might still seem to be the need of God to set the mechanism working ... But when He had done this, and decreed the law of gravitation, everything went on by itself without further need of divine intervention' (Russell, 1972, 537). This led to a profound change in the conception of man's place in the universe. Building upon Bacon's hostility toward nature, writers in the Tudor period displayed an absolute anthropocentric belief in the centrality of humanity. Sir Matthew Hale, one of the founding fathers of classical common law theory, said that '[a]ll creatures were made for man, subjected to his government and appointed for his use' (1677, 78). Samuel von Pufendorf argued that vegetables could have no rights, since they were deprived of sense and thus were incapable of injury. Thomas Hobbes agreed that there could be no obligation toward animals, because 'to make covenants with brute beasts is impossible' (1651, 125). Pascal summed this novel version of human exceptionalism in his *Pensées*: '[m]an is only a reed, the frailest thing in nature, but he is a thinking reed. To crush him it does not take the whole universe in arms: a breath of wind, a drop of water is enough to kill him. But were the universe to crush him, man would still be nobler than his killer. For he knows that he is dying and that the universe has the better of him. But the universe knows nothing of this' (1670, 231).

At the same time, the complete removal of metaphysical considerations objectivized and normalized science (as well as its unstated premises and bias, what Bacon called 'idols') as the *only* acceptable truth. '[P]urpose, which had since Aristotle formed an intimate part of the conception of science, was now thrust out of scientific procedure. Any one might still believe the heavens exist to declare the glory of God, but no one could let this belief intervene in an astronomical calculation. The world might have a purpose, but purposes no longer enter into scientific explanations' (Russell, 1972, 538).

The mechanistic architecture of modern science is fully realized in René Descartes's attempt to establish a full philosophical system, an attempt that is often considered the beginning of modern philosophy. Descartes famously began as a radical sceptic, doubting everything. But since no one can deceive themselves of the fact of their self-existence that led him to proclaim *cogito ergo sum* ('I think therefore I am'). The *cogito* famously led to a distinction between *res cogitans* (the thing that thinks, the *mind*) and *res extensa* (matter). He also introduced *res divina*, God, as the necessary counterbalance to the scepticism with which he started, and the only way to ultimately justify any knowledge of the world. While the *cogito* is an epistemological argument against doubt, it connects existence and rationality. The mind, significantly, becomes more important than matter—and mind is connected to rationality. Descartes's *cogito* 'brought to completion, or very near to completion, the dualism of mind and matter which began with Plato and was developed, largely for religious reasons, by Christian philosophy' (Russell, 1972, 567). By fully separating mind and matter, and by assigning mind only to humanity, he fully realized human exceptionalism, regarding 'the bodies of men and animals as machines; animals he regarded as automata, governed entirely by the laws of physics, and devoid of feelings and consciousness' (Russell, 1972, 561). From this point onward, Copleston writes, '[t]he whole material world can be treated as a mechanical system' (2003 ed, vol IV, 137). Nature, since Descartes, is nothing but a machine.

Science's mechanistic materialism soon entered political theory. Niccoló Machiavelli introduced the idea of pure ethical consequentialism, by looking at the most efficient means of obtaining certain ends. Not long after, the individualism engendered by the more personal approach to religion in Luther, Calvin and the Reformation was naturalized by the birth of liberalism. Thomas Hobbes proclaimed a thorough-going materialism. To him '"[l]ife" ... is nothing but a motion of the limbs, and therefore automata have an artificial life' (Russell, 1972, 548). He reasserted Machiavelli's ultimate individualism and egoism in 'scientific' terms, noting, with Bernardino Telesio, that the ultimate 'law of nature' is the individual instinct of self-preservation. This individualism, which would notoriously lead to a war of all against all, making life 'nasty, brutish and short', depicts a view of humanity at war not only with nature (as Bacon had contended) but also with itself. As the previous chapter highlighted, Hobbes's thought experiment of the 'state of nature' still influences many contemporary narratives of imagined environmental apocalypses. Thomas Hobbes's *Leviathan* formed the political basis for the figure of the absolute ruler, what he called the Sovereign (Jean Bodin, in his *Six livres de la république*, had already defined sovereignty as the 'supreme power over citizens and subjects, unrestrained by law'). The absolute power of the State, in turn, allowed the emergence of positivism and the idea of absolute arbitrariness of human laws (against the belief in natural law that had continued until Aquinas). With the solipsistic belief in human arbitrariness, issues of 'nature' progressively disappeared from ethical, political and legal concerns. Notwithstanding his articulation of 'natural law', Hugo Grotius made it very clear that 'the human relationship to the environment was not a subject for ethical concern' (Nash, 1989, 17).

The idea of self-interest as the driver of human societies was further articulated by Locke, for whom property is the chief reason for the institution of governments—[t]he great and chief end of men uniting into commonwealths, and putting themselves under government, is the preservation of their property; to which in the state of nature there are many things wanting'—and later by Adam Smith's novel 'political economy', who argued that, in the long run, individual self-interest coincides with the general interest of, and the best outcome for, society.

David Hume (building upon George Berkley's denial of the existence of matter) developed empiricism to its final form and conclusion: in *Essay on Miracles* he rejected any historical evidence for miraculous or supernatural events, establishing a fully mechanistic and materialistic conception of nature that can be fully, and exclusively, appraised empirically. Ideas, with Hume, lost their metaphysical value and became just a fainter version of sensory 'impressions'. He banished the conception of *substance* from psychology as Berkeley had banished it from physics. There can be no idea of self, he argued, as there is no impression of the self. The consequence of such view is the abolition of any conception of the 'soul', thus paving the way for the full application of materialism not only to the world, but even to humanity.

Rationality reigned triumphant in the Age of Reason, as the Enlightenment is often called. A rationalist came to be understood, Copleston suggests, as 'a thinker who denies the supernatural and the idea of the divine revelation of mysteries' (2003 ed, vol IV, 16). Another description, however, is that of a thinker who applies mathematics and logic to a series of premises about a world that can only be seen in mechanistic and materialistic terms. Yet, this idea of empirical 'facts' existing somewhat in the world, to be appraised by the observing self, is, as Barbara Shapiro shows (2000), a historical development. Shapiro shows that the concept of 'fact' developed in the legal arena during the fifteenth and sixteenth century. Such a concept shaped and sharpened 'the epistemological assumptions and methods of a wide range of intellectual enterprises', from history, through chorography and travel narratives, to the emerging science, and thus 'played a key role in the development of English empiricism' (Shapiro, 2000, 3). Far from being neutral *data* to be appraised via the senses, 'facts' are thus already charged with a degree of epistemological normativity. 'What began as a professional category for dealing with legally relevant events and became somewhat extended by historians was to be transformed into a common way of thinking about an increasingly wide range of events, occurrences and things, human, natural and divine' (Shapiro, 2000, 63). Furthermore, 'If well-reported "facts" were modifying the nature of political and economic knowledge, they also created a new body of knowledge dealing with the manners, customs and religious practices of human populations, both foreign and domestic, familiar and exotic' (82).

The Enlightenment reached its apotheosis with Denis Diderot's and Jean le Rond D'Alembert's *Encyclopedie*, and its promise of cataloguing all that is known (continuing and expanding upon Linnaeus's categorization of the *genera* and *species* of the natural world, still in use today), while science assumed an almost forcibly optimistic attitude, as exemplified by Gottfried Leibniz's belief that we live the best possible world (something Voltaire caricatured through his fictional Doctor Pangloss in *Candide*). One only needs to look at Julien Offray de La Mettrie *L'homme machine—Man a Machine* (1748) to see how fully realized the mechanistic idea of the world had become. La Mettrie was intent in showing that 'man's psychical processes, no less than his physical processes, could be explained in terms of a mechanistic and materialistic hypothesis' (Copleston, 2003 ed, vol IV, 13). Similarly, the Baron Paul-Henri Dietrich d'Holbach, rejecting and yet expanding upon Descartes's dualism, maintained that the mind is nothing more than an epiphenomenon of the brain, with a human being just a physical body, thus asserting that the belief in the soul's immortality is just a superstition. Enlightenment authors expound an extreme, even crude, form of materialism, as exemplified by Pierre Jean Georges Cabanis's extreme focus on the physiological bases of physical life. It is among these authors that the idea of progress can be fully found. Robert Jacques Turgot introduced a positivist interpretation of history, in the sense that 'the intellectual achievements of one generation are taken over, widened and surpassed by the next' (Copleston, 2003 ed, vol IV, 57), and '[t]he thinkers of the period ... manifested a strong belief in progress and in the dependence of progress on intellectual enlightenment ... and in the growth of civilization' (41). Ultimately, however, Max Weber described the 'disenchantment of the world' as directly caused by the rise of the 'instrumental rationality' that began in the Renaissance and culminated with the Enlightenment (Devall & Session, 2007, 45).

3.1.5 Romanticism and Modernity

As Russell points out, '[a] new movement, which gradually developed into the antithesis of liberalism, begins with Rousseau and acquires strength from the romantic movement and the principle of nationality'. In this movement, 'individualism is extended from the intellectual sphere to that of the passions, and the anarchic aspects of individualism are made explicit. The cult of the hero, as developed by Carlyle and Nietzsche, is typical of this philosophy' (1972, 600). During the Romantic period, individualism reached its apotheosis, manifesting partly as hatred of the ugliness of industrialism (for aesthetic, more than ethical, reasons), partly as nostalgia of a mythical past (particularly the middle ages), partly as hatred of the modern world and partly as an assertion of the right of individual rebellion in the name of nationalism and of the mythicized splendour of war in defence of 'liberty'.

In *Eloise,* Jean-Jacques Rousseau proposed a radical individualism based on freeing an individual's passions, which are restrained by social constructs that are ultimately alien and antithetic to humanity's 'true nature'—a far cry, this, from Aristotle's definition of 'man' as a political animal. The apotheosis of one's life is to be free from social bonds and to reassert their individuality within the wild nature they inhabit: '[t]he mystic becomes one with God, and in the contemplation of the Infinite feels himself absolved from duty to his neighbour. The anarchic rebel does even better: he feels himself not one with God, but God' (Russell, 1972, 681). For the Romantics, human beings have become gregarious because of self-interest, but they remain, ultimately and by instinct, solitary and individualistic. This view is later seen in Thoreau and in the grandiose (and racist) construction of a mythical 'wild other' in Edgar Rice Burroughs's *Tarzan*. The fundamental aspiration is to free oneself from society *and* to become one with a socially alien nature that somehow re-awakens some primal instinctive part of the solitary and individualist human. This particular myth of a liberating nature persists to this day: D H Lawrence's *The Man Who Loved Islands* is, after all, but a precursor of the more recent feature film *Into the Wild*.

At the same time, the past (particularly the Middle Ages) is mythicized. Samuel Coleridge's *The Ancient Mariner* and *Kubla Khan* are perfect examples of this. Romantic authors such as Coleridge, Percy Bysshe Shelley and Lord Byron emphasized the strange, the magical and the mystical (as can be seen in the *Mysteries of Udolpho* or Mary Shelley's *Frankenstein*). The fascinating monstrous that emerges in *Frankenstein*, or in John Polidori's *The Vampyre*, reflects a larger wild and aw-inspiring nature. William Blake's poem *Tyger*, or Caspar David Friedrich's *Wanderer above the Sea of Fog* fully capture a novel enamorement with a previously alien 'wilderness'.

As Russell suggests, '[t]he romantic movement is characterized, as a whole, by the substitution of aesthetic for utilitarian standards ... The morals of the romantics have primarily aesthetic motives' (1972, 678). This preference extends to Gothic architecture and to a particular view of 'wild' nature. In Rousseau's stories 'we find wild torrents, fearful precipices, pathless forests, thunderstorms, tempests at sea, and generally what is useless, destructive and violent' (Russell, 1972, 678). As we will further discuss later, this view of a 'wild' but pure nature, untouched by and unbending to humanity still dominates the idea of nature to this day.

In parallel, however, Roussau's *Emilio* epitomizes a pessimistic view of society, which corrupts that which is otherwise natural. Although sharing an ultimately positive belief in the *fundamental* nature of humanity with Locke, Rousseau presented an ultimately opposite view to him, stating that the 'origin of civil society and of the consequent social inequalities is to be found in private property' (Russell, 1972, 688). To undo this evil, Rousseau asserted, one must abandon civilization. For Rousseau, 'everything that distinguishes civilized man from the untutored barbarian is evil' (Russell, 1972, 687). Rousseau's admiration for the 'noble savage', who he professed having inherited from Plutarch's *Lives* and in particular from Lycurgus's Sparta, has had a profound legacy, through nineteenth century anthropological assumptions, on the idea of the colonized Other, with urban-dwelling or technology-adopting Indigenous people being cast as a corrupted version of a mythical 'pure' Indigeneity. The myth of the 'good savage', the 'uncivilized', the 'poorer' and yet 'purer' being is thus born. However, it is important to note that '[t]he poor, to the romantics, were never urban and never industrial; the proletariat is a nineteenth century conception, perhaps equally romanticized, but quite different' (Russell, 1972, 676).

Rousseau anticipated Max Horkheimer and Theodor Adorno's argument, in *Dialektik der Aufklärung,* that scientific progress was an enslavement rather than a liberation of humanity, and that Nature was perceived to possess a darker, more threatening dimension, analogous to the non-rational elements of the human psyche. In any case, by introducing a new natural religion, for the first time in centuries religious belief was no longer coupled with, or required, reason, but rather emerged from, and was justified by, a well of emotions. This, however, made belief an entirely private (and ultimately solipsistic) pursuit. With the Romantics, metaphysics appears to have become a fully individualistic affair. As Russell writes, the '[r]evolt of solitary instincts against social bonds is the key to the philosophy, the politics and the sentiments, not only of what is commonly called the romantic movement, but of its progeny down to the present day' (1972, 682).

German idealism began with Immanuel Kant (and continued with Georg Wilhelm Friedrich Hegel) as an attempt to escape the solipsistic subjectivism that empiricism (with Locke, Berkeley and ultimately Hume) had created. To resolve the scepticism about the nature of knowledge that had led, through empiricism, to the solipsism of Berkley and Hume, Kant proposed reality to be located *outside* the system of cognition (in the sense later indented by Ferdinand de Saussure). While 'the outer world causes only the matter of sensation, ... our own mental apparatus orders this matters in space and time, and supplies the concepts by means of which we understand experience' (Russell, 1972, 707). As a result, things-in-themselves, or *noumena,* which are the ultimate causes of our sensations, are inherently unknowable: they are not substances, nor do they exist in space or time. Space and time are, instead, subjective and objective at the same time: they are, a priori, part of our individual apparatus of perception. Importantly, these a priori 'categories' of knowledge (such as space and time) are not individual, but are instead universal and inherently rational. In this sense, Platonic *ideas* are now normalized in accordance with the universal reason inherited by the Enlightenment, and, in so doing, the ontological assumptions espoused the burgeoning scientific community are normalized and crystallized into a set of beliefs about what the world ultimately *is*.

Kant's rationalism was further expanded upon by Hegel. Notwithstanding deeply pantheistic and mystical tendencies, Hegel asserted that the real is rational and the rational is real, noting that 'the nature of Reality can be [logically] deduced from the sole consideration that it must be not self-contradictory' (Russell, 1972, 731). Bernstein (2003) notes how Hegel begins *The Spirit of Christianity* with the story of Noah and the flood, interpreting it as the mythological moment of rupture between Western consciousness and the 'state of nature'. Cast against such a destructive and invincible force, Peter Burdon writes, 'Western rationality emerges in response to this event and is generated as a means to human survival against a cold and indifferent natural world' (2015, 25). Although Hegelian logic didn't *necessarily* entail it, Hegel's conception of time as progress toward cosmic perfection enshrined in philosophy the idea of progress that had emerged over the previous centuries (since the rise of science). Hegel's notion of history further led to the absolute glorification of the nation-state, an idea that still dominates the political world of today (Hegel's glorification of war, which echoed Heraclitus as his declared intellectual predecessor, is very much the apotheosis of the Romantic turn from rebellious individualism to state totalitarianism).

Following Hegel, the focus on the *will* replaced the focus on knowledge. Johan Gottlieb Fichte posited that Ego is the only ultimate reality that can be said to exist, because it posits itself. Notwithstanding Coleridge's accusation against Fichte's 'boastful and hyperstoic hostility to Nature, as lifeless, godless, and altogether unholy' (1817, 78), Fichte and Friedrich Schelling's philosophy led to extreme subjectivism. Max Stirner (pen name of Johan Kaspar Schmidt) took the individual ego to the extreme. Reminiscent of Protagoras, Stirner argued that the single individual is the only valid measure of everything, thus justifying an absolute moral egoism (Gordon Gecko's modern assertion that 'greed is good' cannot fail to evoke Stirner's philosophical arguments). Nietzsche took this turn to its logical conclusion, praising the triumph of the individual will, turning Hobbes's hypothetical and violent 'natural' state of humanity into something to be glorified and actively pursued. Not only egoism, but active prevarication of the other becomes philosophically justified. His justification for power was related to his perceived value of individual existence as located in the capacity to be 'better' than others. This Nietzschean obsession with competitive fame and status informs us to the present day.

During the nineteenth century, the emergence of the industrial age had a profound effect on humanity: 'machine production profoundly altered social structure, and gave men a new conception of their powers in relation to the physical environment' (Russell, 1972, 719). Furthermore, Russell continues, '[t]he most important effect of machine production on the imaginative picture of the world is an immense increase in the sense of human power. This is only an acceleration of a process which began before the dawn of history, when men diminished their fear of wild animals by the invention of weapons and their fear of starvation by the invention of agriculture'

(728). As Swimme and Berry suggests, '[a] newly developed mystique of our plundering industrial society is committed to moving out of the Cenozoic, not by entry into the Ecozoic, but by shaping an even more controlled order of things that might be designated as the *Technozoic* era' (1994, 249).

Just as nature was now seen as raw material for the full expression of humanity's power (which had been unlocked by the technological mastery humans believed to have attained), so was that section of humanity that did not actively participate in government to be seen as but a mere source of impersonal labour. While the labour theory of value had already been introduced by Locke, Adam Smith and David Ricardo, it is with Karl Marx that the theory was fully articulated. While for the mercantilists, as the theories of Sir William Petty in the late seventeenth century show, value was connected to trade and valuable metals, with a focus on the accumulation of the latter by selling more product to foreign entities via the former, Adam Smith, breaking away also from the physiocratic belief that value came from the land rather than mercantile exchanges, gave birth to the modern labour theory of value, placing industrial workers (rather than farmers) at the centre of the production boundary. Smith argues that key to the idea of an economy is the concept of 'surplus'.[11] With this, the idea of growth entered economic parlance. Building upon Ricardo's concept of the exchange value as a crystallization of the value inherent in commodities, Marx found an invariable measure of value in the workers themselves. Continuing along the socialist tradition (the term socialism was first used in 1827 to describe the followers of Robert Owen), Marx brought together a renewed materialism (influenced by Ludwig Feuerbach's materialist revolt against Hegel's idealism) and the rationalist and system-building philosophy of Hegel (his mentor). According to Marx's dialectical materialism, 'the bare object, apart from the activity of the percipient, is a mere raw material, which is transformed in the process of becoming known' (Russell, 1972, 783). For Marx, matter, and the way in which matter is altered by human activity (Marx's *mode of production*), is the driving force behind history. 'In this way, Marx's materialism, in practice, becomes economics' (Russell, 1972, 785).

Emerging at the same time, Darwin's theory of evolution indirectly (and somewhat against Darwin's own writings, which emphasized the superiority of co-operation over competition for survival) emphasized the survival of the fittest as a violent competition for survival. Although Darwin himself did not think of evolution in hierarchical terms (he explicitly wrote '[n]ever use the words *higher* or *lower*', and referred to animals as 'our fellow brethren'), others interpreted the 'struggle for existence' and the 'survival of the fittest' in very different terms. Thomas Huxley (1893) noted that human relationship with nature was essentially amoral, with no ethical responsibilities possible toward any nonhuman entity, while American philosopher William James paralleled existence to a war to conquer nature and urged young people

[11] Mazzucato explains that 'many productive workers produce the equivalent of more grain that they need to feed themselves to survive'; the growth of wealth of a nation, therefore, 'Instead of "wasting" the surplus on paying for unproductive labour, he argued, it should be saved and invested in more production so that the whole nation could become richer' (Mazzucato, 2018, 38).

to become 'part of the army enlisted against Nature' (McDermott, 1977, 669). While the *scala naturae* was denied in a teleological sense, the theory of evolution provided a scientific justification for one's position of power by virtue of the self-evident recognition of one's survival as proof of one's 'fitness'. This darker implication of Darwin's theory led to social Darwinism, the deeply racist, colonial and self-serving practice of placing societies on an evolutionary scale that justified the racist colonial attitudes of the following century and a half (well into the present day), as exemplified by Lucien Lévy-Bruhl's *Les fonctions fondamentales dans les sociétés inférieures* and Herbert Spencer's application of evolution to human societies and his idea of social progress, with 'primitive' societies located *below* industrialized European ones. Furthermore, the idea of human progress became even more crucial to an otherwise meaningless universe. Progress, in this sense, is '[t]he idea of history not as a series of cycles but as a process of progressive development toward an ultimate goal' (Copleston, 2003 ed, vol VI, 151). Departing from the previous theological nature of progress entailed by the Messianic elements of Jewish and Christian thought, with Jacques Bénigne Bossuet's *Discours sur l'histoire universelle* (*Discourse on Universal History* 1681), a novel philosophy of history that is more in line with a natural *and* eschatologically agnostic idea of progress had already emerged. The Eurocentric nature of those novel histories of social progress is almost a given. Progress was seen through 'stages', each placed on steps located in a linear ladder that justified the primacy of Europeans as the pinnacle of such progress.

Positivism is perhaps the inevitable evolution of empiricism combined with the Enlightenment's materialism and rationalism and with the implications of the industrial revolution. With positivism, science posed itself as the only legitimate manifestation of the infinite. For John Tyndall, for example, 'as far as knowledge is concerned, science is omnicompetent. Problems which cannot be answered by science are [simply] unanswerable in principle' (Copleston, 2003 ed, vol VIII, 109). Auguste Comte developed positivism as a 'positivist philosophy'. For Comte, '[p]ositive knowledge [was necessarily] restricted ... to knowledge of observed facts or phenomena and to the coordinating and descriptive laws of phenomena' (Copleston, 2003 ed, vol IX, 77). Emile Littré, a disciple of Comte, marked the ascent of positivism by asserting that beyond matter and force positive science knows (nor can ever know) nothing. Any lingering idea of the soul is abandoned, only matter remains, only a material world of objects and atoms. The world consists exclusively of matter and of the forces immanent in matter. Claude Bernard, another of Comte's disciples, asserted that determinism is an absolute (and foundational) principle of science. Rationalist scientism (rather than science) became the dominant and hegemonic epistemological perspective. Nothing remains of the ethical responsibilities of the past toward a world of mere matter and random forces. Furthermore, with Feuerbach's 'substitution of anthropology for theology, man becomes [perhaps definitively] his own highest object, and end to himself' (Copleston, 2003 ed, vol VII, 298), The combination of science and politics became the new religion, and atheism (the inevitable conclusion of material determinism) became the necessary pre-condition for such a new religion.

3.1.6 The Human Condition

What Georges-André Malraux has described as the 'human condition' occupied a central place in the French philosophical tradition of the twentieth century. In the twentieth century, existentialism, particularly with Jean-Paul Sartre, was still focused on human exceptionalism: '[t]here is at least one being whose existence comes before his essence, a being which exists before it can be defined by any conception of it. That being is man' (Sartre, 1974, 66). Human freedom precedes the essence of man and makes it possible. As Kenny explains, '[w]hereas an oak tree has to follow a particular life pattern because that is the kind of thing it is, human beings do not belong to a kind in this way: it is for each person to decide what kind of thing to be. Human freedom creates a fissure in the world of objects' (Kenny, 2010, 823). Sartre's argument led to ethical solipsism: 'I have not, nor can I have, recourse to any value against the fact that it is I who maintain values in being' (Sartre, 1974, 66). This sense of ethical solipsism, supported by the nihilistic consequences of positivist atheism (or, more appropriately, of the positivist rejection of any metaphysical consideration) is fully exemplified by Albert Camus's sense of the absurb, *le sentiment de l'absurd*. The world in itself, for Camus, is not absurd, it just is. However, '[t]he absurd arises from this confrontation between man's appeal and the irrational silence of the world' (1942, 15).

The emergence of neoclassical economics in the twentieth century, and the new theory of value known as 'marginalism', still dominates today's economic theory. Mazzuccato explains that, according to neoclassical economics, value 'is based on the notions of utility and scarcity and is subjective: the value of things is measured by their usefulness to the consumer. There is, therefore, no "objective" standard of value, since utility may vary between individuals and at different times' (2018, 62). Value, with neoclassical economics, became *only* what the self-referential market says it is. Furthermore, '[b]ecause things exchanged in a monetary market economy have prices, price is ultimately the measure of value' (Mazzuccato, 2018, 65). This led both to the dephysicalization of value, and to the monetization of everything. In describing neoclassical and neoliberal capitalism, Donald Worster writes that

> [t]he capitalists … promised that, through the technological domination of earth, they could deliver a more fair, rational, efficient, and productive life for everyone … Their method was simply to free individual enterprise from the bonds of traditional hierarchy and community, whether the bondage derived from other humans or the earth … People must … think constantly in terms of making money. They must regard everything around them – the land, its natural resources, their own labour – as potential commodities that might fetch a profit in the market … As wants multiplied, as markets grew more and more far-flung, the bond between humans and the rest of nature was reduced to the barest instrumentalism. (1988, 11–2)

As Swimme remarks, '[c]onsumerism is based on the assumption that the universe is a collection of dead objects' (1996, 33). The consequence is, as Karl Polanyi argued in his classic *The Great Transformation,* that 'creating a fully self-regulating market economy requires that human beings and the natural environment be turned into pure commodities, which assures the destruction of both society and the natural environment' (2001, xxv).

The assumptions necessary for this transition are significant. Firstly, humans have to be conceived of as hyper-rational utility maximizers who know at all times what is best for themselves, what price to pay for any given commodity, and how to make an economically rational choice. Secondly, no interference from monopolies can exist in the process of price-setting. Such assumptions are easily supported by the novel view of humanity inherited from nineteenth century positivism. The results of this particular normative view of how humans *ought* to behave economically are well exemplified by Friedrich August von Hayek's emphasis on individualism and free-market capitalism, as well as his depiction of competition as a tool to produce a better society at the expenses of co-operation. The Bretton Woods agreements and the introduction of the International Monetary Fund, the World Bank and the World Trade Organization, are all hallmarks of an international economic system designed to increase not global prosperity but rather monetarily measurable economic growth. The idea of endless growth based on increased consumptions (which is why most economic reporting notes increased consumption as a positive outcome) is encoded in the words of former economic advisor to the President of the USA, Paul McCracken: '[t]he action most urgently needed in the world economy is for the stronger economies to be willing to accept higher levels of living' (1975, 16). Unless the rich reject their 'Calvinistic' restrain on increased and pantagruelic consumptions, the poor will never be able to sell their products and thus will not be able to develop. This is the view underpinning the establishment of Gross Domestic Product (GDP) as the marker of an economy's health and wealth. However, the problem with GDP, as Mazzucato notes, is that it 'can be measured as the total amount of products produced, the total amount demanded, or the total income earned … [but] how sectors are valued influences our calculation of growth rates, and this may in turn decide to steer the economy. In other words, how we measure GDP is determined by how we value things, and the resulting GDP figure may determine how much of a thing we decide to produce' (2018, 76). The normative and pedagogical results are, according to Swimme and Berry, rather perverse, and we (as willing or unwilling adherent to the worldview described thus far) 'must consider that we are into a deep cultural pathology' (1994, 251):

> [a]dvertisements are where our children receive their cosmology, their basic grasp of the world's meaning, which amounts to their primary religious faith, though unrecognized as such. I use the word "faith" here to mean cosmology on the personal level … we live in a culture that has replaced authentic spiritual development with the advertisement's crass materialism. … In the propaganda of the ad the ideal people, the fully human humans, are relaxed and carefree – drinking Pepsi around a pool – unencumbered by powerful ideas concerning the nature of goodness, undisturbed by visions of suffering that could be alleviated if humans were committed to justice. (Swimme, 1996, 17–8)

As Berry wrote, '[w]e lose our intimacy with the natural world once we take on a secular life attitude' (1999, 24). Such an attitude has been fully realized in the twentieth century as a result, I believe, of the accretion of distinct and yet interconnected ideas presented thus far. After all, the metaphor of the computer to explain the mind speaks to a complete materialism that sees the human as just a machine. This metaphor emerged with Allen Newell and Herbert Simon, who considered any intelligent system nothing more than an organic machine that manipulates symbols according to a set of formal rules. Descartes' automata are thus extended to the totality of the universe, no *res cogitans* remains. Even the otherwise visionary R Buckminster Fuller in *An Operating Manual for Spaceship Earth* 'likens the Earth to a machine, [and] asserts that there is no world population problem and says that the world's problems can be solved by computers' (Devall & Sessions, 2007, 139). The consequences of a thoroughly materialistic, ethically self-referential, and monetarily driven worldview are for many to see. Freya Mathews writes that

> [b]y draining matter of any animating principle, science has ensured that the world itself could no longer be regarded either as morally significant in its own right or as the lodestar for human meaning and purposes: henceforth, we would have to find our ends and meanings in ourselves, by means of our innate power of reason. ... with this deanimation of nature, rendered the world a mere backdrop to questions concerning the meaning of life and the nature of the good. From the viewpoint of science, the answers to such questions must lie in the existential datum of humanity itself. (2003, 4)

This deep psychological distancing from matter is well captured by Annie Leonard: '[y]ou're unlikely to hear someone wax sentimental about rocks. They're not grand, awe-inspiring living creatures or a serene, healing, cleansing substance like water. You don't hear appeals form non-profits to save the poor silver or uranium from being removed from its native habitat.' And yet, showcasing the somewhat schizophrenic approach of modernity to matter, '[y]ou *are* likely to run in to people who are emotionally attached to their rock-based Stuff, though. Threaten someone's wedding ring, cell phone, and car, and you're likely to wind up underground yourself' (2010, 25). Furthermore, Maria Mies and Vandana Shiva note how 'modern natural science, particularly mechanics and physics, are based above all on the destruction and subordination of nature as a living organism—and indeed an organism understood as female'. As a result, 'at the end of this process nature is considered only as dead raw material, which is dissected into its smallest elements and then recombined by the great (white) engineer into new machines which totally obey his will', and, consequently, 'this new domination over Mother Earth of necessity went hand in hand with violence' (1993, 44).

The reader will hopefully forgive this journey through the history of philosophy, which was, by necessity, at the same time too brief and too detailed. And yet, I wanted to show that the common reference to the *anthropocentrism* of modernity, against which the theories discussed in the following chapter are often cast, is much more complex and nuanced than it may *prima facie* appear. Of course, by choosing to cast a bird's eye view upon the history of Western philosophy, I have necessarily excluded a host of distinct markers. The arts, literature, the history of architecture and even music would have been equally valid sources to explore the emergence of a worldview that is defined as 'anthropocentric'. Raymond Williams (1980), for example, provides a thorough account of the evolving ideas of nature and the arts, whereby there exists a wide range of cultural meanings for nature: 'nature as a primitive condition before human society; nature as a state of original innocence from which there has been a fall and a curse requiring redemption; nature as a quality of birth (i.e. our "original nature"), through to themes of nature as a personified goddess—"Nature herself" (Jagtenberg & McKie, 1997, 6). The changing ideas of nature, from the arcadian, bucolic and pastoral depictions of Horace and Virgil in classical times to the walled gardens of the Renaissance, from the profound anthropocentrism of the Tudor era to the imagined wilderness of the romantics, are powerful artistic renditions of an imagined nature throughout the ages. The representation of the natural world in art is, after all, a powerful window into the way past cultures viewed the world they inhabited. Thus, the Paleolithic art of Altamira and Lascaux, with their animal representations devoid of any other context than their own dynamism, was replaced by the diagrammatic rock carvings in Val Camonica in Italy and Mount Bego in France, as well as the Minoan art of Crete. Bronze Age Art was then superseded by the initially more geometric (and progressively more naturalistic) art of the Iron Age, until, at the end of the third century BC, landscapes began to feature in Hellenistic art (Almago-Gorbea, 2000). The myth of a pastoral Arcadia in Philip Sidney's poetry (*Arcadia*, 1590), and the benevolent feminine symbolism of bucolic nature in Sandro Botticelli's *Birth of Venus* (1482) and *Primavera* (1477–8) or Lucas Cranach's *The Nymph of the Spring* (1518) are powerful counternarratives to the romantic poetry of Walt Whitman and William Wordsworth, the *Sturm und Drang* movement in Germany, or the first ascent of Mont Blanc in 1786. However, although a very fascinating pursuit in its own right, the artistic and literary depiction of the birth of an anthropocentric worldview had to be, by necessity, eschewed in favour of a more textual and philosophical genealogy. While not novel (Carolyn Merchant, for example, offers a paradigmatic historical reconstruction of the historical conceptions of nature in the Western tradition in her 1983 classic *The Death of Nature*), this brief foray into the history of Western philosophy will hopefully provide the reader with the necessary context for a description of what an 'anthropocentric' worldview is. With this—admittedly brief—contextual introduction in mind, we can now cast our gaze upon the impact that this worldview has had on the theory and practice of law, so that we can finally provide an answer to the question of what it was that made the environmental damages, in *Sierra Club v Morton, legally invisible,* or at least legally *irrelevant.*

3.2 Anthropocentrism: A Primer

The reader will likely have noticed that I have not attempted to actually define 'anthropocentrism' until this point. This was a deliberate choice, as I wanted a provisional definition to emerge from the (Foucauldian) archaeological efforts of the previous section, rather than being pre-emptively and normatively guided by a pre-existing definition. It is now apparent, I hope, that the environmental predicament described in the previous chapter is not the result of general and generic 'human' actions, but rather of the specific actions that some cultures and some worldviews have engendered. There exists, for example, a clear connection between capitalism, colonialism, patriarchy, imperialism and climate change: '[t]he idea that climate breakdown is not the doing of humanity as a homogenous unit, but rather of specific imperial projects', Naomi Klein shows, was highlighted by the recent hypothesis that 'the period of global cooling known as the "Little Ice Age", which took place in the 1500–1600 s, was partly caused by the genocide of Indigenous peoples in the Americas following European contact'. As a result of the initial violent impact of colonization, 'with millions dead from disease and slaughter, huge swaths of land that had previously been used for agriculture were reclaimed by wild plants and trees, sequestering carbon and cooling the entire planet' (2019, 159). Moreover, the very idea of the 'human', Agamben argues (2004), emerges from a necessary philosophical, practical and political caesura between the human and the animal. He writes of 'anthropogenesis', the juncture of distinction (rather than a purportedly objective biological description) from which the idea of humanity itself emerges.

If, then, the environmental predicament described in the opening chapter of this book is the result of a particular worldview (or, more accurately, of a particular convergence of a number of worldviews interacting—and at times conflicting—with each other), and this worldview has been heuristically defied as 'anthropocentrism', how is it to be defined in light of the historical genealogy of the previous section? The Oxford Dictionary defines it as 'a worldview that sees humans as the source of all value, since the concept of value itself is a human creation, and that sees nature as of value merely as a means to the ends of human beings.' However, some authors have provided a more nuance description. Ben Mylius (2017), for example, distinguishes between *ontological* anthropocentrism (the idea that humans cannot help but act and think anthropocentrically by virtue of being human), *analytic* anthropocentrism (the idea that there is something about humans that makes them separate or different from the rest of the universe) and *moral* anthropocentrism (the idea that human beings are *superior* to everything else). Bosselmann (2011), instead, has developed the acronym 'DAMAGE' to refer to the current environmental law approach: Dualism (nature/humanity or culture), Anthropocentrism, Materialism, Atomism, Greed (individualism gone mad) and Economism (the myth of perennial growth). In light of both the rich critical scholarship on anthropocentrism and of the previous section, the definition requires a fuller articulation.

For the purpose of defining *anthropocentrism* as the worldview against which the emergence of an ecological jurisprudence will be later cast, such a worldview is construed as the result of genealogically interlocked, at times conflicting, but ultimately interdependent ideas primarily inherited from Greek philosophy, Roman political and legal universality, Judeo-Christian and Scholastic theology, humanistic and scientific aspirations, Enlightenment and modernist constructions, all combining to display the following intertwined markers:

1. *Anthropocentrism stricto sensu*: the idea that humans are the central referent of existence, ontologically and, or, ethically, either because of a divine justification of their centrality or because of an existentialist self-referentiality. The immediate corollary of this idea is that humans are superior to, and somewhat separate from, the rest of existence. While a degree of 'social' anthropocentrism appears

to be common among all human groups (who tend to privilege their extended families, clan affiliations and, by a much later extension, national allegiances, in determining their ethical priorities), this particular view emphasizes humanity's centrality as *qualitatively* distinct from the rest of the existence. While humanity is at the centre of the universe, no other entity in that same universe is conceptually entitled to a similar self-referential perspective.

2. *Human Exceptionalism*: the idea that humans are radically distinct from the rest of existence. This may be justified by reference to a theological mandate (as in Genesis 1:28), because of a number of purportedly unique biological or social features (language, the capacity for technology, hyper-sociality, et cetera), or because of pure ethical egoism.
3. *Scala Naturae*: the belief in the hierarchical structure of all matter and life, divided into discrete and separate parts, with the non-living world at the bottom, the plants located above it but inferior to animals, and humans above all the rest. Although this 'great chain of being' has multiple permutations (in medieval times, angelic beings and God were located above humans on the ladder, whereas gradations of 'animality' have been more recently introduced in zoological terms), at its core it divides all of existence in hierarchical, vertical terms.
4. *Materialism*: the idea the universe is comprised *exclusively* of matter, without any spiritual or extra-material component. This entails the corollary that both mental and spiritual beliefs and phenomena can be explained by reference to their material components alone. A modern synonym for this idea is *physicalism*.
5. *Mechanicism*: the idea that a (materialistic) universe can (and must) be explained by reference to mathematical and logical rules, laws or models. All is measured and quantified, or at least measurable and quantifiable, with physical (material) laws ultimately able to be described in objective, logical and mathematical terms.
6. *Determinism*: metaphysically, determinism refers to the necessary assumption that any given event requires a pre-existing condition that makes it logically impossible for the event not to occur. In this context, however, determinism additionally refers to the idea that no external causes other than the material ones exist. Furthermore, while incomplete knowledge of the universe currently prevents humanity, so the theory goes, from fully understanding all laws of the universe, there is nothing that, at least in theory, stops a sufficiently advanced scientific civilization from one day being capable of predicting the ultimate trajectory of all material components of the universe. This idea is in direct conflict with the idea of free-will that most versions of human exceptionalism predicate.
7. *Rationality*: the idea that the universe can be understood by the application of mathematical-logical, 'mental' faculties. Furthermore, such faculties are universal (i.e. they are the same across all of humanity, or even all of the universe) and, or, they are objective (i.e. they do not depend on the subjective state—emotional or otherwise—of the rational subject). Rational knowledge, in epistemological terms, is attained *propositionally* and *empirically* via the application of strict linguistic-mathematical-logical parameters, rather than *experientially* and *intuitively*. Copleston writes that '[t]he rationalist divides the human psyche into distinct faculties or powers, reason, will, feeling, imagination, and by reason he

means the understanding as concerned with grasping logical connections between abstract concepts. Other faculties or powers of the human being, such as Pascal's 'heart', are regarded as irrelevant in this respect. Further, reason recognizes no authority except its own. What reason cannot prove to be true the rationalist refuses to be true' (2003 ed, vol X, 59). Rationality, it is important to note, is distinct from *rationalism*, the philosophical belief in some form of a priori way to categorize and appraise any form of knowledge of the world.

8. *Empiricism*: the idea that knowledge is inextricably linked to sensory experiences and measurements appraised through the application of mathematical-logical interpretive parameters. According to empiricist philosophy, as Aquinas stated, *nihil in intellectu nisi prius in sensu,* 'nothing exists in the mind that has not previously been perceived by the senses'. The Oxford Dictionary defines experience, in this context,

> either as the sensory contents of consciousness, or as whatever is expressed in some designated class of statements that can be observed to be true by the use of the senses. Empiricism denies that there is any knowledge outside this class, or at least outside whatever is given by legitimate theorizing on the basis of this class. It may take the form of denying that there is any *a priori* knowledge, or knowledge of necessary truths, or any innate or intuitive knowledge or general principles gaining credibility simply through the use of reason; it is thus principally contrasted with rationalism.

9. *Scientism*: the 'mythological ideology that has grown up around the simple but powerful logic of the scientific method' (Greer, 2009, 207). While the scientific *method* is displayed by virtually all knowledge-system across the world, the scientific revolution claimed it as its own exclusive domain, leading to a conflation of particular, historically situated, and ultimately contingent theories with the universal objective nature of the scientific method itself. Scientism, in other words, is the conflation of *process* (the scientific method) with *content* (the historically situated theories that have emerged within Western science as a result of the application of the scientific method over the past few centuries). A corollary of this view has been the removal of all metaphysical considerations form socially authorized and discursively legitimized scientific pursuits.
10. *Objectivity*: the belief that scientific truths, by virtue of their methodological production can be treated as 'objective', factual and universal.
11. *Progress*: the idea that (human) knowledge and welfare advance in a linear trajectory toward ever-superior states of being.
12. *Technological fideism*: the belief that scientific technological powers grant absolute and unbridled mastery over nature. A corollary of this idea is the belief that all problems (as well as all predicaments) can be ultimately solved by the appropriate application of technology.
13. *Industrialism*: the application of technology to modes of production both in manufacturing and agriculture in order to rationalize and maximize such production. While capitalism (below) is strictly intertwined with the development of the industrial age, the two concepts are distinct. Moreover, industrialism is deeply marked by factory production, technological mechanization, division of labour and bureaucracy.

14. *Capitalism*: the belief in an economic system where the factors of production are privately owned and the owners have complete discretion to use them as they choose. Within a capitalist system, a strict division of labour is believed to allow resources to be optimally allocated and exchanged according to economic rules of supply and demand. Finally, the individual ownership of vast sections of limited resources (such as land, minerals, or others) are seen as both necessary and desirable.
15. *Monetization* and *market value*: the idea that the value of everything is ultimately determined by market exchanges. Furthermore, such value is encoded in a quantifiable and monetized form and is thus ultimately disconnected from the physical world.
16. *Competition*: the idea that economic (and social) competition is beneficial for the growth of the economy and the ultimate betterment of both society as a whole and the competing individuals.
17. *Growth*: the belief that an ultimately de-physicalized economy can grow endlessly, because of the introduction of new and more efficient technologies, because of the discovery (or novel technological exploitation) of new resources, or, more recently, because of the possibility to decouple economic growth from the material physical world.
18. *Consumerism*: the belief in the continued increased consumption of goods and services as an inherent social and economic good to be actively pursued, in extreme cases through *planned* and socially manufactured (with the help of advertisements and lifestyle narratives) *perceived* obsolescence.
19. *Individualism*: the belief that the interests of the individual have primacy over that of any social group (be it a family or a society). Introduced by early liberalism, the romantic movement amplified the focus on the individual ego to unprecedented levels. Two significant corollaries of this view, particularly when combined with the belief in competition as a beneficial social value, are the almost pathological pursuit of fame and status as central to the validation of one's identity: to be different from, and superior to, others is seen as the ultimate marker of an individual's success.
20. *Psychological* and *ethical egoism*: connected to the emphasis on individualism, the belief that individuals are ultimately motivated by self-interest (a belief known as *psychological* egoism) is a common feature of modern philosophy, as exemplified by Hobbes's depiction of the fundamental law of nature as the pursuit of individual self-preservation. *Ethical* egoism is the belief that, whether or not individuals are motivated by self-interest, they *ought* to behave accordingly, since rational behaviour requires the maximization of self-interest. A corollary of this is the deep social pessimism displayed by its proponents.
21. *Violence*: the belief in the inevitability of inter- and intra-species violence as the inevitable 'state of nature'. This view, which was first proposed by Heraclitus's idea of Strife, was further advanced by Machiavelli and by Hobbes's thought experiment on the 'state of nature', and was ultimately glorified by Nietzsche, remains a central feature of much of today's popular narrative in a plethora of media.

22. *Racism, colonialism* and *imperialism*: racism refers to the (now thankfully rejected) idea that human groups—defined by reference to their 'ethnic' traits—are placed on a scale of progress, with European-derived societies at the pinnacle. Such a view, which justified the colonialist and imperialist projects of the last few centuries, has more recently morphed in a more subtle form of intellectual and moral colonialism, whereby the old colonial powers now assert a degree of moral superiority and 'freedom' that ought to be universalized, often via military intervention. Even within post-colonial European societies, the idea remains in the form of a strict adherence to the idea of social hierarchies. The contemporary impact of colonialism and imperialism is aptly captured by Amitav Gosh, who writes that '[t]he Anthropocene has reversed the temporal order of modernity: those at the margins are now the first to experience the future that awaits all of us; it is they who confront most directly what Thoreau called "vast, Titanic, inhuman nature"' (2016, 62–3).
23. *Hierarchy*: the belief in the necessity or appropriateness of rigid vertical hierarchies, and the consequent organization of society in vertical structures of dominance and power.
24. *Sovereignty* and *statehood*: the belief in relatively centralized nation-states as the absolute, hegemonic and exclusionary seat of power and social control, with an absolute monopoly on the use of force.
25. *Persons, things* and *rights*: inherited from the Roman tradition, the belief that all entities can be categorized as 'legal *persons*' (or *subjects, personae*), 'things' (*res*) or legal relations (*actiones*).
26. *Legal formalism*: the belief in law as a logical structure of propositional norms, with a strong emphasis on the 'rule of law', and on hierarchical and bureaucratic legal institutions.
27. *Public* and *private*: the rigid separation between two spheres of social existence, with the corollary emphasis on the profound protection of the private sphere against its intrusion from the public.
28. *Discretionary property*: the idea of exclusionary property over 'things', and the absolute and unfettered dominion over that which is the object of one's property.
29. *Patriarchy*: the domination of society by generally heterosexual, and still mostly Caucasian, males. A corollary of this is the heteronormative belief in some form of gender and sexual universality.
30. *Nature* and *Culture*: the belief that human cultures exist in a separate realm from that of nonhuman 'nature'.
31. *Wilderness* or *Arcadia*: either the classical and neoclassical idea of an idyllic 'natural' reality or the romantic and transcendentalist aspiration toward an untamed 'wilderness'. In either case, the belief is accompanied by a degree of rejection of, alienation toward, and even hatred for, the urban and industrial world that is seen as the opposite of the imagined 'natural' world. The ideas of 'conservation' (which relies on the idea of a 'wilderness' deprived of humans) and of 'development' (which sees the natural world as a collection of resources to be exploited to fulfil o human needs, as a merely unrealized potential until

fully and properly 'developed') are both a direct consequence of these last two points.

In conclusion, an *anthropocentric* worldview, I contend, is more than the mere belief that humanity is the central or focal point of its own existence. While not all traits are displayed at all times by those worldviews, practices and perspectives that are generally defined as anthropocentric, their intertwined development represents a fuller spectrum of deeply interdependent beliefs. This enlarged and more articulated account of an anthropocentric worldview is necessary, I believe, to fully appraise the reactions to it that have led to the emergence of an ecological jurisprudence over the last few decades.

3.3 Law, Nature and Property

Anna Grear contends that any 'ethically responsible future engagement with '"anthropocentrism" and/or with the "Anthropocene" must explicitly engage with the oppressive hierarchical structure of the anthropos itself—and should directly address its apotheosis in the corporate juridical subject that dominates the globalized order of the Anthropocene age' (2015, 225). The contingent nature of a culturally and historically situated *anthropos*, it is my hope, has been made abundantly clear throughout the previous sections. Within its contingent and at times internally conflicting constraints, however, the anthropocentric worldview has been made visible in the current dominant mode of life of a great portion of humanity. The natural world itself has been shaped and moulded by it. As Roland Barthes writes, '[o]ne could answer with Marx that the most natural object contains a political trace, however faint and diluted, of the more or less memorable presence of the human act which has produced, fitted up, used, subjected or rejected it' (1973, 143–4).

The ontological possibilities entailed by the development of an anthropocentric worldview have turned the nonhuman world (and, for a portion of European history, other part of the human world as well) into nothing more than something to be exploited, transformed and used at will for and by the alleged uniqueness of human ingenuity. The transformation however did not happen by itself.

Weaving together all practices, irrespective of their ontological stance, are distinct normative, regulatory and legislative regimes. After all, as environmental lawyer and activist James Thornton pointed out to me in a private conversation, law is the current language of international institutions and thus acts as the fundamental axis around which all possible responses to the environmental predicament revolve. 'Civilization has grown to depend on the law to the extent that the fate of whole ecosystems now hangs on the use of such linguistic niceties', and 'corporations speak in the grammar of money ... Since they are very happy to violate the environmental laws, if you want them to take those laws seriously you need to speak to them in the grammar of money' (Goodman & Thornton, 2017, 19–21).

Worldviews and legal structures are both intertwined and co-dependent. European societies first and then the rest of the globalized world articulated the horizon of ontological possibilities granted by an anthropocentric worldview within legal and normative structures and mechanisms that allowed natural landscapes to be physically changed by the collective effort of humans, groups and institutions. Normative structures permitted 'wild' places to be plied and shaped according to the conquering ontological ideals exposed above. Simon Schama, in his visually compelling *Landscape and Memory*, notes that '[e]ven the landscapes that we supposed to be the most free of our culture may turn out, on closer inspection, to be his product' (1995, 9). Landscapes, therefore, 'are culture before they are nature; constructs of the imagination projected onto wood and water and rock' (61). Such is the insight of Nicole Graham (2011), who calls this interplay of law and landscape a *lawscape*, arguing that there is no place in the world that is merely a landscape, that the very possibility of a piece of land void of human inhabitation is the deliberate result of a particular set of legal relations. 'Natural' landscapes do not merely exist as a background upon which human activities are cast, but rather are shaped, even created, by the dominant legal paradigm, which, through the subtle operation of property regimes, imposes a set of parameters that define the spectrum of environments allowed to exist. In this sense, there is no distinction between *natural* and *human-made* environments, as every single landscape is, in fact, an authorized *lawscape*.

Moreover, Graham continues, '[p]lace or the physical, "natural" world, is predominantly conceived, experienced and articulated anthropocentrically, as something separable and "other" to human subjectivity' (5). In fact, the 'absence of place is the condition of the possibility of a universal and universalizing law that extends "across the Whole globe, like a coinage reducing all things to a common measure"' (8).

If such is the case, it is then immediately apparent how a particular philosophical legacy encoded within a particular legal structure made it possible for the environmental damages decried by the Sierra Club and Christopher Stone as legally invisible or legally irrelevant. If 'nature' is nothing more than matter, then 'nature' is nothing more than a collection of inert objects (a concept that still includes today all plants and most of the animal world). If 'nature' is a collection of inert objects, then there is no (nor can there be any) moral responsibility toward it. After all, as the Parmenidean introduction of the possibility of the 'void', the 'nothing' it entailed, there can be no moral responsibility toward nothing, and once the world enters the ethical equivalent of the ontological void, then humanity's moral responsibility toward the world disappears. If such is the case, and 'nature' is nothing more than a collection of inanimate objects, then 'nature' can be, at law, nothing more than an *object* of another *subject's* rights. And if that subject possesses unfettered property rights against a portion of 'nature' such as an old growth forest, then such a subject is allowed to dispose of their property as they see fit, including by destroying the object of their rights. Therefore, the clearly evident environmental destruction of an old growth forest in the Sierra mountains of southern California, is, indeed, irrelevant, if not necessarily invisible, to the law.

I have purposely included the term 'nature' in quotation marks, as I will explore the contested meaning of nature in the following chapters. The reader will already know, and this chapter has hopefully confirmed, that 'nature' is far from a self-evident concept, and I am cognisant of such an issue, to which I will attend again in a brief while. For the time being, I have used the term to refer to that which is not considered a legal subject for the purpose of the Western legal tradition. This entails a brief reminder of the concept of *subjectivity* and *objectivity* at law.

The *Corpus Iuris Civilis*, a combination of the codification willed by the Byzantine Emperor Justinian in the sixth century CE (known as *Codex Justinianus*), the *Digests* (codified Roman case law) and the *Institutes* (educational texts) divided the books of private law (*civilis* for civil or private law, as opposed to canonical laws of the Christian Church) in three: *personae* (persons), *res* (things) and *actiones* (actions or procedures). Leibniz further developed the Roman trifurcation of person, thing and action, by calling them *subject*, *object* and *cause* of a *right*. Leibniz also divided subjects (persons) between natural (*naturalia*) and artificial (*artificialia*), noting that only subjects have the capacity to hold rights (*iura*). William Blackstone incorporated this tripartite distinction in the *Commentaries on the Laws of England* (1765). In Germany, Von Savigny used the *Digests* (or *Pandectae*, from which the name of the German school, *Pandektenwissenschaft*, was derived) to build a closed system of legal concepts, while the Napoleonic *Code Civil* influenced the rest of Europe with a codification built around the original division: persons (natural and artificial), their goods and their dealings with them. Kaarlo Tuori asserts that the division between persons and things is part of the 'deep structure of law' of the Western legal tradition, since concepts like 'legal subjectivity' (i.e. legal personhood) and 'subjective rights' are the basic legal categories that underpin 'the conceptual space for modern law' (2002, 186–8). By 'Western legal tradition', it may be important to add, the author and myself refer to the major synchronic and diachronic grouping of legal systems commonly articulated by comparative legal scholars.

3.3.1 The Nature of Property

The property regimes of the Western legal tradition are thus a direct response to the anthropocentric worldview the development of which was discussed above. Peter Burdon argues that 'law is deeply anthropocentric and directed toward maintaining hierarchical structures for the protection of [private] property and economic growth' (2015, 5). To highlight the anthropocentric undertones of contemporary property law in the anglosphere, Burdon examines four periods in the development of private property: antiquity, the scientific revolution, the Industrial revolution and the influence of modern liberal and neoliberal political philosophy. Property is seen as central to the engagement with 'nature' and the nonhuman environment, because, as English jurist Lord Scarman notes, '[f]or environment, a traditional lawyer reads property' (1975, 59). Eric Freyfogle adds that '[w]hen lawyers refer to the physical world, to this field and that forest and the next-door city lot, they think and talk in terms of property and ownership' (1993, 49). Burdon describes such an approach as 'the conceptualization of the environment as human property' (2015, 16).

Indeed, most of the world's land today is either state-owned or private property, with a few (very minor) exceptions (such as Marie Byrd Land in Antarctica and Bir Tawil, between Egypt and Sudan). The oceans and high seas, while not under the sovereign claims of any particular state, are nonetheless global commons, highly regulated for human usage and exploitation. The same is true of most (if not all) animal and vegetal life on the planet. As former United Nations Special Rapporteur on Human Rights and the Environment David Boyd writes, '[w]e have divided the diversity of life on Earth into two categories—people and things ... To say that we share this planet with millions of other species is ecologically incontrovertible, but legally incorrect' (2017, xxviii–xxix). Moreover, '[i]f we are the only species with rights, we are the only species that really matters' (xxix).

This approach was far from accidental. Richard Posner, for example, posits that '[i]f every valuable resource were owned by someone, ownership connotes the unqualified power to exclude everybody else from using the resource as well as to use it oneself, and ownership rights were freely transferable ... value would be maximized' (1986, 32). For Carl Schmitt, the idea of property is nomothetic: that is, it precedes and creates the entire artifice of the law. For him, the original act from which law emerges is in the occupation of land, the conscious acquisition of a particular territory (*Landnahme*). This is contained in the Greek word *nomos*, a term he derives from the verb *nemein*, in the triple meaning of conquer (*nehmen*), divide (*teilen*) and cultivate/produce (*weiden*). Keith Thomas concurs, since, '[a]s Karl Marx would note, it was not their religion, but the coming of private property and a money economy, which led Christians to exploit the natural world in a way that the Jews had never done; it was what he called the "great civilizing influence of capital" which finally ended the "deification of nature"' (1983, 23).

The evolution of the concept of property in Western legal thoughts is aptly traced by Kelly (1992), whereas legal historian Plucknett (2010) maps the idea of property throughout the English legal tradition. The Roman *Lex Aquilia* expressly treated animals (as well as slave) as property of their owner, and any damages to such property ought to be compensated in purely monetary terms. Gaius' *Institutes* (or Institutions) engaged with damages caused by animals and the responsibility of their owners, but no action could be taken by or against animals themselves. Underpinning the absolute power over the object of one's property is located in the Roman power awarded to the *pater familias,* which was further articulated among distinct powers: *potestas* over children and slaves, *manus* over women, *mancipium* over children alienated from their original *pater*, and the power over things, the *dominium.* The latter represented the idea of the object 'belonging' to its subject, with an original concept of 'property-sovereignty' directly derived from the absolute power of the *pater familias.* This led 'objects in the external world to be exposed to the domination and economic discretion of man [sic]' (Grosso, 1993, 132).[12] It is here that the origin of the concept of *res*, the legal 'thing' that is at absolute disposal of the power-holder over it, is to be found.

---

[12] In the original: 'esposizione degli oggetti del mondo esteriore alla dominazione e disposizione economica dell'uomo'.

The feudal influence on the idea of property was marked by the peculiarity of land law, whereby the vassal held the land of the lord. Simon Winchester explains that '[d]uring its prime, Anglo-Saxon England did … create a system of landownership, and it is fair to say that during the period leading up to the Norman invasion just about all the land in Old England was owned by someone' (2021, 165). A fact, this, that led to the Domesday Book, the great survey of the newly formed kingdom by William the Conqueror in his late years. While the *Decretum* of Gratian (ca 1140) explicitly asserted that the wealth of the earth was naturally the common property of humanity, and that private property was the direct result of the original Fall into sin, the idea of private property in the middle ages was nonetheless justified by recourse to natural law, by authors such as William of Auxerre and Alexander of Hales. It is, however, with Thomas Aquinas that the first elaborate justification of private property can be found. Aquinas built upon Aristotle's distinction between 'natural' and 'legal' justice and provided a number of caveats to the exclusive nature of private property, but nonetheless provided a theological justification of the idea in Western legal thought. Prior to the Industrial revolution, Burdon notes, the English courts articulated and reasserted the notion of 'natural use or incidents':

> What then is the right of land its owner or occupier? It is to have all natural incidents and advantages as nature would produce them. There is a right to all the light and heat that would come, to all the rain that would fall, to all the wind that would blow, a right to the rain which would pass over the land should not be stopped and made to fall on it, a right that the heat from the sun should not be stopped and reflected on it, a right that the wind should not be checked but should be able to escape freely; and if it were possible that these rights were interfered with by one having no right, no doubt an action would lie (Bryant v Lefever, 1879)

William Blackstone also asserted that '[t]he Earth, and all things therein, are the general property of mankind, exclusive of other beings, from the immediate gift of the creator' (Boyd, 2017, xxvi). Burdon notes how this older conception of property, however, stood in the way of rapid economic growth, and that 'the [new] idea of private property entailed to use the land more intensely that had been practised by previous generations' (2015, 33).

Graham traces the conceptual origin of modern property law to the enclosure of the English commons, 'the name given to the process of enclosing and appropriating land—hitherto worked and enjoyed by a peasant community in common—usually with a hedge, fence or other physical boundary' (2011, 51). The commons referred to the common rights of the peasants who, although not holding title over pastures and forests, nonetheless had the common law right to roam them and to what they produced. The English enclosures were effected with more than 3280 bills passed by Parliament between 1770 and 1830 to enact the enclosure of the commons (under common law, enclosure of a common previously required the unanimous consent of the entire community and no authority had the common law right to alienate and enclose the commons). The commons, Vandana Shiva suggests (2005), soon became commodities, with colonialism itself seen as a large-scale enclosure of the entire planet. The mindset of the enclosure, Shiva suggests, still underpins most of the current regulatory regimes in relation to agriculture, water and intellectual property, all under the aegis of free-market rationalization. Shiva also counters Garreth

Hardin's so-called 'tragedy of the commons' (the idea that when each user of a common is faced with a choice, they will rationally choose what will bring individual gain at the cost of collective well-being, leading to the inevitable deterioration of an unregulated common, which is thus to be seen as an inherently wasteful space), by stating that 'what Hardin does not see is that the very existence of the commons implies the reality of cooperative management and ownership' (2005, 54), citing the traditional Indian land distribution practice of *bahiachara* (or 'custom of the brothers). Shiva's is not an isolated example, as the Andean concept of the *ayllu* also demonstrates.

The marriage between unshackled private property and liberal individualism was, for Burdon, unavoidable, for 'private property is *the* key mechanism through which liberals promote their platforms of individual freedom and choice' (2015, 42). The problem, of course, is that 'a conception of private property that focuses exclusively on individual freedom fails to account for the vast network of social and ecological relationships within which human beings exist' (43). 'The paradigm of modern European property relations', Graham summarizes, 'is anthropocentric. It is a dichotomous model of the world that separates people from everything else, placing people in an imagined centre, their environment literally surrounds and is peripheral to them' (2011, 4).

Graham further argues that Western property regimes have led to the process of 'dephysicalization', the 'removal of the physical "thing" from the property relation and its replacement with an abstract "right"' (xiii). This process creates a 'paradigm of placelessness' (5): by de-physicalizing nature, and thus engendering a cognitive dissonance between the economic implications of property law and its ecological consequences, it led to the normalization of the alienation of the property owner from the physical object of their property rights. As Wade Davis points out,

> [w]e accept it as normal that people who have never been on the land, who have no history or connection to the country, may legally secure the right to come in and by the very nature of their enterprises leave in their wake a cultural and physical landscape utterly transformed and desecrated ... we place no cultural or market value on the land itself. The cost of destroying a natural asset, or its inherent worth if left intact, has no metric in the economic calculations that support the industrialization of the wild (2009, 118–9)

Perhaps unsurprisingly, Marx writes in 1843 in *On the Jewish Question* that 'the view of nature which has grown up under the regime of private property and of money is an actual contempt for and practical degradation of nature' (in Bellamy Foster, 2000, 74). The alienation form nature, for Marx, was realized via the fetishism of money: '[m]oney is the universal and self-constituted *value* of all things. It has therefore deprived the entire world—both the world of man and of nature—of its specific value' (1975 ed, 239). Christopher Stone also noted that '[w]herever it carves out "property" rights, the legal system is engaged in the process of *creating* monetary worth' (1972, 476).

This conception, albeit dominated by its focus on property law, is by no means limited to it. David Farrier notes that, similarly to property law, environmental law regards the environment anthropocentrically, as 'a "resource" to be used by human beings' (1999, 1). Moreover, while most cultures, for Shiva (2005, 22), see the earth as *terra mater* (mother earth), the colonial category of *terra nullius* (land of no one, or empty land) is what allowed the dispossession of large sections of the earth from the cultures that originally inhabited it, with an intergenerational trauma carrying to the present day.

This chapter will have, hopefully, made apparent the interplay between the anthropocentric worldview that came to dominate Western thought over the centuries and the legal regimes that actualized it into norms and practices that permitted the land itself to be shaped according to human individual desires. That environmental damages exist and that they threaten the very fabric of human society (if not humanity's very survival), as the first chapter has shown, is beyond doubt. That such damages are rendered *legally* irrelevant by the interplay of a complex and entangled anthropocentric worldview and the legal regimes and institutions within which such a worldview is articulated is also very apparent, as this chapter has endeavoured to demonstrate.

The next chapter, however, will show that there have always been *other* ways to conceive of the cosmos. It is such ways that form the basis for the philosophical counter to the anthropocentric worldview this chapter has construed.

References

Agamben, G. (2004). *The open. Man and animal* (K. Attell, Trans.). Stanford University Press (First published in Italian 2022).
Almago-Gorbea, M. (2000). Images of hunting and farming in prehistoric art. *Naturopa, 93*, 6–7.
Baird Callicott, J. (1994). *Earth's insights. A multicultural survey of ecological ethics from the mediterranean basin to the Australian outback*. University of California Press.
Barthes, R. (1973). *Mythologies* (A. Lavers, Trans.). Hill & Wang (First published in French 1957).
Bellamy Foster, J. (2000). *Marx's ecology. Materialism and nature*. Monthly Review Press.
Bennett, J. (2010). *Vibrant matter. A political ecology of things*. Duke University Press.
Bernstein, J. (2003). *Classic and romantic German aesthetics*. Cambridge University Press.
Berry, T. (1988). *The dream of the earth*. Sierra Club Books.
Berry, T. (1999). *The great work*. Three Rivers Press.
Bookchin, M. (1991). *The ecology of freedom. The emergence and dissolution of hierarchy*. Black Rose Books (First published 1982).
Bosselmann, K. (1995). *When two worlds collide. Society and ecology*. RSVP.
Bosselmann, K. (2011). From reductionist environmental law to sustainability law. In P. Burdon (Ed.), *Exploring wild law: The philosophy of earth jurisprudence*. Wakefield Press.
Boyd, D. R. (2017). *The rights of nature. A legal revolution that could save the world*. ECW.
Braun, O., & Bauer, J. (Eds.). (1911–13). *F D E Schleiermacher works*. Leipzig.
Bryant v Lefever. (1879). Common Pleas Division 172.
Burdon, P. D. (2015). *Earth jurisprudence. Private property and the environment*. Routledge
Burnet, J. (1920). *Early greek philosophy* (3rd ed.). A & C Black.

Camus, A. (1942). *Le mythe de Sisyphe.*
Charlton, A. (2011). Man-made world. Choosing between progress and planet. *Quarterly Essay, 44*, 1–72.
Copleston, F. (2003). *A history of philosophy* (Vol. I–XI). Continuum (First published 1946–1986).
Darwin, C. (1871). *The descent of man and selection in relation to sex.* John Murray.
Darwin, F. (Ed.). (1888). *The life and letters of Charles Darwin.* John Murray.
Davies, M. (2022). *EcoLaw: Legality, life, and the normativity of nature.* Routledge.
Davis, W. (2009). *The wayfinders. Why ancient wisdom matters in the modern world.* House of Anansi Press.
Descola. P. (2013). *Beyond nature and culture* (J. Lloyd, Trans.). University of Chicago Press (First published in French 2005).
Devall, B., & Session, G. (2007). *Deep ecology.* Gibbs Smith.
Diamond, J. (1997). *Guns, germs and steel.* W W Norton.
Farrier, D., Lyster, R., & Pearson, L. (Eds.). (1999). *The environmental law handbook: Planning and land use in New South Wales* (3rd ed.). Redfern Legal Centre Publishing.
Freyfogle, E. T. (1993). *Justice and Earth: Images of our planetary survival.* Free Press.
Gaaker, J. (2016). "Sua cuique persona?" A note on the fiction of legal personhood and a reflection on interdisciplinary consequences. *Law and Literature, 28*(3), 287–317.
Gillespie, A. (1997). *International environmental law policy and ethics.* Oxford University Press.
Goodman, M., & Thornton, J. (2017). *Client Earth.* Scribe.
Gosh, A. (2016). *The great derangement. Climate change and the unthinkable.* University of Chicago Press.
Graham, N. (2011). *Lawscape. Proeprty, environment, law.* Routledge.
Grear, A. (2015). Deconstructing anthropos: A critical legal reflection on 'anthropocentric' law and anthropocene 'humanity.' *Law and Critique, 26*, 225–249.
Greer, J. M. (2009). *The ecotechnic future. Envisioning a post-peak World.* New Society Publishers.
Grosso, G. (1993). *Lezioni di Storia del Diritto Romano* (5th ed.). Giappichelli.
Harari, Y. N. (2011). *Sapiens. A brief history of humankind.* Vintage.
Hardin, G. (1968). The tragedy of the commons. *Science, 162*, 1243–1248.
Harris, M. (1977). *Cannibals and kings.* Random House.
Harrison, P. (2006). Having dominion: Genesis and the mastery of nature. In R. J. Berry (Ed.), *Environmental stewardship: Critical perspectives—past and present.* T&T Clark International.
Huxley, T. (1893). *Evolution and ethics.*
Jagtenberg, J., & McKie, D. (1997). Eco-impacts and the greening of postmodernity. In *New maps for communication studies, cultural studies, and sociology.* Sage Publications.
John, J. (2011). And finally … humans! In P. Burdon (Ed.), *Exploring wild law: The philosophy of Earth jurisprudence.* Wakefield Press.
Kelly, J. M. (1992). *A short history of western legal theory.* Clarendon Press.
Kenny, A. (2010). *A new history of western philosophy.* Oxford University Press.
Klein, N. (2019). *On fire.* Simon & Schuster.
Kuhn, T. (2012). *The structure of scientific revolution* (4th ed, Vol. 121). University of Chicago Press (First published 1962).
Laertius, D. (1972). *Lives of the philosophers* (R. D. Hicks, Trans.). Harvard University Press.
Latour, B. (2017). *Facing Gaia: Eight lectures on the new climatic regime.* John Wiley & Sons.
Lee Humphreys, W. (1971). Pitfalls and promises of the biblical texts as a basis for a theology of nature. In G. C. Stone (Ed.), *A new ethic for a New Earth.* Andover.
Leonard, A. (2010). *The story of stuff.* Constable.
Lovejoy, A. (1961). *The great chain of being: A study of the history of an idea.* Harvard University Press (First published 1936).
Marx, K. (1975). *Early writings.* Vintage.
Mathews, F. (2003). *For love of matter. A contemporary panpsychism.* State University of New York Press.

Matthews, D. (2021). *Earthbound. The aesthetics of sovereignty in the anthropocene*. Edinburgh University Press.
Mazzucato, M. (2018). *The value of everything. Making and taking in the global economy*. Penguin.
McCracken, P. (1975). *Wall street journal*. September 17, 1975.
McDermott, J. J. (Ed.). (1977). *The writings of William James*. University of Chicago Press.
Merchant, C. (1983). *The death of nature. Women, ecology, and the scientific revolution*. HarperSanFrancisco.
Mies, M., & Shiva, V. (1993). *Ecofeminism*. Spinifex.
Mylius, B. (2017). Earth jurisprudence. In *Encyclopedia of the anthropocence*. Elsevier. https://doi.org/10.1016/B978-0-12-409548-9.10449-X
Nash, R. (1989). *The rights of nature. A history of environmental ethics*. University of Wisconsin Press.
Plucknett, T. F. (2010). *A concise history of the common law*. Liberty Fund (First published 1929).
Polanyi, K. (2001). *The great transformation. The political and economic origins of our time*. Beacon Press (First published 1947)
Posner, R. (1986). *Economic analysis of law*. Aspen.
Robinson, O. F. (1997). *The sources of roman law. Problems and methods for ancient historians*. Routledge.
Rogers, N. (2020). *Law, fiction and activism in a time of climate change*. Routledge.
Russell, B. (1972). *The history of western philosophy*. Simon & Schuster (First published 1945)
Sartre, J. P. (1974). *Existentialism is a humanism*. Methuen Publishing (First published in French 1945).
Scarman, L. (1975). *English law: The new dimension*. Stevens Publishing.
Schama, S. (1995). *Landscape and memory*. Vintage.
Schmitt, C. (2006). *The nomos of the Earth*. Telos Press (First published in German 1950).
Shapiro, B. J. (2000). *A culture of fact. England, 1550–1720*. Cornell University Press.
Shiva, V. (2005). *Earth democracy. Justice, sustainability, and peace*. South End Press.
Stone, C. D. (1972). Should trees have standing?-Towards legal rights for natural objects. *Southern California Law Review, 45*, 450–501.
Swimme, B. (1996). *The hidden heart of the cosmos. Humanity and the new story*. Orbis Books.
Swimme, B., & Berry, T. (1994). *The universe story. From the primordial flaring forth to the Ecozoic Era*. HarperCollins.
Swimme, B., & Tucker, M. E. (2011). *Journey of the universe*. Yale University Press.
Thomas, K. (1984). *Man and the natural world. Changing attitudes in England 1500–1800*. Penguin.
Tudge, C. (1998). *Neanderthals, Bandits and farmers*. Weidenfeld and Nicholson.
Tuori, K. (2002). *Critical legal positivism*. Ashgate.
Wells, S. (2010). *Pandora's seed. The unforeseen cost of civilisation*. Random House.
White, L., Jr. (1967). The historical roots of our ecological crisis. *Science, 155*, 1203–1207.
White, L. (1973). Continuing the conversation. In I. G. Barbour (Ed.), *Western man and environmental ethics*. Longman.
Williams, R. (1980). *Problems in materialism and culture*. Verso.
Winchester, S. (2021). *Land. How the hunger for ownership shaped the modern world*. William-Collins.
Worster, D. (Ed.). (1988). *The ends of the earth*. Cambridge University Press.

Chapter 4
Deus Sive Natura

All Things Are Full of Gods
Thales of Miletus

The previous chapter has introduced an enlarged definition of *anthropocentrism* as a heuristic device against which the emergence of an ecological jurisprudence will be cast. *Anthropocentrism* thus construed refers to the belief that modern human beings are located—in an ontological, and, or, in an ethical sense—at the centre of the cosmos and at the pinnacle of progress and evolution. Anthropocentric perspectives vary widely, but most consider humans as central, superior, and somewhat separate from the rest of the universe. Consequently, since (as Protagoras suggested) humans are the measure of all things, then the value of everything other than human is in turn measured against human values, desires and utility. Against anthropocentric narratives of dominance, individualism and separateness, however, other counternarratives of interdependence can be found.

Many authors have linked the environmental damages so apparent today to the particular worldview that has enabled them to occur and have challenged such a worldview as a consequence. John Seed, for example, defines the idea that 'humans are the crown of creation, the source of all value, the measure of all things' as a form of 'human chauvinism' (1988), and J. Baird Callicott famously wrote that 'the extent of misanthropy in modern environmentalism may be taken as a measure of the degree to which it is biocentric' (1980, 326), suggesting a radical departure from anthropocentric hegemony. Thomas Berry wrote that the '[p]hysical degradation of the natural world is also the degradation of the interior world of the human', while Roderick Nash asserted that '[t]he emergence of th[e] idea that the human-nature relationship should be treated a s a moral issue conditioned or restrained by ethics is one of the most extraordinary developments in recent intellectual history' (1989, 4).

A. Pelizzon, *Ecological Jurisprudence*, Contemporary Environmental Law and Policy,
https://doi.org/10.1007/978-981-96-0173-8_4

In opposition to an *anthropocentric* perspective, a *biocentric* approach acknowledges the inherent value of all living organisms, irrespective of their utility for human goals. An *ecocentric* approach goes even further and values the entirety of the natural world independently of (and potentially even contrary to) any value it may hold for human desires. According to Bill Devall and George Sessions, the work of cultivating these approaches, what they define as an 'ecological consciousness', is found in a 'minority tradition' of Western philosophy (2007, 18), as well as in other cultures (notably Indigenous cultures) and philosophical and religious traditions (notably Eastern traditions such as Taoism or Buddhism). This chapter will, therefore, begin by looking at these ecologically conscious counternarratives, firstly by casting the (once again necessarily brief) gaze upon the 'minority traditions' of Western philosophy, and then upon other worldviews, which, it is important to remember, have often suffered the violent colonial and imperialistic impact of the anthropocentric worldview described in the previous chapter, as the nonhuman environment has; after all, as Thomas Jagtenberg and David McKie point out, many social ecologists 'see the alienation and domination of nature—its otherness—as a reflection of problematic relations between human beings' (1997, 7). The next chapter will then turn to the emergence of an explicitly environmental or ecological ethical tradition, which forms the basis for the emergence of an equally ecologically oriented jurisprudence. Aldo Leopold famously wrote that 'one of the penalties of an ecological education is that one lives alone in a world of wounds'. Hopefully, this chapter and the next ones will show, it does not have to be necessarily so.

4.1 Imagined Nature

As noted in the previous chapter, I have not, thus far, engaged with the multifaceted and often uncertain concept of 'nature'. I will indeed return to it more in-depth in later chapters, due to its particular relevance for some of the critiques advanced against many of the eco-jurisprudential initiatives that I will later discuss. I do want, however, to prefigure the contested terrain occupied by purportedly objective notions of 'nature', and for the time being note that the idea of 'nature' is often cast against, and emerges in opposition to, the idea of 'culture'. While Alfred Kroeber and Clyde Kluckhohn (1952) have famously created an inventory of more than 164 accepted definitions of culture, the canonical formulation of 'culture' was proposed by Edward Taylor (1871), who described it as follows: 'Culture or Civilization … is that complex whole which includes knowledge, belief, art, morals, law, custom, and any other capabilities and habits acquired by man as a member of society' (vol I, 1). In the twentieth century, through the work of Franz Boas, Philippe Descola suggests, 'emerged the idea that each people constitutes a unique and coherent configuration of material and intellectual features sanctioned by tradition, that tradition being typical of a certain mode of life, rooted in the specific categories of a language and responsible for the specificity of the individual and collective behaviour of its members' (2013, 73).[1] Furthermore, Descola continues, '[t]here can be no doubt that the notion of culture (in the singular) derives much of its fertility from its opposition to nature' (still in the singular). While nature remains in the singular, however, cultures are discussed in the plural. This is what Descola describes as the dualism of 'natural monism and cultural relativism' (79). For many classical anthropologists, therefore, 'even if the environment in which [cultures] have developed certainly does constitute an important dimension in the peculiarities ascribed to them, from a culturalist point of view their manner of adapting to nature is but one means among others that helps us to understand them' (75).

It follows that 'nature' is already cast as both the singular 'via negativa' against which all cultures are defined, and the plural imaginary of each culture in relation to that which each culture identifies as *outside* its own boundaries. To contextualize the counternarrative of interdependence of the Western philosophical tradition, therefore, it may be useful to engage with the changing attitudes toward the imagination of nature within it. 'Nature', in this sense, becomes a comprehensive and all-encompassing term to refer to all that is not comprised within the boundaries of culture, the entire cosmos of things that are and that are not, the great non-human other against which 'culture' (particularly 'Western' culture) defines itself. Naturally, the imagination of nature throughout history is neither singular nor it is unchanging. Nor is this imaginary a mere backdrop against a tautological history of ideas. Indeed, in referring to the technological developments of the last few centuries, Maurice Merleau-Ponty once said that '[i]t is not scientific discoveries that brought about a change in the idea of Nature. Rather it is the change in the idea of Nature that has made those discoveries possible' (1994, 25).

4.1.1 The Invention of the Wilderness

The classical Greco-Roman conception of nature can be evinced from the idea of an idyllic state of nature cast against the urban life of the *polis* (πόλις) or the *urbs*, which can be found in the Homeric Golden Age as well as in Virgil and Juvenal bucolic landscapes. The Roman idea of nature, however, was inherently dichotomic. A less idyllic version of nature, in fact, is the one introduced by Tacitus in *Germania*, deeply connected to the idea of a dark, alien, 'wild' place. The modern translation of the English term 'wild' in Romance languages (*sauvage, selvaje, selvaggio* and so on) comes from the Latin *silva*, 'the great

[1] Furthermore, in the same passage Descola notes that the word *civilisation* 'is itself relatively recent. I appeared for the first time in French in 1757, penned by Victor Riqueti de Mirabeau, and about ten years later in England, used by Adam Ferguson with an equivalent sense. It meant the state of civilized society, which had resulted from constant progress in virtue and civic skills, in contrast to the mere urbanity of civil behaviour.'

European forest that Roman colonization was gradually to erode' (Descola, 2013, 48–9).The concept of the *silva* refers an uncultivated space to be cleared, 'a place for the beasts and plants found there and the rough people who inhabit it, for individuals seeking refuge from the laws of the city, and, hence, for those possessed of fierce temperaments and who are recalcitrant to the discipline of social life' (Descola, 2013, 48–9). The chthonic attributes of the Roman *silva* were cast against the positive qualities otherwise represented by the *domus*, not necessarily a geographical unit as the *silva*, but rather 'an environment for living, originally involving agricultural exploitation, in which, under the authority of the paternal head of the family and the protection of the household deities, women, children, slaves, animals and plants all found conditions that favoured the realization of their true natures' (Descola, 2013, 48–9). Descola argues that this antithetical pair of characteristics inherited from the Roman conception of the 'natural' world was to continue, in its original essence, throughout more recent colonial times. 'The Tupinamba of Brazil and the Indians of New France would take the place of the Germans and the Britons described by Tacitus, while domestication would undergo a change of scale and turn into civilization … [this] opened up the possibility of the inversion that Montainge and Rousseau were to exploit' (48–9).

However, the 'wild' forests of the Germanic world were not merely an embodiment of the tangled mass of untamed forces cast against the spread of civilization, but also a *foresta,* 'the gigantic park filled with game that the Carolingian dynasty, as early as the ninth century, took measure to protect by edicts limiting grazing rights and deforestation' (Descola, 2013, 51). The *foresta* represented the fascinating counterpart to the threatening *silva*, the embodiment of all that lay beyond the reach of Rome, 'the limit of the state's jurisdiction, a reminder of the impenetrable tangle of vegetation into which the Etruscans had withdrawn to escape the consequences of their defeat, or, in its concrete form, the vast wooded expanse to the east of Latinised Gaul, where the last savages of Europe still held out against the legions' (Descola, 2013, 54). Within this dichotomic portrayal of the 'wild', Tacitus's depiction of the ancient Germans introduced a protean view of the 'wild human' as a (yet unnamed) 'noble savage', a view further embraced in the late Renaissance and fully realized by Rousseau. Whereas, throughout the middle ages, wild men and women had represented the hairy, violent, sexually predatory antithesis of Christian values (Brenheimer 1982), wild men became exemplars of the virtues of natural life now purged of previous images of bestiality in the later part of the fifteenth century (at the same time that Tacitus *Germania* was rediscovered). During the Renaissance, the primeval and hostile view of nature as the *silva* (and even the *foresta*) had begun to merge with the imagery of a more positive (although still exotic) woodland, influenced by the myth of the forest-dwelling Germans Tacitus had described more than a millennium earlier.

William Cronon, however, notes that the *idea* of wilderness in its modern sense is a relatively recent creation:

> [g]o back 250 years in American and European history, and you do not find nearly so many people wandering around remote corners of the planet looking for what today we could call "the wilderness experience". As late as the eighteenth century, the most

> common usage of the word "wilderness" in the English language referred to landscapes that generally carried adjectives far different from the ones they attract today. To be a wilderness then was to be "deserted", "savage", "desolate", "barren" – in short, a "waste", the world's nearest synonym. Its connotations were anything but positive, and the emotion one was more likely to feel in its presence was "bewilderment" – or terror … (1995, 300)

While the more positive idea of the 'wilderness' was yet to develop in its modern form, during the late Middle Ages and early Renaissance, the constant growth (or regrowth, given the pre-existing sizes of ancient Roman *urbes*) of cities and urbanization across Europe altered the perspective of where people were meant to live, as historian G M Trevelyan notes: '[i]n Renaissance times the city had been synonymous with civility, the country with rusticity and boorishness. To bring men out of the forests and to contain them in a city was to civilize them' (1946). Keith Thomas adds, '[t]he town was the home of learning, manners, taste and sophistication. It was the arena of human fulfilment' (1984, 243), and '[w]hen heaven or utopia were imagined, they were predominantly in the form of cities', as was the case with Augustine's *City of God*, Tommaso Campanella' *Città del Sole*, or Thomas More's *Utopia*. However, this focus on urbanization as the pinnacle of human realization was always contrasted not only by the imagination of a threatening 'wilderness', but also by Arcadian, bucolic or rural landscapes, always (it is important to add) agrarian in nature. 'The cult of the countryside was … in many ways a mystification and an evasion of reality' (Thomas, 1984, 251). A tripartite distinction between a civilized urbanity, a bucolic agrarian nature and a threatening, violent and hostile wilderness was thus being crystallized in European imagination. The Arcadia theme was eulogized, for example, in the poetry of Philip Sidney (*Arcadia* 1590) and Edmund Spenser (*The Shepheard's Calendar* 1579). In the arts, it was captured by paintings such as Sandro Botticelli's *The Birth of Venus* (1482) and *Primavera* (1477–8) or Lucas Cranach's *The Nymph of the Spring* (1518). In these depictions, the backdrops are idyllic, with open fields ripe with fruits and abundance, with grazing animals and singing birds, but with predators, decay and diseases nowhere to be seen. Throughout the Renaissance, the idyllic aspect of nature was often represented as female, as Carolyn Merchant notes, 'an escape backward into the motherly benevolence of the past. Here, nature was a refuge from the ills and anxieties of urban life through a return to an unblemished Golden Age' (1983, 7). However, the contemporary position of women in Renaissance society meant that the representation of nature as a benevolent female also contained the implication that it could be used as a commodity and manipulated as a resource.

Furthermore, during the Middle Ages, Jean-Pierre Babelon shows, 'although the Crusades failed to bring western soldiers face to face with the Hanging Gardens of Babylon, one of the Seven Wonders of the Ancient World, they did reveal the unsuspected splendours of those in the Near East', with the Alhambra showcasing the Islamic passion for, and marvellous creation of, 'walled gardens and secret areas enlivened by the music of water' (2000, 26–7). Walled gardens were thus introduced in France at the end of the Middle Ages, and took new forms in the more urban Italy during the Renaissance. The landscape gardens of Europe and England (one needs only to think of Versailles or the English castles) speak to this emerging version of the bucolic and rural imagery. However, the new taste for nature was not 'an intuitive affair', Thomas notes:

> [j]ust as the appreciation of the English landscape garden in the early eighteenth century required a classical education and some knowledge of history and literature, necessary to catch all the references to Horace and Virgil, or the allusions to Poussin and Claude, so the attraction to unimproved nature was initially a sophisticated business, reflecting the highly literary and intellectual inspiration of the new sensibilities. (1984, 265)

Thus, nature became increasingly construed, through the subtle pedagogy of a new artistic and architectural sensibility, as an imagined reality removed from the daily life of a 'civilised' (which Rousseau will later define as 'unnatural') urban world, with nature both admired in its idyllic depiction and feared in its primal and wild (and at times terrifying) state. Always, however, at a distance. The concept of a 'landscape' that emerged from its roots in the *jardin anglais* and in the later wave of thought inspired by Jean-Jacques Rousseau and the first ascent of Mont Blanc in 1786 became the expression of '[a] new relationship between people and nature: landscape was a slice of nature as perceived by an observer, it implied an aesthetic ordering of nature and its purpose was to offset the deeply felt loss of a direct connection with the cosmos' (Ramos, 2000, 10). The effect of this veritable 'ordering' of nature was that 'Arcadia', Simon Schama shows (1995), was increasingly placed under glass, located in zoos and cages, and under observation glasses. The nostalgic view of an idyllic and bucolic countryside as an idealized place of yearning and escape has continued well into the twentieth century: Tolkien's depiction of the hobbits' Shire in *The Lord of the Rings* is, perhaps, one of the most visible fantastic metaphors for such a view.

Just as the hobbits' bucolic lifestyle is threatened by the growing power of 'wild' and primeval orcs, however, a similar conception of a hostile 'wilderness' continued, throughout the Middle Ages, in parallel with the bucolic imaginary described above. Such 'wilderness' entails, throughout the ages, an ambivalent attitude. On the one hand, the myth of the greenwood took political connotations, via the English imagery of the rebellious (but staunchly and idealistic royalist) Robin Hood, as described in the original *Lyttel Gest of Robyn Hode*. On the other hand, attitudes toward animals and plants in the Tudor age are well documented by Keith Thomas in *Man and the Natural World* (1984). The choice of the gendered subject is very apt, as it reflects a hierarchical attitude that places humanity above animals (and the rest of nature), with non-white men, women and the poor portrayed as closer to the animal kingdom than men, whose mastery over an untamed natural creature is a physical representation of their perceived power over reality itself. In Tudor England, for example, 'contemporary hunters betray uninhibited delight in the capture and killing of wild animals. When James I hunted the stag, he would personally cut his throat and daub the faces of his courtiers with blood, which they were not permitted to wash off' (Thomas, 1984, 29). The pursuit of mastery over the natural world, fully captured by Bacon's words quoted in the previous chapter, is tragically epitomized by Melville's *Moby Dick,* where the ever-increasing manic Ahab obsessively embarks in an ultimately self-destructive attempt to conquer and dominate nature (in the form of the leviathan-like Moby Dick).

Carolyn Merchant (1983) depicts the domination of man over nature and women as deeply intertwined throughout the history of philosophy and art. Against the benign maternal depiction of an agrarian and bucolic nature, Merchant notes, is that of nature as a chaotic witch. The chaos and sexuality of nature (as the untamed feminine) is exemplified, for example, by Louis-Ernest Barrias's sculpture *Nature Reveals Herself* (1899). The Mother Earth image is thus always countered by the idea to the uncontrollable wild, both representations of the feminine: 'woman was both virgin and witch: the Renaissance courtly lover placed her on a pedestal; the inquisitor burned her at the stake' (Merchant, 1983, 127).

During the Romantic and Industrial periods, the imagination of the countryside changed. 'By the eighteenth century', Thomas points out, 'a combination of literary fashion and social facts had created a genuine tension between the relentless progress of urbanization and the rural longing to which an increasing number of people were subject. These longing provided a clear indication that there were many who felt that, although the natural world should be tamed, it ought not to be completely dominated and suppressed' (1984, 254). While the ancient pastoral idea had survived into the modern industrial world, it was then reshaped, with the pastoral depiction of an idyllic 'nature' supplanted 'by a novel admiration for the untamed "wilderness", and a "growing reaction against the relentless advance of cultivation"' (1984, 254). The new taste for a 'wild' nature, this 'semi-religious devotion to wild landscapes' was, of course, a European phenomenon, 'whose prophets included Rousseau and Alexander von Humboldt. But it was the English who went furthest towards has been called "the divinisation of nature"' (1984, 261).

The more recent myth of 'nature' as the place where the 'true' human 'nature' could be realized is the hallmark of the Romantic period, prefigured by authors such as William Blake and fully embraced by authors such as William Wordsworth, Samuel Taylor Coleridge, and Robert Frost. It is captured by painters such as John Constable, Joseph Turner and Caspar David Friedrich, and by composers such as Edward Elgar, Frederick Delius and Gustav Holst. The mythical stature awarded to mountain climbing (a previously unheard-of activity) emerged in England in that period, inspired by Percy Bysshe Shelley's 1816 *Mont Blanc*. The forest itself became 'romantic'. In fact, 'Gothic architecture was widely regarded as an attempt to reproduce in stone the branching of a forest walk' (Thomas, 1984, 216), and trees were seen to provide 'a link with eternity' (217). English oaks were found to be over 700—sometimes even 1500—years old, and older trees around the world were later discovered in other parts of the world. The newly imagined reality of the Alps as places of lyrical escape from the urban world is captured in Albrecht von Holler's poem *Die Alpen*, published in 1732.

The Romantics enacted a radical reversal of the relationship between 'nature' and 'culture'. For them, Timothy Morton writes, the changing idea of nature became 'a way of healing what modern society had damaged ... the damage ...

ha[d] sundered subjects from objects, so that human beings are forlornly alienated from their world. Contact with nature, and with the aesthetic, will mend the bridge between subject and object' (2007, 22). For the Romantics, therefore, the perceived value of nature was as much aesthetical as it was ontological or ethical. Connected to the idea of the wilderness was a new appreciation for solitude and even loneliness. 'Perhaps the growth of population', Thomas suggests, 'helped to foster [an] anti-social feeling. For, in previous less populated centuries, it had been conventional to regard loneliness as a human misfortune' (1984, 268). However, the trouble with the Romantic idea of 'wilderness', Cronon posits, is that 'it quietly expresses and reproduces the very values its devotees seek to reject. The flight from history that is very nearly the core of wilderness represents the false hope of an escape from responsibility, the illusion that we can somehow wipe clean the slate of our past and return to the *tabula rasa* that supposedly existed before we began to leave our marks on the world' (2008, 300–1). Moreover, he adds, '[o]nly people whose relation to the land was already alienated could hold up wilderness as a model for human life in nature, for the romantic ideology leaves precisely nowhere for human beings actually to make their living from the land' (301–2). The 'wilderness' of 'nature' is thus as removed from the life of 'culture' as the tamed Arcadia of gardens, zoos and landscapes is, and such an image, Cronon concludes, 'may teach us to be dismissive or even contemptuous of … humble places or experiences. Without our quite realizing it, [the idea of] wilderness tends to privilege some parts of nature at the expense of others' (303).

The American 'wild west' tradition, from Daniel Boone and Davey Crockett to Huckleberry Finn, constitutes a particular embodiment of the imagination of 'the wild', still deeply steeped in European conceptions of what such a 'wild' is actually constituted of. Such idea of 'wildness' in the American tradition is fully described by Roderick Nash in *Wildness and the American Mind* (1967). Hausdoerffer and Horn (2017) distinguishes the terms 'wilderness' from 'wildness', both more common in American English usage and without literal translations in most other languages. The former, he argues, refers to undeveloped habitats, void of human intervention and artefacts, whereas the latter refers to the capacity of self-renewal of a being, a system or a community. Such an idea is fully captured by the US *Wilderness Act* of 1964, which legislates that the wilderness, 'in contrast to those areas where man and his own works dominate the landscape, is hereby recognised as an area where the earth and its community are untrammelled by man, where man himself is a visitor who does not remain'.

This radically exclusionary idea of 'nature' is a marked departure from the Germanic *foresta* of Tacitus, one that does not take into account how other cultures have embedded themselves within (and radically altered) the landscapes they inhabited. Never was the impact of such an imagined nature as visible in the colonial imposition of an English idea of nature in Australia, for two centuries depicted as a land untouched by human intervention—a myth, this, that has been radically rejected by works such as Bill Gammage's *The Greatest Estate on Earth* (2010) and Bruce Pascoe's *Dark Emu* (2014). This idea of 'wilderness' seems to imply that humanity is equated with its modern technological tools and machinery, and does not consider more complex ecological techniques displayed by most human cultures throughout history. This is not to say that exclusionary zones are not needed today. Indeed, among the socio-technical choices we must make today, such an exclusion may be necessary for biodiversity to survive in the radically altered ecological landscape of today, as Edward O Wilson suggests in *Half-Earth* (2016). However, such choices should be seen as a completely novel innovation, not a return to a mythical (culturally projected and historically non-existent) 'wild state of nature' untouched by humans.

The depiction of 'nature' in European history from the Greco-Roman times to the present thus displays three main intertwined themes: urban and domestic life (that of the *urbs* and the *domus*, where 'culture' is to be found and human potential is fully realized) cast against an agrarian benevolent Arcadia urban dwellers always somewhat yearn to return to (as an escape from the 'unnatural' and constraining aspects of 'civilisation'), and surrounded by an untamed and uninhabited 'wilderness' that is, at the same time, fascinatingly alluring (the Roman *foresta* and the Romantic idea of the 'wild'), and frighteningly hostile (the Roman *silva* and the Mediaeval conception of the 'wilderness' as 'wasteland'). This tripartite relationship with the imagined natural world still dominates today's view of 'nature', as well as the ethical attitude toward it. After all, the task of making a home in nature is what Wendell Berry has called 'the unfinished lifework of our species'. Importantly, he adds that '[t]he only thing we have to preserve nature with is culture; the only thing we have to preserve wildness with is domesticity' (1987, 138). Cronon concurs, by stating that '[c]alling a place home inevitably means that we will *use* the nature we find in it' (1995, 303). The imagination of 'nature' is thus strictly intertwined with any ethical choices made in relation to it. It is not possible to imagine how one normatively *ought* to engage with 'nature' without an articulation of what 'nature' is. Before casting our gaze upon the emergence of an environmental or ecological ethics in the nineteenth and twentieth centuries, then, and following upon the imagination of nature described in this section, it is now possible to look at the 'minority narratives' of the Western philosophical tradition, cast against the *anthropocentric* ones described in the previous chapter and that have impacted both the ecological imagination of 'nature' that emerged in more recent times and the ethical stances toward it that followed.

4.2 Counternarratives of Interdependence

To cast once again our gaze toward the earliest texts on record, the idea of 'nature' among ancient pre-Abrahamic religions is, as Bertrand Russell suggests, deeply connected to fertility cults: '[t]he earth was female, the sun male. … In Babylon, Ishtar, the earth-goddess, was supreme among female deities. Throughout western Asia, the Great Mother was worshipped under various names'. In fact, 'Christianity transformed her into the Virgin Mary, and it was a Council at Ephesus that legitimated the title "Mother of God" as applied to Our Lady' (1945, 5). Some traces of the animism of these fertility cults can be found in the Bible, as in Job 12:7–8: 'But ask now the beasts, and they shall teach thee; and the fowls of the air, and they shall teach thee; or speak to the earth, and it shall teach thee; and the fishes of the sea shall declare unto thee'. The Leviticus also reminded people that the surface of the land belonged to Yahweh, and that it 'shall not be sold for ever: for the land is mine, and ye are strangers and sojourners with me'. Some caesura from a maternal 'nature' within whose womb humanity exists, however, was already lamented in the *Epic of Gilgamesh,* where the author 'bemoans the destruction of the Mesopotamian forests, and wonders ... how humankind will ever be able to answer to God for the wounds inflicted on His world' (Winchester, 2021, 227).

4.2.1 Physis and Kosmos

Starting this diachronic journey throughout Western philosophy, once again, with ancient Greek philosophy, Frederick Copleston notes that 'there is no supernatural in Homer, for the Homeric god is part of nature' (2003 ed, vol I, 60). Homer's ultimate cause of all events is, indeed, Fate, represented by the Μοῖραι (*moirai*), rather than the Olympian gods. Russel (1945) suggests that, for the Greeks, the idea that creation out of nothing is impossible inevitably led to pantheism, the belief that the divine (or the One) and the world are one, and that everything in the world is part of God (a view fully realized, two millennia later, in Spinoza). However, while it is certain that pre-Socratic philosophers saw the One and the world as one (unlike the dichotomy introduced by the latter neo-Platonic and Christian idea of transcendence), Copleston describes them more accurately as monists rather than pantheists, defining 'a pantheist [a]s a [person] who, while denying a Transcendent Principle of the universe, makes the universe to be ultimately Thought (unlike the materialist, who makes it Matter alone)' (2003 ed, vol I, 59). Nonetheless, Aristotle famously recorded Thales expressing the view that 'everything is full of gods'.

The fundamental hylozoism (the idea that all matter is alive, that primordial matter contains an intrinsic animating principle) of the Milesian schools led them to believe, Fritjof Capra explains (1975), that there is no distinction between animate and inanimate, spirit and matter. In fact, they did not even have a word for matter, since they saw all forms of existence as manifestations of the "physis", endowed with life and spirituality' (24–5). The view that a divine essence pervades all things led Anaximander to suggest that entire universe is supported by *pneuma* (πνεῦμα), conceived of as air or the cosmic breath (an idea possibly akin to the breath of the *dharma* in Hinduism). Anaximander contended that all things come from a single primal substance, that is both infinite and eternal, encompassing all worlds and differentiating into distinct basic substances. The primal element, the 'urstaff', is, and must be, boundless (the ἄπειρον, *apeiron*), often rendered as the Infinite. Moreover, Anaximander (and later Heraclitus) connected the fundamental unity of nature (against its apparent multiplicity) to the unity of the laws that govern it. Thus, the pre-Socratic hylozoist conception of matter contains an unavoidable (yet often ignored) *normative* quality.

Following Anaximander, Heraclitus also believed that all things emerge from a single unity, formed by the combination of all multiplicities in the world. Heraclitus was the first to speak of a divine 'law' that trumps human laws (while the concept was not novel, Heraclitus was the first to speak in terms of an inherent principle or 'law', rather than in terms of the gods' commands). Anaximander's and Heraclitus's view of a *necessary* 'balance' among all physical (bounded) elements as the basis for natural law certainly prefigures the modern idea of homeostasis and autopoiesis developed in the twentieth century. Parmenides expanded upon this inherently *normative* quality of matter by making it an essential component of the nature of being. The Parmenidean being, the One, moreover, is a whole from which the distinction human/nature is entirely absent.

The very concept of the 'world' as a cohesive and self-bounded entity emerged early within Greek texts, who, anticipating Parmenides, defined the world (or better, the entirety of existence) as *kosmos* (κόσμος). Pythagoras was the first to call *kosmos* the totality of all things in existence, 'because of the order (*taxis*) that reigns in it' (Brague, 2004). 'Pythagoras's central conviction', Brian Swimme and Mary Evelyn Tucker assert, 'was that the essence of the universe is not water or air or fire or anything concrete like that. The essence of the universe is number; the heart of the universe is revealed in pattern' (2011, 58). Notwithstanding the quantification of the world that this view introduced, however, Pythagorean philosophy maintained an ecstatic quality, and mathematics itself was originally connected with a peculiar form of mysticism (something still very much present in the Jewish tradition of the הַלָּבַק, the Kabbalah). To Pythagoras is also attributed to the idea that all things born with life ought to be treated as kindred, and he was known to preach to animals like Saint Francis centuries later: Pythagorean cults (which entailed a common way of life, common property, and equal treatment of men and women) maintained a strict vegetarianism, treating animals (if not necessarily the entirety of the world) with the same respect owed to humankind. Not long thereafter, Anaxagoras considered the 'mind' as qualitatively identical in humans, animals and plants, with the only difference being a bodily one (Anaxagoras argued that the superiority of humanity over the rest of the animal world is due exclusively to the fact that humans possess hands, which animals do not).

Later pre-Socratic philosophy progressively shifted away from the holistic and mystical tendencies discussed thus far. Thus, the atomists purposely avoided engaging with the notion of *purpose* or *cause*, arguing instead that they looked at the world 'as is' (and thus obscuring the ontologically normative implications of their own observations), while the sophist Prodicus suggested that the worship of the gods is really the worship of the natural forces they represent (hence, e.g., the worship of Hephaestus is the worship of fire, and that of Demeter the worship of bread). However, a less materialist undercurrent was still present, albeit in a less overt manner, in later Greek philosophy. Contrary to the Socrates of Aristophanes, for example, Xenophon's stories about Socrates indicate that Socrates suggested it to be arrogant to think that we humans are the only site of the Mind (*nous*), attributing it instead to the cosmos as a whole.

Plato's mysticism, the idea that true knowledge is ultimately supra-sensible, is, perhaps unfortunately, coached in a language that later led to the rejection of the sensible world. However, it can be suggested that Plato instead spoke of mystical experiences, akin to those produced by trance-like states or the use of psychotropic plants.[2] In any case, as Copleston states, Plato was 'neither materialist nor epiphenomenalist, but an uncompromising spiritualist' (2003 ed, vol I, 207), and in the *Timaeus*, he articulated the idea of a world-soul, an *anima mundi*, as the intrinsic connection between all living beings.

For Aristotle, all celestial bodies are living, intelligent entities, comprised of souls as well as bodies (an idea more recently at the core of Doris Lessing's *Canopus in Argos* series). Aristotle also proposed the idea of the world as an ordered and harmonious whole in which all parts have a purpose or *telos*, with each thing tending toward its own perfect ultimate state or realization, or *entelechy* (ἐντελέχεια).[3]

Diogenes of Sinope, arguably the most famous of the Cynics and a very early precursor of Thoreau, held up the life of animals as the model for humanity, rather than the other way around. He advocated a 'return to nature' and proclaimed his brotherhood to animals, leading Russell (1945) to equate him to the Taoists, as well as Rousseau and Tolstoy. A similar, albeit more moderate, attitude toward animals, demanding their kind treatment, was later to be found in a number of Roman authors as diverse as Ovid, Seneca, Porphyry and Plutarch (Lecky, 1869).

The Stoics occupy a special place in Roman philosophy, for they believed that

> [a]ll things are parts of one single system, which is called Nature; the individual life is good when it is in harmony with Nature. In one sense, *every* life is in harmony with Nature, since it is such as Nature's laws have caused it to be; but in another sense a human life is only in harmony with Nature when the individual will is directed to ends which are among those of Nature. *Virtue* [therefore] consists of *will* which is in agreement with Nature. (Russell 1945, 254)

The Stoics' position introduces a dichotomy between that which is 'natural' (simply by virtue of being) and that which is 'unnatural' (by being in antithesis to natural 'ends'), as well as an identification of Reason (from which such natural ends can be derived) with Nature. Notwithstanding the Stoics' rationalism, however, their approach aspired to a harmony with the universe, rather than pre-eminence over it. While materialists, the Stoics nonetheless conceived of what Elizabeth Grosz defines as four 'incorporeals', which 'cannot be understood as

[2] Some suggest that the effect of such psychoactive plants (and altered states of consciousness in general) is to remove bodily and sensory distraction, allowing the mind to appraise a fuller form of knowledge.

[3] An entity's *entelechy* is also complemented by the same entity's state of perfect 'being-at-work' or *energeia* (ενέργεια, the origin of the modern – and rather different – scientific idea of 'energy'), and is contrasted, as 'actuality', by an entity's 'potentiality', or *dynamis* (δύναμις).

qualities, generalities (or universals), or even as quasi objects: they neither act nor are acted upon … They are more conditions for the possible and actual existence of bodies (and their expression), an imperceptible yet unimposed and constitutive field of cohesion … that enables bodies, objects, to come into being, and to come to mean something' (2017, 32). These four incorporeal are void (*kenon*, κενών), place (*topos*, τόπος), time and *lekta* (λεκτά, what can be said about a thing). The Stoics' rationalism was challenged by the sceptics, who argued against the idea of a universal 'reason' that allows for an irrefutable deductive or inductive logic. In *De Rerum Natura*, Lucretius asserted a continuity of existence within the cosmos, stating that nothing proceeds from nothing, nor passes into nothingness (*res quoniam docui non posse creari de nilo neque item genitas ad nil revocari*, 'since I have taught that things cannot be born from nothing, cannot when begotten be brought back to nothing').

4.2.2 'Fratello Sole, Sorella Luna'

Building upon the neo-Platonic rejection of the atomists' materialism, Christian philosophy was very early on marked by a spiritualist conception of the world, albeit not necessarily a mystical one. Indeed, Copleston notes how Christian mysticism was often subterranean, such as in the writings of the Pseudo-Dionysus. Early Christianity was marked by the emphasis on transcendence, and a quasi-rejection of the corporeal world. The Gnostics suggested that the Yahweh of the Old Testament was instead the Demiurge, whereas the serpent in the Garden of Eden had warned Eve against the Demiurge's deceptions. While still embodying the fullest rejection of the sensible world, such an interpretation speaks of an otherwise uncommon connection with the animal world, in this instance symbolized by the serpent. Similarly, some less-known early Christians expressed some concerns for animals. Notable are a prayer written by Basil of Caesarea and a remark by John Chrysostom urging kindness toward animals. Others, like Neot, acted as early eco-saboteurs, sabotaging hunts by rescuing trapped animals (Linzey, 1976; Passmore, 1975).

Overall, while the Platonic distinction of soul and body suggested that the soul can be truly happy only when stripped of its bodily constraints, the Christian idea of the immortality of the *body* as well as the soul (which Christianity inherited and continued from the Old Testament) suggests an element of relevance of the bodily realm that, even hidden under the Christian insistence on 'sin', was absent in Platonic philosophy. In the late second century, Origen of Alexandria suggested that there is nothing incorporeal other than God (perhaps suggesting a non-Platonic corporeality of the soul) and that the stars are living rational beings (who can, as a consequence, sin). Origen's world was, without a doubt, one of sentient relations.

The later emergence of a monastic tradition is paralleled by their advanced skills as expert agriculturalists. Benedictine monks combined spiritual, intellectual, and physical exercises to remain in close contact with nature and establish a harmonious relationship with it (Dubos, 2006). The notorious replacement of the temple of Apollo in Monte Cassino by the first Benedictine monastery is, likely, a strong example of the physical continuity of more geographically connected nature of ancient places of worship (which still maintained some degree of ecological connection to place) with a more impersonal and more abstract religiosity, which, nonetheless, shows that under the Christian churches often remained (and likely still remains) the physical reminder of a sense of reverence for natural places.

John the Scot categorized nature into four distinct classes: what creates and is not created (God), what creates and is created (the Platonic ideas), what is created but does not create (all things in space and time) and what neither creates nor is created (God as the End and Purpose of all things). Russell (*contra* Copleston) defines him as a pantheist, due to his belief that the ultimate end of all material things is ultimately the same as their beginning, with all things emanating from God and yet striving to return to Him. A likely precursor of Spinoza's monism, in *De Divisione Naturae*, he refers to 'Nature' as both the natural world and the supernatural sphere, all Reality being ultimately conceived of as one.

Even the 'doctor angelicus', Thomas Aquinas, wrote, in almost panentheistic terms in the *Summa Theologica*, that God is at the same time above all things (*supra omnia*) and yet in all things (*in omnibus rebus*), and that while God is in all things, yet all things are in God. Since the divine whole 'could not be adequately represented by one creature alone, he produced many and diverse creatures, [so] that what was wanting to one in the representation of the divine goodness might be supplied by another. For goodness, which in god is simple and uniform, in creatures is manifold and divided; and hence the whole universe together participates the divine goodness more perfectly and represents it better than any single creature' (in Berry, 1988, 79). Thomas Berry suggests that Aquinas thus proposes a form of 'ultimate universal socialism'. Moreover 'despite some fundamentally anthropocentric statements', Berry continues, he also 'appeared to recognize the stewardship ethic. He suggested that Nature honours God, and that, consequently, studying the world is better than consuming it' (1988, 79). Building upon Augustine's proclamation that all creatures ultimately reflect the 'goodness of the Creator', Aquinas 'rejected an earlier perspective that any creature could be essentially evil', and, a precursor of modern ecological thought, he noticed 'the connections between Nature and used metaphors to speak of harmony and equilibrium' (Gillespie, 1997, 69).

Among other scholastic thinkers, Robert Grosseteste, prefiguring modern physics, famously argued light (*lux*) to be the first corporeal form. The hyper-realist Odo of Tournai believed in a form of sheer monism, in the sense that 'all objects to which we apply the term substance are modifications of one substance and, more comprehensively, that all beings are modifications of one Being' (Copleston, 2003 ed, vol II, 141). Odo is another likely precursor of Spinoza, along Maimonides,

David of Dinant (a thirteenth-century materialistic pantheist criticized by Thomas of Aquinas for suggesting that God is the same as primary matter) and Almaric of Bene (who had already identified God, as the essence of all things, with space and time themselves).

Of all Christian thinkers, however, the most striking counternarrative to an otherwise profoundly anthropocentric tradition is that of Francis of Assisi, whose *Canticle of Brother Sun, Sister Moon* famously refers to 'our sister, Mother Earth'. Francis, Russell contends, 'loved all things, not only as a Christian or a benevolent man, but as a poet. His hymn to the sun, written shortly before his death, might *almost* have been written by Akhnaton the sun-worshipper' (1945, 450).

Fourteenth-century mysticism (and, later the sixteenth-century one of Teresa of Avila and of John of the Cross) appeared as a somewhat pantheistic reaction to the metaphysical rationalism of the previous centuries, particularly of Scholastic Aristotelian logic. This is well symbolized by Eckhart von Hochheim (generally known as Meister Eckhart)'s conception of time, with creation said to occur in the 'now' (*nunc*) of eternity, which suggests an idea of originary creation that exists *beyond*, not *before* time (an idea that cannot fail to remind the reader of the Australian Aboriginal—far older—concept of the 'Dreaming', a concept that will be further discussed in a later chapter). Furthermore, Meister Eckhart displays a panentheist concept of the soul, whose essence or 'spark' (*vünkelin* or *scintilla*), he argued (although he had later to refuse it in order to avoid an accusation of heresy), is uncreated, and whose 'citadel' (*bürgelin*) can ultimately unite with God as 'being' (*esse*). John Tauler further identified a connection between the deeper essence of the soul and the human faculties that emanate from it, a link called *das Gemüt*, which points to some kind of universal 'nature' shared by all souls, while John Ruysbroeck wrote of the 'most high and super-essential Unity of the Divine Nature' (Copleston, 2003 ed, vol III, 197). The Neoplatonic Renaissance alchemist Robert Fludd, in his *Utriusque Cosmi Majoris Scilicet et Minoris Metaphysica* (1617–21), portrays 'the world soul as a woman connected by her right hand to God, represented by the Hebrew tetragrammaton—the four consonants JHVH—transmitted by a golden chain to the terrestrial world below' (Merchant, 1983, 11).

4.2.3 *Natura Naturans and Natura Naturata*

Roger Bacon, who introduced the idea of a *scientia experimentalis*, the renewed emphasis on scientific empiricism, included in such science a wide range of religious visions and mystical states of raptures, thus displaying a lack of the extreme and exclusionary scientism of later modernity. Among the early natural philosophers, Pico of Mirandola saw human beings as totipotential beings at birth, containing the seeds of many forms of life. Depending on which seeds are cultivated, he posited, one can become a vegetable, a brute, a rational spirit, or a son of God. While still influenced by the *scala naturae*, this perspective speaks of a far deeper interconnection among distinct natural forms. Pietro Pomponazzi similarly wrote that beasts share with humans some degree of self-knowledge: 'nor must we deny that the beasts know themselves. For it seems altogether stupid and irrational to say that they do not know themselves, when they love themselves and their species' (in Copleston, 2003 ed, vol III, 223). Nicholas of Cusa proposed an almost Heraclitean idea of unity as the harmonious synthesis of differences, the *coincidentia oppositorum*. A deep undercurrent of pantheism (something he himself denied) can be evinced from his idea of God containing all things within Himself (*omnia complicans*), while at the same time being the source of all multiple things that reveal something of Him (*omnia explicans*).[4] Cusa overtly challenged the *scala naturae*, by emphasizing the importance of individual things each as a unique manifestation of God. Giordano Bruno similarly spoke of God as *Natura naturans* insofar as He is distinct from His manifestations, and *Natura naturata* insofar as He is considered in His self-manifestation.[5] A protean panentheist rather than a pantheist, for Bruno the greatest and highest achievement of philosophical speculation is not Plotinus's ecstatic mysticism, the abandonment and union with God, but rather the magical vision of Nature in its ultimate unity. For him, the ultimate goal of humanity is the identification with Nature, as exemplified by the myth of Acteon and Diana: when the hunter Acteon saw Diana (taken as the symbolic representation of Nature) in its full nakedness, he was transformed into a stag. Far from being a punishment, Bruno interprets this transformation as a reward, as a way of becoming an integral part of Nature himself. Nicola Abbagnano suggests that Bruno's is a 'dyonisiac religion of the infinite' (2003, vol II, 148).[6] Tommaso Campanella, in *The City of Sun*, actually imagined and proposed such a natural religion (ultimately leading to a communist state not too dissimilar from Plato's Republic).

Among Renaissance thinkers arose the idea of Nature as a 'self-sufficient unity, as a system unified by all-pervading forces of sympathy and attraction and animated by a world-soul' (Copleston, 2003 ed, vol II, 248), a cosmos, that is, whose value is found within itself rather than by reference to its usefulness for human flourishing. These late Renaissance 'organicist' thinkers anticipated the more recent Gaia theory, and saw Nature essentially as an organism 'in regard to which the sharp distinctions, characteristic of mediaeval thought, between living and non-living and between spirit and matter, lost their meaning and application' (Copleston, 2003 ed, vol II, 248). Henry More defined the *Anima Mundi*, the Soul of the World, as the Spirit of Nature (Worster, 1977). Not much later, both Campanella and Savinien de Cyrano (better known as Cyrano de Bergerac) described the universe as a gigantic animal, with stars being at the same time parts

---

[4] *Deus ergo est omnia complicans, in hoc quod omnia in eo; est omnia explicans, in how quia ipse in omnibus:* 'Therefore, God is the unfolding of all things in that all things are in Him; and He is the unfolding of all things in that He is in all things' (De docta ignorantia, 2–3).

[5] Notably, Bruno denied that the Earth and the solar system occupy a privileged place in the universe, and instead proposed the idea of multiple universes.

[6] In the original: 'una religione dionisiaca dell'infinito'.

of this being and worlds in and of themselves for beings such as ourselves (who, in turn, function as worlds for a host of other creatures), while Gerolamo Cardano saw the world as an organism animated by a world-soul clearly inspired Plato's *Timaeus*.[7] Importantly, these organicist philosophers viewed the world, in contrast with the Heraclitean Strife, as a self-organizing and ultimately harmonious whole, and they increasingly placed great emphasis on the idea of natural law and of Nature as a unified, law-governed system.

Philippus Aureolus Theophrastus Bombastus von Hohenheim, better known as Paracelsus, perhaps most famously combined this organicist tendency with a spiritualist ontology, by suggesting that the world at large is animated by an immanent vital principle, the *archeus*, which also animates each individual. Therefore, the task of the physician, he argued, is spiritual inasmuch as material: it is to assist Nature to do her work, by stimulating that vital principle and thus allowing it to heal the individual of any ailment they may have. Similarly, the 'Cambridge Platonists' (such as Lord Herbert of Cherbury, Emmanuel College, Ralph Cudworth and Henry More) became concerned, against the growing materialistic interpretation of the universe, 'with defending a spiritualist interpretation of the universe as a foundation for the Christian moral life' (Copleston, 2003 ed, vol V, 57). Merchant traces back the more recent origin of 'vitalism' from the organicist (and animistic) idea of an organic unity of Campanella or the English astrologer John Dee, through the Neoplatonic natural magic of Marsilio Ficino and Pico della Mirandola, to the Naturalism of Bernardino Telesio, Tommaso Campanella and Giordano Bruno, and to the proto-vitalism of Paracelsus and Anne Conway's monistic vitalism (from whom Leibniz derived—or possibly, Merchant argues, appropriated) the term *monad*. The term *vitalism*, Merchant notes, 'designates the unity of matter and spirit as a self-active entity, in which the spiritual kernel is considered the real substance and the material "cover" a mere phenomenon' (1983, 117).

The philosophy of Baruch Spinoza possibly embodies the most notable counterargument to the growing materialism and mechanical determinism that accompanied the rise of science in the seventeenth century. His monism, inherited directly from Parmenides and likely influenced by the naturalist philosophers who preceded him, suggested that there can only be one substance, 'God or Nature' (*Deus sive Natura*). Souls and matter are not separate things, he argued, but merely aspects of the divine Being. As such, they are merely 'adjectival' (Russell 1945, 571). David Abram writes that '[t]o Spinoza, every sensible phenomenon had its own mental aspect; every tangible body within the material world was also an idea within the vast, encompassing intelligence that was known inwardly (to

[7]One of the most interesting organicist-spiritualist explanations of the origin of differences from an original undifferentiated *Ungrund*, which is 'neither light nor darkness, neither love nor wrath', an 'incomprehensible will that is neither evil nor good' is that offered by Jakob Böhme in *Von der Gnadenwahl*. (Copleston 2003 ed, vol III, 271). Böhme argued that individual entities emerge from a process of self-manifestation arising from the will to self-intuition; Nature, in its ideal or spiritual state called the *mysterium magnum*, emerges in visible and tangible form in the actual world, which is thus animated by the *spiritus mundi*.

some) as God and outwardly (to all) as nature' (2010, 109). Spinoza believed in the absolute logical necessity (almost the predestination) of existence: it is logically impossible for events not to be what they are, he argued, and thus there is no metaphysical space for free will. He regarded time as unreal and suggested that the wise person ought to see the world as God sees it, *sub specie aeternitatis,* under the aspect of eternity. Such a perspective resulted in the suggestion that '[w]e are part of a universal nature, and we follow her order. If we have a clear and distinct understanding of this, that part of our nature which is defined by intelligence, in other words the better part of ourselves, will assuredly acquiesce in what befalls us, and is such acquiescence will endeavour to persist' (in Russell 1945, 574). Thus, Spinoza argued, each thing (*res*) strives (*conatur*) to persevere in its own being. The scholastic *conatus*, originally seen as the impulse to self-*preservation*, is seen by Spinoza as the impulse to self-*realization*. Intelligence, or Reason, is both, therefore, a manifestation of the universal *conatus* shared by all things, and is universal in its manifestation. Abram notes that '[h]e alone saw that the human mind could never be reconciled with the human body unless intelligence was recognized as an attribute of nature in its entirety' (2010, 109). Russell writes that Spinoza's panentheistic notion that every being or object is nothing more than a temporary manifestation of a common divine substance, is 'the best example of what may be called "logical monism"—the doctrine, namely, that the world as a whole is a single substance, none of whose parts are logically capable of existing alone' (1945, 577).

Gottfried Leibniz attempted to reconcile Spinoza's monism with the atomistic view that deeply influenced the rise of science. He introduced the idea of an infinite number of substances, which he called 'monads'. Since whatever is complex is made up of what is simple, he argued, and what is simple in unextended (otherwise it could be further divided), there must be simple immaterial elements. These are the monads. However, while monads may have the physical properties of a point (as the atomist suggested), each monad (following Spinozean monism) is, in fact, a 'soul'. Each *monad* is distinct from all others, and 'expresses the universe after its own manner' (Kenny, 2010, 555), encapsulating the world from a particular viewpoint. Where for Spinoza there was a single substance, for Leibniz there are infinite substances, all, however, with identical properties. As a result, Leibnitz discarded any qualitative distinction between humans and nature, and rejected any ontological separation between 'living' and 'non-living'.

4.2.4 A 'New Science'

While science was driven toward (and by) an increasingly materialistic conception of the universe, the introduction of telescopes suggested that 'the earth was hardly the centre of the universe', while the introduction of microscopes 'revealed a complex community on which people seemed to depend rather than the other way around' (Nash, 1989, 21). As a result, Nash suggests, '[t]he more humans learned about nature, the more difficult it became to entertain the notion that the universe, or even the vacant field down the street, existed *for* humans' (1989, 21). Copernicus heliocentric theory[8] had the effect of 'dethron[ing] … earth from its geometrical pre-eminence. In the long run, this made it difficult to give to man the cosmic importance assigned to him in the Christian theology' (Russell 1945, 526). At the same time, the biophilosophies of flow described by Michel Serres in *The Birth of Physics* (2000) clearly rejected the machine model of nature, with is idea of inert matter existing in the void. As a result, while some of the most salient aspects of anthropocentrism became an inextricable part of the modern dominant worldview, the challenge to that very same worldview also gained momentum. Giambattista Vico, in his *Nova Scientia*, reintroduced a cyclical view of history and challenged the rationalist approach to all knowledge Particularly in *De Antiquissima italorum sapientia—Ancient Wisdom of the Italians* (1710), he emphasized the importance of poetry and mythology, and of all those other 'sciences' (such as history, politics, language and jurisprudence) that had been neglected by the rationalist pursuits of the emerging scientific period. At the same time that reason was universalised, its pre-eminence above all other forms of knowledge production was being equally challenged. Pascal's most famous aphorism, that 'the heart has its reasons of which reason knows nothing', suggests an 'instinctive, immediate, unreasoned apprehension of … truth' (Copleston, 2003 ed, vol IV, 165).

Against the Cartesian idea that animals are nothing more than *automata,* in Thomas More's *Utopia*, the killing of animals was to be done by bondsmen, to avoid free citizens learning cruelty. While not necessarily a direct precursor of Peter Singer's argument, more presented a degree of ethical respect toward animals greater than many of his contemporaries. Similarly, Michel de Montaigne attributed considerable importance to the idea of 'nature'. For Montaigne, Copleston explains, 'nature' gives each individual 'a dominant type of character which is fundamentally unchangeable; and the task of moral education is to awaken and preserve the spontaneity and originality of this endowment of nature rather than attempt to mould it into a stereotyped pattern' (2003 ed, vol III, 228). Nature, through Montaigne, increasingly refers to an external, nonhuman, reality, and to an internal 'essence' unique to each individual. In the *Apology for Raimond Sebond* (1435), Montaigne also questioned whether humans are indeed superior to animals. 'When I play with my cat', he mused, 'who knows whether she is passing her time with me no less than I am passing my time with her?' He further noted that '[a]nimals of different kinds have individual senses sharper than ours; they can acquire by swift intuition information that humans have to work out laboriously. They have the same needs and emotions as we have, and they display, often to a more remarkable extent, the same traits and virtues that human take pride in'. In reflecting on why a fox would cock his head to find the best way across a frozen river, '[s]urely', he concluded 'we have therefore reason to judge that there

[8] Copernicus did not seem to be aware of Aristarchus of Samo's equal theory from antiquity.

passes through his head the same discourse as would run through ours, reasoning from sensation to conclusion: what makes a noise, moves; what moves, is not frozen; what is not frozen is liquid; what is liquid gives way' (in Kenny, 2010, 512). Montaigne concluded that the power to reason must be extended beyond the human. In fact, he went even further, ascribing two eminently human activities—theology and philosophy—also to animals.

In political science, Machiavelli advanced an implicitly evolutionary and ecological conception of a community as 'an organic growth, which statesmen can only affect to a limited extent' (Russell 1945, 511), while the idea of unrestricted legal dominion over the rest of the universe found its opponents in both Thomas Hobbes and John Locke. Hobbes argued that in the 'state of nature' there is no property, and that property is exclusively created by government. While this, in his formulation, gives absolute power to dispose of property to the sovereign, it created a distinction between the idea of property as an *inherent* right toward the world and a merely legal construct (and thus subject to any sort of discretionary limit). There is nothing *necessary* about the claim to property, Hobbes argued. Moreover, the idea of natural laws regulating trade and the economy made its way into economic theory with the 'physiocrats', most notable among them François Quesnay and Anne Robert Jacques Turgot, Baron de Laune. For Quesnay, often credited as the 'father of economics', 'national wealth depends on agricultural productiveness. … Manufacture and commerce merely give new forms to the wealth produced … and transfer wealth from one hand to another. They are therefore "sterile", not "productive", though to say this is not to say that they are not useful' (Mazzucato, 2018, 28). A physician, Quesnay saw the economy as a 'metabolic' system, and since in a metabolic system everything must come from somewhere, he argued that this included wealth. Breaking away from the mercantilists, for whom value was in exchanges and the gold they produced, he pointed out that, 'unlike humans, Nature actually produced new things: grain out of small seeds for food, trees out of saplings and mineral ores from the earth … Since agriculture, husbandry, fishing, hunting and mining … bring Nature's bounty to society, Quesnay called them the "productive class" … he … linked value creation inextricably with production' (Mazzucato, 2018, 29). Although the movement he initiated was later described as the 'physiocrats' (literally 'the wealth of nature') they themselves self-identified as 'Les Économistes'.

At the same time, the impact of Spinoza's monism extended well beyond the modest confines in which the unassuming author had developed his philosophy. Denis Diderot, one of the greatest contributors to the Enlightenment via the *Encyclopédie*, adopted a Spinozian view of the world as a single organism (with God as its world-soul), displaying an unusual degree of panpsychism and attributing perception to atoms, interpreted as Leibniz's monads. Gotthold Ephraim Lessing reasserted the idea of the Spinozian One, the immanent Divinity in the world, 'the One and All' (Eν καὶ Πᾶν).

4.2.5 Sturm Und Drang

Spinoza's influence further extended well into the Romantic period. The *Sturm und Drang*'s (a movement named after Maximilian Klinger's 1776 homonymous drama) fundamental theme of the union between Nature and the Spirit is aptly captured by Friedrich Schiller's work. The parallel aspiration toward the infinite is highlighted by Friedrich Hölderlin's *Hyperion* (1797–9). Copleston suggests that Hölderlin's poetry embodies the idea of Nature 'as a slumbering spirit and the human spirit as the organ of Nature's consciousness of herself' (2003 ed, vol VII, 16).

Furthermore, the Romantics tended to conceive of the infinite totality aesthetically, with 'the means of apprehending this unity being intuition and feeling rather than conceptual thought' (Copleston, 2003 ed, vol VII, 18). Knowledge, for the Romantics, is sensorial and experiential (if not necessarily mystical), rather than mental, logical, propositional. The Romantic reaction to the hyper-rationality and rationalism of the Enlightenment led to the emphasis on extreme passions uninformed by thought. Friedrich Schelling is often considered the direct precursor of both transcendentalism and deep ecology, seeing nature as having fundamental value in and of itself. Schelling rejected the burgeoning idealism of his contemporaries, arguing that 'transcendental philosophy, which takes the subjective as primary, is only one part of philosophy, the other being nature-philosophy (*Naturephilosophie*), which takes the objective as primary' (Gare, 2017, 52). Blurring the distinction between organic and inorganic matter, for this nature-philosophy, '[t]he concept of *nature* does not entail that there should also be an intelligence that is aware of it. Nature, it seems, would exist, even if there were nothing that was aware of it' (Schelling, 1978 ed, 18). Schelling also predicted the ultimate unification of humanity into a single civilization, one where the development of a global world consciousness would require the parallel development of a 'philosophical religion' to replace the parochialism of the specific religions of particular civilizations.

In England, Samuel Coleridge expressed a Spinozian pantheism, for example in *Frost at Midnight* (1798):

So shalt thou see and hear.
The lovely shapes and sounds intelligible.
Of that eternal language, which thy God.
Utters, who from eternity doth teach.
Himself in all, all things in himself.

Coleridge displayed a profound sympathy for Schelling's philosophy of Nature. For Coleridge, the ultimate principle of reality was to be sought in the identity of subject and object. Similarly, Thomas Carlyle, whose characteristic was 'his vivid sense of the mystery of the world and of its nature as an appearance of, or veil before, supersensible reality' (Copleston, 2003 ed, vol VIII, 156), argued that the fundamental truth of the world is apprehended by the intuition of humanity's inmost nature. As mentioned in the previous chapter, Jean-Jacques Rousseau, in

Nouvelle Héloïse, saw progress as a return to a mythical state of nature (conceived as an inner world inasmuch as an outer one), with a natural religion (although shaped by reason) to guide such return. It is Rousseau's mythical conception of a purer rural life that will later inform the transcendentalist poets of America, and yet, it is important to remember, '[t]he poor, to the romantics, were never urban ànd never industrial; the proletariat is a nineteenth century conception, perhaps equally romanticized, but quite different' (Russell 1945, 676).

A student of Schelling, Georg Wilhelm Friedrich Hegel maintained a belief in the 'unreality of separateness; the world, in his view, was not a collection of hard units, whether atoms or souls, each completely self-subsistent. The apparent self-subsistence of finite things appeared to him to be an illusion; nothing, he held, is ultimately and completely real except the whole' (Russell 1945, 731). However, unlike Parmenides and Spinoza, Hegel conceived the whole not as a simple or single substance, but rather as a complex system, a kind of an organism. In this sense, Hegel enacted a mélange of Heraclitan and Parmenidean philosophies, enriched by everything that had developed in the two intervening millennia and a half: 'the apparently separate things of which the world seems to be composed are not simply an illusion; each has a greater or lesser degree of reality, and its reality consists in an aspect of the whole, which is what is seen to be when viewed truly'. The whole, for Hegel, is the Absolute. Hegel's subsequent difficulty in dealing with this Absolute (and his resort to logic and Reason to engage with such a profound epistemological difficulty) cannot but remind of the opening line of the *Tao Te Ching*: 'The Tao that can be spoken of is not the enduring and unchanging Tao. The name that can be named is not the enduring and unchanging name'.

The reversal of the relationship between nature and culture affected by the Romantics also entered political and economic theory. François Marie Charles Fourier anticipated Marx in proposing a socialist society as an answer to the evil brought into existence by civilization. What is particularly interesting in Fourier's work is the assertion that 'human social regeneration would have remarkable effects not only in the animal kingdom but even among the heavenly bodies ... he saw a real problem ... namely that of humanizing industrial society and labour and overcoming what is described as alienation' (Copleston, 2003 ed, vol IX, 54–5). Marx's dialectical materialism was extended, by Friedrich Engels, to all of nature. In this sense, the industrial product of humanity is seen as part of a natural process, thus dissolving the distinction between 'nature' and 'culture', even though, Copleston asserts, Engels 'was laying the foundation of a mechanistic version of dialectical materialism, in which the movement of history would be regarded as simply a continuation of the necessary movement of autodynamics matter' (2003 ed, vol VII, 319). According to John Bellamy Foster, Marx's notion of the alienation of human labour 'was connected to an understanding of the alienation of human beings from nature' (2000, 9). In fact, Marx's very first work was his doctoral thesis titled *Difference Between the Democritean and the Epicurean Philosophy of Nature* (1841). Bellamy Foster explores the philosophical underpinnings and context of Marx's theory, showing a direct lineage (through Hegel and, to an extent, Feuerbach) to Epicurean philosophy and its conception of justice. Contained in such lineage is the recognition that 'it was in *Capital* that Marx's materialist conception of nature became fully integrated with his materialist conception of history' (2000, 141). Marx employs the concept of 'metabolism' (*stoffwechsel*) to define the labour process as 'a process between man and nature, a process by which man, through his own actions, mediates, regulates and controls the metabolism between himself and nature' (1976 ed, vol I, 283). Yet, 'an "irreparable rift" had emerged in this metabolism as a result of capitalist relations of production and the antagonistic separation of town and country' (Bellamy Foster, 2000, 141). Marx asserted that this 'rift' in the balance of exchanges (or metabolism) that connects human societies and natural systems is deeply connected to the emergence of a capitalist society:

> [c]apitalist production collects the population together in great centres, and causes the urban population to achieve an ever-growing preponderance. This has two results. On the one hand, it concentrates the historical motive force of society; on the other hand, it disturbs the metabolic interaction between man and the earth, I.e. it prevents the return to the soil of its constituent elements consumed by man in the form of food and clothing; hence it hinders the operation of the eternal natural condition for the lasting fertility of the soil... All progress in capitalist agriculture is a progress in the art, not only of robbing the worker, but of robbing the soil (1976 ed, 637)

The idea of the 'ecological rift' introduced by Marx is taken further by Bellamy Foster, Clark and York (2010), who apply it to the current environmental predicament. In addition to revisiting the Jevons Paradox (introduced in a previous chapter), for example, they highlight the 'Paperless Office Paradox', according to which 'the development of a substitute for a natural resource is sometimes associated with an increase in consumption of that resource' (they note that the introduction of digital alternatives to the use of paper, such as email and other digital storage devices, has in fact *increased* the use of paper). Unhappily vindicating Marx's insight, Christian Parenti ominously concludes that '[t]he metabolism of the world economy is fundamentally out of sync with that of nature. And that is a mortal threat to both' (2012, 225).

Virtually contemporary to Marx's *ouvre*, Charles Darwin's theory of evolution somewhat diminished the mechanistic approach to the world, reintroducing a justification for, and a belief in, some cosmic purpose (however unintentional in the author's formulation). Moreover, the conception of the 'organism' substituted the metaphor of the 'machine' or 'automaton' to describe the world and its creatures. The overarching concept that emerged from Darwin's theory was the unity and continuity of life. Species might have changed often, but the process itself ran back, in an unbroken chain, to the first lifeforms. At this point Darwin stopped: he referred to the origin of *species*, not of *life*. He referred to animals as 'our fellow brethren' and remarked that 'we may be all melted together'. While he described fierce and merciless competition, he also saw equality among the competitors, living and dying together over the eons. Darwin also stated that moral sensibilities were a product of evolution, recognised rudimentary ethics in the social qualities of animals, and argued that cooperation or mutual aid within a species had direct survival value and hence was naturally selected. However, Darwin also understood that the greater the biological differences between humans and other lifeforms, the longer the time lag before we (humans) would regard them as morally considerable. To counter that, a note scribbled to himself urged him never to use the words higher and lower in discussing evolution (Nash, 1989, 42).

For some interpreters of Darwin, the phrase 'struggle for existence' or 'survival of the fittest' (a phrase later coined by Herbert Spencer) meant that might made right. Thomas Huxley wrote in 1893 that ethics ended at the boundary of civilization: human relationship to nature was inherently a-moral. William James urged the American youth to conquer nature, enlisting in the army *against* Nature (an echo of this fearful and oppositional approach to the natural world remains in more recent popular culture, in televised programmes such as *Man vs Wild*). The most extreme Social Darwinists even removed less advantaged humans from the ethical circle that ultimately contained only the rich and powerful (tautologically seen as the 'fittest'). However, others disagreed. Thomas Hardy, for example, believed that Darwinism 'logically involved a readjustment of altruistic morals, by enlarging … [their] application from the area of mere mankind to that of the whole animal kingdom' (Nash, 1989, 43). Writing in 1945, almost three decades before Stone, Russell noted that

> [t]here is a further consequence of the theory of evolution, which is independent of the particular mechanism suggested by Darwin. If men and animals have a common ancestry, and if men developed by such slow stags that there were creatures which we should not know whether to classify as human or not, the question arises: at what stage in evolution did men, or their semi-human ancestors, begin to be all equal? Would *Pithecanthropus erectus*, if he had been properly educated, have done work as good as Newton's? Would the Piltdown Man have written Shakespeare's poetry if there had been anybody to convict him of poaching? A resolute egalitarian who answers these questions in the affirmative will find himself forced to regard apes as the equals of human beings. And why stop with apes? I do not see how he is to resist an argument in favour of Votes for Oysters. An adherent of evolution may maintain that not only the doctrine of the equality of all men, but also that of the rights of man, must be condemned as biological, since it makes too emphatic a distinction between men and other animals. (1945, 727)

Philosophy at the turn of the twentieth century was (some would say finally) influenced by other worldviews. Schopenhauer overtly acknowledged the influence of Eastern philosophies and suggested that Kant's *noumena*, rather than being the logically unattainable horizon of possible knowledge, are the 'veil of Maia', and that such a veil can be pierced (by the Will). Schopenhauer's starting point (possibly an evolution of George Berkeley's philosophy) was that the world is, at its core, *representation.* As Russell explains, for Schopenhauer, '[t]he distinction between one man and another is part of the phenomenal world, and disappears when the world is seen truly. To the good man, the veil of Maya (illusion) has become transparent; he sees that all things are one, and that the distinction between himself and another is only apparent … When the veil of Maya is lifted, a man takes on the suffering of the whole world' (1945, 756). The panpsychist Gustav Theodor Fechner, in *Elemente der Psychophysik* (*Elements of Psychophysics*, 1860), 'leaves the purely scientific sphere and … becomes a kind of poet of the universe', says Copleston (2003 ed, vol VII, 376). Fechner 'contrasted what he called the day-view with the night-view, to the detriment of the latter. The night-view, attributed not only to the materialists but also to the Kantians, is the view of nature as dumb and dead and as affording no real clue to its teleological significance. The day-view is the vision of nature as a living harmonious unity, animated by a soul. The soul of the universe is God, and the universe considered as a physical system is the divine externality' (370). At the same time, for Wilhelm Dilthey, any human being stands 'in a living felt unity with Nature, and his primary experience of his physical milieu are personal lived experiences (*Erlebnisse*)'.

Russian philosophy in the nineteenth and early twentieth centuries seemed to be undertaking an even stronger turn away from anthropocentrism. Already in the eighteenth century, Ivan Kireyevsky had profoundly critiqued what he defined as Western rationalism inherited by Aristotle through the Christian middle ages. Against this exclusionary belief in reason as the *only* way of attaining truth, he proposed a form of integral knowledge, asserting that the 'endless, wearisome game of concepts which was continued for seven hundred years, this useless kaleidoscope of abstract categories incessantly revolving before the mind's sight, inevitably produced a general blindness in regard to those living convictions which lie above the sphere of reason and logic' (in Copleston, 2003 ed, vol X, 61). Instead, these living convictions, he argued, can only be attained by a 'union of all spiritual forces', by bringing together the distinct powers of the human psyche into 'one indivisible whole' that includes aesthetic experience or perception. Similarly, Peter Yakovlevich Chaadaev had a vision of unity that was not limited to unity between human beings alone. In his third *Letter* he wrote that the goal of progress could only be 'a complete fusion of our nature with the nature of the whole world', a 'great fusion of our being with universal being' (1969, 84–5). Moreover, Leo Nikolayevich Tolstoy (influenced by Rousseau's view of humanity) had already argued that the abolition of the state would not lead to a Hobbesian violent 'state of nature', but rather to a good one (importantly, Tolstoy's principle of non-resistance was later taken up by Mahatma Gandhi).

4.2.6 The Twentieth Century

In the twentieth century, Edmund Husserl's *epoche* (the suspension of judgement about the existence of extra-mental reality) cast an agnostic gaze toward the existence (or lack thereof) of an external reality, focusing instead on phenomena as they are appraised by consciousness (irrespective of their external reality). However, David Abram suggests that

> [a]lthough Husserl at first wrote of the nonmaterial, mental character of experienced reality, his growing recognition of intersubjective experience, and of the body's importance for such experience, ultimately led him to recognize a more primary, corporeal dimension, midway between the transcendental "consciousness" of his earlier analyses and the utterly objective "matter" assumed by the natural sciences. This was the intersubjective world of life, the *Lebenswelt*, or "life-world." The life world is the world of our immediately live experience, *as* we live it, prior to all our thoughts about it. (1996, 40)

Building upon Husserl's phenomenology, Martin Heidegger articulated the concept of *Dasein*, of 'being-in-the-world'. *Dasein* is not a substance, but rather the inherently temporal unfolding of a life. Importantly, 'our life is not a self-contained, self-developing entity: from the outset we find ourselves thrown into a physical, cultural and historical context. This "thrownness" (*geworfenheit*) is called … the "facticity" of *Dasein*' (Kenny, 2010, 819–20). *Dasein* is, moreover, discursive: 'that is to say, it operates within a world of discourses, among entities that are articulated and interpreted for us by the language and culture that we share with others'. Kenny explains that *Dasein* leads to a 'caring about' (*besorgen*): '*Dasein* is not a *res cogitans* [thinking is only one way of being in the world], but a *res curans*: not a thinking thing, but a caring thing. Only if I care about, or have interest in, the world will I go on to ask questions about it and give answers to those questions in the form of knowledge-claims' (819). Heidegger's idea of *Dasein* thus (re-)introduces a subjective ethical element to otherwise purportedly neutral claims to knowledge, engendering a positionality and responsibility of the knowing subject ignored since Socrates.

The richness of the many philosophical strands that in the twentieth century were highly critical of the anthropocentric worldview described in chapter three is far too great to summarize, however concisely. Suffice it to say that these many nuanced philosophical reflections evolved in parallel with the emergence of an environmental ethics, and were often explicitly interwoven with it. Among them, as a few examples among many, Maurice Merleau-Ponty strove 'for a new way of speaking that would express this consanguinity of the human animal and world it inhabits' (Abram, 1996, 66). Francis Herbert Bradley postulated 'an original experience of the unity of reality, of the One, on the level of feeling of immediacy, a unity which analytic reflection breaks up or fragments but which metaphysics tries to restore' (Copleston, 2003 ed, vol IX, 333). James Ward (1920) rejected both materialism (in the sense of a mechanical theory of nature) and dualism, rather orienting himself toward what he called 'spiritual monism', not in the classical Spinozian sense of a single substance of being, but rather that all entities are in some sense spiritual. Jules Lachelier claimed that the deeper form of spiritualism consists 'in seeking in spirit that explanation of Nature and in believing that the thought which operates unconsciously in Nature is the same as the thought which becomes conscious in man [sic]' (Copleston, 2003 ed, vol IX, 164). William James argued that there exists only one primal material, out of which everything is composed. However, rather than substance, he calls such material 'pure experience', the 'immediate flux of life which furnishes the material to our later reflections' (in Russell 1945, 813), with knowledge emerging as a set of relations between two portions of pure experience, and the subject-object relation being just derivative. James Edwin Creighton adopted a more pragmatic form of personal idealism, distinguishing two forms of idealism. The first, mentalism, is the antithesis of materialism: '[w]hile the materialist interprets the psychical as a function of the physical, the mentalist reduces material things to psychical phenomena, to states of consciousness or to ideas. And as the material world cannot without absurdity be reduced to any given finite individual's states of consciousness, the mentalist is inevitably driven to postulate an absolute mind' (Copleston, 2003 ed, vol VIII, 293). The second type is objective or speculative idealism, 'which does not attempt to reduce the physical to the psychical but regards Nature, the self and other selves as three distinct but coordinated and complementary moments or factors within experience'. Furthermore, 'though Nature is irreducible to mind, the two are mutually related. Nature, therefore, cannot be simply heterogenous to mind; it must be intelligible' (Copleston, 2003 ed, vol VIII, 293–4). Charles Sanders Peirce introduced the concept of *synechism*, the idea that the universe exists as a continuous whole of all of its parts, with no part being fully separated. Emmanuel Lévinas's doctrine of Alterity, and of an innate ethical disposition toward the endless and boundless other, speaks to a different ethical rapport with the cosmos. Thomas Berry and Brian Swimme show how Aristotle teleological *entelechy* has now pervaded all sciences in the twentieth century: 'to use Heisenberg's terminology, each thing has a field of "tendencies" associated with itself, a spectrum of potentialities out of which the future will unfurl' (1994, 43). Indeed, 'there is ... the tendency in all things toward fulfillment of their inner nature. In physics, this is referred to as the quantum tendencies that hover within any physical situation. In cybernetics this is referred to as the autopoiesis of a coherent system, such as a developing star or a mature ecosystem. In biology this is referred to as the epigenetic pathways folded into a particular ontogeny' (53). The world (for modern scientists) is, once again, full of purpose.

It may be apt to conclude a propositional account of the non-anthropocentric 'minority tradition' of Western philosophy by gesturing toward a more experiential appraisal of the world. Semyon Frank, in *The Object of Knowledge* (1915) and *The Unfathomable* (1939), advocated for a 'metalogical unity',

> the ultimate all-embracing reality [which] obviously does not belong to the empirical world of determinate things. Though presupposed by them, it is not one of them and cannot, therefore, be found among them. It transcends them. Further, it transcends conceptual though, inasmuch as it is unique and this cannot be grasped by universal or abstract concepts. It can only be approached through the process of negation and is known only indirectly through what Nicholas of Cusa called *docta ignorantia* ... The world of the "fathomable" is the world of objects, the world which is graspable in concepts and to which the basic principles of logic are applicable. The all-embracing unity, however, the ultimate reality, is not and cannot be an object. For by trying to objectify it, one sets it over against oneself, as something which one can contemplate. And that which is set against oneself is not the all-embracing unity. As therefore the ultimate reality is not and cannot be an object of knowledge, it is the unfathomable. It is the unity of being or existence and truth, and it can be experienced. But as this experience is not an experience of an object but a lived experience in which experiencer and experienced are one, it is inexpressible. (Copleston, 2003 ed, vol X, 357-8)

This section has, hopefully, shown the undeniable existence of a rich minority tradition cast in direct opposition against the anthropocentric worldview that currently underpins Western legal thought. Such a tradition has fully blossomed in a complex environmental ethics, the lineaments of which are the ultimate necessary piece of information to explore before embarking in an appraisal of the emergence of an ecological jurisprudence. Before doing so, however, it is also necessary to briefly mention the many other worldviews and philosophical traditions that, albeit often silenced throughout the colonial process, have not embraced the anthropocentric elements summarized in the previous chapter.

4.3 The Tao that You Can Speak of

In 1975, physicist Fritjof Capra sets himself the task of exploring the parallels between twentieth-century physics and millennia-old Eastern traditions. The result was the bestseller *The Tao of Physics.* In it, Capra wrote that.

> [f]or Eastern mystics, all things and events perceived by the senses are interrelated, connected, and are but different aspects or manifestations of the same ultimate reality. Our tendency to divide the perceived world into individual and separate things and to experience ourselves as isolated egos in this world is seen as an illusion which comes from our measuring and categorizing mentality. It is called *avidya*, or ignorance, in Buddhist philosophy and is seen as the state of the disturbed mind which has to be overcome (29).

Capra noted that '[a]lthough the various schools of Eastern mysticism differ in many details, they all emphasize the basic unity of the universe'. Furthermore, '[t]he highest aim for their followers—whether they are Hindus, Buddhists or Taoists—is to become aware of the unity and mutual interrelation of all things, to transcend the notion of an isolated individual self and to identify themselves with the ultimate reality'. Capra concludes that '[t]he emergence of this awareness—known as "enlightenment"—is not only an intellectual act but is an experience which involves the whole person and is religious in its ultimate nature' (29). Of course, this section does not attempt to discuss Eastern philosophies in any detail, but rather aims to show that the 'minority tradition' discussed above has many parallel (as well as having been profoundly influenced by) a great number of distinct—and often antithetical to it—worldviews.

Tu Wei-Ming (2008) summarizes traditional Chinese cosmology, with its central belief in *ch'i* (the vital force that pervades all of existence) and the continuity and wholeness of the world. Taoism, 'an ecologically-oriented Chinese traditional philosophy', originated around 2500 years ago with the *Tao Te Ching* by Lao-Tsu. Richard Sylvan and David Bennett argue that Taoism is 'throughout ecologically oriented; a high level of ecological consciousness is built into it, and it provides the practical basis for a way of life whose main tenet is "Follow Nature"' (1988, 148). Central to Taoism is the notion of 'Effortless Action' (*Wu Wei,* 無為), which, J Baird Callicott explains, 'literally and paradoxically means not-doing. *Wu-wei* and its correlative notions, *wu-chih* (not-knowing) and *wu-yu* (not-desiring) … suggest … a doing that proceeds from one'e own *te* [the disposition of a particular—dynamic, not static—being] and respects the myriad *tes* of one's surrounding' (1994, 73). Ling Feng explains that, 'p]roperly understood … Effortless Action is participative and inclusive rather than passive and anthropocentrically instrumental' (2009, 58). Laozi wrote that '[m]an takes his law from the Earth; the Earth takes its law from Heaven; Heaven takes its law from the Tao. The law of the Tao is its being what it is' (the Taoist word for Nature, *tzu-jan*, 自然, is translated as 'of itself so'—what spontaneously happens by itself, what is not pushed but just pops up). The parallel with Aquinas's quadripartite formulation of natural law is certainly striking. Thomas Berry wrote that

> [i]n China, the Taoists sought to create an interior consciousness of the omnipresent and all-pervading Tao. Humans must present themselves in a condition of total passivity to the immanent activity of the Tao. For while the absolute principle in the yogic world of India is in itself completely quiescent, the absolute principle of the Taoist world is the dynamic of reality and it is attained by an attitude of human receptivity described as nonactive, as *wu wei*. Nonbeing and nonaction are exalted as the conditions by which humans attain their authentic reality and remove all self-alienation on the modality of their lives. (2009, 40)

The concept of *wu wei* thus articulated is strikingly akin to the north-western Australian Aboriginal concept of 'waiting time' articulated to me by Nyikina Warrwa scholar Anne Poelina.

The *Bhagavad Gita* and the *Rig Veda*, two of the texts most sacred to the Hindu tradition, introduce the concept of *brahman* (ब्रह्मन्), the ultimate reality that is the 'soul' or essence of all things. While *prima facie* similar to Plato's *ideas* or Kant's *noumena*, the key difference is that in Hinduism such reality cannot be comprehended by the intellect, nor can it be adequately described in words. Rather, it can be apprehended through non-rational mystical experiences and practices, and thus, as a result, the language of myth and metaphor is consistently used to describe it. Therefore, the Heraclitan endless *becoming*, the Parmenidean *being*, and Spinozian *monism*, are reconciled in the combined ideas of *brahman*, *atman*—the individual soul, which is one with the Divine and ultimate *brahman*—*lila* (लीला, the creative activity of the Divine whereby the ultimate reality 'becomes the world which, in the end, becomes again' the Divine (Capra, 1975, 100)—*maya*—माया, the creative power of *brahman* in transforming itself into the myriads forms of the world—and *karma*—कर्म, literally 'action'—which is 'the active principle of the play, the total universe in action, where everything is dynamically connected with everything else' (Capra, 1975, 101). Over time, the term *maya* shifted from the original meaning of creative power, and 'came to signify the psychological state of anybody under the spell of the magic play' created by *brahman*' (Capra, 1975, 100). *Maya*, therefore, 'does not mean that the world is an illusion, as is often wrongly stated. The illusion merely lies in our point of view, if we think that the shapes and structures, things and events, around us are realities of nature, instead of realizing that they are concepts of our measuring and categorizing minds. Maya is the illusion of taking these concepts for reality, of confusing the map with the territory'. As long as our view of the world is fragmented, Capra concludes,

> as long as we are under the spell of *maya* and think we are separated from our environment and can act independently, we are bound by *karma*. Being free from the bond of *karma* means to realize the unity and harmony of all nature, including ourselves … To be free from the spell of *maya*, to break the bonds of *karma* means to realize that all the phenomena we perceive with our senses are part of the same reality. It means to experience, concretely and personally, that everything, including our own self, is *Brahman*. This experience is called *moksha*, or 'liberation' in Hindu philosophy and it is the very essence of Hinduism (100).

The experience of transcendence advocated by Hinduism, therefore, is an invitation to abandon the exclusionary nature of rationality (Heidegger concurred deeply with such prospect). This form of Eastern transcendence, therefore, is radically distinct from Platonic, neo-Platonic, Gnostic or Christian forms of mysticism in that the rational mind is seen as an obstacle rather than as the (only) path to knowledge. This rejection of rationality has led, according to many, to a different ethical stance toward the universe. In fact, Callicott asserts, it is in Jainism, even more explicitly than in philosophical Hinduism, that one can find 'the conceptual grounds for and the development of an environmental ethic' (1994, 53). Descola notes that, 'in Sanskrit texts, *jāngala*, from which the Anglo-Indian "jungle" is derived, has two main meanings. First … an uninhabited place long abandoned and fallow. But—and this is the first paradox, *jāngala* also designates dry land—that is to say, the exact opposite of what "jungle" has evoked for us ever since Kipling' (2013, 47).

Mahayana Buddhists speak of the *dharma* (धर्म), or Buddha-nature, of every object. According to the writings of D T Suzuki, for Zen Buddhism, 'Nature is a seamless continuum, in which each momentary and unsubstantial event arises conditioned by the whole and, in turn, conditioning the whole. Self and whole fuse in a field of relationships' (Callicott 1994, 101). According to Suzuki, 'Zen proposes to respect Nature, to love Nature, to live its own life; Zen recognizes that our Nature is one with objective Nature, not in the mathematical sense but in the sense that Nature lives in use and we in Nature' (1959, 351–2). The process of enlightenment (called *satori,* 悟り) requires a transcendence of the 'ethical gulf between humans and nature' (Nash, 1989, 113).

Descola suggests that in Shintoism, the term *shizen* (自然, a transliteration of the Taoist *tzu-jen*), by which the concept of nature is translated, conveys 'only one of the meanings of "nature" in the West, the closest to the original notion of *phusis*, namely the principle according to which a being is what it is in itself: it develops according to its "nature"'. However, Descola continues, '*shizen* by no means covers the idea of a sphere of phenomena that are independent of human action, for in Japanese thought, there is no place for a conscious objectivization of nature or for such a withdrawal of humanity from all that surrounds it' (2013, 30). All things are permeated with divine power or spirit (*kami,* 神).

Seyyed Hossein Nasr argues that '[t]he Quran depicts nature as being ultimately a theophany which both veils and reveals God' (2008, 580), with an inherent human responsibility toward it. Pakistani geographer Zaidi (1981) concurs, stating that environmental attitudes are embedded in the *Quran*, emphatically requiring that humanity's relationship with nature should be one of stewardship rather than mastery. A group of Saudi scholars also assert that humanity is 'a mere manager of the earth and not a proprietor; a beneficiary, not a disposer or ordainer' (Nasr, 2008, 13). Moreover, the 'whole world and all its parts are understood in Islam as "signs" … indicative of the greatness, the goodness, the subtlety, the richness … of the creator. … The Islamic prohibition of environmental abuse … is therefore quite clear' (Callicott 1994, 32–3).

Hawaiian scholar Lilikala Kame'eleihiwa explains that the Hawaiian concepts of *aloha'aina* (love of the land) and *malama'aina* (serving and caring for the land) are essential to Hawaiian identity, with the land identified as humanity's older brother. 'It is the duty of Hawaiians to *malama'aina*, and as a result of this proper behaviour the land will *malama* Hawaiians. In Hawaiian this perfect harmony is known as *pono*, which is often translated into English as "righteousness", but really refers to the universe being in perfect balance' (in Callicott 1994, 113).

While most (if not, indeed, all) Indigenous philosophical and metaphysical traditions parallel (and deepen) many of the ideas briefly introduced in this section, they are too many to be fully covered with any justice. However, it is not for this reason that I omit them from this section, but rather because I will return to them in much greater depth in the latter part of the final chapter.

Even within Christianity, elements of a protean environmental ethics can be glimpsed. Mesolithic and Neolithic images of a fertile female figure 'with pendulous breasts and rotund hips' (Callicott 1994, 37) point, for Baird Callicott, to an ancient Earth-worshipping Goddess religion diffused throughout Europe. Such a religion was likely incorporated in the latter cults of the Virgin Mary by the syncretic power of Christianity. Jason John, in offering a different interpretation of Genesis 2:4–2:25, notes that Adam is a derivative Hebrew word for earth (*adamah,* המדא), making 'Adam' an 'inherently earthly creature'; at the same time, the word 'till' is overwhelmingly translated, in the rest of the scriptures, as 'serve', while 'keep' attracts elsewhere the meaning of 'keep safe', 'protect' (John, 2011, 118). Bill McKibben asserts that '[t]he Old Testament contains ... especially in the book of Job, one of the most far-reaching defences ever written of wilderness, of nature free from the hand of man' (2006, 64). René Dubos pointed to Benedict of Nursia as a pioneer of what he called a 'theology of the earth' (1972). Lynn White Jr called Francis of Assisi 'the patron saint for ecologists' (1967, 1205). The idea of St Francis as the patron saint of all those Christians who loved nature had indeed been introduced by zoologist Bates (1960) and was officially adopted the by the Vatican in 1980. Pope Francis adopted his name upon becoming elected and wrote an Encyclical, *Laudato Si'*, predicated on his work. Francis notably used the adjective 'mother' to characterize the earth.

Wendell Berry, in *The Gift of Good Land* (1987), attempted to refute Lynn White's argument on the inherently harmful influences of Judaism and Christianity on the natural world, and the most common Christian response to Lynn White Jr's accusation is that of 'stewardship' of the earth. The 'dominion' in Genesis, it is argued, connotes not despotism, but rather trusteeship. The support for such a view is to be found in Genesis 2:15, whereby humanity was placed in the Garden of Eden 'to till it and keep it'. The bottom line is that the world, belonging to God, is to be seen as holy, and thus must be revered accordingly. Walter C Lowdermilk, in the 1930s, used stewardship to justify the growing resource conservation movement, calling for an 'Eleventh Commandment': 'Thou shalt inherit the holy earth as a faithful steward, serving its resources and productivity from generation to generation' (in Nash, 1989, 97). An emerging ecotheology began, in the 1950s, with Joseph Sittler, who argued that all things, not just human souls, are potential objects of God's salvation. Richard Baer Jr asserted that since the world belongs to God and God likes his creation (as stated in Genesis 1: 31), then humans should never forget that they live on earth as guests (the earth is property that does not belong to humanity) and thus should fulfil their obligations as its faithful trustees.

The ecological mandates of all these traditions are undeniable. Be they the Abrahamic religions, Eastern spiritual traditions, Indigenous metaphysical philosophies, ancient Earth-centred creeds, and even neo-paganism and the 'return of the goddess' cults, they all display a fare more ecologically restrained (and astute) approach to the relationship of humanity with the universe. 'Do not dump waste in any place from which it could be scattered by the wind or spread by flooding', commands Maimonides's *Mishneh Torah.* The 180 Precept of Lord Lao asserts that 'You should not burn [the vegetation of] uncultivated or cultivated fields, nor of mountains and forests. You should not wantonly fell trees. You should not throw poisonous substances into lakes, rivers, and seas. You should not wantonly dig holes in the ground and thereby destroy the earth'. 'Do not cut trees, because they remove pollution', says the *Rig Veda* (6:48:17), while the *Yajur Veda* states 'Do not disturb the sky and do not pollute the atmosphere' (5:43). Vandana Shiva notes that, according to the *Isopanishad,* '[a] selfish man over-utilizing the resources of nature to satisfy his own ever increasing needs is nothing but a thief, because using resources beyond one's needs would result in the utilization of resources over which others have a right'. This relationship between restraint in the use of resources and social justice, Shiva argues, 'was also the core element of Mahatma Gandhi's political philosophy: "The Earth provides enough for everyone's needs, but not for everyone's greed"'. This principle of 'not taking more than you need' 'ensures that enough resources are left in the ecosystem for other species and that sustainability is maintained by preserving essential ecological processes' Diversity and pluralism are the necessary characteristics of an *ahimsa,* or non-violent economic order, that 'combines justice and sustainability at a deep level' (Shiva, 2000, 131).

What all these traditions show is that there are other ways of thinking and being in the universe that have not, for whatever reason, entailed the same ecological devastation underpinned by the anthropocentric worldview described in the previous chapter. While it would be both reductionist and incorrect to assert that no other worldview has led to significant environmental damage, it would be equally simplistic to assume that in all those cases where the same extent of destruction did not occur, it was merely by accident and no conscious choices were made to prevent it. All these other ways of seeing are, therefore, a powerful background against which the rise of environmental ethics within the Western philosophical tradition must be cast.

References

Abbagnano, N. (2007). *Storia della Filosofia* (Vol. I–V). UTET

Abram, D. (1996). *The spell of the sensuous*. Vintage Books.

Abram, D. (2010). *Becoming animal*. Doubleday.

Ba Kader, A. B. A., Al Sabbagh, A.L.T.E.S., Al Glenid, M.A.S. and Izzidien, M. Y. S. (1983). *Islamic principles for the conservation of the natural environment*. International Union for Conservation of Nature and Natural Resources.
Babelon, J.-P. (2000). Garden art in Europe. *Naturopa, 93*, 26–27.
Bates, M. (1960). *The forest and the sea*. Vintage.
Bellamy Foster, J. (2000). *Marx's ecology*. Monthly Review Press.
Bellamy Foster, J., Clark, B., & York, R. (2010). *The ecological rift*. Monthly Review Press.
Berry, T. (1988). *The dream of the Earth*. Sierra Club Books.
Berry, T. (2009). *The sacred universe*. Columbia University Press.
Berry, W. (1987). *Home economics*. North Point.
Brague, R. (2004). In trans T.L. Fagan (trans.), *The wisdom of the world: the human experience of the universe in western thought*. University of Chicago Press.
Brenheimer, R. (1982). *Wild men in the middle ages: A study in art*. Cambridge University Press.
Burkett, P. (2014). *Marx and nature*. Haymarket Books.
Baird Callicott, J. (1980). Animal liberation: A triangular affair. *Environmental Ethics, 2*(4), 311–326.
Baird, C. J (1994). *Earth's insights. A multicultural survey of ecological ethics from the Mediterranean basin to the Australian outback*. University of California Press.
Capra, F. (1975). The Tao of physics. Shambala.
Chaadaev, P. (1969). In R.T. McNally (trans.), *The major works of Peter Chaadaev*. Notre Dame.
Copleston, F. (2003). *A history of philosophy (Vol. I–XI)*. Continuum (First published 1946–1986).
Cronon, W. (1995). The trouble with wilderness; or, getting back to the wrong nature. In G. Adelson, J. Engell, B. Ranalli, & K.P. Van Anglen (Eds.), *Environment, an interdisciplinary anthology*. Yale University Press.
Descola, P. (2013). In J. Lloyd (trans.), *Beyond nature and culture*. University of Chicago Press (First published in French 2005).
Devall, B., & Session, G. (2007). *Deep ecology*. Gibbs Smith.
Dubos, R. (1972). *A god within*. Macmillan.
Dubos, R. (2006). Franciscan conservation versus Benedictine stewardship. In R.J. Berry (Ed.), *Environmental Stewardship: Critical perspectives—Past and present*. T&T Clark International.
Feng, L. (2009). Effortless action. In A. Stibbe (Ed.), *The handbook of sustainability literacy. Skills for a changing world*. Green Books.
Gammage, B. (2010). *The greatest estate on Earth*. Allen & Unwin.
Gare, A. (2017). *The philosophical foundations of ecological civilization. A manifesto for the future*. Routledge.
Gillespie, A. (1997). *International environmental law policy and ethics*. Oxford University Press.
Grosz, E. (2017). *The incorporeal. Ontology, ethics, and the limits of materialism*. Columbia University Press.
Hausdoerffer, J., & Van Horn, G. (2017). *Wildness*. University of Chicago Press.
Jagtenberg, J., & McKie, D. (1997). *Eco-impacts and the greening of postmodernity. New maps for communication studies, cultural studies, and sociology*. Sage Publications.
John. J. (2011) And finally … humans! In P. Burdon (Ed.), *Exploring wild law: The philosophy of Earth jurisprudence*. Wakefield Press.
Kame'eleihiwa, L. (1994). *Land and the promise of capitalism: A dilemma for the Hawaiian chiefs of the 1848 Mahele* (Unpublished University of Hawaii Ph.D. dissertation). In J. Baird Callicott. (1994) *Earth's insights. A multicultural survey of ecological ethics from the Mediterranean basin to the Australian outback*. University of California Press.
Kenny, A. (2010). *A new history of western philosophy*. Oxford University Press.
Krober, A., & Kluckhohn, C. (1952). *Culture: a critical review of concepts and definitions*. Harvard University Press.
Lecky, W. E. H. (1869). *History of European morals from Augustus to Charlemagne*. Longmans.

Lessing, D. (1979). *Shikasta*. Alfred J Knopf.
Linzey, A. (1976). *Animal rights: A Christian assessment of man's treatment of animals*. SCM Press.
Marx, K. (1976). *Capital*. Vintage (First published in German 1867).
Mazzucato, M. (2018). *The value of everything. Making and taking in the global economy*. Penguin, London
McKibben, B. (2006). *The end of nature*. Random House (First published 1989).
Merchant, C. (1983). *The death of nature. women, ecology, and the scientific revolution*. HarperSanFrancisco.
Merlau-Ponty, M. (1994). *La nature: Notes et cours du Collège de France*. Éditions du Seuil.
Morton, M. (2007). *Ecology without nature*. Harvard University Press.
Nash, R. (1970). The American invention of national parks. *American Quarterly, 22*, 726–735.
Nash, R. (1989). *The rights of nature*. University of Wisconsin Press, Madison.
Nasr, S. H. (2008). Sacred science and the environmental crisis—An Islamic perspective. In G. Adelson, J. Engell, P. Ranalli, & K.P. Van Anglen (Eds.), *Environment, an interdisciplinary anthology*. Yale University Press.
Parenti, C. (2012). *Tropic of chaos*. Bold Type Books.
Pascoe, B. (2014). *Dark Emu*. Magabala Books.
Passmore, J. (1975). The treatment of animals. *The Journal of the History of Ideas, 36*, 195–218.
Ramos, J. (2000). Romantic landscapes in Europe. *Naturopa, 93*, 10.
Russell, B. (1972). *The history of western philosophy*. Simon & Schuster (First published 1945).
Schama, S. (1995). *Landscape and memory*. Vintage.
Schelling, F. W. J. (1978). In P. Heath (trans.), *Systems of transcendental idealism* . University Press of Virginia (First published 1800).
Seed, J. (1988). *Beyond anthropocentrism*. In J. Seed et al. (Eds.), *Thinking like a mountain: Toward a council of all beings*. New Society Publishers.
Serres, M. (2000). *The birth of physics*. Clinamen.
Shiva, V. (2000). *Tomorrow's biodiversity*. Thames & Hudson.
Silver, L. (1999). Nature and nature's god: landscape and cosmos of Albrecht Altdorfer. *The Art Bulletin, 81*(2), 194–214.
Suzuki, D. T. (1959). *Zen and Japanese culture*. Princeton University Press.
Swimme, B., & Berry, T. (1994). *The universe story. From the primordial flaring forth to the ecozoic era*. HarperCollins.
Swimme, B., & Tucker, M. E. (2011). *Journey of the universe*. Yale University Press.
Sylvan, R., & Bennett, D. H. (1988). Taoism and deep ecology. *The Ecologist, 18*, 148.
Taylor, E. B. (1871). *Primitive culture: Researches into the development of mythology, philosophy, religion, language, art and custom*. Murray.
Thomas, K. (1984). *Man and the natural world. Changing attitudes in England 1500–1800*. Penguin.
Trevelyan, G. M. (1946). *English social history* (3rd ed.). Longmans.
Wei-Ming, T. (2008). *The continuity of being: Chinese visions of nature*. In G. Glenn Adelson, J. Engell, B. Ranalli, & K.P. Van Anglen (Eds.), *Environment, an interdisciplinary anthology*. Yale University Press.
Ward, J. (2010). *The realm of ends or pluralism and theism*. BiblioBazaar (First published 1923).
White, L., Jr. (1967). The historical roots of our ecological crisis. *Science, 155*, 1203–1207.
Wilderness Act 1964 16 USC 1131-6.
Wilson, E. O. (2016). *Half-Earth*. Liveright.
Winchester, S. (2021). *Land. How the hunger for ownership shaped the modern world*. WilliamCollins.
Worster, D. (1977). *Nature's economy: The roots of ecology*. Sierra Club.
Zaidi, I. H. (1981). On the ethics of man's interaction with the environment: An Islamic approach. *Environmental Ethics, 3*(1), 35–47.

Chapter 5
Wild Law

When we try to pick out anything by itself, we find it hitched to everything else in the universe
John Muir (1911)

'What would happen to the world', Steb Fisher asks (2013), 'if, with the snap of our fingers, we shifted all our energy supplies to renewable sources overnight? You might be surprised at the answer: not much, at least for biodiversity and ecosystems'. Bill McKibben also notes that '[t]he diminished availability of fossil fuel is not the only limit we face. In fact, it's not even the most important. Even before we run out of oil, we're running out of planet. One of the consequences of nearly three hundred years of rapid economic growth has been the stress on the natural world: we've dug it up, eroded it away, cut it down' (2007, 18). Fisher and McKibben point out that the current climate predicament is only one problem among many, and that the technological and economic responses that have been proposed to this day would fail to address some of the more deeply rooted assumptions that underpin them. Perhaps, even the most miraculous technology would fail to halt the rate of over-consumption of Earth's resources (caused, as it is, by a particular view of the economic system), and even the most frugal and sustainable approach to resource consumption would fail to address the fundamentally ethical issue of the welfare, well-being and ultimate fate of earth's biodiversity, if such biodiversity was seen as nothing more than a resource in and of itself.

A deeper answer to the current environmental predicament, therefore, is to be found in the emergence of environmental ethics since the early part of the twentieth century, an emergence rooted in the 'minority traditions'—as well as the many non-anthropocentric traditions—discussed in the previous chapter. 'Without biodiversity in all its forms', Fisher reminds us, 'which creates the complex web of interrelated systems that hold the biosphere in homeostasis, things that we take for granted such as temperature, the level of oxygen in the atmosphere or the even concentration of salt in the sea, will no longer support the life we know'. Even a utilitarian approach to our own very survival as a species would entail a radical change of the way the

A. Pelizzon, *Ecological Jurisprudence*, Contemporary Environmental Law and Policy,
https://doi.org/10.1007/978-981-96-0173-8_5

dominant system of relationships with the non-human world is currently conceptualized. However, environmental ethics has gone further and has challenged that very utilitarian approach to its core.

5.1 Welcome to the Revolution: Enter the Environment

Roderick Nash claims that 'environmental ethics is revolutionary; it is arguably the most dramatic expansion of morality in the course of human history' (1989, 7). Before introducing a brief overview of environmental ethics, it is important, I believe, to temper Nash's enthusiasm (which, I am sure, many readers will share) by acknowledging that such an extension of morality is only seen as an extension against the backdrop of the particular worldview reconstructed in the previous chapters, and such worldview, as the immediately preceding chapter will have hopefully shown, is by no means a universal human constant. Worster (1977) notes that there were ecologists well before the birth of ecology. William Houck concurs, describing a progression over time, whereby 'Western conservation policy rose from more pragmatic roots, took seed well before the birth of Christ, and became a self-imposed restraint on empire'. At the same time, '[e]arly Hawaiian cultures managed coral reef fisheries on a sustained yield basis as did the Dutch for herring ... Spain guarded the forests of its widely flung empire in order to equip ships for its navy', and 'Peter the Great ... also preserved the great forests on his western border as a barrier to (recurring) invasion'. However, in all those instances, Houck contends, 'environmental' actions were consistently predicated on human use. A second stage in environmental considerations followed the revelation that humanity was (and still is) at risk not only to consume the ultimately limited amount of natural resources, but also of contaminating the world beyond its capacity to recover. 'The evidence was everywhere ... the Great Smog of London, the deaths of Lakes Erie and Baikal, rivers literally on fire, and the rise in airborne diseases, waterborne diseases, and cancers from substances with complex molecular structures and unpronounceable names, the precursors to Rachel Carson's *Silent Spring*'.The final stage, for Houck, was the introduction of regulatory regimes that initially protected nature for utilitarian, anthropocentric reasons, but that, over time, shifted the protection (of nature) *for* human purposes to the protection *of* nature per se. This stage, yet in the process of unfolding, is directly connected to the development of a new environmental sensibility, to the shift from the innovative science of eco*nomy* in the eighteenth century to the novel science of eco*logy* two hundred years later.

Jedediah Purdy (2010) chronicles the emergence of the conservation movement in the USA, and its radical transformation (through Aldo Leopold's *land ethics,* and Rachel Carson's publication of *Silent Spring*) into the environmental movement of the 1960s. Rachel Carson's book, published in 1962, is thus seen by many as the milestone that marks the birth of the environmental movement. As John Dryzek (1997) points out, however, basic concepts about the environment have changed quite dramatically over time, hence it would be inappropriate to think of environmental politics before such a date in strictly normative terms and judge past perspectives in accordance with current beliefs. Equally, we should be cautious against the idea of progress toward a more 'enlightened' environmental or ecological consciousness, lest we replicate the myth of 'progress' discussed in previous chapters. Rather, we should remember that the environmental discourse 'begins in industrial society, and so has to position itself in the context of the long-dominant discourse of industrial society, which we call industrialism'.

The term 'ecology' (*oekologie*) was originally coined, in 1866, by German biologist Ernst Haeckel, who defined it as 'the science of relations between the organism and the surrounding outer world' (in Maren-Grisebach, 1982, 32). The word, like its cognate 'economy' is based on the Greek *oikos* (οἶκος), meaning 'home', and *logos*, in its meaning of 'knowledge' or 'study' (as distinct from *nomos*—νόμος—hereby used in the sense of 'rule' or 'organization'). The concept was not new, of course. Theophrastus, a disciple of Aristotle, had first described the interrelationships between organisms, and between organisms and their environment, and '[t]he idea that the many parts of nature fit together into a single unit—or so were fitted by a creative God—appeared frequently in scientific and religious circles since the seventeenth century' (Nash, 1989, 36). Linneus had written, in 1749, the treatise *The Oeconomy of Nature*, popularizing the phrase preferred by pre-ecologists. Holistic thinkers such as Henry More and John Ray are clear examples of parallel precursors of Haeckel's term. The term, nonetheless, came to symbolically encompass all those different ideas, and its modern English spelling was introduced in 1890, by which time it meant 'the study of how organisms (of any sort) interact with each other and with their total environment' (Nash, 1989 55). Wolfgang Sachs has suggested that since the 1960s, '[t]he scientific term [ecology] has turned into a worldview. And as a worldview, it carries the promise of reuniting what has been fragmented' (1999, 63).

For Donald Worster, 'the Age of Ecology began on the desert outside Alamogordo, New Mexico on July 16, 1945, with a dazzling fireball of light and a swelling mushroom cloud of radioactive gases' (1977, 339–40). In other words, the idea of ecology is inherently intertwined with the fear and the (very real) possibility of environmental collapse. It is also important to note, however, that the very idea of the 'environment' in a contemporary sense did not exist until the 1960s (although, naturally, many concerns for particular aspects of what we now call 'the environment' predate that).[1] The very word 'environment' was introduced into English in 1827 by Thomas Carlyle, as an adaptation of the word *umgebung* used by Goethe.

Underpinning much of the modern environmental movement is the 'minority' philosophical tradition discussed in the previous chapter. A particular place is occupied, of course, by monistic pantheism, the belief that a single continuous force or energy permeates all beings and things. Its main exponent, as we have seen, was Spinoza, with Leibnitz, Schelling and Hegel all contributing distinct perspectives to Spinoza's idea. However, Nash argues that 'it would be a mistake to read an environmental ethic into the work of seventeenth- and eighteenth-century organicists. Although they questioned anthropocentrism, they remained convinced of the

[1] Similarly, the idea of a 'population' did not exist until 200 years ago.

legitimacy of human control [over] the natural world' (1989, 22). Nonetheless, their influence extended well into many subsequent philosophical and practical pursuits, from Henry More's idea of a 'Soul of the World' or 'Spirit of Nature', to British poet Alexander Pope's definition of 'Nature's children' as everything that is alive, and that all living things '[a]re all but parts of one stupendous whole, Whose body Nature is, and God the soul' (1966, 249). More's pupil, botanist John Ray, wrote, in *The Wisdom of God Manifested in the Works of Creation* (1691), that animals and plants had an intrinsic value that did not depend on human utility, but rather that they exist 'to enjoy themselves' (128), thus rejecting the commonly received opinion that the visible world was created for 'Man', the idea that 'Man is the end of the Creation, as if there were no other end of any creature but some way or other to be serviceable to man' (127–8). Philosophy, arts and science became increasingly intertwined in this pre-ecological journey. Anticipating the idea of the 'Anthropocene' by more than a century, Catholic priest and geologist Antonio Stoppani proposed the 'Anthropozoic' as the name of a new Earth-historical period impacted by 'human relicts', such as tools, weapons and buildings.

5.1.1 Animal Suffering, the Reverence for Life and the Omega Point

The increasingly ecological view of the cosmos was not, however, limited to philosophy. Nash notes how Jeremy Bentham's utilitarianism 'contained the potential of transcending a narrowly anthropocentric sense of the term' (1989, 23) and understood how extending the 'felicific calculus' (the maximization of happiness) to slaves would constitute the basis for further extension: 'the blackness of the skin is no reason why a human being should be abandoned without redress to the caprice of a tormentor. It may come one day to be recognized that the number of the legs, the villosity of the skin or the termination of the *os sacrum* are reasons equally insufficient for abandoning a sensitive being to the same fate ... The question is not Can they *reason*? nor Can they *talk*?, but Can they *suffer*?' (Bentham, 1789, 311). Although both for him and for John Stuart Mill 'cruelty to people, whose nervous systems were the most refined, was [still] worse than cruelty to lower forms of life' (Nash, 1989, 23), this was only a *quantitative* difference, not a *qualitative* one.

Not long after, in 1824, Richard Martin and other humanitarians established the (later Royal) Society for the Prevention of Cruelty to Animals, now known as RSPCA.[2] In 1866, the American Society for the Prevention of Cruelty to Animals (ASPCA) was created, containing a *Declaration of the Rights of Animals*. The humane movement was born, with many prominent figures joining in a very short period of time. Nash warns, however, that '[t]he ethical principle behind nineteenth-century humanitarianism was that it is wrong for humans to be cruel, rather than that cruelty

[2] Interestingly, many of its founders, such as William Wilberforce, had been leaders in the English movement to abolish slavery and the slave trade.

violates the rights of animals' (1989, 48). In 1876, England passed the *British Cruelty to Animals Act* to regulate vivisection. The English humane movement, cast against cruelty to animals (such as vivisection and cock-fighting), albeit inherently anthropocentric and dualistic, and unquestioning of the existence of animals for human's benefit, 'did call for the human dominion to be as gentle as possible' (Nash, 1989, 19). In 1891, Henry S Salt wrote *Animals' Rights Considered in Relation to Social Progress*, where he asserted that '[i]f we are ever going to do justice to the lower races [by which he meant animals], we must get rid of the antiquated notion of a "great gulf" fixed between them and mankind, and must recognize the common bond of humanity that unites all living beings in one universal brotherhood' (in Nash, 1989, 28). As previously remarked, Charles Darwin had described fierce competition among creatures, but he also 'saw a commonality among all the competitors' (Nash, 1989, 43). He 'recognized rudimentary ethics in the "social qualities" of animals, and argued that cooperation or "mutual aid" within a species had direct survival value and hence was naturally selected ... Over time ... humans broadened their ethical circle to include "small tribes," then "larger communities", and eventually "nations" and "races"' (Nash, 1989, 44).

Edward P Evans (1898), who had been focused on the historical symbolism of animals and the prosecution of animals in medieval courts, became highly critical of the 'tyrannical mandate' in Genesis to conquer the earth and anticipated a later trend in unfavourably comparing the Judeo-Christian tradition to Eastern religions such as Buddhism and Brahmanism. Evans argued that any attempt to set humankind apart from nature is 'philosophically false and morally pernicious'. John Howard Moore argued that 'all the inhabitants of the planet Earth' are related 'physically, mentally, morally' and are all bound by what he, independently anticipating Thomas Berry and Cormac Cullinan, called 'the Great Law ... a law ... applicable ... to *all* men; and not to men only, but to *all being*' (1906, 273). Extending Kantian morality, he stated that all beings are *ends*, never *means*. His ethical circle, however, ended with *consciousness* and did not extend to plants, which were still considered 'outsiders', 'mere things' and not beings or creatures. Moore also displays the fundamentalist (and possibly bizarre) view that some ethicists have at times displayed by arguing against meat eating even by wild animals (contradicting the ecological processes later discovered as depending on the cycles of predation).

In 1915, American horticulturalist Liberty Hyde Bailey urged to ethical considerations toward the 'holy earth', while English metaphysician Alfred North Whitehead articulated the most advanced theory of interdependence. For him, 'the identity and purpose of every object in the universe arose from its relationship to everything else' (Nash, 1989, 60). Naming him the most important British metaphysical philosopher since Bradley, Copleston asserts that Whitehead 'assumes that the universe is an organic system, and ... attempts to show that the universe is in fact a unified dynamic process, a plurality-in-unity' (2003 ed, vol VIII, 401).

In 1915, Albert Schweitzer introduced the idea of 'Reverence for Life', or *Ehrfurcht,* which, in the original 'has the connotation of awed humility in the face of a vast and mysterious power' (Nash, 1989, 60). His theory of value was based on the 'will-to-live' (clearly reminiscent of the medieval *conatus*) that he believed all beings to possess, and thus right conduct means for a human being to give 'to every will-to-live the same reverence for life that he gives to his own' (Schweitzer, 1933, 188). Schweitzer extended such ethical attitude to encompass all matter, not only the biotic world. An ethical person, he said, 'shatters no ice crystal that sparkles in the sun, tears no leaf from its tree, breaks off no flower, and is careful not to crush any insect as he walks' (1923, 254). Ethically, Schweitzer argued, one is compelled to 'widen the circle from the narrowest limits of the family first to include the clan, then the tribe, then the nation and finally all of mankind' and '[b]y reason of the ... universal idea ... of participation in a common nature, [one] is compelled to declare the unity of mankind with all created beings' (1936, 261–2).

Jesuit priest, scientist, paleontologist, theologian and philosopher Pierre Teilhard de Chardin (1959) argued that atop all other physical spheres of our planet (lithosphere, biosphere and atmosphere) rest what he called the 'noosphere', the realm of the mind, the greatest system of all that leads to an ultimate sphere of ultra-mentality he called the 'Omega Point', which evolution leads toward, 'one single, hyper-complex and conscious arch-molecule coextensive with the planet itself' (in Sessions, 1981, 277). Teilhard de Chardin developed an idea of cosmogenesis, of the world as 'an evolutionary movement in which any dualism between matter and spirit is dissolved. Matter is not simply the opposite of spirit, but spirit emerges from matter, and the movement of the world is towards the further development of spirit' (Copleston, 2003 ed, vol IX, 319). In *The Phenomenon of Man,* Theilard de Chardin famously stated (somewhat following Hegel, and building upon Julian Huxley's assertion two years prior) that humanity is evolution becoming conscious of itself (1959, 221).[3]

5.1.2 *Transcendentalism and Conservationism*

Not long prior, transcendentalist philosophy had developed in New England, in the USA. The movement, owing much to contemporary idealism, was introduced by Ralph Waldo Emerson, who asserted that '[t]he materialist takes his stand on sense-experience and on what he calls facts, whereas the idealist takes his departure from his consciousness, and reckons the world an appearance' (1866, vol II, 280). For Emerson, however, the world is not a creation of the mind, but rather is the product of 'that Unity, that Over-Soul, within which every man's particular being is contained and made one with all other' (1866, vol I, 112).

Henry David Thoreau's holism, similarly, 'stemmed from his belief in the existence of an "Oversoul" or godlike moral force that permeated everything in nature. Using intuition, rather than reason and science, humans could *transcend* physical

[3] Julian Huxley famously noted said that '[a]s a result of ... of evolution, the universe is becoming conscious of itself, able to understand something of its past history and its possible future. This cosmic self-awareness is being realized in one tiny fragment of the universe—in a few of us human beings' (Huxley, 1957).

appearance and perceive "the currents of the Universal Being" binding the world together' (Nash, 1989, 36). Thoreau wrote '[t]he earth I tread on is not a dead, inert mass; it is a body, has a spirit, is organic and fluid to the influence of its spirit' (Torrey, 1906, vol III, 165). His idea of community extended well beyond the boundaries of the human and was profoundly ecological (and non-hierarchical): '[w]hat we call wildness is a civilization other than our own' (Torrey, 1906, vol XI, 450). His starting assumption was that 'every creature is better alive than dead, men and moose and pine trees' (Torrey, 1906, vol IV, 422). Thoreau invented (or at least established in the modern mind) the modern idea of the 'wild', and famously stated that '[i]n wildness is the preservation of the world' (1854, 644).

George Perkins Marsh, in *Man and Nature; Or, Physical Geography as Modified by Human Action* (1864), offered 'the first comprehensive description (in English) of the destructive impact of human civilization on the environment' (Nash, 1989, 38). While, unlike Thoreau, Marsh did not challenge anthropocentrism or an enlightened dominion of humanity over nature, he noted the intricate balance of nature and warned that the interconnectedness of 'animal and vegetable life is too complicated a problem for human intelligence to solve, and we can never know how wide a circle of disturbance we produce in the harmonies of nature when we throw the smallest pebble into the ocean of organic life' (2003, 46).

John Muir also recognized humans as part of an integrated and holistic community. He famously once wrote that '[w]hen we try to pick out anything by itself, we find it hitched to everything else in the universe' (1911, 211). Consequently, respect for nature is due in recognition of its holistic and integrated essence. 'What good are rattlesnakes for?', he asked, answering that '[they are] good for themselves, and we need not begrudge them their share of life' (1911, 57–8). His ethical stance extended beyond animals, to encompass a much wider circle. 'Nature's object in making animals and plants might possibly be first of all the happiness of each one of them, not the creation of all for the happiness of one' (1917, 324). 'Why', he continued,

> should man value himself as more than a small part of the one great unit of creation? ... A numerous class of men are painfully astonished whenever they find anything, living or dead, in all God's universe, which they cannot eat or render in some way ... useful to themselves. These people never thought that Nature's object in making animals and plants might possibly be first of all the happiness of each of them, not the creation of all for the happiness of one ... I have never yet happened upon a trace of evidence that seemed to show that any one animal was ever made for another as much as it was made for itself (in Nash, 1989, 39–40).

For Muir, 'Nature was his church, the place where he perceived and worshipped God' (Nash, 1989, 41). Building upon Thoreau's idea of wildness and of a vanishing one at that, he championed the idea of national parks, which led to the establishment, in 1890, of the Yosemite National Park. In his later years, Muir argued that nature possesses aesthetic value for people, for their rest and recovery, for aesthetic pleasure and for spiritual nourishment. His variety of conservation is better termed 'preservation'.

The transcendental movement has been criticized for its allegedly exaggerated positive portrayal of nature. Bill Devall and George Sessions note that, according to Santayana, 'while Calvinism saw both man and Nature as sinful and in need of redemption, Transcendentalism, with Ralph Waldo Emerson, saw Nature as "all beauty and commodity". Transcendentalism', Santayana argued, 'was a "systematic subjectivism", a "sham system of Nature"' (2007, 47).

As a result of Muir's efforts, the Sierra Club (so-called from 1908) was established in 1892, originally to protect the recently established national park. Conservation (and preservation) evolved separately from the humane movement. The idea of conservation (and the ensuing idea of management of nature) had emerged a couple of centuries prior, at the time of raising impact of humanity on its surrounding environment through emerging technologies. John Evelyn wrote *Silva. A Discourse of Forest Trees and the Propagation of Timber in His Majesty's Dominions* in 1662, whereby he analysed the destructive impact of wasteful land practices and the lack of conservation methods, instead calling for sound conservation practices. A 'marriage of the practical and the fantastical', *Silva* is considered 'the greatest of all forestry books ever published in English' (Schama, 1995, 159) and explicitly harkens back to an imagined mythical past, imagining the Druids in their oak groves as the direct ancestors of modern Britons.

Renowned American geologist William McGee wrote that conservation was a way to 'round out the American revolution' (1909, 379). While the first national park in the world setting land aside for nature, the Bogd Khan Uul, had been established in Mongolia in 1778, the Yellowstone National Park and Banff National Park, created a century later, marked the beginning of what became known as 'progressive conservationism'. The 'conservation' movement, so-called by the first Chief of the US Forest Service, Gifford Pinchot in 1907, represents a direct predecessor of the environmentalist movement that emerged in the 1960s. Progressive conservation reached its apex with the US *Wilderness Act* of 1964, which imposed an unprecedented 'hands-off' approach to areas 'where the earth and its community of life are untrammelled by man, where man himself is a visitor who does not remain'.

The Wilderness Society was created in 1935. Robert Marshall, one of its co-founders, used the word *wilderness.*

> to denote a region which contains no permanent inhabitants, possesses no possibility of conveyance by any mechanical means, and is sufficiently spacious that a person in crossing it must have the experience of sleeping out. The dominant attributes of such an area are: first, that it requires anyone who exists in it to depend exclusively on his own effort for survival; and second, that it preserves as nearly as possible the primitive environment (1930, 288).

Nash (1989), likely the first 'historian' of the idea of the 'wilderness', lists its values as a reservoir of normal ecological processes, a sustainer of biological diversity, a formative influence on national character, a nourisher of arts and letters, a church, a guardian of mental health, a sustainer of human diversity, and an educational asset in developing environmental responsibility.

The 'conservationist' approach, however, has been heavily criticized for its ultimately anthropocentric perspective. Nash noted that '[t]ime and again Pinchot ... pointed out that conservation did not mean protecting or preserving nature. The idea was to control nature and serve the material interests of humankind but with an eye to long-term needs' (1989, 9). Simon Winchester challenges the view of the 'wilderness—a word that suggests the overwhelming power of nature against which mankind has failed to struggle with success', rather calling it 'a landscape of *dereliction*, in which mankind was a dominant and in later times a malevolent force, and whose agents left a legacy of ruin and despair and chocked the life from the place' (2021, 188). Moreover, Winchester argues, the conservation of the 'wilderness' has been, from the beginning, exclusionary, since 'there are many places of inestimable and churchly beauty in the world in which the wildlife includes not just elk, deer, bears, eagles, bluebirds, salmon and alligators—but [also] human beings' (375). A prime example is the Yosemite Valley itself, which the creation of the National Park closed off to the human inhabitant, the Indigenous peoples who had lived in deep connection with and within it for thousands of years. The shift from conservationism to environmentalism that occurred in the mid-twentieth century, therefore, marks a shift from what Hays (1959) calls a 'gospel of efficiency' to what Roderick Nash defined a 'gospel of ecology' (1989, 225).

5.1.3 Vitalism, Organicism and Ecology

The shift was assisted, in great measure, by science. In biology, ahead of the organicist movement, scientists went through a phase known as 'vitalism'. Similar to the subsequent organicist movement, vitalism was opposed to the reduction of biology to mere physical and chemical components, believing that the whole is more than the sum of its parts. Moreover, vitalism asserted that some 'nonphysical entity, force, or field must be added to the laws of physics and chemistry to understand life. [In contrast] organismic biologists maintain that the additional ingredient is the understanding of "organization" or "organizing relations"' (Capra, 1997, 25), what Arthur Koestler (1967) later called the 'ghost in the machine'.

Hans Driesch (a direct precursor of the Gaia hypothesis) extended the idea of the organism to the world as a whole. He then articulated the idea of a supreme *entelechy*, a word derived from Aristotle to describe the 'autonomous active principle which directs the vital processes and which cannot be accounted for by a purely mechanistic theory of life' (Copleston, 2003 ed, vol VII, 383), or, more simply, God. Henri Bergson introduced the idea of the *élan vital* ('vital impetus' or 'vital force'), the 'tremendous internal push to life ... the primitive impetus of the whole ... which thrusts life into the world' (1998 ed, 132).

Capra (1997) chronicles the emergence of a number of theories in the twentieth century that challenged the mechanistic view of the universe and rather aligned with an ecological worldview. Among them are quantum physics, gestalt psychology, systems thinking and ecology. Quantum physics showed that the solid materiality of objects dissolves at the subatomic level into wavelike patterns of probabilities—probabilities of interconnections, rather than of things. Therefore, quantum physics suggests, 'we cannot decompose the world into independent existing elementary units' (Capra, 1997, 30), *pace* Democritus. Gestalt (a German word for 'organic form') is closely connected to the assertion that the whole is more than the sum of its parts, the key formula adopted by subsequent system thinkers.

Johan Wolfgang von Goethe had already started to use the term 'morphology' to study biological forms from a developmental and dynamic point of view, defining nature's 'moving order' (*bewegliche ordnung*) and conceiving of 'form as a pattern of relationships within an organized whole' (Capra, 1996, 21). He wrote that '[e]ach creature is but a patterned gradation [*schattierung*] of one great harmonious whole'. In his *Scientific Studies,* he further asserted that '[w]e conceive of the individual animal as a small world, living for its own sake, by its own means. Every creature has its own reason to be. All its parts have a direct effect on one another, a relationship to one another, thereby constantly renewing the circle of life' (in Shiva, 2000, 127). A century later, Aldo Leopold wrote that '[a]ll ethics rest upon a single premise: that the individual is a member of a community of interdependent parts' (1949, 203). Early ecologists such as Frederic Clements went into the field and noticed that living things functioning together resembled a single greater being, leading to the recognition that they were all mutually dependent for their continued existence. Austrian geologist Edward Seuss introduced the term *biosphere* in 1875 to describe the layer of life surrounding the Earth. The term was translated in the English translation of *the Face of the Earth* in 1909 and was further expanded upon by Russian geochemist Vladimir Vernadsky, who (anticipating James Lovelock and Lynn Margulis) saw life as a geological force that both creates and controls the planetary environment. Physiologist Walter Cannon, refining Claude Bernard's principle of the consistency of an organism's internal environment, introduced the idea of *homeostasis*, a self-regulating process by which biological systems maintain stability while adjusting to changing external conditions. Scottish biologist John Arthur Thompson first described this quality in 1914 with the phrase 'web of life', an idea often attributed to the famous speech by Suquamish Chief Sealth in 1854, and first used by Dutch Lutheran minister John Bruckner (Thompson, 1920). Horticulturist Bailey (1915) coined the idea of a 'biocentric' approach to the study of ecology, while Clements and Shelford (1939) introduced the idea of a 'biotic community' or 'biome'. Charles Elton, in 1927, coined both the idea of an ecological 'niche' (the specific place a species occupies in a biotic community) and the phrase 'food chain' to refer to the nutritional intertwining of the sun, plants, plant eaters and carnivores (often using the metaphor of a pyramid to represent it). His research showed incontrovertibly that the least sophisticated lifeforms, far from being insignificant, were the most vital to the continued existence of a biome. Ecology led to the idea of interdependence. Harvard biologist William Morton Wheeler called, in 1910, creatures working together a 'superorganism', arguing that there in 'an inexplicable "social" tendency [in nature] for wholes to combine ... with wholes to form wholes of higher orders' (1926, 433), leading to enlarged ecological communities. Among the emerging concepts within the science of ecology were ideas of 'community', 'network', 'organism' and 'superorganism', 'biota'. In 1935, English ecologist Arthur G Tansley substituted the idea of a 'community' with that of an 'ecosystem'.

Jakob von Uexküll suggested that all organisms inhabit a *umwelt* (often translated as 'self-centred world') distinct from their *umgebung*, the objective space in which they move. This *umwelt* represents each individual's perceived and inhabited environment. Margaret Davies suggests that 'this ... *[u]mwelt* is an extension of Kant's view that space and time are produced by the "unity of apperception" through which "different qualities are constantly being associated into unities"' (2022, 65). Uexküll theorized that individual organisms have distinct and unique *umwelten*, even though, Davis explains, 'shared biological capacities and locations in the world mean that there are significant overlaps between individuals of the same and even of different species'. All *umwelten*, Agamben adds, 'though they are uncommunicating and reciprocally exclusive, are all equally perfect and linked together as if in a gigantic musical score' (2004, 40).

Systems thinking emerged in the twentieth century with Austrian biologist Ludwig von Bertalanffy's theory of 'open systems' and his 'general systems theory', rooted in the work of process philosophers such as Alfred North Whitehead and a number of disparate sources, such as Russian medical researcher Alexander Bogdanov's 'tektology' (generally translated as the study of structure, from the Greek word *tekton*, τέκτων, 'builder'). The traditional Cartesian view intimated that the whole can be understood entirely from the properties of its parts. However, Capra writes, the 'great shock of twentieth-century science has been that systems cannot be understood by analysis. The properties of the parts are not intrinsic properties but can be understood only within the context of the larger whole' (1997, 29). It was the philosopher Broad (1925) who coined the term 'emergent properties' in the 1920s to describe those properties that emerge at a certain level of complexity but do not exist at lower levels. For Donella Meadows, a system is 'an interconnected set of elements that is coherently organized in a way that achieves something' (2008, 11). A system is thus comprised of three parts: distinct elements, interconnections among all those elements and a particular function or purpose. 'One of the central insights of systems theory', Meadows further articulates, 'is that systems with similar feedback structures produce similar dynamic behaviors, even if the outward appearance of these systems is completely dissimilar' (51). What is important in system thinking is the identification of precise and specific *leverage points*, 'places in the system where a small change could lead to a large shift in behavior' (145).[4]

In the 1940s, Ilya Prigogine and Paul Glansdorff studied non-equilibrial systems and found that such nonlinear systems produce new ordered structures on the far side of instability, as long as they receive a steady flow of energy from 'outside' them, and rather than degenerating into randomness they become self-organizing. Prigogine calls them 'dissipative structures'.[5] Vernadsky had already refused any distinction between life and matter, emphasizing the continuity of life between water, rocks and complex biological organisms. Russian biochemist Alexander Oparin, in 1929, built

[4] Meadows also notes how embedded in myth the idea of a leverage point is: the hero's moment, the silver bullet, the magic word.

[5] A dissipative structure is a system that has a dynamical regime that is in some sense in a reproducible steady state, and can be reached by natural evolution of the system, by artifice, or by a combination of these two. A dissipative system (in contrast to a conservative system)is a thermodynamically open system that operates out of, and often far from, thermodynamic equilibrium in an environment with which it exchanges energy and matter (Prigogine 1967).

upon Vernadsky's idea, by introducing the concept of prebiotic evolution (the idea that life originates from inanimate matter via a continuous evolutionary process). As Harold Morowitz also explains, '[s]ustained life is a property of an ecological system rather than a single organism or species' (1992, 59). Russian philosopher Peter D Ouspensky stated that 'there can be nothing dead or mechanical in Nature … life and feeling … must exist in everything' (1981, 166).[6] Ouspensky believed that everything had a phenomenal or visible appearance and a noumenal essence, and while cells functioned together to create organs, and organs made organisms possible, more organisms [and more species] working together in the broader context (air, water and soil) constituted a superorganism with its own noumenon. As a consequence, he concluded, earth itself was alive.

Building upon the pioneering work of French mathematician Jules Henri Poincaré, American meteorologist Edward Lorenz introduced *chaos theory* in 1961. Chaos theory states that, within the apparent randomness of complex systems, there are underlying patterns, interconnection and feedback loops suggesting a process of self-organization, Lorenz introduced the theory via the 'butterfly effect', which describes how an apparently insignificant change in one state of a deterministic nonlinear system results in large differences in a later state. The common metaphor to explain this effect is a butterfly flapping its wings in Brazil and causing a tornado in Texas. Fractal geometry, which was developed independently of chaos theory by French mathematician Benoît Mandelbrot, soon became deeply intertwined with the latter. Chilean neuroscientist Maturana and Varela (1980), coined, together with Francesco Varela, the term *autopoiesis*. According to this principle, living systems are organized in a closed circular process that allows for evolutionary change to occur in the way such circularity is maintained, but not for the loss of the circularity itself. Circular systems, Maturana and Varela asserted, are not only self-organizing ('autopoietic') but also self-referential. According to Maturana, 'perception, and more generally cognition, do not *represent* an external reality, but rather *specify* one through the nervous system's process of circular organization' (Capra, 1997, 86).

Maturana and Varela also presented the idea that cognition is a biological phenomenon and then identified cognition with the process of life itself. Their Santiago Theory of Cognition suggests that all autopoietic systems undergo structural changes while preserving their weblike patterns of organization. The organism, Capra explains,

> couple to its environment *structurally* … through recurrent interactions, each of which triggers structural changes in the system. The living system is autonomous, however. The environment only triggers the structural changes; it does not specify or direct them. Now, the living system not only specifies these structural changes, it also specifies *which perturbations from the environment trigger them*. … The structural changes in the system constitute an act of cognition. By specifying which perturbations from the environment trigger its changes, the system "brings forth a world" … Cognition is not a representation of an independently existing world, but rather a continual *bringing forth of a world* through the process of living. The interactions of a living system with its environment are cognitive integrations, and the process of living itself is a process of cognition … "To live is to know" (Capra, 1997, 267),

[6] Ouspensky also wrote about the 'mind of a mountain', certainly influencing Leopold's work.

While distinct from cognition, consciousness (defined as a narrower subset of cognition) also underwent an expansion in the 1990s. Together with that, the idea of embodiment, that is, the idea that human reason, cognition and consciousness cannot transcend the body (and thus, by extension, the ecological milieu in which it is located), is later presented by cognitive linguists George Lakoff and Mark Johnson: '[t]he mind is inherently embodied. Thought is mostly unconscious. Abstract concepts are largely metaphorical' (1999, 3). Jurgen Habermas formulated a 'theory of communicative action', according to which social phenomena can be understood as an interplay between social systems (with an institutional focus on the ways social structures shape, constrain and enable people's individual actions) and 'life-worlds' (*lebenswelt*), focused on meaning and communication. Niklas Luhmann (1990) developed a theory of 'social autopoiesis', while Norbert Wiener developed the idea of 'cybernetics' (from the Greek *kybernetes,* κυβερνήτης, 'steerman') as the science of 'control and communication in the animal and the machine' (1948). One of the offshoots of the emerging science of cybernetics was the computer model of mental activity.

As Nash writes, '[e]cology after World War II became increasingly abstract, quantitative, and reductionist. Crop yields and mathematical modelling, not the ethical implications of the organic wholeness of life and matter, dominated the new research agenda. Interdependence gave way as an organizing concept to production efficiency' (1989, 73). However, the science of ecology had still much to offer. Joseph Wood Krutch developed one of the main tenets of ecology, the suggestion that the problem of modern humanity is its 'too successful participation in the struggle for existence' (1954, 302). By not having predators that keep humanity in check, 'the modification of nature was beneficial up to the point where it did not interfere too drastically with the ecosystem as a whole. Everything in nature had limits, even human progress' (Nash, 1989, 75–6), and if humanity 'insists upon trying to go beyond those limits, nature will have the last word' (Wood Krutch 1954, 305). René Dubos (1970) introduced a sort of an 'ecological theodicy' of disease, noting that germs are overall necessary to the healthy functioning of human bodies (although not necessarily from the point of view of a specific individual), and thus diseases are an actual part of the overall ecological 'harmony'. Importantly, Dubos introduced a distinction between 'crude' anthropocentrism (the idea that humanity 'is the only value to be considered in managing the world') and what he called 'enlightened anthropocentrism'. The latter acknowledges that, over the long run, 'the world's good always coincides with [humanity]'s own most meaningful good' (1970, 16), thus leading to a call for an effective earth stewardship predicated on loving nature 'for her own sake' (1972, 45). Dubos's point was that a holistic ethics is ultimately utilitarian, and, at the same time, ultimately more effective. Dubos's point was further articulated by Rachel Spring, for whom ethics, 'as a restraining device on technological man, was a means to [an] end' (Nash, 1989, 81), that of a more balanced integration of human practices within the ecological web of interconnectedness. Vandana Shiva suggests that the ultimate lesson from biodiversity 'is co-operation, not competition; the big depends on the small and cannot survive by exterminating the small … it is the relational approach to biodiversity that is important, not the arithmetical approach' (2000, 14).

The term 'Anthropocene' (literally the 'Epoch of Man'), as previously mentioned, was coined by aquatic biologist Eugene F Stoermer in the early 1980s and was then popularized by atmospheric chemist Paul Crutzen in 2000. In the 1970s, two authors, British physicist James Lovelock and American microbiologist Lynn Margulis, proposed the 'Gaia Hypothesis'. That is, the idea that the Earth itself could be considered a giant self-regulating super-organism (which they named after the Greek goddess Gaia, one of the primordial beings in Greek mythology). The Gaia Hypothesis postulates that 'the physical and chemical condition of the surface of the Earth, of the atmosphere, and of the oceans has been and is actively made fit and comfortable by the presence of life itself. This is in contrast to the conventional wisdom which held that life adapted to the planetary conditions as it and they evolved their separate ways' (2000 ed, 144). Lynn Margulis writes that '[s]imply stated, the [Gaia] hypothesis says that the surface of the Earth, which we've always considered to be the *environment* of life, is really *part* of life. The blanket of air—the troposphere—should be considered a circulatory system, produced and sustained by life'. Furthermore, '[w]hen scientists tell us that life adapts to an essentially passive environment of chemistry, physics, and rocks, they perpetuate a severely distorted view. Life actually makes and forms and changes the environment to which it adapts. Then that 'environment' feeds back on the life that is changing and acting and growing in it' (in Capra, 1997, 106). The result, Callicott underscores, is that 'Earth is an organic whole, greater than the sum of its parts' (1994, 39). As Daniel Matthews points out, '[o]ne of the novelties in Lovelock's early account of Gaia was the role he assigned to organic life in the functioning of geochemical processes, something that until the 1990s was rejected by mainstream geochemists who understood life as little more than a "passenger" on earth and simply subject to the evolutionary pressure of the environment'. Instead, Lovelock's hypothesis made Gaia 'metabiotic', suggesting that organic life has '*the capacity to shape* geochemical forces, rather than simply be subject to them' (Matthews, 2021, 34). Lovelock further proposes that we, humans, as a species, constitute a 'Gaian nervous system' a sort of an over-brain 'which can consciously anticipate environmental changes' (Lovelock, 1979, 139). It is important to note that Lovelock's Gaia Hypothesis 'is a theory about biogeochemical processes, not a postulation about some new age Goddess or "Mother Earth". Lovelock does not posit any agency *in addition to* the interactions between various elements within the biosphere, lithosphere and so on; these interactions simply are what he calls "Gaia"' (Matthews, 2021, 34).

5.2 Land Ethics and Modern Environmentalism

Aldo Leopold has been called 'the father or founding genius of recent environmental ethics' (Callicott 1980, 311), and his quest for a holistic and biocentric 'land ethic' in the 1940s marks the introduction of a novel ethical approach to the environment. His passion for the burgeoning idea of the 'wilderness' is undeniable. 'Wilderness', he wrote, 'is the raw material out of which man has hammered the artefact called civilization' (1949, 188). Leopold expanded humanitarian concerns previously limited exclusively to living things to the entirety of the cosmos. He believed that humans are part of a complex community of beings:

> [t]he wild things that live on my farm are reluctant to tell me, in so many words, how much of my township is included within their daily or nightly beat. I am curious about this, for it gives me the ratio between the size of their universe and the size of mine, and it conveniently begs the much more important question, who is the more thoroughly acquainted with the world in which he lives? (1949, 78).

As Ouspensky before him, Leopold rebelled against the idea of a 'dead earth' (Nash, 1989, 65). Since the earth as a whole was not dead, but alive, and the whole was greater than the sum of the parts, the 'indivisibility of the earth' was a sufficient reason to respect it 'not only as a useful servant but as a living being' (Hargrove, 1979, 131–41). In a 1933 paper, he decried the fact that the progress of civilization still entailed 'the enslavement of the earth', with land still conceived of as property. He concluded that '[w]e abuse land because we regard it as a commodity belonging to us. When we see land as a community to which we belong, we may begin to use it with love and respect'. Leopold said that 'when we attempt to say that an animal is "useful", "ugly" or "cruel", we are failing to see it as part of the land. We do not make the same error in calling a carburettor "greedy". We see it as part of a functioning motor' (in Nash, 1989, 64).

Leopold's profoundly organic conception of nature led him to suggest that we must learn to 'think like a mountain' to understand interconnectedness of all things. In thinking about the role of wolves, until then seen as dangerous beings to be eliminated, he was led to the realization that 'wolves and other predators were necessary for the healthy herds of game animals human prized. This was a utilitarian viewpoint, but Leopold transcended it to understand that the wolf was a legitimate part of the southwestern ecosystem. Its presence had ecological and ethical, if not economic, justification' (Nash, 1989, 64–5). Leopold was the first to introduce a 'land ethic' driven by an 'ecological conscience' focused on the entirety of the system, rather than on any individual component. For Leopold, practices such as hunting and meat eating, and even 'the alteration, management and use' of ecosystems are acceptable as long as any human action is undertaken as 'to prevent the deterioration of the environment'. As a result, a land-use decision 'is right when it tends to preserve the integrity, stability, and beauty of the biotic community. It is wrong when it tends otherwise' (in Nash, 1989, 71). The end goal is always the 'healthy functioning' of the 'biotic mechanism'. Quite poetically, Leopold described humans as 'fellow voyagers with other creatures in the odyssey of evolution' (1949, 204).

The concept of ecological and biological integrity originated in the wake of Aldo Leopold and filtered through domestic legislation with the early US environmental Acts. Laura Westra suggests that 'a true understanding of ecological integrity', as introduced by Leopold, 'reconnects human life and the wild, and the rights of the latter with those of the former' (2008, 33), and the modern Global Ecological Integrity Project is an articulation of this approach (2000).

5.2.1 A Silent Spring

Building upon Leopold's 'land ethics', modern environmentalism is said to have officially begun with Rachel Carson's publication of *Silent Spring* in 1962. Carson wrote that.

> the world of systemic insecticides ... is a world where the enchanted forest of the fairy tales has become the poisonous forest in which an insect that chews a leaf or sucks the sap of a plant is doomed. It is a world where e flea bites a dog, and dies because the dog's blood has been made poisonous, where an insect may die from vapors emanating from a plant it has never touched, where a bee may carry poisonous nectar to its hive and presently produce poisonous honey (33).

Moreover, 'the earth's vegetation is part of a web of life in which there are intimate and essential relations between plants and the earth, between pants and other plants, between plants and animals. Sometimes', she agreed with Leopold, 'we have no choice but to disturb these relationships, but we should do so thoughtfully, with full awareness that what we do may have consequences remote in time and place' (64). Much of her work prefigured the modern understanding of ecological homeostasis, as well as the modern appreciation of the precautionary principle, both ground-breaking ideas in the early 1960s.

> In some quarters nowadays it is fashionable to dismiss the balance of nature as a state of affairs that prevailed in an earlier, simpler world ... but [although] the balance of nature is not the same as in Pleistocene times, ... it is still there: a complex, precise, and highly integrated system of relationships between living things which cannot safely be ignored any more than the law of gravity can be defied with impunity by a man perched on the edge of a cliff. The balance of nature is not a *status quo*; it is fluid, ever shifting, in a constant state of adjustment. Man, too, is part of this balance. Sometimes the balance is in his favor; sometimes – all too often through his own activities – it is shifted to his disadvantage. ... The trouble is that we are seldom aware of the protection afforded by natural enemies until it fails. Most of us walk unseeing through the world, unaware alike of its beauties, its wonders, and the strange and sometimes terrible intensity of the lives that are lived about us (246-9)

Carson's work inspired a novel generation of thinkers. Ruth Harrison coined the term 'factory farming' in *Animal Machines,* in 1964. Writing shortly after, theologian Ivan Illich (1973) suggested that many technological tools have been artificially restricted by the radical monopoly of elite professional groups through some institutional arrangement, rather than maintaining their inherently convivial nature. Murray Bookchin further argued that 'the domination of nature by man stems from the very real domination of human by human' (1982). Bookchin wrote *The Ecology of Freedom* 'with a very clear purpose in mind: to advance a holistic, socially radical, and theoretically coherent alternative to the largely technocratic, reformist, and single-issue environmental movements that were holding centre stage at that time' (1991 ed, xiii). To do so, he introduced the idea of a *social ecology* and proposed the creation of an *ecological society* (one aptly captured, perhaps, by Callenbach's *Ecotopia*). In apocalyptic terms, he predicted 'the end of humanity's tenure on the planet' without revolutionary changes leading to the dismantling of America's 'institutional and ethical framework', leading to the establishment of an anarchist 'ecological society'

(1982, 366). His focus was on dismantling the very concept of 'hierarchy', defined as the 'cultural, traditional and psychological systems of obedience and command, not merely the economic and political systems to which the terms class and State most appropriately refer' (1991 ed, 4). He argued that '[h]ierarchy is not merely a social condition; it is also a state of consciousness, a sensibility toward phenomena at every level or personal and social experience' (4). Calling for a 'revolutionary change' steeped in environmentalism, he stated that, '[a]fter some ten millennia of a very ambiguous social evolution, we must re-enter natural evolution again—not merely to survive the prospects of ecological catastrophe and nuclear immolation but also to recover our fecundity in the world of life' (1991 ed, 315).

5.2.2 *Deep Ecology*

In 1941 Peter Zapffe had outlined a non-anthropocentric theory of human-natural relations called 'biosophy', whereas Norwegian Sigmund Kvaloy had coined the term 'ecophilosophy' in 1974. However, the full articulation of a non-anthropocentric ecological philosophy is generally attributed to Arne Naess and the introduction of a 'deep ecology'. According to Duvall and Session, Naess was attempting.

> to describe the deeper, more spiritual approach to Nature exemplified in the writings of Aldo Leopold and Rachel Carson. He thought that this deeper approach resulted from a more sensitive openness to ourselves and nonhuman life around us. The essence of deep ecology is to keep asking more searching questions about human life, society and Nature ... The foundations of deep ecology are the basic intuitions and experiencing of ourselves and Nature which comprise ecological consciousness. Certain outlooks on politics and public policy flow naturally from this consciousness (2007, 65).

Central to Naess's theory was the equal right of every form of life 'to live and blossom' (1973, 96). If Gandhi had argued that, in extending aid to others, 'altruism was unnecessary because [the] self embraced the whole village', deep ecologists simply defined the new village as 'global, coterminous with the planet' (Nash, 1989, 151). Deep ecology was thus defined by its quest for 'ecological egalitarianism' (Naess, 1973, 96). For Warwick Fox, deep ecology 'is the idea that we can make no firm ontological divide in the field of existence: That there is no bifurcation in reality between the human and the non-human realms' (1978, 194). For deep ecologists, who thought in terms of processes, environmental impacts are acceptable as long as they are required to satisfy 'vital' needs, as opposed to 'peripheral', 'excessive' or 'nonvital' ones. They argued that the central problem of modern technological civilization is its inability to distinguish between them. As a result of the disconnection of modern civilization from its natural substratum, environmental ethics becomes, therefore, essential as a restraining device on humanity's excesses. Consequently, Naess proposed that ecologists and philosophers should form a disciplinary alliance around a new discipline he called 'ecosophy' (from the Greek *sophia*, σοφία, the Platonic principle of knowledge higher than both *logos* and mere *techne*, τέχνη, craft).

Holmes Rolston (1986) interestingly argued, against the emerging idea of the wilderness charted in the previous chapter, that humans did not create the wild world, but rather that *it* created them. For him, wilderness became a 'generating matrix' with intrinsic and existential value. Gary Snyder, at the same time, worked on 'an ethic that combined Buddhist and Native American principles with American natural-right ideology. The result was explicit personification of nature and its inclusion in a Lockean social contract' (Nash, 1989, 114). David Ehrenfeld (1978) stretched environmental ethics, arguing that the base for ethical respect ought to be 'existence value', what Nash describes as an 'ecological because-it-is-there attitude', extending the protection of the right to life of even an organism whose only function is to prey on humanity.

Often cast against the extensive land ethics proposed by deep ecologists are those ethicists focused on the welfare and well-being of individual creatures. Among them, Peter Singer's call for an 'animal liberation' movement certainly stands out. Singer argued that the interests of any being capable of experiencing pain and pleasure had to be considered equal to those of any other beings. The creatures included in Singer's moral community, however, had to possess a nervous system of sufficient sophistication to feel pain, a criterion that philosophers define as 'sentience'. Singer somewhat jokingly stated that, based on this criterion, ethics ceased to apply 'somewhere between a shrimp and oyster' (1975, 188). Tom Regan (1982), instead, argued that a more meaningful approach to extending ethics toward nonhuman animals is to be found in natural-rights philosophy. Since animals, like humans, are creatures capable of valuing their lives, they possess 'intrinsic worth' and 'an equal right to life', leading him to conclude that 'the animal rights movement is a part of the human rights movement' (1983, xiii). In a perhaps harsh critique of the focus on animal welfare and animal rights, Callicott, however, declared that

> the animal liberation movement was not even allied with environmental ethics. The former was "*atomistic*"; it emphasized the rights of individual organisms. The land ethic, on the other hand, was "*holistic*" and had as its highest objective "the good of the community as a whole". This constituted a revolutionary new perspective because traditional ethics located moral value only in individuals. Natural-rights philosophy was a good example … The whole … carried more ethical weight than any of its component parts (in Nash, 1989, 153).

5.2.3 A Pluralist Environmental Landscape

Toward the latter part of the twentieth century, interdisciplinary studies incorporating an ecological perspective became increasingly more common. In addition to the already mentioned 'social ecology', the fields of 'bioethics', and 'ecotheology' emerged in the 1970s and 1980s, as well as journals such as *Environmental Ethics* and *Ecology Law Quarterly*. Texts such as George Kieffer's *Bioethics* (1979), Robert Elliot and Arran Gare's *Environmental Philosophy* (1983), Tom Regan's *Earthbound* (1984) and Holmes Rolston's *Philosophy Gone Wild* (1986) expanded the field of 'ecophilosophy'. A powerful attempt to 'find a metaphysical and ethical expression for the intuition of "oneness"' (Matthews, 1991, 3) in philosophy is represented by

Freya Matthews's *The Ecological Self* (1991), where she explores the intersection between worldviews, philosophy, myths and science and develops 'geometrodynamics' as a novel form of scientific metaphysics. 'Environmental humanities' draw on a wide range of environmental sub-disciplines—such as (in addition to the above) environmental literature, environmental history and environmental anthropology—to bridge traditional divides between science, arts and the humanities. Over the last two decades, Indigenous scholarship became increasingly interested in depicting non-anthropocentric Indigenous worldviews, while biosemiotics emerged as a field of semiotics studying the systems of signs and codes within the biological realm. 'Ecosemiotics' extends the study further, to all aspects of ecosystems, and, ultimately, Tom Jagtenberg and David McKie call for an 'ecoculturalist postmodernism' (1997, 36).

Ecofeminism was born in France in 1972, with the formation of Ecologie-Féminisme by Françoise d'Eaubonne (Mies & Shiva, 1993). Ariel Kay Salleh argues that 'most systems of morality that concern nature are weakened by a masculine preference for a hierarchy of rights of competing individuals. Ecofeminism, she asserts, is deeper than deep ecology' (in Nash, 1989, 146). Val Plumwood argues that the collision between reason and nature mimics the master–slave relationship in how the former's power assigns the latter to the status of the inferior other. In *The Death of Nature*, Carolyn Merchant (1983) presents a through depiction of the philosophical history of the representation of Nature as feminine (positive, as well as negative) throughout the history of Western philosophy. Ynestra King writes that '[t]he hatred of women and the hatred of nature are intimately connected and mutually reinforcing' (1983, 118). At the heart of this analogy is the image of the natural environment as a divine feminine, Mother Earth (the Gaia of ancient Greece). The threat to both Earth and women is rooted in male dominance, the patriarchy and particularly 'the tendency of male sexists to conquer, master, manipulate oppress, and exploit what they fear, hate, and perceive to be less powerful than themselves' (Nash, 1989, 144). Carolyn Merchant argues that the nurturing maternal image of nature was substituted, in the seventeenth century from a conception of nature as threatening and uncontrolled, 'wild' in the pejorative sense of the term. While most authors stress the feminist understanding of life as deeply systemic and interconnected, however, Plumwood suggests that many ecofeminist cultivate the myth of a female 'angel in the ecosystem' (1993, 9). Ecofemisit critiques, finally, did not develop in isolation. For example, Vandana Shiva, in *Earth Democracy* (2005), highlights the complex interplay between colonialism, patriarchal structures, modern enclosure and rationalism. Ecofeminism defines as *androcentrism* the 'centering of men on themselves, to the detriment of women, the home, and the family as well as the Earth and everything on the Earth' (Berry, 1999, 181).

Many other authors inhabit the theoretical landscape that has emerged since Carson's *Silent Spring*, too many to present even in an introductory manner. Among them can be found authors as diverse as Lester Brown, Garret Hardin (with his impactful, albeit highly critiqued, *The Tragedy of the Commons*), Amory and Hunter Lovins, Wendell Berry, David Suzuki and his notable 'Declaration of Interdependence (2007), Thom Hartmann, and R Buckminster Fuller. Edward O Wilson, who recently renewed a call for conservationism in *Half-Earth* (2017), applied the insights of evolutionary theory to the study of ethics. He argued that, like everything else in the biota, ethics too should be explained in evolutionary terms (we could apply the same insight to the study of legal orders: that is, maladaptive legal orders simply collapse). His first assumption is that 'modern technological humans' survival is threatened by their ability to reduce biological diversity' (Nash, 1989, 83). The first argument, defined as 'surface ethic', is instrumental: it is wrong to eliminate species as they may be found to be useful in future. Therefore, conservation works because ethics is based on ultimately selfish reasons. But he also spoke of a 'deep conservation ethic' based on 'biophilia' (1984), which he defined as 'the tendency of the human mind to "affiliate" with other forms of life and with the life process ... His definition of community ranged not only across the entire contemporary ecosystem but backward in time to the beginning of evolution. Humans belonged, physical and psychologically, to both past and present ecosystem' (Nash, 1989, 83). For Wilson, '[t]he key to saving one-half of the planet is the ecological footprint, defined as the amount of space required to meet all of the needs of an average person. It comprises the land used for habitation, fresh water, food production and delivery, personal transportation, communication, governance, other public functions, medical support, burial, and entertainment' (2017, 189). His proposal, straddling Progressive Conservationism and Callenbach's Ecotopia, identifies keystone areas for biodiversity conservation.

Herbert Marcuse (1972) called for a 'liberation of nature' connected to a broader revolution against American economic and political traditions. Similarly, Charles Birch and John Cobb Jr called for the 'liberation of life', and in the 1983, Michael J Cohen wrote of human 'prejudices against nature'. Bill McKibben in *The End of Nature* posited that 'human beings had become so large that they altered everything around us. That we had ended nature as an independent force, that our appetites and habits and desires could now be read in every cubic meter of air, in every increment of the thermometer' (1989, xviii).

> By the end of nature I do not mean the end of the world. The rain will still fall and the sun shine, though differently than before. When I say "nature", I mean a certain set of human ideas about the world and our place in it. But the death of those ideas begins with concrete changes in the reality around us – changes that scientists can measure and enumerate. More and more frequently, these changes will clash with our perceptions, until, finally, our sense of nature as eternal and separate is washed away, and we will see all too clearly what we have done (1989, 7).

The ecological turn also influenced the world's religions. As mentioned in the previous chapter, Fritjof Capra popularized, in 1974, the views of many non-Western perspectives, in *The Tao of Physics*. A specular version of the *Tao of Physics* is the Dalai Lama's *The Universe in a Single Atom* (2006), which bridges current scientific epistemology and traditional Buddhist spirituality. Gloria Schaab notes that '[s]ome Christian theologian have attempted to use the notion of *imago dei* [the image of God] to redeem the Christian tradition with regard to the environment by proposing that the human being in the image of God shares God's creative love and responsibility for the sustenance of the planet' (2011, 108). H Paul Santmire writes of 'Brother Earth', interestingly choosing the metaphor of 'brother' rather than the more commonly used one of 'mother' (1970, 132). Changes in Christian beliefs begin with Pope John Paul II's call to 'respect for the beings which constitute the natural world', stating that '[t]he dominion granted to man by the Creator is not an absolute power, nor can one speak of a freedom to "use and misuse", or to dispose of things as one pleases ... When it comes to the natural world, we are subject not only to biological laws, but also to moral ones, which cannot be violated with impunity' (1988, sec 34, 73-4). Most significantly, Pope Francis solidified the Christian stewardship argument in the 2015 Papal Encyclical *Laudato Si'*, noting that '[t]he creation accounts in the Book of Genesis contain, in their own symbolic and narrative language, profound teachings about human existence and its historical reality. They suggest that human life is grounded in three fundamental and closely intertwined relationships: with God, with our neighbour and with the earth itself' (47). In the document, Pope Francis explicitly rejects the interpretation of Genesis according to which humanity is given 'dominion' over the Earth, rather emphasizing the duty of care for the earth, derived directly from God.

With roots in John Locke and John Stuart Mills' limits to property, Marx's 'metabolic rift', and Malthus (and later Ehrlich)'s population limits, economy too was influenced by ecological considerations. British economist Ernst F Schumacher, in his 1973 *Small is Beautiful*, argued that the modern economy is unsustainable since natural resources are treated as expendable income rather than (as they should) as capital. His theory of 'enoughness' (in consumption, but also in all other economic considerations) was later termed 'Buddhist economics' (Brown, 2017). Building upon Schumacher's work, Karl Polanyi, in his classic *The Great Transformation* (1944) argued that 'creating a fully self-regulating market economy requires that human beings and the natural environment be turned into pure commodities, which assures the destruction of both society and the natural environment' (Polanyi 2001 ed, xxv).

John Michael Greer goes so far as to call many of the assumptions of contemporary economics 'modern day superstitions' (2011, 7). In *Prosperity without Growth* (2009), Tim Jackson remarks that, traditionally, prosperity is connected to the pursuit of economic growth. However, he further argued, such view has now become unravelled. 'Perhaps it worked better when economies were smaller and the world was less populated', he posits (2009, 35). Whatever the case, prosperity must be redefined, while the idea of growth as a necessary precondition or functional to prosperity must be challenged. Applying system thinking to economic growth, Heinberg (2011) predicts the inevitable 'end of growth'. At the same time, the idea of 'rational utility maximization' has been challenged by authors such as Robert Costanza, who noted that 'short-term behavior can get out of kilter with longer broad-term goals' (in McKibben, 2007, 31), and the school of 'behavioral economics' pioneered by Daniel Kahneman, for whom 'the orthodox economist's premise that we can figure out what constitutes a good economy by summing the *rational individual* actions of consumers is suspect' (McKibben, 2007, 32). In his classic *Steady State Economics*, Herman Daly wrote that '[o]nce we have replaced the basic premise of "more is better" with the much sounder axiom that "enough is best", the social and technical problems of moving to a steady state become solvable. But *unless* the underlying growth paradigm and its supporting value are altered, all the technical prowess and manipulative cleverness in the world will not solve our problems and, in fact, will make them worse' (1991 ed). Daly's work was the basis for the emergence, in the 1980s, of environmental (or ecological) economics, with many contemporary offshoots such as the Degrowth movement. Oscar Wilde once quipped that an economist is a man who knows the price of everything and the value of nothing. It may not be the case any longer.

In 1969, Paul Shepard suggested that, due to the anthropocentric assumptions that underpin liberal ideology, it was perhaps unsurprising that 'the ideological status of ecology is that of a resistance movement. Its [members] are subversive' (1969, 9). While this is unlikely to be the case any longer, the idea of ecological movements as revolutionary and dominated by disruptive activism carries to this day. A corollary of this view is the often puzzling and scientifically suicidal attacks on environmentalism and ecological considerations launched by some members of the political right, who view such movements as politically situated and located within the political left. Even though significant changes in perspectives have occurred over the past ten years (with many political elections won over climate change concerns), the spectre of the politicization and radicalization of environmental concerns (not only of their ensuing movements) remains.

Inspired by organizations such as the RSPCA, the Sierra Club, and the Wilderness Society, Friends of the Earth was established in 1969. Two years later, Greenpeace became the first organization to represent the interests of radical environmentalists. Famously, Greenpeace adopted the 'traditional Quaker method of nonviolent "witnessing" of injustice' (Nash, 1989, 181). The Worldwatch Institute, established in 1974 by Lester Brown, produced its last *State of the World Report* in 2017, after which date it closed down. Dissatisfied with what he perceived to be a lack of meaningful action on the part of Greenpeace, Paul Watson, often defined as 'the most famous eco-radical in the world' (Nash, 1989, 171), went on to found the Sea Shepherd Conservation Society in 1979, justifying the use of violence 'against property, but never against life, human or otherwise' (Watson, 1982, 155). Ronnie Lee and his colleagues, after making news in 1974 for breaking into laboratories conducting experiments on animals, established in 1978 the Animal Liberation Front. Alex Pacheco co-founded in 1980 People for the Ethical Treatment of Animals (PETA). Also founded in 1979, Earth First! rallied behind the slogan 'No Compromise in Defense of Mother Earth!', and had the explicit goal of 'translating the biocentric paradigm of Deep Ecology into political action' (Nash, 1989, 189), which led to a number of instances of ecological sabotage (with one of his main founders, Dave Foreman, trying to systematize environmental militancy in 1985 in *Ecodefense: A Field Guide to Monkey-wrenching*). Earth First! adopted a practice known as 'monkeywrenching' (adopted from Edward Abbey's 1975 novel *The Monkey Wrench Gang*, which explicitly defended environmental sabotage). The radical and militant environmentalism of Earth First! inspired the establishment in England, in 1992, of the Earth Liberation Front.

More modern movements are embodied by the Rewilding movement or the Greenbelt movement in Kenya, for which Wangari Maathai won the Nobel Prize in 2004.

The world's first political party to campaign on an environmental platform was the United Tasmania Group in the state elections of Tasmania, in Australia, in 1972. The choice of the name 'Green' was derived from the 'green bans', a form of strike action taken by a trade union (or other labour group) for environmentalist or conservationist purposes. The political expression of the Green movement was well documented, in 1984, by Fritjof Capra and Charlene Spretnak in *Green Politics*. With this, ecological considerations fully entered the political discourse and became a common feature of both legal theory and initiatives, as the next section will discuss.

5.2.4 Beyond Anthropocentrism

It is my hope that these first two sections will have fully presented the complex, rich, nuanced and intricate reaction against—and rejection of—the 'anthropocentric' worldview discussed in the previous chapter. Be it embodied in system theory or the Gaia Hypothesis, in a relationist ethos or an ecological self, be it advanced by Earth Democracy or ecopsychology, there is no doubt that biocentrism and ecocentrism now define a huge range of spheres of knowledge and practices. For Capra, this new paradigm may be called

> a holistic worldview, seeing the world as an integrated whole rather than a dissociated collection of parts. It may also be called an ecological view, if the term 'ecological' is used in a much broader and deeper sense than usual. ... Shallow ecology is anthropocentric, or human-centered. It views humans as above or outside of nature, as the source of all value, and ascribes only instrumental, or 'use', value to nature. Deep ecology does not separate humans – or anything else – from the natural environment. It sees the world not as a collection of isolated objects, but as a network of phenomena that are fundamentally interconnected and interdependent. Deep ecology recognizes the intrinsic value of all living beings and views humans as just one particular strand in the web of life. ... Deep ecological awareness recognizes the fundamental interdependence of all phenomena and the fact that, as individual and societies, we are all embedded in (and ultimately dependent on) the cyclical processes of nature (1997 6–7).

The explicit challenges to the anthropocentric worldview are multifaceted. Stephen Jay Gould outspokenly denies the idea of progress, asserting that it is a 'noxious, culturally embedded, untestable, nonoperational idea that must be replaced if we wish to understand the patterns of history'. Richard Leakey adds that '[i]t is noxious ... because of the social context in which progress has been used to justify racism and the suppression of the poor and socially disadvantaged'. (Leakey, 1996, 93). Technological fideism is equally rejected as a modern Pascal's wager: '[t]he growthmania position rests on the hypothesis that technological change can become entirely problem solving and not at all problem creating and can continually perform successively more impressive encores as resources are depleted. There is sufficient evidence to make reasonable people quite doubtful about this hypothesis' (Daly, 1991 ed 115). However, Daly continues, if we were to take an agnostic position, '[w]e can err in two ways: we can accept the omnipotent technology hypothesis and then discover that it is false, or we can reject it and later discover that it is true.

Which error do we most wish to avoid?' he rhetorically asks. 'If we accept the false hypotheses, the result will be catastrophic. If we reject the true hypothesis, we will forgo marginal satisfactions and will have to learn to share, which, though difficult, might well be good for us'. Even assuming a technologically successful future, however, Loren Wilkinson wrote that 'a society which meets all the subsistence and development needs of its people but which destroys or tortures all living things under its control is not a just society'. This does not imply that 'the needs of a tree, a wolf, or a cow are to be equated with the needs of a human', but 'neither are they to be ignored' (1980, 246–9).

John Dryzek categorizes all environmental discourses according to a matrix defined by two sets of opposite positions: reformist and radical, and prosaic and imaginative. There exist four possible broad categories of environmental discourses. The first is *environmental problem solving*, (reformist and prosaic) 'defined by taking the political-economic *status quo* as given but in need of adjustment to cope with environmental problems, especially via public policy' (1997, 13). Its mechanisms range from administrative rationalism—with professional resource-management bureaucracies, pollution control agencies, regulatory policy instruments, environmental impact assessment, expert advisory commissions—and democratic pragmatism—with public consultations, alternative dispute resolutions, policy dialogue, public inquiries, and right-to-know legislation, and economic rationalism—from private market resolution to carbon taxes). The second is *survivalism*, (radical and prosaic) born out of the efforts of the Club of Rome in the 1970s (and preceded by Malthus and accompanied by Ehrlich's population concerns and general resource scarcity considerations). Its basic idea is that 'continued economic and population growth will eventually hit limits set by Earth's stock of natural resources and the capacity of its ecosystems to support human agriculture and industrial activity' (14). It is radical because it seeks a wholesale reorientation of power within the industrial political economy, and a wholesale reorientation away from perpetual economic growth' (14). The opposite of the survivalist discourse is the *promethean* or *cornucopian* discourse, the one that contends that limits either do not exist or can always be overcome by technological and/or socio-political ingenuity. The third is *sustainability*, (reformist and imaginative) which begins in the 1980s with the publication of the Brundtland Report in 1987 and is defined by 'imaginative attempts to dissolve the conflicts between environmental and economic values that energize the discourses of problem solving and limits' (14). This entails sustainable development, ecological modernization and the 'greening' of the economy. The fourth is *green radicalism* (radical and imaginative), which rejects 'the basic structure of industrial society and the way the environment is conceptualized therein in favor of a variety of quite different alternative interpretations of humans, their society, and their place in the world' (15). This goes from green romanticism—including deep ecology, cultural ecofeminism, lifestyle greens, eco-theology and eco-communalism—to green rationalism—green political parties, social ecology, environmental justice, social ecofeminism, bioregionalism, animal liberation movements.

The spectrum presented by Dryzek ranges from social ecologists with pastoral visions to deep ecologists who prefer landscapes without humans. If, on the one hand, rests what Dubos defined as 'enlightened anthropocentrism', the other extreme of the ecological perspective leads to actual misanthropy, with Edward Abbey's famous statement that 'he would rather kill a man than a snake' (Nash, 1989, 153). J Baird Callicott stated that '[t]he extent of misanthropy in modern environmentalism may be taken as a measure of the degree to which it is biocentric' (in Nash1898, 154). Paul W Taylor argued that the complete disappearance of humanity would not be a moral catastrophe, but something that the rest of the 'community of life' would welcome with 'a hearty "Good Riddance"' (1981, 209). He argued that humans have.

> the responsibility of calculating their own "basic" and "nonbasic" needs as well as those of other life-forms. As a life-form themselves, humans had a biotic right to eat and create shelter and also to realize their own special potential in such activities as the arts, medicine, and technology. But respect for nature meant according to all beings a similar opportunity ... [as a result] humans were ethically obligated to restrain their environmental impact. This meant choosing "a way of life that minimize habitat destruction" ... [and they] should also "control their own population growth, change their habits of consumption, and regulate their technology (Nash, 1989, 156).

Tom Regan characterized this misanthropic version of holism as 'environmental fascism', meaning that, 'just like some twentieth-century totalitarian governments, the ecocentrists favour a system in which the good of the community, group, or nation-state supersede[s] that of the individual' (cited in Nash, 1989, 159). Equally, against Taylor nihilistic and misanthropic assertion of the insignificance of human survival, Nyikina Warrwa scholar Anne Poelina proposed, in a private conversation with me, the perspective that if humans were to disappear, Mother Earth would be as saddened as if whales, or polar bears, or old growth forests were to vanish, and she would miss the human rhythmic steps when dancing on her skin.

The shift from (and rejection against) an anthropocentric worldview, therefore, takes many forms, and thus I purposely avoid identifying a specific list of points to counter the list proposed at the end of Chap. 3. Indeed, among the main axioms of this shift are the recognition of ecological interconnectedness, the acknowledgement of ecological principles that regulate humanity's biological existence within the web of life, and the notion of ecological embodiment or embeddedness of human social constructs. The 'Age of Ecology' has indeed influenced the totality of humanity's many theories and practices, and today, as Stuart Hall once stated, 'the natural is political' (Jagtenberg & McKie, 1997, 148).

5.3 Ecology and Legal Theory

The previous two sections have highlighted the emergence of a rich and variegated environmental movement, as well as a complex and nuanced ecological consciousness in politics, economics, sociology, science, and all other fields of human endeavour. The present section (perhaps finally) brings its attention entirely to the field of law and thus begins to focus on the emergence of a jurisprudence (intended both as a theory *and* a practice of law) that parallels the growing consciousness described above. I term this jurisprudence, marked by the same ecological sensibility, an 'ecological jurisprudence'.

The emergence of an ecological jurisprudence, its many advocates contend, is entailed by the recognition that the environmental predicament described in chapter one has created a novel status quo, and thus a continuation of—or a return to—the 'normal' status quo (intended as the anthropocentric practice that has guided the dominant cultural practices over the past few centuries) is no longer possible. Law, in this sense, is observed in light of its evolutionary adaptability: that is, those legal systems that are incapable to adapt to the environmental conditions within which they are inscribed are historically replaced by other, more adaptive systems. As Nicole Rogers note, '[l]egal systems as we know them today evolved against a backdrop of predictable weather patterns, largely manageable natural disasters and seemingly limitless natural resources: the Holocene era' (2020, 32). If the most striking feature of humanity as a species is, as Israeli historian Yuval Harari suggests (2011), the collective capacity for flexible cooperation mediated by symbolic structures, unsurprisingly, then human social structures evolve from an interplay with environmental conditions and constraints, by creating a symbolic epistemological and ontological framework that underpins normative precepts and political-legal institutions.

If that is the case, however, the journey toward an ecological jurisprudence is beset by many challenges. Some of them are very practical. Richard Lazarus, for example, writes that climate change, due to its diffuse spatial and temporal dimensions, is 'environmental lawmaking's worst nightmare' (2009, 1174). Arran Gare notes the interplay of socio-political inequality and the current ecological predicament:

> [t]he most important problem that has to be overcome if an ecological civilization is to be achieved is the hypercoherence of the ruling elites of the core zones of the world economy, channelling exponentially increasing amounts of energy and nutrients of the global ecosystem and global economy into its further growth, empowering themselves at the expense not only of humanity, but the ecological conditions for humanity's flourishing. As noted, these ruling elites can now be recognized as a component of a cancerous tumour within the current global ecosystem, an ecosystem peculiarly suited to human life. A remission will require slowing the flows of energy and nutrients to this tumour. From this perspective, the goal of politics should be defined as eco-poiesis – making and augmenting homes and households of "people", whether the "People" are individuals, local communities, nations or humanity as a whole (2017, 182-4).

Gare's emphasis on egalitarianism, which echoes the work of Murray Bookchin, is further asserted by the work of Wilkinson and Picket (2009), who show the correlation between inequalities in society and a range of social ills. Gare calls for a 're-enchantment of science' (in Griffin, 1988) and a radical rethinking of law itself, following Roberto Unger's exposition of 'the perilous state of jurisprudence' (1983, 561). Gare suggests that, against traditional legal positivism, which argues that justice is measured by positive law, 'a synthesis of Aristotelian, republican and neo-Hegelian legal theory through speculative naturalism can reinstate the notion of justice as proper recognition as the core of legal systems, through which positive law can be judged' (2017, 188). Gare's argument highlights that most of the challenges faced by an emerging ecological jurisprudence—perhaps the most interesting—are theoretical. How is law to be reconfigured in a way that is cognizant of the ontological, epistemological and axiological standpoints introduced by an ecological consciousness? While at first daunting, these challenges are ripe with possibilities. Klaus Bosselmann gestures toward the day when 'we may be able to bring the laws of society and the laws of nature into reconciliation' 1995, 73).

Deontological, utilitarian and metaphysical considerations intersect and overlap within the emerging field of ecological jurisprudence. Ethical standards (i.e. the attribution of moral values—right or wrong—to human actions and overall behaviour) are, inevitably, at the forefront of both the theory and the practice of ecological jurisprudence. Perhaps equally importantly, these ethical standards are inseparable from the ontological positioning upon which they are based. To examine an ecological jurisprudence, therefore, is to examine, at the same time, its ethical and metaphysical orientation. The ultimate goal, however, is far more reflective than messianic. The goal, as Thomas Berry once wrote, is not to 'save the planet', but rather to realise that '[t]o save the planet is to save ourselves' (2009, 84).

In his classic *The Rights of Nature* (1989), Roderick Nash presented the historical evolution of ethics from what he termed a 'pre-ethical' past into a 'wider' ethical future. According to Nash, history shows a linear progression toward an extension of moral responsibilities from the self toward the cosmos. From a 'pre-ethical past' focused on the self, humanity's ethical attitude advanced through an 'ethical past' marked by responsibilities toward one's family, tribe and region, through an 'ethical present' where one's locus of ethical responsibility becomes one's nation, one's 'race' [sic] and then humanity as a whole, to finally enter an 'ethical future' where ethical responsibilities extend, in an ever-expanding manner, toward animals, plants, all of life, rocks, ecosystems, the entire planet, and, ultimately, the entire universe. Nash advanced the argument building upon William E H Lecky's *History of European Morals* (1869), and Henry Salt, who had argued that '"every great liberating movement" had progressed from a vague sense of sympathy to a clear conception of rights' (Nash, 1989, 31). The representation of a linear ethical progression may better be thought of as a powerful thought experiment (after all, stoic cosmopolitanism was replaced by regional and even tribal concerns only a few centuries later, showing that the progression is far from historically inevitable or linear), with the 'pre-ethical past' and the 'ethical future' marking the ends of a possible ethical spectrum rather than specific moments in time (the pernicious idea of *progress* that we explored in the previous chapters seems to affect Nash's work).

5.3.1 The Extension of Rights

Notwithstanding the lack of an inevitable sense of 'progress' toward an aspirational 'ethical future', the extension of the right discourse to beyond the boundaries of the human can certainly be mapped historically. Much of Western legal history is purely anthropocentric, with the natural world being absent from legal considerations. However, challenges to such an anthropocentric legal worldview exit. Ulpian defined the *ius animalium* (which could be loosely translated as 'animal law') as an integral part of the *ius naturale,* containing the idea of what later philosophers would call natural 'rights' (Passarin d'Entreves, 1951). Shiva notes that the *Institute of Justinian* indicated that 'water and other natural resources are public goods: "by the law of nature these things are common to mankind—the air, running water, the sea, and consequently the shore of the sea"' (2002, 19–20). Equally', [t]he *sharia,* which originally connoted the "path to water", provides the ultimate basis for the right to water"' (20). Klaus Bosselmann notes how '[f]orest management scholars in Germany proclaimed the wisdom of replacing every tree felled with planting a new one. They cited the medieval land use system ("*Allmende*") as the mother of sustainable economies' (2011, 207). The idea of natural rights contained in the Roman concept of the *ius naturale* was further articulated in the Magna Carta, which asserted that the barons 'possessed rights by virtue of their existence, independent of the will of the king' (Nash, 1989, 14). Throughout the Middle Ages, there are occasional reports of English courts conducting criminal trials of animals that had killed humans (Evans, 1906). However, the earliest general law with respect to the treatment of animals (and thus, by extension, of the non-human world) in Anglo-American jurisprudence is the *Body of Liberties* in the Massachusetts Bay Colony, authored by Nathaniel Ward in 1641. Its list of 'rites' (i.e. rights) contains the stipulation that 'no man shall exercise any Tyranny or Crueltie towards any bruite Creature which are usuallie kept for man's use'. Not long prior, *Aldred's case* of 1610 was the first case where an ordinary person was given a right of action for public nuisance caused by environmental harm against his immediate neighbour.[7] However, Tony Zelle et al. note, '[n]uisance proved to be inadequate to address the mounting environmental problems that followed in the wake of the industrial revolution' (2021, 12).

John Locke argued that the humane treatment of animals (notwithstanding their categorization as property) was morally necessary and that any unnecessary harm done to animals was morally wrong. The argument was one of debasing humanity by the harm being committed, more than that of an inherent right of animals not to be harmed. Locke had also already placed limits on the natural right to private property:

> Whatsoever, then, a man removes out of the state that nature hath provided and left it in, he hath mixed his labor with it, and joined to it something that is his own, and thereby makes it his property. But how far has God given property to us to enjoy? As much as anyone can make use of to any advantage of life before it spoils, so much may he by his labor fix his property in. Whatever is beyond this is more than his share, and belongs to others (in Daly, 1991 ed, 55).

John Stuart Mill equally wrote that 'Private property, in every defense made of it, is supposed to mean the guarantee to individuals of the fruits of their own labor and abstinence'. However, he continued, '[t]he guarantee to them of the fruits of the labor and abstinence of others, transmitted to them without any merit or exertion of their own, is not of the essence of the institution, but a mere incidental consequence,

[7] In that case, William Aldred claimed that his neighbour maintained a pigsty too close to Aldred's house, making occupancy unbearable. A right of action also came into being for public nuisance when a person's actions unduly affected the health or welfare of a class of the public (Zelle et al., 2021, 12).

which, when it reaches a certain height, does not promote, but conflicts with, the ends which render private property legitimate' (in Daly, 1991 ed, 54).

Mill also suggested that the crime for parents to abuse their children should 'apply not less strongly to the case of those unfortunate slaves and victims ... the lower animals' (1948, vol II, 952). In 1796, John Lawrence had written *A Philosophical Treatise on Horses and the Moral Duties of Man towards the Brute Creation*, where he rejected the Cartesian view of animals as automata without rights and rather argued that 'life, intelligence, and feeling necessarily imply rights', and that 'the essence of justice is not divisible', proposing that 'the Rights of Beasts be formally acknowledged by the state, and that a law be framed upon that principle, to guard and protect them from wanton cruelty' (in Nicholson, 1879, 79–81). Less than three decades later, in 1822, Richard Martin (one of the founders of what is now known as the RSPCA) pushed the adoption, in England, of the *Ill-Treatment of Cattle Act* (also known as *Martin's Act*). This was followed, in 1876, by the *British Cruelty to Animals Act*. Edward B Nicholson argued that, while animals' 'functions of mind are fewer and [their] feelings more limited than that of a man', the same is true of a 'human idiot' [sic], and thus, as no ethical person would deny the latter the right to life, the same ought to be true of animals. And, since animals do have nervous systems, 'animals have the same abstract Rights of Life and Personal Liberty with man' (1879, 19). What was particularly interesting in Nicholson's argument is that animals weren't warranted a lower order of natural rights, but the same as humans. It is important to note that the existence of a nervous system is still considered as essential by many in the animal rights movement today, thus somewhat arbitrarily shifting from anthropocentrism to zoocentrism. Henry Salt's argument about the universal brotherhood with the animal world led to his call for the 'perfection of democracy' by including 'all living things within its scope' (1894, 92). In 1867, John Muir had proposed respect for 'the rights of all the rest of creation' (Muir, 1917, 324). Muir was inspired by Darwin's novel theory of evolution, which he considered an enormously humbling idea. To Muir, evolution implied that every creature on the planet had a right to exist, or at least a right to struggle to exist, equal to that of every other creature. Aldo Leopold, in *The Land Ethic*, extended the suggestions of a 'right to continued existence' of not only animals and plants, but of waters and soils as well.

In 1964, Clarence Morris published a revolutionary essay on 'nature's 'legal rights'. Conservation laws, to him, should be assumed to express 'a presumption in favor of the natural'. He suggested that it would help to curtail human impact on the environment to assume that environmental laws 'confer primary legal rights on nature' that could be advocated by lobbyists and enforced by the courts' (1964, 189). Not long after, Paul Santmire, one of the most radical ecotheologians of the Faith-Man-Nature Group, argued that 'the Kingdom of God validates the rights of both nature and civilization' (1970, 98), and that 'man's dominion is limited by the rights of nature' (149). Humanity must 'not only to respect nature's rights but to *act to preserve and to defend* those rights' (160). Santmire advocated the 'inalienable rights' of all the 'citizens' (i.e. the entire of existence) in a universal Kingdom of God expanded to the entire ecosystem, a sort of anew Augustinian *City of God* that becomes co-terminous with the whole of nature. These latter arguments, together with Earl F Murphy's, 1971 essay titled 'Has Nature Any Right To Life?' (the title of which, however, was more provocative than its content), represent the immediate precursors to Christopher Stone's provocative question with which I began this book.

Stone adopted an evolutionary approach to the extension of rights.

> Throughout legal history, each successive extension of rights to some new entity has been, theretofore, a bit unthinkable. We are inclined to suppose the rightlessness of rightless "things" to be a decree of Nature, not a legal convention acting in support of [the] status quo ... The fact is, that each time there is a movement to confer rights onto some new "entity" the proposal is bound to sound odd or frightening or laughable. This is partly because until the rightless thing receives its rights, we cannot see it as anything but a *thing* for the use of "us" – those who are holding rights at the time (1972, 453-5).

Stone's argument was, perhaps for the first time in legal theory, explicitly not *anthropocentric*, but rather *biocentric* or *ecocentric*, even if such an approach was legally utilitarian. To answer the puzzling question of how to address the environmental damage caused against the old growth forest in *Sierra Club v Morton*, Stone proposed 'going beyond gathering up the loose ends of what most people would presently recognize as economically valid damages' and establish a system of guardianship: '[t]he guardian would urge before the court injuries not presently cognizable—the death of eagles and inedible crabs, the suffering of birds, the disappearance of a wilderness area' (475). Stone's proposal influenced the dissenting opinion of Justice Douglas, which, for the first time, marks the emergence of an alternative legal consciousness within a Western court. Douglas's opinion, likely one of the most poetic judgments of the twentieth century, warrants its extensive reproduction.

> The critical question of 'standing" would be simplified and also put neatly in focus if we fashioned a federal rule that allowed environmental issues to be litigated before federal agencies or federal courts in the name of the inanimate object about to be despoiled, defaced, or invaded by roads and bulldozers and where injury is the subject of public outrage. .... This suit would therefore be more properly labeled as Mineral King v. Morton.
>
> Inanimate objects are sometimes parties in litigation. A ship has a legal personality, a fiction found useful for maritime purposes. The corporation sole - a creature of ecclesiastical law - is an acceptable adversary and large fortunes ride on its cases. The ordinary corporation is a "person" for purposes of the adjudicatory processes, whether it represents proprietary, spiritual, aesthetic, or charitable causes. So it should be as respects valleys, alpine meadows, rivers, lakes, estuaries, beaches, ridges, groves of trees, swampland, or even air that feels the destructive pressures of modern technology and modern life. The river, for example, is the living symbol of all the life it sustains or nourishes - fish, aquatic insects, water ouzels, otter, fisher, deer, elk, bear, and all other animals, including man, who are dependent on it or who enjoy it for its sight, its sound, or its life. The river as plaintiff speaks for the ecological unit of life that is part of it. Those people who have a meaningful relation to that body of water - whether it be a fisherman, a canoeist, a zoologist, or a logger - must be able to speak for the values which the river represents and which are threatened with destruction. ...
>
> With all respect, the problem is to make certain that the inanimate objects, which are the very core of America's beauty, have spokesmen before they are destroyed. It is, of course, true that most of them are under the control of a federal or state agency. The standards given those agencies are usually expressed in terms of the "public interest." Yet "public interest" has so many differing shades of meaning as to be quite meaningless on the environmental front.

> The voice of the inanimate object, therefore, should not be stilled. That does not mean that the judiciary takes over the managerial functions from the federal agency. It merely means that before these priceless bits of Americana (such as a valley, an alpine meadow, a river, or a lake) are forever lost or are so transformed as to be reduced to the eventual rubble of our urban environment, the voice of the existing beneficiaries of these environmental wonders should be heard. Perhaps they will not win. Perhaps the bulldozers of "progress" will plow under all the aesthetic wonders of this beautiful land. That is not the present question. The sole question is, who has standing to be heard? ... That is why these environmental issues should be tendered by the inanimate object itself. Then there will be assurances that all of the forms of life which it represents will stand before the court - the pileated woodpecker as well as the coyote and bear, the lemmings as well as the trout in the streams. Those inarticulate members of the ecological group cannot speak. But those people who have so frequented the place as to know its values and wonders will be able to speak for the entire ecological community (Sierra Club v. Morton, 405 U.S. 727).

Stone's argument and Justice Douglas's dissenting opinion were soon followed, not long thereafter, by Laurence Tribe's now classic 'Ways Not To Think About Plastic Trees' (1974). In the article, Jedediah Purdy explains, Tribe argued that '[w]e are always taking two very different attitudes toward value at the same time. On the one hand, we *decide* what we value ... On the other hand ... we *acknowledge* value, in other people, institutions and nature, and our choices are part of this acknowledgement' (2013, 865). This distinction prefigures the distinction between rights *for* Nature or rights *of* Nature that dominates the present rights of Nature discourse. The former perspective flows directly from Stone, 'arguably a legalist at heart' (Naffine, 2012, 82), whereas the latter is more representative of Tribe's and (later) Berry's approaches.

As early as 1973, Godofredo Stutzin penned articles calling for the rights of nature in Chile. Stutzin was driven by what he called an 'ecological imperative': '[e]very day it becomes more obvious', he wrote, 'that if we want sustainable and long-lasting solutions to the ecological problems we have created, we cannot continue ignoring the existence of a nature with its own interests' (1984, 97) and argued that granting nature rights 'implies overcoming the anthropocentric bias of law'. Mihnea Tănăsescu writes that for Stutzin—who independently agreed with Tribe (and later Berry)—'nature's rights are formulated as *recognized*, not invented or granted by humans. The role of the human', Tănăsescu continues, 'is not of creating a legal mechanism, but rather of using legal mechanisms to translate what is already the case' (2022, 25).

Against the growing calls for an extension of rights, John Passmore argued, in 1974, that rights are simply not applicable to nonhumans, because of their inability to communicate and to 'recognize mutual obligations'. However, calls for an extension of rights beyond the boundaries of the human continued. In the English-speaking world, John Lilly suggested that human individuals and groups ought to 'be given the right to sue on behalf of ... cetacean individuals placed in jeopardy by other humans' (1976, 67–8). Gary Snyder 'explicitly applied natural-rights liberalism to the human relationship with nature ... [and i]n a 1976 interview he returned to the idea of being a spokesman for the rights of nature' (Nash, 1989, 115). He argued that poets were specially positioned to 'hear voices from the trees' (Snyder, 1980, 72) and could be the vehicle for nature's expression that Stone was advocating for. In 1979, David Favre proposed to enact a new constitutional amendment on behalf of wildlife, arguing that humans must not 'deprive any wildlife of life, liberty or habitat without due process of law' (279). Favre explained that 'human survival interests could override wildlife rights, and he knew enough about ecology to recognize that in the absence of natural predation people might need to check excessive wildlife populations in the interests of those creatures' (Nash, 1989, 133). Joseph Petulla suggests that the *Marine Mammal Protection Act 1972* and the *Endangered Species Act 1973* already represent the idea that 'a listed nonhuman resident of the United States is guaranteed, in a special sense, life and liberty' (1980, 51). The language of life and liberty (which echoes both Locke and the American Constitution) is particularly present in these early US formulations of rights of nature.

The calls for rights to be granted to non-human beings extended, in the 1980s, beyond the zootic boundaries to which many of these calls were limited. Michael W Fox wrote, in 1978 that 'if a human has a natural right, by virtue of his being, to be free … then surely this right should be accorded to all other living creatures' (118). Calls for rights of the planet emerged in the late 1970s (Lovelock, 1979; Roszak 1980), and in the 1980s they were extended to the entire solar system (Hargrove, 1986). Theodore Roszak understood 'the rights of the planet' as deriving directly from 'the personhood of the Earth' (1978, 32).

5.3.2 Earth Jurisprudence

The many calls for the extension of rights to the nonhuman world represent a powerful insertion of ecological ontologies and ethics within the realm of Western jurisprudence. However, these calls were not given a cohesive theoretical articulation until the introduction of an 'Earth Jurisprudence' with the writings of Thomas Berry and Cormac Cullinan. A catholic priest influenced by deep ecology, and a self-professed 'geologian', Thomas Berry argued that 'extreme anthropocentrism and dedication to consumerism [are] causing the exploitation and devastation of the planet, supposedly for human advantage' (2009, 36). However, he continued, the development of an ecological sensibility had begun to shine a light on the self-destructive nature of such an approach. 'Until recently', he stated, 'few people have realized the extent to which human fulfillment depends on the integral functioning of the Earth in all the grandeur of its natural landscapes—the forests, mountains, woodlands, rivers, and lakes—and in the wonder of its wildlife: animals, insects, fish, and songbirds' (2009, 36). Yet, that had changed over the previous decades, with a growing awareness of the necessary interdependence and interconnectedness of all things. Berry preferred to speak of the emergence of a new 'Ecozoic Era' (2009, 47), preferring the term 'Ecozoic' to 'ecological', since the former term could refer to a coming geobiological era: the sequence he proposed moved from the Paleozoic (from six hundred to 220 million years ago), to the Mesozoic (from 220 to sixty-five million years ago), to the Cenozoic (the past sixty-five million years), and now to the Ecozoic.

Central to Berry's overall theory was the notion that '[t]he universe is not a collection of dead objects but is, rather, a seamless whole community made up of cosmos-creating subjects' (Swimme, 1996, 103). 'That the universe is a communion of subjects rather than a collection of objects', Berry wrote, 'is the central commitment of the Ecozoic. Existence itself is derived from and sustained by its intimacy of each being with every other being of the universe. We might even suggest', he continued, 'that the Earth functions as an organism, provided we understand that we are here using the term *organism* as an analogous expression since the Earth is not simply an enlarged organism at the same level as a tree or a bird' (Swimme & Berry, 1994, 243). Berry spoke of an 'Earth community' (1988) as the total sum of all the beings and phenomena that interact within it. The influence of deep ecology and of a revised Gaia hypothesis is immediately apparent, as are the transcendentalist undertones of Berry's writing. However, against the accusation of an over-emphasis on the harmonious elements of an 'Earth community', Berry never directly referred to any form of homeostasis or of planetary 'balance' in static or purely positive terms. Rather, his description of a healthy and functioning Earth Community is more similar to that offered by many of the system theorists discussed in the previous chapters, devoid of any inherently benign connotation toward its individual components (albeit the overall system is, indeed, seen in a benevolent manner).

The immediate corollary of the idea of an Earth Community is that all the various components of the universe exist primarily 'for the integrity of the universe' (Swimme & Berry, 1994, 243), rather than for their own benefit. Indeed, were that not the case, the Earth Community would eventually cease to exist, cannibalized by the needs and interest of one of its individual components. If that is the case, then '[t]he well-being of the planet is a condition for the well-being of any of the component members of the planetary community' (243). This insight applies not only to nature as a whole, but also to humanity: '[t]he human, however noble in itself, exists for the integrity of the universe and for the Earth more than these exist for the human' (Berry, 1999, 77). It then follows that '[w]e [meaning humanity as a whole] need to move from our human-centred to an earth-centred norm of reality and value' (56), and '[t]o preserve the economic viability of the planet must be the first law of economics' (Swimme & Berry, 1994, 243).

Berry effects a very interesting conjoining of enlightened anthropocentrism and deep ecology. If we, humans, are indeed part of an interconnected and interdependent system of beings and phenomena, and the well-being of each member of the system is connected to, and dependent from, the well-being of the system as a whole, then the safeguard of the well-being of the system is more important than that of each individual member of the system—including humans. In other words, a *biocentric* or *ecocentric* perspective is not only preferable, in long-term ecological terms, to an *anthropocentric* one, but these perspectives are, ultimately, indistinguishable. The preservation of the functioning of the system is necessary, in a very utilitarian sense, for the preservation of humanity (at least, in its current form), but this becomes co-terminous with a deep ecological approach that sees an inherent value of the nonhuman world and the Earth Community, irrespective of any human utility. In fact, Berry stated, '[t]his re-enchantment with the earth as a living reality is the condition for our rescue of the earth from the impending destruction that we are imposing upon it. To carry this out effectively', he continued, 'we must now, in a sense, reinvent the human as a species within the community of life species. Our sense of reality and of value must consciously shift from an anthropocentric to a biocentric norm of reference' (1988, 21).

Reminiscent of words later used both by Pope Benedict XVI and Pope Francis, Berry stated that to undertake such a shift, '[t]he historical mission of our times is to reinvent the human' (1999, 159). This shift, which undoubtedly inserts a high degree of humility to balance the *hubris* of modernity, he called the 'Great Work' of our times:

> [t]he Great Work now, as we move into a new millennium, is to carry out the transition from a period of human devastation of the Earth to a period when humans would be present to the planet in a mutually beneficial manner. This historical change is something more than the transition from the classical Roman period to the medieval period, or from the medieval period to modern times. Such a transition has no historical parallel since the geobiological transition that took place 67 million years ago when the period of the dinosaurs was terminated and a new biological age begun. So now we awaken to a period of extensive disarray in the biological structure and functioning of the planet (1999, 3).

To undertake this Great Work, he argued that human governance needs to change from its self-referential, anthropocentric focus, and rather function 'within the context of Earth's governance, just as our economic functioning needs to be an extension of Earth's economy' (2009, 96–7). This would happen, first of all, by introducing a 'bioregional' form of governance, since '[e]verywhere life is established on a functional community basis' (1988, 67–8). He defined these bioregions as 'regions with mutually supporting life systems that are generally self-sustaining' (67–8). The extension of the theory of autopoiesis to human governance will certainly have not escaped the reader. Moreover, Western 'ethical traditions know how to deal with suicide, homicide and even genocide; but these traditions', he remarked, 'collapse entirely when confronted with biocide, the extinction of the vulnerable life systems of the Earth, and geocide, the devastation of the Earth itself' (1999, 104).

With Berry, the focus thus shifts entirely on the third element of the current environmental predicament—that of the fate of life itself, irrespective of any technological and economic response that may curtail the current environmental degradation and the exhaustion of available resources. The attention is no longer on environmental degradation or resources depletion (or even on biodiversity loss in an instrumental sense), nor it is about technological or economic responses. Berry introduced a very explicit focus on the ethical responsibility of humanity toward the rest of the cosmos.

To enact such responsibility, Berry concluded, 'we need a jurisprudence that would provide for the legal rights of the geological and biological as well as human components of the Earth community. A legal system exclusively for humans is not realistic. Habitats of all species, for instance, must be given legal status as sacred and inviolable' (1999, 161). Berry denounced what he called '[a] pervasive flaw in Western civilization', the limitation of rights to humans. 'The attitude that the primary purpose of the nonhuman is its use by humans can no longer be accepted. This attitude has contributed to our devastation of the natural world' (2009, 133).

Instead, he argued that all beings possess three basic rights: 'the right to be, the right to habitat, and the right to fulfill its role in the great community of existence' (133). He added that 'every being has the right not to be abused by humans, a right not to be despoiled of its primary dignity whereby it gives some manner of expression to the great mystery of existence, and a right not to be used for trivial purposes' (133).

Berry's views on the issue of rights from an Earth-centred perspective are clearly and succinctly set out in a short pamphlet titled *The Origin, Differentiation and Role of Rights* (reproduced in Cullinan 2002, 103). When questioned on the use of the term 'right', Berry said that by that he meant 'the freedom of humans to fulfil their duties, responsibilities and essential nature and by analogy, the principle that other natural entities are entitled to fulfil their role within the Earth Community' (Cullinan 2002, 97). The most obscure passages in Berry's articulation of rights is his sixth point, which seems to suggest a separate normative (and possibly legal) order for different members of the Earth Community, which then leaves open (and unresolved, at least in explicit terms) the question of commensurability and inter-communicability of these rights. I will return to this question in a later chapter. For the time being, it is useful to present Berry's 'Bill of Rights for the Planet Earth' in full:

A Bill of Rights

For the Planet Earth

1. Rights originate where existence originates. That which determines existence determines rights.
2. Since it has no further context of existence in the phenomenal order, the universe is self-referent in its being and self-normative in its activities. It is also the primary referent in the being and activities of all derivative modes of being.
3. The universe is a communion of subjects, not a collection of objects. As subjects, the component members of the universe are capable of having rights.
4. The natural world on the planet Earth gets its rights from the same source that humans get their rights, from the universe that brought them into being.
5. Every component of the Earth community has three rights. The right to be, the right to habitat, and the right to fulfill its role in the ever-renewing process of the Earth community.
6. All rights are species specific and limited. Rivers have river rights. Birds have bird rights. Insects have insect rights. Humans have human rights. Difference of rights is qualitative not quantitative. The rights of an insect would be of no use to a tree or fish.

7. Human rights do not cancel out the rights of other modes of being to exist in their natural state. Human property rights are not absolute. Property rights are simply a special relationship between a particular human "owner" and a particular piece of "property" *for the benefit of both.*
8. Species exist in the form of individuals and groupings–flock, herds, schools of fish and so forth. Rights refer to individuals and groupings, not simply in a general way to species.
9. These rights as presented here establish the relationships that the various components of the Earth have toward each other. The planet earth is a single community bound together with interdependent relationships. Every component of the Earth community is immediately or mediately dependent on every other member of the Community for the nourishment and assistance it needs for its own survival. This mutual nourishment, which includes predator–prey relationship, is integral with the role that each component of the Earth has within the comprehensive community of existence.
10. In a special manner humans have not only a need for but a right of access to the natural world, not only to supply their physical needs but also to provide the wonder needed by human intelligence, the beauty needed by human imagination, and the intimacy needed by the human emotions.

Cormac Cullinan built upon Berry's work not long thereafter. Cullinan explains that he 'learned from Thomas Berry … that reforming our governance systems will require us to entirety reconceptualise our *idea* of law from a biocentric or Earth-centred perspective' (2011 ed, 29). Cullinan realized that it was necessary to do more than simply list a new set of rights for the nonhuman world, but rather a deep reimagination of legal theory itself was needed to align law and the world's legal systems with the ecological insights advocated by Berry. Cullinan's focus was thus not only on the extension of rights but on reimagining *jurisprudence* itself. Jurisprudence, in this sense, was seen as the theory, not only the practice, of law. 'While the regulatory function of law is easy to see', he noted 'we often overlook the fact that law plays an equally important role in constituting and forming society itself' (2011 ed, 55). In his seminal 2002 book *Wild Law* he openly followed in the footsteps of Thomas Berry and argued that.

> in order to change completely the purpose of our governance systems, we must develop coherent new theories or philosophies of governance ('Earth Jurisprudence') to supplant the old. This Earth Jurisprudence is needed to guide the realignment of human governance systems with the fundamental principles of how the universe functions (which I refer to … as the 'Great Jurisprudence') (2011 ed, 31).

Cullinan later described this Earth Jurisprudence as 'a philosophy of law and human governance that is based on the idea that humans are only one part of a wider community of beings and that the welfare of each member of the community is dependent on the welfare of the Earth as a whole' (2011b, 13). He also confirmed that '[f]rom this perspective, human societies will only be viable and flourish if they regulate themselves as part of this wider Earth community and do so in a way that is consistent with the … "Great Jurisprudence"' (2011b, 13). The concept of a 'Great Jurisprudence' is thus the architrave of Cullinan's articulation of an Earth Jurisprudence.

> On the one hand, there are the 'Laws" or principles that govern how the universe functions. These are timeless and unified in the sense that they all have the same source. This "Great Jurisprudence" is manifest in the universe itself … "Earth Jurisprudence" refers to legal philosophies developed by humans that are to a large extent derived from, and consistent with, this "Great Jurisprudence". … The Great Jurisprudence is like the mountains. It is what it is, and our descriptions of it are abstract approximations. It is neither right nor wrong, and it is inherent in all things by virtue of the fact that they are part of the universal whole. In this sense it is better understood as a quality of the universe rather than as a rule or principle that governs it. … [yet] If we are to be guided by the Great Jurisprudence in developing a viable Earth Jurisprudence for our species, we need to start by trying to discern the nature and content of that Great Jurisprudence (2011 ed, 78).

To further articulate the emergence of Earth Jurisprudence, Cullinan proposes the term 'wild law'. The provocative use of the idea of 'wildness', albeit linguistically located in the tradition initiated by Thoreau, is somewhat distinct from the common usage of the term. The idea of the 'wild', for Cullinan, is in direct opposition to the homosphere. Ian Mason describes wild law as 'lawyers' law 'drawn from and reflecting the intimate human-Earth relationship and recognising the limitations of formal law' (2011, 41). For Mason, 'wild law' is marked by 'Earth Centredness'—that is, rather than formulating laws from a purely human perspective and for purely human purposes, 'laws are formulated from the perspective of the whole of nature epitomised by Earth', (41)—by the consideration that the whole natural world must be regarded as a commons that cannot be reduced to private property, by a system of remedies based on restorative—rather than retributive—justice, and by community-based ecological governance.

Begonia Filgueira and Ian Mason also define 'Earth Jurisprudence' as 'the philosophy of law and regulation that gives formal recognition to the reciprocal relationship between humans and the rest of nature' (2011, 192), while Judith Koons, describes it as 'an emerging legal theory based on the premise that rethinking law and governance is necessary for the well-being of Earth and all of its inhabitants. Earth Jurisprudence is an inclusive and systems-based theoretical perspective that supports robust environmental regulation and recognizes a kinship with the field of environmental ethics' (2011, 45). Furthermore, 'Earth Jurisprudence embraces the connection between Earth justice and social justice' (45). Koons also describes some of the key principles that define Earth Jurisprudence, such as the 'principle of subjectivity' (the idea that the Earth has intrinsic value), the 'principle of communion and relational responsibility', and the 'principle of differentiation' (which she refers to, borrowing Vandana Shiva's term, as Earth Democracy). She writes that 'the functioning of the universe is not reflected in hierarchy or separation, but in a circling dance of spheres, orbits and rotations' (51).

The idea of Earth Jurisprudence has been used in different contexts and for different purposes. It operated as the basis for much of the rights of Nature movement that will be discussed shortly and in the next chapter, and it offered the opportunity for further theoretical inquiries. However, the implications of the introduction of a concept such as the 'Great Jurisprudence' received relatively little theoretical consideration for quite some time, even though it represents the most difficult and yet fertile space in which to interrogate the very concept of jurisprudence in ecological terms. I will return to some of these implications in the final chapter of the book, suffice it here to say that the introduction of Earth Jurisprudence and Wild Law opened the terrain to a host of related theoretical pursuits informed by an ecological sensibility.

5.3.3 Ecological Law

Steven White noted that '[t]he extent of the similarities between the challenges to the status quo posed by Wild Law, and that posed by a progressive animal law, is striking' (2014, 247–8). However, the two theories are also marked by clear differences, the first being the extent of the challenge to property law doctrine, which, in most animal law theory, is far less radical than that posed by Wild Law. Another key difference and potential tension concerns 'what should be understood as "nature" or the "environment". Should animals be understood as just one aspect of the wider category of "nature" or do they need to be considered in their own right?' (247–8).

What White points to is that, from the onset, the emerging theory of Earth Jurisprudence was cast against a host of distinct and yet related theories, all informed by different ecological and environmental ideas. This led to the proliferation of terms at times used synonymically and at times in opposition to each other. Earth Jurisprudence and Wild Law were soon complemented by the use of the term, or terms, 'Earth Law' and 'Earth Laws', adopted both by the Australian Earth Laws Association (AELA—formerly the Australian Wild Law Association) and the Earth Law Center in the USA. Anthony Zelle and others assert that 'Earth Law takes an ecocentric approach to environmental law' (2021, 3). Other terms commonly used, introduced by a variety of scholars such as Klaus Bosselmann, Louis Kotzé, Geoffrey Garver and Margaret Davies (and many others, too numerous to enumerate exhaustively) are 'Earth-Centered Law', 'Ecocentric Law', EcoLaw', 'Ecocentric Governance', 'Ecological Social Contract' (a further articulation of Michel Serres's 'Natural Contract'), 'Earth-centric approach', 'Earth system law', 'Earth Governance', 'Earth system law' and 'Earth system governance', 'Ecological rule of law', and 'Ecological Sovereignty'. The concept of 'Ecological Law' (or 'Ecological Law and Governance') occupies a special place in this list, and I will return to it shortly. In parallel to the proliferation of these many terms (which do not necessarily mean, or purport to mean, the same thing), other, more distinct, perspectives have also emerged, such as 'Earth trusteeship' and 'Ecofeminist jurisprudence', and even more traditional environmental law is now interpreted under the new lens offered by an 'environmental rule of law'.

To exemplify the growth of literature in the field, at the time of the establishment of the Global Alliance for the Rights of Nature (GARN) in Quito in 2010, the number of scholarly publications on the idea of rights of Nature alone was limited to, at most, a few dozens of direct and related texts. Little over a decade after, in 2023, an attempt to establish a dedicated 'eco-jurisprudence library' by GARN's Academic Hub soon revealed that a rapid Google Scholar search of 'rights of Nature' would yield more than 18,000 results. Less than a year later, in early 2024, the number had grown by more than 15% in a single year.

While it is no longer possible to offer an exhaustive overview of all these disparate perspectives outside of a dedicated monograph, many of them still warrant special consideration. Klaus Bosselmann (2016) preceded Thomas Berry in articulating a number of ecological legal principles, in particular what he calls the 'principle of sustainability' and the 'principle of ecological integrity'. Writing in German, Bosselmann argued for 'ecological fundamental rights' (*ökologische grundrechte*) in 1998. Against what he calls environmental reductionism, Bosselmann further proposes the sustainability principle as the basic architrave for ecological law (2010), and the principle of ecological integrity as a novel *grundnorm* of international law (2014). Bosselmann also advocates for state trusteeship of the global commons (2015b).

At the same time, a number of non-English authors either preceded or followed Berry in calling for an articulation of law that would take into account ecological considerations: from Italian novelist Italo Calvino's *The Baron in the Trees* (1957) to Uruguayan writer Eduardo Galeano's *La Naturaleza no Es Muda* (2008); from Brazilian theologian Leonardo Boff's *Constitucionalismo Ecologico in Latino America* (2013) to French environmentalist Valerie Cabanes's *Un Nuveau Droit Pour la Terre* (2016); from Ecuadorian Alberto Acosta and Esperanza Martinez's *El Buen Vivir* (2009) to Uruguayan biologist Eduardo Gudynas's *Extractivismo: Ecologia, economia y politica de un modo de entender el desarrollo y la naturaleza* (2015).

Michael M'Gonigle and Paula Ramsay propose a 'Green Legal Theory' that reaches beyond environmental law 'to understand the root of unsustainable dynamics in a systemic way, particularly by looking at how environmental law is embedded in liberalism' (2004, 333). Nicholas A. Robinson puts forth a proposal for 'identifying new legal principles based upon instinctive norms, which have evolved within all humans' (2013, 46). In particular, he focuses on what he describes as three 'evolved norms': cooperation, biophilia and resilience. Laitos (2012), another proponent of an ecocentric rights-based approach, advocates for a 'rule of law for nature' that recognizes 'rights of nonuse' for nature. De Lucia (2015) subsumes under the expression 'ecosystem approach' the 'entire spectrum of ecosystem-oriented frameworks existing within environmental law and policy', as located at the transition from anthropocentrism to ecocentrism.

Former UN Special Rapporteur on Human Rights and the Environment, David Boyd, calls for a 'sustainability law', arguing that four fundamental 'system conditions', based on the laws of nature, 'establish the normative basis for sustainability law'. These 'system conditions' are the 'concentrations of substances extracted from the Earth's crust, ... the concentrations of substances produced by society, ... the degradation by physical means, and [the premise that] people are not subject to conditions that systematically ... undermine their capacity to meet their needs' (2004, 369–70). Afshin Akhtar-Khavari's work (2019) focuses on ecological restoration law, defined as 'an intentional activity that initiates or accelerates the recovery of an ecosystem with respect to its health, integrity and sustainability'. Building upon Michel Serres's *Natural Contract*, the author argues that 'human beings have to help the natural world to recover from the violence which, by not listening to it, we inflict upon'.

Ugo Mattei and Fritjof Capra look at the 'ecology' of law, using the term 'to refer to a legal order that does not see the law as a separate social field independent from politics, economics, justice, religion, social norms of good behaviour, morality and so forth. Nor does this conception separate the law into a domain of facts—how the law *is*—and a domain of clauses—how the law *ought to be*' (2015, 14). They provide an account that describes in the detail the parallel development of the scientific and the legal method, and, as a result, they call for a profound shift toward an ecological order informed by ecological literacy:

> [o]nce we have achieved some degree of ecoliteracy, we must make urgently needed shifts in law and economics. Human laws, like the laws of nature, need to be understood as manifestations of a relational order in which the individual is not alone but is connected to and shares power with other living inhabitants of the planet, who are entitled to equal access to the global commons. These inhabitants are not only other human beings but also other animals, plants, and in general all the Earth's ecosystems. ... To be sustainable, human laws should serve, rather than exploit and plunder, the web of life (29).

The result, for Capra and Mattei, is that by applying an ecological lens to the world of legal practice, 'we would consider the extractive legal institutions of modernity—state sovereignty and private property—as "algal blooms" of human laws' (155), a direct parallel with the process of eutrophication—excessive plant growth stimulated by high nutrient concentrations. This would radically alter the way in which property, sovereignty and contract are conceived (even though the categories *themselves* are maintained). 'An ecolegal order', they conclude,

> would recognize the fundamental interconnectedness of our global problems and enable us to find appropriate, mutually supportive solutions that, instead of distinguishing law, politics, and economics at the local, state, or even international level, would mirror the interdependence of the problems they address. By looking at the example of owning a private jet, they argue that '[e]cologically literate lawyers, politicians, and people will find it completely reasonable to invert the relationship between the rule and the exception; the burden to prove the social acceptability of a given property scheme will be reversed. No commoner perceives the limit of the use of a private aircraft as a limitation on the property freedom of the 1 percent. Rather, owning such an aircraft will be an unacceptable limitation on the freedom of the community to happily survive and reproduce itself on the planet (185).

Bruce Jennings distinguishes 'governance' from 'government': governance is 'the overall process of coordinating, shaping, and directing individual and collective agency. [It] is inherently normative and value-laden ... [It] embodies the character of the collectivity, representing the kind of society an association of people aspires to be or become' (2016, 173–4). For Jennings, ecological governance is affected in three distinct ways: ecological authoritarianism, ecological discursive democracy and ecological constitutionalism. In her recent book *The Constitution of the Environmental Emergency* (2018), Jocelyn Stacey frames the current predicament well within the dangerous terrain of the language of 'emergency', although carefully arguing for a revised and democratic rule of law informed by deliberative-democratic principles. She argues that 'the exercise of public authority can be governed by a democratic conception of the rule of law, elaborated, as it needs be, for the special challenges posed by environmental issues' (1). She explicitly asserts that 'the best way to understand the challenge that environmental issues pose for law is through the lens of an ongoing emergency. Like emergencies, environmental issues require decisions to be taken under conditions of deep uncertainty where the possibility of a catastrophe cannot be reliably eliminated in advance'. Her argument is based on the fact that.

> [t]he concept of the environmental emergency reveals that the epistemic features of emergencies are inherent in environmental issues. The complex, adaptive nature of ecological systems means that our understanding of environmental issues and their potential regulatory solutions is necessarily limited. We cannot reliably distinguish in advance between sound policy choices and catastrophic choices, and this undermines our ability to govern environmental issues through *ex ante* legal rules (39).

While the language used may raise some of the risks identified in the first chapter, Stacey is very aware of those dangers and brings them to the fore of her argument. The most paradigmatic historical example she uses is that of Roman constitutional dictatorship, adhering to Ferejohn and Paquino's suggestion that '[m]odern emergencies are, to a greater or lesser extent, modelled on the ancient model of the Roman dictatorship' (2002, 211), 'which provided for the temporary appointment of a constitutional dictator solely for the purpose of bringing the emergency to an end' (Stacey, 2018, 30). She also acknowledges the risks of emergency powers acting, as Dyzenhaus suggested, as 'legal black holes' (2006, 3): that is, legislative attempts to create a sphere of action not governed by the rule of law. However, she draws on Lon Fuller's insight (1969) that compliance with the requirements of the rule of law is an essential trait of what law *is*, suggesting that principles of environmental law, such as sustainable development and precaution, are to be interpreted in line with ideals of deliberative democracy and the rule of law, informing basic common law principles such as reasonableness and fairness.

In *Earthbound* (2021), Daniel Matthews sets himself the task of 'understanding sovereignty as a *framing device* and a *mode of perception*'. Furthermore, '[i]n developing an account of the *aesthetics of sovereignty*, [he aims to] demonstrate that sovereignty has the capacity to shape our sense perception, rendering us sensitive, attentive or attuned to certain phenomena, while bracketing or keeping "offstage" a range of other seemingly "non-political" forces, spaces and actors' (7). In *Law as if Earth Really Mattered* (2017), Nicole Rogers and Michelle Maloney asked their contributors to reformulate existing judgments using an Earth-centred perspective, a task that 'involved the critique and reshaping of principles within a number of different areas of law', beyond the confines of environmental law.

Garver (2013) notes that David Boyd's notion of 'sustainability law' (2004), Klaus Bosselman's 'principle of sustainability' (2008) and Cormac Cullinan's 'wild law' all distinctly capture Berry's ecological conception of law. He himself proposes the notion of 'the rule of ecological law' as a way to combine 'the notion of ecological law with the notion of the rule of law'. And call into question 'the current insistence on perpetual economic growth' (Garver, 2013, 318). Garver also notes that use of the term 'ecological law' has been historically rare. Indeed, the term 'ecological law' was used in the late 1980s to refer to the Soviet development of a legal system informed by ecological principles (Kolbasov 1988), but was not much used thereafter. The modern re-emergence of ecological law, for Garver, arguably represents the most advanced articulation of legal theory in relation to legal pursuits informed by ecological principles. Ecological law, Garver explains, 'is emerging as a field of law founded on systems thinking and the need to integrate ecological limits, such as planetary boundaries, into law' (Anker et al., 2020). He further articulates the term with reference to Berry's 'ecologically imbued notion of law', which views law as an extension of ecology. The term is also selected to avoid the ambiguity of the term 'sustainability', due to its prioritization of economic concerns over ecological ones. Instead, Garver chooses 'ecological law' as a term that 'emphasizes [the primacy of ecological integrity] by making clear that global ecological limits constrain the economic and social spheres' (2013, 318–9). Like Cullinan, he argues that 'the scientific laws that govern how the Earth works necessarily constrain the legal architecture for ecological law' (318–9).

Carla Sbert's definition of ecological law is similar, albeit slightly narrower:

> [e]cological law is a radical approach to understanding, critiquing and imagining law, and is also the norms and legal frameworks that this approach aims to bring about. It is not a new area of law, or a "reform" of environmental law, but law that is conceived with an ecological basis regardless of its specific subject matter. Ecological law responds to two fundamental concerns: 1) an immediate need to prioritize ecological integrity over economic interests, constraining economic activity within ecological limits to avoid ecological collapse; and 2) a broader need to shift from anthropocentric to ecocentric legal systems as a foundation for an ecologically just society. The objectives of ecological law are thus to provide legal tools that can help constrain the economy within ecological limits and restore ecological integrity, and to develop legal frameworks that will enable an ecologically just society. I thus propose (and use herein) the following tentative definition: *Ecological law is an emerging approach to law aimed at constraining economic activity within ecological limits, restoring and preserving ecological integrity, and building and supporting an ecologically just society.* (2019, 56).

Klaus Bosselmann identifies four concepts at the core of ecological law: the principle of sustainability, ecological justice, ecological human rights and ecological integrity. He defines the *principle of sustainability* 'as the duty to protect and restore the integrity of the Earth's ecological systems' (2008, 22). Another important concept for ecological law articulated by Bosselmann is that of *ecological justice*, since 'conventional theories of justice have been insufficient to conceptualize the environmental dimension of justice' (2006), and thus 'concern for the non-human-natural world' is required 'for a theory on ecological justice as distinct from mere social justice' (2008, 99). Bosselmann also argues for an 'ecological approach to human rights [that] acknowledges the interdependence of rights and duties' (143), proposing that *ecological human rights* are human rights that are constrained by ecological limits. The parallels with Cullinan's theory of an Earth Jurisprudence are immediately apparent, and both Bosselmann and Cullinan agree on the need for law to establish limits on the ability of humans to affect nature and to foster their responsibility towards the natural world. However, Bosselmann advocates a focus on human responsibilities, while Cullinan favours a rights-based approach, as discussed above. The final concept at the core of ecological law, for Bosselmann, is that of 'ecological integrity', which, he argues, 'is emerging as a common conceptual denominator' in international law as 'more than a dozen multilateral environmental agreements contain some reference to the integrity of ecosystems in their preamble or the operative part' (Kim & Bosselmann, 2015, 194).

Sbert, instead, identifies three key principles of ecological law. Firstly, 'ecocentrism', which 'recognize[s] and respect[s] the value of all beings and the interconnectedness among them, equitably promoting the interests of human and nonhuman members of the Earth community' (2019, 95). Secondly, 'ecological primacy', which '[e]nsures that social and economic behavior and systems are ecologically bound, respecting Planetary Boundaries' (102). Thirdly, 'ecological Justice', which '[e]nsure[s] equitable access to the Earth's sustaining capacity for present and future generations of humans and other beings, and avoid the inequitable allocation of environmental harms' (112). Importantly, Sbert defines ecological law in direct opposition to environmental law, focusing on the alleged failure of the latter, generally ascribed to the maintenance of an economic growth paradigm over other social and ecological goals. Ecological law, she asserts, is not an 'evolution' from environmental law, but rather a radical departure from law's role in mitigating the negative effects of economic activities to addressing its root causes, and thus it represents a paradigm shift from anthropocentrism to interconnectedness and ecocentrism. While it is certainly true that ecological law (or, for that matter, Earth Jurisprudence and all the theories discussed thus far) did not emerge in a genealogically linear manner from environmental law, the distinction may be less absolute, as I will explain shortly.

5.3.4 Ecological Jurisprudence

I originally proposed the term 'ecological jurisprudence' in 2012, in a phone conversation with Cormac Cullinan. Cullinan and I were at the time discussing the negative reception of the term 'wild law' in some Australian contexts. The term was seen, by many Indigenous scholars and activists in Australia, as evocative of the pejorative connotations of the term 'wild', historically used in Australia to refer to pre-colonial Aboriginal cultures in detrimental sense. As a result, Cullinan and I wanted to find an alternative that did not carry such unintended connotations. Furthermore, I also wanted to transcend the planetary boundaries entailed by the term 'Earth' (used in '*Earth* Jurisprudence'). After all, the delicate and dynamic homeostatic balance of Earth is dependent on the planetary configuration of the other planets, moons and asteroids in the solar system. Without Jupiter and the asteroid belt, the chances of meteoric impacts would increase significantly, thus making the current state of life on earth far more precarious. It would be, therefore, more appropriate to talk of a 'Cosmic Community', rather than limiting it to the planet alone. Reading Berry, it was clear to me that such was the intention behind his holism. I thus proposed the term 'ecological' jurisprudence (rather than the undoubtedly bizarre 'cosmic' jurisprudence) and began to use it thence.

To the best of my knowledge, Peter Burdon used the term 'ecological jurisprudence' in the title of an early article published a year later (2013), and Vito De Lucia adopted, in the same year, the term 'ecological philosophy of law' to refer to the same theoretical pursuit. Ben Mylius (2017) further suggests that the term is rooted in a number of publications from the 1980s, such as Ilich's 'Silence is a commons' (1983) and Lisityn's 'Information and environmental legislation' (1988). That notwithstanding, the term, in its usage I ascribe to it, arose independently from the conversation with Cullinan in 2012.

Initially, I used the term as an extended synonym for 'earth jurisprudence'. The term, however, soon evolved in its usage and scope, bursting beyond not only the semantic but also the conceptual boundaries from which it emerged. Not content to consider it any longer a wider extension of earth jurisprudence, I started to use it to encompass a wide range of theories, of which earth jurisprudence was only one. In this sense, and at its core, *ecological jurisprudence* refers to the theory and/or practice of law that aspires and attempts to be aligned to ecological principles.

However, while the term has entered scholarly parlance since and is often used along similar lines as the ones described in the previous paragraph, there was a third reason for its usage, which became apparent to me over the decade since its original introduction. Initially, as mentioned, the term was at times used as a direct synonym for 'earth jurisprudence', which was, at the same time, accused of being a novel version of natural law theory. While it would be absolutely legitimate for it to be so, I have always felt, since my first encounters with it a decade and a half ago, that the horizon of possibilities entailed by the 'ecologizing' of law extends well beyond the confines of traditional natural law theory, both in its classical and its modern permutations. Rather, the process transcends the traditional divide between legal positivism and natural law theory that still dominates Western jurisprudence. I will return to this point much more in-depth in a subsequent chapter. Suffices it to say, at this point, that I increasingly felt that 'ecological jurisprudence' was not merely an extended synonym for 'earth jurisprudence' at a theoretical level, but rather captured something else, a theoretical *zeitgeist* that, it later became apparent, was indeed in the process of emerging.

Earth Jurisprudence undoubtedly constitutes a novel articulation of legal theory informed by ecological sensibilities in direct and explicit opposition to the anthropocentric worldview construed above. The same is true of the many other 'ecological' legal theories briefly mentioned above, with 'ecological law' undoubtedly presenting the latest and most extensive example thus far. All such theories are marked by a particular positioning, be it by reference to the 'Great Jurisprudence' or the key principles of ecological law proposed by Bosselmann and Sbert. In some cases, the theoretical position of one of such theories is cast in contrast (or perhaps even in opposition) to another. However, while the specific formulation of the key tenets of each theoretical approach may vary (at times even only slightly), what all these theories have in common is an explicit rejection of an extreme anthropocentric worldview (which I endeavoured to construct in the initial chapters of this book, a view often referred to as 'crude' anthropocentrism), replaced by an 'ecological' worldview (which I have, again, endeavoured to construct in the previous chapters). As a result, and to articulate further, an 'ecological jurisprudence' is the theory and practice of law that is informed, positively, by the injection of 'ecology' into legal theory, and, negatively, by the rejection of an extreme anthropocentric view that is seen as both self-destructive in a utilitarian sense and as deontologically untenable.

The term 'ecological jurisprudence', then, is offered not as a singular theoretical construct, but rather as a spectrum of theoretical possibilities. All those theories and practices of law that are informed by ecological considerations and articulate themselves in opposition to an anthropocentric worldview fall, I propose, within the confines of an 'ecological jurisprudence'. At the one hand of the spectrum is the more 'crude anthropocentric' worldview that is seen as the ontological underpinning of the current environmental predicament. Naturally, it is important to note, such a worldview does not exist in some absolute, self-evident sense, but rather is discursively created and contextually construed. I have endeavoured to construe, in previous chapters, *one* construction of such view that could heuristically capture the range of diverse and heterogeneous concepts contained in the term 'anthropocentrism'. Such a construction does not intend to be (nor can it ever be) definitive, but it can hopefully provide a clear theoretical structure against which to articulate the broad spectrum of 'ecological' legal theories.

Moreover, the worldview thus construed forms, as Dubos noted, an *extreme* anthropocentric perspective. Many of the authors discussed thus far also note how an *enlightened* anthropocentric perspective distinguishes itself from its more extreme version, and Berry (and Gandhi before him) pointed out that altruism and enlightened self-interest become one and the same when the conceptual barrier between the self and the other is removed. I will return in a later chapter to the consideration of whether it is ever possible (or even desirable) to transcend or abandon anthropocentrism altogether. For the time being, however, it is sufficient to note the distinction between an *extreme* anthropocentric perspective—which constitutes one of the theoretical boundaries of the spectrum of theories and practices captured by the term 'ecological jurisprudence'—and a more *enlightened* anthropocentric perspective that many of the 'ecological' authors discussed thus far have embraced.

At the other end of the spectrum, an 'ecological jurisprudence' ceases to exist wherever either the idea of jurisprudence or the idea of the human disappears. The rejection of jurisprudence itself as a conceptual category (as some of the above authors have proposed) makes it inherently impossible for *any* form of jurisprudence to exist. Equally, the most misanthropic implications of some versions of ecocentrism, which view the human as a nuisance to be eradicated, are likely to represent a threshold that cannot be meaningfully crossed if any form of theorizing desire to maintain its purpose. Within such a broad spectrum, however, lie the many paths toward an ecological jurisprudence.

As long as its two core, interdependent and inextricably intertwined components—the rejection of extreme anthropocentrism and the pursuit of an ecological worldview—are accepted, ecological jurisprudence is not, therefore, a *specific* theory, but rather a trend, a tendency, a striving toward. Within the spectrum of 'eco-jurisprudential' pursuits, it follows, it is possible to see a huge range of approaches, from more radical ecocentric proposals to more moderate initiatives driven by an enlightened anthropocentrism. Therefore, while useful in certain contexts, the internal distinctions between specific attempts and approaches may be less relevant in a broad theoretical sense. Few (if any) of the existing theoretical proposals or practical initiatives reject anthropocentrism in its totality. As a result, the *qualitative* distinction between, for example, environmental law and ecological law may best be conceived of as a *quantitative* one. Indeed, many of the animating principles behind environmental law also reject some aspects of anthropocentrism, while very few eco-jurisprudential initiatives reject *all* elements that combine to form an anthropocentric worldview. While this is true, however, what becomes relevant is *in what sense and for what reason* the rejection of specific elements occurs. Ontological and axiological considerations, therefore, can never be assumed or obscured in any meaningful eco-jurisprudential discussion, but rather must be explored explicitly as the necessary premise to contextually locate the specific discourse being advanced.

The emergence of an ecological jurisprudence has been historically marked by the theoretical milestones that I have covered (necessarily briefly) over the previous chapters. I have elected to identify a few thresholds that marked its emergence, noting that such thresholds are (as thresholds always are) inherently arbitrary:

- The publication of 'Should Trees Have Standing?' by Christopher Stone in 1972, which marked the full articulation of a novel invitation to extend the boundaries of legal subjectivity beyond the human alone.
- The articulation of an Earth Jurisprudence by Thomas Berry and Cormac Cullinan, and the publication by the latter of *Wild Law* in 2002, as the first coherent and cohesive articulation of a legal *theory* to answer Stone's invitation.
- The 2008 Constitution of Ecuador, which, for the first time, recognized Nature as a subject *of* and *with* rights (I will explore this further in the next chapter).

While at the time of Stone's question the actual constitutional, legislative or judicial examples of initiatives that would fall within the broad definition of an ecological jurisprudence were extremely few (if any at all), such is not the case any longer. The next chapter will focus on these initiatives, to examine them in light of the theoretical lens developed thus far, and then, in the immediately following chapter, I will analyse and appraise many of the specific critiques and unresolved issues that have emerged over the last few decades of eco-jurisprudential initiatives. However, I am also cognizant that the overall process of 'ecologizing' jurisprudence and the subsequent emergence of an ecological jurisprudence contain a number of yet-unexplored challenges to the very *idea* of law. What *is* law in an eco-jurisprudential sense? Cullinan and Berry refer to the interplay between the 'Great Law' and 'human laws', but are the two categories still meaningfully separable? Is there a *qualitative* difference between 'human' and 'nonhuman' law? I will engage with such questions in the final chapter of this book, not in an attempt to definitively answer questions that have exercised the mind of legal theorists for (at the very least) the better part of two millennia, but to expand (together with many colleagues) the theoretical confines of the existing theoretical discourse even further. The expansion, responding to Naess's invitation, may even lead to the development of a deeply *ecosophical* jurisprudence.

References

Agamben, G. (2002). In A. K. Stanford (trans.), *The open. Man and animal*. University Press.

Akhtar-Khavari, A., & Richardson, B. J. (2019). *Ecological restoration law. Concepts and case studies*. Routledge.

Anker, K., Burdon, P. D., Garver, G., Maloney, M., Sbert, C. (Eds.) (2020). *From environmental to ecological law* . Routledge.

Bailey, L. H. (1915). *The holy Earth*. Scribner.

Baird Callicott, J. (1980). Animal liberation: A triangular affair. *Environmental Ethics, 2*(4), 311–338.

Baird, C. J. (1994). *Earth's Insights. A multicultural survey of ecological ethics from the Mediterranean basin to the Australian outback*. University of California Press.

Bentham, J. (1789). *An introduction to the principles of morals and legislation*.

Bergson, H. (1998). In A. Mitchell (trans.) *Creative evolution*. Henry Holt & Co. (First published in French 1907)

Berry, T. (1988). *The dream of the Earth*. Sierra Club Books.

Berry, T. (1999). *The great work*. Three Rivers Press.

Berry, T. (2006). *Evening thoughts*. Catapult.

Berry, T. (2009). *The sacred universe*. Columbia University Press.

Berry, W. (1977). *The unsettling of America: Culture and agriculture*. Sierra Club Books.

Birch, C., Cobb, J. B., Jr. (1981). *The liberation of life: From the cell to the community*. Cambridge University Press.

Bloch, E (1986). In D.J. Schmidt (trans.), *Natural law and human dignity*. MIT Press.

Bookchin, M. (1971). Ecology and revolutionary thought. In M. Bookchin (Ed.), *Post-scarcity anarchism*. Ramparts Press.

Bookchin, M. (1980). *Toward an ecological society*. Black Rose Books.

Bookchin, M. (1982). *The ecology of freedom*. Cheshire Books, Melbourne.

Bosselmann, K. (1998). *Ökologische Grundrechte: zur Verhältnis zwischen individueller Freiheit und Natur*. Nomos.

Bosselmann, K. (1995) *When two worlds collide: society and ecology*. RSVP.

Bosselmann, K. (2006). *Ecological justice and law*. In B.J. Richardson, & S. Wood (Eds.), *Environmental law for sustainability: A reader*. Hart Pub.

Bosselmann, K. (2008). *The principle of sustainability: Transforming law and governance*. Ashgate Publishing Co.

Bosselmann, K. (2010). Losing the forest for the trees: Environmental reductionism in the law. *Sustainability, 2*, 2424–2448.

Bosselmann, K. (2011). From reductionist environmental law to sustainability law. In P.D. Burdon (Ed.), *Exploring wild law: The philosophy of earth jurisprudence*. Wakefield Press.

Bosselmann, K. (2014). The rule of law grounded in the Earth: Ecological integrity as a Grundnorm. In L. Westra & M. Vilela (Eds.), *The Earth charter, ecological integrity and social movements*. Routledge.

Bosselmann, K. (2015a) The rule of law in the anthropocene. In: P. Martin et al. (Eds.), *Search of environmental justice*. Edward Elgar.

Bosselmann, K. (2015b) *Earth governance. Trusteeship of the global commons*. Edward Elgar.

Bosselmann, K. (2016). *The principle of sustainability* (2nd ed.). Routledge.

Bosselmann, K. (2020). The framework of ecological law. *Environmental Policy and Law, 50*, 479–486.

Boulot, P. (2012). A new legal paradigm: Towards a jurisprudence based on ecological sovereignty. *Macquarie Journal of International and Comparative Environmental Law, 8*(1), 1–15.
Boyd, D. R. (2004). Sustainability law: (R)Evolutionary directions for the future of environmental law. *Journal of Environmental Law Practice, 14*, 357–385.
Boyd, D. R (2017). *The rights of nature. A legal revolution that could save the world*. ECW.
Broad, C. D. (1925). *The mind and its place in nature*. Routledge.
Brown, C. (2017). *Buddhist economics. An enlightened approach to the dismal science*. Bloomsbury.
Brown, L., et al. (1988). *State of the World, 1988: A worldwatch institute report on progress toward a sustainable society*. Worldwatch Institute.
Burdon, P. D. (2013). The Earth community and ecological jurisprudence. *Oñati Socio-Legal Series, 3*(5), 815–837.
Callenbach, E. (1975). *Ecotopia*. Heyday.
Capra, F. (1997). *The web of life*. Anchor Books, Palatine.
Capra, F. (2002). *The hidden connections*. Anchor Books, Palatine.
Capra, F., & Mattei, U. (2015). *The ecology of law: Toward a legal system in tune with nature and community*. Berrett-Koehler.
Carson, R. (1962). *Silent spring*. Houghton Mifflin.
Catton, W. R., Jr. (1982). *Overshoot: The ecological basis for revolutionary change*. University of Illinois Press.
Clements, F., & Shelford, V. (1939). *Bio-ecology*. Wiley.
Cohen, M. J. (1983). *Prejudice against nature: A guidebook for the liberation of self and planet*. Freeport.
Cullinan, C. (2011a) *Wild law* (2nd ed.). Chelsea Green Publishing, White River Junction (First published 2002)
Cullinan, C. (2011b). A history of wild law. In P.D Burdon (Ed.), *Exploring wild law: The philosophy of earth jurisprudence*. Wakefield Press.
His Holiness the Dalai Lama. (2006). *The universe in a single atom. How science and spirituality can serve our world*. Abacus.
Daly, H. E. (1991). *Steady-state economics* (2nd ed.). Island Press (First published 1977)
Davies, M. (2022). *EcoLaw: Legality, life, and the normativity of nature*. Routledge.
Devall, B., & Session. G. (2007). *Deep ecology*. Gibbs Smith.
Dubos R (1970–1971) The Despairing Optimist. American Scholar 40:16–20
Dubos, R. (1972). *A god within*. Scribner.
De Lucia, V. (2013). Towards an ecological philosophy of law: A comparative discussion. *Journal of Human Rights and the Environment, 4*(2), 167–190.
De Lucia, V. (2015). Competing narratives and complex genealogies: The ecosystem approach in international. *Environmental Law, 27*(1), 91–117.
Dryzek, J. S. (1997). *The politics of the Earth: Environmental discourses*. Oxford University Press.
Dyzenhaus, D. (2006). *The constitution of law: Legality in a time of emergency*. Cambridge University Press.
Ehrenfeld, D. (1978). *The arrogance of humanism*. Oxford University Press.
Elton, C. (1927). *Animal ecology*. McMillan Co.
Emerson, R. W. (1866). Complete works. Bell & Daldy.
Evans, E. P. (1898). *Evolutional ethics and animal psychology*. Appleton & Co.
Evans, E. P. (1906). *The criminal prosecution and capital punishment of animals*. E P Dutton.
Favre, D. F. (1979). Wildlife rights: The ever-widening circle. *Environmental Law, 9*, 279.
Ferejohn, F., & Pasquino, P. (2002). The Law of exception: A typology of emergency powers. *International Journal of Constitutional Law, 2*, 210–235.
Filgueira, B., Mason, I. (2011). Wild law: Is there any evidence of earth jurisprudence in existing law? In P.D Burdon (Ed.), *Exploring wild law: The philosophy of Earth jurisprudence*. Wakefield Press.

Fisher, S. (2013). Our sustainability crisis didn't start and doesn't stop at climate change. In *The conversation*. http://theconversation.com/our-sustainability-crisis-didnt-start-and-doesnt-stop-at-climate-change-17471
Fox, M. W. (1978). Man and nature: Biological perspectives. In R. Knowles Morris, & M.W. Fox (Eds.), *On the fifth day: Animal rights and human ethics*. Acropolis.
Fuller, F. (1969). *The morality of law*. Yale University Press.
Gare, A. (2017). *The philosophical foundations of ecological civilization. A manifesto for the future*. Routledge.
Garver, G. (2013). The rule of ecological law: the legal complement to degrowth economics. *Sustainability, 5*, 316–337.
Gordon, R. B., & Wood Krutch, J. (1954). Conservation is not enough. *American Scholar, 24*(1), 127–128.
Greer, J. M. (2011). *The wealth of nature*. New Society Publishers, Gabriola.
Griffin, D. R. (Ed.). (1988). *The re-enchantment of science*. SUNY Press.
Harari, Y. N. (2011). *Sapiens. A brief history of humankind*. Vintage.
Hargrove, E. C. (1979). Some fundamentals of conservation in the southwest. *Environmental Ethics, 1*, 131–141.
Hargrove, E. C. (Ed.). (1986). *Beyond spaceship Earth: Environmental ethics and the solar system*. Sierra Club Books.
Hartmann, T. (1998). *The last hours of ancient sunlight: The fate of the world and what we can do before it's too late*. Three Rivers Press.
Hays, S. P. (1959). *Conservation and the gospel of efficiency: the progressive conservation movement, 1890–1920*. Cambridge University Press.
Hays, S. P. (1987). *Beauty*. Cambridge University Press, Cambridge.
Heinberg, R. (2011). *The end of growth*. New Society Publishers, Gabriola.
Huxley, J. (1957). *New bottles for new wine*. Harper and Row.
Ilich, I. (1983). Silence is a commons. *The Coevolution Quarterly, 40*, 5–9.
Ilich I,. (1973). *Tools for conviviality*. Harper & Row.
Jackson, T. (2009). *Prosperity without growth. Economics for a finite planet*. Earthscan.
Jagtenberg, J., & McKie, D. (1997). *Eco-impacts and the greening of postmodernity. New maps for communication studies, cultural studies, and sociology*. Sage Publications.
Jennings, B. (2016). *Ecological governance: Toward a new contract with the Earth*. West Virginia University Press.
Jessop, R. (2012). Coinage of the term environment: a word without authority and carlyle's displacement of the mechanical metaphor. *Literature Compass*. https://doi.org/10.1111/j.1741-4113.2012.00922.x
King, Y. (1983). Toward an ecological feminism and a feminist ecology. In J. Rothschild (Ed.), *Machina Ex Dea: Feminist perspectives on technology*. Elsevier.
Kim, R. E., & Bosselmann, K. (2015). Operationalizing sustainable development: Ecological integrity as a grundnorm of international law. *Reciel, 24*(2), 194–208.
Koestler, A. (1967). *The ghost in the machine*. Hutchinson.
Kolbasov, O. S. (1988–9). The concept of ecological law. *Conn. Journal of International Law*, 4, 267.
Koons, J. E. (2011). Key principles to transform law for the health of the planet. In P.D. Burdon (Ed.), *Exploring wild law: The philosophy of earth jurisprudence*. Wakefield Press.
Kotzé, L. J., & Kim, R. E. (2019). Earth system law: The juridical dimensions of earth system governance. *Earth System Governance, 1*, 1–12.
Kvaloy, S. (1974). Ecophilosophy and ecopolitics. *North American Review, 259*, 17–28.
Laitos, J. G. (2012). *The right of nonuse*. Oxford University Press.
Lakoff, G., & Johnson, M. (1999). *Philosophy in the flesh*. Basic Books.
Lazarus, R. J. (2009). Super wicked problems and climate change: Restraining the present to liberate the future. *Cornell Law Review, 94*, 1174–1176.
Leakey, R. (1996). *The sixth extinction*. Anchor Books, Palatine.

Lecky, W. E. H. (1869). *History of Eurpoean morals from Augustus to Charlemagne*. Appleton & Co.
Lecky, W. E. H. (1910). *The history of the rise and influence of the spirit of rationalism*. Appleton & Co.
Leopold, A. (1933). The conservation ethic. *Journal of Forestry, 31*, 634–635.
Leopold, A. (1949). *A sand county Almanac and sketches here and there*. Oxford University Press.
Lilly, J. (1976). The rights of cetaceans under human laws. *Oceans, 9*, 67–68.
Lovelock, J. (1979). *Gaia: A new look at life on Earth*. Oxford University Press.
Luhmann, N. (1990). The autopoiesis of social systems. In N. Luhman (Ed.), *Essays on self-reference*. Columbia University Press.
Luttenberger, L. R., & Luttenberger, A. (2012). Earth-centric approach in environmental protection. *Scientific Journal of Maritime Research, 26*(1), 27–44.
Lisityn, E. N. (1988). Information and environmental legislation. *Connecticut Journal of International Law, 4*(2), 429–440.
M'Gonigle, M., & Ramsay, P. (2004). Greening environmental law: From sectoral reform to systemic re-formation. *Journal of Environmental Law and Practice, 14*, 333–361.
Maren-Grisebach. M. (1982). *Philosophie der Grünen*. Olzog.
Margoulis, L., & Sagan, D. (2000). *What is life?* University of California Press.
Marcuse, H. (1972). *Counterrevolution and revolt*. Beacon Press.
Marsh, G. P. (Ed.) (2003). *Man and nature; or, physical geography as modified by human action*. University of Washington Press (First published 1864)
Marshall, R. (1930). The problem of the wilderness. In G. Adelson, J. Engell, B. Ranalli, & K.P. Van Anglen (Eds.), *Environment, an interdisciplinary anthology*. Yale University Press.
Mason, I. (2011). One in all: Principles and characteristics of earth jurisprudence. In P.D. Burdon (Ed.), *Exploring wild law: The philosophy of earth jurisprudence*. Wakefield Press.
Mathews, F. (1991). *The ecological self*. Routledge.
Matthews, D. (2021). *Earthbound. The aesthetics of sovereignty in the anthropocene*. Edinburgh University Press.
Maturana, H., & Varela, F. (1980). *Autopoiesis and cognition: The realization of the living*. Reidel.
McGee, W. J. (1909–10) The conservation of natural resources. In *Proceedings of the Mississippi Valley Historical Association* (Vol. 3, p. 379).
McKibben, B. (1989). *The end of nature*. Random House.
McKibben, B. (2007). *Deep economy. The wealth of communities and the durable future*. St Martin's Griffin.
Meadows, D. H. (2008) *Thinking in systems*. Chelsea Green.
Merchant, D. (1983). *The death of nature. Women, ecology, and the scientific revolution*. HarperSanFrancisco.
Mies, M., & Shiva, V. (1993) *Ecofeminism*. Spinifex.
Moore, J. H. (1906). *The universal kinship*. Charles Kerr & Co.
Moore, J. H. (1909). *The new ethics*. Ernest Bell.
Morowitz, H. (1992). *Beginning of cellular life*. Yale University Press.
Morris, C. (1964). The rights and duties of beasts and trees: A law teacher's essay for landscape architects. *Journal of Legal Education, 17*, 189–191.
Muir, J. (1909). *Our national parks*. Houghton Mifflin.
Muir, J. (1911). *My first summer in the Sierra*. Houghton Mifflin.
Muir, J. (1917). *A thousand-mile walk to the Gulf*. William F Bade.
Murphy, E. F. (1971). Has nature any right to life?'. *Hastings Law Journal, 22*, 467–484.
Mylius, B. (2017). *Earth jurisprudence*. Elsevier. https://doi.org/10.1016/B978-0-12-409548-9.10449-X
Naess, A. (1973). The shallow and the deep, long range ecology movement: A summary. *Inquiry, 16*, 95–100.
Naffine, N. (2012). Legal personality and the natural world: On the persistence of the human measure of value. *Journal of Human Rights and the Environment, 3*, 68–83.

Nash, R. (Ed.). (1976). *The American environment*. McGraw Hill.
Nash, R. (1989). *The rights of nature*. University of Wisconsin Press.
Nicholson, E. B. (1879). *The rights of animals: A new essay in ethics*. Kegan Paul & Co.
Ouspensky, P. D., & Kadloubovsky, E. (1981). *Tertium organum: The third canon of thought, a key to the enigmas of the world*. Routledge (First published 1923)
Pinchot, G. The birth of conservation. In G. Glenn Adelson, J. Engell, B. Ranalli, K.P. Van Anglen (Eds.), *Environment, an interdisciplinary anthology*. Yale University Press.
Passarin d'Entreves, A. (1951). *Natural law: An introduction to legal philosophy*. Hutchinson.
Passmore, J. (1974). *Man's responsibility for nature: ecological problems and western traditions*. Scribner.
Petulla, J. (1980). *American environmentalism: Values, tactics*. Texas University Press, College Station.
Plumwood, V. (1993). *Feminism and the mastery of nature*. Routledge.
Polanyi, K. (1944). *The great transformation. The political and economic origins of our time*. Farrar & Rinehart.
Pope Francis. (2015). *Laudato Si'. On care for our common home*. Libreria Editrice Vaticana.
Pope John Paul, I. I. (1988). *Sollicitudo Rei Socialis*. St Paul Publications.
Pope, A. (1966). Essay on man. In H. Davis (Ed.), *Pope: Poetical works*. Oxford University Press, University
Prigogine, I. (1967). *Dissipative structures in chemical systems*. In S. Claesson (Ed.), *Fast reactions and primary processes in chemical kinetics*. Interscience.
Prigogine, I., & Stengers, I. (1984). *Order out of chaos*. Heinemann.
Purdy, J. (2013). Our place in the World: A new relationship for environmental ethics and law. *Duke Law Journal, 62*(4), 858–932.
Purdy, J. (2010). The politics of nature: Climate change, environmental ale, and democracy. *Yale Law Journal, 119*(6), 1122–1209.
Ray, J. (1691). *The wisdom of god manifested in the works of creation*.
Regan, T. (1982). *All that dwell therein*. University of California Press.
Regan, T. (1983). *The case for animal rights*. University of California Press.
Regan, T. (2010). Holism as environmental fascism. In J.E. White (Ed.), *Contemporary moral problems* (10th ed.). Wadsworth (First published 1985).
Robinson, N. A. (2013). Evolved norms: A canon for the anthropocene. In C. Voigt (Ed.), *Rule of law for nature*. Cambridge University Press.
Rogers, N. (2020). *Law, fiction and activism in a time of climate change*. Routledge.
Rogers, N., & Maloney, M. (Eds.). (2017a). *Law as if Earth really mattered: The wild law judgment project*. Routledge.
Rogers, N., & Maloney, M. (2017). The wild law judgment project. In N. Rogers, & M. Maloney (Eds.), *Law as if Earth really mattered: The wild law judgment project*. Routledge.
Rolston, H. (1986). *Philosophy gone wild: Essays in environmental ethics*. Prometheus.
Roszak, T. (1978). *Person/planet: The creative disintegration of industrial society*. iUniverse.
Sachs, W. (1999). *Planet dialectics*. Zed Books.
Salleh, A. K. (1984). Deeper than deep ecology: The eco-feminist connection. *Environmental Ethics* 339–345.
Salt, H. S. (1894). *Animals' rights considered in relation to social progress*. George Bells & Sons.
Santmire, H. P. (1970). *Brother Earth: Nature, god and ecology in time of crisis*. Nelson.
Sbert, C. C (2019). *Mining from the lens of ecological law: Obstacles and opportunities for reformation* (Ph.D. thesis). University of Ottawa.
Schaab, G. L. (2011). Beyond dominion and stewardship. In P. Burdon (Ed.), *Exploring wild law: The philosophy of earth jurisprudence*. Wakefield Press.
Schama, S. (1995). *Landscape and memory*. Vintage.
Schweitzer, A. (1923). In A. John Naish, & C Black (Eds.), *Philosophy of civilization: Civilization and ethics*.
Schweitzer, A. (1933). *Out of my life and thought: An autobiography*. H Holt.

Schweitzer, A. (1936). In C. E. B Russell & H. Holt (trasns.), *Indian thought and its development*. New York
Shepard, P. (1969). ecology and man—A viewpoint. In P. Shepard, D. McKinley (Eds.), *The subversive science: essays toward an ecology of man*. Houghton Mifflin.
Shiva, V. (2000). *Tomorrow's biodiversity*. Thames & Hudson.
Shiva, V. (2002). *Water wars*. India Research Press.
Sierra Club v. Morton, 405 U.S. 727.
Singer, P. (1975). *Animal liberation: A new ethics for our treatment of animals*. HarperCollins.
Skolimowski, H. (1981). *Ecophilosophy: Designing new tactics for living*. Marion Boyars.
Snyder, G. (1980). *The real work: Interviews and talks, 1964–1979*. New Directions Publishing.
Stacey, J. (2018). *The constitution of the environmental emergency*. Hart.
Stone, C. D. (1972). Should trees have standing?—Towards legal rights for natural objects. *Southern California Law Review, 45*, 450–501.
Stuart Mill, J. (1848). *Principles of political economy*. John Parker.
Stutzin, G. (1984). Un imperativo ecológico: Reconocer los derechos de la naturaleza. *Ambiente y Desarrollo, 1*(1), 97–114.
Suzuki, D., McConnell, A., & Mason, A. (2007). *The sacred balance. Rediscovering our place in nature—Updated and expanded*. Greystone Books.
Swimme, B. (1996). *The hidden heart of the cosmos*. Orbis Books.
Swimme, B., & Berry, T. (1994). *The universe story. From the primordial flaring forth to the ecozoic era*. HarperCollins.
Tanasescu, M. (2022). *Understanding the rights of nature*. Transcript Verlag.
Tansley, A. G. (1935). The use and abuse of vegetational concepts and terms. *Ecology, 16*, 284–307.
Taylor, P. W. (1981). The ethics of respect for nature. *Environmental Ethics, 3*, 209.
The Body of Liberties 1641
Theilard de Chardin, P. (1959). In W.B. Harper (trans.), *The phenomenon of man*, Torchbooks.
Thompson, J. A. (1920). *The system of animate nature*. Williams and Northgate.
Thoreau, H. D. (1854). *Walden*. Ticknor and Fields.
Torrey, B. (Ed.). (1906). *The writings of Henry Thoreau*. Houghton Mifflin.
Tribe, L. H. (1974). Ways not to think about plastic trees: New foundations for environmental law. *Yale Law Journal, 83*, 1315–1348.
Unger, R. M. (1983). The critical legal studies movement. *Harvard Law Review, 96*, 561–675.
UN Environment Programme. (2019). *Environmental rule of law, First global report*. UN Envrionment Programme.
Vernadsky, V. (1986). *The biosphere*. Synergetic Press (First published 1926)
Watson, P. (1982). *Sea shepherd: my fights for whales and seals*. Norton.
Westra, L. (2000). The global integrity project and the ethics of integrity. In P. Crabbe A. Holland L. Ryszowski, & L. Westra (Eds.), *Implementing ecological integrity: restoring regional and global environmental and human health*. Kluwer Academic Publishers.
Westra, L. (2008). *Environmental justice and the rights of indigenous peoples. International and domestic perspectives*. Earthscan.
Wheeler, W. M. (1926). Emergent evolution of the social. *Science, 64*, 433–440.
White, S. (2014). Wild law and animal law. In M. Maloney & P.D. Burdon (Eds.), *Wild law–In practice*. Routledge
Wiener, N. (1948). *Cybernetics*. MIT Press.
Wilderness Act, 16 U.S.C. § 1131 2(c) (1964)
Wilkinson, L. (Ed.) (1980). *Earthkeeping: Christian stewardship of natural resources*. Eerdmans.
Wilkinson, R., & Pickett, K. (2009). *The spirit level: Why more equal societies almost always do better*. Allan Lane.
Wilson, E. O. (1984). *Biophilia*. Cambridge University Press.

Wilson, E. O. (2017). *Half-Earth*. Liveright Publishing.
Winchester, S. (2021). *Land. How the hunger for ownership shaped the modern world*. William-Collins.
Worster, D. (1977). *Nature's economy: The roots of ecology*. Sierra Club.
Zelle, A.R., Wilson, G., Adam, R., & Greene, H. F. (Eds.). (2021). *Earth law. Emerging ecocentric law—A guide for practitioners*. Wolters Kluver.

Chapter 6
Rights of Nature

We begin to understand that there already exists a governance of the Earth, a governance too subtle for us to understand. This governance enables the Earth to bring forth the immense variety of its living forms that interact so intimately and extensively with one another. The well-being of each is fulfilled in the well-being of the whole. This governance has capacities far beyond anything humans are capable of. Yet this primordial governance remains the context into which we must insert our human governance.
Thomas Berry, The Sacred Universe, 2009
Nature, or Pacha Mama, where life is reproduced and occurs, has the right to integral respect for its existence and for the maintenance and regeneration of its life cycles, structure, functions and evolutionary processes.
Art 71, Ecuadorian Constitution 2008.

There are, the authors discussed in the previous chapter have shown, many distinct ways to make law less anthropocentric and more ecocentric: to some, this means the extension of rights to nature and, or, granting nature legal personhood and standing to nature; to others, it means a stronger application of the precautionary principle, the adoption of notions of sustainability and ecological integrity as guiding principles, both jurisprudentially and legislatively; to others still, it means the reimagination of the current theoretical and practical approach to property. However, before the rise of these many proposals, their often fragmented implementation and the many theoretical articulations of the shift, within law and legal theory, from anthropocentrism to ecocentrism, there was, of course, environmental law.

To fully capture the import and impact of the existing initiatives that represent, collective, the emergence of, and the aspiration to, an 'ecological jurisprudence', it is necessary to reconstruct a diachronic evolution of all its initiatives from the early introduction of environmental law within the dominant Western legal discourse to the many contemporary initiatives that are aptly captured by the Global Alliance for the Rights of Nature's *Eco-Jurisprudence Monitor*.

A. Pelizzon, *Ecological Jurisprudence*, Contemporary Environmental Law and Policy,
https://doi.org/10.1007/978-981-96-0173-8_6

6.1 The Rise of Environmental Law

Environmental law refers, in a broad sense, to the body of law that regulates human impact on the environment. The management of 'natural resources', albeit distinct, is strictly related to this body of law. As a result, environmental law acts as an umbrella term for categories such as environmental protection, conservation, regulation of pollution, mining, fisheries, natural resource management, cultural heritage, environmental impact assessment and planning and development laws.

Environmental law, Klaus Bosselmann suggests (2010), was born in the 1960s. Of course, there are many precursors to the US Acts that are generally seen as the beginning of environmental legislation. Roman laws protecting Rome's supply of clean water can be traced back to the first-century CE, while fourteenth-century England prohibited the burning of coal in London, and the disposal of waste in London's waterways. Tokugawa-era Japan (Diamond 2005) and late Renaissance Germany (Bosselmann, 2011) are very explicit examples of advanced forestry management. In the early years of the USA, Benjamin Franklin led numerous campaigns to stem the wanton disposal of waste, while the British government repeatedly attempted to curtail the damaging effects of coal burning and chemical waste on both public health and the environment. The progressive conservation movement was driven by an explicit attempt to curtail the human impact on the environment, and the Russian Federation, from 1917 onward, began the creation of *zapavedmka* (заповедники, literally 'sacred, prohibited from disturbance'), 'nature preserves in which humans themselves are not allowed to enter save as scientific purposes, creating in effect the largest and most protective wilderness system in the world' (Weiner, 1999). The 1952 'Great Smog' of London led the UK Parliament to pass the *Clean Air Act 1956* (UK).

6.1.1 Modern Environmental Law

Notwithstanding these historical precursors, Klaus Bosselmann writes that '[t]he year 1969, when the US *National Environmental Policy Act* came into force, is often referred to as a landmark in modern environmental law' (2010, 2424). Environmental law is indeed considered to be born with a number of US Acts in the 1960s and the milestone 1972 'Stockholm Conference' (to which I will return to below). The US *Clean Air Act* of 1963 was the first piece of legislation to enable the US Federal government to take direct action to control air pollution. This act was soon followed by the *Wilderness Act* in 1964 (as a result of which more than 107 million acres of federal public land in the USA have since entered the statutory category of 'wilderness'), the *Clean Water Act* in 1972, the *Marine Mammal Protection Act* of 1972, the *Endangered Species Act* of 1973 and the *Pollution Protection Act* of 1990. The US Environmental Protection Agency (EPA) was established in 1970.

The trend initiated by US legislation was soon followed by the rest of the world. In 2019, the United Nations Environment Programme released the first-ever global assessment of what it defined as the 'environmental rule of law'. The report found that, as of 2017, 150 countries have enshrined environmental protection or the right to a healthy environment in their constitutions, 176 countries have environmental framework laws and 164 countries have created cabinet-level bodies responsible for environmental protection. The report also identified enforcement as the greatest obstacle to the full effectiveness of many of these environmental law regimes, 'exacerbating environmental threats, despite prolific growth in environmental laws and agencies worldwide over the last four decades' (and the backlash against implementation, in many cases, included the harassment, arbitrary detention and murder of environmental advocates and activists).

Glenn Adleson and others note that '[a] corollary to environmental law is the concept of environmental justice, which is not subject to the same degree of formalization and is often without systemic remedy' (2008, 747). The pursuit of environmental justice is particularly visible in the emergence of environmental constitutionalism, which entails 'the recognition that the environment is a proper subject for protection in constitutional texts and for vindication by constitutional courts worldwide' (May & Daly, 2015, 1). The emergence of environmental constitutionalism (the incorporation of environmental rights, procedures and policies into national Constitutions), Erin Daly and others claim,

> is nothing short of astonishing. Arguably owing its genesis to the 1948 Universal Declaration on Human Rights, and 1966's twin international covenants on Civil and Political and Economic, Social and Cultural Rights, it entered the lexicon at 1972's Stockholm Convention on the Human Environment, which is widely considered to be the global impetus that sparked the exponential growth of international, regional and national environmental law regimes. (2017, 30)

Klaus Bosselmann mapped the emergence of environmental constitutionalism in 2015: Portugal was the first country to include an environmental provision within a national constitution in 1976, with many countries following since (to the above reported total of over 150 countries at present). Among them, perhaps the most striking is the Constitution of Bhutan of 2008, which included a new measure, 'gross national happiness' (GNH) to substitute GDP, and that includes a host of environmental measures to accompany such novel measurement.

Given the rapid expansion of environmental law over the past six decades, it is perhaps unsurprising that many of the authors discussed above are highly critical of its actual impact and would rather position themselves in a theoretically distinct position. Rebecca Bratspies notes that '[t]he starting point for most critics of environmental law and sustainable development is that the growing global ecological crisis signals the overall failure of these approaches despite many successes in tackling specific (mostly pollution) issues' (in Sbert, 2019, 16). Lowe (2014), even more strongly, argued a decade ago that environmental laws and regulations have not fundamentally changed the rate of environmental destruction, despite over 60 years of awareness of environmental issues and over 50 years of environmental law. Devall and Session would concur, stating that, overall, environmentalism 'is frequently seen as an attempt to work only within the confines of conventional political process of industrialized nations to alleviate or mitigate some of the worst forms of air and water pollution, destruction of indigenous wildlife, and some of the most short-sighted development schemes' (2007, 2). Vito De Lucia writes that, 'while environmental law has been able to save many trees, it may well have lost sight of the forest, which is being lost at an ever more alarming rate. Environmental law', he continues, 'has predominantly functioned as a mitigating instrument whose strategic aim is that of *containment*: the ecological disruption of economic and industrial activities is to be mitigated, contained or otherwise reduced *to the extent possible*' (2013, 169). As a result, Holder contends, environmental law has a 'business as usual tone' (2000, 165). Michael M'Gonigle and Paula Ramsay define environmental law as 'an especially ironic form of self-regulation that asks a benevolent state to regulate against its own long history of economic growth and expansion, and its own (self-conceived) self-interest' (2004, 12). Even more critically, M'Gonigle describes 'environmental law as a prop to an unsustainable political economy' and 'an essentially technical discourse operating within the very forces it should be challenging' (2008, 335). The same degree of deep criticism of environmental law is voiced by Mari Margil, who contends that environmental law is not conducive to the protection of the environment, but rather is a form of regulatory administrative law focused on regulating the *quantum* of extraction: 'environmental laws are put in place to determine *how much* [emphasis added] we can harm or exploit nature' (2021). Peter Burdon also asserts that 'the only thing regulated by environmental law are the environmentalists. The laws regulate the way environmentalists respond, and make them predictable' (2009).

The alleged reasons for the failures of environmental law are multifaceted. Geoffrey Garver suggests that

> [a] key flaw of contemporary environmental law is its reductionist tendency to focus on environmental problems as discrete and isolated, which impedes the full integration of a systems-based ecological approach into the entire legal infrastructure. ... A second flaw is the tendency in environmental law, as with environmental economics, to favour monetization as the way to normalize social preferences and to regulate the relationship between environmental problems and the development pressures that create them. Environmental law relies too heavily on assessments of monetized costs and benefits and an enduring allegiance to a reactive, non-precautionary approach that gives primacy to economic constraints instead of ecological ones. (2013, 320-1)

Bossellman concurs, asserting that environmental law is hampered by a reductionist approach to its subject: the environment, or, more precisely, the human–nature relationship. This relationship is misconceived through the domination of certain philosophical and cultural traditions in European history. As a consequence, he concludes, since 'modern legislation to protect the natural environment has developed in a compartmentalised, fragmented, economic and anthropocentric manner ... [t]he inherent design flaw is the absence of a fundamental rule to not harm the integrity of ecosystems. Such a rule requires the acceptance of sustainability as an overarching legal principle' (2011, 204). Bratspies also argues that there exist two key problems or 'fallacies' that must be addressed to turn environmental law into a more effective tool for sustainability. The first, or 'Marginal Fallacy' is 'the belief that we can achieve sustainability by tinkering at the margins of the existing social, economic, and legal systems'. The second, or 'Splintered Fallacy' is 'the tendency to splinter each problem into discrete pieces to be dealt with one at a time (the Splintered Fallacy)' (Sbert, 2019, 16). Environmental law is also criticized for its strong degree of anthropocentricity. Bosselmann points out that '[t]raditionally, legal relationships ... are perceived as relationships purely between people: people have no legal obligations towards nature and nature has no rights towards people' (2008, 80).

For this reason, a number of authors see environmental law as existing in theoretical *opposition* to many of the more ecocentric theoretical approaches discussed in the previous chapter. Nicole Rogers states that '[e]nvironmental law generally does not resemble wild law' (2011, 186). Bosselmann asserts that '[f]or environmental legislation to become effective ... broader coverage and better enforcement are not enough' (2011, 204). The 'Oslo Manifesto' concurs: '[t]he difference between environmental law and ecological law is not merely a matter of degree, but fundamental. The former allows human activities and aspirations to determine whether or not the integrity of ecological systems should be protected. The latter requires human activities and aspirations to be determined by the need to protect the integrity of ecological systems' (2016, 5). Some authors even assert that 'environmentalism's love affair with science, technology, and law ful (has failed to put the brakes on the biospheric crisis'. Even further, 'it has ... contributed to the ... problem' and 'has become a cause for reform-minded tinkerers who imagine eco-alternatives and fixes of every kind—save those that would wrest power from the few and democratize the web of life', thus becoming a veritable tool of the powerful (Moore, 2024).

While many of the critiques are certainly warranted, the question, I believe, remains open as to whether there exists an actual *qualitative* difference between environmental law and the other proposed approaches. After all, the same critique of a lack of effectiveness could be labelled against the latter too, given their decade-long experimentation (as in the case of the rights of Nature initiatives) or their lack of actual implementation in any legal initiative. Furthermore, David Boyd (2015) notes how much more positive many of the environmental measurements are today (than they would likely be), perhaps, he contends, as a result of the emergence of environmental laws and regulations over the past few decades.

The distinction between environmental law and a more ecocentric legal theory, while certainly true to a certain extent, appears to replicate the distinction between utilitarian environmental reasons informed by enlightened anthropocentrism and deep ecological and holistic reasons informed by a more ecocentric aspiration. However, as mentioned above, not even the most ecocentric arguments appear to reject the totality of anthropocentrism. As the 'Oslo Manifesto' itself shows, the document limits itself to an ecological reimagination of the *approach* to law marked by a focus on the principle of ecological integrity, rather than reimagining *law* itself in a deeper normative sense. As a result, while it is undoubtedly necessary to appraise the effectiveness as well as the discursive implications of environmental law, I wonder whether the deep *theoretical* hostility toward its alleged failures is, in fact, theoretically warranted, or at least effectively useful.

6.1.2 Environmental Litigation

Environmental litigation occupies a special place in relation to the rise of environmental law, both domestically and internationally. A number of specialized entities have been set up with the goal of undertaking (often public) environmental litigation in accordance with the relevant domestic environmental law regime. Among the most notable examples are the Environmental Defender's Offices (EDOs) in Australia, with the first one established in NSW in 1985 in response to the perceived need 'for a dedicated organization of environmental lawyers to provide support to conservation organizations' (Sydes, 2014, 60). Equally significant is the Community and Environment Legal Defense Fund (CELDF) in the USA, which has been instrumental in supporting some of the first rights of Nature initiatives worldwide. James Thornton, the founder of ClientEarth, possibly the most famous environmental litigation firm in Europe, is indeed unashamedly optimistic about the role of environmental law. 'Law becomes about saving civilisation', Thornton proposes. 'It offers the opportunity to delay the impacts of our past actions, and release our creativity to build a positive future together. … Environmental law tries to capture, in a snapshot, the best science that can be turned into policy, and then into rule of law' (Goodman & Thornton, 2017, 30–1).

In some cases, litigation has relied on domestic legal doctrines that have been then transplanted elsewhere. In the USA, in particular, the 'public trust doctrine' has been widely used to impose obligations on the government to protect and manage public assets responsibly and appropriately. While more common in the USA, the public trust doctrine has antecedents in law dating back to the Roman Institutes of Justinian and the Carta and Wilkinson (1989) explains. The public trust means 'that the public owns in common certain property interests in natural resources and land within the territory, and that the government is the people's designated trustee with the obligation to protect such property on behalf of the citizens' (429). Traditionally, the doctrine applied to the protection of large watercourses and their banks for navigation, fishing, drinking water and other uses by the public. According to Joseph Sax, the doctrine imposes three types of restrictions on governmental authority: 'first, the property subject to the trust must not only be used for a public purpose, but must be held available for use by the general public; second, the property may not be sold, even for a fair cash equivalent; and third, the property must be maintained for particular types of uses' (1970, 477).

In 2019, the Supreme Court of Holland established, in *The State of the Netherlands v. Urgenda Foundation* (*Urgenda*), the Dutch government's legal duty to address climate change. The Court ordered the Dutch government to slash greenhouse gas (GHG) emissions to 25% below 1990 levels by the end of 2020 in enforcement of the European Convention on Human Rights and other legal standards. The *Urgenda case* represents the world's first case in which citizens successfully established a legal duty to address climate change on the part of a national government.

The full exploration of the many cases of environmental litigation is, naturally, well beyond the scope of the present text, as it is thoroughly and carefully explored by a host of dedicated scholars and monographs elsewhere.

6.2 International Law and the Environment

Bosslemann points out that we can—and should—think of the environment as 'a universal concern. Arguably, the environment is even more fundamental than human rights as it represents the natural conditions of *all* [emphasis added] life including human beings' (2015, 173). As a result, while '[t]he prospect of a global environmental constitution may not be realistic for many years to come ... the health of the entire planet is at stake. This requires global awareness wherever people live and act ... Therefore, it is worth pondering whether global values can be identified and incorporated into some form of a world constitution' (182). Whether a comprehensive global constitution can ever be achieved, notwithstanding its undeniable desirability, a number of international law principles have emerged over the past century.

Philippe Sands and Jacqueline Peel point out that '[e]arly attempts to develop international environmental rules focused on the conservation of wildlife ... and, to a limited extent, on the protection of rivers and seas' (2012, 23). As early as 1872, Switzerland proposed an international regulatory commission for the protection of migratory birds, whereas the first international treaty aimed at the protection of wildlife was the 1900 *Convention Destinée à Assurer la Conservation des Diverse Espèces Animales Vivant à l'Etat Sauvage en Afrique qui sont Utiles à l'Homme ou Inoffensive.* The first whaling convention was adopted in 1931. The *Pacific Fur Seal* dispute between the USA and Great Britain arbitrated the alleged exploitation of the latter of fur seals in areas beyond national jurisdiction, whereas the more well-known arbitral award of the *Trail Smelter* case emerged from a dispute between the USA and Canada over the emission of polluting sulphur fumes from a Canadian smelter causing damage in the US state of Washington.

The UN Charter did not originally include any provision in relation to the environment or the conservation of natural resources. However, the 1947 *United Nations Conference on the Conservation and Utilisation of Resources* (UNCCUR) took place not long thereafter. In 1954, under the auspices of the International Maritime Organization (IMO), the first *International Convention for the Prevention of Pollution of the Sea by Oil* was adopted, and the 1971 *Ramsar Convention* became the first environmental treaty addressing the conservation of a particular ecosystem. The International Union for the Conservation of Nature and Natural Resources (IUCN) was established in 1948, under the auspices of UNESCO and the guidance of its first Director General, British biologist Julian Huxley. In 1970, in direct response to the Santa Barbara oil spill in California, the first Earth Day was celebrated on 22 April.

However, it is only with the 1972 *United Nations Conference on the Human Environment* (the 'Stockholm Conference') that environmental issues truly came to the fore at the international level. Emerging from the 'Biosphere Conference' organized by UNESCO in 1968, where it was expressly stated that '[u]ntil this point in history the nations of the world have lacked considered, comprehensive policies for managing the environment' (in Sand & Peel, 2012, 30), the Stockholm Conference was attended by 114 states and a large number of international organizations and non-governmental participants and observers. The outcomes of the Conference and of the ensuing *Declaration of the United Nations Conference on the Human Environment* (the 'Stockholm Declaration') were 109 'Recommendations' to define the framework for future actions on the part of the international community (which were accepted by general consensus), a set of general guiding 'Principles' and the establishment of a number of institutions to coordinate existing states and international entities (the 'Action Plan').[1] The Action Plan included the establishment of Earthwatch to monitor the environment via a Global Environmental Monitoring System (GEMS) and an International Referral System (subsequently named INFOTERRA). The most important institution that emerged from the Conference was the 193 member states-strong United Nations Environment Programme, the first international organization to be headquartered in the 'global south' (in Nairobi, Kenya). In calling for an increased international cooperation among states in developing environmental law, Principle 24 required the international community 'to effectively control, prevent, reduce and eliminate adverse environmental effects resulting from activities conducted in all spheres, in such a way that due account is taken of the sovereignty and interests of all states'. Principle 1 linked, for the first time, human rights and environmental protection, asserting all of humanity's 'fundamental right to freedom, equality and adequate conditions of life, in an environment of a quality that permits a life of dignity and well-being, and [humanity] bears a solemn responsibility to protect and improve the environment for present and future generations'. Additionally, the *Stockholm Conference* introduced the concept of 'environmental impact assessment', an 'established international and domestic legal technique for integrating environmental considerations into socio-economic development and decision-making processes' (Sand & Peel, 2012, 601). The explicit attempts to move beyond crude anthropocentrism entailed by the Stockholm Conference are undeniable.

Two important follow-ups to the Stockholm Conference were the 1982 *United Nations Convention on the law of the Sea* (UNCLOS) and the 1978 UNEP *Draft Principles on Shared National Resources*. In 1977, UNESCO published a Universal Declaration of Animal Rights, stating that wild animals have the rights to life, liberty and procreation in their natural environment. In 1982, ten years after the Stockholm Conference, the UN General Assembly adopted the *World Charter for Nature*, a much more explicitly ecological instrument (prepared by the IUCN) that emphasizes the protection of nature as an end in and of itself, establishing 'principles of conservation by which all human conduct affecting nature is to be guided and judged' (UNGA

[1] These four institutional arrangements were an intergovernmental Governing Council for Environmental Programmes, an Environmental Secretariat, an Environmental Fund (to provide financing for environmental programmes), and an interagency Environmental Co-ordinating Board to ensure cooperation among all the existing UN agencies.

Res 37/7). The World Charter for Nature (which is reproduced in full in Appendix 1) presented a protean version of the precautionary principle, demanding that 'actions causing "irreversible" damage be avoided; those posing "significant risk" not proceed until impacts were "fully understood"; that damaged areas be "restored"; and that non-renewable resources ... be developed compatibly with "the functioning of natural systems"'.

In 1981, UNEP established the Montevideo Programme for the Development and Periodic Review of Environmental Law (Montevideo Environmental Law Programme), now in its fifth iteration. This programme is a sequential ten-year intergovernmental programme dedicated to the development and periodic review of environmental law globally. The 1980 *World Conservation Strategy*, a collaboration of IUCN, UNEP, the United Nations Educational, Scientific and Cultural Organization (UNESCO), the Food and Agriculture Organization (FAO) and the Worldwide Fund for Nature (WWF), began to introduce the idea of 'sustainable development'. Its 1991 follow-up, which led to a document titled *Caring for the Earth: A Strategy for Sustainable Living*, solidified an international commitment to sustainable living. The idea of 'sustainability', however, was fully embraced by the 'Brundtland Report', the document (published in 1987) that followed the work conducted by the *World Commission on Environment and Development* (WCED), established by the UN General Assembly in 1983 and chaired by Norwegian Prime Minister Gro Harlem Brundtland. The Report made specific recommendations on a range of matters (population, food security, biodiversity loss and the loss of genetic resources, energy, industry and human settlements), acknowledging their deep and inextricable interconnectedness. Most importantly, the Report fully introduced the idea of 'sustainable development', defined as 'development that meets the needs of the present without compromising the ability for future generations to meet their own needs'. In the same year, the only Protocol to the 1985 *Vienna Convention*, the 1987 *Montreal Protocol* was introduced to protect the highly threatened ozone layer (the region of the Earth's stratosphere that absorbs most to the Sun's ultraviolet radiation), by phasing out the production of the substances that had been identified as responsible for ozone depletion. To this day, the *Montreal Protocol* arguably represents the most successful international effort to reign in environmentally harmful human activities, with ozone levels not only stabilizing in the mid-1990s but even beginning to recover in the 2000s.

The Brundtland report was a major catalyst for the 1992 *United Nations Conference on Environment and Development* (UNCED), also known as the 'Earth Summit' (or the 'Rio Summit' or 'Rio Conference') held in Rio de Janeiro in June 1992, twenty years after the Stockholm Declaration and a decade after the adoption of the *World Charter*. The *Rio Declaration* that followed 'represents a series of compromises between developed and developing countries and a balance between the objectives of environmental protection and economic development' (Sand & Peel, 2012, 42). Principle 1 of the Declaration still reflects a rather anthropocentric perspective, declaring that humanity is 'at the centre of concerns for sustainable development', and, while falling short of declaring a right to a clean and healthy environment, is nonetheless 'entitled to a healthy and productive life in harmony with nature'. The idea of harmony with nature will re-emerge almost two decades later, but, in the meantime, UNCED was followed, a decade later, by the *World Summit on Sustainable Development* held in Johannesburg in September 2002. Twenty years later, the *United Nations Conference on Sustainable Development* known as 'Rio + 20' took place once again in Rio and contributed significantly to the development of the 'Sustainable Development Goals' (which will be introduced shortly). The *International Conference for Sustainable and Inclusive Urban Development*, the 'Rio + 30 Cities' anniversary follow-up to the Earth Summit was then cancelled 'to prevent an event of this magnitude from interfering with [the 2022] electoral process', a clear and dire indictment on the state of environmental concerns in Brazil under the Bolsonaro government.

One of the most significant outcomes of the Earth Summit was the 'Agenda 21' (the number refers to the twenty-first century), a non-binding action plan in relation to sustainable development. Chapter 38 of Agenda 21 proposed the establishment of a UN Commission on Sustainable Development, as well as the central role of the UN General Assembly[2] and the Economic and Social Council (ECOSOC), and a further development of both UNEP (notably only a 'programme', rather than a specialized agency) and the United Nations Development Programme—UNDP, established in 1965 as the principal mode of providing technical and investment assistance to developing countries—recognizing the interplay between the conservation and management of resources for sustainable development and a host of social and economic dimensions related to combating poverty, particularly in developing countries. A second significant outcome of the Earth Summit was the adoption of the 1992 *Convention on Biological Diversity*, focused on the comprehensive conservation and sustainable use of biological diversity. The language of biological and genetic diversity as a 'resource' is further affirmed in the 2010 *Nagoya Protocol on Access to Genetic Resources and the Fair and Equitable Sharing of Benefits Arising from Their Utilization*, whose objective, under Article 1, is 'the fair and equitable sharing of the benefits arising from the utilization of genetic resources, including by appropriate access to genetic resources and by appropriate transfer of relevant

[2] As well as a host of specialized agencies, such as the Food and Agriculture Organization (FAO—established in 1945 to collect, analyse and disseminate information on nutrition, food and agriculture), the United Nations Educational, Scientific and Cultural Organization (UNESCO—established in 1945 to promote international collaboration through education, science and culture), the International Maritime Organization (IMO—established in 1948), the International Labour Organization (originally established in 1919), the World Meteorological Organization (WMO—established in 1947 to facilitate worldwide co-operation in meteorological observation and other hydrological and geophysical observations related to meteorology), and other agencies and organizations, such as the International Civil Aviation Organization (ICA), the United Nations Industrial Development Organization (UNIDO), the World Health Organization (WHO), the International Atomic Energy Agency (IAEA), the World Bank—comprising the International Bank for Reconstruction and Development (IBRD), the International Development Association (IDA) and the International Finance Corporation (IFC)—the International Monetary Fund (IMF), and the World Trade Organization (WTO). Regional organizations outside the United Nations, such as the European Union and the Organization for Economic Co-operation and development (OECD) also play a major role in the dialogue.

technologies … contributing to the conservation and sustainable use of biological diversity and the sustainable use of its components'.

The third significant outcome of the Earth Summit was the *United Nations Framework Convention on Climate Change* (UNFCCC), initially signed by 154 states (it now comprises 198 member states) to combat 'dangerous human interference with the climate system'. The UNFCCC holds yearly conferences (Conferences of the Parties—COP) to assess the international progress in dealing with climate change (since 2005, the COPs also serve as the formal Meetings of the Parties to the Kyoto Protocol—CMP—and since 2016 as the formal Meetings of the Parties to the Paris Agreement—CMA). The work of the UNFCCC is heavily informed by two international legal instruments. The first is the Joint Group of Experts on the Scientific Aspects of Marine Environmental Protection (GESAMP). The second is the highly influential Intergovernmental Panel on Climate Change (IPCC), a body established in 1988 by the World Meteorological Organization (WMO) and UNEP to advance knowledge on human-induced climate change. The IPCC (through its three working groups—on Physical Scientific Aspects, Impacts Vulnerability and Adaptation and Mitigation—and a task force on Greenhouse Gas Inventories) has since produced six Assessment Reports, which have significantly contributed not only to the UNFCCC, but also to both the Kyoto Protocol and the Paris Agreement. In 1997, the third Conference of the Parties adopted the *Kyoto Protocol to the Climate Change Convention*. The *Kyoto Protocol* committed state parties to the UNFCCC to reduce greenhouse gas emissions (acknowledging both that global warming is indeed occurring and that anthropogenic CO_2 emissions are its main contributors), according to Article 2, to 'a level that would prevent dangerous anthropogenic interference with the climate system'.[3] Notably, the *Kyoto Protocol* was based on the principle of common but differentiated responsibilities on the part of the states.

Some further progress was made at the COP 15 (the 15th Conference of the Parties) held in Copenhagen in 2009 in regard to the financing of climate mitigation and adaptation activities, including measures to reduce emissions from deforestation and forest degradation and the role of conservation, sustainable management of forests and enhancement of forest carbon stocks in developing countries (REDD +). It was in 2015, however, that significant international agreement was reached at COP 21, held in Paris. The Paris Agreement (*Accord de Paris*), often referred to as the Paris Accords or the Paris Climate Accords, which opened for signature on Earth Day 2016 in New York, introduced the clear goal of keeping the rise in mean global temperature to well below 2 °C above pre-industrial levels and preferably limit the increase to 1.5 °C. To significantly reduce the effects of climate change, the Accord decided, emissions should be reduced as soon as possible and reach net-zero by the middle of the twenty-first century, with a reduction of 50% by 2030 if there is any hope to stay below 1.5 °C of global warming.

[3] Annex A lists seven gases to which such reduction ought to apply: carbon dioxide (CO_2), methane (CH_4), nitrous oxide (N_2O), hydrofluorocarbons (HFCs), perfluorocarbons (PFCs), sulfur hexafluoride (SF_6), and nitrogen trifluoride (NF_3).

Following the UN Millennium Summit in 2000, the UN established the Millennium Development Goals, eight goals established for the year 2015. On that year, at the UN Sustainable Development Summit in 2015, and following the Post-2015 Development Agenda, which had been developed from 2012 to 2015 to define the future global development framework that would succeed the Millennium Development Goals, a new framework called Sustainable Development Goals was introduced. These goals, whose introduction officially launched the 2030 Agenda for Sustainable Development, are the following: no poverty, zero hunger, good health and well-being, quality education, gender equality, clean water and sanitation, affordable and clean energy, decent work and economic growth, industry, innovation and infrastructure, reduced inequality, sustainable cities and communities, responsible consumption and production, climate action, life below water, life on land, peace, justice and strong institutions and partnerships for the goals. In 2017, Oxford economist Kate Raworth combined the Sustainable Development Goals and the concept of Planetary Boundaries (discussed in chapter one) to create what she termed 'doughnut economics', the doughnut-shaped space between the two frameworks were humanity is neither in overshoot nor in shortfall, but rather thrives.

In 1990, the Sub-Commission on Prevention of Discrimination and Protection of Minorities of the UN Commission on Human Rights appointed a Special Rapporteur on Human Rights and the Environment. In 2009, the Plurinational State of Bolivia introduced a Resolution that, endorsed by over 50 member states and approved by the General Assembly, designated 22 April (Earth Day) as International Mother Earth Day. In his speech to the General Assembly, Bolivian President Evo Morales Ayma expressed the hope that, 'as the twentieth century had been called "the century of human rights", the 21st Century would be known as "the century of the rights of Mother Earth"' (in Cullinan, 2011 ed, 186). He also called upon the member states to begin developing a 'Declaration on the Rights of Mother Earth', which was then taken up by civil society a year later. In 2012, in participation with the United Nations Earth Summit of 2012, the Bolivian government submitted a proposal titled 'Harmony With Nature' to define a platform for sustainable development. The General Assembly, with resolution 73/235, established the Harmony with Nature Programme. Led by Maria Mercedes Sanchez, the programme organizes interactive yearly dialogues on harmony with nature issues to commemorate International Mother Earth Day every year. Additionally, the programme offers a yearly report to the UN Secretary-General, with a wide list (as comprehensive as possible) of all harmony with nature initiatives that have occurred throughout the year.

Among other initiatives, it is worth noting that, in 1990, the United Nations Development Programme (UNDP) introduced the 'Human Development Index' to measure human welfare and publishes annually a *Human Development Report*. At the same time, Wackernagel et al. (1999) had introduced the idea of the 'human ecological footprint' to measure the amount of land necessary to provide for a particular individual, community, nation or humanity as whole's way of life. Although not an international document, the 2006 Stern Review on the Economics of Climate Change was presented to the Government of the UK. The report (briefly mentioned in chapter one) is perhaps the most well-known report on the impact of climate change on the world economy, stating that (at the time of writing the report), inaction on climate change would equate to a perennial annual loss of 5% of the global GDP.

6.2.1 *International Environmental Legal Principles*

A number of principles have emerged from the international frameworks briefly introduced above. Many such principles are located along the spectrum previously identified. Some, like many of the Sustainable Development Goals, are representative of a (slightly) more enlightened anthropocentrism, whereby self-restraint is mandated by the need for long-term survival of humanity in its current civilizational form (and thus rejecting the absolute faith either in yet-to-be-developed technology or the invisible hand of the market). Others, like the Harmony with Nature programme, embody a far more ecocentric perspective. First among these principles is the idea of a human right to a healthy environment. Atapattu (2002) charts the emergence of a human right to a healthy environment, noting that the Stockholm Declaration already recognized the link between environmental protection and human rights. This right, however,

> cannot be conceived as implying or condoning indifference towards the non-human world since in requiring that the non-human environment should be preserved in the condition that is adequate for human health and wellbeing it implies – especially in a world as disrupted by anthropogenic environmental harms as this one is now – rather stringent demands of environmental protection. Moreover, part of its core rationale is to oppose the unbridled pursuit of those rights that do manifest the most "strongly" anthropocentric tendencies. (Haywood, 2005, 33)

At least 155 national governments have presently recognized that humans possess a right to a healthy environment (Knox & Pejan, 2018). More recently, a team of experts convened by the Sierra Club at the request of the Special Rapporteur on Human Rights and the Environment prepared a series of Draft Principles on Human Rights and the Environment, whereas the IUCN drafted a set of Draft Articles on Environment and Development in 1995. Another core principle of the international legal framework is comprised the rights of future generations, whose advocate argue that today's population 'owes a legal obligation to future generations who should therefore be granted standing in court' (Charlotte Unruh 2016).

Sand and Peel (2012, 187–237) list additional core principles of the international legal regime as the following:

- The responsibility not to cause damage to the environment of other states or to areas beyond national jurisdiction, set out in Principle 21 of the *Stockholm Declaration*, which provides that 'States have, in accordance with the Charter of the United Nations and the principles of international law, the sovereign right to exploit their own resources pursuant to their own environmental policies, and the responsibility to ensure that activities within their jurisdiction or control do not cause damage to the environment of other States or of areas beyond the limits of national jurisdiction'. Principle 2 of the *Rio Declaration* only added the words 'and developmental policies' after 'their own environmental'. It is important to note how this principle is strictly connected to the reaffirmation of the principle of exclusive state sovereignty.

- The related principle of cooperation and 'good-neighbourliness', enunciated in the Article 74 of the UN Charter.
- The principle of 'preventive action', the obligation to prevent damage to the environment, or at least 'to reduce, limit or control activities that might cause or risk such damage' (Sand & Peel, 2012, 200), as recognized by the arbitral tribunal in the *Iron Rhine* case.
- The principle of 'sustainable development' introduced by the Brundtland Report. In the report, sustainable development was defined as 'development which meets the needs of the present without sacrificing the ability of the future to meet its needs'. Daly (1977) calls for substituting the principle of a sustainable *development* with that of sustainable *evolution*: the latter represents the natural way in which all systems function, the former merely reflects the endless growth myth.
- The principle of guardianship of the Earth's resources for the benefit of future generations. The idea that 'as members of the present generation, we hold the earth in trust for future generations' (Brown Weiss, 1990, 199), originally introduced by the USA in the *Pacific Fur Seal* arbitration in 1893, has informed a large number of international documents (as exemplified by the above definition of 'sustainable development' in the Brundtland Report).
- The 'precautionary principle'. While this principle had appeared in domestic legal systems before (notably in West Germany), it was featured in international legal instruments only from the mid-1980s onward. Principle 15 of the *Rio Declaration* encapsulates it as follows: '[w]here there are threats of serious or irreversible damage, lack of full scientific certainty shall not be used as a reason for postponing cost-effective measures to prevent environmental degradation'. Atus Mariqueo-Russell proposes that, white there is no single definitive articulation of the precautionary principle, 'when we encounter uncertain yet plausible threats of severe harm to the environment or public health, scientific uncertainty *should not be used as a reason for failure* to take protective or preventative action. Rather, *uncertainty about the potential of harm should be a reason for implementing* regulation'. In other words, the precautionary principle should transfer the burden of proof: 'instead of one party having to prove that an action of another is potentially harmful, the burden is on those who wish to pursue the allegedly harmful action to demonstrate sufficient evidence of safety' (2017, 21–30).
- The 'polluter pays principle', according to which 'the costs of pollution should be borne by the person responsible for causing the pollution' (Sand & Peel, 2012, 228), and the principle of 'common but differentiated responsibility', contained in Principle 7 of the *Rio Declaration*, according to which 'States shall co-operate in a spirit of global partnership to conserve, protect and restore the health and integrity of the Earth's ecosystem', albeit noting that '[i]n view of the different contributions to global environmental degradation, states have common but differentiated responsibilities.'

The concept of 'ecosystem services', defined as 'the conditions and processes through which natural ecosystems, and the species that make them up, sustain and fulfil human life', is derived by the work of economists like Robert Costanza. The ensuing economic calculus which establishes the monetary value of these 'services' is heavily criticized for its strong anthropocentric connotations.[4] Finally, as a result of many of the above principles, 'environmental considerations are increasingly addressed in regulatory and voluntary schemes designed to identify the environmental effects of the activities of companies or industrial sites' (Sand & Peel, 2012, 659). These take the form of 'eco-labelling', the practice of labelling the environmental impact of good and services, and of environmental auditing, or 'eco-auditing', and accounting, the techniques that allow 'a company or a state to assess the impact of its activities on the environment, which includes procedures beyond the scope of a traditional financial audit that can be performed by an internal consultant or by an independent third person' (659).

6.3 The Rights of Nature

While domestic and international environmental law and principles appear to be located still within a rather anthropocentric worldview (or, at least, closer to the anthropocentric end of the theoretical spectrum identified in the previous chapter), the attribution of rights to Nature (often abbreviated as RoN by their advocates) is the most notable instance of articulating more ecocentric proposals. Well before the establishment of the first RoN initiatives in the twenty-first century, Nash had already pointed out that the use of the term 'rights' was bound to create 'considerable confusion. Suffice it to say for now', he proceeded to clarify, 'that while some use the term in a technical philosophical or legal sense, others take it to mean that nature, or parts of it, has intrinsic worth which humans ought to respect' (1989, 4). I will return more specifically to the issue of rights in the next chapter, and for the time being I will adopt Nash's provisional clarification.

In *Noah's Second Voyage: The Rights of Nature as Law*, Oliver Houck (2017) provides a comprehensive history of Nature's rights, noting that, historically, rights were first extended to individual nonhuman creatures. Similarly, Kresten (2017) offers an articulated list of the possible reasons for extending rights to nature.

- Firstly, nature can be construed as possessing no legal status of its own, but is protected indirectly by the subjective rights of humans. He defines this indirect protection a '"legal reflex": human subjects have rights to life, to physical integrity and to property. If nature is polluted or destroyed in a way that would affect one

[4] The most important of these services are: purification of air and water, water absorption and storage, mitigation of droughts and floods, decomposition and detoxification, sequestering of wastes, reparation and build-up of soil structure, pollination, pest control, seed and nutrient dispersal, provision of a wide variety of agricultural, medical and industrial products, evolution and maintenance of the biotic gene pool, aesthetic, intellectual and spiritual uplift.

of these rights, the affected human subjects have the right to be protected—and nature is protected indirectly by this legal mechanism, too' (10).

- Secondly, nature can be seen as the common heritage of humanity. This concept, derived from international law and first developed with respect to the ocean floor and the Antarctic, leads to the establishment of international institutions for the protection of nature and the governance of knowledge. The difficulties with this concept, Kresten notes, are that, as a concept, it is often 'limited to charismatic parts of nature and it does not protect nature or its resources from being exploited' (11).
- Thirdly, nature can be protected as a result of constitutional provisions aimed to protect the environment (what was described above as environmental constitutionalism).
- Fourthly, nature can obtain a degree of legal status as a result of a human right to a healthy environment.
- Finally, Nature (Kresten capitalizes the term in this fifth instance), is granted independent legal status as a legal subject and person.

6.3.1 Animal Rights and the Rights of Species

In limited circumstances, rights have been historically extended to some nonhuman animals and species. The animal welfare movement focused on granting five fundamental freedoms for animals: from hunger, thirst and malnutrition; from fear and distress; from physical discomfort; from pain, injury and disease; and to express normal patterns of behaviour. The animal rights movement, on the other hand, focused on granting basic rights to individual animals. Both movements saw, Boyd points out (2017), an exponential increase in the twentieth century. The idea emerged from the extension of rights to nonhuman physical entities, in particular the 1925 Indian case of *Mullick v Mullick*, whereby counsel was appointed for an idol (the custody of which was contested in a family dispute) on retrial. In two early-twentieth century Californian cases (*People v Fimbres* and *Ex parte Ackerman*), the issue arose as to the idea of a dog having 'rights' (an idea that was summarily dismissed by the courts).

However, the discussion of extending rights beyond the confines of the human world did not meaningfully advance any further until after Stone's article and *Sierra Club v Morton*. After a number of lawsuits were filed, generally unsuccessfully, in US federal circuit courts, the first case in which a nonhuman became a plaintiff in Court is the 1979 US *Palila* case (*Palila v Hawaii Department of Land and Natural Resources*). In this instance, the Sierra Club Legal Defense Fund and the Hawaiian Audubon Society entered a suit (and won) on behalf of a few hundred's remaining palila birds and stopped the grazing of cattle, sheep and goats in the bird's endangered habitat. Twenty years later, the 1998 *Loggerhead Turtle* case (*Loggerhead Turtle v County Council of Volusia County*) is perhaps the most successful case where a court permitted to add the Leatherback Sea Turtle as a party to the case. In the immediately subsequent 1999 *Coho* case (*Coho Salmon v Pacific Lumber Company*) and in the

2004 *Cetacean Community* case (*Cetacean Cmty.v Bush*) the court allowed standing for nonhumans but 'based it expressly on the claims of the human co-plaintiffs'. In 1991, Steven Wise filed a lawsuit on behalf of Kama, a six-year-old dolphin, against the New England Aquarium, but the court ruled that the dolphin didn't have standing. More recently, in 2013, Wise filed habeas corpus lawsuits on behalf of four chimpanzees held in captivity in the state of New York. While unsuccessful, these lawsuits elicited sympathetic responses from a number of the judges who made the decisions. Two years prior, the People for the Ethical Treatment of Animals (PETA) had filed a lawsuit on behalf of five orcas against SeaWorld in Orlando and San Diego, arguing that SeaWorld was in violation of the US Constitution thirteenth amendment prohibiting slavery. While the lawsuit was certainly provocative, Judge Jeffrey Miller of the US District Court for Southern California interpreted the thirteenth amendment as applicable exclusively to humans. A more important case was the one decided in Argentina in late 2016 on behalf of a chimpanzee named Cecilia, for whom the lawyers from the Argentinian Association of Professional Lawyers for Animal Rights (AFADA) filed a habeas corpus case to have her transferred from the small concrete enclosure in which she was kept at the Mendoza Zoo to the Sorocaba chimpanzee sanctuary in Brazil. Judge María Alejandra Mauricio, citing both the Argentinian Constitution and the Universal Declaration of Animal Rights, ordered the release of Cecilia. The Judge remarked that, '[g]iven that neither provincial regulation nor national law contemplate a process for evaluating the condition of caged animals, I consider that a petition of habeas corpus is appropriate for an animal deprived of their essential rights' (Tercer Juzgado de Garantias, case no. P-72.254/15, 44). In 2018, New York Court of Appeals Judge Eugene Fahey stated, in *Nonhuman Rights Project v Lavery*, that '[w]hile it may be arguable that a chimpanzee is not a "person", there is no doubt that it is not merely a thing', and as such should have 'the right to liberty protected by habeas corpus'.

While individual animal rights cases certainly grab the media attention, the extension of rights to entire species has possibly had more significant legal implications. In 1973, Professor Zygmunt Plater began what was then to become known as the *Snail darter* controversy (*Tennessee Valley Authority v Hill*). The case entailed the application of the recently released US *Endangered Species Act* to the discovery, in 1973, of an endangered species of snail that was threatened by the construction of the Tellico Dam on the Little Tennessee River, a project that had been authorized and had begun before the passage of the Act. The US Supreme Court stated that 'the plain intent of Congress in enacting [the Act] was to halt and reverse the trend toward species extinction, whatever the cost', asserting that the legislation under review 'indicate[d] beyond doubt that Congress intended endangered species to be afforded the highest of priorities', and thus stopped the project (which was, unfortunately, then completed through a series of legislative circumventions of the Act).

In addition to the US *Endangered Species Act* and the 1973 *Conventions on International Trade in Endangered Species of Wild Flora and Fauna* (CITES), there has been a rise in the idea of the intrinsic value of species (as already introduced in the World Charter, the Earth Charter and the Convention on Biodiversity). The Indian Constitution, for example, imposes a 'fundamental duty' on all citizens to 'protect and improve the natural environment … and to have compassion for all living creatures'. Intrinsic value of species has been incorporated in laws in Costa Rica, Canada, Bangladesh, Japan, Tanzania, New Zealand and the European Union. Costa Rica's 1998 *Biodiversity Law* is the first to promote 'respect for all forms of life', stating that '[a]ll living things have the right to live, independently of actual, or potential economic value'. Section 6.2 of Canada's *Northwest Territories' Wildlife Act* of 2013 states that '[w]ildlife is to be conserved for its intrinsic value and for the benefit of present and future generations', while Israel's 2010 *National Biodiversity Plan* asserts that 'it is incumbent upon humankind to respect and protect biodiversity, also (or even mostly) due to its intrinsic and existence value' (Boyd, 2017, 88).

While the extension of rights to individual animals represents a clear attempt to transcend the anthropocentric confines of Western jurisprudence—which has traditionally seen rights as vested in human beings and their artificial constructs—it is with the articulation of rights of entire *species* that a more ecocentric approach enters the scene. Such an approach is fully realized by the many (and diverse) RoN initiatives that have emerged over the past two decades.

6.3.2 Rights of Nature and Legal Personhood for Nature

While animal rights and the rights of species have emerged somewhat separately in distinct jurisdictions, the development of rights for all of nature presents a more cohesive international picture, with many initiatives linked across different jurisdictions and legal traditions. The discussion below, it is important to not, is not (and cannot be) a comprehensive review of all cases. Since this is impossible, given the sheer number of initiatives, this section will only identify the paradigmatic ones and chart the relevant milestones in the emergence of RoN to date.

The reader may have noticed that, throughout the entirety of the preceding chapters, the term 'nature' was at times written in lower case, and times was capitalized. From this point onward, I will capitalize the term Nature, in line with the common practice among rights of Nature advocates and with the Harmony with Nature programme. The choice reflects the recognition of Nature as an ontological, even before becoming a legal, subject (albeit construed in different ways in different circumstances). This choice does not exhaust the reflection of that 'Nature' *is*, however, and I will return to the contested *idea* of Nature in the next two chapters.

Co-founder and CEO of the Pachamama Alliance, Bill Twist, in 2010, at the initial gathering of the Global Alliance for the Rights of Nature held at the feet of the Tungurahua volcano in Ecuador, quoted Victor Hugo, saying that 'nothing … is so powerful as an idea whose time has come'. He later explained, in a personal interview with me in 2019, that, while the idea was on the verge of becoming in 2010, there was no doubt that its time had come a decade later. Twist's words have certainly been confirmed by the rapid growth in number and jurisdictional spread of RoN initiatives around the globe. Initial attempts to map the emergence RoN initiatives were provided by Linda Sheehan and later by Kauffman (2020). The

Harmony with Nature reports list rights of Nature initiatives among all the various Harmony with Nature initiatives, and, in 2020, the list was amplified into a full supplement that catalogued 170 cases of Earth Jurisprudence initiatives. In 2022, Alex Putzer and others provided a first comprehensive map of RoN initiatives together with an analysis of the data collected. The authors identified 409 initiatives related to 430 documents (the discrepancy being comprised of 'failed attempts'). Ninety % of the initiatives they identified were from 39 countries spread across all continents, with 10% transcending national boundaries. Thirty-eight % of these initiatives were local regulations, particularly because of countries like the USA and Brazil, where close to three-quarters of all initiatives (74.8% and 70%, respectively) are local. Ecuador and Colombia presented a majority of court decisions (respectively, 79% and 88.9%). Eighty % of country initiatives the authors identified were clustered in the American continents, predominantly in the USA, making it the country with the highest number of initiatives (although, due to their local nature, not necessarily the most impactful in terms of outcomes). All texts identified were written in 10 different language, with 91.0% written in either English or Spanish.

Kauffmann and Martin (2021) provided the first large comparative analysis of RoN provisions in 2021. In it, they identify two distinct models of construing RoN provisions. The first, which they define as the 'Nature's rights' model, is found in Bolivia, Ecuador and the USA. In this model, they propose,

> rights-bearing Nature is defined extremely broadly: all of Nature (within the legal jurisdiction) is recognized as having rights. Most important, these laws recognize unique substantive rights, including the right to exist, to maintain the functioning of ecosystem cycles, and to be restored when damaged, among others. Procedurally, these laws empower any person to speak for Nature, but doing so is voluntary; no person is obligated to so speak. Consequently, the model tends to address RoN reactively, with people seeking to defend Nature's rights in court when violations are imminent or have occurred (18).

The second model they identify is what they call the 'legal personhood' model, illustrated by legal provisions in Colombia, India and New Zealand. In this model, rather than recognizing rights for all of Nature, particular ecosystems are recognized as legal persons. In many of the initial cases they examined, there is no recognition of unique substantive rights for ecosystems, and instead general personhood rights are extended to them. Moreover, in many instances, legal personhood granted ecosystems the same rights and liabilities held by all other legal persons. Specific guardians—often embedded in new governance institutions charged with managing an ecosystem in a way that ensures its health and well-being—are generally appointed to speak on behalf of an ecosystem (and are, in fact, obliged to do so). Naturally, there is nothing inherently *necessary* about this particular construction of personhood, as many advocates have pointed out. I will return to the issue of personhood in the next chapter.

Kauffmann and Martin also highlight that explicit diffusion mechanisms are evident in more recent RoN laws (in Bangladesh, Brazil, Colombia, India, Mexico and Uganda), while they were absent in the world's earliest RoN laws (in Ecuador, New Zealand and the USA). They explain the simultaneous emergence of 'normatively similar but structurally distinct' RoN laws by reference to convergent evolution theory in evolutionary biology, 'as well as research on norm construction and pragmatist theories of institution building' (19–20). Convergent evolution theory suggests the independent development of features that are functionally similar because they evolve in response to similar functional needs, but the features look different because the evolution takes place in different contexts. In a similar fashion, they argue, functionally similar RoN laws (their similarity determined by their embodiment of common underlying principles of Earth Jurisprudence) emerged independently in response to common environmental pressures.

Finally, at the time of their writing, they identified 1,189 individuals and organizations that either self-identified as RoN advocates or were identified by advocates as partners in projects to advance RoN. They further identified major organizations (and, in some more limited cases, specific individuals) as 'network nodes'. While few government agencies are active nodes, 'a handful of governments have played an important role in inserting RoN into global policy debates regarding sustainable development' (43). The overall network, Kauffmann and Martin conclude, is quite large, although most nodes are only connected to one or a few other nodes in the network. On average, the shortest path between two nodes in the network involves three to four degrees of separation. The network structure showed that over a decade 'a sizable number (more than one hundred) RoN-focused organizations have formed a dense and cohesive transnational network dedicated to promoting RoN legal provisions globally' (50). By far the most central node is that of the Global Alliance for the Rights of Nature (GARN), with the greatest number of direct ties of any node in the network, and with the second most central node in the global RoN network being the UN Harmony with Nature Programme, 'one of the most truly global hubs in the network' (50). The third most central node in the network is, notwithstanding its primarily domestic focus, the US Community and Environment Legal Defense Fund (CELDF).

The most advanced map to date of RoN provisions is the Ecological Jurisprudence (or Eco-Jurisprudence) Tracker, the central component of the Ecological Jurisprudence (or Eco-Jurisprudence) Monitor, an initiative of the Academic Hub of the Global Alliance for the Rights of Nature launched in late 2022. The Tracker adopts a narrower definition of ecological jurisprudence than the one defined in this book. The choice is deliberate and strategic, rather than theoretical, and it stems from the desire to meaningfully identify and code all existing initiatives (within the boundaries of its definition) worldwide, with the view to expand the scope of the Tracker at a later stage. For the purpose of the initial mapping, the Tracker identified initiatives that are defined by 'ecocentrism' (i.e. initiatives that recognize and respect the value of all beings and the interconnectedness among them, equitably promoting the interests of human and nonhuman members of the Earth community) and 'ecological primacy' (initiatives ensuring that social and economic behaviour and systems are ecologically bound, respecting planetary boundaries and the limits of ecosystems' carrying capacity). Moreover, many initiatives also pursue 'ecological justice', by ensuring equitable access to the Earth's sustaining capacity for present and future generations of humans and other beings, and avoid the inequitable allocation of environmental harms. Examples of the theoretical framing within which the initiatives are located (either directly or indirectly) are rights of Nature, legal personhood for Nature, ecocide, ecosystems as sacred natural sites, ecosystems as living spiritual beings, Earth trusteeship, extinction crisis, Earth democracy, ecological civilization, ecological governance and planetary boundaries. The Tracker's codebook explicitly includes in the current dataset all the following initiatives:

- Those recognizing rights of nature.
- Those recognizing rights of animals.
- Those recognizing ecocide as a crime.
- Those recognizing the rights of future generations to healthy functioning ecosystems.
- Those applying Indigenous traditional ecological knowledge.
- Those emphasizing ecological sustainability, intended as the need (and responsibility) to maintain the functioning of ecological systems and preventing actions that threaten their ability to function. These initiatives tend to frame Nature as a community of life and emphasize ecological science, the need to live within ecosystem and planetary boundaries, the responsibility of individuals and, or, states to ensure the functioning of ecological systems, and the importance of social justice. These are often referred to using terms such as 'ecological civilization', 'Earth democracy', and 'ecological governance', among others.

The Tracker explicitly excludes, at this stage, any initiative involving the public trust doctrine but no other element of ecological law, any involving payment for ecosystem services and other market systems that commodify nature, as well as more generic environmental law provisions. Furthermore, the Tracker focused on actual initiatives as its unit of analysis, including formal law provisions as well as citizen tribunals and civil society soft law. It does not include general statements in support of ecological law, conferences, publications, or statements of recognition or support of ecological jurisprudence in political party platforms. Among the initiatives coded are international documents, Constitutions, Indigenous and Tribal Constitutions and legislation, statutes and direct legislative documents, local and delegated legislative initiatives, policies and regulations, government and other official statements, declarations and resolutions, cases, citizen tribunals and soft law (i.e. documents that are adopted or endorsed by a collective of civil society organizations). These initiatives can be drafted, submitted, approved (or passed, decided, signed), stayed, on appeal, rejected, overturned or repealed. At its launch in 2022, the Tracker was able to identify a total of 430 initiatives across 42 countries plus the international level. Of these, 302 were, at the time, approved, 57 rejected, 53 drafted or submitted, 15 overturned and 3 on appeal. Twist's assertion was certainly vindicated. The exponential growth in just over a decade from a single piece of legislation in 2006 suggests that the time for this idea has certainly arrived.

6.3.2.1 First Initiatives and US Ordnances

As Marsha Moutrie writes, the '[l]egal recognition of Nature's rights began about fifteen years ago in the mountainous woodlands of Pennsylvania's Southern Coal Region, in Tamaqua, a community of about 7000 residents. Raw sewage, being dumped into an abandoned open-pit mine within the borough limits, threatened the drinking water supply' (2020, 6). On the 19th of September 2006, the Tamaqua Borough of Schuylkill County passed the Tamaqua Borough Sewage Sludge Ordinance, 'an Ordinance to protect the health, safety and general welfare of the citizens and environment of Tamaqua Borough by banning corporations from engaging in the land application of sewage sludge; ... by removing constitutional powers from corporations within the Borough; [and] by recognizing and enforcing the rights of residents to defend natural communities and ecosystems' (in Boyd, 2017, 113). The borough or any of its residents may file a lawsuit on behalf of a local ecosystem to recover compensatory and punitive damages for any harm done by sewage sludge. Damages recovered in this way must be paid to the borough and must be used to restore those ecosystems and natural communities. The ordinance was prepared with the assistance of the Community Environmental Legal Defense Fund (CELDF). Although not directly inspired by Berry's or Cullinan's writing, Mari Margil writes that there is a clear move from the '*idea* of Rights of Nature to the *codification* of those rights ... In Tamaqua, for the first time, we see a move from *discussion* to *practical application*' (2014, 153). Chris Morrison, mayor of Tamaqua Borough at the time of the ordinance's adoption, stated: 'If you are taking away my clean soil or my clean drinking water or my clean air to breathe, you're actually just taking my civil right away. By damaging the ecosystem, you're damaging me' (in Margil, 2014, 153).

For many, this represents the first instance of recognition of rights of Nature in any legal document. This is, however, slightly incorrect. In 2003, three years before the Tamaqua ordinance, the Navajo Tribal Council had amended the Navajo Nation Code to recognize certain 'fundamental laws', including the rights of Nature. The code declared 'all creation, from Mother Earth and Father Sky to the animals, those who live in the water, those who fly and plant life have their own laws, and rights and freedom to exist' (in Moutrie, 2020, 40). The first recorded case of rights of Nature instantiated in law is thus located within US tribal legislation, an important point I will return to later in this and in subsequent chapters.

The impact of the Tamaqua Borough ordinance extended well beyond its municipal confines, thus triggering a subsequent cascade of similar initiatives. The move to extend rights to local ecosystems via local ordinances was soon followed by many other municipalities across the USA. In Grant Township, a small rural community located 130 kms west of Pittsburgh, the community enacted, in 2014, a community bill of rights guaranteeing the people of the township the right to clean air, clean water and a sustainable energy future, by recognizing the rights of natural communities and ecosystems (including, among others, rivers, streams and aquifers). This led, in 2014, to a burgeoning legal battle between the township and a company called Pennsylvania General Energy (PGE), which had obtained a permit to convert an existing oil and gas well into a wastewater injection well. The lawyers for PGE used derogatory language toward the community bill of rights, noting that standing for a watershed ought to be considered ludicrous given its nature as a fiction lacking consciousness, intelligence and cognition (abysmally failing to note that the same lack of characteristics apply to a corporation such as PGE and is not necessary to grant it legal personhood, as will be discussed in the following chapter). As David Boyd notes, '[]it is remarkable that PGE's lawyers could describe watersheds as "artificial constructs" while simultaneously believing that corporations are real persons to whom rights naturally belong' (2017, 119). Grant Township and PGE settled the dispute before trial, 'agreeing that PGE would dismiss with prejudice its remaining claims and request for damages in exchange for the township's token payment of $1.00 in damages on the constitutional claims which had been decided in PGR's favour on summary judgment' (Moutrie, 2020, 26–7).

In March 2006, Barnstead, in New Hampshire, became the first community in the USA to ban corporations from privatizing their water and one of the very first to recognize RoN. Section 5.1 of the Barnstead law dictates that '[n]atural communities and ecosystems possess inalienable and fundamental rights to exist and flourish within the Town of Barnstead. Ecosystems shall include, but not be limited to, wetlands, streams, rivers, aquifers, and other water systems' (Margil, 2021). Neighbouring Nottingham passed the Nottingham Water Right and Local Self-government Ordinance to prevent USA Springs to take over one million litres per day from the local aquifer for bottled water destined to be shipped overseas. Since 2007, multiple communities have passed local laws that codify Nature's rights. Among them are Pittsburgh (Pennsylvania), Santa Monica (California), Mora County (New Mexico), Athens and Broadview Height (Ohio), Mountain Lake Park (Maryland). Pittsburgh became, in 2010, the first large city to ban fracking. Two Vermont municipalities have adopted resolutions urging the state legislature to amend the Vermont Constitution to include the rights of Nature. In 2012, the Santa Monica City Council adopted the *Sustainability Rights Ordinance*, which recognizes the 'fundamental and inalienable rights' of 'natural communities and ecosystems' in the City to 'exist and flourish'. The resolution is deeply inscribed in the rise of Nature's ecocentric legislation:

> our legal system classifies the natural world as human property, which may be used by its human owners for their own, private economic benefit, generally with minimal regard to the health of the environment … worldwide, national and local environmental communities are urging governments to adopt a new paradigm based upon recognition that people have fundamental environmental rights, as do natural communities and ecosystems, that the health of the world's populations and ecosystems depend on the full protection of these rights, and that asserted corporate rights cannot take precedence over these rights to human and environmental health and well-being … the City of Santa Monica supports local recognition of the fundamental rights of natural communities and ecosystems to exists, thrive and evolve, and supports effectuating these rights by modifying local law and policy as needed to better protect and sustain, for future generations, the natural environment upon which we all depend. (Santa Monica Municipal Code Art 12 Ch 12.02–03)

The first implementation of the Resolution occurred in August 2018, when the City Council adopted the *Santa Monica Sustainable Groundwater Management Ordinance*, which addresses the local aquifer (the city's main water supply) and its inherent rights, banning the construction of new, private water wells. Santa Monica is a small dense city surrounded by the megalopolis of Los Angeles, and yet, Moutrie writes, '[d]espite its urban character, the city is strongly connected to Nature by its location, with the downtown situated atop bluffs overlooking the beaches of Santa Monica Bay, which sweep in a crescent connecting the Santa Monica Mountains to the north with the headlands of the Palos Verdes Peninsula to the south' (2020, 45-6). Importantly, in this instance the ordinance 'does not address any specific environmental threat; nor does it seek to diminish or strip away corporate rights. Instead, it expresses an environmental ethic that serves as the philosophical foundation for the City's environmental laws, policies and programs' (48-9).

In 2013, Mora County, which encompasses almost 2000 square miles of New Mexico's western landscape, passed the *Mora County Community Water Rights and Local Self-Government Ordinance* (Ordinance 2013-01) to stop corporate oil and gas drilling operations. The ordinance expressed in particularly poetic terms the community's 'strong emotional bond with Nature and recognition of human responsibilities to Nature:' the ordinance's preamble asserts that 'We, the residents in Mora County, are a multicultural community with indigenous roots of Many, and. … recognize the Earth, water, and air as a source of life for all living in Mora County' (in Moutrie, 2020, 16). In 2017, an unsuccessful lawsuit was brought on behalf of the Colorado River Ecosystem against the State of Colorado for violating its constitutional rights. Matthew Miller (2019) notes that the lawsuit's advocates were seeking to establish in US Federal courts, albeit unsuccessfully, two of the fundamental doctrines of the rights of Nature movement: environmental personhood and standing for Nature. In 2018, the small subalpine town of Crestone in Colorado, long a spiritual refuge home to twenty-three religious and spiritual centres, formally recognized Nature as a unitary, living entity with rights:

> Whereas, an abiding reverence for nature defines and unites the Town of Crestone, whose residents share a deep spiritual connection to the natural world around them (...) the Sangre de Cristo Wilderness, the high alpine desert valley, the old growth cedar and pinon forests, the abundant wildlife, and the life-sustaining waters of the North Crestone Creek; and
>
> Whereas, Town residents have long understood that humans are part of and dependent upon the natural world, which provides the necessities of life – air, water, food and home – and also nourishes the human spirits, thereby enabling humans not merely to exist, but also to flourish; and
>
> Whereas, special recognition of the primacy of this relationship exists in the region long before the Town of Crestone was founded, when Native American Tribes considered the area to be sacred land and journeyed here for rites of passage, seeking insight and rejuvenation; and
>
> Whereas, today, as in the past, visitors and residents alike receive nourishment, inner peace and spiritual renewal from the religious pristine sacred land, and Town residents reciprocate these gifts by serving as stewards of the natural environment; and
>
> Whereas, the understanding that humans must protect the natural world, though felt with particular intensity in Crestone, is widespread in society, as is demonstrated by the existence of both state and federal laws protecting in environment in general and clean, plentiful water in particular; and

> Whereas, the Board of Trustees therefore wishes to join the growing number of communities, cities and nations around the world that have recognized nature's rights,
>
> Now, therefore, be it resolved (...) that consistent with this widespread understanding and in furtherance of Crestone's particular commitment to environmental stewardship, the Town of Crestone does officially recognize that nature, natural ecosystems, communities, and all species possess the intrinsic and inalienable rights which must be effectuated to protect life on Earth. (Resolution 005–2018, 9 August 2018)

In early 2019, the citizen of Toledo, Ohio (in the USA) voted to amend the city's charter to establish the *Lake Erie Bill of Rights* (LEBOR) and grant the Lake Erie ecosystem the legally enforceable 'right to exist, flourish and naturally evolve'. A complaint was filed by a local farm partnership, claiming that the LEBOR's enactment exceeded the city's authority, and State Governor Mike DeWine only five months later signed a provision into law expressly stating that 'Nature or any ecosystem does not have standing to participate in or bring an action in any court of common pleas' (2020–2021 Fiscal Year Budget H.B. 166). This led some authors to ask whether legal personhood for Nature was to be considered 'dead in the water' (Berman, 2019, 15). Others, however, argued that the case managed to bring RoN to the attention of the public awareness in the USA.

Virtually all US RoN initiatives to date (2024) are drafted in the form of municipal ordinances (which are subordinate to state and federal laws) and home rule charters. Tribal initiatives, which will be discussed below, operate differently. Although these local provisions vary widely, Moutrie (2020, 8–9) identifies the following characteristics as common among them. They generally:

- Recognize the peoples' right to local, self-government.
- Prohibit or target corporate activities that threaten the local environment.
- Diminish or nullify legal rights of corporate violators.
- Elevate local authority to control use of the local environment over state and federal authority.
- Recognize that natural communities and ecosystems have legal rights to, e.g. exist, flourish and naturally evolve.
- Confer legal 'personhood' (and thus the ability to sue) upon elements of Nature.

One immediately apparent problem of these local initiatives is that they can be easily overruled by State legislation. Another problem is their focus on countering the negative influence of corporate rights on local ecosystems. In emphasizing the ultimate freedom of the local community to determine its own legislative destiny, this focus runs the risk of potentially destructive environmental outcomes—indeed, what if the local community *wants* to frack and pollute its own waterways?

6.3.2.2 The 2008 Ecuadorian Constitution

In 2008, the Constitutional Assembly of Ecuador met in Montecristi and passed the new Constitution of Ecuador, which became the first Constitutional document ever to recognize the rights of Nature. Due to its particularly authoritative nature (far greater than that of the US local ordinances), the document also marked the symbolic beginning of the rights of Nature shift from an *idea* to actually legislated *reality*. In 2008, the newly elected President Rafael Correa appointed Alberto Acosta to lead the drafting of the new Constitution. Acosta had just authored the Yasuní-ITT proposal, where Ecuador had promised to permanently refrain from exploiting the Ishpingo-Tambococha-Tiputini (ITT) oilfield beneath the Yasuní National Park if the global community donated half of the oil's value to Ecuador. The Constitutional drafting process was a highly democratic one, with more than 3000 proposals submitted and reviewed by the Constitutional Assembly. Assisted by the Fundación Pachamama and, through it, by CELDF, Acosta and Uruguayan writer Eduardo Galeano identified the possibility for Ecuador to become the first country to inscribe rights of Nature in a Constitution. Among the main proponents of including rights of Nature were the Ecuadorian Indigenous peoples, united under the Confederation of Indigenous Nationalities of Ecuador (CONAIE), a body created in 1980 and that had since evolved into a powerful political force. The result was the new Constitution of Ecuador, and its momentous recognition of the rights of Nature, or Pachamama. The Constitution's preamble refers to the intention of the people of Ecuador 'to build a new order of cohabitation for citizens, in its diversity and in harmony with nature, to achieve well being [which is defined both by the Spanish term "el buen vivir" and the Indigenous Quichwa term "sumaqkawsay"]'. Three Constitutional articles fully articulate the rights of Nature:

Chapter Seven

Rights of Nature

Article 71. Nature, or Pacha Mama, where life is reproduced and occurs, has the right to integral respect for its existence and for the maintenance and regeneration of its life cycles, structure, functions and evolutionary processes.

All persons, communities, peoples and nations can call upon public authorities to enforce the rights of nature. To enforce and interpret these rights, the principles set forth in the Constitution shall be observed, as appropriate.

The State shall give incentives to natural persons and legal entities and to communities to protect nature and to promote respect for all the elements comprising an ecosystem.

Article 72. Nature has the right to be restored. This restoration shall be apart from the obligation of the State and natural persons or legal entities to compensate individuals and communities that depend on affected natural systems.

In those cases of severe or permanent environmental impact, including those caused by the exploitation of nonrenewable natural resources, the State shall establish the most effective mechanisms to achieve the restoration and shall adopt adequate measures to eliminate or mitigate harmful environmental consequences.

Article 73. The State shall apply preventive and restrictive measures on activities that might lead to the extinction of species, the destruction of ecosystems and the permanent alteration of natural cycles.

The introduction of organisms and organic and inorganic material that might definitively alter the nation's genetic assets is forbidden.

Article 74. Persons, communities, peoples, and nations shall have the right to benefit from the environment and the natural wealth enabling them to enjoy the good way of living.

Environmental services shall not be subject to appropriation; their production, delivery, use and development shall be regulated by the State.

6.3.2.3 Ecuadorian Court Cases

In 2011, an appeal for an *acción de tutela* (an 'action for protection'), filed by Eleanor (Norie) Huddle and Richard Wheeler on behalf of the Vilcabamba River in Ecuador, led to the first successful rights of Nature case in the world (*Wheeler* et al. *v Director de la Procuraduria General del Estado en Loja*), now known as the *Vilcabamba* case. The provincial government of Loja, one of Ecuador's southernmost provinces near the Peruvian border, underwent the widening of the Vilcabamba-Quinare road without a prior environmental impact study. The construction debris dumped in the Vilcabamba river altered the river's path and caused an increase in its flow, in turn leading to an upsurge in flooding, with consequent damages both to local ecosystems and to local landowners' properties. In 2010, two of those landowners, Huddle and Wheeler, sued the provincial government of Loja. However, rather than suing for damages caused to their property, the plaintiffs invoked constitutional rights of Nature and sued on behalf of the river. While the judge dismissed the action on the ground that the river lacked standing, on appeal, the Loja Provincial Court of Justice ruled in favour of Nature in this case instantiated in the Vilcabamba River. Although a relatively short and protean judgement, its symbolic impact is certainly undeniable (Cristy et al., 2019), as is the importance awarded to Nature as whole, the references to which easily overshadow the Vilcabamba River itself in the text of the judgement.

A second successful 2011 Ecuadorian rights of nature case involved illegal shrimp farming in coastal mangrove forests. In 2012, the Ecuadorian government had signed a contract with Chinese-owned mining company Ecuacorriente to establish the country's first large-scale, open-pit mining project in a sector of the Amazonian province Zamora-Chinchipe known as 'Condor-Mirador', one of the most biodiversity-rich areas of the planet, and home to several endangered species. The company's own environmental impact study showed that the impacts would be in violation of RoN Constitutional provisions. In January 2013, a collection of Indigenous movements, environmental and human rights NGOs and communities jointly filed a lawsuit for protective action to the Pichincha provincial Civil Court. The judge, however, ruled that the project did not violate RoN for two main reasons: firstly, it did not affect a protected area (an argument that contravened both the actual research showing the impact and the fact that RoN provisions in Ecuador are extended to *all* of Nature, not just to protected areas); secondly, since the claimants were putting forward a (collective) private interest, whereas the project was acting in favour of a public interest (development), the judge ruled that the public interest took precedence and ruled against the claimants. The appeal to the Provincial Court of Pichincha was also lost, with an allegation of political pressure on the judges on the part of the Presidency, suggesting an 'illegitimate abuse of protective action provided for in the Constitution' (Kauffman & Martin, 2017, 135).

Still in 2011, the Ecuadorian Coast Guard busted a major illegal shark fishing activity conducted by the fishing boat *Fer Mary I* and its six smaller accompanying crafts in Galapagos National Park and Marine Reserve. Pressured by the Conservation Sector, the Galapagos district attorney's office and Galapagos National Park filed a criminal lawsuit against the boat captain and crew for crimes against Nature. The Conservation Sector lead attorney, Hugo Echeverria, filed a lawsuit on behalf of the sharks' interests on the basis of the constitutional rights of Nature, an attempt rejected by the initial judge. The case was moved to Guayaquil and, in July 2015, the court ruled in favour of the sharks, leading to the first criminal conviction of an environmental crime under the new RoN provisions in Ecuador.

In 2014 a young people's environmental organization, YASunidos, filed a lawsuit in the local court of Chimborazo against a large pine tree plantation authorized in the fragile *páramo* ecosystem of Tangabana, alleging that the constitutional rights of the ecosystem were violated by the plantation. In November 2014, a collection of RoN activists represented by YASunidos Chimborazo and Acción Ecológica filed a lawsuit for protective action in the Judicial Court of Colta. The judge ruled against the claimants on the basis that the claimants did not own the land (not a requirement for constitutionally enshrined RoN in Ecuador), nor were they directly harmed (again, an irrelevant point according to RoN Ecuadorian provisions). The judge's argument seemed to echo *Sierra Club v Morton*, fully ignoring the very letter of constitutional RoN provisions. The appeal to the Provincial Court of Chimborazo refused to consider new evidence and thus ruled the claim inadmissible.

In late 2021, the Constitutional Court revoked the mining concessions that the Ecuadorian government had granted to the state-owned ENAMI mining company in partnership with Canadian mining company Cornerstone Capital Resources to two thirds of the Los Cedros Protected Forest, in particular in relation to the Río Magdalena. The court reviewed the appellate decision of the Provincial Court of Justice of Imbabura in an action for injunctive relief filed by the GAD of Santa Ana de Cotacachi on behalf of the Los Cedros Protected Forest, alleging that the rights of nature, the right to a healthy environment, the right to water and the right to an environmental consultation were violated. The court held that the Forest's constitutional rights had been violated by the mining activities, setting a much stricter framework of requirements for the development of future extractive projects in Ecuador. The case is particularly significant, as it constitutes the first instance of a clear victory of rights of Nature provisions against extractivist, minerary and commercial interests.

In 2017, Kauffman and Martin explored a decade of RoN litigation in Ecuador to determine the effectiveness of 13 cases they identified as paradigmatic. They looked at four primary tools used in those cases, as well as four ways in which the cases had been initiated. The four tools used are, firstly, constitutional lawsuits seeking protection of Constitutionally guaranteed RoN processed through civil and constitutional courts asking for damaged ecosystems to be restored and, or, for preventative action to be taken to avoid future violations. Secondly, constitutional lawsuits seeking to overturn laws and executive orders that contradict the Constitution's RoN clauses. Thirdly, criminal lawsuits, made possible by the passage of 2014 new Penal Code of Ecuador, whose Chap. 4 specifies various 'crimes against the environment, Nature or Pachamama' (including against biodiversity and natural resources), with lawsuits seeking to prosecute and punish guilty parties. Fourthly, and finally, an administrative action (not a lawsuit) by a government agency to uphold RoN. The cases could also be initiated via norm-driven civil society pressure, through instrumental government action, via bureaucratic institutionalization, and, or, as a result of professional interpretation by judges. Their finding, somewhat surprisingly, indicated that civil society pressure was the least effective. Among the 3 protective actions, 1 challenge to law's constitutionality and 1 criminal lawsuit, more than half of the cases failed. The authors found that '[t]he idea that individual and corporate property rights must be curtailed in some cases to uphold Nature's rights was not only foreign to most judges, but ran counter to their legal training. As a result, judges in civil society lawsuits have generally ruled that economic development activities are protected by individual rights (e.g. property rights, right to work) that supersede Nature's rights' (2017, 134). All other pathways, on the other hand, had a success rate of 100%.

An example of State-initiated lawsuits (all successful to the date of the analysis, and including protective actions, criminal lawsuits and administrative actions) is the government's use of RoN to combat unauthorized mining, such as in the provinces of Esmeraladas and Zamora-Chinchipe. Another approach is the Ministry of Environment invoking RoN 'to justify routine administrative actions that are part of its institutional mission of environmental protection' (Kauffman & Martin, 2017, 137), such as the Cayapas shrimper case, whereby a number of shrimp companies, which had been previously allowed to continue operations in the newly established and mangrove-rich Cayapas Ecological Reserve, were forcibly removed. While the lower courts ruled against the Ministry, the Constitutional Court ruled, in 2015, that RoN, due to the centrality to the Constitution, are to be considered 'transversal', meaning that they affect all other rights, including property right. As a result, the Constitutional Court acknowledged that this reflects a 'biocentric vision that prioritizes Nature in contrast to the classic anthropocentric conception in which the human being is the center and measure of all things, and where Nature was considered a mere provider of resources' (Corte Constitucional del Ecuador, 2015 *Sentencia No 166-15-SEP-CC, 10*) and ruled in favour of the Ministry.

Finally, equally successful were attempts by the judiciary itself to implement RoN provisions, such as in the case of unilateral application of RoN in Santa Cruz, Galapagos, where an lawsuit by a number of citizen to stop the construction on a main boulevard during high tourist season based on procedural reason was extended by the judge to include RoN in his decision, noting that the construction would occur on the habitat of marine iguanas and other species, halting the construction until an environmental licence base on an environmental impact assessment that would guarantee the protection of the species were to be obtained. In the end, Kauffman and Martin conclude that 'the Ecuadorian cases demonstrate the power of "weak laws"—legal provisions adopted by governments as "cheap talk" because they see little cost and have no intention of enforcing them' (2017, 131).

In 2024, a local court in Quito recognized the Machángara River, which runs through the country's capital, as a subject of rights. The case had been filed as an *acción de tutela* (a 'protection action') by the Kitu Karu Indigenous people to address the river's pollution caused by the city's wastewater. The Constitutional Court of Ecuador had already previously recognized, in 2022, that rivers are indeed protected under Chap. 7 of the Constitution, and the local court further argued that since the river is considered alive, it is a subject of rights under the Ecuadorian Constitution, including the right to protection and restoration. The decision marks the clearest foray of Ecuadorian jurisprudence into the clearer identification of *specific* natural features as legal subjects (rather than Nature, or Pacha Mama, in its entirety). The stage for a more instantiated discussion of legal personhood for Nature, a more recent evolution in the rights of Nature movement (as I will discussed later) is thus set in Ecuador.

6.3.2.4 Bolivia: The Laws of Mother Earth

Although the 2009 Bolivian Constitution does not include rights of Nature provisions, a section called Environmental Rights states that '[e]veryone has the right to a healthy, protected, and balanced environment. The exercise of this right must be granted to individuals and collectives of present and future generations, as well as to other living things' (Art 1). Similar to the Ecuadorian Constitution, Bolivia focuses on the concept of *sumaj kamaña* (in Aymara, whereas in Ecuadorian kichwa the same concept is expressed as *sumak kawsay*), or *buen vivir*, which 'recognizes the intimate human relationship with nature and implicitly condemns the excessive exploitation of natural resources' (Boyd, 2017, 191). The 2009 Constitution abolished the pre-existing republic and in its place created a 'plurinational' state, which recognized the 36 indigenous nations that constitute part of the country's socio-political fabric. In its Preamble, the Constitution acknowledges Nature in the form of Mother Earth, or Pachamama:

> [i]n ancient times mountains arose, rivers moved, and lakes were formed. Our Amazonia, our swamps, our highlands, and our plains and valleys were covered with greenery and flowers. We populated this sacred Mother Earth with different faces, and since that time we have understood the plurality that exists in all things and in our diversity as human beings and cultures. Thus, our peoples were formed, and we never knew racism until we were subjected to it during the terrible times of colonialism.

Paola Villavicenzio Calzadilla and Louis Kotzé note that, even though the Bolivian Constitution 'does not constitutionalize the rights of Mother Earth, it recognizes at the highest constitutional level the importance of ecological integrity, which enables people to create a new future for themselves through a new constitutional framework: without the integrity of nature, a new constitutional democracy will be impossible' (2018, 403).

In 2010, Bolivia passed the *Law on the Rights of Mother Earth* (*Ley 071 de Derechos de la Madre Tierra*) based on a draft prepared by the Pact of Unity, a coalition of Indigenous and campesino (small farmer) organizations. The law defines Mother Earth as 'a dynamic living system comprising an indivisible community of all living systems and living organisms, interrelated, interdependent and complementary, which share a common destiny. Mother Earth is considered sacred' (Art 3). Article 7 further articulates seven broad rights of Mother Earth:

Mother Earth Has the Following Rights

1. **To life**: The right to maintain the integrity of living systems and natural processes that sustain them, and capacities and conditions for regeneration.
2. **To the diversity of life**: It is the right to preservation of differentiation and variety of beings that make up Mother Earth, without being genetically altered or structurally modified in an artificial way, so that their existence, functioning or future potential would be threatened.
3. **To water**: The right to preserve the functionality of the water cycle, its existence in the quantity and quality needed to sustain living systems, and its protection from pollution for the reproduction of the life of Mother Earth and all its components.
4. **To clean air**: The right to preserve the quality and composition of air for sustaining living systems and its protection from pollution, for the reproduction of the life of Mother Earth and all its components.
5. **To equilibrium**: The right to maintenance or restoration of the inter-relationship, interdependence, complementarity and functionality of the components of Mother Earth in a balanced way for the continuation of their cycles and reproduction of their vital processes.
6. **To restoration**: The right to timely and effective restoration of living systems affected by human activities directly or indirectly.
7. **To pollution-free living**: The right to the preservation of any of Mother Earth's components from contamination, as well as toxic and radioactive waste generated by human activities.

In 2012, the Plurinational Legislative Assembly of Bolivia adopted the Framework Law 300 of Mother Earth and Integral Development for Living Well (*Ley Marco de la Madre Tierra y Desarrollo Integral para Vivir Bien*). In 2013, Bolivia established the Plurinational Mother Earth Authority, which includes an ombudsperson for Nature. Kauffmann and Martin (2021) note that, notwithstanding the many similarities between Ecuador and Bolivia, in the latter case, there has been no evidence of

RoN being invoked in any lawsuit, nor of being inserted into administrative policy. Much of the work of the Plurinational Mother Earth Authority is focused on the international arena, following the *World People's Conference on Climate Change and the Rights of Mother Earth* held in 2010, the result of which was the drafting of the *Universal Declaration on the Rights of Mother Earth* (further discussed below).

6.3.2.5 New Zealand: Rivers, Forests and Mountains

New Zealand became the first country to recognize specific parts of Nature as legal persons. The road to such an achievement was independent of the USA or the Andean developments and was instead paved by Treaty Settlements between the Crown and Māori *iwis* (tribes). A precedent is found in the *Te Arawa Lakes Settlement Act* 2006, which transferred ownership of a series of lakebeds to a newly created Te Arawa Lakes Trust (who is mandated to put the lakes' interests first) and the *Waikato-Tainui Raupatu Claims (Waikato River) Settlement Act* 2010, which articulated a very different cosmology from the colonial one. To the Waikato-Tainui people, David Boyd explains, the Aikato River is 'a *tupuna* (ancestor) that possesses *mana* (prestige) and in turns represents the *mana* and *mauri* (life force) of the tribe. Respect for *te mana o te awa* (the spiritual authority, protective power and prestige of the Waikato River) is at the heart of the relationship between the *iwi* and their ancestral river' (2017, 135).

In 2014, the *Te Urewera Act* was adopted in New Zealand, recognizing the forest Te Urewera as a legal person with rights. The Act emerged from treaty settlement negotiations resolving Treaty of Waitangi claims from the Ngāi Tūhoe *iwi* (which had not signed the Treaty of Waitangi in the nineteenth century) in relation to Te Urewera. The Act recognizes that Te Urewera has intrinsic value and possesses 'all the rights, powers, duties, and liabilities of a legal person'. Importantly, some of the concepts in the Act are written only in Māori, since it was believed that they could not be directly translated in English. This represents a novelty for any colonial Act worldwide.

The Whanganui *iwi* initiated a lawsuit in 1938 for alleged breaches on the part of the Crown of the Treaty of Waitangi, among which one of the issues to be resolved was the question of guardianship over the Whanganui River. In the dispute between the interpretation of the Treaty of Waitangi, it is important to note, the English version of the Treaty suggests that Māori chiefs 'ceded sovereignty to the British Crown in exchange for a broad-ranging guarantee of property rights', whereas the Māori version suggested that they ceded *kawanatanga* (or 'government') but retained their *tino rangatiratanga* (or 'sovereignty') (Jones, 2016, 42). The issue was finally resolved with the passing, in 2017, of the *Te Awa Tupua (Whanganui River Claims Settlement) Act*. The Act recognized the Whanganui River, known in Māori as Te Awa Tupua, as an entity that reflected the iwi's unique ancestral relationship with the river. The Act declared Te Awa Tupua to be a legal subject with 'all rights, powers, duties, and liabilities' of a legal person. Te Awa Tupua is represented in the human world by the office of Te Pou Tupua, the self-described '*human face* of Te

Awa Tupua', which 'act[s] in [its] name[.]' As Sect. 19 of the acts outlines, Te Pou Tupua's functions are many and diverse, including acting and speaking on behalf of Te Awa Tupua, upholding and protecting Te Awa Tupua's status, values, health and well-being and overseeing Tu Awa Tupua's lands. Te Pou Tupua is comprised two natural persons, one nominated by the New Zealand Crown and one by local iwi. Below Te Pou Tupua lies a hierarchy of descending power and influence, first an advisory group, *Te Karewao*, then a strategy group, *Te Kōpuka*, and finally a looser 'collaboration of persons with interests in the Whanganui River', *Te Heke Ngahuru*. Clark and others write that the Whanganui Claims Settlement Act.

> is ground breaking in its *legislative* declaration of a river as a legal person. The Act not only embodies in law what Māori have always known, but it does so in a way that seamlessly melds the everyday prosaic with the otherworldly sacred. In its administrative and regulatory detail, the Whanganui River legislation serves as a useful model for paradigmatic change—away from the vicissitudes of judicial interpretation seen in the preceding and following case studies. Above all, the Act is grounded in cultural and physical context, the unique relationship of particular peoples with their particular river. (2019, 804-5)

6.3.2.6 Indian Juristic Persons

In 2014, Mohammad Salim, a resident of Kuhlal in the Indian State of Uttarakhand, complained about encroachments on the banks of a canal that connected to the Ganga in the state capital, resulting from illegal mining and stone crushing operations. State authorities ordered the removal of the encroachments, but the private actors refused and sought an injunction against the order. In March 2017, the High Court of Uttarakhand granted legal personhood to the Ganges and Yamuna Rivers and their tributaries (*Mohd Salim v State of Uttarakhand & Others*, the *Ganges and Yamuna case*) and to their glaciers and surrounding environmental features (*Lalit Miglani v State of Uttarakhand & Others*, the *Glaciers case*). In the *Glaciers* case, the court declared the '[g]laciers, including Gangotri and Yamunotri, rivers, streams, rivulets, lakes, air, meadows, dates, jungles, forests, wetlands, grasslands, springs and waterfalls, legal entity/legal person/juridical person/moral person/artificial person having the status of a legal person, with all corresponding rights ... of a living person, in order to preserve and conserve them' (at 64). In granting legal personhood to the rivers and the surrounding natural environment, the court described them as 'breathing, living and sustaining the communities from mountains to sea' (*Ganges and Yumuna* case, at 17) and relied on existing theories of legal personhood, including corporate personhood, which grant legal personality, rights and obligations to 'any subject matter other than a human being' (*Glaciers* case, at 63). Justice Sharad Sharma argued:

> A juristic person can be any subject matter other than a human being to which the law attributes personality for good and sufficient reasons. Juristic persons being the arbitrary creations of law, as many kinds of juristic persons have been created by law as the society require[s] for its development. (*Ganges and Yumuna* case, at 16)

Erin O'Donnell argues that one of the problems of these two judgements was that the court expanded 'the definition of *legal* person significantly by conflating it with *living* person' (2018, 138). This is indeed an apt insight into the reasons as to the subsequent failures of these two cases. Indeed, in this instance the court applied the principle of *parens patriae*, and Articles 48-A and 51A(g) of the Constitution of India, and appointed the Director of the NAMAMI Gange Project, the Chief Secretary of the State of Uttarakhand and the Advocate General of the State of Uttarakhand as '*persons in loco parentis* as the human face to protect, conserve and preserve Rivers Ganga and Yamuna and their tributaries'. The court held that '[t]hese Officers are bound to uphold the status of Rivers Ganges and Yamuna and also to promote the health and well-being of these rivers' (*Ganges and Yumuna* case, at 19). In May 2017, the State of Uttarakhand and others filed a petition with India's Supreme Court to overturn the ruling naming them as the rivers' legal guardians. The primary complaint was that Uttarakhand authorities did not wish to be held accountable for the Ganga and Yamuna Rivers.

Although ultimately unsuccessful, however, the symbolic value of the decisions reverberated powerfully on the international scene. Sam Campbell and Laura Gurney note that 'the Ganges, or Gangā, is both *divine subject* and *agent*, a goddess who plays a significant role in the daily lives and practices of millions of Hindus' (2020, 7). The decision states that '[a]ll the Hindus have deep Astha [faith] in rivers Ganga and Yamuna and they collectively connect with these rivers … rivers ganga and Yamuna are breathing, living and sustaining the communities from mountains to sea' (*Ganes and Yumuna* case, at 17). In fact, the Ganga and Yamuna are seen as 'sister rivers and daughters of the Lord Himalaya' (Kedzior, 2015, 561). Their Himalayan sources, Gangotri and Yamunotri, 'are included in the Himalayan pilgrimage to the four divine *dhāms*, or abodes, and there are many *tīrthas*, or sacred crossings between heaven and earth, along their banks' (Campbell & Gurney, 2020, 8). The Gangā Mātā, or Mother Ganges, is both a goddess and a river, whose 'waters are said to be the liquid embodiment of *sakti* as well as the sustaining immortal fluid (*amrta*) of mother's milk' (Eck, 1996, 137). Although unsuccessful, the judgement, according to Yates and others, nonetheless instantiates the 'potential of embracing ontological plurality in water governance' (Yates et al., 2017, 797).

In April 2018, the Uttarakhand High Court issued another ruling recognizing the rights of Nature in regard to the abuse of horses used to transport cargo from Nepal to India. In this ruling (*Narayan Dutt Bhatt v Union of India & Others*), the court recognized rights for the entire animal kingdom, by describing all members of the animal kingdom as legal entities with all the rights, duties and liabilities of a legal person. However, unlike the previous cases, this judgement mandated a different guardianship arrangement:

> The entire animal kingdom, including avian and aquatic, are declared as legal entities having a distinct persona with corresponding rights, duties and liabilities of a living person. All the citizens throughout the State of Uttarakhand are hereby declared persons in loco parentis as the human face for the welfare/protection of animals (at 99).

6.3.2.7 Colombian Judicial Activism

Directly inspired by the legislative initiatives in New Zealand, in 2016, the Constitutional Court of Colombia declared the Atrato River as a legal entity and a subject of rights, to be represented by a 'commission of guardians of the Atrato River' (*comisión de guardianes del río Atrato*), composed of both a representative of the Colombian government and a representative nominated by the local Indigenous and afro-Colombian communities (*Center for Social Justice Studies* et al. *v Presidency of the Republic* et al., known as the *Atrato River Case*). The Atrato River, one of the most extensive, economically significant and culturally relevant of all Colombian rivers, is home to both one of the most biodiverse ecosystems of Colombia and to a number of local communities, both Indigenous and afro-Colombian. Due to extensive (ad primarily illegal) mining in the region, the Tierra Digna Center, on behalf of a number of community councils and Indigenous and afro-Colombian organizations,[5] filed, in 2016, an *acción de amparo* (or *acción de tutela*), an action guaranteed by Section 86 of the Colombian Constitution for the protection of constitutional rights, against both the local and national institutions. The Constitutional Court also inscribed its judgement within a jurisprudential tradition that, for well over two decades, had articulated the idea of an 'Ecological Constitution', whereby the protection of the environment is seen as a primary collective interest superior to other fundamental rights and is guaranteed by over thirty constitutional provisions. The court also directly referred to international environmental legislation and expressly acknowledged the arguments embodied in the 2008 Ecuadorian Constitution, the 2009 Bolivian Constitution and the more proximate recognition of legal personhood to the Whanganui River in New Zealand. Notably, the court argued that, in order to protect those fundamental environmental rights, an *ecocentric* perspective is to be preferred. The court articulated very explicitly an ontological spectrum marked by three distinct positions: firstly, a classical anthropocentric perspective, whereby the environment is seen as exclusively instrumental to human survival. Secondly, a biocentric perspective, where Nature is to be protected to prevent an environmental catastrophe. Thirdly, an ecocentric perspective, whereby 'the earth does not belong to humans, but rather it is humans who belong to the earth', with the consequence that Nature is articulated as a legal subject recognized and protected by the State through its legal representatives. The court asserted that 'only an attitude of profound respect for and humility toward nature, its component elements, and its integrated cultures allow[s]... engage[ment] with them in just and equal terms, abandoning all concepts limited to the utilitarian, the economic or the efficient' (*Atrato* case, at 43). Clark and others note that 'the court's argument in recognizing the Atrato River as a legal entity is interesting in being ontologically motivated, while strategically employing rights of Nature' (2019, 810). In July 2017, Colombia's

[5] Centro de Estudios para la Justicia Social 'Tierra Digna', on behalf of the Foro Interétnico Solidaridad Chocó (FISHC), and the Consejo Comunitario Mayores de la cuence del Atrato (Consejo Comunitario Mayor de la Organización Popular y Campesina del Altro Atrato – COCOMOPOCA, Consejo Comunitario Mayor de la Asociación Campesina Integral del Atrato – COCMACIA, Asociación de Consejos Comunitarios del Bajo Atrato – ASCOBA).

President appointed the Ministry of Environment as the government's designee to the Guardian Council for the Atrato River, which was subsequently formed in May 2018, containing 14 community members from the Choco regions. Representatives of the Chocoano communities chose these guardians based on their leadership in their communities.

In 2018, 25 Columbian young people (aged 7 to 25), representing the future generations that will have to face the major implications of climate change and supported by the NGO Dejusticia, filed an *acción de tutela* demanding the protection of their constitutional rights, which, they alleged, were threatened by the accelerated deforestation of the Colombian Amazon basin. The court found in favour of the plaintiff, noting that.

> it can be preached that the fundamental rights of life, health, minimum subsistence, freedom, and human dignity are substantially linked and determined by the environment and the ecosystem. Without a healthy environment, subjects of law, and sentient beings in general, will not be able to survive, much less protect those rights, for our children or for future generations. Neither can the existence of the family, society, or the State itself be guaranteed. (*Future Generations v. Ministry of Environment et al*)

Importantly, the court went beyond the grounds raised by the plaintiffs and, following the precedent established in the *Atrato case*, recognized the Amazon rainforest as a subject of rights. Following the success of the *Atrato* and of the *Amazon* cases, a number of regional courts have since begun to apply an ecocentric perspective in their decisions. In all cases, two main actions were used: the *acción de tutela* (which is simpler and does not require a lawyer), created by the Colombian Constitution of 1991 and applicable to protect fundamental constitutional rights, including the right to a healthy environment; and the *acción popular* ('popular acion'), enshrined in the Constitution for the protection of collective rights and interests related to the environment and public health (among others).

In 2018, the Administrative Tribunal of Boyacá declared that the Páramo (a unique alpine tundra ecosystem) of Pisba was a subject of rights, making it the third recognized rights-bearing ecosystem in the country. The recognition raised the explicit question as to whether *all* Colombian ecosystems are indeed subjects of rights. In 2019, the local Ombudsman began a popular action in the central-western province of Tolima in the Coello, Combeima and Cocora Rivers case, whereby the Regional Court of the Province of Tolima recognized the rights of these three rivers. In 2019, in response to an *acción de tutela* filed by Senator Juan Luis Castro and activist Diego David Ochoa, the Superior Court of Medellín recognized the Cauca river, its basin and its tributaries as a subject of rights and ordered their protection, conservation and maintenance by the State of Medellín. Still in 2019, the Colombian Municipal Civil Court of La Plata recognized the rights of the Plata River, while the Third Court of Enforcement of Sentences and Security Measures of Cali did so for the rights of the Pance River Basin. The RoN movement in Colombia seems to be led, at present, by a high degree of environmentally conscious judicial activism.

6.3.2.8 Jurisdictional Explosion: Mexico, Australia, Bangladesh, Uganda, Brazil, Canada

While the above cases show a relatively consistent RoN approach within each particular jurisdiction, more isolated examples abound across the planet. The isolated nature of these instances may indicate a lack of maturity in relation to RoN considerations in each individual jurisdiction, but, when taken together, they certainly gesture toward a growing global sensibility. Although the examples are too many and too disparate—and thus, at this stage, not capable of being grouped together according to any discernible patterns or categories—it is worth highlighting some of the more paradigmatic initiatives.

In 2013, the Federal District of Mexico, inspired by the Ecuadorian and Bolivian innovations, amended its main environmental law to be called the *Environmental Law for the Protection of the Earth*, while the more recent Constitution of Mexico City includes a rights of Nature provision, as does that of the state of Guerrero. The Constitution of Brazil explicitly recognizes the importance of an ecologically balanced environment, even though the value of Nature is justified solely in anthropocentric terms for its benefit to humans. That notwithstanding, Brazil is home to a rapidly growing body of scholarship and of judicial interest in relation to the rights of Nature. In 2023, the Rio Laje, in Rondônia, was the first natural entity in the country to have a set of rights recognized (by a Guajará-Mirim City Council by law), while, in 2019, the city of Florianopolis had already enacted local legislation recognizing rights of Nature. More recently, the sense of urgency to save the Vermelho river from rapid degradation led the Goiás City Council to approve a bill recognizing the river's rights. Once more, as was the case in Ecuador, Colombia, India and New Zealand, rivers seem to be spearheading the rights of Nature movement in relation to discrete natural entities.

The Australian State of Victoria, in 2017, passed the *Yarra River Protection (Wilip-gin Birrarung murron) Act 2017* (Vic). Co-named in both English and the traditional Woi-wurrung language, the Woi-wurrung name for the Act, *Wilip-gin Birrarung murron*, means 'to keep the [Birrurung or] Yarra alive'. While purposely avoiding declaring the river a 'legal person', the Act nonetheless identifies the river as 'one living and integrated natural entity' and establishes the Birrarung Council, a statutory body to be the 'independent voice' not *of* but '*for* the river' (O'Bryan, 2017, 49). In 2016, the Martuwarra Fitzroy River Council, a body that represents the many Aboriginal communities that extend along the banks of the long Martuwarra/Fitzroy River in north-western Australia, issued the Fitzroy River Declaration, in which the river is declared 'a living ancestral being' with 'a right to life' that 'must be protected for current and future generations, and managed jointly by the Traditional Owners of the river.'. In 2021, the Federal Court of Australia ruled that the Australian environment minister has a duty to protect children from future injury caused by climate change.

In 2019, the Turag river in Bangladesh was recognized as a living entity and a legal person by the High Court Division of the Supreme Court of Bangladesh (*Human Rights and Peace for Bangladesh v Government of Bangladesh and others,* the *Bangladesh Rivers* case). In response to a report by Bangladesh national newspaper *The Daily* that declared the Turag river dead, the non-government organization Human Rights and Peace filed a petition invoking the writ jurisdiction of the High Court Division of the Supreme Court of Bangladesh to save the river. The court asked for a judicial investigation into the matter, as a result of which it felt compelled to declare the river to be a 'legal person' and to be recognized in law as a living entity. The Court extended the argument to apply to *all* rivers in Bangladesh, stating that 'all other rivers flowing in and through the territory of this country will also enjoy the same status' (directive 2). The Court appointed the National River Protection Commission as the legal guardian in *loco parentis*, further charging it with the obligation to 'free all rivers of pollution and encroachment and to ensure their natural navigability along with their protection, conservation, beautification and associated developments' (at 278–9). The court relied primarily on the public trust doctrine and on a number of constitutional human rights, including the right to a healthy environment. In its judgement, the court explicitly acknowledged the 'law of nature' as the 'supreme law' and stated that all laws contrary to nature are simply void (although it did not provide any criteria to determine how such law is to be construed to be contrary to the law of nature), stating that human existence depends on the environment and that 'if we destroy nature, it will take revenge on us' (at 258). The argument clearly brings to mind Berry and Cullinan's idea of a 'Great Law', as well as the natural law stoic principle *lex iniusta non est lex* applied to the physical environment. The court explicitly referred to the 'rights of Nature', indicating that natural entities abide by the laws of nature but to not need to comply with human laws. Islam and O'Donnell argue that '[b]y placing humanity within nature, rather than separate to it, the Court explicitly adopted an *ecological jurisprudence*' (2020, 166).

Section 6.4 of Uganda's 2019 *National Environment Act* addresses the rights of Nature, stating that 'Nature has the right to exist, persist, maintain and regenerate its vital cycles, structure, functions and its processes in evolution'. Advocates who had sought inclusion of such language observed that 'Ugandans' right to a healthy environment cannot be realised unless the health of Nature herself is protected' (Gaia Foundation, 2019), a sentiment that is aligned with Berry's conflation of human needs and an ecocentric perspective.

In 2021, a joint declaration by the Innu Council of Ekuanitshit and the Regional Municipality of Minganie in the Canadian Province of Quebec recognized the Mutehekau Shipu (or Magpie River), situated within the *Nitassinan* (the ancestral territory) of the Ekuanitshit community of the Innu people, as a legal person. The recognition places particular emphasis on traditional culture, spirituality and practices, such *ushashameku* (Atlantic salmon) fishing, as well as explicitly inscribing the decision within the global paradigmatic change of the rights of Nature movement within a legal pluralistic context. The recognition proceeds to list the river's fundamental rights in its capacity as a living entity, with a shared Guardianship system comprised of members appointed both by the Innu First Nation and the Minganie Municipality. Two years later, in 2023, the Assembly of First Nations Quebec-Labrador (AFNQL) unanimously adopted a resolution to confer legal personality to the St Lawrence River.

The proposed 2022 Chilean Constitution (which was rejected at the plebiscite held in September 2022) contained an entire Chapter (Chapter III) dedicated to the rights of Nature. In addition to articulating Nature as a holder of rights, it would have recognized animals as sentient beings subject of special protection. In 2024, the Nauta provincial court of Peru, located in the Loreto region, recognized the Marañón River's intrinsic value, as well as the river's right to exist, flow and be free from pollution. The decision marks the entrance of the last of the central Andean countries (tougher with Ecuador and Bolivia) into the realm of the rights of Nature (or, to be more aligned with Andean terminology, the rights of Pacha Mama).

Still in 2022, during the 15th Conference of the Parties to the Convention on Biological Diversity, around 200 countries approved a non-binding accord, known as the Kunming-Montreal Global biodiversity framework. The document explicitly acknowledges the 'important roles and contributions of indigenous peoples and local communities as custodians of biodiversity' (8), accepts that 'Nature embodies different concepts for different people, including biodiversity, ecosystems, Mother Earth, and systems of life' (9), advocates for a conservation of 30% of terrestrial, inland water, coastal and marine areas—managed through 'ecologically representative, well-connected and equitably governed systems of protected areas' (Target 3)—and recognizes the fundamental role of rights of Nature in achieving the accord's goals, with the ultimate aim of living in 'harmony with nature'. The international journey toward an ecological jurisprudence is thus aptly captured by the language of the accord.

6.3.2.9 Europe: The Latest to the Table

Europe's adoption of rights of Nature initiatives occurred late relative to other continents. A European Citizens' Initiative to include rights of Nature provisions within European legislation was launched in 2014. Not long after, in 2016, the Green Party of England and Wales adopted a rights of Nature policy platform, though the adoption did not translate into any actual initiative being passed. In 2017, members of the European Parliament, representatives from key EU environmental institutions, NGOs and international experts met at the European Parliament in Brussels for a conference exploring the adoption of rights of Nature, legal personality and rights for ecosystems and species in EU law and policy. The conference, titled *Nature's Rights: The Missing Piece of the Puzzle*, also aimed to inform participants about the European Citizen Initiative to propose a Draft EU Directive on the right of Nature to the European Union's legislative agenda.

In 2022, the Spanish Senate approved the *Mar Menor Act* (Ley 19/2022, de 30 de septiembre, para el reconocimiento de personalidad juridica a la laguna del Mar Menor y su Cuenca). The Mar Menor, one of the most unique ecosystems in Spain, located in the south-eastern region of Murcia, had been suffering from environmental degradation for a number of years, as the largest saltwater European lagoon, once teeming with life and biodiversity, was increasingly impacted by unrestrained agricultural and commercial exploitation. After a Popular Legislative Initiative led by professor of legal philosophy Vicente (2023) triggered the legislative process by collecting over 600,000 signatures, the Law 19/2022 recognized the lagoon's own right 'to exist as an ecosystem and to evolve naturally', as well as additional rights to protection, conservation, maintenance and restoration. Furthermore, the Law establishes a Committee of Representatives, a Monitoring Commission and a Scientific Committee who jointly act as Guardians of the Mar Menor. While the Law was met by a (still pending) constitutional challenge allowed by Spain's Constitutional Court in 2013, the Mar Menor initiative undoubtedly represents the injection of rights of Nature within the fabric of European legal practice, shifting the emergence of an ecological jurisprudence from the realm of thoughts and speculation it had occupied for more than a decade (since the emergence of the America initiatives) to the terrain of actual legislative praxis. For a continent still deeply steeped in the philosophical milieu from which anthropocentrism (mainly) evolved (as discussed in the initial chapters of this book), the Mar Menor initiative is nothing short of a profoundly revolutionary step.

6.3.2.10 US Tribal Law

While initially hesitant (and with good reason, as I will discuss in the final chapter of the book), the direct involvement of Indigenous people in rights of Nature initiatives has steadily increased over the past decade. Tribal Law in the USA warrants a special place. The reader will remember that the first recorded instance of rights of Nature legislation is indeed the Navajo Tribal Council amendment to the Navajo Nation Code to recognize certain 'fundamental laws', including the rights of Nature (in Moutrie, 2020, 40). The number of US tribal initiatives in relation to rights of Nature has grown steadily since.

In 2017, the Ponca Nation adopted an anti-fracking measure including rights of Nature in their formal enactments as a strategy for stopping fossil fuel projects near tribal land. The resolution gives the Ponca Tribal Court the power to enforce penalties for crimes against Nature, punishable by up to one year in prison and US$5,000 for each day of each offense. If a crime against Nature is committed by a corporate entity, the resolution states that the chairman of the board of the corporation should be held personally responsible for the crime. Casey Camp-Horinek notes that '[i]In passing the RoN into Ponca tribal law, for the first time we saw our Indigenous values and rights reflected in Western law. We are not people protecting Nature, we are Nature protecting itself. This is a powerful way to create system change' (in Kauffman & Martin, 2021, 11).

In 2018, the Ho-Chunk Nation, a US Tribal Nation based in Wisconsin, added a clause acknowledging the rights of Nature to the bill of rights portion of its constitution, the first to do so at a tribal constitutional level. The amendment states that '[e]cosystems and natural communities within the Ho-Chunk territory possess an inherent, fundamental, and inalienable right to exist and thrive' (in Boyd, 2017, xxxi).

In response to the threats caused by increasing levels of sulphates released by mining into the local aquatic ecosystem, which comprises over 47 lakes and 500 other bodies of water and is home to both the Ojibwe or Anishinaabeg people and to the 'food that grows on water', the wild rice or Manoomin (the spiritual and economic pillar of their culture), the White Earth Band of the Chippewa Nation and the 1855 Treaty Authority passed a resolution recognizing the rights of Manoomin itself, modelling the resolution on similar enactments in Ecuador, Bolivia and New Zealand. The resolution describes Manoomin as a gift from the Creator, a 'central element of the culture, heritage, and history of the Anishinaabeg people' with an inherent right to 'exist, flourish, regenerate, and evolve'. The Chippewa's right to harvest Manoomin by using traditional practices is thus preserved.

In 2019, the Yurok people, settled along the banks of the Weroy (the Klamath River), one of the 'least known, least populated, wildest, and most remarkable natural regions of California' (Moutrie, 2020, 42), adopted a 'Resolution Establishing the Rights of the Klamath River'. The resolution asserts that '[t]his whole land, this Yurok country, sated in balance, kept that way by our good stewardship, hard work, wise laws, and constant prayers to the Creator'. In declaring the rights of the river, the resolution recognizes that the Yurok's rights to harvest sustainably and protect the river are intertwined sovereign and inalienable rights of the Yurok people, protected by international norms contained in the *United Nations Declaration on the Rights of Indigenous Peoples* (UNDRIP). As a result, to secure 'the highest protection of the Klamath River through recognition of legal rights', the following rights must be recognized for the Klamath River: 'to exist, flourish, and naturally evolve; to have a clean and healthy environment free from pollutants; to have a stable climate free from human-caused climate change impacts, and to be free from contamination by genetically engineered organisms'. The resolution concludes by proclaiming the Yurok's intention to adopt an ordinance to this effect. The Yurok Tribe in California passed a resolution in 2019 to allow cases to be brought in the name of the Klamath River in tribal courts.

By January 2021, at least nine Tribal Nations in North America—the ʔEsdilagh First Nation of Canada, the Ho-Chunk Nation, the Menominee Tribe, the Navajo Nation, the Nez Perce Tribe, the Passamaquoddy Tribe, the Ponca Nation, the White Earth Band of Ojibwe and the Yurok Tribe—had recognized RoN in their constitutions or tribal law, with more Tribal Nations following since. Marsha Moutrie notes that 'Native Americans have been leaders on this pathway [of emphasizing human's bond to Nature and responsibility for Nature's welfare], a status reflecting a cosmology in which humans are part of Nature, rather than its proprietors' (2020, 40). Indeed, '[w]hile the U.S. community rights enactments focus mainly on local communities' right to control local environments, Native American resolutions emphasize human unity with Nature, dependence upon Nature, and responsibility for Nature's welfare' (45). Against the relative failure of local rights of Nature initiatives in the USA, often cast aside by State legislation, tribal law in the USA appears to have become both the guardian and champion of the movement in the USA.

6.4 Ecocide and Ecocrimes

If rights of Nature initiatives have undoubtedly dominated the eco-jurisprudential landscape over the past decade and a half, another approach to curtailing harmful human behaviour exists. That is, the direct prohibition (and related criminalisation) of actions that are seen as ecologically harmful and destructive. Scottish lawyer Polly Higgins wrote that.

> [t]he development of a green perspective in criminology has drawn attention to crimes and harms affecting the environment, human and non-human life and the planet itself. Examples of such crimes and harms include: industrial pollution; corporate criminality and its impact on the environment; health and safety in the workplace where breaches have environmentally damaging consequences; involvement of organised crime and official corruption in the illegal disposal of toxic waste; and the impact and legacy of military operations on landscapes, water supply, air quality and living organisms populating these areas. Despite this breadth of impact, the plundering of the earth's resources and degradation of the environment have only relatively recently been thought of as activities that might be considered criminal or at least seriously harmful with intergenerational consequences and transnational impacts. (Higgins et al., 2013, 251)

Higgins also distinguished between 'crime' and 'harm', the latter considering the question of whether to embrace 'those activities that lie within lawful practice but evidently, at least to some and by some measures of evidence, have harmful consequences that might merit legal proscription and response' (252). Among the activities that clearly cause environmental damage (although they are *legally* invisible to criminal law regimes) are: water pollution, air pollution, deforestation and spoiling of the land and harmful actions against animals and nonhuman species.

Wijdekop (2016) reports that the term 'ecocide' was coined in 1970 by American biologist Arthur Galston at the Conference on War and National Responsibility. Not long after, in 1972, Swedish Prime Minister Olof Palme explicitly referred to the Vietnam War as 'ecocide' in his opening speech for the United Nations Conference on the Human Environment, by arguing that '[t]he immense destruction brought about by indiscriminate bombing, by large scale use of bulldozers and herbicide is an outrage … which requires urgent international attention' (in Wijdekop, 2016, 2).In 1987, Michael Allan Fox argued that nuclear war could result in ecocide. Mark Gray used the term to describe the 'causing or permitting [of] harm to the natural environment on a massive scale', reflecting a 'breach of duty of care owed to humanity in general' (1996, 215). Lynn Berat (1993) had used the term Geocide in a similar way, to provide a means in international law to preserve the right to a healthy environment. Higgins recalled that a protean draft International Convention on the Crime of Ecocide to be submitted to the UN International Law Commission (ILC) was prepared by Richard Falk and was introduced as part of a review process which sought to evaluate the effectiveness of the Genocide Convention. The proposal was to include, in an amended Convention, 'a law against ecocide that could address both direct ecological crimes and ancillary cultural ecocide' (Higgins et al., 2013, 251). Falk argued that it was necessary to recognize 'that we are living in a period of increasing danger of ecological collapse … and that man has consciously and unconsciously inflicted irreparable damage to the environment in times of war and peace' (1973, 93). However, at the 1996 meeting of the ILC, the then Chairman, Ahmed Mahiou, unilaterally chose to remove the crime of ecocide completely as a separate provision without putting it to a vote.

In 2010, Higgins once again proposed to the International Law Commission to amend the Rome Statute, arguing that ecocide should be an international crime for which offenders could be prosecuted at an international level, even if their behaviour was permitted (or even facilitated) at the domestic level. 'For the purpose of international law, I propose the following definition for ecocide: the extensive destruction, damage to or loss of ecosystem(s) of a given territory, whether by human agency or by other causes, to such an extent that peaceful enjoyment by the inhabitants of that territory has been severely diminished' (2011, 306). An emerging social movement through a number of organizations, notably End Ecocide on Earth, has since contributed to the dialogue, with End Ecocide on Earth drafting their own amendment to the Rome Statute, focused on protecting ecosystem services and the global commons. According to Wijdekop, the recognition of an international crime of Ecocide would 'catalyse a transition to a green economy [by] alert[ing] corporations and states that there are legal consequences to serious damage and destruction of ecosystems, and establish[ing] a normative threshold which is illegal to cross' (2016, 4).

At present, only one provision in the Rome Statute of the International Criminal Court, related to war crimes, explicitly mentions damage to the environment. Article 8(2)(b)(iv) makes it a crime to

> [i]ntentionally launch an attack in the knowledge that such attack will cause incidental loss of life or injury to civilians or damage to civilian objects or widespread, long-term and severe damage to the natural environment which would be clearly excessive in relation to the concrete and direct overall military advantage anticipated.

Higgins lamented that '[f]or now, in law outside of wartime, it is not a crime to cause mass destruction or loss of ecosystems' (2013, 264). Ecocide, therefore, constitutes the missing 5th crime against peace. Nonetheless, in 2013, a committee of eleven citizens from nine EU countries officially launched the 'European Citizen Initiative [a tool created by the Lisbon Treaty to promote participative and direct democracy] to End Ecocide in Europe'. The 2022 statement by the World Council of Churches (the world's largest ecumenical organization whose Assembly is held every eight years), titled *The Living Planet: Seeking a Just and Sustainable Global Community*, unanimously voiced its support for ecocide law as a new and strengthened form of environmental accountability. In 2023, the European Union approved the strengthening of its directive on the protection of the environment through criminal law. While the text does not include the word 'ecocide', both the overall sentiment and the wording of the directive echo the aspirations of those who like to include ecocide and similar legislation within international, transnational and domestic legislation.

At present, at least ten countries, including Armenia, Belarus, Georgia, Kazakhstan, Kyrgyzstan, Moldova, Russia, Tajikistan, Ukraine, Uzbekistan and Vietnam, have designated ecocide as a crime against peace under their criminal legislation.

For example, Article 278 of Vietnam's Penal Code states that 'destroying the natural environment, whether committed in time of peace or war, constitutes a crime against humanity' (in Boyd, 2017, 214). Additionally, in 2021 the French National Assembly approved the creation of an ecocide offence as part of a battery of measures aimed at protecting the environment, while Ecuador, although not referring specifically to a crime of 'ecocide', has made possible a number of criminal lawsuits with the passage of its new 2014 Penal Code, whose Chap. 4 specifies various 'crimes against the environment, Nature or Pachamama'. However, Higgins remarks, '[a] law of Ecocide should recognise human-caused environmental damage and degradation (whether committed during or outside of war-time), as a crime of strict liability (in other words, without intent). Of the ten countries that have already included Ecocide in their criminal penal codes, not one of them sets out a test of intent' (2013, 262). The road to an international crime of ecocide, as well as to a domestic criminalisation of the same harmful activities, is clearly yet to be taken in earnest.

6.5 The Ecological Civilization

The notion of an 'ecological civilisation' came to the fore in November 2007, when the term was incorporated into the Central Commission Report to the Chinese Communist Party's 17th National Congress and embraced as a central policy objective by the government. In 2012, the Party included the goal of achieving an ecological civilisation in its constitution and included this goal in its five-year plan. In 2017, then, the 19th Congress of the Party called for an acceleration of the establishment of an ecological civilisation (Gare 2021, 37).

The original notion of an 'ecological civilization' had actually been coined in the Soviet Union in 1984, when environment experts proposed the term in an article entitled 'Ways of Training Individual Ecological Civilization under Mature Socialist Conditions', published in the second volume of *Scientific Communism* (Arran Gare, 2009, 167). It was, however, two decades later in China that the concept was taken up, developed and vigorously and successfully promoted, most importantly by Pan Yue, the Vice-minister of China's State Environmental Protection Administration (Gare, 2012; Pan, 2016). Arran Gare highlights the unfolding of this radically progressive vision 'put forward by radical Chinese environmentalists and embraced, at least in principle, by the Chinese government, first as a goal of government policy in 2007, and in 2012, written into their constitution' (2017, 10).

James Thornton writes that '[f]acing the ruin of their environment, the Chinese looked hard and amended their constitution ... If we are going to thrive into the future,' the argument ran, 'it will be as an ecological civilisation' (Goodman & Thornton, 2017, 45). To enact this project, the China Council for International Cooperation on Environment and Development had the mandate to foster cooperation in the area of environment and development between China and the international community. The Council consisted of 25 Chinese members and 25 from the international community, 'chosen for their experience, expertise, and influence' (Goodman & Thornton, 2017,

221–2). With this mandate, Chinese officials sought out global leaders in public interest environmental law, among whom was James Thornton, the main lawyer behind ClientEarth (perhaps the most famous public interest environmental law firm in Europe). In the summer of 2014, one panel of Chinese policy advisers, headed by Wang Yuqing, former Deputy Environment Minister of China, reached Brussels. Wang Yuqing argued that the many lawyers that are emerging from China's Schools of Law 'have been charged with supporting one of the most fundamental societal shifts in human history'. Humans have progressed through 'primitive civilization, agricultural civilization, and industrial civilization' (Pan, 2016, 40), the latter 'now at the end of a 300 year run of unsustainability' (Goodman & Thornton, 2017, 217). Wang Yuqing explained, as Thornton recalls,

> China has decided to articulate and force into being the next era of humanity's planetary existence. It has pledged to bring into being "ecological civilisation". The phrase was coined by the agricultural economist Qiang Ye in 1984 ... retrieved the concept from Ancient Chinese religious and philosophical discourse ... entered politics in a report to the 17th National Congress of the Chinese Communist Party in 2007. The then President Hu Kintao explained, "building ecological civilisation, in essence, is building a resource efficient and environmentally friendly society that is based on resource and environment carrying capacity, complies with natural laws, and aims at sustainable development." ... the phrase became enshrined in the Chinese Communist Party's Constitution in 2013, at the Third Plenary Session of the 18th Central Committee. A 12000 character document followed in April 2015: *Central Document Number 12* fixed a programme of actions and targets ... Officials would bear lifelong accountability for the impact of their decision making on the environment, while economic growth would no longer be "the only criterion in government performance assessment." ... The progress in bringing fresh environmental laws had already been huge and "in many ways unprecedented in history". (Goodman & Thornton, 2017, 221-2)

Since its introduction in 2007, and especially after President Xi Jinping endorsed it in 2013 as a major framework for the country's environmental laws and policies, the concept has gained traction both in Chinese society and in neighbouring Asian countries, and in 2018 it was elevated to a more prominent position in the constitution. Mette Halskov Hanse and others note that, since 2007, 'more than 4000 published Chinese articles and books have included eco-civilization as one of their key words, and more than 170,000 articles in mainstream press-media in China have invoked the concept' (2018, 195). The public impact of the concept is undeniable. Thornton shares that he 'was struck by hearing from senior Chinese officials that they were proud of raising more people from poverty than anyone else in history, but that they got the balance wrong. They drew down the environment too much and now would do whatever is necessary to restore the balance' (Goodman & Thornton, 2017, 274).

Halskov Hanse and others suggest that, while scholars have approached ecocivilization as 'an ideology and as a political framework, plan and vision', it may be best understood as 'a socio-technical imaginary' (2018, 196). While in its early stages the concept was formulated mainly in terms of cultural principles and ethics about human beings and nature—with limited discursive space for science and technology—since the endorsement by President Xi Jinping, science and technology have become major components of the vision, and 'the driving force towards what is perceived as "the green future." In this way, ecocivilization has developed from a largely philosophical endeavour into a full-fledged socio-technical imaginary with political backing' (198). The cultural and ethical imaginary, however, remains central to the discourse on ecological civilisation.

Overall, ecological civilisation (or ecocivilization) is envisioned as 'a cultural ethic of complete harmony (*hexie gongsheng,* 和谐共生) between humankind and nature, among human beings themselves, and in their relation to society' (Halskov Hanse et al., 2018, 197). Tao (2005), senior official of the Policy and Law Department of the Ministry of Environmental Protection writes that 'China is one of few countries in the world to have a long history in drafting environmental laws and regulations', a history that stretches back three millennia'. In support of this claim, he cites a mention in the Han Feizi, written 475–221 BCE, of a law on public loitering under the Shang Dynasty (1600–1046 BCE). The Chinese ecological tradition, Pan Yue insists, has not only taught the philosophy of ecological ethics long before the time of Confucius, but also the *practice* of environmental protection. Long before the emergence of its parallel in global public discourse in the 1960s, China already had its own 'environmental culture' (*huanjing wenhua,* 环境文化). During the Xia dynasty 4000 years ago, Pan notes, felling trees in spring was prohibited, as was catching fish, killing young wild animals and collecting bird eggs in summer. During the Zhou dynasty 3000 years ago, hunting for animals, catching birds, fishing, logging and burning fields were strictly regulated according to the climate and season. During the Qin dynasty 2000 years ago, similarly, harvesting young sprouts and catching young wild animals were strictly prohibited, and it was forbidden to kill fish and turtles with poison. 'For every dynasty and every epoch there were explicit laws and prohibitions to protect the environment' (Pan, 2003). Halskov Hanse and others note that, although Pan 'mainly draws on Confucianist texts and ideas to create a specific Chinese version of traditional ecological culture, he also seeks to integrate it with both Taoist and Buddhist elements. In Taoism, according to Pan, heaven (or *tian*) does not represent a moral or political authority, but rather, 'the Way (*dao* 道) is modeled on nature (*ziran*)' and the loftiest principle is humanity's respect for the laws of nature' ((2018, 196). Similarly, Pan claims, Buddhism teaches that 'Buddha nature' (*foxing,* 佛性) is the unity and the essence of all things in the universe. It implies that all living things are equal and that all have the right to exist, affirming an intrinsically ecocentric view of humankind and nature. To Pan, Chan Buddhism in particular represents a distinct Chinese interpretation of Buddhist philosophy, one that has been influenced by Confucian ethics, Chinese philosophical ideas of unity between heaven and man, and the Daoist ideal of the simplicity of life' (196).

In the official English translation of then President Hu Jintao's speech for the 18th Party Congress in 2012, the Chinese term *shengtai wenming* (生态文明), was translated as 'ecological progress' (rather than 'ecological civilization'), 'possibly in order not to confuse an international audience unfamiliar with using the term "civilization" in this way' (Halskov Hanse et al., 2018, 195). Gare highlights that, in Chinese, 'the words for "culture" (*wenhua*) and "civilisation" (*wenming*) are sometimes seen as synonymous, and the way the word "civilisation" is used in China corresponds more closely to the way the word "culture" is used in Russia' (2021, 39). Gare also notes that the advent of an ecological civilisation is heralded to follow the industrial civilisation. This could be interpreted to mean that China must first fully industrialize before it can afford to fully deal with ecological problems. 'It can also be interpreted as dealing with ecological problems generated by industrialisation by utilising technological solutions, much as in Western capitalist countries' (Gare, 2021, 38). Halskov Hanse and others are equally cautious, noting that, against the argument that China has historically displayed 'a unique tradition of economic self-restraint that can also serve as a model to overcome contemporary consumerism created by Western philosophical tradition and industrial civilization', nonetheless, 'in the dominant versions of eco-civilization continued economic growth is never argued against, and no documents suggest radical alternative means of, for instance, redistributing wealth and slowing production in order to prevent further environmental degradation' (2018, 196). Gare concludes by noting that '[a] more radical view is that the centralisation of power engendered by capitalism and industrialisation needs to be challenged, and that ecological civilisation requires institutions to subordinate markets and empower people at local levels' (2021, 38).

6.6 Soft Law and Eco-Jurisprudential Organizations

While the many initiatives described in this chapter already represent a varied palette of instances in which ecological sensibilities have entered the political and legal discourse, there are many additional examples of 'soft law' of equal importance. GARN's Eco-Jurisprudence Tracker refers to 'soft-law' as documents that are adopted or endorsed by a collective of civil society individuals and organizations with the view to influence public policy and legislation.

Among them, the *Earth Charter* (which is fully reproduced in Appendix 2) occupies a special place. The idea of the Earth Charter originated in 1987, with Maurice Strong and Mikhail Gorbachev as members of the Club of Rome and following the UN World Commission on Environment and Development's call for a new charter leading the transition to a sustainable development. With the support of the Dutch government, the Earth Charter Commission led a global consultation process, with an international drafting committee chaired by Steven Rockefeller and comprised of members such as Amadou Toumani Touré and Leonardo Boff, among others. The Charter was then adopted, in 1998, by the IUCN and was finally approved and launched in 2000. The Charter contains an articulated declaration of fundamental values and principles considered useful for building a just, sustainable and peaceful global society. Peter Burdon argues that the Earth Charter represents 'the most visible attempt to fuse concepts such as Earth community with democracy' (2014, 26).

Following the underwhelming results of COP15, held in Copenhagen in 2009, Bolivian President Evo Morales Ayma called for—and then, on 22 April 2010, hosted—a 'Peoples' World Conference on Climate Change and Mother Earth Rights'. The conference, held in the small Bolivian town of Cochabamba, was attended by over 35,000 people (two times the number of people originally expected) and concluded with President Morales adopting a declaration that was then to be presented to the United Nations. Drafted with the support of many Earth Jurisprudence advocates, such as Cormac Cullinan, and drawing inspiration from the Universal Declaration of Human Rights and the Earth Charter, the *Universal Declaration of the Rights of Mother Earth* (reproduced in full in Appendix 3) expressly acknowledges humanity's profound dependence on, and relationship with, the Earth. It also asserts that the Earth is an 'indivisible community of diverse and interdependent beings with whom we share a common destiny and to whom we must relate in ways to benefit Mother Earth'. Mother Earth, as a consequence, has the right 'to exist, to persist and to continue the vital cycles, structures, functions and processes that sustain all beings'. Similar fundamental rights are recognized for all beings, who all possess:

- The right to exist.
- The right to habitat or a place to be.
- The right to participate in accordance with its nature in the ever-renewing processes of Mother Earth.
- The right to maintain its identity and integrity as a distinct, self-regulating being.
- The right to be free from pollution, genetic contamination and human modifications of its structure or functioning that threaten its integrity or healthy functioning.
- The freedom to relate to other beings and to participate in communities of beings in accordance with its nature (in Burdon, 2011).

The most innovative element of the Declaration is the linguistic shift away from Nature toward the use of the term 'Mother Earth'. While the Ecuadorian Constitution had already paired the term 'Nature' with the Andean term 'Pachamama', the Declaration moved further and chose to abandon the more impersonal and less relational concept of 'Nature' altogether.

Of equally profound significance, among soft law documents, is the Papal Encyclical Letter *Laudato Si'*, released by Pope Francis in 2015. The encyclical—a specific type of papal document, representing a pastoral letter to clarify Catholic doctrine and usually addressed to patriarchs, archbishops and bishops who are in communion with the Holy See—represents an authoritative document on theological and ethical matters. Concern for the environment was not novel in the Vatican. Pope Paul VI, in the 1971 Apostolic Letter *Octogesima Adveniens*, had written that '[d]ue to an ill-considered exploitation of nature, humanity runs the risk of destroying it and becoming in turn a victim of this degradation' (416-7). Pope John Paul II, 20 years later, called for an ecological conversion to 'safeguard the moral conditions for an authentic *human ecology*' (*Centesimus Annus* 1991, 841) and his successor Benedict XVI proposed 'eliminating the structural causes of the dysfunctions of the world economy and correcting models of growth which have proved incapable of ensuring respect for the environment' (*Address to the Diplomatic Corps* 2007, 73). However, it is only with Pope Francis's *Laudato Si'* that the Holy See (and thus, by extension, Catholic Christianity) fully addressed current environmental concerns. The encyclical would not be amiss among the most radical texts of deep ecology, as well as acknowledging and speaking to the current scientific consensus on the state of the planet. Its title explicitly harkens back to Francis of Assisi's poetic devotion for 'our Sister, Mother Earth', noting how the Saint patron of modern ecological thought (Saint Francis, from whose literary work the title of the encyclical was derived) 'invites us to see nature as a magnificent book in which God speaks to us and grants us a glimpse of his infinite beauty and goodness' (Francis, 2015, 13).

The number of soft law initiatives is, naturally, far too great to comprehensively capture here. Among these many other, however, some are of particular note. In 2012, the IUCN, the only international observer organization to the UN General Assembly with expertise in the environment, adopted a resolution specifically calling for a Universal Declaration of the Rights of Nature. In 2014, on its fiftieth anniversary, leaders of the Group of 77 (a coalition of developing countries) and China met in Bolivia and adopted the Declaration and Plan of Action of Santa Cruz de la Sierra titled *Towards a New World Order for Living Well*. The declaration repeatedly calls for 'living well in harmony with nature' and consistently refers to the recognition of rights of Nature. Past Presidents Rafael Correa of Ecuador and Evo Morales of Bolivia have repeatedly called for a new International Court of Climate Justice, whereas there have been ongoing calls for a 'Green Amendment' to the US Constitution, with an enshrined right to a healthy environment. In November 2015, the Club des Juristes released a report recommending the adoption of a universal pact to 'merge international environmental law in a binding instrument that would (1) impose environmental obligations on states and non-state actors, (2) confer environmental rights to citizens, and (3) create an inviolable legal instrument in national courts' (Aguila, 2017). In 2017, the network of experts now known as the International Group of Experts for the Pact (IGEP) published a white paper, *Toward a Global Pact for the Environment* (GPE), 'to further advance governmental and civil society support for the Global Pact' (Zelle et al., 2021, 432). The Earth Trusteeship Initiative (ETI) was established in 2018 in the Hague, the Netherlands, on the 70th anniversary of the adoption of the *Universal Declaration of Human Rights*. With the support and endorsement of many human rights, environmental and professional organizations, the ETI launched the *Hague Principles for a Universal Declaration on Responsibilities for Human Rights and Earth Trusteeship* (reproduced in Appendix 5). While not an example of soft law, the replacement of the Gross National Product and Gross Domestic Product, 'which defines production based on its geographic location rather than its ownership' (Heinberg, 2011, 255), as the measure of a country's economic well-being is particularly significant. The small Himalayan kingdom of Bhutan substituted those measures with its novel Gross National Happiness index (a phrase introduced by the incoming King Jigme Singye Wangchuck upon ascending to the throne at the age of 16 in 1972) in its new Constitution of 2008. In 2021, the then Prince of Wales (now King Charles III) launched, as part of the Sustainable Markets Initiative, the 'Terra Carta'—a charter that aims to place sustainability at the heart of the private sector. The document, which explicitly derives its name from the Magna Carta, aims to offer 'the basis of a recovery plan that puts Nature, People and Planet at the heart of global value creation – one that will harness the precious, irreplaceable power of Nature combined with the transformative innovation and resources of the private sector'. Its Statement of intent explicitly aims to 'provide an integrated roadmap toward an inspiring, inclusive, equitable, prosperous and sustainable future for the sake of present and future generations; one that will harness the power of Nature combined with the transformative power, innovation and resources of the private sector'. The document places great emphasis on sustainability at the core. While the language and aim seem to be operating within an enlightened anthropocentric paradigm, some of the later comments seem to gesture toward a more ecocentric sensitivity.

6.6.1 Organizations

In parallel with the official organizations mentioned above (such as the IUCN and the Harmony with Nature programme, for example), there have been a few that have played a major role in the development of an ecological jurisprudence over the past two decades. The London-based Gaia Foundation was inspired by the writings of Thomas Berry and collaborated with him to hold the first international conference on Earth jurisprudence in 2001. Over the following years, the Gaia Foundation then facilitated numerous workshops to further advance the nascent theory of Earth Jurisprudence. These meetings produced the Earth Justice Network, 'a community of activists working to develop a common understanding of a new, Earth-centered legal paradigm' (Kauffman & Martin, 2021, 32–3). In 2007, Sisters Patricia Siemen and Margaret Galiardi established the Center for Earth Jurisprudence (CEJ), which offers seminars in Earth Jurisprudence at the Barry University Law School in Florida.

The first major organization dedicated to the direct advocacy, analysis and pursuit of rights of Nature, however, was the Global Alliance for the Rights of Nature (GARN), established at the feet of the Tungurahua in Ecuador in 2010, with the *Tungurahua Volcano Declaration*, which states the following:

> Recognizing that exploitation, abuse, and contamination have caused great destruction, degradation and disruption of Mother Earth, putting all life at risk through phenomena such as climate change … Convinced that in an interdependent living community it is not possible to recognize the rights of only human beings without causing an imbalance within Mother Earth … Believe that the universal recognition and effective implementation of the Rights of Nature is essential to avert catastrophic harm to humanity and the life as we know it … calls upon all organizations and people of the Earth … to bring forth the universal adoption and effective implementation of the Rights of Nature. (in Margil, 2014, 154)

As Kauffmann and Martin note, GARN frames its purpose as 'creating a system of jurisprudence that sees and treats nature as a fundamental, rights bearing entity and not as mere property to be exploited at will' (2021, 34). Not a single organization, GARN is, instead, an alliance of distinct entities, such as (among many others) the Pachamama Alliance and Fundación Pachamama, the African Biodiversity Network, the UK Environmental Law Association (UKELA), the Gaia Foundation, as well as the previously mentioned Community and Environmental Defense Fund (CELDF), the Earth Law Center, the Australian Earth Laws Alliance (AELA), the Women's Earth and Climate Action Network (WECAN), the Center for Earth Jurisprudence,

End Ecocide Earth, CEDENMA, Movement Rights, the Center for Earth Jurisprudence, Nature's Rights, Lodyn and the Indigenous Environmental Network. Indeed, throughout the first two decades of the twenty-first century (and particularly in the 2010s), a great number of organizations focused on Earth Jurisprudence formed in Australia, Botswana, Brazil, Kenya, South Africa, the UK, the USA and elsewhere. The networked nature of the movement meant that ideas circulated rapidly among new entities and organizations, allowing for the growth of a relatively cohesive global discourse. In fact, the Commission on Environmental Law of the International Union for Conservation of Nature (IUCN) and the Harmony with Nature programme are also heavily populated by lawyers and academics involved in many of these organizations.

In 2013, GARN established the first International Rights of Nature Tribunal. The tribunal is inspired by the International War Crimes Tribunal created by Bertrand Russell to investigate alleged human rights abuses committed against Vietnamese peoples by US military. The tribunal is comprised lawyers and leaders from indigenous, social justice and environmental communities and works within a self-codified set of rules. Its mandate is to hear cases and determine whether violations of rights of Nature have occurred, identify the individual or entity responsible for the violation and prescribe actions to prevent further harm and restore damaged ecosystems and communities, with regional tribunals being established around the world. 'The founders of these tribunals', David Boyd points out, 'hope to shine a spotlight on acts that violate the rights of nature, even where the activities causing these harms are legal under today's laws. More broadly, by critiquing the current legal system, participants seek to illustrate the structural flaws and weaknesses in the obsessive pursuit of economic growth and today's anthropocentric laws' (2017, 213). The first cases were heard in Quito in 2014, with Alberto Acosta presiding over the hearing, and in December of the same year a second tribunal was held in conjunction with the COP in Lima, Peru, presided by Vandana Shiva. The trend continued in 2015 in Paris, with Cormac Cullinan this time presiding over the tribunal. Among the 'prosecutors' are many of the key members of the Global Alliance for the Rights of Nature or its allies: Alberto Acosta, Cormac Cullinan, Vandana Shiva, Tom Goldtooth, Nnimmo Bassey, Linda Sheehan, Osprey Orielle Lake, Atossa Soltani, Blanca Chancoso and more. A common critique of these tribunals is alleged bias and one-sidedness, with predetermined outcomes and no attention paid to procedural fairness. Boyd writes that

> [c]ritics argue, with reason, that the tribunal lacks legitimacy because it was not established by any law, and does not ensure that defendants are represented. Many of the countries in which alleged violations of the rights of nature are occurring do not legally recognize these rights. Most judges are activists drawn from within the international rights of nature movement. Therefore, it is not surprising that, in every case decided to date, the judges determined that the rights of nature had been violated. Given its lack of authority, there are no legal consequences for the perpetrators "found guilty" of violating nature's rights. (2017, 217-8).

While that is true, however, the value of these tribunals is twofold. On the one hand, they are a publicity activity, one designed to draw attention to the rights of nature. Just like the citizens' tribunals before them, they 'contribute to public education, raising the profile of human rights abuses,' and while the citizens' tribunals 'had no authority to impose sanctions or hold anyone accountable ... one could argue that these tribunals set a precedent for the eventual establishment of the International Criminal Court in 2002' (Boyd, 2017, 215). Moreover, these tribunal also present a unique theatrical opportunity in which to workshop how rights of Nature can be operationalised, highlighting the strengths and weaknesses of the arguments provided in the light of existing legal structures.

Among many other important institutional initiatives are the Great Transition Network, the Chipko movement in northern India, which draws on the political-action principles of Gandhi and the foundational ideas of Hindu philosophy, the Sri Lanka Sarvodaya ('awakening of all') movement and Earth Democracy, the term used by Vandana Shiva to describe both a world view and a political movement promoted by the organization Navdanya in India. A more recent network that is rapidly growing in influence is the Ecological Law and Governance Association (ELGA), which was formed in 2017, one year after the launch of the 'Oslo Manifesto', a document titled *From Environmental Law to Ecological Law: A Call for Re-Framing Law and Governance* designed to overcome the existing flaws and shortcomings of current environmental law by calling for an ecological approach to law based on ecocentrism, holism and intra/intergenerational and interspecies justice. The document (which is reproduced in full in Appendix 5) was adopted at the IUCN WCEL Ethics Specialist Group Workshop at the IUCN Academy of Environmental Law Colloquium held at the University of Oslo.

6.6.2 Activism

In parallel with soft law documents and institutional entities, there exists a wide range of organized activists devoted to pursuing a political and legal system informed by ecological considerations. These individuals and groups carry out what Karen O'Brien and others call 'dutiful dissent' (2018, 1), which involves 'working with existing systems and institutions, drawing upon existing norms and rules, but with an emergency tendency toward more disruptive (if not necessarily dangerous) strategies' (Rogers, 2020, 76). Nicole Rogers points out that many of these active forms of resistance disrupt existing tropes and create novel memes, by adopting traits typical of the 'trickster' figure, such as 'dark play' (2020, 156–60). Examples are the Australian 'Knitting Nannas', the most unlikely of protesters, or the UK practice of 'Brandalism'. The most notable are, without a doubt, the members of the group Extinction Rebellion.

Of great significance is youth activism, something prophetically prefigured by Doris Lessing in her novel *Shikasta*. Following the 2018 March for Our Lives, then 15-year-old Greta Thunberg launched the 'School Strike for Climate' by sitting alone in protest outside the Swedish Parliament. Her example inspired the Fridays for Future, Youth for Climate and Youth Strike for Climate, an international movement of school students who skip Friday school classes to participate in demonstrations and demand action on climate on the part of governments. Young protestors and plaintiffs, akin to those who launched the successful *Amazon case* in Colombia, have spread in many jurisdictions. In the US case of *Juliana v United States*, (the *Juliana case*), 21 young people, along with the NGO Earth Guardians and on behalf of 'future generations', sued the US government for allowing CO2 rises above dangerous levels. The plaintiffs, in addition to arguing the public trust doctrine, alleged that the right to a stable climate is protected under the Ninth Amendment and that climate stability is essential to the effective protection of the Fifth Amendment. In 2020, the US Ninth Circuit Court of Appeals dismissed the lawsuit, however, arguing that 'the plaintiffs' impressive case for redress must be presented to the political branches of government'.

One of the common strategies used by protestors in many of these cases, particularly in the US, is to invoke the defence of necessity, which.

> permits people to break the law in order to prevent a greater evil. Thus, the unlawful can be lawful ... The defence serves both a conservative function, as a legal mechanism for accommodating catastrophe, and a radical one, as a point of rupture for legal norms. Acknowledging the necessity of law-breaking is to concede that the normative framework is not all-encompassing ... the defence recognises a lacuna in law ... and can be viewed as a stabilising device, preventing more fundamental challenges to the existing structure of norms by conceding that the exceptional sometimes lies outside the capacity of such norms to tame and subsume. (Rogers, 2020, 169)

Like self-defence or the insanity defence, the defence of necessity is usually considered an affirmative defence, one 'in which the defendant accepts the prosecution's facts but offers additional facts that warrant a not-guilty finding' (Zelle et al., 2021, 358). Its 'vigilante nature' and its location at the boundaries—and beyond—law's empire, makes it rarely palatable to judges. Although the specific nature of the defence differs, it usually requires the following elements:

- The defendant faced an imminent harm to themselves or others.
- The defendant's actions were less harmful than the harm to be avoided.
- The defendant reasonably thought that their actions would be effective in avoiding or mitigating the imminent harm.
- The defendant had no reasonable legal alternatives to violating the law.

As Zelle and others report (2021, 359), since the mid-2000s, climate activists have used the defence to justify their acts of civil disobedience. Generally, the defendants argue the following:

- Climate change is not only imminent, but it is occurring now and is causing severe harms to the planet and its people.
- Their acts of civil disobedience are much less harmful than the harms caused by climate change.
- Civil disobedience is demonstrably effective in mitigating or avoiding specific climate change harms, in building public support for climate change policy and in influencing political decision-makers.

- Traditional alternatives such as voting, lobbying and organizing have failed to prevent climate change harms, making civil disobedience necessary.

In *People v Gray*, the defendants, who were protesting the dangers of air pollution to bikers and pedestrians on the Queensboro Bridge in New York City and were charged with disorderly conduct for blocking the entrance of a bridge roadway, the judge acquitted the defendants in a non-jury trial, finding that they had proven all elements of the necessity defence.

Indigenous protests also demonstrate a different articulation of ecological demands. In 2010, the Units'ot'en clan od the Wet'suwat'en Nation occupied and established themselves on their ancestral lands in Canada's British Columbia, to oppose a number of proposed gas and oil pipelines. Conscious that '[t]he integration of Indigenous philosophies into hegemonic institutions can often lead to distortion, erasure and co-optation, a new form of epistemic violence' (Temper, 2018, 15), they shifted their focus from rights to responsibilities, by explicitly rejecting 'a rights-based discourse that can only be accorded to them by what they perceive as an occupying power, and actively assert their responsibilities to the territory and their ancestral and natural law' (Temper, 2018, 15). Perhaps the most famous protest led by Indigenous activists and their many allies is the one that took place a few years back at Standing Rock. Also known as the Dakota Access Pipeline Protest, it began in 2016 as a grassroot opposition to the construction of the Energy Transfer Partners' Dakota Access Pipeline, designed to cross beneath part of Lake Oahe near the Standing Rock Indian Reservation in the USA. The protestors established many 'water protectors camps' and started chanting *Mní Wičóni* ('water is life' in Lakota) protests, gathering thousands of people around the initial camp. Conflict between protestors and law enforcement escalated, leading heavily militarized police to enter the camps and conduct a number of arrests. While, in 2020, an order was made to suspend operations and for the US Army Corps of Engineers to conduct a new environmental impact review, the decision was later overturned, and while the environmental review was to continue, the pipeline was to resume operations.

6.7 Reflections

The purpose of this chapter was to demonstrate the broad range of legal initiatives that have occurred, over the past six decades, in parallel with the emergence of an environmental ethics, and that unequivocally point to the progressive emergence of an ecological jurisprudence over the past few decades. The theoretical aspirations discussed in the previous chapter, I hope it will have now become apparent, are not purely aspirational any longer. They are not confined to the texts of scholars and utopian writers alike, nor are they figments of imagined possibilities. Instead, they are very present in the lived experiences of legislators, judges, lawyers, legal scholars and activists across a number of jurisdictions around the world. In fact, former UN Special Rapporteur on Human Rights and the Environment, David Boyd

(2017), defines the rights of Nature movement (and, I would expand, the entire trend toward an ecological) as the fastest growing legal movement of the twenty-first century. Ecology, which has become central to both science and philosophy, has most certainly entered in profound ways the legal discourse, both theoretically and practically. Of course, both theory and practice are still infused with a host of unresolved and evolving questions, However, while I will engage with many of the critiques and problems in the next chapter, I believe this chapter shows unequivocally the emergence of what I have defined an 'ecological jurisprudence'.

Such an emergence has taken many forms, from the slightly enlightened anthropocentrism of many environmental law provisions to the far more ecocentric approaches displayed by some of the rights of Nature initiatives. The question, therefore, once again arises as to where are the boundaries of an ecological jurisprudence to be found among the vast landscape of initiatives presented here. If an ecological jurisprudence is marked, as I have argued, by a rejection of an extreme anthropocentric worldview, then environmental law presents a fluid boundary, one where some provisions (for example, the introduction of the precautionary principle or the World Charter for Nature) certainly fall within the confines of an ecological jurisprudence, whereas others (such as the commodification of natural resources for human usage) do not. However, the question remains as to whether a *qualitative* difference in the theoretical positions discussed in the previous chapter exists in a clear and incontrovertible manner in the many practical and distinct examples of eco-jurisprudential initiatives. In other words, can environmental law and ecological law be cast in a fundamentally irreconcilable opposition to each other? To do so, one would have to argue that the former is still anthropocentric, whereas the latter is not. However, none of the initiatives described above seem to abandon the *entirety* of the anthropocentric worldview presented in the initial chapters of this book. It may even be argued that it may not be necessary (or even desirable) to do so and that rather, some elements of that worldview can (or are to) be maintained. Whether that is the case or not, however, the many legal and political initiatives inspired by environmental ecological concerns are far more theoretically intertwined than an apparent opposition may suggest. That is, at the very least, because of many of the legal and political assumptions that underpin these initiatives.

Furthermore, the lack of *practical* effectiveness of much environmental law does not necessarily entail the need for a *theoretical* distancing and differentiation from it. Moreover, writing decades after his initial article, Stone (2010, 145) proposed to assess claims about the lack of effectiveness of environmental law (and environmentalism in general) against a number of indicators: environmental literacy, general attitudes and preferences, willingness to contribute to environmental groups, environmentally sensitized individual actions, influence of lawmaking, public sector funding, litigation and direct indicators of environmental health. Apart from the last indicator, all others seem to be increasing, thus revealing a far more optimistic figure for the environmental movement and for environmental law in general. Naturally, the last of the indices is also the most important, indicating that the current trend is not *sufficient* to reverse the current environmental degradation. This is not to say, however, that it is not *necessary*. Environmental law, therefore, has a direct role to play in the current ecological trajectory of human governance systems.

While a different, more ecocentric, approach may be desirable, such an approach has found no complete historical realization (so far) in any of the initiatives discussed, and thus it may not be truly necessary to establish theoretical oppositions within the many movements, theories and advocates of an ecological jurisprudence. Rather, it may be more useful to think of any of the above initiatives as located within a spectrum underpinned by a distinct degree of rejection of extreme anthropocentrism. In fact, even the idea of this spectrum ought to be considered not in a scalar or linear manner, but rather in terms of degrees of intensity and self-reflection. Moreover, the emergence and evolution of law toward an ecological jurisprudence over the past few decades is remarkable in that it does not present a reactive response to an emerging crisis, but rather displays a veritable journey, a homeostatic trajectory toward a dynamic balance between anthropogenic and non-anthropogenic forces to maintain existing goldilocks environmental conditions, from a crude quantification of emission regulation toward a much deeper interrogation of legal theory itself, by gesturing toward an epistemological normativity that pushes beyond the traditional confines of Western legal theory.

Leaving aside some of the theoretical considerations (which will be investigated in the final chapter of this book), and by looking at all the above initiatives holistically and in the light of their theoretical underpinning, it becomes immediately apparent that many of these initiatives range from ecosystem services (located at the uncertain boundaries of an ecological jurisprudence) to the more progressive rights of Nature proposals. In other words, on the one hand, protection of and respect for Nature occurs primarily (or even exclusively) for the long-term benefit of humans (early conservationism and much of 'old' environmental law are examples of this position). This is a utilitarian or prudential approach, marked by the precautionary principle. On the other hand, Nature is seen as having intrinsic value and thus possesses, at least, the right to exist unhindered from human exploitation. In other words, one can either think that humans have a right to a healthy ecosystem or that the ecosystem itself possesses rights. If that is the ethical spectrum within which these initiatives are located, in terms of actual initiatives after environmental law (both domestically and internationally), rights of Nature initiatives are the ones that feature most prominently.

Linda Sheehan (2019, 229) notes that there are three ways to implement Nature's rights: firstly, by enforcing them through court action (which requires a sufficient degree of judicial education); secondly, by adopting 'follow-up laws that advance specific elements of broader, rights-based legislation'. Thirdly, by implementing rights of Nature law through administrative law (i.e. by developing regulations that recognize nature's rights). Moreover, the history of the rights of Nature movement has shown either a distinct articulation of legal subjectivity or an increase in litigation. Nicole Rogers calls the latter the 'human rights "turn" in climate litigation' (2020, 33) and describes how litigation occurs either against States or against corporations. She privileges the term 'climate justice' to link climate change effects on human rights infringements, both present and future. Rogers concludes her analysis by noting that '[i]t is arguable that there are inherent dangers in constructing a legal narrative of blame focused upon corporations. This narrative deflects attention away from the complicity of all carbon users, the daunting challenge of global transformative change, and the need for effective, transnational, mitigation policies' (53).

In summary, and leaving aside the history of environmental law (which has been successfully mapped elsewhere), even within the global rights of Nature movement there has been a very clear evolution, with three phases marking the movement:

- The first decade of the movement, from the first initiatives in the mid-2000s to the mid-2010s, marks the first phase of the movement, with a greater focus on the issue of 'rights', and the recognition of Nature (as a whole) as a legal subject *with* (or *of*) rights.
- A second phase emerged from the mid-2010s until the end of the decade, with a shift of focus from the issue of Nature's rights to the identification of the legal subject (or subjects) of those rights. Nature as a legal person became the focal point of many initiatives, with rivers initially taking centre stage (perhaps due to their being the essential arteries of fresh water along which human civilisations exist, as well as being relatively easy to identify in geographical terms). This phase also saw the development of much of the initial rights of Nature litigation.
- A third phase began, toward the end of the 2010s, with a rejection of the limitations that the extension of statutory personhood and of the right discourse entailed for much of the movement. This phase saw the emergence of much more nuanced theoretical scholarship in relation to the movement.

Furthermore, the movement also displays six distinct trends:

1. Firstly, an emphasis on local, municipal, 'bottom-up' initiatives, as typified by the US ordinances and municipal rules.
2. In parallel, the legal idiosyncrasies of the USA have also seen an increase of rights of Nature provisions being adopted by Tribal legal entities as a tool to convey Native American worldviews *for the benefit of the colonial collective.*
3. A very different, 'top-down' approach is the one adopted in Ecuador, with its corollary usage of constitutionally enshrined and legislated provisions on the part of institutional actors being the most effective way to implement these provisions.
4. A fourth trend is embodied by the Treaty settlements in New Zealand. While the *strategic* element displayed by Native American tribes is also present in New Zealand, its resolution is instead encapsulated in *negotiated* documents that operate as a synthesis of distinct legal ontologies (and are, undoubtedly, still a work in progress).
5. A fifth trend is captured by the judicial activism of the Colombian judiciary, whereby the shift toward an ecological jurisprudence is enacted not by civil society, the legislative or the executive, but rather by an ecologically inclined judiciary.
6. The final trend is the one adopted by the Plurinational State of Bolivia and focuses on the establishment of a global eco-jurisprudential framework. Of all the trends, this may be at the same time the most aspirational and yet, at the same time, the most symbolically powerful.

Kaufmann and Martin (2017) have also mapped and comparatively evaluated the emergence of rights of Nature in relation to a number of indicators. They argue that.

> RoN meta-norms have emerged globally over the last decade, expressed in governmental and nongovernmental institutions, from the UN General Assembly and IUCN to the GARN. These expressions share general normative beliefs regarding the intrinsic value of Nature, the need for humans to see themselves as part of Nature, and humans' obligations to live in harmony with Nature (59).

In their comparative analysis of three of the main jurisdictions involved in RoN over the first decade (the USA, Ecuador and New Zealand until then), they focused on a few key indicators, such as who the rights-bearing subject is, which rights are identified, what type of legal tool is used, where are RoN located within the domestic hierarchy of rights and who represents Nature. Their finding is as follows:

	Ecuador	USA (while acknowledging the wide variation of US RoN laws, they present the most common characteristics)	New Zealand
Who is the rights-bearing subject	All of Nature or Pachamama	Municipal ecosystems (the local 'natural community')	Specific natural entities (Te Urewera and Te Awa Tupua)
Which rights are identified	To exist and maintain ecosystem integrity	To exist and 'flourish'	Legal personhood status, with rights and duties
What type of law/ standing is adopted	Constitution	Municipal ordinances and home rule charters	Acts of Parliament
Where are RoN placed in the hierarchy of rights	RoN are declared as transversal	RoN are considered superior to corporate rights	n/a
Who represent Nature (and whether they have a mandate to do so)	Everyone (and they have no mandate)	City/municipal citizens (and they have no mandate)	Appointed guardians (and are mandated to represent the identified entities)

The indicators selected by Kauffmann and Martin operate well to identify many of the keystone concepts within the rights of Nature movement and will thus become the main foci of the next chapter. While emerging from the critiques against (and responses from) the rights of Nature movement, these points are central to the entirety of all eco-jurisprudential initiatives and can thus be adopted as the reference points to provide a protean analysis of the pragmatic aspects of the movement. I emphasize that the next chapter will focus mostly on the *praxis* of an ecological jurisprudence (even though it will do so from a theoretical standpoint), while the subsequent chapter will engage with more purely theoretical considerations. This is because, as Margaret Davies notes,

> [t]he change of orientation required by ecological thinking inspires a second set of … connections, that is, concerning the material entanglements of humans and all of their institutions with the nonhuman world. Meanings emerge from the material world and humans also emerge as beings from this world. Everything human belongs to material ecologies; as first and foremost physical beings we are entirely reliant on our habitat and environment … Thinking ecologically requires a repositioning, a flattening, of the subject and object: no longer in charge, no longer unique, no longer essentially individual, the human circulates in distributed networks in which are always becoming rather than being. We are ontologically object as much as subject, although we assume the position of subject and reify it through social forms and legal institutions. (2022, 18)

References

1855 Treaty Authority Resolution. Resolution No. 2018–05. adopted December 5, 2018.

2020–2021 Fiscal Year Budget, H.B. 166, 133rd Gen. Assemb., Reg. Sess. Ohio.

Address to the Diplomatic Corps Accredited to the Holy See. 8 January 2007: AAS 99

Adelson, G., James Engell, J., Ranalli, B., Van Anglen, K. P. (Eds.), *Environment, an interdisciplinary anthology*. Yale University Press.

Aguila, Y. (2017). La Adopción de un Pacto Internacional para la Protección del Medio Ambiente. *Mision Juridica: Revista De Derecho y Ciencias Sociales, 13*, 431.

Apostolic Letter Octogesima Adveniens (14 May 1971) 21: AAS 63: 416–417.

Arran Gare, A. (2009). Barbarity, civilization and decadence: Meeting the challenge of creating an ecological civilization. In M. Weber, R. Desmet, V. Chromatikon (Eds.), *Yearbook of philosophy in process*. Presses Universitaires de Louvain.

Atapattu, S. (2002). The right to a healthy life or the right to die polluted: the emergence of a human right to a healthy environment under international law. *Tulane Environmental Law Journal, 16*, 65–126.

Berat, L. (1993). Defending the right to a healthy environment: Towards a crime of geocide in international law. *Boston University International Law Journal, 11*, 327–348.

Berman, D. A. (2019). Lake Erie Bill of rights gets the Ax: Is legal personhood for nature dead in the water. *Sustainable Development Law and Policy, 20*(1), 15–16.

Bosselmann, K. (2008). *The principle of sustainability: Transforming law and governance*. Ashgate Publishing Co.

Bosselmann, K. (2010). Losing the forest for the trees: Environmental reductionism in the law. *Sustainability, 2*, 2424–2448.

Bosselmann K (2011) From reductionist environmental law to sustainability law. In P.D. Burdon (Ed.), *Exploring wild law: The philosophy of earth jurisprudence*. Wakefield Press.

Bosselmann, K. (2015). Global environmental constitutionalism: Mapping the Terrain. *Widener Law Review, 21*, 171–186.

Brown Weiss, E. (1990). Our rights and obligations to future generations for the environment. *American Journal of International Law, 84*, 198–207.

Boyd, D. R. (2015). *The optimistic environmentalist: Progressing towards a greener future*. ECW Press.

Boyd, D. R. (2017). *The rights of nature. A legal revolution that could save the World*. ECW.

Burdon, P. (2009). *Toward an earth-friendly legal system*. Eureka Street. http://www.eurekastreet.com.au/article.aspx?aeid=13932

Burdon, P. (2011). Earth rights: The theory. *IUCN Academy of Environmental Law eJournal, 1*, 1–2. https://566259-1852283-raikfcquaxqncofqfm.stackpathdns.com/wp-content/uploads/2021/09/EarthRights-ATheory.pdf

Burdon, P. (2014). Earth jurisprudence and the project of Earth democracy. In M. Maloney, P. Burdon (Eds.), *Wild law—In practice*. Routledge.
Campbell, S., & Gurney, L. (2020). Mapping and navigating ontologies in water governance: The case of the Ganges. *Water International*. https://doi.org/10.1080/02508060.2020.1812268
Cano Pecharroman, L. (2018). Rights of nature: Rivers that can stand in court. *Resources, 7*(13), https://doi.org/10.3390/resources7010013
CBD/COP/15/L25 18 December 2022 ('Kinming-Montreal Global biodiversity framework').
Center for Social Justice Studies et al. v Presidency of the Republic et al. Judgment T-622/16 (The Atrato River Case), Constituional Court of Colombia (10 November 2016) trans Dignity Rights Project, Delaware Law School, USA.
Cetacean Cmty. V. Bush, 386 F.3d 1169, 1173 (9th Cir. 2004).
Clark, C., Emmanouil, O., Page, J., & Pelizzon, A. (2019). Can You hear the rivers sing? Legal personhood, ontology and the nitty gritty of governance. *Ecology Law Quarterly, 45*, 787–844.
Charlotte Unruh, C. (2016). Present rights for future generations. *Kriterion, 30*(3), 77–92.
Clean Air Act 1956 (UK).
Clean Air Act 1963 42 U.S.C ch. 85 (7401-7671q).
Clean Water Act 1972 (USA)
Coho Salmon v Pacific Lumber Company, 61 F. Supp. 2d 1001 (N.D. Cal. 1999).
Constitution of the Plurinational State of Bolivia (2009).
Constitution of the Republic of Ecuador (2008).
Constitution of Portugal.
Constitucion Politica de la Ciudad de Mexico.
Constitucion Politica del Estado Libre y Soberano de Guerrero.
Constitutional Court of Ecuador, Ruling No. CASE No. 1149-19-JP/20 Reporting Judge: Agustín Grijalva.
Corte Constitucional del Ecuador. (2015). Sentencia No 166-15-SEP-CC Caso No 0507–12-EP p10.
Convention Destinée à Assurer la Conservation des Diverse Espèces Animales Vivant à l'Etat Sauvage en Afrique qui sont Utiles à l'Homme ou Inoffensive London 8 November 1933, 172 LNTS 242.
Convention on Biological Diversity (Rio de Janeiro) 5 June 1992, in force 29 December 1993, 31 ILM 822 (1992) (1992 Biodiversity Convention).
Convention for the Protection of the Ozone Layer (Vienna) 22 March 1985, in force 22 September 1988, 26 ILM 1529 (1985) (1985 Vienna Convention).
Convention for the Regulation of Whaling (Geneva) 24 September 1931, in force 16 January 1935, 155 LNTS 349.
Cullinan, C. (2011). *Wild law* (2nd ed.). Chelsea Green Publishing (First published 2002).
Cullinan, C. (2008). *If nature had rights. What would people need to give up?*' Orion Magazine. https://566259-1852283-raikfcquaxqncofqfm.stackpathdns.com/wp-content/uploads/2021/09/If-Nature-Had-Rights.pdf
Daly, E., Kotze, L., May, J., & Soyapi, C. (Eds.) (2017). *New frontiers in environmental constitutionalism*. UNEP.
Daly, H. E. (1991). *Steady-state economics* (2nd ed.). Island Press (First published 1977).
Davies, M. (2022). *EcoLaw: Legality, life, and the normativity of nature*. Routledge.
Devall, B., & Session, G. (2007). *Deep ecology*. Gibbs Smith.
De Lucia, V. (2013). Towards an ecological philosophy of law: A comparative discussion. *Journal of Human Rights and the Environment, 4*(2), 167–190.
Diamond, J. (2005). *Collapse. How societies choose to fail or succeed*. Penguin.
Draft Principles on Shared National Resources, 17 ILM 1094 (1978).
Eck, D. L. (1996). Gangā: The Goddess Gang4s in Hindu sacred geography. In J.S. Hawley, & D.M. Wilff (Eds.), *Devī: Goddesses of India*. University of California Press.
ELGA. (2016). *Oslo manifesto' (2016) ELGA our mission, Our vision*. https://elgaworld.org/oslo-manifesto. Accessed December 11, 2020.

Encyclical Letter Centesimus Annus (1 May 1991), 38: AAS 83 (1991), 841.

Endangered Species Act 1973 (USA).

Falk, R. A. (1973). Environmental warfare and ecocide—Facts, appraisal, and proposals. In T. Marek (Ed.), *Bulletin of peace proposals*. Universitersforlaget.

Fitzroy river declaration. https://static1.squarespace.com/static/5e86add4e98f7421bace70f1/t/5e9fcc157dedb86cbb06a2e9/1587530798453/fitzroy-river-declaration.pdf

Fox, M. A. (1987). Nuclear weapons and the ultimate environmental crisis. *Environmental Ethics, 9*, 170.

Gaia Foundation. (2019). *Rights of nature gain ground in Uganda's legal system*. Gaia Foundation. Accessed January 16, 2022.

Gare, A. (2012). China and the struggle for ecological civilization. *Capitalism Nature Socialism, 23*(4), 10–26.

Gare, A. (2017). *The philosophical foundations of ecological civilization. A manifesto for the future*. Routledge.

Gare, A. (2021). The eco-socialist roots of ecological civilisation. *Capitalism Nature Socialism, 32*(1), 37–55.

G.A. Res. 37/7, World Charter on Nature (Oct. 28, 1982).

GARN. (2022). *Eco-jurisprudence monitor*. https://ecojurisprudence.org

Garver, G. (2013). The rule of ecological law: the legal complement to degrowth economics. *Sustainability, 5*, 316–337.

General Assembly resolution 177 (II) of 21 November 1947.

Goodman, M., & Thornton, J. (2017). *Client Earth*. Scribe.

Gray, M. A. (1996). The international crime of ecocide. *California Western International Law Journal, 26*, 215–271.

The Hague Principles' (Earth Trusteeship, 2020). www.earthtrusteeship.world/the-hague-principles-for-a-universal-declaration-on-human-responsibilities-and-earth-trusteeship/. Accessed 11 December 2020

Halskov Hanse, M., Hongtao Li, H., & Svaervurd, R. (2018). Ecological civilization: Interpreting the Chinese past, projecting the global future. *Global Environmental Change, 53*, 195–203.

Haywood, T. (2005). *Constitutional environmental rights*. Oxford University Press.

Heinberg, R. (2011). *The end of growth*. New Society Publishers, Gabriola.

Higgins, P. (2011). Towards a garden of Eden. In P. Burdon (Ed.), *Exploring wild law: The philosophy of earth jurisprudence*. Wakefield Press.

Higgins, P., Short, D., & South, N. (2013). Protecting the planet: A proposal for a law of ecocide. *Crime Law Social Change, 59*, 251–266.

Holder, J. (2000). New age: Rediscovering natural law. *Current Legal Problems, 53*(1), 151–179.

Human Rights and Peace for Bangladesh v Government of Bangladesh and others (201)] HCD (Writ Petition No 13989 of 2016, judgment declared on 3 February 2019, translation from Banlga by MS Islam) (Bangladesh Rivers case).

Houck, O. (2017–2018) Noah's second voyage: The rights of nature as law. *Tulane Environmental Law Journal, 31*(1), 1–49.

Innu Council of Ekuanitshit, No 919-082, Dossier No. 919-01-18, 12 January 2021

International Climate Justice Network 2002 Bali Principles of Climate Justice

International Convention for the Prevention of Pollution of the Sea by Oil London, 12 May 1954, in force 26 July 1958, 327 UNTS 3.

Islam, M. S., & O'Donnell, E. (2020). Legal rights for the Turag: Rivers as living entities in Bangladesh. *Asia Pacific Journal of Environmental Law, 23*(2), 160–177.

International Union for Conservation of Nature. (2012). Incorporation of the Rights of Nature as the organizational focal point in IUCN's decision making (Resolution WCC-2012-Res-100) (Report).

Jones, C. (2016). *New treaty: New tradition*. UBC Press.

Juliana v United States, 217 F. Supp. 3d 1224, 1260-61 (D Or, No 6:15-cv-01517-TC).

Kauffman, C. M. (2020). *Mapping transnational rights of nature networks & laws: New global governance structures for more sustainable development* (Unpublished). Harmony with Nature. http://files.harmonywithnatureun.org/uploads/upload924.pdf

Kauffman, C. M., & Martin, P. L. (2017). Can rights of nature make development more sustainable? Why some Ecuadorian lawsuits succeed and others fail. *World Development, 92*, 130–142.

Kauffman, C. M., & Martin, P. L. (2019). How courts are developing river rights jurisprudence: Comparing guardianship in New Zealand, Colombia, and India. *Vermont Journal of Environmental Law, 20*(3), 260–289.

Kauffman, C. M., & Martin, P. L. (2021). *The politics of rights of nature*. MIT Press.

Kedzior, S. B. (2015). Pollution and the renegotiation of river goddess worship and water use practices among the Hindu devotees of India's Ganges/ganaga River. In S.D. Brunn (Ed.), *The changing world religion map: Sacred places, identities, practices and politics*. Springer.

Knox, J. H., & Pejan, R. (2018). Introduction to the human right to a healthy environment. In J.H. (Ed.), *The human right to a healthy environment*. Cambridge University Press.

Kotari, A., & Bajpai, S. (2017). We are the river, the river is us. *Economic & Political Weekly, 52*(37), 103–109.

Lake Erie Bill of Rights (USA).

Lalit Miglani v. State of Uttarakhand & Others. (2017). MCC 139/2017 (India).

Ley 071 de Derechos de la Madre Tierra (Bolivia).

Ley 19/2022, de 30 de septiembre, para el reconocimiento de personalidad juridica a la laguna del Mar Menor y su Cuenca. BOE-A-2022-16019. Spain.

Loggerhead Turtle v County Council of Volusia County, Fla. 148 F.3d 1231 (11th Cir. 1998).

Lowe, I. (2014). Wild law embodies values for a sustainable future. In M. Maloney & P.D. Burdon (Eds.), *Wild law—In practice*. Routledge.

M'Gonigle, M. (2008). Green legal theory: A new approach to the concept of environmental law. *Okologisches Wirtschaften*, 4.

M'Gonigle, M., & Ramsay, P. (2004). Greening environmental law: From sectoral reform to systemic re-formation. *Journal of Environmental Law and Practice, 14*, 1–27.

Margil, M. (2014). Building an international movement. In M. Maloney & P.D. Burdon (Eds.), *Wild law—In practice*. Routledge.

Margil, M. (2021). *Los Derechos de la Naturaleza: Rights-Based Protection for Pachamama*. Global Alliance for the Rights of Nature. https://566259-1852283-raikfcquaxqncofqfm.stackpathdns.com/wp-content/uploads/2021/09/Margil_Rights-Based-Protection_Pachamama.pdf

Marine Mammal Protection Act 1972 (USA).

Mariqueo-Russell, A. (2017). Rights of nature and the precautionary principle. *Transformations in Environment and Society, 6*, 21–30.

May, J. R., & Daly, E. (2015). *Global environmental constitutionalism*. Cambridge University Press.

Menominee Indian Tribe of Wisconsin Resolution no. 19–52: Recognition of the Rights of the Menominee River. (2020).

Miller, M. (2019). Environmental personhood and standing for nature: Examining the Colorado River case. *University of New Hampshire Law Review, 17*, 355–377.

Mohd. Salim v. State of Uttarakhand & Others. (2017). Uttarakhand HC 126 (India).

Moore International Arbitral Awards. (1893).

Moore, J. (2024). *The fear & the fix: How environmentalism serves the powerful*. The Baffler. https://thebaffler.com/latest/the-fear-and-the-fix-moore

Moutrie, M. J. (2020). The rights of nature movement in the united states: Community organizing, local legislation, court challenges, possible lessons and pathways. *Barry Environmental and Earth Law Journal, 10*(1), 5–63.

Mullick v Mullick L.R 52 Ind. App. 245 (Privy Council 1925).

Narayan Dutt Bhatt v. Union of India & Others Uttarakhand High Court Writ Petition No. 43 of 2014.

Nez Perce Tribe Resolution SPGC20-02 on the Snake River. (2020).

Nonhuman Rights Project, Inc. v Lavery 100 N.E.3d 846. (2018). at 849.

O'Brien, K., Selboe, E., & Hayward, B. M. (2018). Exploring youth activism on climate change: dutiful, disruptive and dangerous dissent. *Ecology and Society, 23*(3), 1–13.
O'Bryan, K. (2017). Giving a voice to the river and the role of indigenous people: Whanganui river settlement and river management in Victoria. *Australian Indigenous Law Review, 20*, 48–77.
O'Donnell, E. L. (2018). At the intersection of the sacred and the legal: Rights for nature in Uttarakhand, India. *Journal of Environmental Law, 30*, 135–144.
Palila v hawaii Department of Land and Natural Resources 471 F Supp 985. (1979).
Jiahua Pan, J. (2016). *China's environmental governing and ecological civilization*. Springer.
Pan, Y. (2003). *Environmental culture and national revival*. Ministry of Ecology and Environment of the People's Republic of China. http://www.mee.gov.cn/gkml/sthjbgw/qt/200910/t20091030_180661.htm
Passamaquoddy Tribe Joint Tribal Council of the St Croix River and Alewife Resolution. (2012).
People v Fimbres 228 P. 19, 20. (1930). Ex parte Ackerman, 6 Cal. App. 5, 13; 91 P. 429, 433 (1907).
People v. Gray 571 N.Y.S.2d 851, 866 (Crim. Ct. 1991).
Pollution Protection Act 1990 (USA).
Pope Francis. (2015) *Laudato Si'. On care for our common home*. Libreria Editrice Vaticana.
Protocol on Access to Genetic Resources and the Fair and Equitable Sharing of Benefits Arising from Their Utilization to the Convention on Biological Diversity (Nagoya) 29 October 2010, not in force, C. N. 782.2010.TREATIES-1 (2010 Nagoya Protocol).
Protocol on Substances that deplete the Ozone Layer (Montreal) 16 September 1987, in force 1 January 1989, 26 ILM 154 (1987) (1987 Montreal Protocol).
Protocol to the United Nations Framework Convention on Climate Change (Kyoto) 11 December 1997, in force 16 February 2005, 37 ILM 22 (1998) (1997 Kyoto Protocol).
Putzer, A., Lambooy, T., Jeurissen, R., & Kim, E. (2022). Putting the rights of nature on the map. A quantitative analysis of rights of nature initiatives across the world. *Journal of Maps*, https://doi.org/10.1080/17445647.2022.2079432
Ramsar Convention on Wetlands if International Importance Especially as Waterfwol Habitat 2 February 1971, in force 21 December 1975, 996 UNTS 245 (Ramsar Convention).
Raworth, K. (2017). *Doughnut economics: Seven ways to think like a 21st-century economist*. Random House.
Report—Our Common Future. (1987).
Report of the UN Conference on the Human Environment, Stockholm, 5–15 June 1972. UN Doc. A/CONF.48/14/Rev. 1.
Republicà de Colombia, Corte Suprema de Justicia (Apr. 5, 2018) STC 4360–2018. Future Generations v. Ministry of Environment et al. TOLOSA VILLABONA, P. J. Supreme Court of Justice STC4360–2018 Bogotá, D.C., April 5th, 2018
Resolution 63/278 https://undocs.org/A/RES/64/196.
Rio+30 Cities Conference on Sustainable and Inclusive Urban Development. https://rio30.rio/en/
Rogers, N. (2011). Where the wild things are: Finding the wild in law. In P. Burdon (Ed.), *Exploring wild law: The philosophy of earth jurisprudence*. Wakefield Press.
Rogers, N. (2020). *Law, fiction and activism in a time of climate change*. Routledge.
Sand, P., & Peel, J. (2012). *Principles of international environmental law* (3rd ed.). Cambridge University Press.
Santa Monica City Council, City of Santa Monica Regular City Council Meeting Agenda. (24 Jan 2020).
Santa Monica, C. Municipal Code art 12 Ch 12.02-03 (added by Ord No 2421 CCS para 1, adopted 4/9/13; amended by Ord No 2611CCS para 10, adopted 6/25/19).
Sax, J. L. (1970). The public trust doctrine in natural resource law: effective judicial intervention. *Michigan Law Review, 68*, 471–566.
Sbert Carlsson, C. (2019). *Mining from the lens of ecological law: Obstacles and opportunities for re-formation* (Ph.D. thesis). University of Ottawa.

Sheehan, L. (2019). Implementing nature's rights through regulatory standards. *Vermont Journal of Environmental Law, 20*(3), 227–242.

Sohn, L. (1973). The Stockholm declaration on the human environment. *Harvard International Law Journal, 14*, 423–515.

Stone, C. (2010). *Should trees have standing? Law, morality, and the environment* (3rd ed.). Oxford University Press.

Sydes, B. (2014). The challenges of putting Wild Law into practice In Maloney M, Burdon P D (eds) Wild Law – In Practice. Routledge, Oxon

Tallis, H., & Kareiva, P. (2005). Ecosystem services. *Current Biology,* 15.

Tao, B. (2005). *Environmental law system in China.* China Daily. http://www.chinadaily.com.cn/english/doc/2005-09/26/content_480788.htm

Te Awa Tupua (Whanganui River Claims Settlement) Act 2017, ss 3, 7(b), 57 (N.Z.).

Temper, L. (2018). Blocking pipelines, unsettling environmental justice: from rights of nature to responsibility to territory. *Local Environment*, 14. https://doi.org/10.1080/13549839.2018.1536698

Tennessee Valley Authority v Hill, 437 U.S. 153 (1978).

Tercer Juzgado de Garantias, case no. P-72.254/15, 44 (Mza.). Argentina

Trail Smelter case, 16 April 1938, 11 March 1941, 3 RIAA 1907 (1941).

Turner, S. J. (2017). Quantitative standards within the environmental provisions of national constitutions—Bhutan and Kenya. In E. Daly, L. Kotze, J. May, & C. Soyapi (Eds.), *New Frontiers in environmental constitutionalism.* UNEP.

UN Charter, San Francisco, 26 June 1945, in force 24 October 1945, 1 UNTS

United Nations Convention on the Law of the Sea (Montego Bay) 10 December 1982, in force 16 November 1994, 21 ILM 1261 (1982) (UNCLOS).

UNEP. (2019). *Environmental rule of law.* United Nations Environment Programme

United Nations Framework Convention on Climate Change (New York) 9 May 1992, in force 24 March 1994, 1771 UNTS 107 (1992 Climate Change Convention).

UNGA Res 37/7, 28 October 1982.

UNGA Res. 42/187 (1987).

UNGA Res. 43/196 (1988).

US Resolution 005-2018, 9 August 2018.

Urgenda Foundation v. Kingdom of the Netherlands, Translation of Summons, 15, ¶ 28 (June 25, 2015), http://www.urgenda.nl/documents/FINAL-DRAFT-Translation-Summons-incase-Urgenda-v-Dutch-State-v.25.06.10.pdf

Van Rossum, M. K. (2017). *The green amendment.* Disruption Books.

Vicente Gimenez, T. (2023). The Mar Menor: an ecosystem with its own rights. In Y. Vega Cardenas, D. Turp (Eds.), *A legal personality for the St lawrence river and other rivers of the world.* Editions JFD

Villavicenzio Calzadilla, P. (2019). A paradigm shift in courts' view of nature: The Atrato River and Amazon Basin cases in Colombia. *Law, Environment and Development Journal, 15*, 1–11.

Villavicenzio Calzadilla, P., Kotzé, J., & L J,. (2018). Living in harmony with nature? A critical appraisal of the rights of Mother Earth in Bolivia. *Transnational Environmental Law, 7*(3), 397–424.

Von Moltke, K. (1988). *The Vorsorgeprinzip in West German environmental policy*. In Royal Commission on Environmental Pollution - Twelfth Report

Wackernagel, M., et al. (1999). National natural capital accounting with the ecological footprint concept. *Ecological Economics, 29*, 375–390.

Wiener, D. R. (1999). *A little corner of freedom: Russian nature protection from Stalin to Gorbachev.* University of California Press.

Wheeler et al. v. Director de la Procuraduria General del Estado en Loja, Corte Provincial de Justicia de Loja, 31 marzo 2011, Judgment 11121–2011-0010.

White Earth Reservation Business Committee Resolution No. 001-19-009, adopted 31 Dec 2018. (Resolution 001-19-009 and Resolution 001-19-010.

Wijdekop, F. (2016). Against ecocide: Legal protection for Earth. *Great Transition Initiative*, 2
Wilderness Act 1964 (USA).
Wilkinson, C. F. (1989). The headwaters of the public trust: Some thoughts on the source and scope of the traditional doctrine. *Environmental Law, 19*, 425.
Yarra River Protection (Wilip-gin Birrarung murron) Act 2017 (Vic) s 1(a) (Australia)
Yates, J. S., Harris, L. M., & Wilson, N. J. (2017). Multiple ontologies of water: Politics, conflict and implications for governance. *Environment and Planning: Society and Space, 35*(5), 797–815.
Yurok Tribe, Resolution of the Yurok Tribal Council No. 19-40 (9 May 2019).), Yurok Tribal Council Resolution 19-40 Resolution Establishing the Rights of the Klamath River.
Zhihe Wang, Z. (2014). The ecological civilization debate in China. *Monthly Review, 66*(6).
Zelle, A. R., Wilson, G., Adam, R., & Greene, H. F. (Eds.) (2021). *Earth law. Emerging ecocentric law—A guide for practitioners*. Wolters Kluver.

Chapter 7
Relationality, Reciprocity and Responsibility

The voice of the inanimate object, therefore, should not be stilled. That does not mean that the judiciary takes over the managerial functions from the federal agency. It merely means that before these priceless bits of Americana (such as a valley, an alpine meadow, a river, or a lake) are forever lost or are so transformed as to be reduced to the eventual rubble of our urban environment, the voice of the existing beneficiaries of these environmental wonders should be heard. Perhaps they will not win. Perhaps the bulldozers of "progress" will plow under all the aesthetic wonders of this beautiful land. That is not the present question. The sole question is, who has standing to be heard? ... That is why these environmental issues should be tendered by the inanimate object itself. Then there will be assurances that all of the forms of life which it represents will stand before the court - the pileated woodpecker as well as the coyote and bear, the lemmings as well as the trout in the streams. Those inarticulate members of the ecological group cannot speak. But those people who have so frequented the place as to know its values and wonders will be able to speak for the entire ecological community.
(Justice Douglas, dissenting opinion, Sierra Club v Morton, 1972)

The previous chapter has shown that human legal and regulatory regimes in relation to the environment have been profoundly influenced by the emergence of ecological thought over the past decades, leading to a wide range of constitutional, statutory, judicial and political provisions and initiatives that challenge the anthropocentric worldview that underpins the current environmental predicament. However, while different theoretical standpoints and distinct initiatives display different ontological and axiological premises, no *actual* constitutional, legislated, judicial, or even civil society-driven initiative has rejected an anthropocentric worldview *in toto*. It is also useful to remember once more that the term 'anthropocentrism' is here used as a heuristic device and defined in an enlarged sense, as the total sum of a reconstructed worldview. Therefore, if actual initiatives do not reject the *entirety* of that world-view (whether that is even possible, is another question that will be explored in the

A. Pelizzon, *Ecological Jurisprudence*, Contemporary Environmental Law and Policy,
https://doi.org/10.1007/978-981-96-0173-8_7

following chapter), then any internal distinction between eco-jurisprudential theoretical perspectives appear to be somewhat arbitrary. However, this does not mean that specific critiques ought to be subsumed under a generic undifferentiated banner. On the contrary, the specific nuances of each argument become even more relevant, since the ontological and axiological position adopted in each particular circumstance, the emergence of an ecological jurisprudence suggests, is central to situating any such particular initiative. As a result, I will focus on some of the key issues of reflection and contention I have identified over the past fifteen years within the movement.

7.1 Environmental Law v Earth Law

As previously mentioned, some critics argue that environmental law and many new eco-jurisprudential initiatives are radically distinct. The former are said to be unsuccessful notwithstanding 50 years of application in stopping environmental changes, whereas the latter are heralded as a solution to the current environmental predicament. While the argument is relevant in focusing on the *philosophical* and *ethical* premises underpinning any of those initiatives, this book, I hope, has shown the very complex ethical and philosophical terrain within which *all* of these initiatives are located. To try and identify a *specific* philosophical and ethical milieu for the *entirety* of environmental law appears too broad (and perhaps simplistic) a task—and ultimately unnecessary if the goal is to challenge the anthropocentric assumptions that are seen as the root of current predicament. In this sense, both environmental law and all the more ecocentric initiatives discussed in the previous chapter are examples of a global tendency toward changes of behaviour facilitated (or even directly caused) by law in relation to the 'natural' world. Moreover, as noted in the concluding remarks of the previous chapter, many indicia of effectiveness seem to have *improved* over the past few decades, apart from any actual changes to measurements pertaining to the state of the environment itself. While such is a legitimate critique advanced toward the operation of environmental law over the past few decades the same critique can be advanced toward all the supposedly more ecocentric initiatives apparently cast against an inherently anthropocentric environmental law. Notwithstanding (in some cases) more than 15 years of experimentation, neither the rights of Nature movement nor any of the other initiatives seem to have stopped the *global* trend toward the current environmental predicament.

As a result, I will leave aside the general critiques advanced toward environmental law and will instead focus more specifically on the critiques advanced toward the more ecocentric initiatives that have been developed over the years. Since, among those initiatives, rights of Nature provisions are by far the most numerous, I will focus more specifically on them. After all, Arturo Escobar notes, rights of Nature have been heralded not just as 'alternative development' but as an 'alternative *to* development' (1992, 20).

7.1.1 The Rights of Nature: A Critical Appraisal

Much of the initial scholarship on rights of Nature is found in Spanish, pioneered by authors such the Ecuadorian Alberto Acosta, Esperanza Martinez and Ramiro Avila and the Uruguayan Eduardo Gudynas. English scholarship, virtually non-existent just over a decade ago, has grown exponentially since the mid-2010s.

Notwithstanding the many advocates of rights of Nature discussed in the previous two chapters, the very *idea* of rights of Nature has attracted a significant degree of criticism. Ariel Rawson and Becky Mansfield, for example, argue that RoN

> recapitulates the precise logic of dualism it seeks to undo. In the name of a nondualist biocentric alternative to the anthropocentric dualism of modernity and western modes of being and living, RoN enacts an elemental division between inside and outside, the west and the rest ... Second ... by treating rights of nature as a natural truth RoN ... naturalizes the colonial history of legal personhood ... RoN enacts a contradictory logic, where in the name of overcoming western human-nature dualism, and its concomitant anthropocentrism, it turns to western notions of rights, personhood, and holism as the solution ... Our argument is that the rights-based approach and holistic models of life that constitute RoN are not just connected to the same western ideas of nature and law it rejects, but through these connections western thought and modes of existence are further universalized as natural. (2018, 100–1)

Julien Bétaille (2019) further argues that many of the problems that RoN tries to cure, such as the difficulty of enforcement, can be replicated and reproduced without careful attention to avoid them. Daniel Matthews writes that, overall, '[m]any commentators see inherent flaws in the Anthropocene terminology, particularly the implication that a unified *anthropos* is responsible for the present climate emergency' (2021, 33). Indeed, as previous chapters will have hopefully shown, such a unified *anthropos* is not a historical reality, but rather the heuristic indicator of a dominant worldview that impacts the overall human relationship with the nonhuman world in a disproportionate way. This critique is entailed by the linguistic choices of many of the early authors. Thomas Berry himself, for example, often speaks of a generic 'humanity' whose task is the current 'Great Work', without consistently noting that this is only one mode of existence that has led to the current environmental predicament. While Berry deeply and consistently acknowledges this to be the case, the language of his writing at times obscures it.

Daniel Matthews's critique of the theory of Earth Jurisprudence is also predicated on the perceived limitation of its '*political aesthetics*', which 'advances themes of *harmony, integrity* and *wholeness* in a way that is utterly disconnected from the messy entanglements to which Latour's reading of Gaia attends' (2021, 37). My personal experience with many activists and proponents of Earth Jurisprudence does not support this critique. The idea of *harmony* and *wholeness* Matthews presents is cast as somewhat static and idyllic, a modern version of a seventeenth-century arcadia, almost a caricature of the ecological principles of *homeostasis* and dynamic balance that the vast majority of the people I have interacted with and interviewed display. Indeed, the idea of 'harmony' is often used in two distinct senses. Firstly, of peaceful co-existence of all that *is*, or secondly, as a general tendency to homeostasis. The former is, in my experience, unlikely to be subscribed to by any serious participant in the movement, whereas the latter is more generally accepted as a 'technical' meaning within the scholarly community that embraces it and that normatively advocates for a degree of respect for relative balance and slow change. Matthews's critique, of course, remains valid (and importantly so) at a theoretical level and ought to be preserved as remainder of the risks of simplistic reduction of a far more complex reality. However, the critique, when cast against the texts themselves, may not be necessarily true. Even Berry's own work, which arguably represents the greatest example of the argument for harmony, integrity and wholeness, displays a far less idyllic understanding of the operation of the nonhuman world: '[v]iolence and destruction are dimensions of the universe', Berry openly admits (Swimme & Berry, 1994, 51).

Another critique, stemming directly from the presentation of a single *anthropos* as the author of the current environmental predicament, takes a different pragmatic turn. Virginia Marshall's argument is less focused on the theoretical implications of the emerging rights of Nature movement and more on the pragmatic political impacts it has on already dispossessed peoples. Marshall begins by recognizing that while '[i]n Aboriginal ontology and law customary water use cannot be decoupled from its relationship with the environment because Aboriginal water concepts are central to community and kinship relationships with "Country" …the removal of Indigenous peoples from holding property rights, for example, to a river, a mountain or land is antithetical to the Indigenous rule of law and their cultural obligation' (2020, 1–2). Marshall then continues by arguing that Indigenous people have spent decades (if not centuries) to obtain the recognition of basic rights inscribed within the colonial legal framework, and thus the eco-jurisprudential pivot in the framework now puts an additional burden on them to pivot as well, both theoretically (having to reconceptualize their relationship with the settler state) and pragmatically (by having to direct resources to such a change). The 'liberation of Nature', she writes, fractures Indigenous inherent rights. The speed of the change means that '[t]he challenge in the construct of the rights to nature ideology is that it is counterintuitive and counterproductive to the … laws, customs and practices of Australia's First Peoples. The construct of nature as a legal entity invariably replaces accepted western concepts of property and also undermines the exercise of Indigenous elf-determination and inherent governance'. I will return to the intersection of Indigenous rights and the rights of Nature movement in the next chapter, but suffice it to say, for now, that the emergence of more ecocentric perspectives in legal theory and practice is not, and cannot be, separate from historical issues of colonialism, dispossession and power differential. Irrespective of the theoretical desirability of a shift toward an ecocentric perspective, the recognition that both the perspective one is shifting *from* (anthropocentrism) and the one they are shifting *to* (ecocentrism) are equally culturally inscribed and should be cautious about universalizing any ensuing proposal without a carefully constructed global dialogue.

Related to the critique of the *anthropos* is the alleged tautological nature of the human legal process. Oliver Houck writes that while trees may have standing, they cannot *talk*, let alone be physically *brought to court*. As a result, they will always 'need a human after all, which leads us back to homocentric litigation' (2017–8,

16–7). In fact, he continues, this 'leads us instead to the conflation of lawyer and client'. I will return to the issue of representation below, but it may be useful to note that Houck concludes by remarking that '[l]awyers represent ships, estates, and other non-people every day. As they could, just as easily, Mineral King. For these purposes, trees don't need tongues, or an IQ of one, for that matter' (27). The issue of representation, however, is certainly a complex one, lest the entities represented are construed as somewhat 'second-class', and as inherently defined by the measure of those representing them. Others critique the *anthropos* and reject the idea of rights of Nature, because, they argue, 'nature' itself no longer exists, either as a conceptual category (as Bruno Latour proposes) or in a very physical sense (as Bill McKibben has suggested): '[w]e are in the Anthropocene, human impacts are everywhere, and there is no natural baseline' (Kareiva et al., 2012).

Another common critique, to which I will return more in depth below, has been the extension of the liberal rights discourse to Nature, seen as an extension of the same liberal limitations contained within the very idea of rights. However, both Stone and Cullinan intimate that the language of rights is entailed *pragmatically*. Since rights are used, extensively, by corporations and fictional entities, then, unless rights are removed from the social discourse *entirely*, it stands to reason that the same discourse is extended to the nonhuman world. Minhea Tanasescu writes that 'rights liberalism has evolved to be a growing kaleidoscope of rights that are incompatible with each other and therefore remain at the mercy of the state for resolution and effective application'. However, he adds, this does not mean that '[t]he rights of nature … *inherently* do this'. Instead, he argues that 'a certain *kind* of rights, enamored with totality and completely un-critical of its own intellectual inheritance, can—perhaps despite themselves—do this. But the rights of nature harbor other possibilities as well' (2022, 119). Peter Burdon writes that 'Earth rights can be seen first and foremost as articulating an ethical demand. They are not principally legal or proto legal and even though they have inspired legislation, this is a further fact, rather than their constitutive character' (2011, 1). In exploring the relationship between the conferral of rights and personhood on rivers in Colombia, India and Aotearoa New Zealand, Elizabeth Macpherson and others ask whether these cases 'might be the result of activists 'learning to play the legal game better' or of judges, lawyers and politicians seeking to 'make their mark' through novel legal mechanisms inspired by alternative value-systems' (2021).

Some ask, given the extent of environmental legislation across the planet, whether rights of Nature (and other forms of ecocentric initiatives) are even necessary. The implication, of course, is that they are not. Houck, however, disagrees and notes that '[t]he record to date is otherwise':

> [f]or one, they reinforce and expand the interpretation of those same laws, adding restoration requirements to some, enforcement to others. They also provide a safety net where existing programs have been overwhelmed by other interests, or because they fail to address the injury at all … More proactively, they provide a seat at the table, in advance of development decisions, for nature rights to appear through the lens of its own needs and not simply the cacophony of competing human interests. … As proactively, they provide a vantage point to demand restoration for past injury and to insist on compensation going forward. … Lastly,

> and perhaps more enduringly, they catalyze a new awareness of our relationship with the natural world, which, in turn, could play a larger role in human survival than many now admit. (2017–8, 94–6)

The self-portrayed *strategic* and *pragmatic* nature of much of the rights of Nature discourse has been one of its fundamental features from the beginning. Many activists and advocates I have interviewed emphasize (and perhaps, at times, over-emphasize) the importance of a 'practical' outcome or implementation of the initiatives they advocate, often at the expenses of more nuanced theoretical considerations. While the desire for immediacy may be motivated by the perceived sense of environmental urgency, it is important to caution against ignoring many of the ontological and axiological implications of any position being taken, lest their obscuration lead to a host of unintended (and undesirable) consequences. Mihnea Tănăsescu (2022) summarizes three key reminders about the emergence of the rights of Nature movement over the past two decades: firstly, '*[t]he rights of nature are not a monolith.* … There has been international diffusion of this idea, to be sure, but this does not mean that all cases can be subsumed under a unifying label propagated by a broad movement'. I will return to this point in the next paragraph below. Secondly, '*[t]he most useful frame for understanding the rights of nature is political, not legal.* One cannot understand what the rights of nature are *doing* without thinking about them in terms of power relations. All too often, strictly legal interpretations forget that legal norms are as good as their implementation, which necessarily passes through political power'. And thirdly, '*[t]he rights of nature are not primarily about nature.* … The rights of nature are neither a universal solution to environmental harm, nor uniquely placed to solve such harm. In fact, they are not primarily about the environment at all, but about creating new relations through which environmental concerns may be differently expressed'. Importantly, '[w]hat "environmental concerns" look like is entirely dependent on the power configuration that births them, [and thus] *[h]ow rights of nature laws/provisions/regulations are drafted matters a lot!*'

Craig Kauffman and Pamela Martin (2021) have interrogated the relatively sudden emergence of rights of Nature from 2006 onward. RoN and Earth Jurisprudence, they argue (and this book has surely shown), had existed as ideas for decades, but had remained philosophical discussions at the margins of law and policy until 2006. 'What', they ask 'explains the timing of RoN's rise as a salient international norm and its institutionalization through law and policy?' (11). Indeed, within the short space of four years, four countries somewhat independently adopted RoN provisions: the USA from 2006 onward, Ecuador in 2008, Bolivia in 2009/2010 and New Zealand in 2012. It would appear, Kauffman and Martin argue, that policy and norm diffusion were at work. Yet, all these early RoN laws 'differ in key ways, including their definition of Nature, the rights granted, enforcement provisions, and their institutional structure. This variation', they conclude, 'contradicts predominant models of policy and norm diffusion, which predict policy convergence' (11). Rather, the authors suggest an initial convergent development (as discussed in the previous chapter) that led to rights of Nature provision emerging independently at the same time. One cannot fail to be reminded of Bill Twist's remark, cited in the previous chapter, that the time for this powerful idea had, indeed, arrived. If the convergent emergence theory is correct, the reasons for timing of this emergence (the mid-2000s) are yet to be further explored. Nonetheless, once the first provisions were established, a movement soon emerged, as Kauffmann and Martin have demonstrated, leading to a deep level of reciprocal influence (*contra* Tanasescu's point above). Furthermore, the two authors then develop a framework to analyse RoN laws along two conceptual axes: scope and strength. '*Scope* refers to the range of rights afforded and how broadly these rights are applied; this has normative implications regarding how Nature is conceptualized and defined in practice. *Strength* refers to enforcement capacity expressed through laws' formal authority and individuals' capacity and responsibility to enforce Nature's right' (14–5).

A similar analysis is offered by Marsha Moutrie (2020) in relation to the local ordinances in the USA. One of the main critiques of these ordinances concerns what is perceived as an excessive focus on combating the alleged evils of corporate interests. While the pervasiveness of profit-driven corporate interests is undeniable, the critics argue, such a focus risks to obscure the effect of other conflicts of rights. Indeed, if the primary purpose of these ordinances is to protect the local communities' rights against their encroachment by external corporate interests—and the rights of the local ecosystems are subsumed within this purview—then, at least hypothetically, communities who choose to destroy and despoil their local ecosystems ought to be able to do so against any external mandate to the contrary. While the issue has been, so far, hypothetical, it remains nonetheless present.

That aside, Moutrie focuses on the legal trajectory of the ordinances that had been passed until the time of her writing (2020). Only a small number of the US community rights laws were challenged in court, particularly Grant Township and Highland Township in Pennsylvania, Mora County in New Mexico, Lafayette in Colorado and Toledo, Ohio. In the case of the first two, the Federal Court determined that the community rights laws were invalid because they violated corporate constitutional rights. In the Grant Township case, the Grant Township and PGE settlement did not end the dispute. PGE sought to recover US$ 500,000 in attorney's fees and costs, claiming that such costs had been incurred as a result of frivolous unfounded claims. The District Court Judge awardee US$ 52,000 against two CELDF attorneys on the basis that '[t]he continued pursuit of frivolous claims and defences, despite [the lead attorney's] first-hand claim of their insufficiency ... substantially and inappropriately prolonged th[e] litigation, and required the Court and PGE to expend significant time and resources eliminating these baseless claims' (*Pa Gen Energy Co v Grant Township* 2018, at 25). PGE also continued to pursue additional attorney's fees as the prevailing party in a federal civil rights action, with the court granting the motion in the negotiated amount plus costs (which was later further negotiated between PGE and Grant Township, with CELDF reportedly covering such costs for the township). A subsequent decision by the Pennsylvania Supreme Court, it is important to note, 'determined that the state Constitution Environmental Rights Amendment imposed a constitutional obligation upon the state to prohibit the degradation, diminution, and depletion of public natural resources, whether those harms might result from state action or the action of private parties, and also act affirmatively, through the adoption of legislation, to protect the environment', and three-judge appellate panel granted the Township 'the right to try and prove the environmental damages caused by hydrofracking and the disposal of its waste, thus reinvigorating the struggle' (Moutrie, 2020, 30–1). In Mora County, when the ordinance was challenged by SWEPI, the Shell Oil Corporation that had acquired a permit from the State of New Mexico to drill for oil and gas in the County, the federal district court judge ruled that the ordinance violated SWEPI's rights, because it was in conflict with the Supremacy Clause and the First Amendment guaranteed by the US Constitution to corporations. However, the court did not completely foreclose the capacity for the County to concurrently regulate oil and field extraction with state authorities.

As mentioned in the previous chapter, the day immediately after the Lake Erie Bill of Rights was adopted, the Drews Farms Partnership challenged its constitutionality (and Toledo's authority to adopt it) in a federal court. Although partly similar to the cases of Grant Township and Mora County, the challenge also alleges a violation of the US Constitution Fifth and Fourteenth Amendment prohibitions 'against laws so vague that they do not provide fair notice of what conduct is punishable or they invite arbitrary or discretionary enforcement' (Moutrie, 2020, 37). At the initial hearing, where Toledo's community filled the courtroom with their numbers and protested outside the courtroom, CELDF commented that 'whatever the outcome, the people of Toledo had already won because they had organized, passed a ground-breaking law, and ensured that meaningful arguments were made in court about the lake's rights and the people's rights to govern locally to protect nature and their health' (Moutrie, 2020, 38). However, the federal district court decided on the unconstitutionality of vague laws, asserting that even '[u]nder the most forgiving standard, the environmental rights identified in LEBOR are void for vagueness' (*Drews Farm Partnership v City of Toledo*).

Moutrie summarizes her analysis by noting three points: firstly, that 'the widespread adoption of community rights laws in the USA demonstrates the potential and power of grassroots organizing to combat local environmental threats; and experience shows that communities remain engaged, despite risks and setbacks'. Secondly, that 'the experiences of adopting and defending the community rights laws shows that the boundary between state and local control of activities impacting the environment may be redrawn through political action and litigation disregarding the attempts to strip corporations of constitutional rights'. And, thirdly, that 'the judicial response to local rights of nature laws provides guidance that can be used in formulating and drafting future laws' (2020, 39). Moutrie notes that, 'though only a relatively small percentage of the community rights laws recognizing Nature's rights have been challenged, those that have been challenged were invalidated'. On the other hand, however, other legislative approaches in the USA have emphasized Nature's rights and human's bond with Nature, 'rather than maximizing local authority or diminishing corporations' legal rights' (40), as has been the case with a number of Tribal initiatives and the Santa Monica case. These approaches have been far more successful. As a result, Moutrie concludes, there exist two distinct modalities in approaching Nature in the US initiatives. On the one hand are the 'positive declarations of the spiritual belief and ethical understanding that all life is one and humans are responsible for Nature's welfare' (53). On the other hand, local laws 'were intended to do much more than stop environmentally destructive activities and promote human respect for the environment. They were intended to enhance local legal authority, diminishing federal and state authority, strip corporations of long-established constitutional rights, and create new legal rights and remedies'. The former path, for Moutrie, has been proven as not only the most desirable, but also the most successful, and thus, emphasis should be given to the human responsibilities toward Nature.

7.2 The Onto-Axiological Spectrum

What Moutrie's conclusion points to (affirming Tănăsescu's argument) is that the ethical standpoint underpinning a particular provision does matter. Of course, individual initiatives can be seen pragmatically, irrespective of the theoretical paradigm being adopted, and, in many cases, the results and the ensuing limitations will be the same. After all, limiting human exploitation of the environment can occur either because of a belief in the sanctity of Nature or to secure long-term human survival, with the results often being pragmatically undistinguishable.

This is not to say, however, that the paradigm within which they are theoretically inscribed is not relevant. In fact, that paradigmatic choice is what constitutes the emergence of an ecological jurisprudence. The ethical spectrum introduced over the previous chapters is thus the necessary start with which to analyse eco-jurisprudential initiatives. Roderick Nash wrote that all emerging authors in the field of environmental ethics and law agreed that

> there was no right and wrong in nature … ethical norms were human constructs. Other forms of life might be the subjects of ethics, but they lacked the mental capacity to think of their behaviour in terms of right and wrong or to enter into a reciprocal ethical relationship with humans. Morals existed in the human mind; they were self-imposed restraint on people's freedom of action. Humans determined ethical eligibility and, in a sense, dispensed rights … Much of the controversy turned on the question of whether environmental ethics were utilitarian and instrumental – derived from human self-interest – or whether nature possessed interests, value, or, perhaps, rights which people ought to respect even at considerable personal sacrifice … Another division concerned moral eligibility. Was everything in the environment to be included in humankind's moral community? If not, where did the ethical cut-off fall? … "deep ecologists" or "ecophilosophers", widened their circle to include all life. Going farther still, some holistic ethicists saw no reason to draw a moral boundary at the edge of life and argued for ethical consideration of rocks, soil, water, air, and the biophysical processes that constitute ecosystems. (1989, 124)

While the issue of whether normativity is limited to the human world remains open (and I will return to it in the next chapter), Nash's summary presents a good overview of the distinct ethical standpoints that can be adopted in engaging with the nonhuman world. These standpoints, furthermore, are necessarily connected to the ontological premise one selects in relation to the rest of existence. I will call this the 'onto-axiological standpoint', to describe the interrelated nature of ontological assumptions and axiological choices. That is, of the particular view one has of the nature of 'being', as well as the particular ethical choices that follow.

7.2.1 From Human Instrumentalism to the Intrinsic Value of Nature

Firstly, one can fully embrace nihilistic materialism and consider the world as nothing more than purposeless and inert matter. No ontological reasons would exist, in this case, to warrant ethical responsibilities toward the world, other than those that can be tautologically selected from within a self-constructed ethical framework. When this ontological standpoint is combined with absolute psychological or ethical egoism, then the hedonistic pursuits of each individual entail no restraint. The glorification of selfishness within popular narratives and much of consumeristic advertisement appears to be fully located within this onto-axiological position, what René Dubos, in a previous chapter, has defined as 'crude anthropocentrism'. No meaningful discussion as to other ways of being in the world can be had with such a position, since the measure of everything is not only the *anthropos,* as Protagoras had suggested, but the individual (and tautologically self-contained) self. It is also important to note, however, that nihilistic materialism does not *necessarily* entail a conjoining with extreme psychological or ethical egoism.

Another ontological position can be that of imagining a transcendent spiritual world from which Nature emerges. In this instance, Nature could be nothing more than inert matter, although its initial origin is nonetheless preter- or super-material. Alternatively, one can imagine a spiritual world that is co-terminous with the whole, as in Spinoza's panentheism or Hegel's idealism. Frederick Copleston writes that, in speculative metaphysics, 'God is the imaginative or intuitive form in which the absolute reveals itself to the religious consciousness ... If we preserve speculative metaphysics', therefore, 'we must admit in the long run that theism is a half-way house between the frank anthropomorphism of polytheism on the one hand and the idea of the all-inclusive Absolute on the other' (2003 ed, vol VII, 24). In this case, materiality is maintained, albeit infused and informed by a more-than-material quality—an *entelechy* or *conatus* that cannot be reduced to its material components. Copleston also notes that '[w]e can eliminate the idea of a spiritual reality, whether unconscious or conscious, which produces Nature, and we can at the same time retain the idea of the Absolute becoming self-conscious. The Absolute then means the world, in the sense of the universe. And we have the picture of man's knowledge of the world and of his own history as the self-knowledge of the Absolute'. In this sense, which represents one of the main interpretations of Hegel's absolute idealism, there is no spiritual reality distinct from the sensible world, but rather the sensible world *is* inherently and entirely spiritual.

The range of ontological options here identified exists as part of an onto-axiological continuum, and thus the philosophical axis around which eco-jurisprudential initiatives are articulated covers a spectrum, from an instrumentalist view of the environment as a web of relations that are the necessary precondition for human sustainability (and even survival), to the idea of the environment as inherently worthy of recognition, respect, and protection irrespective of (and potentially in opposition to) human needs. While the most radical view of anthropocentrism entails a profoundly utilitarian, materialistic and deterministic view of nature—as worthy of consideration only for human purpose, particularly in an economic sense—a more moderate version of anthropocentrism exists that does not see itself in contradiction with an ecological approach. While the former supports an economic approach in which nature is seen as a collection of resources to be exploited at will to further potentially endless economic growth (limited only by human technological ingenuity), the latter acknowledges that the well-being of humans is both connected to and dependent from the well-being of the environment within which humans are located. In this sense, environmental protection is paramount to human survival, even though the environment is not recognized as necessarily possessing any intrinsic value per se. In this instance, human goods are still central, but rather than being monetary and economic goods, they are rather articulated around principles of health, well-being and sustainability. Such an approach was implicit, for example, in the Declaration of the United Nations Conference on the Human Environment in 1972 (the 'Stockholm Declaration'), which stated that '[b]oth aspects of man's environment, the natural and the man-made, are essential to his well-being and to the full enjoyment of fundamental rights, including the right to life itself'.

Alexander Gillespie (1997) presents a comprehensive picture of the possible ethical standpoints that can be adopted in relation to the environment. He sets out to examine 'the reasons *why* the environment is protected and how these ideas are represented in the international environmental arena of policy and law'. This is juxtaposed 'against what is broadly known as the theories of "radical ecology". Radical ecology devolves into two parts. The first is known as "deep ecology" and the second as "social ecology". Very briefly, deep ecology is concerned with *why* the environment is protected, whereas social ecology is concerned with *how* to achieve this end' (1). In both cases, however, all the relevant theorists agree that environmental protection must be based 'upon the inherent (or intrinsic) value of non-human Nature. This is in contrast to what is known as "shallow environmentalism" which justifies environmental protection on the grounds that Nature has instrumental value for humans. This position, which revolves around anthropocentrism, proclaims that only humanity has inherent value. It is this shallow environmentalist that forms the predominant basis of international environmental law and policy'. This is not to suggest, however, that non-anthropocentric justifications are to be cast as the salvific position against more traditional anthropocentric considerations, as they are indeed, 'also besieged by a number of faults and limitations that will prevent deep ecology, in its present form, from being the panacea for all environmental considerations' (2). It is also important to note once again the distinction between 'crude anthropocentrism' and 'enlightened anthropocentrism previously introduced by Dubos (2006). The former refers to the more extreme connotations of materialism and ethical egoism, whereas the latter recognizes the importance (if nothing else for one's own survival) of ethical respect toward the nonhuman world.

7.2.2 *Ethical Justifications*

7.2.2.1 Self-interest

Gillespie thus identifies three forms of justification for any form of ethical responsibility toward the nonhuman world. The first is the self-interest justification, noting that most forms of anthropocentric environmental protection are derived from some form of self-interest' (1997, 19). In this case, the 'self' to be preserved is humanity as a whole rather than a particular individual. In 1973, UNEP stated that its first policy objective was to 'anticipate and prevent threats to human health', and the Brandt Reports of 1980 (*A Program for Survival*) and 1983 (*Common Crisis*) both recognized the risks for human survival. The 1982 *World Charter for Nature* asserted that '[l]asting benefits from nature depend upon the maintenance of essential ecological processes and life support systems, and upon the diversity of life forms' (Preamble). As a result, prudent self-interest may thus lead to a form of 'enlightened anthropocentrism' (Gillespie, 1997, 22), which combines the good of humanity with the good of the biosphere. Nonetheless, in this instance, as John Passmore suggested, '[a]n ethic dealing with man's relation to land, and to the plants and animals growing on it would not only be about the behaviour of human beings, as is sufficiently obvious, but would have to be justified by reference to human interests' (1974, 19). The problem of doing so is that species and natural 'things' that do not appear to provide any benefit to humanity become ethically invisible. As Robyn Eckersly stated, '[i]f we restrict our perspective to a human welfare ecology perspective we can provide no protection to those species which are of no present or potential use or interest to humankind' (1992, 37). Not only it is the case that many parts of Nature cannot be demonstrated to have utilitarian value, and not only such value may become apparent only at a later stage, once they have been irreversibly damaged, but also 'once the preservation of a piece of Nature is justified solely by human self-interest, its protection is only required for as long as that need is believed to be present. Once the interest is gone, so too is the reason to preserve the environment' (Gillespie, 1997, 22).

Three main approaches have been used in articulating the self-interest justification. First among them is the use of an economic rationale as the justification for the protection of the environment. This approach achieved great prominence with the publication of the Brundtland Report *Our Common Future* in 1987, and the economic valuation of the environment generally proceeds from a cost–benefit analysis. 'Such an approach compares inherently different interests, values, and components, and attempts to overcome their dissimilarity by reducing everything to a common medium: money' (Gillespie, 1997, 29). The problem, as William Nordhaus's argument that it would have been more cost effective *not* to cut the emission of greenhouse gases below the target of 2% show (1991), is that such analyses may prove myopic in the long term. Furthermore, economic justifications for environmental protection face the problem of value, in that many values exist that do not neatly fit within economic logic and, or, are not easily (if ever) monetized, a fact that Adam Smith himself had acknowledged in noting that economic self-interest does not provide all the justifications for human activity. Moreover 'economic values cannot always be established and even if they are, they may change' (Gillespie, 1997, 47). Such a change may be due to changing social perspectives, or to the late recognition of values that were previously seen as non-existent. As a result, species may be wiped out, or damages may be caused before it is realized that such damages are irreversible, leading to a host of unintended consequences. The final problem is connected to the use of markets to regulate the environment, since '[i]t has been calculated that quick profit from immediate exploitation are often greater than a sustained, lower use of an intact resource over a long period' (Gillespie, 1997, 57). As a result, in a market economy that is deeply monetized, it is unlikely that the markets will lead to optimal long-term ecological decisions.

A second suite of self-interest justifications is the religious ones. Such is the case, for example, with the 'stewardship' interpretation of Genesis 1:26 and Genesis 1:28 in the Bible, which can lead to 'an approach which is beneficial from an environmental perspective' (Gillespie, 1997, 67). The inherent goodness of creation and the importance of creation for God, which leads to the responsibility of humans to act as stewards (rather than as absolute masters), derives from such an interpretation. The problem with religious justifications is that they can easily lead to fundamentalist positions. For example, 'in a contemporary setting, many fundamentalists explicitly reject the new environmental approach that is shown by some of their brethren. ... For example, Steven Schwarzschild argues from a traditional Jewish standpoint that he is obliged by the commands in the Bible (Genesis 1:28–30) to actually dislike, despise, and conquer the natural world' (Gillespie, 1997, 72). Such a view is similar to the one professed by Francis Bacon and Descartes. Not only sacred textual interpretations clearly change over time, and not only some of these interpretations carry an explicit hostility toward environmental concerns, but sometime the problem is mere indifference, which can be seen even with influential environmentalists, as in the case of Ralph Waldo Emerson, '[f]or despite the influence of transcendental pantheism upon his eco-centric outlook, he was still indifferent towards the vast initial plundering of the American countryside. In his opinion the recoupable powers of Nature were a sufficient guarantee that the destruction of Nature would not lead to any form of final devastation' (Gillespie, 1997, 79). Another problem with religious justifications is that of misplaced optimism and fideism. Such fideism can be seen not only in the alleged salvific powers of a particular religion, but also in the expected powers of technological marvels.

A third version of the 'enlightened anthropocentric' self-interest argument is that for which environmental protection stems from aesthetic, cultural and/or recreational justifications. Aesthetic justifications, for example, can be seen in Article 2 of the 1933 *Convention Relative to the Preservation of Fauna and Flora in their Natural State*, according to which national parks must be set up 'for the propagation, protection and preservation of ... objects of aesthetic importance', as well as the 1962 United Nations Educational, Scientific, and Cultural Organization (UNESCO) *Recommendation Concerning the Safeguarding of the Beauty and Character of Landscapes and Sites*. Obviously, the subjectivity (both individual and cultural) of aesthetic considerations (which was explored briefly in relation to the imagination of nature) makes such an argument very uncertain. The cultural justification for environmental protection poses other problems. Indeed, '[t]he preservation of culture is recognized as a legitimate and worthy pursuit by the international community' (Gillespie, 1997, 99). However, as Gillespie argues in relation to the issue of contemporary whaling, 'just because something is derived from, or common within, culture does not make it [automatically] ethically defensible. Indeed, cultural relativism cannot be seen as an absolute excuse for any actions that cultures may wish to condone' (101), as is the case at present with genocide, slavery, cannibalism, infanticide, female circumcision, racism and sexism. At the moment, he writes,

> there is often a choice between interfering with a way of life of an important and distinct culture, or allowing the extinction of a species. If a species is on the verge of extinction and the choice is between killing it off completely in the present because it is important for a culture to do so, or allowing it to survive and perhaps recover in the distant future, the surely the culture will also be saved in the future. To kill off a species now in the name of cultural tradition is to kill off the culture. The tradition either dies completely now, or continues in a different form ... [Therefore], [t]he survival of entire species and ecosystems should override cultural considerations. (101)

The final justification, that of recreational values and the importance of the wilderness for recreational purposes as a justification for environmental protection, is often predicated on an imagined idea of nature and the wilderness explored in previous chapters.

An interesting corollary of the self-interest justification, since science has increasingly shown that the collective self-interest and broader ecological considerations for the *present* state of Nature are becoming ever-more indistinguishable, is that such an enlarged version of 'self-interest' ultimately encompasses the Gaia community. Indeed, bar the pursuit of immediate, individualist pleasure, a self-interest justification is either motivated by one's well-being over time in a highly disturbed environment or by the survival of one's direct family and kin. Richard Watson argued that it is indeed possible to attain 'ecologically responsible behaviour without assuming the intrinsic value or rights of nonhuman life. All humans need to know [is that] their own survival depend[s] on the preservation of the integrity and health of the ecosystem. Enlightened self-interest, in other words, would bring about the same results'. However, since some life-forms and ecosystems were perceived to have ... no value for human survival, more than enlightened self-interest was necessary if they were to retain their rightful place in the ecosystem. ... [and secondly] the idea that identity of the individual was indistinguishable from the identity of the whole, interrelated cosmos. Therefore selfishness, rightly understood, could embrace the interests and rights of all life and matter' (in Nash, 1989, 151). For practical purposes, in other words, the results of an enlarged self-interest justification are indistinguishable from other justifications. What happens is that 'an inchoate sense of obligation towards natural objects then develops, which is flattened into an aspect of self-interest'. In summary, self-interest operates as somewhat of a threshold concept, a conceptual boundary for the emergence of an ecological jurisprudence. The most conservative forms of self-interest, perhaps defining nature based on a set of 'ecosystem services', that measure an overall 'natural capital' (Costanza, 1996), may not be examples of an emergence of an ecological jurisprudence, while others might.

7.2.2.2 The Rights of Future Generations and Ecocentrism

A second justification advanced to support ethical respect for the nonhuman world is that of the rights of future generations. This approach was already contained in the 1946 *International Convention for the Regulation of Whaling*, which recognizes (albeit in very anthropocentric language) 'the interests of the Nations of the world in safeguarding for future generations the great natural resources represented by whales' (Preamble, para 2). This justification is generally hampered by motivational limits on the part of the present generation to restrain itself for the benefit of future ones. Moreover, some authors 'foresaw a problem with the argument for the consideration of the interests of future generations ... there must be limits on how far considerations of the future can be taken owing to a limited knowledge of the certainties with which it is currently possible to obtain and how it may affect the future generations' (Gillespie, 1997, 119).

A third justification for the respect and protection of the nonhuman world is the ecocentric one. The overall ethical approach to the nonhuman (or, perhaps more aptly, 'more-than-human') world has changed significantly over time. While the 1972 *Stockholm Declaration* recognized, in anthropocentric terms, that 'man has a special responsibility to safeguard and wisely manage the heritage of wildlife and its habitat' (Chapter II, Principle 4), just one year later the 1973 *European Ministerial Conference on the Environment* noted that 'the environment must be taken care of because of its own value, as a part of the world's heritage' (Resolution 1, Preamble), and the 1982 *World Charter* stated that '[e]very form of life is unique, warranting respect regardless of its worth to man, and to accord other organisms such recognition, man must be guided by a moral code of action'. This shift has been very visible in the increased protection of endangered species, both at a domestic and at the international levels, with a marked shift to focus upon ecosystems rather than on specific individuals. Gillespie writes that there are 'three major philosophical positions which a non-anthropocentric approach could adopt in attempting to extend the basis of human ethical concerns to the non-human world' (1997, 135). Firstly, the moral considerability of animals. Secondly, a concern for all entities that are alive. And thirdly, an approach 'known broadly as deep ecology or land ethic, [which] places its ethical focus upon the welfare of the whole, at both an ecosystem and biosphere level'. Importantly, Gillespie notes, these approaches 'are not, prima facie, complementary and cannot easily be joined together in a form of moral pluralism. Rather, they are based upon different conceptions of moral monism'.

The moral considerability of animals is predicated upon Peter Singer's arguments in *Animal Liberation* (1975) about sentience and Tom Regan's 'subject of life' argument (1983). The argument is a utilitarian one, based on the avoidance of suffering. Since 'all humans from infants to imbeciles [sic] and "normal" functioning people have an interest in the avoidance of physical suffering, [and since] this is a characteristic of all sentient creatures, and not just humans, [t]herefore, membership of the human species cannot justify a difference in moral treatment' (Gillespie, 1997, 137). Inherent value, previously limited exclusively (or at least pre-eminently) to humans, is thus extended to all sentient beings. The problem with this approach, of course, is that if an entity is not sentient, then it cannot be the subject of direct moral consideration. Therefore, '[o]nly creatures that are sentient ... have inherent value, everything else possesses only instrumental value' (146).

A more enlarged version of this argument is 'the idea behind the respect for life theories', which suggests that there is something 'about the essence of living organisms [that] requires concern and respect. The basic proposal is that non-sentient beings with life, who possess an inherited biological propensity towards natural growth and existence are not mere "things", but rather have independent value' (150). This position rejects Singer and Regan's criteria of feeling pleasure and pain or being a 'subject of life' as inherently anthropocentric. Albert Schweitzer has generally been credited with advancing this life-oriented approach, based on his basic rule that '[i]t is good to maintain and promote life; it is bad to destroy life or obstruct it' (1929, 246). Life has been described as a 'disenthropic enterprise': a living being 'has structures for maintaining a disenthropic equilibrium for availing itself of forms of energy, which it is capable of using for resting change incompatible with tis continuing functioning'. The outcome of this position, 'that it is usual to value living entities above non-living things, has caused some to question how far our ethical precepts should reach' (Gillespie, 1997, 151). Indeed, the novel science of plant consciousness suggests a far greater attention to entities traditionally ignored (plants), suggesting that we may need to extend this criterion to what we currently identify as 'inanimate' (but which may prove to be something else upon closer and future reflection). There is an inherent arbitrariness in creating a boundary of what 'life' is, hence some ask whether such a boundary would best be altogether abandoned.

The individualism of the sentience and reverence for life approaches is often at odds with holistic ecocentric ideals. 'Holistic environmental ethics, deep ecology or the land ethic' (Gillespie, 1997, 159), starts from a rejection of 'the human-in-environment image, in favour of the relational, total-field image' (Fox, 1984, 194). This approach is exemplified by the writings of Aldo Leopold and Arne Naess, and it underpins much of the rights of Nature movements to date. A first problem with ecological and holistic theories is with 'postulations about the stability or equilibrium of ecosystems. This is a common theme for many holistic environmental theorists. However, ... [c]hange, rather than continual, harmonious equilibrium, is generally recognized as a common biospheric (non-human) quality. Consequently, it has been asserted that the balance of nature "does not exist" and that such ideas are "outmoded biological concepts as everything changes over time"' (Gillespie, 1997,

167). However, whether holistic ethicists espouse such a monolithic view has been questioned.

> [T]he absoluteness of this view, namely that change is constant, has been challenged for over one hundred years. In a modern context it has been argued that stability with slow change, rather than uncontrolled rapid change, is the basic feature of the living world. The natural world is seen as primarily constant and conservative with regard to change, and tends toward stability. Change occurs not because it is desirable *per se*, but because in certain conditions it is necessary as a means of preventing larger and more disruptive change. (101)

Indeed, 'quite clearly, natural systems are not geared towards change but towards the avoidance of change' (Margalef, 1989, 225), and '[h]omeostasis is the objective of living things. ... This is not suggesting that homeostasis is stagnant and immobile. Rather, it is still a dynamic process but with the underlying objective of stability or overall limitation of dramatic change. ... Although the idea of a perfect state of equilibrium can be challenged, an underlying basic regularity still exists' (Gillespie, 1997, 167–8). Cullinan writes that it 'would be wise to bear in mind that natural systems exhibit what Edward Goldsmith calls "whole-maintaining" characteristics. In other words, each aspect of a properly functioning system acts in a manner that contributes to the health and integrity of the whole. If thus were not the case, then the whole system would begin to deteriorate with adverse consequences for all the component parts' (2011 ed, 81). The key question, of course, is how to identify what is "whole-maintaining" and what is not. 'This', Cullinan concludes, 'is where communion is vitally important. Communion can be understood as the web of relationships or the dance between different aspects of the universal whole' (83).

A second problem with holistic ethics, particularly when it is articulated in terms of rights, is both the individuation of the subjects of those rights in a holistic sense, and the resolution of conflicts when the rights of distinct natural entities enter into conflict *among themselves* (rather than against human interests and rights). I will return to the issue of rights more in details in the next section.

A third problem with the deep ecological, ecocentric and holistic view is its potential misanthropic tendency. Arne Naess wrote that '[t]he flourishing of human life and cultures is compatible with substantial decrease of the human population' (1989, 29). Some may also argue that such a slightly misanthropic view may still be anthropocentric, as it fails to see the ecological role of humanity on the planet. To circumvent this problem, 'it has been suggested that the land ethic does *not* hold everything as possessing unbreachable equality. Thus, absolute ecological egalitarianism is not subscribed to within the holistic framework offered by deep ecology, Rather, the emphasis is upon *appropriate* treatment, and not necessarily *equal* treatment' (Gillespie, 1997, 172). As such, human needs and rights are still prioritized, just with different priorities. Indeed, Gillespie notes, a land ethic 'does not imply the "passive surrender" of humanity, as humans, like other species, are recognized as special in their own unique ways and are entitled to modify ecosystems in which they live in order to survive and blossom. Humanity would be allowed to keep life-threatening organisms in check, "where there is no alternative" and it is necessary to satisfy vital human needs, provided any such actions are carried out with minimum harm (173). Descola offers a resolution, in noting that

> holistic ethical systems seem closer to animism, for they lay the emphasis not on individuals or species endowed with particular properties, but on the need to preserve the common good and not inconsiderately upset the relations of interdependence that unite all the organic and abiotic components of an environment. ...The ecosystem comes to transcend its elements and these, both human and nonhuman ... are stripped of any ontological substance and so become mere cogs in a network of relations in a constant state of reorganization. Nature and culture lose their raison d'être in such a cosmology, which is no longer biocentric or anthropocentric. Instead, it is ecocentric, that is, subject to the regulatory mechanisms of energy in the environment. (2013, 195–7)

If this onto-axiological spectrum allows us to identify more clearly the ontological and axiological assumptions that underpin all eco-jurisprudential initiatives, then, by inference, 'ecological jurisprudence' can be identified more clearly. On the one hand, it encompasses anything that is not underpinned by ethical (or even psychological) egoism as well as extreme anthropocentrism. On the other hand, it is equally bounded by the more extreme misanthropic tendencies of holistic ethics, which, I contend, sit outside its confines. These two boundaries are both porous and uncertain, but, I believe, they nonetheless identify ecological jurisprudence as both a *field* and a *horizon* of possibilities. In this sense, an ecological jurisprudence is an *aspiration* rather than a *definition*. As I have previously suggested, all the initiatives presented in the previous chapter, from the discourse on sustainability, through conservationism, to the articulation of the Rights of Mother Earth, sit on this complex and interwoven onto-axiological continuum and are best understood in relation to it. In this sense, I contend that all such initiatives are best thought of not as separate, but as representing a large overall shift, one that is not merely pragmatic (i.e. the protection of the environment) but rather is much more radical and ontological, and gestures toward our own collective identity as a species, as well as our pluriversal imagination of both the normative and the legal.

7.3 Rights and Duties

Peter Burdon writes that 'outside of human moral or legal analysis, nature does not have rights and it is unable to recognize the rights of others. Thus, a landslide that uproots a small pine forest does not violate the rights of the tree community. Even if the landslide kills human beings,' he continues, 'it does not violate human rights. The mountain is not guilty of reprehensible behaviour and one cannot bring it to be shamed in a court of law. Legal rights correspond with legitimate claims and entitlements' (2011, 1). Burdon concludes by saying, with Homes Rolston III, that 'rights are a uniquely human construct and entail a multiplicity of bilateral jural relations'. The emergence of rights of Nature initiatives has undoubtedly raised a host of questions that did not impact (at least not to the same extent) traditional environmental law (and that do not appear to impact the many ecocide proposals or the ecological civilization discourse). A common argument behind the extension of rights to Nature has been to inscribe such an extension within a trajectory of enlargement of the boundaries of the entities possessing legal rights. As Nash notes (1989), rights have extended, in a linear fashion, from white privileged males, to include all of humanity, and beyond, to include first some elements and then the whole of Nature. Similarly, Tanasescu describes the 'moral evolutionism of liberal rights ... in terms of the existence of different rights generations' (2022, 41). The first-generation human rights focused on political and civil claims. The second extended to economic, social and cultural rights. The third, termed solidarity rights, encompasses everything that did not fit in the first two generations. Oliver Houck (2017), in his comprehensive review of rights of Nature history, also depicts an almost linear progression from individual creatures (soon extended to species as a whole), to natural features such as rivers and forests, to Nature as a whole.

Tănăsescu, however, also notes that 'the expansion of human rights discourses has choked out other ways of conceiving of radical emancipation while being quite easily incorporated within liberal and capitalist status quos' (in Houck, 2017, 1). Many of the critiques commonly advanced against the rights discourse in general extend to the rights of Nature movement as well. Burdon (2011), for example, points to the limitations of individualizing rights discourses in the absence of broader market reforms. Tanasescu asserts that, in the case of rights of Nature, 'scholars have al- ready started to point out how they further legitimize rights discourses without any guarantee that this will actually translate into more substantive human or nature rights' (2022, 42). Rawson and Mansfield (2018a, 2018b) propose that, rather than guaranteeing rights for the natural world, rights of Nature instead accomplish the *naturalization of rights*.Erin O'Donnell very aptly notes that the rights discourse is an inherently individualizing one, and thus, as a result, the emphasis on the *rights* of Nature (as opposed to human *responsibilities toward* Nature) enacts a further separation from and within the natural world, creating a world of expectations and demands rather than one of relationality and accountability. Daniel Matthews writes that '[t]he history of rights ... is unthinkable apart from the history and theory of the modern state, with the "age of rights" progressing hand in glove with the celebrated account of sovereignty in early modernity. Rights, therefore, are inextricably tied to modern law and its various entailments'. As a result, '[i]n expanding the scope of rights—to include non-human actors—we therefore tacitly acknowledge that such claims ought to be recognised and enforced through existing state structures, juridifying any claims made in their names' (2021, 40).

It is important to note that, while Matthews's insight is very accurate, Stone himself did not hide the *strategic* nature of his proposed enlargement of rights to the nonhuman world. Stone's—and many of the rights of Nature activists'—argument is that *as long as* the state persists, and *as long as* the rights discourse continues, then their usage *necessarily* requires an extension beyond their existing confines. Naturally, one may argue, with Bookchin, for a far more radical dismantling of the state structure, but such an abandonment of rights would not be limited to the rights of Nature discourse, and would rather extend to the rights discourse in general. As David Boyd points out, '[r]ights are symbolically and politically powerful as the history of the civil rights, women's rights, Indigenous rights, and gay rights movements demonstrates ... they are a proven means of securing progress in the way society embraces previously mistreated communities' (2017, xxxiii). Furthermore, irrespective of whether the focus ought to be on rights or responsibilities, history shows, at present, a rapid and significant growth of rights initiatives, and not of others. Leaving aside the judgment of whether this *ought* to be, it is, therefore, important to acknowledge the social appeal of this approach as privileged to all others. Anna Grear, who is equally critical of an uncritical extension of the rights discourse, writes that there is 'something to be salvaged from rights discourse all the same—if we can find a way to deploy the idea of "rights" while decentring "the human"' (2022). The result, Astrida Neimanis concurs, is that, perhaps, 'we can find ways of understanding ourselves as entangled partners, and sometimes co-sufferers, with nonhuman animals, beings and systems in a "more-than-human world"' (2014, 5).

7.3.1 Rights 'of' Nature or Rights 'to' Nature?

The most fundamental issue in regard to the rights of Nature is whether rights are *recognised 'of'* Nature (such is Thomas Berry's position, influenced by a novel form of natural law) or instead are statutorily *attributed 'to'* Nature (such is Stone's position). Margaret Davies writes that

> [r]ight claims for nature that are less persuasive (in my view) are those based on the Western natural law tradition, which has been used to argue that nature has universal and essential qualities and therefore intrinsic rights. Legal rights can be said to flow from the nature of nature, so to speak. (Nature already has rights, and the law should recognise them.) This claim for the rights of nature suffers from many of the problems of the natural law tradition. ... the idea of a universal natural law (whether framed around god or human nature or physical nature) has always suffered from a lack of agreement about what this "law" consists of and where the "rights" (an essentially Eurocentric notion) are located. (2017 ed, 472)

On the other hand, Davies continues, 'Stone's approach is primarily pragmatic, legalistic, and instrumental. It does not rely on nature *having* any essential qualities or characteristics that necessarily translate into natural rights in the way that human beings are sometimes said to have natural rights by virtue of essential human qualities such as the capacity to reason, our inherent dignity, or our alleged possession of a soul' (476). Indeed, Stone had said that 'an entity cannot be said to hold a legal right unless and until *some public authoritative body* is prepared to give *some amount of review* to actions that are colourably inconsistent with that "right" ... But for a thing to be a *holder of legal rights*, something more is needed than that some authoritative body will review the actions and processes of those who threaten it ... first, that the thing, can institute legal actions at its behest, *second, that in determining the granting of legal relief, the court must take injury to it* into account; and third, that relief must run to the *benefit of it*' (1972, 458). The issue of rights, Stone noted, was directly connected to 'standing'. He also noted that '[i]t is no answer to say that streams and forests cannot have standing because streams and forests cannot speak. Corporations cannot speak, either; nor can states, estates, infants, incompetents, municipalities, or universities' (464). Instead, a form of guardianship ought to be instituted, and 'we should have a system in which, when a friend of a natural object perceives it to be endangered, he can apply to the court for the creation of a guardianship. Perhaps we already have the machinery to do so' (464–5). However, Stone added, the central challenge is the identification of these rights. Rather than *beginning* with a comprehensive enumeration of those rights, however, Stone argued the opposite. 'To flesh out the "rights" of the environment', he suggested, 'demands that we provide it with a significant body of rights for it to invoke when it gets to court' (482).

7.3.1.1 Rights of/to Nature Critiques

Houck (2017–8) presents a comprehensive overview of many of the critiques as to the theoretical possibility of rights of (or to) Nature. Firstly, many of the critics, he observes, suggest that laws are uniquely human constructs and, therefore, 'ineluctably homo-centric'. Houck counterargues that 'the observation, while true on its face, claims too much. Nothing has impeded humans from recognizing rights in non-human things, and in an increasingly complex world, we do it with some frequency' (31). I will also return on the issue of whether law *is* indeed homo-centric in the next chapter. Houck then notes that a more theoretical critique is that rights 'necessarily imply reciprocal duties, and it would be foolish to say that nature had to return the favor'. However, he also counter argues, rights are not contracts, and in many existing cases certain types of protections (for the mentally unable or the infant, for example) 'are considered rights in order to assure their needs, not because they owe us something in return' (32–3). Moreover, '[o]ne might go further to recognize that nature indeed does reciprocate, in myriad ways that benefit us in our interconnected worlds. There is no signed contract, but the providing of "consideration" (if such is required) is clear to anyone, and, if anything, an order of magnitude more forthcoming from the nature side'. Finally, rights-holders do not need 'to be aware of their status, any more than a ship is, or an infant, or an adult in the throes of dementia'. A final objection, which reflects the dichotomy of rights being 'recognised' or 'attributed', is that the rights of Nature, being declared by humans, would be inherently and originally anthropocentric, thus leading to an internal contradiction. However, such a critique is more valid in the case of recognition than in the case of attribution, as any kind of rights can be statutorily attributed to any kind of entity. Moreover, the recognition of rights, Houck concludes, does not make them any 'less real, nor does it make them perforce human-centered. If we acknowledge that other living things have rights to be, to continue to be, then it is simply false to claim to say that these rights as ours; they are theirs and focused on their needs, which is the definition of ecocentricity. In many instances, of course, anthropomorphic and ecocentric interests marry … but this is a far cry from contending that only one is valid' (33).

To proceed further with the contextual positioning of the idea of rights within the rights of Nature discourse, therefore, it is necessary to briefly engage with the complex liberal idea of natural rights. First of all, while the idea of 'natural' rights is inextricably connected to liberalism, the idea of 'rights' per se (intended as expectations and counterparts to responsibilities), is far more ancient. Ronald Dworkin firstly introduced the idea that legal and moral theories can be right-based, duty-based or goal-based, further arguing, with his 'rights thesis' of 'rights as trumps', for the primacy of rights over all other considerations. Waldron provides an example to illustrate this tripartite distinction. The opposition to torture may occur because we want to prevent the suffering of the victim (this is a *right*-based approach), because we believe that torture debases the torturer (a *duty*-based approach), or because torture may negatively impact upon society as a whole (a *goal*-based approach).

7.3.1.2 The *Idea* of Rights

There are two general competing theories about the nature of rights. The first, espoused by Hart (1955), is known as the 'will' or 'choice' theory. Such a view sees 'the purpose of law as being to grant the widest possible means of self-expression to the individual, the maximum degree of self-assertion' (Freeman, 2014 ed, 335). This theory identifies the right-bearer by virtue of the power that they have over the right in question. As a result, '[i]ndividual discretion is the single most distinctive feature of the concept of "rights"' (Flathman, 1976). The will theory is rather problematic, because, from a moral standpoint, some rights are considered as inalienable (for example the right to life or not to be tortured), but also, from a practical standpoint, because some right-holders lack either the standing or the capacity to articulate such rights. This is often the case with children, and it is easily visible in the case of animals and natural entities, 'for what will can animals, let alone mountain peaks have?' (Freeman, 2014 ed, 336). In reality, the problem is not what will they may have, but how such will is to be known and articulated. Joel Feinberg asks what sort of beings or things could be said to possess rights. His answer depends on the 'interest principle'. Something must 'possess the ability to be harmed or benefited (and to be aware of such treatment) in order for people to think meaningfully about its rights' (Nash, 1989, 126), and 'without awareness, expectation, belief, desire, aim, and purpose, a being can have no interests; without interests, he cannot be benefited; without the capacity to be a beneficiary, he can have no rights' (Feinberg, 1974, 61). This principle necessarily restricts the category of right-possessors to humans and to some animals. The latter are not 'moral "agents" but they d[o] have an interest and a right to its satisfaction' (Nash, 1989, 126). Plants are excluded because they lack sufficient 'cognitive equipment'.

The second theory is known as the 'interest' (or 'benefit') theory and is found in Bentham's writing, as well as being espoused primarily by Neil McCormick (1982), Joseph Raz and others. According to this theory, the purpose of a right is not to protect individual desires, but certain individual interests. Rights are thus conceived of as 'benefits secured for persons by rules regulating relationships' (Freeman, 2014 ed, 336). 'One version of the benefit theory says', Freeman explains, 'that X has a right whenever he stands to benefit from the performance of a duty ... Another ... says that X can have a right (whether in moral theory or within a legal system) whenever the protection or the advancement of an interest of his is recognised (by moral theory or the legal system, as the case may be) as a reason for imposing obligations, whether they are actually imposed or not' (337). One issue that arises from the 'interest' theory of rights is whether such interests could be protected by a rule that doesn't require the conferral of rights, as O'Donnell questions.

Within the language of rights, furthermore, there are internal differentiations. Bentham distinguished between 'rights' and 'liberties', whereas Windscheid distinguished between 'rights' and 'powers' (Freeman, 2014 ed, 337). It is, however, Wesley Newcomb Hohfeld (1913) who fully categorized the different types of 'rights' typologies. Firstly, he noted that the sentence that 'X has a right' is different from 'X has a book': the first is a normative statement which can be established only by reference to a set of rules (legal or not), whereas the second is a descriptive statement. However, even the sentence 'X has a right' indicates a number of distinct 'legal relations'. He then proceeded to clarify them, by creating a schema of 'jural correlatives' and 'opposites'. *Stricto* sensu, the sentence 'X has a right to R' means that Y (and everyone else) has a 'correlative' 'duty' to allow X to do R. But the sentence may also mean that X is simply free to do or to refrain from doing something. In this case, the issue is not what Y must do, but what X is free to do. Hohfeld called this a 'privilege' (later authors preferred the term 'liberty') and described its correlative 'no-right' on the part of Y to prevent such a privilege from being exercised (importantly, Y has no 'duty' toward X's exercise of their 'privilege'). A third sense of the word is to refer to a 'power': in this case, X has the ability to change legal relationships (for example by making a contract or a will). Generally speaking, 'powers' (and their correlative 'liabilities') are attached to 'rights' and, or, 'privileges', but they can exist independently of other typologies. Finally, the term can refer to an 'immunity'. Where Y lacks the power to produce a change in X's legal relations (Y's correlative 'disability'), then X is said to have an 'immunity'. 'Reflecting on the types of rights identified by Wesley N. Hohfeld,' Burdon asserts, 'it is clear that the most suitable legal category for nature is a claim right, defined as claims correlative to other persons' duties' (Burdon, 2011, 1).

7.3.1.3 Rights, Duties and Symbolic Power

Within most of the rights of Nature discourse, rights are often used—a fact that is very apparent to the many rights of Nature advocates and lawyers I have interviewed—in a very pragmatic sense: i.e. to bring forth their jural correlatives. By recognizing (or granting) rights to Nature, any correlative duty can be judicially evaluated, thus incorporating Nature within the adjudicating process. The invocation of Nature's rights—as well as human's correlative duties—brings the interests of nonhuman entities *within* human political-legal frameworks. Tanasescu writes, that '[a] nature with rights becomes, first and foremost, a *political* subject' (2022, 139). Rights of Nature are thus a strategic way to counter human harmful behaviour in an indirect and diffused way, by giving the power and responsibility to do so to the community in the form of court actions that can be articulated *on behalf* of a rights-holding natural subject.

The choice of engaging with a rights discourse in relation to Nature, however, is not only strategic and pragmatic, but it is also, at the same time, psychological and symbolic. Stone had already noted this. Why arguing in terms of rights, he asked? He asserted that

> [i]ntroducing the notion of something having a "right" (simply *speaking* that way), brings into the legal system a flexibility and open-endedness that no series of specifically stated legal rules ... can capture. Part of the reason is that 'right" ... have meaning – vague but forceful – in the ordinary language, and the force of these meanings, inevitably infused with our own thought, becomes part of the context against which the "legal language" of our contemporary rules is interpreted (1972, 488).

As a result, 'a society in which it is stated, however vaguely, that "rivers have legal rights" would evolve a different legal system than one which did not employ that expression' (Stone, 1972, 488). Houck concurs, noting that a common argument was that Mineral King-as-plaintiff would *add* anything unless the system articulated human duties more clearly. However, '*Sierra v Morton* was about the very existence of a high mountain valley that even the majority characterized as "pristine". What legal recognition also adds is honesty. Yes, weekend hikers may be offended, but this is the real injured party-long after the hikers have gone-this special place and its many interlocking components'. Moreover, he concluded, '[w]hen the Sierra Club brought two later suits on behalf of the Palila and the Northern Spotted Owl (two endangered birds), it placed them first on the plaintiff list and brought stuffed specimens to counsel table, every day. Coincidentally, it won both cases. With recognition, minds begin to change' (2017–8, 32–3).

The symbolic power of rights of Nature, perhaps significantly greater than their legal effectiveness, is very apparent to rights of Nature advocates. Kauffman and Martin note that their analysis suggests 'that rights of nature and, in Bolivia's case, rights of Mother Earth have significant potential (especially symbolically, but also otherwise) to frame political, legislative and academic debates on ways to confront the persistent anthropocentrism of law that legitimizes and perpetuates the neoliberal development model the world over' (2021).

7.3.1.4 Which Rights? To Whom? And Against Whom?

If the pragmatic and strategic significance of the adoption of 'rights' within the rights of Nature movement has been contextually and theoretically situated, the issue remains as to what rights specifically have been recognized, or granted. Houck points out that '[i]n the field of environmental ethics, they are essentially three: the right to *exist,* the right to *continue* to exist, and the right, if degraded, to *be restored'* (2017–8, 31). Houck's tripartite list is generally reflected in many of the initiatives presented in the previous chapter, as well as being included in the list of rights proposed by Berry (and by many subsequent rights of Nature advocates). The rights of Nature are thus often cast in opposition to human rights. However, this does not necessarily have to be the case, and Walter Mignolo (2014) has suggested a new category of rights to replace both human rights and the rights of Nature, what he calls 'life rights'.

Another question that emerges in relation to the extension of rights to Nature is the extent of their attribution. If all of Nature were to be granted rights, what would that in turn mean for human behaviour? As Margaret Davies asks, '[a]re property rights even possible, without a clear sense of differentiation between subjects and objects and the power that attaches to the hierarchical superiority of subjects over objects? Does it make any sense at all to speak of post-human property?' (2022, 46). At what point would a human being be entitled to encroach upon the rights of Nature? In other words, the issue of the *conflict* of rights follows suit from the identification of Nature's rights.

The issue of conflict of rights is twofold. On the one hand, it concerns the conflict of rights of Nature with human rights. On the other hand, it concerns the conflict of rights of Nature *between different parts of Nature*. In the first instance, as Marshall has remarked in relation to Indigenous perspectives on the rights of Nature, one of the problems is that rights are inscribed within networks of uneven power relations, and thus a number of dispossessed and underprivileged individuals may have their (relatively basic) rights curtailed by the introduction of rights of Nature. It may be, for example, as is the case in Bangladesh, that millions of people live in informal settlements along the banks of rivers whose rights have been recently recognized, and is now being evicted as a result of that recognition. While such an action may be at times justified, it is impossible not to be cautious against the influence that Foucauldian governmentality can have in many such instances. It may be best, as Cullinan once suggested to me, to think of rights of Nature as guidelines for behaviour, with courts making individual assessments in each specific case. It may also be the case that, over time, rights of Nature legislation will include explanatory sections on how to address the issue of such conflicts.

Another issue of conflicting rights concerns potential conflicts *within* Nature, once Nature is recognized (either in its component parts, or as a whole) as a rights-bearing subject. Which parts of Nature are to be recognized as subject-holders, of course, matters a great deal. Naturally, the issue becomes more complicated when the application shifts from specific individual natural objects, to species, to bounded natural entities (such as rivers), and even to unclear entities such as the climate (let alone all of Nature). As Stone himself noted, 'the "climate" makes for a shifty client—"it" is more a set of parameters than a thing' (2010, 34). Moreover, the allegations in *Sierra Club v Morton* were directed to a uniquely situated 'wrongdoer', but in the case of the climate (and maybe of Nature as a whole), the issue is far too complex: '[b]y contrast, the risks of climate change fall everywhere on everyone, globally. And we are all, as well as prospective complainants, prospective defendants' (Stone, 2010, 34).

Even when the rights-bearing subject is identified, however, the issue arises as to what happens when the rights of two natural entities, equally subjects of rights, become in conflict. Is there a duty on the part of humans to intervene? Thus far, the issue has not emerged in any actual case, nor has it been explored by the literature. It may be that Nature's rights, like Santmire says (2020), are best conceived of as ways to preserve and defend Nature. What this implies is that such a defence is construed *against other humans* rather than against itself. This point requires further considerations, in order to avoid any absurdist renditions of the rights of Nature movement. In *Staying Alive*, published in 1989, Vandana Shiva *assumes* the standing of trees, but argues for a more nuanced situatedness of natural objects, one that is cognisant of place, situation and circumstance. Building upon Shiva's argument, Lorrain Code asks '[w]hich trees? Where? And to what ends?' (2012, 84), by pointing to the case of *eucalyptus* trees in India, whose cultivation for marketable timber is, as Shiva asserts, related to water-related and food scarcity problems that plague India's arable land (and thus, *these* trees should not have standing). Code does not suggest that standing ought to be granted exclusively to indigenous species in their natural habitat, but rather that the issue of standing may require a degree of contextual specificity. Mary Warnock asks 'if trees had standing, it is easy to imagine the situation that might arise in a managed forest, where some trees had to be felled for the good of the forest as a whole, and the question arose as to "which trees?"' (2012, 65).

7.3.1.5 Rights and Responsibilities

Finally, Nature may not demand—nor have any intrinsic—rights. However, Nash wrote, '[h]umans are the moral agents who have the responsibility to articulate and defend the rights of the other occupants of the planet. Such a conception of rights means that humans have duties or obligations toward nature'. One of the things that emerge from above is the tension between *rights* and *responsibilities*. Rather than *rights*, Daniel Matthews proposes to focus one's attention on the issue of *responsibilities*, citing one of the exercises that Andreas Philippopoulos-Mihalopoulos proposes to his students in his 'Law of the Environment' classes, a walking meditation not on '*rights of or for the city* but on the *urban obligations* that constitute the city as an associative form' (2021, 167). This claim echoes Simone Weil's critique of the inadequacy of *rights*, rather recognizing the *priority of obligations*: '[t]he notion of obligations comes before that of right which is relative and subordinate to it' (2001, 2). Zelle and others note that '[c]onventional environmental law is generally based on human responsibilities. Humans are responsible for acting in such a way that they do not harm other people by damaging their environments in ways prohibited by law'. However, they continue, echoing the Hoefeldian notion of jural correlative, 'Rights versus Responsibilities cannot, however, always be seen as opposing approaches because rights and responsibilities are often interrelated. Rights, once recognized, impose responsibilities on others with respect to those rights. And, in many situations, responsibilities imposed are grants of rights to others' (2021, 83).

The approach to engaging with Nature via responsibilities or obligations has been pursued (legally) primarily via ecocide proposals, but with less success than rights of Nature proposals. Thus far, actual examples of an ecological jurisprudence have articulated fewer instances of *obligations* and *responsibilities* than *rights*. It is hard not to agree with the underlying sentiment of the above critique, however. And while it does not diminish the value of the pursuit of rights, it is desirable that an ethical sensitivity driven by a sense of obligation will continue to be pursued. Catherine

Iorns Magallanes writes that '[a]ll rights come with responsibilities; it is time for our environmental responsibilities to come out from under the shadow of our human rights' (2017, 247). She suggests to move from 'systems based on human property rights over nature, to a system that is based on responsibilities for nature and includes respect for all life forms and systems ... Despite the anthropocentric nature of human rights, a human rights-based approach can help achieve the shift necessary for such system changes'. Burdon notes that, in discussing human obligations,

> Immanuel Kant drew a helpful distinction between perfect and imperfect obligations. A perfect obligation is a direct and immediate duty to take a course of action or refrain from a particular enterprise. However, there are also less specific responsibilities in the general form of what Kant called "imperfect obligations". Earth rights entail both of these types of obligation and their legislative recognition would impose on individuals a duty to consider ways through which environmental harm can be prevented (or minimized) and then decide on a reasonable course of action. (2011)

While rights and correlative responsibilities (or duties, or obligations) are certainly two sides of an intertwined whole, it may be argued that the focus could even shift toward *relationships,* rather than *rights* and *responsibilities.* The latter, after all, continue to engender an idea of separateness in their individual construction. The idea of *relatedness,* instead, may engender a sense of obligation that is derived not by obligation but by the active desire to be the creative and constitutive part of a collective. Fisher notes that '[t]he attribution of personality or status to nature as a subject within the law implies that nature is capable of legal relationships with other subjects' (2014, 98). A relational approach would entail what Zelle and others (2021) identify as '*reciprocity*, a norm whereby a positive action carried by an individual entails the duty to undertake a positive action in return, but without the necessary expectation that such an action is carried out at a particular time. In other words, reciprocity is an ethical attitude toward the world encoded in norms and protocols'.

Such an approach, some rights of Nature activists contend, is already present in some of the Andean concepts that have accompanied the development of rights of Nature in Bolivia and Ecuador. In Bolivia, the advancement of ecological jurisprudence revolves around the concept of *Suma Qamaña,* the Aymara original of *Buen Vivir (Living Well).* This is the main goal of the new Constitution of 2009. María Itatí Dolhare notes that the original meaning of the word *Qamaña* is 'to dwell'. Its root *qama* refers to energy/existence, force or strength of the soul, as well as 'to create or to organise'. The word *Suma* (in aymara, in quechua with the addition of the letter q or j at the end) 'denotes something that is good, pleasant and amenable' (2019, 83). The quechua equivalent is *Allin Kawsay* (*allin* denotes something that is good in a general sense, with *sumaq/j/k* having a more superlative sense, in relation to something that is excellent or exceptional), with Ecuadorian quechua preferring the term *Sumaq Kawsay.* As a result, the Andean concept of *Vivir Bien* portrays 'a culture of life' (Huancuni Mamani, 2010, 3), a 'complementary coexistence' (Oviedo Freire, 2013, 259), a 'paradigm of life' (Yampara Huarachi, 2011, 1), a principle of 'living well together' (Albó, 2011) under principles of 'conviviality and reciprocity or solidarity' (Itatí Dolhare, 2019, 84). While the parallels with Aristotle's *eudaimonia* are immediately apparent, the Andean concept is marked by a degree of reciprocity and responsibility that is absent *prima facie* in Greek philosophy (albeit the discussion of the relationship between *eudaimonia* and *areté*—or virtue—seems to be pointing in a similar direction). The concept of *Vivr Bien* is thus defined by the principles of 'integrality', 'complementarity', 'relationality' and 'reciprocity/solidarity'. The main explicit aim of the *Vivir Bien* principle is that of a 'harmonious and balanced coexistence between all the communities of Mother Earth' (Itatí Dolhare, 2019, 95).

7.4 Personhood, Representation and Agency

If the issue of articulating the idea of rights in relation to Nature was the focus of the previous section, the problem of individuation remains: who is to be the rights-holder, in the case of rights of Nature? If the answer is 'all of Nature', the problem is that humanity is not ultimately separate from it, it is not an external observer to the unfolding of a natural legal subjectivity separate from itself. As a result, 'all of Nature' leads to the practical impossibility to determine the boundaries of the rights-holder subject. If not, however, which elements ought to be privileged, and why? Kevin Schneider (2018) suggests that 'keystone species' could act as 'rights umbrella', as legal pivots or leverage points that could affect the entire system. Without any doubt, the existence of rights presupposes the existence of a subject of those rights. As George Deiser notes, '[a] right is inconceivable without corresponding relations between some individual and the community to which he is subject. If we find a right, such as that of ownership, in existence, we must discover a subject for that right. If the rights attach to a human being, he is the subject; if it attaches to a name used to designate the collective will of a group of men, the name or collective will is the subject' (1908, 137).

The identification of elements of Nature as legal subjects, or legal *persons*, has caused, over the first instances, a degree of controversy. In the *Ganges and Yamuna case*, Kauffman and Martin note, the concern stemmed from the use of the *in loco parentis* doctrine, since in its conventional application, court-appointed *parentes* do not simply speak for their charges, but are also responsible for them. As a result, they argue

> [m]aking guardians of natural ecosystems liable for damage done to humans in the course of regular ecosystem functioning is, of course, problematic. It contradicts the logic behind Earth jurisprudence by reproducing the problematic view of humans as controlling Nature and possessing greater authority than natural ecosystems, rather than viewing humans as one cog within the ecosystem. And it reverses the natural order of things by embedding Nature within human economic and governance systems rather than the other way around. (2021, 205)

Similarly, Akshita Jha and Adrija Ghos lament that, 'on closely examining such a grant of personhood to the Ganga and Yamuna in India, it may be noted that such arbitrary attribution of personhood achieves nothing but the creation of an avenue for the State to divest itself of its duties of preservation and conservation of these rivers' (2018, 469). Sara Rodrigues notes that, interestingly, it is not 'nature', but rather 'natural communities' and 'ecosystems' that are more commonly cited and defined in the US ordinances. 'In several ordinances, for example, "natural community" and "ecosystem" are understood as one and the same thing "including, but not limited to, wetlands, streams, rivers, aquifers, and other water systems' (2014, 174). Such a narrow definition of 'natural community', she argues, 'is problematic because it does not recognise that mutuality, symbiosis and interdependence are often integral to the preservation of an ecosystem. Thus, it may inadvertedly allow corporations to circumvent the terms of the ordinance if its activity endanger other entities in the community but does not endanger the entity that is protected'.

7.4.1 Nature's Personhood: Critiques

Three critiques are generally advanced against the attribution of personhood to Nature. Firstly, that it is set *against* the rights of Nature. Secondly, that the attribution of personhood to natural entities explicitly or implicitly recognizes their *liabilities*, leading to paradoxical consequences. And thirdly, that problems of precise identification follow in the case of natural features with more uncertain boundaries.

In the first instance, Kauffman and Martin argue that 'the most important difference between the Nature's rights model and legal personhood model is that the former recognizes ecosystems as possessing unique rights, while the latter extends human rights to ecosystems' (2021, 219). The mere extension of pre-existing, undefined rights to a statutorily created artificial person is not, however, *intrinsic* to the idea of personhood. Michelle Maloney (2018) proposes a distinction between 'Rights of Nature laws and Legal Personhood for Nature laws'. She presupposes a distinction and separateness between the two concepts based on the premise that rights of Nature laws 'recognise that the living world has a right to exist … and is a subject of the law', whereas legal personhood for nature laws 'make certain elements in the living world … a *subject* of the law … and *give nature the same rights as a legal person*'. As a result, Maloney argues, legal personhood 'extends the human-centred notion of "personhood" to "nature", which by its very definition, is not human [and, moreover] in legal terms, nature has legal rights and legal *liabilities*'. Therefore, 'using "legal personhood" constructs to protect nature "misses the point" of changing the legal system to respect nature, and simply tries to extend the same rights to nature that people have'. The argument, which has been reproduced with me in a similar form by a number of rights of Nature activists, appears to conflate the idea of the natural and the artificial person within a single construct, while at the same time indirectly pointing to some of the inherent limitations that the articulation of legal personhood for Nature has displayed thus far. As a result, it is necessary to disentangle the underlying confusion that such a conflation may carry and delve a little further into the concept of personhood.

7.4.2 The Legal Persona

According to Richard Mohr, '[t]he personal sense of identity, that we feel *ourselves* to be the same person we were yesterday, is closely bound to our sense of physical integrity, our embodied-ness' (2008, 41). The idea of the 'person' is thus intricately connected to the very flesh it represents. However, such is not the legal meaning of the concept. The idea of the 'legal person' is derived from the *Institutes* of the Justininan Code, which divided the books of civil law between *personae* (persons), *res* (things) and *actiones* (actions or procedures). Leibniz further developed the Roman trifurcation of persons, things and actions, by calling them *subjects*, *objects* and *causes* of a *right*. Furthermore, Leibniz also divided subjects (persons) between natural (*naturalia*) and artificial (*artificialia*), noting that only subjects have the capacity to hold rights (*iura*).

Alexis Dyschkant (2015) notes that the first legal conception of the Legal Person is as a human: the "natural' person. 'Even though corporations are clearly not natural persons, the concept of humanity has been fundamental for attributing personhood to corporations ... The extension of personhood to corporations was described in light of the role of human beings in corporations. Corporations are "constituted by and encompass large numbers of other legal persons", including the natural persons that control them. It is the capabilities of the human beings that control the corporation that actually constitute the personhood of the corporation' (2084–5). However, Hannah Arendt insists that personhood is *always* something *artificial*: '[i]t is the product of laws, regulations, practices, and discourses that create distinctions between persons (citizens) and "mere" members of the human species—natural men—who lack such personhood. Because of this artificiality, its constructed, mask-like nature, it can also be "affixed" to groups and corporations, and even to "a common and continuing purpose"' (Horsman, 2016, 320). Hannah Arendt expands upon the artificially constitutive nature of the *persona* in *On Revolution*:

> [i]n its original meaning it signified the mask ancient actors used to wear in a play ... The mask as such obviously has two functions: it had to hide, or rather to replace, the actor's own face and countenance, but in a way that would make it possible for the voice to sound through. At any rate, it was in this twofold understanding of a mask through which a voice sounds that the word *persona* became a metaphor and was carried from the language of the theatre into legal terminology. The distinction between a private individual in Rome and a Roman citizen was that the latter had a *persona*, a legal personality, as we would say; it was as though the law had affixed to him the part he was expected to play on the public scene, with the provision, however, that his own voice would be able to sound through. The point was that "it is not the natural Ego which enters a court of law. It is a right-and-duty-bearing person, created by the law, which appears before the law". Without this *persona*, there would be an individual without rights and duties, perhaps a "natural man" – that is, a human being or homo in the original meaning of the word, indicating someone outside the range of the law and the body politic of the citizens, as for instance a slave – but certainly a politically irrelevant being. (1976 ed, 106–7)

The origin of the *idea* of the person is thus found in the classical precursor to the social theatre of public speaking, the *persōna* (from the Greek πρόσωπον, 'mask', or 'character', to the Latin *per-sonare*, 'to sound through') which provided the actor with license to speak. Maria Bettetini (2004) notes that Aristotle used the term (originally derived from a word for the prow of a ship) to refer to the theatrical mask as well as the character which the mask portrayed, while 'the Greek bible used the term *prosopon* for the face of God which Moses dared not look at, and … *kata prosopon* referred to the presence of God' (Mohr, 2008, 37). Bettetini posits that the Latin *persona* 'may also have derived from "*per-sonat*", the capacity of the mask to resonate to the actor's voice'. The theatrical origins of the term survived in the concept of 'the "dramatis personae" of Shakespearean and later theatre, and in the notion that we can adopt a "persona", in the sense that we may play a role'. Pier Francesco Savona notes that 'the actor of the Greek theatre put on the "mask" that turned the actor into a "persona" also to signify that there was no intention to challenge the gods by this conduct but only to play a "role", which could be done with impunity just because this a conduit between the divine and the human' (2005, 105). The Greek actor, by wearing a mask, signified that there was no challenge to the Gods by his (all Greek actors were male) action. The *prosopon* thus allowed to avoid *hubris* and acted as a conduit between the human and the divine.

The theatrical meaning of the term shifted in the Roman word, particularly with Cicero and Livy, who used the word *persona* to refer to 'the functions or roles played by a Roman citizen' (Mohr, 2008, 37). This marks the beginning of the 'persona' as a legal role and, or, function, as a legal category in Roman legal life. Terry Pinkard describes Roman *personae* as 'bearers of legal rights in which the individual communal self-identity is fully exhausted by this legal status' (1996, 147). The reason for the creation of the 'persona' as a legal category was already articulated by Hegel, Paul Baumgardner suggests (2016), in his contrast between the Greek 'way of life', marked by social cohesion and the idea of the *polis* as the fulcrum of identity in which individuals are subsumed, and the Roman way of life, marked by the geographical impossibility of such cohesion. Some authors further argue that 'the category of legal personhood could assimilate the broadening imperial population and ease governance: the geographical reach of the ballooning empire required to deal with questions of pluralism: how could such a large swathe of land be united, and made to flourish together? As the first pluralistic empire, the Roman required a substitute for the normative cohesion of the Greek way of life', and they found it in the legal construct of the *persona*, the emergence of which coincides with the emergence of the idea of *Romanitas*, of belonging *as a citizen* to an abstract political entity. 'With legal personhood came a sort of moral and political licence, a freedom to act in accordance with one's own values and commitments, so long as those actions did not collide with the law' (Baumgardner, 2016, 20).

Cicero emphasized that '[w]e must realize also that we are invested by Nature with two characters [*personae* in the original], as it were; one of these is universal, arising from the fact of our being all alike endowed with reason and with that superiority which lifts us above the brute. … The other character is the one that is assigned to individuals in particular' (1968 ed, book I, xxx, 107–9). Jeanne Gaaker writes that '[a]s far as the former *persona* is concerned, the distinction between humans and non-human beings that has proved to be detrimental to innovation of legal personhood in our present age is prominent. The latter *persona* refers to both social and legal roles that may or may not overlap, each with corresponding duties' (2016, 291).

The notion of personhood, from a legal category, morphed into a socio-biological one with stoicism, which, in conjunction with the rise of Christianity, led to the creation of the idea of a universal 'humanity' (an idea never encountered before). From a legal category, thus, the *persona* morphed into an ontological category of being. The term soon 'took centre stage in many theological debates, including the mystery of the Holy Trinity (Mohr, 2008, 38). Marcel Mauss (1979) points to the role of the Council of Nicaea (325 CE) in resolving questions of the unity or diversity of the divine substances. The word to define the substance of the three distinguishable Father, Son and Holy Spirit (ὑπόστασις, *hypostasis* in the original Greek) was translated as *persona* in Latin: *unitas in tres personas, una persona in duas naturas* ('unity in three persons, one person with two natures'). Mohr notes that, '[b]y 500 CE a Christian definition of *persona* was required, and was famously supplied by Severinus Boethius as "*naturae rationalis individua substantia*": rational nature in an individual substance … It is possible to see in this theological definition the seeds of Descartes' later distinction between mind and matter' (2008, 38).

During the middle ages, an ecclesiastical *collegium* (most medieval corporate bodies had a religious or caritative purpose) or a *universitas* 'could not be excommunicated or be found guilty of a civil or criminal offence … on the view that the *universitas* did not have a corporal body and neither did it have a soul or a free will, being only a legal name, *nomina sunt juris et non personarum*' (Gaaker, 2016, 292). However, in 1155, Gaaker recalls, Emperor Frederick Barbarossa

> awarded the schools in Bologna that were devoted to the study of law a special status. These schools were private schools, small *societates*, each grouped around a *magister*. Students of different schools began to unite depending on their geographical roots, i.e. *citramontanas* and *ultramontanas*, that is, from the Italian side of or from beyond the Alps. Thus two *universitates* were formed … local authorities in 1270 recognized the *universitas* as a separate entity, an autonomous corporation with specific privileges for the students such as tax exemptions … its corporate personality offered protection against both secular and clerical intrusions. (2016, 292)

The modern, extended and *artificial* concept of the *persona* was thus born. Visa Kurki (2019) notes that Hughes Doneau was the first to use the term *persona* in a modern sense in the sixteenth century, soon followed by the German jurist Hermann Vultejus who distinguished between *homo* (a physical human being) and *persona* (a human being with civil standing). Leibniz, noting that only subjects (persons) have the capacity to hold rights (*iura*), divided them between natural (*naturalia*) and artificial (*artificialia*). As Gaaker notes, the popularity of artificial personhood 'for practical, commercial reasons is obvious: unlike the human body to the natural person as a legal person, the artificial person does not die, *universitas non moritur*' (2016, 292). Mohr concurs, by noting that '[t]he modern legal person, born of this edifice of fictions, is an identifiable unit, to whom may be allocated responsibility, blame, entitlement or obligation' (2008, 38–9). Personhood, in a legal sense, became the technical personification of a complex of norms, rights and duties: i.e. the *subject* of them all.

To further articulate the *artificial* person, a number of theories on corporate personality have emerged since the Enlightenment: the 'fiction theory' (primarily expressed from Savigny) which identified legal/artificial/corporate persons as legal fictions: any entity capable of exercising right and obligations as established by law. John Dewey said that 'for the purposes of law, the conception of a "person" is a legal conception; put roughly, 'person' signifies what law makes it signify' (1926, 656). The second theory, known as the 'purpose theory', argues that property is not necessarily owned by any 'person', but rather belongs to a 'purpose'. The third theory, 'realist theory', suggests that corporations and legal entities exist as objective realities, and the law merely recognizes them (rather than creating them). Finally, the 'formalist theory' identifies three distinct meaning of personhood: a biological one (a person as a rational being) a philosophical one (a rational being capable of proposing and carrying out objectives) and a legal one (a subject of law with rights and obligations). Overall, the civil law appears more comfortable with the idea of an artificial person being simply identified in codification, whereas the common law seems to require a 'bundle' of identifiers.

It is the latter of the above theories that fully captures the multifaceted meaning of the term 'person'. It is thus apparent that the critique that personhood extends to nature the same rights as a human being would be valid only if the concept of the persona were to be limited to humans, but that, as we have seen, is not *legally* the case. Within the Western legal tradition, there is no difficulty in attributing the idea of personhood to nonhuman constructs, and, by extension, entities. Moreover, it is not possible to think of any right without conceiving of a subject holding them, and the legal definition of the subject is that of a person. Furthermore, there is nothing *essential* about the type of rights to be extended to a legal person (and thus the extension of generic rights and liabilities to natural persons is a contextual accident rather than a universal mandate). Conversely, however, a legal person is a *necessary* legal pre-requisite for the identification of a holder of rights. However, it is important to note, some authors suggest that a legal subject is not *necessarily* a legal person.

7.4.3 Nature as a Persona

Visa Kurki (2019) provides a nuanced analysis of personhood in relation to natural entities and human collectives. The fundamental distinction he proposes is between 'natural persons', which he describes both *extensionally* ('the set of beings who are natural persons rather than what actually qualifies them as legal persons') and *paradigmatically* ('the set of individuals whose legal personhood is definitely not in dispute'). Paradigmatically, natural persons are human beings, who have been born, who are currently alive and who are sentient (thus excluding, for example, anencephalic infants). These criteria are only sufficient for what the civil law tradition designates as 'legal capacity' (*rechtsfähigkeit* in German, or *capacité de jouissance* in French, or *capacitá giuridica* in Italian), often defined as the capacity to hold rights and bear duties, as distinct from the 'legal competence' (*geschäftsfähigkeit*, *capacité d'exercise, capacitá di azione*), the ability to enter into legal relations. Kurki defines the former as *passive* legal personhood and the latter as *active* legal personhood. In relation to the theory of personhood, Kukri identifies four possible positions. The first position, 'Rights-or-Duties' maintains that an entity must hold at least one right or bear one duty to qualify as a legal person. The second position, 'Rights-and-Duties' maintains that one must hold at least one right *and* bear at least one duty to qualify. The third position, 'Capacity-for-Rights' identified legal personhood as the legal capacity to *hold* rights and bear duties. The fourth position is that of 'explaining legal persons as the only possible parties of legal, or jural, relations' (56).

Kurki argues that '[c]ases such as those of the Whanganui River ... are mentioned as examples in support of the proposition that legal personhood can be extended to just about anything'. However, he proceeds to argue 'many of these "everything-goes" claims are actually based on a conflation of two different senses of "legal person": ... a bundle of legal positions and an entity that holds these legal positions' (127–8). He further distinguishes between a legal *platform* (the bundle of legal positions) and a legal *person* (the holder of such positions). An important aspect of being a legal person is that 'one corresponds to at least one legal platform ... I call this *attachment*: legal platforms attach to legal persons' (135). Furthermore, a '[w]eak attachment of a platform to an entity means that the existence of the platform is dependent on the existence of the entity,' and thus, while the 'legal arrangement pertaining to the Whanganui River is in this regard different from a typical corporation, [t]his weak attachment of a legal platform to a physical object does not ... yet constitute legal personhood for the purpose of attribution' (139). Kurki further argues that, '[a]lthough a legislator can create a virtually infinite number of legal *platforms*—each of which comprises an array of legal positions—it does not follow that absolutely anything could be a legal *person.* ... the incidents of legal personhood can only be attributed to entities that can hold claim-rights or perform acts' (128).

Importantly, he proceeds to explicitly acknowledge that his ontological position is explicitly non-animistic, rejecting the possibility that rivers can be considered as living entities. He says that '[w]e can owe duties to adults, children, and nonhuman animals, but not, for instance, to rivers. Rather, our duties can *pertain* to rivers. This distinction relies on a moral distinction: sentient beings are of ultimate value, and bodies of water are not' (141). He concludes by unequivocally stating that 'animals can be passive legal persons because the duties pertaining to a legal platform could be borne *towards* an animal [whereas n]atural objects such as rivers, on the other hand, cannot hold claim-rights and consequently cannot be passive legal persons' (151).

Kurki's highly nuanced argument shows the direct relationship between the onto-axiological position he adopts (his situated worldview) and the legal arguments that he articulates. The impact of the explicitly anthropocentric perspective he adopts has an immediate consequence on the legal argument he proposes. However, there is nothing *essential* about the argument itself that *necessarily* entails the conclusion he reaches. Indeed, *contra* Kurki's theory of personhood, Ngaire Naffine (2012) notes how humanistic precepts of what constitutes a 'person' inherently define the limits of personhood, but are, by no means, inherently objective or universal.

7.4.3.1 Environmental Personhood

The above discussion provided a (necessarily brief) answer to the first two critiques advanced toward the extension of legal personhood to natural entities. The extension is a *necessary* pre-requisite for the existence of a subject of rights (of Nature, in this instance), while there is nothing *necessary* about the type of rights (Kurki't *platform*) being attributed to the person (in this case, there is no inherent requirement to extend the same rights and liabilities as a natural person). A third and distinct problem, however, is that of identifying more clearly the boundaries of the natural person. A key issue is jurisdictional. Many natural features, such as rivers, do not obey borders and often traverse multiple countries. The issue arises, then, whenever a natural feature that extends across a number of jurisdictions (be they international or domestic) that adopt different regimes in relation to it.

The problems thus identified (the *type* of rights to be identified, the existence of related *liabilities* and the problems of geographical/jurisdictional identification) have led some advocates to propose that the existing distinction between natural personhood and artificial (or juridical or juristic) personhood (of which corporate personhood is an example) is currently insufficient to capture the *sui generis* nature of natural entities as legal persons. After all, such entities are corporeal and (generally) clearly identifiable (as a natural person) and yet, due to their inherent communicative inability within an inherently and inevitably anthropocentric legal system (which requires a human representative for their rights to be articulated in court), they exist as legal constructs more than a natural person ever would (and thus they are, in this sense, more akin to an artificial person). The conundrum, these advocates suggest, requires the emergence of a novel category of personhood, one that may be provisionally called 'environmental' or 'ecological' personhood. Gwendoline Gordon introduces the term 'environmental personhood' not (yet) to refer to a novel category of personhood, but to indicate the attribution of personhood to environmental entities. She notes that 'one weakness in environmental personhood as it is currently articulated is what appears to be a widespread political commitment to a holistic ecocentrism functionally equivalent to real entity theories of the corporation' (2018, 83).

Furthermore, she notes that some countries, like New Zealand, have 'long taken the corporation to be a concession of the state … But the legal personhood of natural objects is not quite so straightforward. The status of these persons is twinned: in the view of the government, concession theory rules, with Parliament able to name whatever it wishes as a person. In the view of the Maori, these are real entities gaining their personhood not merely from government grant but also from the spiritual ties of *whakapapa*, genealogy' (86). As a result, she concludes, the statuses of the Whanganui River and the Te Urewera forest 'are thus conceptualized in New Zealand as a new kind of personhood in addition to that of the natural person and the artificial person – the corporation. This duality is useful in escaping political binds and encouraging compromise. It is also useful in normalizing environmental personhood, giving it simultaneous legal and cultural heft' (87). She also wonders, following Lawrence Tribe, whether 'legislating around natural rights might disintegrate the positive feelings toward nature that would motivate someone to act or to care for nature in the first place ... [and thus the creation of environmental personohood] may erode overarching respect for and commitment to the environment' (89). However, the constitutive nature of many relations has not *necessarily* eroded their psychological and sociological origin. An immediate counter-argument that many would (hopefully) make, for example, is that the creation of the legal institution of marriage has not eroded the feelings of love.

Gordon's analysis also highlights the strategic rather than genealogical, relationship of many Indigenous groups with the rights of Nature. Her point shows that the concept of legal personality for Nature is not and cannot be a direct translation of Maõri (and, by extension, Indigenous) legal concepts. Instead, as Tănăsescu writes, they are a 'potential straitjacket for Indigenous emancipatory politics. The radical character of Indigenous ontologies is not fully reflected in the concept of legal personality' (2020, 429). Miranda Johnson equally questions 'the assumption that the legal fiction of personality is an accurate translation of what Whanganui people believe and practice ... The legislation is better interpreted as a strategic compromise reached between Iwi and the New Zealand state, as these distinct political entities negotiate settlement packages for long-standing grievances' (2017). Furthermore, she adds, '[i]n the context of a settler state seeking to further enhance a distinctive policy of biculturalism in a post-imperial world, using the "vehicle" of legal personality carries with it a particular kind of politics'. That notwithstanding, James Morris and Jacinta Ruru had argued, in 2010, that 'applying Stone's idea to afford legal personality to New Zealand's rivers would create an exciting link between the Maori legal system and the state legal system. The legal personality concept aligns with the Maori legal concept of a personified natural world. By regarding the river as having its own standing, the mana (authority) and mauri (life force) of the river would be recognized, and importantly, that river would be more likely to be regarded as a holistic being rather than a fragmented entity of flowing water, river bed and river bank' (2010, 50).

The negotiated and politically fluid nature of the adoption of rights of Nature discourses and the attribution of legal personhood to natural entities thus constitute a creative space of interaction between asymmetrically situated legal orders, those of Indigenous peoples and those of their colonial counterparts. This has already led to a number of alternative proposals that extend the concept of the 'environmental' person even further. Members of the Martuwarra Fitzroy River Council and a number of Australian and New Zealand legal scholars (including myself) have recently proposed the concept of an *ancestral* person as 'an invitation to challenge the hegemonic and deeply held legal orthodoxy, while at the same time articulating First Law in terms that are recognisable within the colonial context. Once embraced in these comparative terms', we have argued, 'law is no longer something that only humans engage with. Rather, law emerges from the endless interplay between humans and non-human "actants", whereby rivers cease to be mere abstract legal persons, and instead become active participants in the very process of legal creation' (RiverOfLife et al., 2021). Similarly, Jana Norman, drawing on emerging insights from contemporary science and from critical theory such as new materialism and posthumanism, proposes the notion of a 'Cosmic Person' as an alternative legal subject that is 'embodied, embedded and entangled' (2022, 59).

7.4.4 Representation and Agency

However legal personhood for Nature and natural entities is to be construed, a fundamental issue that remains is that of representation. For Nature as a legal person to act within a court of law, it necessarily requires a human representative. As Herman Greene notes, '[a] cosmology of meaning and purpose leads to a biocentric, geocentric or universe-centric orientation, but it does not change the fact that humans make the judgments concerning the rights of nature. In a legal sense, neither the universe, nor Earth, nor any other-than-human creature can represent itself. In this representative function humans will weigh the rights of nature and of humans' (2011, 134). Stone wrote that

> [t]he guardianship approach, however, is apt to raise two objections, neither of which seems to me to have much force. The first is that a committee or guardian could not judge the needs ot the river or forest in its charge; indeed, the very concept of "needs", it might be said, could be used here only in the most metaphorical way. The second objection is that such a system would not be much different from what we now have: is not the Department of Interior already such a guardian for public lands, and not most states have legislation empowering their attorneys general to seek relief – in a sort of *parens patriae* way – for such injuries as a guardian might concern himself with? As for the first objection, natural objects can communicate their wants (needs) to us, and in ways that are not terribly ambiguous' [to exemplify this, Stone uses the example of his lawn wanting water on a dry summer day]. (1972, 471)

In response, Stone suggested a separate system of guardianship, uninfluenced by the political processes and vagaries of any particular time, to prevent the undue influence of corporations and other lobbying groups. He proposed the establishment of a system of Guardians for Nature and natural entities, such as Guardian for the Oceans, for example, or even more a Global Commons Guardian and a related Global Commons Trust Fund. The role of such Guardians would be to *monitor* as well as being involved in the complex web of global policymaking, and as appearing as a special '*intervenor-counsel* for the unrepresented environmental "victim"' (2010, 131). Similarly, at the 1992 *Rio Summit*, the Maltese delegation submitted a proposal to establish an official Guardian to represent the rights of future generations. At present, four different models of representation, agency or guardianship have been adopted (Zelle et al., 2021):

- Everyone can speak on behalf of Nature. This is the model adopted under Art 71 of the Ecuadorian Constitution.
- A specific public office is either specifically established or is granted specific powers to represent Nature. An example of this is the National Ombudsman's office (*Defensoría del Pueblo*), under Articles 38 and 39 of Ecuador's 2015

General Organic Code of Processes. Zelle and others note that the office is responsible 'for handling all allegations brought by people and communities alleging a violation of the rights of nature. Claims for remedial and restorative measures, and the subsequent implementation, are submitted for the approval of the national environmental authority (Ministry of Environment)' (2021, 164).
- Specific Guardians are appointed. This is the case in the New Zealand Te Awa Tupua Act, which appointed a dedicated Office of the Guardian called Te Pou Tupua and established with all the powers necessary to protect and preserve the river, and in the Colombian Atrato river case, whereby Colombia's President appointed the Ministry of Environment as well as 14 community members from the Chocó region as the joint representatives for the river.
- The legal doctrine of *in loco parentis* is used to make government bodies and officers responsible for acting on behalf of the natural entity. This was the path proposed in the Ganges and Yamuna case.

The approaches thus vary widely, from a mere abstract connection between human agents and the natural world they are entitled to represent as is the case in Ecuador, to a sense of profound identity with the natural feature a few select humans are to represent, as is the case between the Whanganui Iwi and the Whanganui river in New Zealand. Naturally, the question arises as to who would best be placed to represent Nature, both as a whole and in specific instances. The generic representation awarded by the Ecuadorian provisions may fail to guarantee the specific needs that local ecosystems and natural features may display. Furthermore, the lack of an explicit epistemic link between the natural entity and its agent or representative risks replicating many of the very onto-axiological projections that are being challenged. At the same time, one may question whether certain natural interests would be better represented by some specifically selected individuals or institutions. Furthermore, the enforced application of the *in loco parentis* doctrine has received a negative response from institutions that resisted the imposition to represent Nature, thus leading to negative unintended consequences whenever such representatives would not be willing to undertake their duties. Moreover, Zelle and other suggest that, '[w]hen rights are recognized for "all of nature" (conceptualized as nested ecosystems), choosing appropriate guardians becomes more complicated as a nested ecosystem encompasses a variety of dynamic characteristics, all of which are interrelated in complex, multiscale connections' (2021, 161–2).

Duvall and Session suggest that, in some instances, a system of stewardship may continue 'the premise of instrumental rationality—the narrowly utilitarian view—of natural resources primarily for human use, and fails to distinguish vital human needs from mere desires, egotistical arrogance and adventurism in technology' (1985, 125). John O'Neill points out that any form of natural representation 'relies on epistemic claims, coupled with care' (2001, 483). O'Neill continues by asserting that, since epistemic claims 'are inextricably linked with processes of power and biopolitical normalisation, any account of nature which purports to stand apart from humanist history and its relation of knowledge and power becomes "profoundly suspicious"'.

As a result, any system of human representation for the natural world must be necessarily cognisant of the asymmetrical power relations that persist in the world, both among distinct human groups and between human and non-human actants. While holistic representations of nature may suggest the existence of a single entity looking after itself, with the result that 'situations of conflicting interests are impossible' (Emmenegger & Tschentscher, 1993, 577–8), the very notion of legal representation must, by necessity, acknowledge that calculations of interests and responsibilities occur within relationships that are 'structurally non-contractual, asymmetrical and rooted in ontological difference' (Turner, 2003, 6). Humanity, particularly given its current historical trajectory, does not encounter most of the non-human world in a symmetrical relationship, and thus issues of power and knowledge are paramount to engender a meaningful discourse surrounding the issue of nature's *representation*. After all, as Mark Sagoff asks, how does any human 'purport to know the interests of a voiceless subject?' (1974, 221–2). In a recent Ph.D. thesis, Oluwabusayo Temitope Wuraola suggests that the 'wider interests of ecosystems [ought to be] internalised by probable representatives for there to be substantive representation as held in political debates' (2022, 125). To do so, she suggests what she terms an 'eco-centred representative model', whereby an ideal representative displays for essential capabilities: to internalise ecosystems' interests, to care for ecosystems morally, to hold knowledge claims, and to engage in substantive representation.

An apt example of guardianship predicated along these principles can be found, at least to an extent, in New Zealand. In 2004 the New Zealand's Environment Court ruled that 'one needs to understand the culture of the Whanganui River *iwi* [tribe] to realize how deeply engrained the saying *ko au te awa, ko te awa ko au* [I am the river, and the river is me] is to those who have connections to the river' (in Boyd, 2017, 134). Kauffman and Martin note that

> [i]n practice, the guardianship arrangement in Te Urewera involves a networked system of governance involving three types of actors. The Te Urewera Board speaks for Te Urewera from a legal and philosophical basis, establishing general principles for people management in Te Urewera. The bush crews speak more directly for Te Urewera, in the sense of living in the forest, observing its natural order and evolution, paying attention to signs the forest is giving them, and communicating this to Te Uru Taumatua operations teams working in each of Te Urewera's four valleys. Te Uru Taumatua then compiles this information into a composite picture of the forest as a whole and uses this information to make operational decisions for the forest as a whole (2021, 578).

In order to implement the Te Urewera Act, it was clear that it was necessary to recover ancestral knowledge, customs and practices to connect the Iwi to the forest and fulfil the responsibilities as *kaitiaki* (guardian, or steward). One of the ways to do this is through the establishment of 'bush crews' led by respected Elders who have maintained the traditional way of life. The first of such crews was created in 2018 in Ruatoki, led by 'Uncle Maynard' Apiata.

The New Zealand example is of particular significance in addressing Sagoff's question. Even assuming that a guardian or representative displays all the capabilities suggested by Wuraola, a fundamental epistemological question remains: how is it ever possible to 'know' what Nature *wants*? The problem of identifying with a nonhuman species, with a radically distinct *umwelt*, was famously introduced by philosopher Thomas Nagel in 1974, in his article 'What Is It Like to Be a Bat?'. While Anne Poelina et al (2020) describe the process of 'Feeling Country' in Australia (i.e. of giving voice to Country through deep empathy with the natural world), such an approach is far from epistemologically available to a worldview still deeply steeped in extreme or crude anthropocentrism. The issue, as Erin O'Donnell remarks, is thus of shifting from a mindset of speaking *for* Nature to one of speaking *with* Nature.

Before such a concept can be further explored (in the following chapter), one last question must be explored, among those that have been raised by the many eco-jurisprudential initiatives and theories discussed thus far. What actually *is* Nature?

7.5 Nature or Natures?

While rights are certainly contested concepts with negotiable meanings, the same is true—even more so in fact—of the very idea of *nature*. What is 'nature',[1] after all? Hume's naturalistic fallacy has definitively shown that we can't *empirically* determine what nature 'is' via observation alone. Furthermore, the term is used to identify a wide range of things: from the idea of untouched wilderness to the fabric of reality (including natural forces, such as gravity as well as natural selection), from the ecologically pristine to the psychological dimension of one's innate tendencies. John Bellamy Foster noted, that '[t]he word *nature* ... is one of the more complex words in modern language, standing as it does in different contexts for the material world and even the universe; the most fundamental domain of existence; the elemental drives of life; the object of natural science; certain timeless, immutable laws; evolution; the non-human and non-social; the non-intellectual and non-spiritual, and so on' (2010, 32). Given such variety of usages, Carolan asks whether one will ever be able to 'unsnarl this terminological quagmire' (2005, 393). Raymond Williams (1980, 68) calls 'nature' one of the most complex words in existence, while Kate Soper (1995) observes that nature is 'a promiscuous concept', and Max Weber referred to the fundamental 'ambiguity of the concept of "nature"' (1977 ed, 95), while Christopher Stone indicated that 'the climate'—and thus, by extension, 'nature' as a whole—'makes for a shifty client ... [being] more of a set of parameters than a thing' (2010, 34).

Is a 'road' natural? Why, or why not? Are breakfast cereals 'natural' in the same sense that an old growth forest is? Soper notes that 'the term "nature" refers to everything which is not human and distinguished from the work of humanity. Thus "nature" is opposed to culture, to history, to convention, to what is artificially worked or produced, in short to everything which is defining of the order of humanity' (2008, 598). Margaret Davies writes that, '[i]n its primary usage relating to external things, "nature" refers collectively to the physical things of the Earth as opposed

[1] For the purpose of this section, I will not capitalise the term, to refer back to the concepts discussed in the initial chapters of this book.

to human beings and human creations'. (2022, 39). Soper argues that nature exists in language in a *realist* sense (as a descriptor of a biophysical reality) and in a *socio-cultural* sense. She further identifies three fundamental concepts of nature: an *external* one (nature as external to, and different from, society); an *intrinsic* one (nature as the Aristotelian essential quality of something for it to be that very thing) and a *universal* one (nature as a global, intertwined, ecological system). The first definition is of particular importance, since structural anthropologists have suggested that the binary of *nature* and *culture* is one by which many human societies organize their conceptual world. Descola writes that '[i]n modern thought … "nature" only has meaning when set in opposition to human works, whether one chooses to call these "culture", "society", or "history", to use the language of philosophy and the social sciences, or "anthropized space", "technical mediation", or "*oikumene*", to use a more specialized terminology' (2013a, 8). Indeed, it can be easily seen how such a dichotomic description of the world, as divided between the *natural* and the *cultural*, is deeply aligned with the anthropocentric worldview underpinning current dominant legal systems described in the above sections. Nicole Graham argues that in English, 'the definition of the word "environment" is "the aggregate of surrounding things" and this reflects, to an extent, a worldview in which people are positioned at its centre and everything else around them. In this view', she continues, 'culture is separate from nature so it is unsurprising that law, being cultural, does not regard itself as derivative of nature' (2011, 263). Bruno Latour argues that 'one of the originary impulses of modernity is the project of "partitioning" or deepening the imaginary gulf between Nature and Culture: the former comes to be relegated exclusively to the scientists and is regarded as being off-limits to the latter' (in Gosh, 2016, 68).

The distinction between nature and culture begs the following question, Descola asks: '[s]hould one consider culture as an adaptive system responding to natural constraints and thus ultimately explainable by mechanisms subject to the laws of matter and of life; or should one see in culture a distinct order of reality which only sustains relationships of a contingent type with the ecological world and the necessities of human metabolism?' (2013a, 12). In the 1950s, Julian Steward introduced the idea of 'cultural ecology', suggesting that ecological constraints shape and define culture. Similarly, Marvin Harris and other partisans of 'ecological determinism' view nature as 'the sum of constraints that a geographical environment allegedly exerts on the development of social life' (Descola, 2013a, 2013b, 19), whereas Lévi-Strauss sees nature as 'the biological framework of the human condition'. Jane Bennett equally points out that 'what we used to call natural is actually the cultural determination of nature. But here the vital materialist points out that culture [itself] is *not* of our own making, infused as it is by biological, geological, and climatic forces' (2010, 115). Indeed, she continues

> we are much better at admitting that humans infect nature than we are at admitting that nonhumanity infects culture, for the latter entails the blasphemous idea that nonhumans … are actants more than objects. … What I am calling vital materiality or vibrant matter is akin to what is expressed in one of the many historical senses of the word *nature*. Though nature can refer to a stable substrate of brute matter, the term has also signaled generativity,

> fecundity, Isis or Aphrodite, or the "Spring" movement of Antonio Vivaldi's *Four Seasons*. (115–7)

Friedrich Schelling had already suggested two centuries ago that 'to philosophize about nature is to produce it'. Peter Knudtson and David Suzuki suggest that 'ecosystems are human constructs to which nature is blind' (1992, 44), while Bruno Latour proposes to dissolve the distinction between nature and culture, positing a world of highly complex relations between humans and nonhumans, both with the same amount of ontological agency, resulting in a symmetrical, non-hierarchical structure. Deep ecology further rejects the inherent dualism of the idea of 'humans in the environment', rather imagining a 'relational total field' (Naess, 1989), whereby all things exist within a field of intrinsic relations in which the nature of any one thing cannot be described independently of its relation to others and ultimately to the field as a whole. Similarly, Timothy Morton advances the notion of a 'dark ecology', suggesting that, to properly develop an ecological view 'we must relinquish the idea of nature once and for all' (2007). To transcend the opposition between nature and culture, Donna Haraway (2003) introduces the concept of 'natureculture'.

Moreover, Descola writes that 'the modern West's way of representing nature is by no means widely shared. In many regions of the planet, humans and nonhumans are not conceived as developing in incommunicable worlds or according to quite separate principles. The environment is not regarded objectively as an autonomous sphere' (2013a, 30). Pope Francis notes that 'in the Judeo-Christian tradition, the word "creation" has a broader meaning than "nature", for it has to do with God's loving plan in which every creature has its own value and significance' (2015, 54)—the deep ecological undertones of the statement will certainly be apparent to many readers—while Carolyn Merchant writes that concepts of nature, just like concept of gender, 'are historical and social constructions. There are no unchanging "essential" characteristics of sex, gender, or nature' 1990 ed, xvi). Wondering whether there indeed exists a universal distinction between familiar, inhabited spaces, and alien, 'wild' ones, Descola answers in the negative.

> Because it is constantly revisited and resocialized, the environment of hunter-gatherers at every turn bears the traces of events that have unfolded there and that revivify old continuities right down to the present. … To claim that hunter-gatherers perceive their environment as a "wilderness" – in contrast to a domesticity that one would be hard put to define – is to deny that they are aware that, in the course of time, they modify the local ecology by their techniques of subsistence (2013a, 35).

Latour writes that '[e]cology clearly is not the irruption of nature into the public sphere but the *end of "nature"* as a concept that would allow us to sum up our relations to the world and pacify them' 2018, 36). This end of nature is distinct from Bill McKibben's 'end of the nature' (1989). For the latter, this represents the end of a state of relative homeostasis in which human societies have flourished over the past millennia. For Latour, it is the end of the very concept of 'nature' as a cultural construct. In fact, Latour goes further, saying that 'for westerners and those who have imitated them, "nature" has made the world uninhabitable', given that the current environmental predicament is dependent on the idea of 'nature' that has co-evolved with the practices that have led to the present moment' 2018, 36).

To briefly summarize the contested definitions of 'nature', Dennis des Chene suggests two meanings: '[t]he first, standardly glossed over as "essence" or "quiddity", is that which defines each individual substance ... The second, glossed as "world", "universe" or "cosmos", is the system of things which have natures in the first sense' (1996, 212). Lisbet Witthøfft Nielsen explains that

> the Western concept of nature can be described through four basic categories. Namely: (1) Nature is the physical whole, everything that constitutes the world, i.e. the physical elements and the 'cosmic' laws/the laws of nature. (2) Nature is that which is not created by Man, or manipulated by Man ... (3) Nature is the essence of a thing or a living being [in the sense that] (a) Nature is what makes a human body human and a tree a tree (the physical state) [and/or] (b) Nature is what makes a person that specific person (the inner/mental state). (4) Nature is what constitutes this world in its difference from others: (a) Nature stands in contrast to the supernatural world (the religious sphere); (b) Nature is what is common/natural in contrast to mutations/unnatural. ... The concept of nature also plays a very important role as a normative frame of reference, where the concept is closely connected to the morally good. (2004, 33–4)

The concept of Nature thus sits at the intersection of the descriptive and the normative. David Hume's naturalistic fallacy introduced the tension between *descriptive* statements (i.e. statements that assert something about the world and that can be *empirically* assessed) and *prescriptive* statements (i.e. statements that dictate how the world must operate).[2] The *idea* of Nature, therefore, exists in a hybrid space between the two. As Witthøft Nielsen notes, '"Nature" is referred to: (a) as the *object (phenomenon)* toward which [a] debate is directed, and (b) as the normative frame of reference that either justifies or rejects a [particular] approach' (2004, 33–4).

The *ideas* of Nature, ranging from the essential *entelechy* of an entity to the empirically observable characteristics of corporeal bodies, and the implications of these ideas for an ecological jurisprudence, are the most vibrant space in which, I believe, the scholarship of ecological jurisprudence is located. I will dedicate part of the next chapter to explore these theoretical implications in more detail. For the purposes of this chapter, however, suffice it to say that the definitions of Nature are immediately relevant for the purpose of identifying Nature—and even more so its individual components—as either the subject of rights or the objects of human responsibilities. It may very well be that, as Fredric Jameson (2009, 23) has stated, the concept of nature indeed represents the fundamental 'ontological rift' in existence, one that poses dialectical oppositions that 'can be fathomed but never fully bridged' (Bellamy Foster et al., 2010, 32). However, for the purposes of an ecological jurisprudence, at the very least, human normativity and legality are expected to align with the scientific constructions of Nature. In other words, an ecological jurisprudence necessarily requires a degree of identification with the science of ecology. While this,

[2] The classic example of the distinction between the two is the statement that 'all crows are black'. If that is uttered as a descriptive statement, then a white crow means that the statement is wrong. On the other hand, if the statement is a prescriptive one, then either the statement is invalid, or the white bird resembling a crow is just not a crow.

prima facie, may appear a confirmation of Berry and Cullinan's notion of the 'Great Jurisprudence', it is important to note that the ecological understanding of the world is neither singular nor static, but it's rather a dynamic and tentatively propositional process. In other words, ecological theories and models are historically and culturally located and are in a constant process of *becoming*. Eco-jurisprudential initiatives can be more or less aligned with this process. In this sense, Nature (or better, the ecological descriptors of the cosmos that can be heuristically defined as 'Nature') becomes, paraphrasing Michele Carducci and Lídia Patrícia Castillo Amaya (2016), not only a new *grundnorm* of global constitutionalism, but also a *grundnorm* for ecological jurisprudence.

Furthermore, the *idea* of Nature that is privileged leads to distinct consequences. Dryzek notes how specific ideas of what Nature *is* (or *ought to be*) have led '[s]ome radical environmentalists [to] believe that any area modified by human activity is no longer worth caring about' (1997, 4). In *The Monkey Wrench Gang*, one of the environmental heroes throws away cans of beer out of the car window, but such litter does not matter to him as it ends up in places already destroyed by human activities. Similarly, Bill McKibben, building upon Carolyn Merchant's title claiming the Death of Nature, argued that 'we have killed off nature—that world entirely independent of us which was here before we arrived and which encircled and supported our human society' (1990, 38). Strong echoes of the idea of the 'wilderness' remain in McKibben's words, as does the idea of humans being external to that world. Anthropocentric reverberances abound. Amitav Gosh questions, in response to Bill McKibben's idea of the 'end of nature' and our life in a 'post-natural world', whether '"Nature" in this sense ever exist[ed]. Or was it rather the deification of the human that gave an illusory apartness from ourselves? Now that nonhuman agencies have dispelled that illusion, we are confronted suddenly with a new task: that of finding other ways in which to imagine the unthinkable beings and events of this era' (2016, 33). To do so, Timothy Morton argues that the very idea of 'nature' must 'wither away in an "ecological" state of human society' (2007, 1).

7.6 Relationality, Reciprocity and Responsibility: Evaluating Nature's Legality

Ecological jurisprudence emerged, as the previous chapters have shown, in the latter part of the twentieth century and the early part of the twenty-first, at a time in which the science of ecology revealed the unprecedented impact that humanity is having on the nonhuman world, an impact that may threaten its very existence in the present form. Rachel Carson wrote that '[t]he question is whether any civilization can wage relentless war on life without destroying itself, and without losing the right to be called civilized' (in Orielle Lake 2013). The rise of ecology firstly permeated all scientific domains and then challenged many long-held assumptions as to the ethical relationships of humanity with the rest of existence, to finally enter the world of human politics and legal structures. Like many social ecologists (such as Carolyn Merchant and Murray Bookchin), as well as both the current Pope and his predecessor, note, the destruction of ecosystems is the direct result of failing human relationships. As a result, it has become clear that ecological impacts are regulated by regulating human relationships. It is those relations that are reconstituted by bringing nonhumans into the human political sphere. The initiatives presented in the previous chapter represent attempts to lead to both the protection of the environment and the sustainability of human societies in as close a homeostatic capacity as possible. Human societies, all these initiatives concur, are maintained by maintaining the integrity of the ecosystems, and such integrity is secured by the strategies and techniques they propose. This goal is achieved by either directly restraining human activities (as in the case of much environmental law and the proposal of ecocide laws) or by bringing nonhuman actants within the realm of the human political and legal arena to indirectly achieve the same outcome. Herman Greene, in numerous conversations with me, has identified the three related concepts of *relationality*, *reciprocity* and *responsibility* as the three fundamental pillars of what he calls 'earth law'. I deeply concur with his tripartite identification and suggest these trinity to capture the essence of an emerging ecological jurisprudence.

7.6.1 Ecological Jurisprudence as the Homeostatic Horizon of Law

The emergence of an ecological jurisprudence, I contend, can be traced through a series of specific milestones: among others, from Stone's article discussed in the Introduction, through the emergence of an Earth Jurisprudence in Thomas Berry and Cormac Cullinan's work, to the many Constitutional, legislative and judicial Rights of Nature initiatives that occurred in a great number of jurisdictions over the last decade. Notwithstanding the relevance of these milestones, the emergence of an ecological jurisprudence cannot be identified with any of these milestones, nor it is a clearly bounded theory, but rather represents a trajectory, a theoretical direction, one that inhabits a complex, pluriversal and adaptive ontological terrain. Furthermore, although some of its exponents may indeed adopt the language of 'crisis' and 'apocalypse', the trend toward an ecological jurisprudence acknowledges the web of historically contingent and ecologically fluid relations within which law is inscribed, and it aims to reconstruct such complexity within a reimagined and *adaptive* legal theoretical identity. In this sense, the emergence of an ecological jurisprudence represents a fundamental counter-narrative to an environmental state of exception, by proposing a 'homeostatic normative alternative' to the eschatological tendencies of apocalyptic narratives.

While it may be true that '[t]he systems of the Holocene are singularly ill-suited to the Anthropocene … in terms of principles, solutions, procedures and strategies to enable the resolution of ethical and other dilemmas associated with climate change exceptionalism' (Rogers 2022, 32), it is the very call to exceptionalism that inscribes such a call within a qualitatively and radically different new reality, as if we had crossed over an invisible threshold in which we are not anymore what we were before, and all that was is now a relic of a past best forgotten. However, and on the contrary, the emergence of an ecological jurisprudence gestures toward a continuity with the past in direct conjunction with a reimagined attitude toward the future, leading to neither a perpetuation of the status quo nor a radical caesura with the past. In this sense, the past is far from being forgotten, but rather informs, as it always does, the present, leaving it to its present interpreters how to make use of it. Rather than constituting a radical transformation, the trend toward an ecological jurisprudence represents a global synthesis, a novel reconciliation of previously distinct legal orders and underlying ontological perspectives that may lead to what Colombian anthropologist Arturo Escobar (2017) calls 'pluriversality', the attempt to bring about, through a collective engagement with ontological politics, a pluriverse, a world comprised of many co-existing ontological worlds, each marked by distinct, and yet ultimately interwoven, ontological and epistemological groundings. It is within this political diversity, which mimics the world's biodiversity, that, Escobar contends, the profound transformation needed to meaningfully engage with the current environmental predicament is to be found.

Humanity is currently faced with a unique environmental predicament, one that is as much a scientific fact as a social narrative. Responses to such a predicament vary, from 'technocures' inscribed within a familiar ontological landscape, to a host of economic, political and ethical suggestions. In the current normatively multifaceted, but ecologically interconnected, world, law acts as its connecting thread, the one around which an investigation of the nature of humanity and its normative place in the cosmos revolves. In the face of a scientifically unanimous environmental predicament that is best *not* described as a 'crisis' or an 'apocalypse'—lest we invoke the ever-present spectrum of an environmental state of exception—law offers, through the emergence of an ecological jurisprudence, a unique synthesis of adaptive (rather than reactive) responses. Naturally, adaptation may need to be rapid and sudden to deal with sudden changes and rapid degrading conditions. However, rather than being framed as a reactive invocation of an environmental state of exception, the emergence of an ecological jurisprudence suggests a homeostatic trajectory, one that strives to align human regulatory systems to the environment within which they exist in a dynamic and pluralist fashion. Ecological jurisprudence thus shows a fundamental shift in the articulation of the current environmental predicament, less construed in terms of an urgent reaction to a pending catastrophe and more in terms of a fundamental moral question: how are we, as humans, to live in relation to the rest of the cosmos? While this may appear, at first, as a purely (or at least primarily) ethical question, its answer lie just as importantly in the very definition of the cosmos (and the understanding of it) that has evolved over the past few millennia. The ontological construction of the idea of 'nature', as well as the underlying interaction between cultural definitions of what constitutes 'nature' and normative, regulatory and legal regimes, are necessary to fully understand the contextual origin of an ecological jurisprudence, its implications and its transformative potential.

7.6.2 Evaluative Matrices

Ecological jurisprudence is thus, on one level, the collection of all disparate initiatives (and their theoretical underpinnings) that range from a very basic rejection of crude anthropocentrism and pure hedonistic egoism through strategic environmental principles in a utilitarian sense, to ecocentrism, stopping short of the more misanthropic consequences of radical ecocentrism (i.e. the view that humans are both irrelevant and deleterious, and, therefore, should disappear). As this chapter has shown, there are four possible ontological positions that inform the philosophical underpinning of an emerging ecological jurisprudence:

1. Pure materialism. The world is considered in materialistic, mechanistic and, or, deterministic manner. Such a materialistic worldview does not *necessarily* entail ethical nihilism, and many forms of instrumentalist restraints are profoundly compatible with it.
2. Nature, the cosmos and corporeal reality emerge from a transcendental non-material (i.e. spiritual) world. While corporeal materiality *may* still be seen in a materialistic, mechanistic and, or, deterministic manner, its initial origin or animating principle is not.
3. The spiritual (i.e. non-material) principle mentioned above is seen as co-existing with, or imbuing, the material world. Such is the case in much philosophical pantheism, in Spinoza's panentheism, and Hegel's idealism.
4. There is no material world, only a spiritual or ideal one, of which 'materiality' is just an interpretive or epistemological accident.

Similarly, there are three main ethical positions that challenge crude anthropocentrism and that underpin all theories and initiatives explored thus far. All of them, it is important to note, are articulated in opposition to a purely hedonistic (and tautological) ethical and, or, psychological egoism.

1. Self-interest: the nonhuman world is to be protected in order to guarantee the ongoing and continued survival and well-being of *present* humanity over the long period. Three different sets of justifications are used in support of this ethical standpoint:

    a. An economic rationale.
    b. Religious justifications.
    c. Aesthetic, cultural and/or recreational justifications.

2. Rights of future generations: the nonhuman world is to be protected in order to guarantee the well-being of humanity not only at present but also into the future.
3. Biocentrism and ecocentrism: the nonhuman world is to be protected for its own sake, irrespective of any utility it may have for humanity. This standpoint entails three main approaches:

    a. The moral considerability of (primarily individual) animals (and, by extension, any other being identified as worthy of consideration).

b. Reverence for life as a whole.
c. Holism, deep ecology and land ethics: the belief that *all* of the nonhuman world is worthy of ethical, normative and legal consideration.

When combined, these positions could constitute a matrix to rapidly locate the underpinning of any particular initiative. A question thus arises as to whether any of these positions are mutually exclusives. Is enlightened anthropocentrism *irretrievably* opposed to ecocentrism? If one assumes an ecological scientific standpoint, and humans do not (and cannot) precisely know in advance the effect of their actions in ecological terms, then a stronger precautionary principle demands humans to behave prudently and with restraint. The result, thus, would be *pragmatically* indistinguishable from a prudent and restrained behaviour motivated by deep ecocentrism. While this is not necessarily always the case, the long-term survival humanity and the respect for the nonhuman world often appear to entail more of a change in *perspective* rather than in mere *praxis*.

Even the recognition of rights to (or for) Nature as a whole may be strategically pursued while still being motivated by instrumentalist mandates. Overall, however, all eco-jurisprudential theories and initiatives acknowledge the necessary pre-requisite of aligning human regulation in relation to the environment with existing scientific scholarship. This, I reiterate (and will explore further in the next chapter), ecological jurisprudence does not emerge by reference to a set of somewhat objective 'laws of nature', but rather as a reconciliation of distinct domains of knowledge, a 'bringing together' of the collective understanding of Nature in scientific (and culturally plural) terms with human laws marked by principles such as the precautionary principle, ecological integrity and sustainability.

With such a matrix of onto-axiological positions in mind, as well as a clear awareness of the goals to be achieved, it is also possible to evaluate all the initiatives discussed in the previous chapter through a more *pragmatic* matrix. If the goal of eco-jurisprudential initiatives is to regulate human behaviour in accordance with an ecological understanding of the world, then such goal can be attained in different ways. John Galbraith (1984) distinguishes between coercive power (which wins submission by threatening sanctions), compensatory power (which offers incentives and rewards) and conditioned power (which changes beliefs through persuasion and education). All eco-jurisprudential initiatives discussed above operate on those levels of power. Behaviour can be changed *directly*, via initiatives that directly and actively effect behavioural change, or *indirectly*. The former could take the form of regulatory incentives, whereas the latter that of taxation mechanisms that indirectly engender behavioural modifications. Equally, behaviour can be changed via *positive* incentives (such as the regulatory incentives just mentioned), designed to generate particular behaviours, or *negative* disincentives (such as the criminalization of environmentally harmful behaviour), designed to prevent specific behaviours. When these two axes are combined, a matrix thus emerges (see Table 7.1), and all initiatives can be aptly located within it. For the sake of simplicity, I will only include some of the main initiatives discussed thus far in the table below.

Table 7.1 Evaluative matrix

	Positive	Negative
Direct	Regulatory incentives Ecological civilization	Ecocide
Indirect	Rights of Nature Ecosystem services	Environmental litigation Taxation (carbon taxes, etc.)

The evaluative matrices offered—both the onto-axiological one and the pragmatic one—can be thus used together to locate any eco-jurisprudential initiative in relation to the pyramid of theoretical relations presented in the Introduction. By reference to these matrices and that pyramid, it is possible to answer a number of questions. What goal (be it normative or legal) is to be achieved by a particular initiative? Why is that goal to be achieved (i.e. what are its onto-axiological premises)? What is the relationship of that initiative with a host of philosophical, ethical, political and jurisprudential considerations? Answers to these questions could be even constructed in the form of comparative tables, such as the hypothetical one below (Table 7.2), which, for the sake of exemplary simplicity, only contains a single row.

The above is not, of course, an attempt to provide the definitive suggestion of what an evaluative matrix of eco-jurisprudential initiatives would look like, but only an attempt to exemplify its possibility. When thus considered, the many initiatives discussed in the previous chapter thus inhabit a far more fluid and less oppositional terrain. Rights of Nature, for example, can be approached either strategically, even with an enlightened anthropocentric approach, or at a deeper ontological level. Of course, at a protean level, the emergence of all these initiatives constitutes the injection of ecology into law, as Fritjof Capra and Ugo Mattei have suggested (2015). More specifically, this occurs at the intersection of the way law conceives of itself

Table 7.2 Comparative table sample

	Ethical goal	Legal goal	Worldview(s)	Immediate effect	Long-term effect	Comments
Rights of nature	Nature as an ethical subject	Nature as a legal subject	Instrumentalist self-interest (enlightened anthropocentrism) or Ecocentrism	Courts can adjudicate on the conflicts between alleged human needs and statutorily-defined rights on nature	Nature is seen as a collection of subjects worthy of respect	Specific rights must be identified – Guidelines for the resolution of conflicts of rights must be developed – The risks of hyper-litigation must be avoided

as a distinct discipline and all the other disciplines law sees as external to itself, as Iris Pitkänen shows in her investigation.

7.6.3 Deep Transformations

Iris Pitkänen, in a yet unpublished paper, adopts Kaarlo Tuoori's (2002) concept of the 'deep structure' or 'deep culture' of law. Conceiving of the law as a 'multi-layered phenomenon', albeit one still inscribed within a legal positivist caesura between the legal and the non-legal, Tuoori suggests that ideas, disciplines and perspectives that are *external* to law 'filter' into law via the relatively porous membranes of adjudication and legal scholarship. These, Tuoori asserts, serve as conduits for external contacts and thus keep the legal order open towards politics and morals, as well as those fields of society which law regulates' (2002, 147). Acting as 'intermediaries' between the internal structure of law and external influences, they establish a 'relation of limitation', whereby external influences are 'filtered through specific receptors, such as the conceptual structure and the principles sedimented into law's sub-surface layers.' (197–9). Tuori calls this process of filtration, whereby external influences 'enter' the space of law, 'relation of sedimentation' (200–1). Pitkänen argues that this process of 'sedimentation' captures the transformative power that eco-jurisprudential initiatives have already displayed on traditional legal practices. Her insights are undeniable, and the transformation that has occurred within the legal community over the past fifteen years is aptly displayed by the hundreds of initiatives and tens of thousands of scholarly artefacts discussed in the previous chapters.

As Vito De Lucia suggests, the transformative power of rights of Nature (and, I would contend, of all other eco-jurisprudential initiatives) is found in their ability to challenge and reconstitute many legal categories (such as rights and subjectivity) as well as many legal ontologies (such as what constitutes an ontological subject) *from within* (2013, 190). Even further, the transformative power of eco-jurisprudential is, continuing with Tuori's construct, bi-directional: while the injection of ecological principles alters—and continues to alter—many orthodox legal categories, these novel categories, in turn, open the space for a novel epistemological and ontological articulation of 'nature', a way to cultivate a novel (or at least renewed for most of the world's population) ecological consciousness. The value of rights of Nature and other eco-jurisprudential initiatives is thus to be found not only in the practical transformation that may engender in direct human behaviours (and the resulting impact on the environmental predicament), but also in the imaginative space they engender. As Pitkänen writes, 'RoN could be seen as a citizen (or at least a trespasser) of both (or many) worlds: the modern Western law and non-Western, Indigenous legalities as well as ecocentric/posthumanistic/new materialistic conceptions of law and subjectivity' (2024, 18).

One important corollary of reconsidering all eco-jurisprudential initiatives in general, and rights of Nature initiatives in particular, in this light is an immediate reimagining of the idea of rights. Far from being seen as merely a vessel for the liberal individualist project, rights become vectors of contestation, instances designed to draw out their jural counterparts, the duties that humans may have toward the nonhuman world (and toward each other in relation to the nonhuman world). Rights, when viewed as part of a process of 'sedimentation' that sees the injection of ecological principles within the realm of legal praxis, are inherently and inescapably relational. Relationality, reciprocity and responsibility, as Greene's proposal implies, are thus deeply enshrined within the ontological and epistemological perspectives underpinning rights of Nature in particular, and ecological jurisprudence more in general. In line with Escobar and others' suggestion (2024), 'relationality' sits at the very ontological core of ecological jurisprudence, and thus suffuses, be it directly or indirectly, the entirety of the discourse, as well as its many distinct initiatives. As a result, whether marked by a weak form of enlightened anthropocentrism or by a deep aspiration of ecocentric considerations, the many initiatives discussed in the previous chapters—and thus, I suggest, the entirety of the current trend toward an ecological jurisprudence—inherently veer toward the focus away from self-focused *rights and expectations* toward individual and collective *reciprocal responsibilities.*

Moreover, the emergence of an ecological jurisprudence operates at an even deeper level as an invitation, for Western jurisprudence, to rethink the normative itself beyond the rationalistic legacy of the last two to three millennia. In other words, while the many implications of a move toward an ecological jurisprudence have been mapped, a question now remains: what does it mean, at a legal *theoretical* level to move toward it? What does the emergence of an ecological jurisprudence mean for the very *idea* of law? The next chapter will interrogate the theoretical implications of an ecological jurisprudence for jurisprudence itself.

References

Albó, X. (2011). Suma Qamaña + convivir bien. Como medirlo? In I. Farah & L. Vasapollo (Eds.), *Vivir Bien: Paradigma no capitalista?* CIMES.

Arendt, H. (1976). *On revolution*. First Published 1963. Penguin.

Baumgardner, P. (2016). Legal rights and personhood in Hegel's phenomenology of spirit. *Birkbeck Law Review, 4*(1), 15–28.

Bellamy Foster, J., Clark, B., & York, R. (2010). *The ecological rift*. Monthly Review Press.

Bennett, J. (2010). *Vibrant matter*. Duke University Press.

Bétaille, J. (2019). Rights of nature: Why it might not save the entire world. *Journal for European & Planning Law, 16*(1), 35–64.

Bettetini, M. (2004). *Figure di verita': La finzione nel Medioevo occidentale*. Einaudi.

Boyd, D. R. (2017). *The rights of nature. A legal revolution that could save the world*. ECW.

Brandt Commission. (1983). *North-south: Common crisis*. Oxford University Press.

Burdon, P. (2011). Earth rights: The theory. *IUCN Academy of Environmental Law eJournal*, 1–12. https://566259-1852283-raikfcquaxqncofqfm.stackpathdns.com/wp-content/uploads/2021/09/EarthRights-ATheory.pdf

Capra, F., & Mattei, U. (2015). *The ecology of law: Toward a legal system in tune with nature and community*. Berrett-Koehler.

Carducci, M., & Lídia Patrícia Castillo Amaya, L. P. (2016). Nature as 'Grundnorm" of global constitutionalism: Contributions form the global south. *Revista Brasileria de Direito, 12*(2), 154–165.

Carolan, M. (2005). Society, biology and ecology: Bringing nature back into sociology's disciplinary narrative through critical realism. *Organization & Environment, 18*, 393.

Cicero, De Officiis, trans Miller W. Harvard University Press.

Code, L. (2012). Ecological responsibilities: Which trees: Where: Why. *Journal of Human Rights and the Environment, 3*, 84–99.

Convention Relative to the Preservation of Fauna and Flora in Their Natural State 1933 1 LNTS Vol 172 (no 3995).

Copleston, F. (2003). *A history of philosophy* (Vols. I–XI). First Published 1946–1986. Continuum.

Costanza, R. (1996). Valuation of ecosystem services and natural capital. In G. Adelson, J. James Engell, B. Ranalli, & K. P. Van Anglen (Eds.), (2008) *Environment, an interdisciplinary anthology*. Yale University Press.

Cullinan, C. (2011). *Wild law* (2nd ed.), First Published 2002. Chelsea Green Publishing.

Davies, M. (2016). Material subjects and vital objects: Prefiguring property and rights for an entangled world. *Australian Journal of Human Rights, 22*(2), 37–60.

Davies, M. (2017). *Asking the law question* (4th ed.). Thomson Reuters.

Davies, M. (2022). *EcoLaw: Legality, life, and the normativity of nature*. Routledge.

De Lucia, V. (2013). Towards an ecological philosophy of law: A comparative discussion. *Journal of Human Rights and the Environment, 4*, 167.

Declaration of the United Nations Conference on the Human Environment, UN Doc A/Conf 48/14/ Rev 1 (1973).

Deiser, G. F. (1908). The juristic person. *University of Pennsylvania Law Review & American Law Register, 57*, 137–138.

Des Chene, D. (1996). *Physiologia: Natural philosophy in late Aristotelianism and Cartesian thought*. Cornell University Press.

Descola, P. (2013a). *Beyond nature and culture* (J. Lloyd Trans.). First Published in French 2005. University of Chicago Press.

Descola, P. (2013b). *The ecology of others* (G. Godbout & B. P. Luley, Trans.). Prickly Paradigm Press.

Devall, B., & Session, G. (2007). *Deep ecology*. Gibbs Smith.

Dewey, J. (1926). The historic background of corporate legal personality. *Yale Law Journal, 35*(6), 655–673.

Drews Farm Partnership v City of Toledo, Case No. 3: 19-cv-0034-JZ Doc#1, filed 27/2/19. Northern District of Ohio, Western Division.

Dryzek, J. S. (1997). *The politics of the Earth*. Oxford University Press.

Dubos. R. (2006). Franciscan conservation versus Benedictine stewardship'. In R. J. Berry (Ed.), *Environmental stewardship: Critical perspectives—Past and present*. T&T Clark International.

Dworkin, R. (1977). *Taking rights seriously*. Harvard University Press.

Dyschkant, A. (2015). Legal personhood: How we are getting it wrong. *University of Illinois Law Review, 5*, 2075–2110.

Eckersly, R. (1992). *Environmentalism and political theory: Towards an ecocentric approach*. UCL Press.

Emmenegger, E., & Tschentscher, A. (1993). Taking nature's rights seriously: The long road to biocentrism in environmental law. *Georgetown International Law Review, 6*, 545–592.

Escobar, A. (1992). Imagining a post-development era? Critical thought, development and social movements. *Social Text, 31*(32), 20–56.

Escobar, A. (2017). *Pluriversal politics*. Duke University Press, Durham.

Feinberg, J. (1974). The rights of animals and unborn generations. In W. T. Blackstone (Ed.), *Philosophy and environmental crisis*. University of Georgia Press.

Fisher, D. E. (2014). Jurisprudential challenges to the protection of the natural environment. In M. Maloney & P. Burdon (Eds.), *Wild law—In practice*. Routledge.

Flathman, R. E. (1976). *The practice of rights*. Cambridge University Press.
Fox, W. (1984). Deep ecology: A new philosophy of our time? *Ecologist, 14*, 105–125.
Freeman, M. D. A. (2014). *Lloyd's introduction to jurisprudence* (9th ed.). Sweet & Maxwell.
Gaaker, J. (2016). "Sua cuique persona?" A note on the fiction of legal personhood and a reflection on interdisciplinary consequences. *Law & Literature, 28*(3), 287–317, 291.
Galbraith, J. K. (1984). *The anatomy of power*. Hamish Hamilton.
Gillespie, A. (1997). *International environmental law policy and ethics*. Oxford University Press.
Gosh, A. (2016). *The great derangement*. University of Chicago Press.
Graham, N. (2011). Owning the Earth. In P. Burdon (Ed.), *Exploring wild law*. Wakefield Press.
Grear, A. (2002). It's wrongheaded to protect nature with human-style rights. Aeon https://aeon.co/ideas/its-wrongheaded-to-protect-nature-with-human-style-rights. Accessed September 6, 2022
Greene, H. F. (2011). *Cosmology and Earth jurisprudence*. In P. Burdon (Ed.), *Exploring wild law*. Wakefield Press.
Gordon, G. J. (2018). Environmental personhood. *Columbia Journal of Environmental Law, 43*, 49–92.
Haraway, D. (2003). *The companion species manifesto: Dogs, people, and significant otherness*. Prickly Paradigm Press.
Hart, H. L. A. (1955). Are there any natural rights? *The Philosophical Review, 64*(2), 175–191.
Hart, H. L. A. (1982). *Essays on Bentham: Studies on jurisprudence and political theory*. Clarendon Press.
Horsman, Y. (2016). Braying, howling, growling for justice: Animal personhood in law, literature, and cinema. *Law & Literature, 28*(3), 319–334.
Hohfeld, W. N. (1913). Some fundamental legal conceptions as applied in judicial reasoning. *Yale Law Journal, 23*(1), 16–59.
Houck, O. (2017–8). Noah's second voyage: The rights of nature as law. *Tulane Environmental Law Journal, 31*(1), 16–17.
Huancuni Mamani, F. (2010). *Buen Vivir/Vivir Bien: filosofía, políticas, estrategias y experiencias regionals andinas*. Coordinadora Andina de Organizaciones Indígenas.
International Convention for the Regulation of Whaling 161 UNTS 72. TIAS No 1849.
Iorns Magallanesm, C. (2017). Using human rights to recognize human responsibilities toward nature. In E. Daly, L. Kotze, J. May, & C. Soyapi (Eds.), *New frontiers in environmental constitutionalism*. UNEP.
Itatí Dolhare, M. (2019). *The concept of Vivir Bien (Living Well) and the constitutional recognition of indigenous epistemologies: Towards a decolonising legal project*. Ph.D. Thesis, University of Queensland.
Jameson, F. (2009). *Valences of the dialectic*. Verso.
Jha, A., & Ghosh, A. (2018). Is being a person essential for the environment to hold rights: Assessing the legitimacy of environmental personhood and alternative approaches. *NUJS Law Review, 11*(3), 469–514.
Johnson, M. (2017). The river is not a person: Indigeneity and the sacred in Aotearoa New Zealand. *The Immanent Frame: Secularism*, religion and the public sphere. https://tif.ssrc.org/2017/06/14/the-river-is-not-a-person/
Kareiva, P., Marvier, M., Lalasz, R. (2012). Conservation in the Anthropocene Breakthrough Journal. https://thebreakthrough.org/journal/issue-2/conservation-in-the-anthropocene
Kauffman, C. K. (2020). Managing people for the benefit of the land: Practicing Earth jurisprudence in Te Urewera, New Zealand. *ISLE: Interdisciplinary Studies in Literature and Environment 27*(3), 578–595.
Kauffman, C. M., & Martin, P. L. (2021). *The politics of rights of nature*. MIT Press.
Knudtson, P., & Suzuki, D. (1992). *Wisdom of the elders*. Allen & Unwin.
Kurki, V. A. J. (2019). *A theory of legal personhood*. Oxford University Press.
Latour, B. (2004). *Politics of nature* (C. Porter Trans.). Harvard University Press.
Latour, B. (2018). *Facing Gaia. Eight lectures on the new climatic regime* (C. Porter Trans.). Polity.

Macpherson, E., Borchgrevink, A., Ranjan, R., & Vallejo Piedrahíta, C. (2021). Where ordinary laws fall short: "Riverine rights" and constitutionalism. *Griffith Law Review*. https://doi.org/10.1080/10383441.2021.1982119

Maloney, M. (2018). *Rights of nature 2018*. Information for Australian Communities. Australian Earth Laws Alliance.

Margalef, E. (1989). Is there a "balance of nature"? In P. Bourdeau (Ed.), *Environmental ethics: Man's relationship with nature*. Official Publications of the European Community.

Marshall, V. (2019). Removing the veil from the "rights of nature": The dichotomy between first nations customary rights and environmental legal personhood. *Australian Feminist Law Journal, 45*(2), 233–248.

RiverOfLife, M., Pelizzon, A., Poelina, A., Akhtar-Khavari, A., Clark, C., Laborde, S., Macpherson, E., O'Donnell, E., & Page, J. (2021). Yoongoorrookoo: The emergence of ancestral personhood. *Griffith Law Review 30*(3), 505–529.

Matthews, D. (2021). Earthbound. The aesthetics of sovereignty in the Anthropocene. Edinburgh University Press.

Mauss, M. (1979). A category of the human mind: The Notion of person, the notion of "self"'. In M. Mauss (Ed.), *Sociology and psychology: Essays by Marcel Mauss*. Routledge.

McCormick, N. (1982). *Legal rights and social democracy: Essays in legal and political philosophy*. Clarendon Press.

McKibben, B. (1989). *The end of nature*. Random House.

Merchant, C. (1983). *The death of nature. Women, ecology, and the scientific revolution*. HarperSanFrancisco.

Mignolo, W. (2014). From "human rights" to "life rights". In C. Douzinas & C. Gearty (Eds.), *The meanings of rights: The philosophy and social theory of human rights*. Cambridge University Press.

Mohr, R. (2008). Flesh and the person. *Australian Feminist Law Journal, 29*, 31–52.

Morris, J. D. K., & Ruru, J. (2010). Giving voice to rivers: Legal personality as a vehicle for recognising indigenous peoples' relationships to water? *Australian Indigenous Law Review, 14*(2), 49–62.

Morton, T. (2007). *Ecology without nature*. Harvard University Press.

Moutrie, M. J. (2020). The rights of nature movement in the United States: Community organizing, local legislation, court challenges, possible lessons and pathways. *Barry Environmental and Earth Law Journal, 10*(1), 5–63.

Naess, A. (1989). *Ecology, community*. Cambridge University Press.

Naffine, N. (2012). Legal personality and the natural world: On the persistence of the human measure of value. *Journal of Human Rights and the Environment, 3*, 68–83.

Nagel, T. (1974). What is it like to be a bat? *The Philosophical Review, 83*(4), 435–450.

Nash, R. (1989). *The rights of nature*. University of Wisconsin Press, Madison.

Neimanis, A. (2014). Alongside the right to water, a posthumanist feminist imaginary. *Journal of Human Rights and the Environment, 5*(1), 5–24.

Nordhaus, W. (1991). To slow or not to slow: The economics of the greenhouse effect. *Economic Journal, 101*, 921–936.

Norman, J. (2022). *Posthuman legal subjectivity: Reimagining the human in the Anthropocene*. Routledge.

O'Neill, J. (2001). Representing people, representing nature, representing the world. *Environment and Planning: Government and Policy, 19*(4), 483–500.

Oluwabusayo, T. W. (2022). *Who should represent ecosystems as legal persons?* Ph.D. Thesis, University of Leicester.

Oviedo Freire, M. (2013). *Buen Vivir vs Sumak Kawsay: una reforma capitalista y revolución alternativa* (2nd ed.). Ediciones Ciccus.

Pa Gen Energy Co v Grant Township, C.A. No. 14-209 (W.D.Pa.) (Opinion and Order, filed 5 Jan 2018).

Passmore. (1974). Removing the rubbish: Reflections on the ecologial craze. *Encounter, 19*.

Pinkard, T. (1996). *Hegel's phenomenology: The sociality of reason*. Cambridge University Press.
Pitkänen, I. (forthcoming). Rights of nature and the ratio of law (with permission to cite from the author).
Poelina, A., Wooltorton, S., Collard, L., Harben, S., Horowitz, P., & Palmer, D. (2020). Feeling and hearing country. *PAN: Philosophy Activism Nature, 15*, 6–15.
Pope Francis. (2015). Laudato Si'. *On care for our common home*. Libreria Editrice Vaticana.
Rawson, A., & Mansfield, B. (2018a). Producing juridical knowledge: "Rights of nature" or the naturalization of rights? *Environment and Planning e: Nature and Space, 1*(1–2), 99–119.
Resolution number 1 of the European Ministerial Conference on the Environment.
Rolston, H. (1993). Rights and responsibilities on the home planet. *Yale Journal of International Law, 18*, 251–279.
SWEPI v Mora County, 81 F.Supp.3d 1075 (D.N.M 2015).
Rawson, A., & Mansfield, B. (2018b). Producing juridical knowledge: "Rights of nature" or the naturalization of rights? *Nature and Space, 1*(1–2), 99–119.
Rodrigues, S. (2014). Localising 'the rights of nature': A critical discourse analysis. *Green Letters: Studies in Ecocriticism, 18*(2), 170–184.
Sagoff, M. (1974). On preserving the natural environment. *Yale Law Journal, 84*(2), 205–267.
Savona, P. F. (2005). *In limine juris: La genesi extra ordinem della giuridicita' e il sentimento del diritto*. Edizioni Scientifiche Italiane.
Schneider, K. (2019). The common law as a critical lever in expanding rights beyond the human: Reflections on the Vermont Journal of Environmental Law's 2018 "Rights of Nature Symposium". *Vermont Journal of Environmental Law, 20*(3), 243–259.
Schwartzchild, S. (1984). The Unnatural Jew. *Environmental Ethics, 6*, 347–362.
Schweitzer, A. (1923). *Philosophy of civilization: Civilization and ethics* (A John Naish & C. Black, Trans.). London.
Shiva, V. (1989). *Staying alive: Women, ecology, and development*. Zed Books.
Soper K (1995) What Is Nature? Culture, Politics, and the Non-Human. In Adelson G, Engell J, Ranalli B, Van Anglen, K. P. (Eds.). *Environment, an interdisciplinary anthology*. Yale University Press.
Stockholm Declaration UN Doc A/CONF 48/14 (1972) 11 ILM 1972. 1416.
Stone, C. D. (1972). Should trees have standing?—Towards legal rights for natural objects. *Southern California Law Review, 45*, 450–501.
Stone, C. (2010). *Should trees have standing? Law, morality, and the environment* (3rd ed.). Oxford University Press.
Swimme, B., & Berry, T. (1994). *The universe story. From the primordial flaring forth to the ecozoic era*. HarperCollins.
Tanasescu, M. (2020). Rights of nature, legal personality, and indigenous philosophies. *Transnational Environmental Law, 9*(3), 429–453.
Tanasescu, M. (2022). *Understanding the rights of nature*. Transcript Verlag.
Tribe, L. H. (1974). Ways not to think about plastic trees: New foundations for environmental law. *Yale Law Journal, 83*, 1315–1348.
Tuoori, K. (2002). *Critical legal positivism*. Ashgate.
Tuoori, K. (2021). *Properties of law: Modern law and after*. Cambridge University Press.
Turner, D. (2020). The animal other: Civility and animality in and beyond Heidegger, Levinas, and Deridda. *disClosure: A Journal of Social Theory, 12*(14). https://doi.org/10.13023/disclosure.12.14
UNESCO Recommendation Concerning the Safeguarding of the Beauty and Character of Landscapes and Sites. (1962). In B. Rusta & B. Simma (Eds.), (1975) *International protection of the environment*. Oceana.
Warnock, W. (2012). Should trees have standing. *Journal of Human Rights and the Environment, 3*, 56–67.
Weil, S. (2001). *The needs for roots*. Routledge.
Williams, R. (1980). *Problems in materialism and culture*. Verso.

Witthøfft Nielsen, L. (2004). The "nature" of nature: The concept of nature and its complexity in a Western cultural and ethical context. *General Bioethics, 17*(1), 31–38.

World Charter for Nature, GA Res. 7, 36 UN GAOR Supp. (No. 51) at 17, UN Doc. A/51 (1982) Preamble.

Yampara Huarachi, S. (2011). Cosmovivencia andina. Vivir y convivir en armonía integral-Suma Qamaña. *Bolivian Studies Journal, 18*, 1–22.

Zelle, A. R., Wilson, G., Adam, R., & Greene, H. F. (Eds.). (2021). *Earth law. Emerging ecocentric law—A guide for practitioners*. Wolters Kluver.

Chapter 8
Neither Natural nor Posited

> *You must teach your children that the ground beneath their feet is the ashes of their grandparents. In order that they may respect the earth, teach them that the earth is full of the life of our ancestors. You must teach your children what we have taught ours: that the earth is our mother. Everything that affects the earth affects the sons of the earth.*
> *(Chief Seattle, 1854 Oration)*

As the previous chapters have shown, all instances of ecological jurisprudence discussed in this book represent attempts (to different degrees) to counter the anthropocentric worldview mapped in the initial chapters of the book. These instances can be analysed pragmatically (as I have done in the previous chapter and as many scholars in the field commonly do). But they can also represent a deeper reinterrogation of legal theory itself, and it is on this aspect of ecological jurisprudence that I will now focus my attention. As mentioned in the previous chapter, an ecological jurisprudence can be seen as a *horizon*, an *aspiration*, a *striving toward*, even more than a *definition*. Ecological jurisprudence is, in a sense, a reactive horizon. Reactive, as it reacts to a dominant anthropocentric tradition deeply encoded in a highly destructive (and self-destructive) lifestyle. A horizon, as it is an aspiration, a tendency, rather than a particular 'thing'. It is an aim, a goal, and maybe a process, rather than a specific outcome. It is, in a sense, akin to Kelsen's *grundnorm* or Harts' rule of recognition (or Kant's *noumena*), in that it is the necessary logical (and ecological) precondition that justifies the wide range of initiatives discussed throughout the book.

The strongest influence of an emerging ecological jurisprudence, therefore, is to be found more in the shifts it engenders than in the techniques it produces. In this sense, an ecological jurisprudence in its multifaceted permutations, represent a novel 'grand narrative' of law, something that has hardly been attempted in a coherent form since the early twentieth century and Kelsen's monumental quest for a General Theory of the Norm. As Arran Gare notes,

> [t]his development of a dialogical grand narrative aiming to create an ecological civilization can be seen as the coming of age of the Radical Enlightenment. It can be characterized as a retotalization after the detotalization of the old grand narratives of emancipation, but a far more complex retotalization than Sartre envisaged, incorporating the interests of the whole

A. Pelizzon, *Ecological Jurisprudence*, Contemporary Environmental Law and Policy,
https://doi.org/10.1007/978-981-96-0173-8_8

> humanity (with its three dialectial patterns driven by the quest for recognition, orientation and empowerment) and most other life forms in their diversity, in their struggle for the survival of civilization and the current regime of the global ecosystem. It is a retotalization based on a comprehensive understanding of the world through speculative naturalism and process metaphysics, orienting people to participate in this retotalization through a new grand narrative committed to averting ecocide. (2017, 208–9)

As a modern 'grand narrative' of law, such is the profoundly transformative power of an ecological jurisprudence. It alters the foundational paradigms upon which legal structures in particular (and social structures in general) currently operate. As Robert Cover states, '[l]aw may be viewed as a system of tension or a bridge linking a concept of a reality to an imagined alternative—i.e. as a connective between two states of affairs, both of which can be represented in their normative significance only through the devices of narrative' (1983, 9). In this sense, '[l] aw … is pedagogic' (13). It is by suggesting alternative possibilities to the current anthropocentric paradigm. Paradigms, Donella Meadows reminds us, are 'the source of systems. … The ancient Egyptians built pyramids because they believed in an afterlife. We build skyscrapers because we believe that space in downtown cities is enormously valuable. [Those] who … manage to intervene in systems at the level of paradigm have hit a leverage point that totally transform systems' (2008. 163). But how is this intervention to occur? It is, I contend, inherently multidisciplinary (i.e., metaphysical, psychological, behavioural, ethical and political), it is theoretical (it alters legal theory), and it is pluralistic and intercultural. I will dedicate the first section to the inherent multidisciplinary tendencies of an ecological jurisprudence, whereas I will cast my gaze to legal theory and on pluiversality in the two following sections.

8.1 The Death of Nature?

The Anthropocene, as mentioned since chapter one, has been adopted as the primary term of reference for the current geological era, one where humanity (as a whole) has become a veritable geophysical force. However, as already noted, many critiques have emerged of this term. Joshua Sterlin argues that the term 'anthropocene' implies a universal humanity, and thus, he suggests, '[w]e do not live in the Anthropocene, but rather [in] the period of time defined by agricultural civilization', a period he describes as 'Civilicene' (2020, 176). This is in line with Malm and Hornborg's assertion that "[r]ealizing that climate change is 'anthropogenic' is really to appreciate that it is *sociogenic*" (2014, 66), i.e. it is caused by a specific social milieu or assemblage rather than humanity per se. Naturally, since some societies have clearly been able to impact the planet (however negatively) more than others, their theoretical standpoints are, by virtue of their impact alone, of crucial importance. These are what Tom Jagtenberg and David McKie call the 'ecoimpacts' of 'a world that is both material and cultural' (1997, 36). A number of names have been proposed to describe these ecoimpacts. Donna Haraway (after dismissing the alternative terms 'plantationocene' or 'capitalocene') coined a new term for the current era, the *chthulucene*. The term is not a reference to the Lovecraftian creature, but rather to its Greek etymology: '[i]t is a compound of two Greek roots (*khthôn* and *kainos*) that together name a kind of timeplace for learning to stay with the trouble of living and dying in responsibility on a damaged earth' (2016, 2). Humans and nonhuman beings, she argues 'are *of* the world as its storied and dynamic substance, not *in* the world as a container' (91). Mihnea Tănăsescu proposes the name 'Ecocene' as an alternative name that 'focuses on the political importance of ecological processes themselves' (2022, 13). John Bellamy Foster and others (2010), building upon Marx's notion of the 'ecological rift', call for a new 'Holoanthropocene'—an epoch of the 'New Whole Human' [from the 'new whole' of the Holocene to the 'new human' of the Anthropocene] based on transcending the alienation of humanity and nature. The rift in ecology and society can only be healed through a new revolutionary transformation in human social and ecological relations'. Glenn Albrecht (2011), who introduced the notion of 'solastalgia' (the sense of environmental distress caused by climate change) proposes the term Symbiocene as a way to aspire to a new era characterized by harmonious interactions between humanity and the rest of the planet.

Unlike most of the authors explored thus far, Clive Hamilton (2017) does not reject anthropocentrism, but rather calls for a 'new anthropocentrism' for the Anthropocene. Rather than abandoning anthropocentrism, Hamilton suggests to fully reclaim the unique position that humanity de facto has in relation to the earth system, by recognizing that we are the only species (at least in recent geological times) that has been capable of acting as a geological force. As a result, it is our responsibility as a species to act accordingly. He argues that if the 'old' anthropocentrism saw humanity's mastery of the Earth as a moral right, a 'new' anthropocentrism should instead acknowledge the fact of such mastery and therefore place humanity in a unique place of responsibility toward the planet:

> [w]e may have acquired it foolishly, but we now have a responsibility for the Earth as a whole and pretending otherwise is itself irresponsible. So the question is not whether human beings stand at the center of the world, but what kind of human being stands at the center of the world and what is the nature of that world. ... Contrary to the comforting expectations that in the Anthropocene we can have "the kind of nature we wish to have," as we enter the new epoch, we will meet an Earth that is further and further from the Earth we might want. And against the belief that "the world we will inhabit is the one we have made," the world we will have to live with is the Earth we have turned against us. (47–8)

Klaus Bosselman similarly suggests that '[t]he word environment is not sufficient to describe our appropriate relationship with nature. The nonhuman world is not something that exists around us but is something that lives with us and we with it'. As a result, "[t]he case in point is not the environment ... but rather our 'with-world', or *Mitwelt*, a term introduced by the German philosopher Klaus Meyer-Abich in 1986" (1995, 11).

8.1.1 Beyond Materiality

The multidisciplinary terrain with which ecological jurisprudence interacts undoubtedly represents the modern quest for an underlying unifying 'principle' rather than an essential and objective 'reality'. This quest is encoded in a number of contemporary philosophical pursuits. Arran Gare (2017) articulates the emergence of what he calls 'speculative naturalism', an attempt to revive the classical tradition of natural philosophy to align science with the humanities. To do so, he reintroduces the Aristotelian concept of *telos* (or purpose) to the concept of an ecosystem. David Abram, on the other hand, pursues an experiential epistemology, one that has been marginalized (if not outright rejected) in the course of Western philosophy and epistemology (be it empiricist/materialist or rationalist/idealist). In *The Spell of the Sensous* (1996), he focuses on the *Lebenswelt*, the life-world of perception (often marked by a degree of synaesthesia, of fusion of the senses), arguing that 'the recuperation of the sensuous is the rediscovery of the Earth' (62). 'As we return to our senses', he argues, 'we gradually discover our sensory perceptions to be simply part of a vast, interpenetrating web of perceptions and sensations borne by countless other bodies' (65). Freya Mathews proposes a "philosophical exploration of a 'reanimated' world, a world that is no longer viewed, in the manner of classical science, as a piece of cosmic hardware, fashioned out of the inherently blind matter of classical physics, but is rather viewed as a subjectival matrix, within the eddies and currents of those dynamics we and other finite creatures stake out our relative identities" (2003, 4). To refer to such a metaphysical approach she readopts the term *panpsychism*: '[w]hen the world is understood in panpsychist terms, the whole spectrum of Western thought undergoes a profound shift, a shift away from the direction in which it has been drifting since the time of the scientific revolution, back toward its original starting point, namely metaphysics'. The result is that, '[w]hen world is resurrected, it becomes a protagonist again in the philosophical drama of human existence' (5).

Slavoj Žižek is concerned with proposing a non-identity of the classic Hegelian One with itself, the 'split which cleaves the One from within, not into two parts: the ultimate split is not between two halves, but between Something and Nothing, between the One and the void of its Place', with the consequence that "the Real is the 'almost nothing' which sustains the gap that separates a thing from itself" (2002, xxvii). Žižek aims to counter the Kantian's view that we are only ever able to access phenomena (appearances) and never the things-in-themselves (reality). Levy Bryant notes that the effect of phenomena appearing as manifestation of an ultimately inaccessible reality 'arises from the split in the object embodied in the relation between the object and the void of its place' (2011, 125). As a consequence, 'in the best case scenario, we are unable to determine whether reality or things-in-themselves are anything like they appear to us, while in the worst case scenario, it is possible that reality or things-in-themselves are entirely different from how they appear to us' (124–5). Žižek instead argues that the crux is not the possibility (or lack thereof) of transcending appearances to appraise reality in itself, but rather that the *apparent* gap between appearance and reality is located within *appearance* itself. As a result, Bryant explains, 'reality is not something beyond or behind appearances, but rather is appearance itself' (2011, 125). While the answer may appear as a novel version of idealism or of Berkley's idea that reality does not exist in a preter-sensorial form, it engenders a novel way to transcend Kant's distinction between *noumena* and *phenomena*. In fact, an object's

> semblance deceives in a Lacanian way: not because it is a deceitful substitute of the Real, but precisely because it invokes the impression of some substantial Real behind it; it deceives by posing as a shadow of the underlying Real … what Kant fails to notice is that *das Ding* is a mirage invoked by the transcendental object … all that "actually exists" is the field of phenomena and its limitation, whereas *das Ding* is nothing but a phantasm which, subsequently, fills out the void of the transcendental object … What we experience as "reality" discloses itself against the background of the lack, or the absence of it, of the Thing … there is nothing – no positive entity – behind the phenomenal curtain, only the gaze whose phantasmagoria assumes different shapes of the Thing. (Žižek, 1993, 36–7)

In other words, 'the real is not something *other* than the symbolic, but rather is a sort of *effect* of the symbolic resulting from the difference that haunts every signifier by virtue of the split between the signifier and its place of inscription' (Bryant, 2011, 127). Žižek's argument opens the space for a new form of philosophical realism, what Graham Harman (2016) calls 'immaterialism', in opposition to what he terms New Materialism—the belief, radically different from the old materialism 'of atoms swerving through the void' (13), that everything, including all 'things', is historically and socially constructed and contingent. His position is equally cast against old philosophical essentialism and 'naïve realism', which 'thinks that reality exists outside the mind and we can know it' (17). Importantly, reality does not exist 'only "outside the mind", as if humans were the only entities with an outside. Instead, reality exists as a surplus even beyond the casual interactions of dust and raindrops, never fully expressed in the world of inanimate relations any more than in the human sphere' (17–8). On the opposite side of Graham's immaterialism sits Elizabeth Grosz's 'incorporeal' (2017). She notes that '[t]he distinction between materialism and idealism, between matter and idea, has pervaded Western philosophy since at least the time of Plato. … From the beginning of the twentieth century to the present, there seems little doubt that the tradition of materialism (whether identified with empiricist epistemologies or not) has apparently overcome the forces of the idealist tradition (whether identified with rationalist epistemologies or not)' (15–6). She explores the 'entwinement of ideality and materiality, how each is the implicit condition for the other' (13). In doing so, she aims to elaborate neither dualism nor a reductionist monism, but rather to reconsider the 'extramaterial' or 'prematerial', what she calls the 'incorporeal, … the direction or trajectory that orients a movement of concepts or thought, that constitutes the possibility of a process of understanding, that enables the creation of a philosophy or a work of art as an emergence from and an entwinement with a material order, planets, stars, constellations, nebulae, and so on … The incorporeal is the dimension of ideality that suffuses all things, enabling them to signify and generate representations' (250). Gilbert Simondon had already noted that '[c]ulture … recognizes certain objects, like the aesthetic object, granting them citizenship in the world of significations, while it banishes other objects (in particular technical objects) into a structureless world of things that have no signification but only use, a utility function' (2017, 16). Simondon aimed to 'replace the study of ontology, of what is, with the study of ontogenesis, the various processes of self-formation that create what is' (Grosz, 2017, 170).

While most of the book thus far has engaged with an attempt to show the legal *subjectivity* of the nonhuman world, a recent philosophical current has taken an apparently opposite route reaching similar ethical and political conclusions. 'Object Oriented Ontology' (Harman, 2002) rejects the privileging of human existence over the existence of nonhuman objects. This movement begins with Graham Harman 'object-oriented philosophy' (2010), often seen as a subset of contemporary 'speculative realism' (Brassier, 2007). Objects come to the fore of any ontological consideration, and Harman cautions against the risk of 'undermining' them, by explaining them in terms of their smaller constituents and thus casting them as manifestations of a deeper (atomistic) reality, or 'overmining' them, by treating them as 'needlessly deep or spooky hypotheses by comparison with their tangible properties, and thus positing no independent reality outside the mind (as in the idealist tradition) or language, discourse or power (as in social constructionism)' (Harman, 2016, 8–10). The movement is well aware of its own nihilistic potential. However, Raymond Brassier writes that philosophy 'would do well to desist from issuing any further injunctions about the need to re-establish the meaningfulness of existence, the purposefulness of life, or mend the shattered concord between man and nature. … Nihilism', he concludes, 'is not an existential quandary but a speculative opportunity'. Quentin Meilassoux challenges what he defines as 'correlationism', the Kantian legacy 'according to which we only ever have access to the correlation between thinking and being, and never to either term apart from each other' (2008, 5). In a very Descartian fashion, Meilassoux begins by stating 'I can only think of myself as existing, and as existing the way I exist; thus, I cannot but exist, and always exist as I exist now' (55). Levi Bryant brings the movement to its realization, by proposing a 'flat ontology' (expanding on Manuel DeLanda's term), one that 'rejects any ontology of transcendence or presence that privileges one sort of entity as the origin of all others and as fully present to itself' (2011, 245). Bryant attempts to bring together the 'tendency to decentralize the human by describing the impact of the nonhuman' and the "speculative tendency … that ranges freely over the 'experience' of nonhuman entities, plumbing the worlds of other entities without being obliged to relate everything back to the human" (248). His is a way of bringing together the human and nonhuman world, transcending anthropocentrism but maintaining a degree of inherent and inevitable epistemological and cognitive anthropomorphism. Rather than being immersed in the intuitive oppositions between objects and subjects, and between objects and events/processes, he strives to think of the '*subjectless* object'.[1] Within his framework of what he terms an 'onticology', 'there is only one type of being: objects' (20). What

[1] His effort is in distinguishing between *epistemological* realism, which 'argues that our representations and language are accurate mirrors of the world as it actually is' and *ontological* realism, which 'is not a thesis about our *knowledge* of objects, but about the being of objects themselves' (18).

is of particular significance is that 'humans are not excluded, but are rather objects *among* the various types of objects that exist or populate the world, each with their own specific powers and capacities'. However, the author is also careful to note that this 'is not a *political* thesis to the effect that all objects ought to be treated equally in human affairs'. Rather, this 'democracy of objects' is the '*ontological* thesis that all objects' (19), as Ian Bogost has so nicely put it, 'equally exist, yet they do not exist equally' (2012, 11). This echoes Slavoj Žižek's reversal of the subject-object relationship:

> [t]he difference between subject and object can also be expressed as the difference between two corresponding verbs, to subject (submit) oneself to object (protest, oppose, create an obstacle). The subject's elementary, founding, gesture is *to subject itself* – voluntarily, of course ... If, then, the subject's activity is, at its most fundamental, the activity of submitting oneself to the inevitable, the fundamental mode of the object's passivity, of its passive presence, is that which moves, annoys, disturbs, traumatizes us (subjects): at its most radical the object is *that which objects*, that which disturbs the smooth running of things. Thus the paradox is that the roles are reversed, in terms of the standard notion of the active subject working on the passive object: the subject is defined by a fundamental passivity, and it is the object from which movement comes. (2006, 7)

Ian Bogost articulates an 'applied' object-oriented ontology through the process of 'ontography', a 'general inscriptive strategy ... that uncovers the repleteness of units and their interdependency' (38). Furthermore, building upon what philosopher of mind Thomas Nagel had described, in his famous 1974 essay 'What is like to be a bat'?, as 'the subjective character of experience' (Nagel, 1974, 436), Bogost introduces the idea of 'metaphorism' as a way for objects to 'try and make sense of each other through the qualities and logics they possess' (Bogost, 2012, 66). In other words, metaphor itself becomes a way to grasp ultimately inherently alien objects' perceptions of themselves and of one another (including through the use of metaphors of selfhood), and for objects to translate other objects' experiences into their own terms. Aldo Leopold's invitation to 'think like a mountain' thus assumes an entirely novel connotation.

8.1.2 The Multicultural and the Multinatural

The recent ontological shift described above has direct implications for an ecological jurisprudence. Since the *idea* of Nature is the key axis around which all eco-jurisprudential initiatives ultimately revolve, then the ontological positioning of the 'object', the 'subject-object relationship', and the ultimate definition of reality directly and deeply affect the onto-axiological standpoint that is adopted. The novel conceptions of Nature (and reality in general) that follow are many. Thomas Berry had lamented (by reference to the Kantian dimensions of time and space) 'a tradition founded on the dominance of our Western time experience of reality over that of an Eastern spatial experience of reality' Instead, he suggested,

> [w]e greatly need to slow down the sequence of time changes by increasing our spatial awareness. Space is complete; time is fragmentary. Space is contemplative; time is active. Space has a present center of rest, time a future goal of attraction. Space is serenity; time is anxiety. The world of space is the world of nature, with its rhythms of rising and falling, its seasonal renewals, which can be easily ritualized and coordinated with the phases of interior renewal in the human. The world of time is the world of history, wherein humans pass through a succession of death-rebirth experiences in the form of historical convulsions, which introduces the fulfilment of the redemptive historical process. (2009, 42)

Bill McKibben (2010) writes of a new planet, which he calls 'Eaarth' to distinguish it from the familiar planet that hosted human civilization for the past 10,000 years, one that we entered once we passed the 350 parts per million of carbon dioxide in the atmosphere one 'with melting poles and dying forests and heaving, corrosive sea, raked by winds, strafed by storms, scorched by heat. An inhospitable place' (1). The apocalyptic meme discussed in the first chapter is very much present here, in the identification of a particular moment of radical change rather than the recognition of an ongoing dynamic process. McKibben adds that it is 'unlucky in the extreme that at precisely the same moment that we've destabilized the climate that underwrote civilization, we've also started to come up short on the fossil fuels that underwrote modernity' (28). Rather than despairing, however, the author calls for new habits to adapt to life in the new planet, calling back to his suggestions in *Deep Economy* for an end of the obsession with growth.

Other authors reject the concept of 'nature' at a more fundamental level. Timothy Morton argues that it is the very *idea* of nature that 'is getting in the way of properly ecological forms of culture, philosophy, politic, and art' (2007, 1). In fact, Morton deconstructs the phrase 'I am immersed in nature', which he describes as the 'metaphorical sum of the endless listing procedures of ecomimesis' (182). That phrase, just like 'I am at one with the cosmos' is a modern version of the Cretan liar paradox.[2] "Even if 'I' could be immersed in nature", Morton argues, 'and still exist as an *I*, there would remain the *I* who is telling you this, as opposed to the *I* who is immersed'. Morton concludes by stating that '[i]f we are even able to achieve ecology without nature, it would be difficult, if not impossible, and even undesirable, to achieve ecology without a subject'.Instead, he introduces the concept of 'hyperobjects' (rather than nature or natural objects) to describe objects (in the sense used by object-oriented ontology) that are so extensively distributed in time and space as to transcend any spatiotemporal individuation. Among such hyperobjects are things like the 'agrilogistic spaces' and 'neighbouring species' (like cats) that emerged with the advent of settled agriculture, and the 'miasma' (or epidemics) that followed (2016, 50). Such hyperobjects both emerge in a time of ecological crisis and alert humanity to the ecological predicament by actually defining it.

Bruno Latour continues the Foucauldian investigation into 'biopower'. In challenging deep ecology (or, at least, its popularized version) as a non-political ecological attempt, Latour suggests that

[2] The Cretan liar paradox is constituted by a sentence, such as 'I am lying', that contains a truth claim that contradicts its semantic form.

> [p]olitical ecology does not speak about nature and has never sought to do so. It has to do with associations of beings that take complicated forms – rules, apparatuses, consumers, institutions, mores, calves, cows, pigs, broods – and that is completely superfluous to include in an inhuman and ahistorical nature. Nature is not in question in ecology: on the contrary, ecology dissolves nature's contours and redistributes its agents … Political ecology does not seek to *protect* nature and has never sought to do so … Political ecology has never claimed to serve nature for nature's own good, for it is absolutely incapable of defining the common good of a dehumanized nature. It does much better than defend nature … It *suspends* our certainties concerning the sovereign good of humans and things, ends and means. (2004, 21)

Instead, political ecology 'proposes to move the role of unifier of the respective ranks of all beings out of the dual arena of nature and politics and into *the single arena* of the collective' (2004, 30). Following Latour's critique of the system theory as applied to Gaia, Daniel Matthews writes that "[t]he system view encourages us to see the earth as something that is already unified and enclosed, something 'over there' from which a human observer can, through a movement of though, detach themselves. [Instead] Gaia insists on an earth that is irreducibly 'down here' in a mess of hybrid interactions with which we humans are always already engaged" (2021, 36). Naomi Klein rather adopts a more pragmatic approach to the ecocentric shift. "Calling the earth 'sacred'", she notes, 'serves a practical purpose … [it] is another way of expressing humility in the face of forces we do not fully comprehend. When something is sacred, it demands that we proceed with caution. Even awe' (2019, 67). Although ecological values are socially construed, 'the natural world provides a rich, variegated, and permanent candidate for induction into the hall of universal and permanent values to inform human action and to give meaning to otherwise ephemeral and fragmented lives' (Harvey, 1993, 10).

At the same time, authors such as Philippe Descola, Eduardo Vivieiros de Castro and Eduardo Kohn attempt to 'render ontology plural without turning it into culture: different worlds instead of different worldviews' (Kohn, 2013, 10). These authors' invitations are strong reminders of the connection between ecological jurisprudence and distinct philosophical and religious traditions, which Capra had already introduced in 1975 with *The Tao of Physics.* The link can be traced back to Werner Heisenberg, who had asserted that '[t]he great scientific contribution in theoretical physics that has come from Japan since the last war may be an indication of a certain relationship between philosophical ideas in the tradition of the Far East and the philosophical substance of quantum theory' (1963, 173). Arturo Escobar, speaking of the 'ontological turn', introduces the concept of the 'pluriverse', a 'world where many worlds fit' (2020, 9). The pluriversal world is not just a collection of human worlds, but extends beyond the boundaries of the human. Ivan Vargas Rocancio advocates a similar shift from the *multicultural* to the *multinatural.* He argues that '[w]ithin a multicultural framework … nature is not cast as a partner in ethical symmetry with the human, but the marginalized *other* to which humans relate differently. The multicultural interpretation of the rights of nature resonates with what legal hermeneutics calls exegesis or literal interpretation'. He suggests that, within the traditional multicultural interpretations of the environment, 'nature is defined as a singular entity that embraces all living beings in a continuum of shared materiality (or physicality), but at the same time affirming the semantic (or internal) discontinuity—ontological difference—between them'. Instead, he proposes that 'a multinatural (Vivieros de Castro) or animist (Descola) interpretation [of the cosmos], on the other hand, restores the ethical symmetry between humans and nonhumans, which the naturalist interpretation seems to cancel out when reducing the latter to their bare materiality' (2017, 80). Vargas Rocancio's invitation recalls what Henri Bergson described as a 'latent belief in the spontaneity of nature' (1998 ed, 45).

Michel Serres calls for a new 'Natural Contract' to replace the foundational myth of the Enlightenment's social contract. 'Henceforth, men come back into the world, the worldly into the worldwide, the collectivity into the physical', he exhorts. 'It's a bit like the era of classical natural law, but with big differences, all of which have to do with the recent passage from the local to the global and with our renewed relationship to the world, which was long ago our master and of late our slave, always and in all cases our host, and now our symbiont. Back to nature, then!' (1995, 38). He states that the word 'politics' 'must now be considered inaccurate, because it refers only to the *polis*, the city-state ... Yet those who live in cities ... know nothing of the world. From now on, those who govern must go outside of the human sciences, outside the streets and walls of the city, become physicists, emerge from the social contract, invent a new natural contract by giving back to the word *nature* its original meaning of our natal and native conditions' (43–4). The natural contract he refers to is the foundational, metaphysical and mythical origin of our interaction in and with the world.

> However mythical it may be, the social contract ... marks the beginning of societies ... [But] [t]he world, which is totally absent from the social contract, as from the social sciences, is slowly permeating collective decisions ... From now on I mean by natural contract above all the precisely metaphysical recognition, by each collectivity, that it lives and works in the same global world as all the others ... the natural contract recognizes and acknowledges an equilibrium between our current power and the forces of the world. (44–6)

Deeply related to object-oriented ontology is the idea of the assemblage (DeLanda, 2016). Nature, humanity, nature and normativity can be seen as a cohesive whole, an 'assemblage' (the common English translation of the original French *agencement*). For Gilles Deleuze, an *assemblage* is "a multiplicity which is made up of many heterogenous terms and which establishes liaisons, relations between them, across ages, sexes and reigns—different natures. Thus, the assemblage's only unity is that of a co-functioning: it is a symbiosis, a 'sumpathy'. It is never filiations which are important, but alliances, alloys: these are not successions, lines of descent, but contagions, epidemics, the wind" (1994, 163). In this sense, the interplay between humanity and Nature is best conceived of as an *assemblage*. This leads Jane Bennett to develop a theory of *distributive* agency, asking her to ask 'how would an understanding of agency as a confederation of human and nonhuman elements alter established notions of moral responsibility and political accountability'? (2010, 21). The kind of distributive agency assigned to human and nonhuman assemblages echoes the Chinese notion of *chi* (as well as the Aristotelian *telos*), conceived of as a 'kind of potential that originates not in human initiative but instead results from the very disposition of things' (Jullien, 1995, 13). Latour (1999), as mentioned before, rejects the categories of 'nature' and 'culture' in favour of the 'collective', which is an ecology comprised of both human and nonhuman elements. By the same token, he argues that we must learn to tell 'Gaia stories' (or at least 'geostories'). Those who decide to tell those stories, he says, are the new 'Earthbound' (2017, 248): '[s]ome are readying themselves to live as Earthbound in the Anthropocene; others decide to remain as Humans in the Holocene'. As Daniel Matthews state, Latour "describes this emergent condition in which the human is conceived neither as *rising above* nor as *situated against* an othered 'Nature' but as intricately enfolded *within* the earth's dynamic systems and processes, as a matter of becoming *earthbound*" (2021, 11).

Equally foundational is what is known as 'Actor-Network Theory', an approach to social theory and political ecology that considers everything in both the social and natural world as constantly and consistently enmeshed in a dynamic and ever-changing network of relationships. Nothing exists outside those relationships, the theory posits. Actor-Network theory 'offers a flat ontology in which anything is real insofar as it *acts*' (Harman, 2016, 2). A corollary of this theory is the notion of the 'actant' (originally derived from semiotics). Jane Bennett describes an actant as 'a source of action that can be either human or nonhuman; it is that which has efficacy, can *do* things, has sufficient coherence to make a difference, produce effects, alter the course of events' (2010, viii). The notion of the 'actant' casts all beings and phenomena as subjects in a pragmatic and corporeal sense, rather than the metaphysical one proposed by Berry. The results are, nonetheless, similar. Bennet attempts to recreate the 'childhood experiences of a world populated by animate things rather than passive objects' (vii). She aims to describe a more 'distributive' agency, including 'the material agency or effectivity of nonhuman or not-quite-human things … my hunch is that the image of dead or thoroughly instrumentalized matter feeds human hubris and our earth-destroying fantasies of conquest and consumption' (ix). Her attempt is to 'shift from environmentalism to vital materialism, from a world of nature versus culture to a heterogeneous monism of vibrant bodies' (121). Against both a 'smooth harmony of parts [and] a diversity unified by a common spirit', she imagines 'a turbulent, immanent field in which various and variable materialities collide, congeal, morph, evolve, and disintegrate' (xi). She builds upon the idea of the actant and of the assemblage of actants. She advances a theory of 'vital materialism' where everything is an expression of 'vibrant matter', and 'in a knotted world of vibrant matter, to harm one section of the web may very well be to harm oneself' (13). She further argues that '[i]f human culture is inextricably enmeshed within vibrant, nonhuman agencies, and if human intentionality can be agentic only if accompanied by a vast entourage of nonhumans, then it seems that the appropriate unit of analysis for democratic theory is neither the individual human nor an exclusively human collective, but the (ontologically heterogenous) "public" coalescing around a problem' (108). However, when faced with the issue of the political (and, we may infer, legal) agency of these assemblages, Bennett asserts that 'while every public may very well be an ecosystem, not every ecosystem is democratic. And I cannot envision any polity so egalitarian that important human needs, such as health or survival would not take priority' (104). She continues by arguing that '[t]he political goal of a vital materialism is not the perfect equality of actants, but a polity with more channels of communication between members'. As a result, she wonders 'whether environmentalism remains the best way to frame the problems … If environmentalists are selves who live *on* [emphasis added] earth, vital materialists are selves who live *as* [emphasis added] earth' (110–1).

The extension of the political collective is the realization of a process that had underpinned the emergence of environmental ethics for over a century. Henry Salt's argument about the universal brotherhood with the animal world had already led to his call for the perfection of democracy by including 'all living things within its scope' (1894, 92). Against David Ritchie's argument that "[b]ecause a work of art or some ancient monument is protected by law from injury, do we speak of the 'rights' of pictures or stones?" (1894, 108), Salt 'was too acute of a thinker really to believe that humans and animals could have reciprocal ethical and political relationships. He knew that right and wrong were human concepts. Animals might have rights in the sense of being the beneficiaries of ethical extension, but they could not be expected to act ethically themselves' (Nash, 1989, 29). Similarly, Vandana Shiva proposes an Earth Democracy to 'connect the particular to the universal, the diverse to the common, and the local to the global. It incorporates what in India we refer to as *vasudhaiva kutumbkam* (the earth family)—the community of all beings supported by the earth … Earth Democracy is the awareness of these connections and the rights and responsibilities that flow from them' (2005, 1). The principles she advocates are as follows: firstly, that 'all species, peoples and cultures have intrinsic worth'; secondly, that 'the earth community is a democracy of life'; thirdly, that 'diversity in nature and culture must be defended'; fourthly, that 'all beings have a natural right to sustenance'; fifthly, that 'Earth Democracy is based on living economies and economic democracy'; sixthly, that 'living economies are built on local economies'; seventhly, that 'Earth Democracy is a living democracy'; eighthly, that 'Earth democracy is based on living cultures'; ninthly, that 'living cultures are life nourishing'; and finally, that 'Earth Democracy globalizes peace, care and compassion'. Shiva's call for an Earth Democracy is reminiscent of other proposals. John Seed and others, building upon Deep Ecology, make an invitation to a 'Council of All Beings', where to 'channel the energies released by despair and empowerment and other rituals into facilitating a profound change to deeply ecological awareness' 2007 ed, 13). Their proposal constitutes a particular fusion of ecological mindset, ritual practices and concrete action.

8.1.3 The Law of the Land

The many theoretical paths that contemporary philosophy and social theory (among others) have taken in relation to the reconceptualization of the human relationship with the cosmos constitute a vibrant, rich and yet largely unexplored terrain for an emerging ecological jurisprudence. Because of the contested notion of 'nature' that is at the core of ecological jurisprudence (both theoretically and pragmatically), this multidisciplinarity is inherently and unavoidably foundational to any eco-jurisprudential project. Ideas of 'actants', 'assemblages' and of 'multinatural' perspectives inform the most nuanced discussions within an ecological jurisprudence.

As the next section will discuss, these ideas are also central in the reimagination of the very *idea* of normativity and law that is entailed by ecological jurisprudence. After all, for Carl Schmitt (2006 trans), the original act from which law emerges is the occupation of land, the conscious acquisition of a particular territory (*Landnahme*). This, he argued, can be evinced from is the Greek word *nomos*, a term he derives from the verb *nemein*, in the triple meaning of conquer (*nehmen*), divide (*teilen*) and cultivate/produce (*weiden*). Schmitt's words make it possible to conceive of the Earth as the 'mother of law', much like Berry and Cullinan have suggested. If that is the case, if the Land, like Christine Black notes (2010), is indeed the source of the Law, what does this mean for the *idea* of law? In other words, Nature may have rights, but can Nature ever be normative?

8.2 Neither Natural nor Posited

It may appear weird that a text focused on ecological *jurisprudence* has purposely avoided fully dedicated jurisprudential considerations until such a late chapter. However, the full horizon of theoretical possibilities entailed by the emergence of an ecological jurisprudence could not be appraised, I contend, without properly setting up the historical and multidisciplinary context in which it is located, as the previous chapters have (hopefully) done. I propose that the legal response to the current environmental predicament represents the deepest engagement with all the theoretical challenges that this predicament introduces. After all, as James Thornton states, '[l]aw suffuses our lives from the public scale to the intimate. Since tribal times, whenever two or more gather, we make rules' (Goodman & Thornton, 2017, 269). Robert Cover, in *Nomos and Narrative* (1983), had introduced the idea of a 'nomosphere' as a relational and all-encompassing field akin to Suess's 'biosphere' and Theilard de Chardin's 'noosphere'. The nomosphere (or, more accurately, the plural nomospheres of different legal traditions) is the total normative and legal field within which all relations are located, categorized and legally construed. Cover distinguishes between two types of law, 'paideic' and 'imperial'. The first is world-creating, 'it implies the existence of a community, the member of which acknowledge a set of common needs and obligations, base their life and worldviews upon these' (Melissaris, 2009, 41), and their 'obedience is correlative to understanding' (Cover, 1983, 13). In the model of imperial laws, instead, 'norms are universal and enforced by institutions. They need not be taught as well, as long as they are effective'. Douzinas suggests that modernity is marked by a sort of 'nomophilia': 'the more the critic denies and decries the law, the more he expresses his subjection and love for the law' (2005, 52).

Law, as the previous chapters have shown, has increasingly turned toward ecology, and ecological principles have entered the legal vernacular. But the fundamental question of what this means *jurisprudentially* remains. Is this turn a modern version of natural law theory? Moreover, Nature can be conceived of as an actant, but can Nature ever be *normative*? These two questions will be the main focus of this chapter.

In the attempt to resolve the issue of scepticism about the nature of knowledge that had led, through empiricism, to the solipsism of Berkley and Hume, Kant relied upon an ontological argument about the nature of reality. In so doing, Kant cast reality (the *noumena*, or thing-in-itself) *outside* the system of cognition in the (clearly Kantian) sense later intended by Saussure. This rejection has been paralleled within legal theory. If Nature is outside the system of cognition, then legal positivism is inevitable, and normativity can only ever be human. Positivism has maintained its supremacy within Western legal theory for the past two centuries. Even after the collapse of legal positivism after World War II, natural law theory has never satisfactorily (at least theoretically) returned. With the emergence of an ecological jurisprudence, however, the issue of normativity of Nature is once again interrogated. What does it *jurisprudentially* mean for Nature to come back as a subject, not just as a Sausseran *referent* or a Kantian *noumena*? While many attempts have been made to transcend the problem of the *noumena* in philosophy, this is the attempt to do so at a *jurisprudential* level. In other words, beyond the pragmatism discussed in the previous chapter, the emergence of an ecological jurisprudence forces jurisprudence to ask itself fundamental questions about the nature of law and normativity. In so doing, it attempts to move beyond both the dichotomy between positivism and natural law *and* the fragmentation of legal theory that followed.

8.2.1 Is Ecological Jurisprudence a New Form of Natural Law Theory?

Ben Mylius describes 'Earth Jurisprudence—sometimes referred to as ecological legal philosophy, Earth law or wild law—[as] an emerging, neonatural law philosophy that synthesizes legal theory, ecology, and environmental philosophy' (2017, 1). He further asserts that 'Earth Jurisprudence is generally considered to be a neonatural law theory, although many of its practitioners incorporate significant elements of legal positivist thought'. However, '[w]here earlier natural law theories asked about the relationship between law and morality, Earth Jurisprudence is interested in the relationship between law and *ecology*: and more specifically, in whether *ecological* norms, principles or laws can and/or should have a bearing on the content, form and validity of human laws' (3). Building upon Peter Burdon's proposal that ecosystems set up a field of 'design parameters', he argues that 'while not specifying the specific positive *content* of any human laws, the larger set of exosystemic contexts nonetheless provides a set of negative limitations (by being selected as limits beyond which the powers or effects of human laws cannot be meaningfully valid)' (4). In this instance, the word 'meaningfully' narrowly avoids the naturalistic fallacy, instead measuring *validity* via its effectiveness.

Zelle and others similarly write that 'Earth Law is related to normative jurisprudence, critical legal studies and natural law' (2021, 69). Vito De Lucia writes that 'EJ [Earth Jurisprudence], particularly in some of its prevailing interpretations, seems to move in the direction of Natural Law, notwithstanding Cullinan's dismissal of Natural Law as being inherently anthropocentric, and other EJ theorists' scepticism toward this movement' (2013, 174). Burdon notes that '[m]any advocates [and critics] of Earth Jurisprudence ... are dismissive of natural law philosophy and have expressed concerns about becoming locked in the unproductive rivalry between positivism and natural law' (2013, 824). Klaus Bosselmann made a similar point almost two decades earlier: 'the ecocentric orientation of values is a turning toward the ideas of Natural law. In this context some authors point toward understanding in a natural law sense. I do not believe that it is necessary to revert in this way, nor that it could be of any help—considering the unproductive rivalry between positivism and Natural law' (1995, 236). Daniel Matthews recently argued that "Earth Jurisprudence offers nothing but a politics of *submission*. It tells us nothing but that *we must obey*, by submitting human law, which can apparently achieve the unlikely task of facilitating both human flourishing and the flourishing of the *entire earth community*—to the 'laws of nature' as defined by the scientific-priests of contemporary ecology. ... In this way, Earth Jurisprudence remains wedded to the staid binaries that have always animated theories of Natural Law" (2021, 39).

It is apparent that many critics and commentators seem to equate some theoretical versions of ecological jurisprudence (particularly Earth Jurisprudence and many of the theoretical underpinnings of the rights of Nature movement) with natural law theory. Yet, this may not be the case as it *prima facie* appears. In commenting on Cullinan's articulation of the Great Jurisprudence, Burdon writes that '[i]t will be clear to anyone familiar with legal philosophy that the basic structure and relationship between these different types of law share resemblance to the Thomist and neo-Thomist natural law traditions' (2015, 82). Once interrogated further, however, the resemblance is more superficial and somewhat linguistically cosmetic than it may appear. Margaret Davies posits that '[t]he key difficulties ... with the natural law inspired version of Earth Jurisprudence are first, that natural law theory does not mesh well with environmental thinking and secondly that Earth jurisprudence has insufficiently developed the core insights of environmental philosophy upon which it is based ... the overtly hierarchical concept of natural law projects something above human knowledge as a higher law and fails to provide guidance about how this is translated into human law' (2017, 490). Yet, she wonders, is her new theory of EcoLaw (which she develops in response to the above shortcomings) "a 'new natural law' theory"? She notes that

> [a]t times, ecologically oriented legal theory has been merged with the anthropocentric and even the theocentric traditions of natural law, without interrogating the vast difference between the constructions of human nature that inform natural law thought and of nature understood as the primarily nonhuman physical world ... Is it possible to wrest the idea of "nature" away from a "human nature" of intrinsic rationality and at the same time to refuse the distinction between nature and human-society-culture? Is it possible for something called "natural law" to be qualitatively plural, place-located, emergent, and transitional?

> Such a move would involve aligning a concept of "natural law" with the emergent form of normativity I have considered, which stands in contrast to the idea of the objective and universal normativity usually associated with natural law … therefore I would hesitate to use the term "natural law" for my endeavour. (2022, 91)

I will endeavour to address the issue of natural law connotations within ecological jurisprudence below, as I believe the theory is far more transformative than a mere inclusion within the confines—however enlarged—of natural law theory would suggest. I being by agreeing with Burdon's intuition (2015, 5) that both legal positivism *and* natural law theory are equally anthropocentric. Conversely, however, ecological jurisprudence is explicitly marked by the attempt to reject an anthropocentric worldview. One of the key ecological principles underpinning all eco-jurisprudential theories and initiatives, as previous chapters have argued, is the recognition that the pure and absolute arbitrariness of law in the face of ecological constraints is impossible. It is not perhaps impossible in an abstract sense (as it may, and does, indeed, occur), but it is certainly untenable in the sense that a legal system that ignores the ecological limits within which it exists will simply fail to sustain itself over time. In other words, the application of the theory of evolution to legal systems shows that a degree of agreement and alignment with ecological principles is a measure of long-term survival fitness for legal principles, structures and institutions. However, this does not entail that such ecological principles are the self-evident embodiment of universal, ahistorical and deeply rational natural laws.

8.2.2 *The Laws of Nature*

In *Wild Law* (2002), Cullinan suggests that human laws *ought* to be aligned 'with the fundamental principles of how the universe functions', which he referred to as the 'Great Jurisprudence' (2011 ed, 31). It is this statement that is seen as particularly problematic by many critics of Earth Jurisprudence, who equate the 'Great Jurisprudence' with a novel form of self-evident, empirically observable and universal natural law principles. However, such is not necessarily the sense in which the concept is intended. In his critique of the concept, Burdon argues that 'human law derives its legal quality from the great law' (2014, 13). However, 'rather than describing the great law with reference to universal laws of nature, [these principles] should be limited to ecological science and measured with respect to concepts such as ecological integrity' (87). Rakhyun Kim and Klaus Bosselmann (2013) had already posited the idea of ecological integrity (which could be the distillation of the 'great law' into a single principle) as a *grundnorm* of international law, the fundamental architrave and keystone of the world's legal order. Burdon further contends that "the Great Law should be defined with reference to 'first principles' uncovered in the scientific discipline of ecology" (2011, 66). Jonathan Crowe, in *Natural Law and the Nature of Law* (2019), presents 'a dynamic idea of natural law, which is partly informed by facts about human nature that change—notably biological facts that change with evolution and social facts that change with history' (Davies, 2022, 94). For Crowe, human biology is central to natural law, and, in this sense, there exists a recognition of the physical world within natural law.

This insight was already present in H L A Hart's 'minimum content' of law (1963), of course, and is explicitly articulated (albeit in non-biological terms) by John Finnis (1980). The shift to ecology in the idea of 'natural law', from the moral and 'inherent nature' of humanity to the idea of 'ecological principles' is undeniable. Ecological Jurisprudence, as Burdon and Bosselmann point out, represents the attempt to align the construct of law with the construct of science—specifically, with the construct of ecology. James Thornton similarly writes that 'Nature ... speaks to us in the grammar of science. So, write laws grounded in science' (Goodman & Thornton, 2017, 275).

The 'Diritto per la Natura' or 'Law *for* Nature' [emphasis added] is a conceptual framework developed by Italian legal philosopher Mariachiara Tallacchini in 1996. Tallacchini 'distinguishes Natural Law from ecological normativity on the grounds that the former establishes a normative relation with morality, the latter with science' (De Lucia, 2013, 176). Moreover, she "grounds the concept of ecological normativity on one fundamental element which—far from being a given—must function as a guiding parameter against which to measure the 'adequacy of law': survival" (De Lucia, 2013, 174). Tallacchini writes that 'from a legal theory point of view, the assumption of limits to respect for the achievement of the human survival is not obvious, since survival, as a goal normally implicit in all legal systems, until recent times has been taken for granted' (1996, 1090). Survival (of humanity as a whole, not necessarily of particular individuals) is thus a—perhaps *the*—normative assumption underpinning the shift to an ecological jurisprudence.

One could extend this and note that such an assumption, couched not in the prescriptive language of normativity, but in the descriptive one of evolutionary science, is present in many authors. Cullinan implicitly speaks of the survival over long periods of time of legal systems. Hart places an emphasis on the *intentionality* of survival to establish the minimum content of natural law. But an evolutionary appraisal of legal systems does not require such an intentionality. It is sufficient to observe that those systems who fail to adapt (or are 'maladaptive', in evolutionary terms) simply vanish over time.[3]

Tallacchini, however, wishes to 'recentre law—as a system of norms and as the formal structure of social organization—around the idea of ecological limits by way of a functionalist interpretation of law' (De Lucia, 2013, 177). She writes that '[a]scribing survival the status of a defining condition of law is a [strong] conception of necessary content in law; one which provides environmental norms with a deep foundation, since it assumes that legislation, which ignores or voluntarily violates the goal of ecological protection (and survival), lack the full status of legal norms, since they contradict a fundamental condition of legal normativity' (Tallacchinni 1996, 1091–2). She explicitly articulates survival not only as an evolutionary precondition for the continued existence of any legal order, but also as a *normative* precondition

[3] This is akin to Eugene Ehrlich's (1936) distinction between *legal norms and legal propositions,* and the assumption that if the latter are in deep contradiction with the former, there will be push back from the former.

for their validity. Vito De Lucia writes that 'this ecological grounding provides the parameter for evaluating legal norms, in terms of their content, through the (external) bio-functional principle of survival. In this manner, the idea of ecological limits and the goal of human survival ... becomes a central legitimizing condition for environmental law' (2013, 177). De Lucia also argues that a 'normativity of uncertainty is predicated on the crucial epistemic role that ignorance has acquired in post-modern accounts of society, where science can no longer provide certainty as regards statements of facts or assessments of risk'.

At a first level, therefore, ecological jurisprudence is marked not by its reference to an absolute conception of self-evident 'natural laws' but rather by its dialogical engagement with scientific principles derived from the science of ecology. The linguistic reference to a 'Great Jurisprudence', therefore, may be misleading, and suggestive of a normative *scala naturae* that is absent from the dialogue between law and science that is rather implicitly embedded in the term. The 'Great Jurisprudence', indeed, appears to be used as a synonym of 'ecology' (as that which is described, rather than the science that describes it). The 'Great Jurisprudence' is, in this sense, a perspectival horizon, not a set of self-evident principles. It is an ongoing process to discern these principles, rather than the static description of a solid reality. This means that legal theory must *assume* the existence of normative patterns in Nature, and must align itself to them. However, these patterns are not self-evident, but rather are ever-moving constructs, and thus the particularities of human laws are not necessarily a mirror of some fixed self-evident 'laws' of Nature, but rather are in constant dialogue with this assumed horizon, this necessary logical precondition for the continuity of human normativity and legality. Nonetheless, even the argument that human normativity and legality is (or ought to be) in alignment with the understanding of the universe may suggest an enlarged conceptualization of ecological jurisprudence as natural law moving from the confines of a 'moral' natural law to an 'ecological' natural law. However, such a description may be inaccurate in the light of the particular connotations of 'natural law' (particularly contemporary natural law) within Western jurisprudence.

Furthermore, the recognition of principles of ecology—and in particular of ecological integrity—as the 'Great Jurisprudence' raises the question as whether these principles have any *normative* value. Does a lack of alignment of human laws with such principles entail a lack of *validity* of those laws? The answer cannot be evinced directly from the literature itself, and it appears that the *ought* used by Cullinan, Burdon and others (i.e. the suggestion that human laws *ought* to be aligned with ecological principles) represents a Kantian hypothetical imperative rather than a normative precept as conceived by Hume. In other words, the alignment between human laws and ecological principles is desirable if a legal system is to continue in an evolutionary sense, but it is not *necessarily* required in a deontic sense.

Moreover, recognizing the evolutionary necessity of ecological principles as foundational to the continuity of a legal order only shifts the epistemic burden from the construct of law to the construct of science, without necessarily avoiding Hume's (and Moore's) 'naturalistic fallacy'. A classical critique in legal philosophy is that any argument that suggests that if a natural behaviour is either observed (by observing patterns of regularity) or logically inferred (e.g. as the need to survive), then humans ought to behave accordingly, 'confuses scientific laws (which *describe* what does occur) with moral and legal ones (which *prescribe* what should occur)' (Freeman, 2014, 77). Michael Freeman notes that

> human laws are not in themselves statements of facts; they are rules or norms, which prescribe a course of conduct, and indicate what should happen in default ... This is, therefore, a particular form or use of language different from that part of language concerned with propositions of fact, ... and, is indeed, related to a whole group of similar "normative" usage, such as commands, exhortations, and moral, ethical or religious codes or rules of conduct. ... Hence, normative rules must be carefully distinguished from physical laws, which state causal connotations. (5)

Statement of facts can be true or false, they are subject to verification, whereas normative statements cannot. This is the fundamental distinction between *sein* (being) and *sollen* (ought) made by Kant and later taken up by Kelsen (Scruton, 1981). Freeman continues by stating that

> [t]he tendency to derive normative rules from physical or natural laws, or to analyse or define them in terms of physical qualities or phenomena, is a pervasive one. Thus, many of the attempts to base positive law on an immutably established natural law governing the universe have involved an attempt to link normative rules directly with what are really conjectural hypotheses of factual character (i.e. in the nature of physical laws). However, in 1740, Hume pointed out the fallacy of trying, as he put it, to derive "ought" from "is", and argued that a normative statement could not be inferred from a purely factual one. So, too, the efforts to define moral norms in terms of something else, which can be ascertained or verified as a fact, such as pleasure or utility, involve a similar confusion which has been stigmatised by G E Moore as the "naturalistic fallacy".

For Hume, the distinction between the world of the *ought* (the normative, and, by extension, the legal) and the world of the *is* (the scientific and empirical) could not be reconciled. The question then arises as to whether a bridge between the *normative* and the *empirical/descriptive* could be found in ecological jurisprudence's suggestion of the necessary alignment between human law and ecological principles. As Alexander Gillespie notes,

> [t]he is/ought problem is recognized as a central problem of moral philosophy [and t]o step from fact to value is to create a "naturalistic fallacy". The fallacy is to state a value conclusion (the ought) that is derived from premises of the fact (the is). David Hume (who first realized the dichotomy) regarded finding values in facts as a very important mistake. For example, the fact is that smoking may cause death. It may therefore be suggested to a smoker that she/he should not smoke, as she/he may die. The fallacy has been committed, as a value (that the smoker does not want to die) has been added to the fact that smoking causes death. (1997, 162)

There are, I believe, two elements that suggest the presence of a conceptual bridge between the *normative* and the *descriptive*. Firstly, HLA Hart spoke of a 'minimum content of natural law', a necessary bedrock of (normatively undefined) principles without which a legal system simply wouldn't exist. These are akin to John Finnis's 'basic goods' (1980) and Eugene Ehrlich's idea of a set of *legal norms* by which the long-term effectiveness of *legal propositions* is measured (1936). Much like Kelsen's *grundnorm*, these principles are not identified (or even identifiable) but are rather the necessary logical (or, in another sense, evolutionary) precondition for the existence of a legal system. Similar principles are those of Bosselmann's ecological integrity, Burdon's principles of ecology, Tallacchini's principle of survival, and, I argue, Cullinan's Great Jurisprudence. In a protean sense, then, ecological jurisprudence aligns itself with a transversal jurisprudential tradition that identifies some principles of validity (either in a pragmatic or a theoretical sense) as located outside the *normative* universe. More importantly, however, science itself, since the nineteenth century, has been imagined as a constructivist project rather than a positivist one, whereby a neutral world is empirically unveiled in its objective appearance. There is a *normative* quality in defining the ontological parameters of science that, as a consequence, blur the irreducible separation of *normative* and *descriptive* statements. Capra and Mattei assert that

> [a] key difference between the laws of nature and human laws seems to be that the former are *descriptive* (giving information about something in the natural world) while the latter are *normative* (prescribing a standard of behaviour for humans). However, as we explore the surprising parallels between how these laws have been conceptualized in science and in jurisprudence, we shall see that this clear-cut distinction must also be modified. On the one hand, a descriptive element occurs in the practice of jurists abstracting the relevant laws from a specific network of social relationships. On the other hand, recent discoveries in science, especially in ecology and climate science, suggest strongly that the ecological principles evolved by ecosystems over billions of years to sustain the web of life must be understood as normative laws for human conducts if we are to overcome tour global environmental crisis. (2015, 19)

As a result, the idea that there exists a *normative* quality in the construction of science itself may suggest that ecological jurisprudence aims to transcend the 'naturalistic fallacy'. According to Martin Curd (1998, 805), two mutually opposed positions occur in relation to nature: the first, or 'necessitarian', argues that there exist in nature inherent necessities that transcend the regularities they produce, and that law statements are but mere descriptions of these necessities. The other position, or 'regularist', argues that there exist no necessities, but only regularities, correlations and patterns in nature, and that the 'laws of nature' are descriptors of such regularities. The engagement with the theoretical tension between the two is a deep (and often unrealized) marker of ecological jurisprudence. As a result, the alignment between law and ecological principles is not one of a static and *normative* discipline (law) with the static and *descriptive* principles of another (science), but rather the alignment of different disciplinary *ways* of ordering and categorizing the world (law and science), both defined by the operation of distinct Foucaldian regimes of truth and techniques of power and governmentality. Pushing the boundaries of the 'Great Jurisprudence'—as defined by Cullinan and, to a lesser extent, by Burdon and Bosselmann—further, *both* law and science are equally and at the same time *normative* and *descriptive*. As a result, it is the dialogue between the two *ways* of knowledge that is brought forward by ecological jurisprudence. It is, in a sense, an attempt to bring a *noumena* that is external to the *normative* system of cognition *within* the confines of that system.

This conjoining may not be entirely novel, after all, as the very origin of the term 'laws of nature' may suggest. Capra and Mattei reveal that

> [t]hroughout the earlier centuries of Western science, various terms were used for the short, concise statements or equations in which scientists like to summarize their theories. They were called propositions, rules, axioms, principles, maxims, and so on. During the second half of the seventeenth century, the expression "laws of nature", which had rarely been used before, came into frequent use, and in subsequent centuries it completely replaced the previously used terms. In the twentieth century ... scientists ... seem to have stopped referring to the regularities they discover as las, except for reference to the well-known "laws" formulated in previous centuries. (2015, 20–1)

Many early scientists were both scientists and lawyers. An apt example is Francis Bacon, not only one of the founders of the modern scientific method, but also a lord chancellor of England. Descartes, Capra and Mattei show, was the first to give the term 'laws of nature' a central place within natural philosophy, but

> Bacon was the first English lawyer to engage in what we could call a total critique of the common-law tradition; he was also the first to draw an explicit analogy between the concept of the laws of nature and the legal realm. In discussing the law, Bacon distinguished between "habits of nature", observed in specific regions, and "fundamental and common laws", which could be discovered and viewed as a background for these local variations ... It is not possible to know whether it was Bacon the lawyers who affected Bacon the scientist whit his idea of torturing nature to extract its secrets, or if Bacon the scientist influenced the law reformer to get rid of formalisms incompatible with the inquiry into truth. (2015, 59–61)

The alignment between human laws and ecological principles suggested by ecological jurisprudence, it follows, is not a simple return to a 'naturalistic fallacy' whereby the normative *ought* of human behaviour is derived from the descriptive *is* of ecology. Instead, the post-modern connotations of ecological jurisprudence suggest a distinct approach to both *normativity* and *empiricism*, with the aspiration to reconcile them within the realm of both theory and eco-jurisprudential praxis. The question remains, however, as to whether this is a novel form, however 'post-modern' of natural law.

8.2.3 Neither Natural nor Posited

Margaret Davies asserts that, '[a]s things stand, the concepts, practices and above all institutional forms of the dominant legal system cannot be abandoned. This system is a critical component of the social glue protecting the so-called democracies of the west from authoritarianism and unchecked corruption'. Moreover, she continues, while '[p]ositivism's value derives from its status as the fiction that enables legal analysis, doctrine and proactive in a certain context ... it fails as a description of law'. However, she concludes, 'there can also be no doubt that both the practice of this law and its concepts are, as they always have been, in transition—at this time away from the image of self-containment that dominated the twentieth century toward a more socially connected image where, increasingly, the normative world includes plants, animals, ecosystems, and entities in the natural environment such as rivers and mountains' (2022, 97).

Developed in parallel with scientific positivism, legal positivism conceived of law as an arbitrary and purely human activity. Casting itself as the theoretical alternative to natural law, legal positivism suggests that there is a logical (and linguistic) quality to the idea of 'law' (in fact, with Kelsen, to the idea of a 'norm') that is purely prescriptive. This concept, already seen in Hume, is fully developed by Jeremy Bentham and John Austin, and is fully codified by Kelsen. Davies notes that

> [t]he dominant assumption, practice, and idea about law, derived from legal positivist theory, is that law is largely conceptual. Despite the inbuilt requirement that law *become* practical at some point, in this perspective law is nonetheless often regarded as having a life of its own as abstract: law's substance, though expressed via the physical medium of language and memorialized in permanent form as documents, is regarded as mental and conceptual. Law may have its origins in social relationships but is conceptually detached from them. (2022, 11)

Freeman remarks that, "[b]y arguing that what 'is' the law is based on a higher law dictated by reason and so is always what the law 'ought' to be, positive law is thought to acquire a sanctity that puts it beyond question" (2014, 75). Naturally, the idea of this complete theoretical and conceptual isolation is now outdated (and rather indefensible) even within the most radical hard positivists. Such prescriptive quality does not and *cannot* tell the appropriateness of the content of a particular norm, only its formal validity (with its ultimate validity, Tallachinni's argument entails, being ultimately socio-biological).

Indeed, legal positivism can authoritatively tell the formal validity of a norm within a particular legal system, but the ultimate principle of validation of that system (the *grundnorm* or rule of recognition) is always located at a liminal boundary that is inherently 'outside' the law (as a system of self-validating norms) and is inscribed in the ecological and social milieu in which its norms exist. Thus, an ecological and social awareness is required not to appraise the mathematical or propositional formal validity of any given norm, but to determine its ultimate legitimacy. The interplay between this ecological sensitivity (at the boundary of legitimacy) and 'law' in a practical sense is a clear strategic hallmark of ecological jurisprudence. As a result, while norms and laws can be seen as arbitrary (as Aristotle had already suggested in its distinction between natural and legal justice), the relationship between their content and their logical form is the terrain where natural law inserts itself, where the idea of an ecological jurisprudence is ultimately located. It is here that the idea of law can remain positivist in its form, but, as Cullinan, Burdon and Bosselmann have intimated, must be informed by an ecological sensibility.

Critical legal scholarly influences promptly inform this perspective. 'By contrast to top-down and conceptual approaches to state-based law, the pragmatic, sociological, and anthropological traditions in legal thought, as well as much of the critical tradition, are more likely to explain law as having a material basis: as emerging from the relationships of humans in their specific communities and located in place and time', Davies suggests (2022, 11).

> So-called moral norms, for instance, can be seen as the product of several intersecting and cumulative factors. These include: evolutionary adaptations that are themselves based on the iterative trial and error of reproduction and finding what works for a particular environment; socio-cultural adaptations that are similarly responsive to place and the environment; historical and economic transitions; intellectual rationalisations of social, political, and other (eg

> religious, economic, etc.) characteristics; and politics and concentrations of power. To dissociate morality from human history, from long-term adaptation to time and place, and from movements between organism and habitat, community and environment, seems to remove the preconditions for any notions of rightness. (12)

Ecological jurisprudence, therefore, is clearly not predicated upon a legal positivist view of law, notwithstanding the very pragmatic attitude of many of its advocates and the strategic adoption of formalist and positivist techniques. However, the question remains, is ecological jurisprudence a representation of an 'enlarged' and 'post-modern' version of natural law theory? Does it merely embody a shift from the presumed normativity of a rationally derived morality to the normativity of the 'laws of nature'? The answer to this question requires a brief overview of natural law theory.

In the Homeric texts and in Hesiod, there exist two divine figures, the relations of whom defines the Greeks' idea of law and justice. *Themis*, a 'word whose force is difficult to grasp, but which is applied to an area at the centre of which is perhaps of a god-inspired decision or directive or finding … It is the word use to convey ruling of the gods as well as of kings' (Kelly, 1992, 7). At her side is her daughter from Zeus, *dike*, 'a word which in the Homeric era had not acquired its later clear senses (abstract justice or a lawsuit or a judgement), but nevertheless had a somewhat sharper edge, a "severer countenance" than *themis*' (7). Köstler writes that '*themis* is a law of the heavens, and *dike* the earthly law which imitates it' (in Kelly, 1992, 7). His etymological analysis suggests that *themis* (from *tithēmi*, τίθημι, 'I place, set') suggests a divine institution, a general direction, whereas *dike* (from *deiknumi*, δείκνῡμῐ, 'I point out, indicate') is a derivative law that comes into effect through a judgement or other process, and that is derived from the former. As Kelly notes, 'of the two concepts, *themis* is the more venerable, the more associated with supernatural beings or their inspirations of human rulers, [while] *dike* … had a set of fully secular and practical senses and derivatives' (1992, 8). The first recorded laws, from Dracon and Solon, are not called *nomoi* (originally, *nomos*, νόμος, had the meaning of custom), but *thesmoi*, (singular *thesmos*, θεσμός), a word cognate with *themis*.

Natural law in its modern connotation was elaborated by the stoics, it was incorporated into Roman law and popularized by Cicero and was then systematized by Aquinas. At its core, natural law thus conceived is the expression of a divine or eternal law that is inherently rational. The Romans conceived of *ius naturale*, an idea of law that predates and transcends human lawmaking (which the Romans described, in regard to the justice overlaid over the natural order, as *ius commune*). It is important to note the use of the more generic term *ius* rather than the more specific *lex*, in this instance. Moreover, the stoics had changed the idea of nature from 'the order of things' to human reason. As a result, "[w]hen man lived according to 'reason', he was living 'naturally'" (Freeman, 2014, 89). Cicero, in *De Republica*, introduced this Stoic principle into Roman law, defining true (natural) law as 'right reason in agreement with nature' (Freeman, 2014, 89). Ulpian defines natural law as follows: *ius naturale est quod natura omnia animalia docuit* ('natural law is that which nature taught to all animals'), that is 'to reproduce, to educate their offspring and the like'. For the Romans, natural law lacked a concept of natural rights in the Lockean sense, nor was positive law subordinate to natural law in the same manner that it later was. Mediaeval and modern natural law, Freeman suggests, 'have little in common' (2014, 76). Although, in truth, they have more in common than it may appear.

Thomas Aquinas, in the *Summa Theologica*, noted that the etymological origin of the word 'law' from the Latin 'binding' (*ligare*), suggesting that 'by it one is bound to a certain course of action'. For Aquinas, law existed in a hierarchical relationship to itself. Firstly, there was a *lex aeterna*, the fundamental norm according to which the whole of creation exists and acts (which Augustine had introduced). Freeman explains that 'the goods disclosed by nature belonged with the *lex aeterna*, God's plan for the universe into which rational man could gain insight through revelation (the *lex divina*) and conscious participation (the *lex naturalis*)' (2014, 77). The *lex naturalis moralis* ('moral natural law') reflects in the individual the prescripts of the *lex aeterna*, and for Augustine, it is constituted of a number of principles imprinted in the soul, heart and mind of humans (Chroust, 1974). The *moralis* is hereby crucial: the *lex naturalis moralis* is a morally binding principle, not a descriptor of natural facts.

Finally, there is the *lex humana,* the positive law created by humans. Aquinas 'strongly asserted that unjust laws are a perversion of law and do not bind human conscience' (Freeman, 2014, 92). Similarly, for Hart (1963), there exists a 'minimum content of natural law' premised on biology and psychology, necessary to ensure our survival: 'there are certain substantive rules which are essential if human beings are to live together in close proximity' (Freeman, 2014, 113). John Finnis takes Hart's concept further, asserting that 'natural law' is 'the set of principles of practical reasonableness in ordering human life and human community' (1980, 280). He argues that there are 'certain basic goods for human beings, objective values, in the sense that every reasonable human being must assent to their value as objects of human striving' (Freeman, 2014, 77). For Finnis, these basic goods are 'objective values in the sense that every reasonable person must assent to their value as objects of human striving' (Freeman, 2014, 117).

Within he Scholastic jurisprudential tradition, under the leadership of authors such as Francisco de Vitoria, the 'highly organized [and ultimately holistic] system of natural law was designed to explain human laws within a holistic theory of God and nature' (Capra & Mattei, 2015, 62). Importantly, the *leges naturae* for Aquinas (as for the Stoics before him) must be cognisable, and they can only be cognisable through reason. This is the modern German concept of *vernunftrecht,* the rational natural law of the seventeenth and eighteenth centuries. For Max Weber, indeed, the most essential characteristic of modern societies was formal rational law. Huig de Groot, often known as Hugo Grotius, articulated in modern terms the idea of natural law indicating, against his imagined Carneades, that humans, as 'superior animals', have a natural tendency toward society, and thus natural law emerges organically from such tendency. The expedient natural justice among States he called 'the law of nations'. Importantly, Grotius played an important role in separating the idea of natural law from theology: 'what we have been saying would have a degree of validity even if we should concede that which cannot be conceded without the utmost wickedness, that there is no God, or that the affairs of men are of no concern to Him', often summarized in a portion of his original Latin articulation: *etiamsi daremus non esse Deum* (1625, para 11). Natural law would exist even if God did not exist, and ‘even if *per impossible* man [sic] were not God’s creation’, he would still be able to interpret natural law, since ‘he would still be a rational creature’. With Grotius, natural law, already rationalistic and objectively universal, becomes mechanistic and materialistic. For Capra and Mattei, with Grotius ‘natural law was reduced to a system of relationships between distinct sovereigns ... governed by a common law based on reason’ (2015, 63).

Thomas Hobbes famously described the ‘state of nature’ as one where there is ‘a war of every Man against every Man’, a condition of unsustainable strife where life would be ‘solitary, poor, nasty, brutish and short’ (1651, Pt 1, Ch 3). The inherent tendency to individual self-preservation, Hobbes argued, is the necessary precondition for the existence of a social contract whereby individuals must abandon their absolute freedom in exchange for certainty and stability. Hobbes’s argument introduces the absolute secularization of *a rational, objective, mechanistic* and now fully *materialistic* natural law, as well as providing the foundations for legal positivism (whereby the will of the sovereign becomes the source of the law). A far less original author in this aspect (he restates many of Aquinas’s ideas, particularly the notion that human law going against the law of nature ceases to be law), John Locke further asserts the connection between natural law and reason: ‘[t]he state of nature has a law of nature that governs it, which obliges everyone: and reason, which is that law, teaches all mankind, who will but consult it, that being all equal and independent, no one ought to harm another in his life, health, liberty or possessions’ (in Russell, 1945, 625). One of the dangers of a universal and purportedly objective natural law—the arbitrariness of its *content* that is ultimately informed by relationships of power—is immediately apparent in Locke’s own writing, as he considers captives in a just war as slaves by the law of nature, and justifies the right to punish attacks against one’s property even by death. Locke turned around Hobbes’s argument, and focused not on duties, but on the correlative right that each individual has to demand others to uphold their obligations. The result was the introduction of the idea of natural rights.

Much of natural law—as legal theory conceives of it today—is thus fully realized, in a theoretical sense, by the seventeenth and eighteenth centuries, and remains thus to the present day. While distancing himself from much of the natural law tradition, and aligning more with Aristotle’s striving for an ideal *telos,* Fuller (1968) still argues that the most fundamental tenet of natural law is the role of reason in legal and social ordering (which he describes, however as a *social* activity, not an *individual* one).

The problem of natural law, Bertrand Russel writes, is that “we may identify ‘natural law’ with moral rules in so far as they are independent of positive legal enactments” (1945, 628). While for Aquinas and Locke this was not a problem, since these moral rules had been spelled out in the scripture, such certainty crumbles when natural law becomes secularized. Davies suggests that

> [p]hilosophers of modern natural law sometimes trace our origin to a social contract that we are said to have signed among ourselves, at least virtually, to enter into the collectivity that made us the men we are ...The same philosophers call natural law a collection of rules said to exist outside of any formulation; being universal, this law would follow from human nature

> … natural law follows from reason inasmuch as reason governs all men … Nature is reduced to human nature, which is reduced to either history or reason. The world has disappeared. Modern natural law is distinguished from classical natural law by this nullification. (2022, 34–5)

Indeed, the concept of 'nature' in the formulation of natural law briefly presented thus far is the realization of an Aristotelian human *entelechy*. The 'nature' of the *lex naturalis moralis* consists "of *human* nature or the 'natural properties of humans' … Thus, natural law of the jurisprudential tradition concerns what Kant called 'the moral law within' rather than the 'starry heavens above' (or anything in between)" (Davies, 2022, 45). As a result, perhaps unsurprisingly, Kaarlo Tuoori writes that "[i]n the era of modern law, the idea of natural law, of eternal principles derived from subjective or objective nature and independent of time and place, has lost its credibility. In 'mature' modern law, there is no place for natural law; all law is human law" (2002, 6).

In summary, the Western conception of natural law is profoundly marked by a number of clear criteria. Natural law is universal, eternal (or at least ahistorical), objective, rational (and it can be deduced by reason), moral, mechanistic and, more recently, materialistic. Therefore, it is hard to define ecological jurisprudence as an enlarged form of natural law that merely exchanges the moral for the ecological. One could argue that Foucauldian considerations of power would suggest the possibility of it being called a 'post-modern' natural law, but I contend that, given the significant and profound differences from much (if not the totality) of natural law as it is conceived of in the Western legal tradition, the *sui generis* term 'ecological jurisprudence' is more appropriate.

If ecological jurisprudence transcends the classical dichotomy of legal positivism and natural law, however, a final question remains as to whether normativity can be reimagined, not just as a human construct, but one *positively* involving nature. In other word, is it possible to move beyond the limits of the 'ecological integrity' *grundnorm* of ecological jurisprudence to the idea of nature being a normative *actant*, or even a normative *agent*?

8.2.4 Is Nature Normative?

Ecological jurisprudence, as discussed above, is an attempt to somewhat bring Nature as a legal *noumena* back *within* the normative and legal 'system of cognition' (rather than being external to it). The question then is whether Nature can become a legal *subject* beyond the strategic way described in the previous chapter. After all, as Davies suggests, '[t]he [Western] tradition of jurisprudence side-lined physical nature as the mere acted upon of law (nature is that which is constituted, determined, coded, categorized and so forth): law, by contrast is understood by th[is] jurisprudential tradition as mental, abstract and subsisting in the realm of ideas' (2022, 40). But nature is also used, in the context of natural law 'to refer to the abstract and even purportedly essential properties or characteristics of human beings … an essence or inherent quality rather than to matter and the physical world'. However, Davies concludes, 'Nature in the sense of an essence that is to be found within the things of physical nature often implies a teleological and—in science—highly controversial resonance' (43). Alessandro D'Entrèves posits that 'many of the ambiguities of the concept of natural law must be ascribed to the ambiguity of the concept of nature that underlies it' (1970, 16). Bruno Latour also writes that '[i]f ecology drives us crazy, it is because it obliges us to plunge head first into the confusion created by reference to a "natural world" that is said to be at once fully endowed and not at all endowed with a normative dimension. "Not at all", since it describes only an order' "fully", since there is no order more sovereign than the order to obey that order' (2017, 34).

I have in the past argued that it may be useful to separate the idea of anthropocentrism between *ontological* and *normative* anthropocentrism. Since the human mind is the term of reference of both observation and theory alike (Barrow & Tipler, 1988), I argued, then it is *ontologically* impossible to transcend and move beyond an inevitably *anthropic* (i.e. *human*) perspective. To paraphrase Leopold's invitation, it may be possible to think *like* a mountain, but it will never be possible to think *as* a mountain. It follows, I argued, that the attempt by many ecological jurisprudence advocates to transcend anthropocentrism does not necessarily entail an attempt to escape an inevitable anthropic perspective but rather it challenges the idea that humanity ought to be considered the only measure of any ethical decision concerning its interaction with the larger environment within which it exists. At the time of writing, I argued that, if it is only human activity that can be truly regulated by human normativity, then human normativity is—and cannot be anything other than—an inherently human-centred activity. Therefore, I distinguished between *ontological* anthropocentrism (which can be theoretically transcended) and *normative* anthropocentrism (which, instead, may be inherently impossible to transcend). My argument was based on two major premises. Firstly, that law is a system of norms made by humans, for humans and *among* humans; and secondly, that it is primarily linguistic and propositional.

However, I now return to that argument to challenge it, and question whether, indeed, normativity is inherently anthropocentric (or, at the very least, anthropic). Thomas Berry wrote that in the case of economics, law and medicine, the planet itself constitutes the 'normative reference' (2009, 127). The idea of normativity has been recently interrogated by Davies who uses the term 'ecolaw' to denote an 'interconnected and plural *nomos*. Ecolaw is not human law that governs the environment or ecosystems. ... It is an attempt to radically expand the referent of 'law' so that it is no longer an exclusively human system or plurality of human systems but unfolds with the matter of the universe (more particularly, of Earth)'. '[R]ather than expand legal subjectivity to animals and other natural objects', she asserts, 'I aim to position law and normativity as ontologically prior to the designation of subjects and objects' (2022, 2). She further writes that

> [t]he laws of nature and human law have in western theory often been regarded as radically different: on the one hand causally deterministic and necessary, and on the other created intentionally and entirely contingent. But these particular meanings of 'law' are extremes. Human and nonhuman nature is more characteristically constituted by patterns that are "normative" in the sense that they are comprised of continually emerging norms. (4)

She acknowledges that "human law clearly cannot be deduced isomorphically from a 'book' of natural meanings like a mediaeval bestiary … nor can natural norms be translated directly into the human socio-legal sphere'. However, '[t]his is not to say that the norms of the natural world are never instructive' (7–8). She argues that her image of a pluriversal "*nomos* refers to the idea that 'nature'—animals, plants, the Earth and so forth—produces its own values and norms, and that human norms are part of this natural *nomos*. … [T]he *nomos*, or normative universe, emerges from material processes but cannot be reduced to them in any mechanical sense … emergent normativity is contingent yet stable and accumulative (or, in social terms, historical) and constantly diversifying' (1). Her argument requires an understanding of what she means by 'norm' and 'normativity'. Davies does not use 'norm' and 'normativity' in the classic Kelsenian sense. In her usage, Nature is 'normative' in the sense that it creates patterns or regularities (or better, that can be understood in terms of patterns and regularities, as Pythagoras had suggested) that can be described as 'norms'. For Davies, a norm is 'a pattern, standard or direction, that is also a guide for action … norms—both legal and non-legal, human and nonhuman—are iterative, connective and teleological. That is, norms are the product of iteration or continued usage—things being done, thought, or spoken the same way repeatedly, though always accompanied by the potential for difference' (4). Furthermore norms 'are pathways created by usage or movement: they guide action but do not mechanically determine it. But norms also arise from exchanges, relationships, and bonds between organisms and between bits of matter' (5). As a result, she concludes, "regularities are embedded in matter and in practices, while explicit standards are abstracted from regularities and/or independently laid down as rules. It is in the transition from the first to the second sense that facts and norms become indistinct. Simply, if something happens regularly, and is 'normal', that is a fact. However, the mere fact that it is normal means that it very often is or becomes a guide for behaviour" (30). Davies's arguments of norms as 'habits' thus both confirms the epistemic bridge between the *normative* and the *descriptive* discussed above and extends the principle of *normativity* (in the sense of norms/patterns-generating regularities) to the entirety of Nature.

All of reality, then, can be described in normative (and normativity-creating) terms. But are these 'norms' in the stronger Kelsenian sense, or are they just ongoing interactions and guidelines, with patterns that can be discerned from those interactions and that suggest future pathways? Do they have 'obligatory' force, are fully 'normative' in an ethical sense? An answer has been provided by Pamela Lyon, who wrote that

> [a]ll organisms maintain themselves far from thermodynamic equilibrium by importing "order" from their surroundings in the form of matter and energy, chemically transforming it to do work, and exporting "disorder" in the form of waste products of various sorts. That they do so seemed to defy the Second Law of Thermodynamics until the crucial distinction was drawn between "closed" and "open" thermodynamic systems, leading the way to the science of dissipative structures and irreversible physical processes. What marks the difference between living systems and other kinds of self-organising complex physical systems that can maintain themselves far from thermodynamic equilibrium – tornadoes and chemical baths, for example – is that (so far) only living systems are capable of acting to circumvent

> the consequences of resource depletion, by seeking resources elsewhere or by changing their own structures to survive stringent conditions. This is the first and most obvious naturally normative fact derivable from biology: *Every organism strives to persist; it is self-preserving* [an echo of Hobbes's first precept of nature, indeed]. Although, technically ... this is an 'attributive' norm rather than a 'prescriptive' norm – which would be of the form *All things considered every organism ought to strive to persist*. ... In order to persist, organisms must establish causal relations with features of their surroundings that lead to exchanges of matter and energy ... This is the third naturally normative fact derivable from biology: *All organisms have one or more mechanisms for assessing value (advantage/harm), namely, how the organism is fairing in the immediate circumstance relative to some biological norm.* (2011, 141–3)

Lyon's words seem to echo Canguilhem's argument in *The Normal and the Pathological* (1992), who, "[i]n speaking of life as normative, was referring to the ways in which life is creative and establishes norms ... 'Vital normativity' is the normativity embedded in biological processes and that is necessary to the continuation and reproduction of life" (Davies, 2022, 58). Normativity, it seems, could be extended to the living world as an evolution of Spinoza's *conatus*, Bergson's *elan vital*, or Aristotle and Driesch's *entelechy*, i.e. an animating force of all living things.

Moreover, Actor-Network Theory, and the recognition of all things as inevitable *actants* equally supports Davies's thesis of Nature's inherent normativity. Davies asks whether the agency of non-living things is 'a *normative* agency—that is, does it create and follow norms? Despite challenges to the life-non-life boundary, a line has nonetheless often been maintained between the laws of nature that ... have nomic necessity and in which purpose or directed action plays no part and the teleological or purpose-driven norms of life. However, even this boundary is now contested' (Davies, 2022, 35). This appears to be an extension of Bennett's idea of a 'vibrant matter', extended to conceive of matter as normative. 'However', Davies also notes, 'the attribution of normativity (as opposed to mechanical-physical laws) to non-living things is not necessarily straightforward. Non-living things clearly act; they are agents, and exert a power and a force on other things'. In other words, they are *actants* in the sense used by Latour and Bennett's. 'But how are these actions normative? In what sense', Davies continues, 'can the forceful actions of non-living matter acting in the absence of life (the flow of water, the dissipation of energy, the bonding and decay of atoms, etc.) be said to be driven by purposes? In what sense are the predictable pathways of matter formed by iterations and connections that are directed and probable (i.e. norm creating) rather than merely mechanical'? (73).

A different answer is provided by some of the more recent philosophical approaches—such as speculative realism—discussed in the previous chapter. The construct of a 'mechanical' world is an onto-axiological interpretive tool, not the reflection of an objective reality. As a result, a world that is seen as normative and agentic allows a different interaction with it, even if the observed normativity is, for all intent and purposes, indistinguishable from a mechanical description of reality. In reflecting upon the distinction between Nature's normative powers and human legal constructs, Davies notes that

> [t]he normative pluralities that form an organism (or superorganism, or holobiont) are not consciously chose or followed. They emerge without reflection. Human law, by contrast,

> can be identified, represented, intentionally followed (or not), and reformed. This workable conceptual distinction between the immanent norm and the representable is not, however, so easily maintained in a material sense, given that all human law is established upon the grounds of both culturally embedded (and therefore neither immanent or external) human norms. (2022, 8)

Similarly, Jane Bennett identifies an agentic power in the world already found in the English notion of the 'deodand' ('that which must be given to God'). In this figure, the nonhuman *actant* involved in harm caused to a human being was surrendered to the Crown to be used or sold in compensation of the damage caused. In summary, it seems that the extension of normativity to the natural world, albeit at the boundaries of Western legal theory, is supported by some degree of existing scholarship and historical examples.

Human normativity, as a result, is enmeshed within a plurality of normative worlds. This plurality of intersecting normative worlds leads Davies to speak of 'normative co-becomigs', 'generative processes occur[ring] at massive evolutionary scales that change the Earth's geology and chemistry' (2022, 68–9), as the Gaia hypothesis has shown. These 'normative co-becomings' may offer a better term of reference for an elusive 'Great Jurisprudence' than any objectively observable 'scientific facts'—and, perhaps, even some fluid 'ecological principles'. Davies concludes by stating that

> [s]ocio-ecological co-becoming concerns the emergence of complex entities as bio-geo-socio-formations (where the "socio-" also includes human law). The idea of *legal* co-becoming on a human plane is nothing new. Throughout the twentieth century, legal autonomy was often seen as a product of a process of normative co-becoming. Eugene Ehrlich's living law, Robert Cover's jurisgenesis in an expansive normative universe, and Patricia Ewick and Susan Silbey's work on legal consciousness are all variations on the theme of state law being produced out of quotidian legal practices and meanings in their interactions with broader socio-political normativities, environments, ideas, and patterns. … What is missing from twentieth-century accounts of legal co-creation within human society is an account of the co-becomings of human *and nonhuman* normativities. (89)

Davies's words appear to be an extension of Michel Serres's natural contract. Their suggestions, however, can be pushed even further. It appears that Nature can indeed be conceived of as normative, at least in a somewhat *passive* sense, as an 'actant' within human relations. Certainly, Nature can also be considered *inferentially* normative: Stone uses the example of a lawn in need of waters in the midst of a dry summer that will communicate its need for waters via the colours of the grass, and any dog owner will intuitively know-how a dog will communicate a desire for food via gestures and behaviour that uncontroversially state 'you must feed me', a definite *normative* canine statement (however valid it may be). But can Nature be thought of as *actively* normative? Is there a conscious or intentional *ought* to be found in nature? And if there is, can it be communicated (to align with Austin's command theory)? And if communicated, does that have legal repercussions?

Philosopher Mark Rowlands (2012), drawing on a number of ethological accounts, argues that animals are not only moral *patients* (i.e. they are recipients of moral considerations on the part of humans, as Peter Singer's and Tom Regan's argument stated in the 1970s and 1980s, that they possess moral rights derived from their status of subjects of a life), but also moral *subjects*—if not necessarily moral *agents*, the latter being a category that invokes the attribution of praise or blame and responsibility, something which, he argues, cannot be extended to nonhuman entities. His argument is based on the recognition that animals display moral emotions; that is, emotions, such as compassion, sympathy, grief and courage (as well as malice, spite and cruelty) that can be called *concern* or *solicitude*, attitudes that have as their focus the welfare or fate of others, and that are, as a consequence, the hallmark of moral attitude. 'The primary thesis ... is that some animals can be moral subjects in the sense that they can be motivate to act by moral reasons. These moral reasons take the form of morally laden emotions—emotions that have moral content. An emotion has moral content in the sense that, if it is not misguided, it guarantees the truth of a moral proposition' (71).

Iván Darío Vargas Rocancio extends the argument further, noting that certain legal orders see all of Nature as agentic and normative, and not just a mere recipient of human normativity. '"*De aquí viene el derecho indígena*" (indigenous law comes from *here*") said the *taita* in the midst of an intense vertigo with the *ayahuasca* (*Banisteriopsis caapi*) brew known as *chuma*. Like a firefly hovering in the background of my memories', Vargas Rocancio notes, 'this enigmatic statement has stayed with me for quite some time' (2020, 246). He then argues that '[t]his agential capacity, however, emerged from the relationship with the human by means of ingestion of the plant. Yet', he asks, 'how can we know if the plant has capacities of intentionality? I suspect that vegetal intentionality revealed itself in the context of the bodily encounter between the human and the plant', as experienced in ceremonial settings. Vargas Rocancio concludes that 'the coca plant was communicating with the human by means of its own speech' (260). Michael Marder suggests that vegetal beings express themselves 'without resorting to vocalization' (2013, 74), and Vargas Rocancio proposes that 'knowledge becomes a matter of eating' (2017, 261), and the word 'language' can be used to describe "plant modes of communication as a form of 'spatialized materiality'".

Rodolfo Sacco had already proposed, in the 1980s, the idea of a legal 'ethology', of the theoretical extension of the phenomenon of law beyond the boundaries of the human. Vargas Rocancio's work seems to vindicate Sacco's intuition, and to suggest a degree of *active* normativity on the part of Nature. While the theoretical (let alone practical) implications of this line of inquiry are yet protean and to be further explored within Western jurisprudence, the notion of an *active* normative natural world has immediate consequences for many of the eco-jurisprudential initiatives discussed in the previous chapters, as the case of Te Pou Tupua (the representative for the Te Awa Tupua, the Whanganui River in New Zealand) shows. In that instance, the Whananui Iwi-appointed representative, as discussed, declare to be speaking *with*, rather than *for*, the river. The normative and legal 'co-becoming' that such a view entails is evidently aligned with a view that considers the river (and, by extension, Nature) not only as a legal *subject* within human legal interactions, but as an active normative agent of its own.

If Nature is normative, then it follows that questions of legal pluralism—the idea that 'human societies live according to plural legal and normative systems, often co-located territorially and forming hybrid normative orders within groups and individuals' (Davies, 2022, 21)—must be asked. Davies notes that 'the concept of legal pluralism has been developed to that it refers not only to relatively autonomous co-existing systems of norms, but to more complex interactions between layered, intersecting, mobile, and heterogenous normative practices. The concept of legal pluralism has not ordinarily been extended to the intersecting plural normative worlds of nonhuman life, but it is an apt translation of pluralism to do so' (21). Emmanuel Melissaris (2009) speaks of an 'ubiquitous law', summarizing the complex discourse of legal pluralism to recognize the comparative universality of the phenomenon of law, and to establish a 'space' (both theoretical and practical) for legal pluralism. Melissaris's 'pluriversality' was arguably not intended to extend beyond the boundaries of human legality. However, in the light of the discussion above, one cannot but wonder whether such extension is theoretically inevitable.

8.2.5 Toward an Ecological Jurisprudence

The emergence of ecological jurisprudence, the scholarship discussed in this section has shown, has done more than pragmatically curtail destructive (and self-destructive) human behaviours for instrumental purposes, or even inscribe Nature (as a whole and in its component parts) within human legal institutions and practices. It has, instead, pushed the theoretical boundaries of what is considered a legal and normative agent to a degree previously unseen within Western jurisprudence. Law is traditionally seen a system of rules encoded within linguistic propositions (laws, judicial pronouncements, et cetera), the validity of which depends on the social legitimacy that such rules exert on individuals. Their prescriptive nature can be considered in the abstract, and their internal consistency can be appraised grammatically through the tools of formal and propositional logic, although their actual effectiveness in the world can only be ascertained by the observation of human behaviour. However, the corporeal inscription of humanity within an interconnected ecological world entails a degree of enmeshment of human laws and abstract rules with a network of nonhuman subjectivities. This means that law, in the light of the emergence of an ecological jurisprudence, can be conceived at multiple levels.

At a first level, law can be considered in an evolutionary sense. Legal systems (defined as a collection of more or less cohesive human regulatory and legal regimes) are exposed to evolutionary forces, and just as entropy defines the economic process (as Georgescu-Rosen suggested), so do evolutionary pressures define the continued survival (or lack thereof) of the many legal systems of the world. As a result, the notion of planetary boundaries and ecological limits act as the theoretical horizon that determines a legal order's continuity over time, even though they may not alter the formal criteria of validity of specific legal provisions. As a result, a '*lex iniusta*' (a law that contradicts ecological principles) may very well still be law, but it is likely to disappear as a result of evolutionary pressures. Such a perspective necessarily entails an enlarged ecological awareness, but does not necessarily engage any further with the *idea* of law. Indeed, law could still be considered in a strictly positivist sense, simply transforming its ultimate *grundnorm* from an abstract apex norm to a set of ecological principles. This approach is visible in Bosselmann's notion of 'ecological integrity', Berry and Cullinan's idea of a 'Great Jurisprudence', and Burdon's interpretation of it as a set of 'ecological principles'. It is also entailed by the strategic adoption of a rights discourse to articulate Nature as a legal *subject*. Notwithstanding its more contained challenge to traditional Western jurisprudence, nonetheless, such an approach to law does not fall easily within the confines of an even enlarged notion of natural law, given the traditional sense in which natural law is understood: that is, as universal, eternal (or at least ahistorical), objective, rational (and able be deduced by reason), moral, mechanistic, and, more recently, materialistic. Instead, it is likely best described as a *sui generis* legal theory.

Beyond such an approach to law, however, ecological jurisprudence entails the reinterrogation of the distinction between *normative* and *descriptive* statements about the world. The distinction between facts and norms, or 'fact-value/fact-norm' is becoming less certain that what Hume's guillotine suggests. As Ruth Anna Putnam suggests, '[t]he notion of a fact ... is hopelessly fuzzy' (2017, 105). Facts, as we have seen, are 'construed' both in law and science, and entail a series of normative ontological assumptions. Moreover, 'as many critical legal theorists have argued, so-called descriptive accounts of law are already or can easily become norm-laden' (Davies, 2022, 28). However, the argument can be taken further, to state that any 'description' of the world is informed by 'pattern-making/describing' (Davies's 'normativity'), and any 'prescriptive' statement about the world is ultimately irrelevant outside of the ecological context in which it exists. In other words, the limits of positivism are found in the fact that norms and laws do not exist in an abstract vacuum, but operate within a pattern of material (ecological) relations. However, those patterns do not exist in a self-evident objective sense. Rather, while they are certainly *assumed,* their formulation is consistently constructed and negotiated. This normative negotiation, this 'ecological normative co-becoming' thus represents the framework within which human laws exist. The myth (or perhaps the hubris) of human arbitrariness is thus constantly faced with the reality of those econormative co-becomings that define its milieu, and ultimately determine the evolutionary continuity of those human prescriptive statements. In this sense, Eugene Ehrlich's work may provide clear guidance, with his proposed tension between legal norms and legal propositions. Legal positivism can definitely continue as a tool for articulating human laws among humans (what I referred to, in the past, as 'normative anthropocentrism'), but it requires to be constantly informed by an ecological awareness in order to determine its fitness (if not for any ethical reason of its alignment with the cosmos, for a very utilitarian reason that without doing so, its existence may very well be jeopardized over a relatively short time). In this sense, there must be an alignment between the normative/descriptive laws of nature (which describe nature but make a series of ontological normative assumptions about what nature 'is') and the normative/prescriptive laws of humans (which are interpreted in positivist terms). It is this approach or tendency that I call an 'ecological jurisprudence'.

A truly ecological jurisprudence is more than the articulation of the relationship between the Great Jurisprudence and human jurisprudence offered by the theory of Earth Jurisprudence, it is something captured to an extent by Davies' 'ecolaw' and Capra and Mattei 'ecology of law'. The core issue raised by ecological jurisprudence, in this sense, is not merely about the alignment of human laws with the laws of nature. Rather, it questions the interplay between the descriptive and the normative, leading to the (certainly post-modern) suggestion that the two are more inextricably intertwined than Hume and Moore's 'naturalistic fallacy' and Kant's distinction of *noumena* and *phenomena* suggest. What Hart and Finnis intuited (but never fully articulated) is that 'natural law' represents a conceptual horizon, not just in the *hypothetical imperative* sense that such a horizon must be respected if the legal system is to survive in the long term, but also in the far more radical assumption that it is in the liminal space of this horizon that the descriptive and the prescriptive, the observational and the normative, meet. The protean and pluripotential capacity to engage with the world is thus both descriptive and normative at the same time, and it is impossible to 'describe' the world without some degree of normative assumptions, nor is it possible to 'prescribe' behaviour without some degree of observation of the adherence (or lack thereof) to these prescriptions.

This approach, articulated by Capra and Mattei in *The Ecology of Law* and by Davies in *EcoLaw*, leads to the assumption of some inherent normativity in the natural world itself. Normativity (and law) are thus not the domain of humanity alone. The normativity of Nature can be considered in two distinct ways. Firstly, 'norms' can be seen as patterns of behaviour and practice that at the same time act as guidelines for future behaviour. Such norms are a function of the pattern-recognition capacity of the observer, of their 'normative instinct', rather than a quality of the process and entities themselves. This approach maintains the idea that, when considered as 'laws of nature', these norms have a nomic quality (i.e. they possess causal necessity) that human laws and norms do not. As a result, the engagement with Nature as a normative 'actant' leads to Davies's idea of an 'ecological normative co-becoming', the idea that the 'norms' of existence are co-created by the interactions of humans and nonhumans. Such an approach necessarily leads to an expanded ecological awareness that is also more critical of its own epistemological standpoint, although it does not necessarily lead to the development of a distinct, non-propositional epistemology. In this sense, rights of Nature—and the idea of Nature's normativity more in general—represent an attempt to have this normative ecological dialogue *reconstructed within the human theatre of law*. The perceived normativity of Nature (which still depends on a human interpreter) is reconstituted, via the legal conceptualization of Nature as a legal subject, *within* the boundaries of human normativity. The results are profound, as they can alter the way in which we establish basic human institutions (perhaps in a horizontal, rather than hierarchical manner, as Bookchin suggested) or even the way we conceive of property or contracts among humans. They can also lead to a representation of the nonhuman within the human legal (positivist) arena through the articulation of rights of Nature, the introduction of environmental personhood, and the existence of a Nature's ombudsman and Nature's representatives.

Another way in which Nature can be considered normative is by casting it as an *active* normative agent whose normativity exits *independently* of humanity. In other words, ecological jurisprudence entails the possibility of transcending not only *ontological* anthropocentrism (as is the case in its multifaceted forms), but also *normative* anthropocentrism. Normativity, in this case, is seen as a universal feature of reality itself, rather than being contained exclusively within human socio-legal confines. This, it is important to note, does not lead to a flat normativity, in which human normativity and nonhuman normativity are treated equally. After all, as Lyon notes,

> all organisms are species-centric. Humans are no different than other animals for privileging their kind in the actions they take. This tendency does not foreclose symbiotic mutualisms or individual animals acting in the interests of individuals of another species. Of all the animals of the Earth, human beings very probably are the only ones capable of understanding why species-centrism is fundamentally illogical and to choose to act in the interests of other organisms in a highly general way. The future of human life on this planet may well depend on activating this capacity. (2011, 144)

The necessary corollary of this approach is that the enlarged ecological awareness entailed by ecological jurisprudence in general requires a radical epistemological shift, one whereby modes of thinking, knowing and being *necessarily* extend beyond the limits of propositional knowledge into forms of experiential knowledge that place the human subject in a (normative) dialogue with the cosmos. Anna Grear has coined the term 'sympoietic normativites' to describe norms that emerge from human-nonhuman interactions, arguing that they may 'ground a renewing legal imaginary for the Anthropocene' (2020, 360–1). While these sympoietic normativities 'are not necessarily translatable—or at least not immediately and directly—into the grand law reform or regulatory efforts of nation-states' (Davies, 2022, 101), they emerge from "human-nonhuman working groups in a wide range of situated endeavours in commons-based, grassroots initiatives, expanded to embrace 'commoners' who are more than simply human" (Grear 2020, 360–1). The result is that they can 'hold space for co-negotiation' and co-created norms can arise. This final approach may even be called, with Arne Naess, an eco*sophical*, rather than eco*logical*, jurisprudence.

8.3 The Land Is the Source of the Law

Within the journey toward an ecological (and even *ecosophical*) jurisprudence, new intercultural possibilities emerge. The shift to the 'multinatural' allows a reconsideration of the 'multicultural'. That the Anthropocene is the result of *one* particular modality of humanity's interaction with the world has been amply discussed. Moreover, such a modality is deeply intertwined with practices of colonialism and dispossession, the impact of which has been geophysical inasmuch as it has been genocidal. Alexander Koch and others, e.g. demonstrate that, as a direct consequence of "the tragic die-off of Indigenous populations in North Americas as a result of war and disease after contact with Europeans, the cessation of their traditional land management practices may have substantially contributed to the global cooling now recognized as 'The Little Ice Age'" (2019, 13). Yet, such a way of being is, by no means, necessarily universal. This is aptly captured by Wade Davis:

> [o]ne of the intense pleasures of travel is the opportunity to live amongst peoples who have not forgotten the old ways, who still feel their past in the wind, touch it in stones polished by rain, taste it in the bitter leaves of plants. Just to know that, in the Amazon, Jaguar shaman still journey beyond the Milky Way, that the myths of the Inuit elders still resonate with meaning, that the Buddhists in Tibet still pursue the breath of the Dharma is to remember the central revelation of anthropology: the idea that the social world in which we live does not exist in some absolute sense, but rather is simply one model of reality, the consequence of one set of intellectual and spiritual choices that our particular cultural lineage made, however successfully, many generations ago. But whether we travel with the nomadic Penan in the forests of Borneo, a Vodoun acolyte in Haiti, a *curandero* in the high Andes of Peru, a Tamashek *caravanseri* in the red sands of the Sahara, or a yak herder on the slopes of Chomolungma, all these peoples teach us that there are other options, other possibilities, other ways of thinking and interacting with the earth. This is an idea that can only fill us with hope. (Davis, 2009, 1–2)

Davis points to a host of distinct cultural strategies, many worldviews to engage with the earth. He calls them *ethnospheres*, and points to a deep symbiosis between these culturally construed *ethnospheres* and the biospheres they inhabit. Without a doubt, as I argued elsewhere, 'the cultural and normative engagement with the welfare of the environment … is not the province of a single legal tradition but rather [is, and] ought to be the collective effort of all distinct legal cultures' (Pelizzon, 2014, 177).

8.3.1 Indigenous Strategies

While I have already repeatedly gestured toward non-anthropocentric (at least not in the heuristic term developed in the initial chapters of this book) traditions located outside the 'Western' philosophical tradition, in this section I will focus primarily on Indigenous philosophical and normative traditions. In this sense, the term Indigenous refers to those peoples identified by the United Nations Declaration on the Rights of Indigenous Peoples (UNDRIP), as well as the International Labour Organization's (ILO) Convention on Indigenous and Tribal Peoples. Among the key defining elements of Indigeneity are ancestrality, political and legal separateness, continuity of connection to the precolonial inhabitation of the land and self-identification. I personally remember the many deep conversations that took place in Geneva in the late 1990s, during the drafting of the UNDRIP, when the definition of what constitutes an 'Indigenous' person was at the centre of the debate. While an agreement was reached to eschew a single binding definition (which was felt to potentially lock Indigenous peoples within another colonial construct), it was also agreed that the term Indigenous (capitalized) was to be used to refer to all those Peoples who would fall within the scope of the Declaration. As a result, the term indigenous (lower case) was to be maintained to refer to anyone's place of origin, whereas the term Indigenous (capitalized) was to refer to a specific political reality, generally marked by colonial dispossession and continuity of identity throughout the colonial event. In this section, I also need to add, I do not wish to speak on behalf of, or 'about', any Indigenous cultures, nor do I claim to represent any form of Indigenous knowledge, which, I acknowledge, can only be spoken of by the traditional holders of that knowledge. Rather, I will only look at the bodies of the existing literature both as an Indigenist scholar and with the eyes of a comparative lawyer and legal anthropologist.

The focus on Indigenous legal orders is of particular significance because of the way in which traditional knowledge has been articulated and sustainably practiced over millennia. The 1992 *Biodiversity Convention*, in Article 8(j), uses the term 'traditional knowledge' to refer to the knowledge and practices of Indigenous and local communities that embody lifestyles that are 'relevant for the conservation and sustainable use of biological diversity'. Patrick Glenn defines Indigenous cultures as the 'chthonic' (from the Greek word *cthon*, χθών, 'earth' or 'soil') traditions of peoples living 'in close harmony with the earth' (2010, 61). For Daniel Wildcat, the term Indigenous peoples 'refers to peoples or nations who take their tribal [collective] identities as members of the human species from the landscapes and seascapes that gave them their unique tribal cultures' (2009, 32). This approach, in the light of the discussions contained in the preceding chapters, suggests a profound recognition of Nature's normativity. However, John Borrows (1997–8) also refers to Indigenous rights based on their traditional relationship to the land as 'frozen rights' and environmental racism—which 'refers to harms perpetrated in and through the environment' (Westra, 2008, 136)—disproportionately affects Indigenous peoples and ethnic minorities, thus making the terrain occupied by ecological jurisprudence a particular important space in which issues of environmental sustainability and social justice are inextricably enmeshed.

When faced with the question as to whether Indigenous Peoples ought to be characterized as inherently environmentalist, while recognizing the Indigenous peoples are neither uniform nor consistent (undoubtedly, Indigenous worldviews vary, often profoundly, and many Indigenous peoples have caused and cause environmental damages), Dennis Martinez and others (2008) point out that traditional ecological knowledge is 'first and foremost *practical* knowledge for survival, not some mystical training for transcendence. Just the fact that so many Indigenous Peoples are still here indicates they have profound ecological knowledge and skills of survival and adaptation' (Nelson, 2008, 13). Thomas Berry wrote that '[t]ribal and village peoples knew their local geographical region well, under the overarching sky, with the sun and clouds by day and moon and stars at night. This familiarity was expressed in mythic forms that accommodated personal experience and traditional environmental knowledge' (2009, 49). The use of the past tense ('knew', rather than 'know') is misleading, since many Indigenous peoples still maintain the same knowledge, but the underlying sentiment is confirmed by the literature, much of which is worth reproducing.

> One of the most striking things about indigenous peoples is that traditionally they live in conscious awareness of the stars in the heavens, the topography of the region, the dawn and sunset, the phases of the moon, and the seasonal sequence. They live in a world of subjects, that is, a world of inner expression shared by every mode of being, not a world of objects.

> Nothing is without its identity, its dignity, its inner spontaneity. Everything has its sacred dimension, which must not be violated. Even today, despite material and social fragmentation stemming … from the colonial encounter, many of the Australian aboriginal peoples still live in a universe that originated in dreamings and was peopled by spirit presences. They live in a topography shaped by song. (Berry, 2009, 88)

> [L]ong-established cultures often display a remarkable solidarity with the lands that they inhabit, as well as a basic respect, or even reverence, for the other species that inhabit those lands. Such cultures, much smaller in scale (and far less centralized) than modern Western civilization, seem to have maintained a relatively homeostatic or equilibrial relation with their local ecologies for vast periods of time, deriving their necessary sustenance from the land without seriously disrupting the ability of the earth to replenish itself. (Abram, 1996, 93–4)

> [I]t appears that certain cultures did manage to evolve laws and other means of regulating human conduct that enabled them to live successfully over very long periods of time as part of a wider community of living and non-living beings. In other words, they appear, by and large, to have succeeded in avoiding degrading their environments aw we have. To me this suggests that they probably know things that we don't and which would be helpful for us to know. (Cullinan, 2011 ed, 88)

While the above sentiment is widely shared within the literature, at the same time, Kirsten Anker explores her own discomfort with the risk of "wrestling with the spectre of the 'noble savage'", what she describes as the 'myth of the ecological Indian' (2020, 3–4). She notes that

> the "noble savage" became a literary trope associated with America's first peoples and other non-Europeans from the seventeenth-century poetry of John Drydon on forming part of a lament for an original and timeless beatific human condition lost through "civilization" … in the mid-nineteenth century one faction of the Ethnological Society of London used evidence of that apparent pitiful state or ignoble tendencies of "savages" in an effort to debunk the idea that Indigenous peoples represent a state of optimal human development or innocent "natural goodness" and thus tried to undermine the more humanist faction of the Society … Muir and Berry had more sympathetic precursors such as the proto-ecologist William Bartram, who in 1771 described intricate adaptations of Creek, Cherokee and other peoples to their environments. (8)

Nonetheless, she also argues that '[i]f the ecological law project aspires to develop law and jurisprudence that are adaptive to specific ecologies and supportive of life on Earth, then it should grasp the opportunity to learn from any communities that, like many Indigenous peoples, have accumulated long-term and intricate knowledge of their local ecosystem' (13). This, she continues, is

> the kind of ecological knowledge that is pertinent to planning for ecological law has roots in long-term conscious participation in specific living places … Produced and actualized by peoples in their territories, this knowledge is necessarily partial, provisional and emergent; it is not only world-learning but world-making …another dimension of embedding the turn to Indigenous knowledges in their legal orders relates to what we think knowledge even *is*. (13–4)

Anker's words are a powerful reminder of the risk of essentializing Indigenous knowledge in a way that serves and perpetrates essentially colonial projects, including ecological ones. Kim Polistina agrees, suggesting that, "[r]ather than learning about other cultures, a deeper and more respectful learning for sustainability can be gained by 'paralleling' different cultural traditions, beliefs and social systems with the consumerist values of the West, and then utilizing this learning as a tool for critical reflection on aspects of learners' own cultures as well as the paralleled cultures" (2009, 118). Similarly, in a book heralded as a modern version of Capra's *The Tao of Physics,* David Peat writes about the collision of paradigms occurring at a Sun Dance. When faced with the question of 'why the ice heals', 'I had to ... let go of everything we had read and had been taught about Western physics. ... I had to discover a new way of entering another space. I had to allow my mind to move into another world, a world with totally different approaches and insights' (2002, 44).

Indeed, despite the 'geographic, social and psycho-cultural' removal experienced by Indigenous peoples worldwide, Wildcat asserts, many of them have maintained 'thousand- and hundred-years-old relationships with specific landscapes and seascapes' (2009, 3). Yet, the threat of a 'fourth removal', one caused by climate change and environmental upheaval now looms large, what the author calls 'global burning'. Laura Westra points out that 'the biological integrity of indigenous peoples ... is dependent upon the ecological integrity of their living environment, and it is their access to environmental regimes that single out their specific habitat conditions' (2008, 9). Three models are generally proposed to secure such integrity: the 'cultural integrity' model, which emphasizes the intrinsic value of traditional cultures themselves, the 'self-determination' model which, according to James Anaya (2004), is the most firmly entrenched in international law, and an 'ecological integrity' model expressly focused on combating what the author defines as 'ecofootprint harms or crimes'.

Notwithstanding the power differential derived from the impact of colonial dispossession, Indigenous peoples have always occupied a special place within the global emergence of ecological jurisprudence. Prefiguring the tribal strategies of more recent times, Vine Deloria Jr presented the idea of legal rights of nonhuman nature in an unpublished 1974 essay (Nash, 1989, 119). Winona LaDuke (1999) shows the present-day struggles of many Indigenous groups in North America, from the Awkesasne's struggle with GM's dumping of toxic waste that contaminated maternal milk, to the Seminole's plea for the few remaining panthers, their totemic ancestors, from the Northern Cheyenne's facing coal-strip mining in their ancestral lands to the Hawai'ian caretakers of traditionl *heiau* (traditional Hawai'ian temple) in the face of the militarization of the Pacific islands. The Ecuadorian Constitution of 2008 was deeply influenced by CEDENMA and the Pachakutik Plurinational Unity Movement (Mijieski & Beck, 2011). The vision of nature contained in Andean cosmology became central to the *Universal Declaration of the Rights of Mother Earth*, while the Māori Iwi are the driving force both the Te Urewara and the Whanganui river initiatives in New Zealand. The Menominee, or 'people of the wild rice'—a name given by their neighbours due to their extensive connection to wild rice to the people who call themselves 'Kaeyas-Machatiwduk' or 'Ancient Ones' (Wildcat, 2009, 86)—have long since developed a successful forestry programme and wood-products manufacturing business. For the Ojjibwes (or Anishinaabeg, how they refer to themselves), rice occupies a central place in their history (LaDuke, 2008, 206). In 2019, the White Earth Band of Ojibwe and the 1855 Treaty Authority jointly adopted the *Rights of Manoomin* law for on and off protection of wild rice and the clean, fresh water resources and habitats in which it thrives. In the second phase of the rights of Nature movement worldwide, and in particular in North America, Indigenous peoples have been central to the strategic advancement of the movement. For example, the Indigenous Environmental Network, a grassroots network of Native communities working on environmental, economic and social justice issues in North America (or Turtle Island) focuses on combined issues of biojustice, bioethcis and the protection of Earth Mother and Sky Father (Goldtooth, 2008, 220–8). When invited to speak about human rights to an international gathering, Chief Oren Lyons Jr, faithkeeper of the Onondaga tribe of the Haudenosaunee (Iroquois) Nation, questioned the very definition of 'nations', by powerfully asking:

> [t]here is a hue and cry for human rights, they said, for all people, and the Indigenous people said: What of the rights of the natural world? Where is the seat for the buffalo or the eagle? Who is representing them at this forum? Who is speaking for the water of the earth? Who is speaking for the trees and the forests? Who is speaking for the fish, for the whales, for the beavers, for our children? (in Boyd, 2017, xxi)

Much of the engagement with eco-jurisprudential initiatives on the part of Indigenous peoples has been essentially strategic. Indigenous activists and trial authorities used the instruments offered by ecological jurisprudence (particularly, though not exclusively, rights of Nature provisions) to advance tribal rights and interests. Incidentally, the adoption of rights of Nature provisions by tribal authorities in the US has protected many of the ideas advocated by the movement from the hostility of most Federal and State courts, who lack jurisdiction on tribal lands and on tribal matters. The strategic adoption of eco-jurisprudential initiatives has been explicitly seen as a way to inject Indigenous worldviews within the (often oppressive) colonial context through the strategic use of legal techniques—such as the ones contained in eco-jurisprudential initiatives—that, albeit liminal, are still located within the confines of the colonial legal order. Casey Camp-Horinek, e.g. admits that after her initial distrust of the idea, she 'realized that colonists need to understand [the Ponca way of life and cosmology] and that was to create a right of nature law in the Ponca Nation' (in Kauffman & Martin, 2021, 179–80).

As a result, Indigenous legal initiatives (and even more so their worldviews) are *not* 'examples' of Earth Jurisprudence, Earth Law, or even ecological jurisprudence. Rather, they are unique cultural, normative and legal expressions of worldviews that may be significantly aligned with many of the ideas advocated within ecological jurisprudence but cannot be assumed to be mere synonyms with them. Within the rich landscape of these worldviews, however, are located many interesting answers to many of the questions raised in relation to most eco-jurisprudential initiatives. Is Nature a legal subject (or a collection of legal subjects)? What *is* Nature? Is Nature normative? Undoubtedly, many Indigenous legal orders have already provided (and continue to provide) many rich and diverse answers to these questions.

8.3.2 *Laws, Knowledge and Ancestral Persons*

It is important to note that, as Westra notes (2008, 59), natural law doctrine is far more commonly invoked in relation to the rights of Indigenous peoples than positivist 'statism' and centralism. However, for the same reasons discussed in relation to ecological jurisprudence in the previous chapter, it would be both simplistic and misleading to assume that Indigenous legal orders operate according to some form of natural law theory, however *sui generis*. Rather, it may be best to consider Indigenous laws as autonomous expressions of distinct legal orders, each marked by a distinct set of jurisprudential principles. While it is not possible (nor is it appropriate) to group the great variety of the world's cultures and legal orders within a single paradigm, if guided by the questions generally asked of ecological jurisprudence, there appear to be some common elements in many Indigenous worldviews, particularly when cast against the particular lineage of culture often referred to as 'the West'.

As previously discussed, a modernist view has tended to singularize nature (*mononaturalism*) while multiplying culture (*multiculturalism*). Yet, once cultures are seen as plural, there suddenly appear many distinct 'natures' as well. Such 'natures' often represent an inextricable relationship between ontology, axiology and praxis, in a way that is advocated (though never quite fully achieved) by more ecocentric proposals within the spectrum of ecological jurisprudence. The very term 'nature', Suzuki and Knudtson (1992) point out, seems incapable of 'enfolding Native notions of a vast, spiritually charged cosmic continuum, in which human society, biosphere, and the entire universe are seamlessly rolled into one'. For the Bunun people of central Taiwan, e.g. there is no single word that translates the Western term 'nature' (Soqluman & Hung, 2010). Rather, two words are used together to convey the meaning of 'nature': *taki*, which describes the totality of the known universe, and *asan*, which describes human interactions with it. *Asan* can be translated literally as 'home', since 'nature', Soqluman and Hung explain, is the place we inhabit, but also as 'escrement', since the place we inhabit is also the place we pollute. 'The combination of these two literal meanings thus indicate that together with the privilege of inhabiting a place comes the responsibility of maintaining it' (Pelizzon, 2014, 183). When asked what it means to be an Indigenous person, Uncle Dootch Kennedy, a Yuin man from the Illawarra region of south-eastern Australia, answered 'it is my nature', and then proceeded to explain

> when I say "that's my nature" I'm talking about the natural environment out there, because *that* is my nature: the ocean, the bush ... People don't look at it in the context, they look at it as my personality. But I say "yes, that's my personality" but understand that my nature also is that natural environment beside you ... When I'm in the bush and I say to people "that's my nature" they understand exactly what I'm saying, because they're in that environment with me and they see how I relate to it ... Indigenous people who are connected to Country, we look at all [that surrounds us] because they're the spirits of our people, the very trees, the very rocks, the mountains that we walk on, we're walking on our spirits ... *That* is my nature. (Pelizzon, 2012, 253)

This sense of identity with 'nature' (or 'Country', as aboriginal people would rather describe it) is encoded in the words with which traditional Hawaiians declared their identity: *I he Hawaii*, 'I am Hawaii' (Taum, 2010). The lack of a specific word for 'Nature' appears to be common among many Indigenous cultures and languages. In Australia, as mentioned in the introduction, 'Country' is the most common term to refer to the interplay between the individual, culture and the environment. Bruno Latour notes that '[n]on-Western cultures *have never been interested* in nature; they have never adopted it as a category'. Instead, 'these cultures offer us indispensable alternatives to the nature-politics opposition, by proposing ways of collecting associations of humans and nonhumans using a single collective clearly identified as political' (2004, 43). Swedish historian of religion Åke Hulktrantz (1987) posits that the term *nature* seems incapable of capturing Native notions of a much broader concept, what Suzuki and Knudtson call a 'vast, spiritually charged continuum, in which human society, biosphere, and the whole universe are seamlessly rolled into one' (1992, 19). As Philippe Descola suggests, "the Amerindian myths do not evoke an irreversible switch from nature to culture. Rather, they portray the emergence of 'natural' discontinuities from an original 'cultural' continuum within which humans and nonhumans were not clearly distinguished" (2013, 132). Descola records that '[f]or the Achuar [of the Ecuadorian Amazon rainforest], technical know-how is indissociable from an ability to create an intersubjective ambience in which regulated relations between one person and another flourish' (5). As a result, Descola wonders whether there is a place for 'nature' in "a cosmology that confers most of the attributes of human beings upon animals and plants? … Can one even describe as a 'wild space' this forest that is barely touched by the Achuar, yet that they regard as an immense garden that is carefully cultivated by some spirit"? (6).

Roderick Nash notes that '[c]entral to most [Native American] Indian religions and ethical systems was [sic] the idea that humans and other forms of life constituted a single society. Indians regarded bears, e.g. as bear *people*. Plants were also people … A complex of rituals and ceremonies reinforced the familial bonds between Indians and their environment. Skins were, in effect, the outer coverings of a common being' (1989, 117). Lakota Elder Luther Standing Bear once noted that 'all things were kindred and brought together by the same Great Mystery' (1933, 193). Augusta Terkildsen explains that such an idea is captured in the expression *Mitákuye Oyásin*, the first word meaning 'relatives', and the latter meaning 'of all kind, everything, every single one' (2019, 26). Similarly, for the Chewong people of Malay Peninsula, "society is not limited to the 260 individuals of which it is composed, for it extends far beyond the ontological frontiers of humanity to encompass a myriad of spirits, plants, animals and objects that are reputed to possess the same attributes as the Chewong themselves and that the Chewong describe collectively as 'our people' (*bi he*)" (Descola, 2013, 22). Frank Forencich writes that "[i]n the Iroquois tradition, people recognize an extended sense of physicality, sometimes referred to as 'the long body'. Even in the modern era, Alexis de Tocqueville wrote about the larger, highly interdependent 'social body'. The body, in other words, is far more than an isolated bag of skin" (2021, 221). David Boyd explains that '[t]here are two important and interrelated concepts at the heart of the Māori relationship with nature that are profoundly different from Western philosophy—*whanaungatanga* and *kaitiakitanga*, loosely translated as kinship and stewardship' (2017, 133).

> *Whanaungatanga* is actually broader than kinship in the sense that it relates not only to relations between living humans, but also to an expansive web of relationships between people (living and dead), land, water, flora and fauna, and the spiritual world of *atua* (gods) – all bound together through *whakapapa* (genealogy). In other words, the Māori believe that all things in the universe, living and the dead, animate and inanimate, are related, going back to Papatūānuku (the Earth) and Ranginui (the sky). That all elements of nature are kin. All are infused with *mauri* (living essence or spirit), and merit the same respect accorded to fellow humans. The people of a particular place are intimately connected to its geographic features – rivers, forests, lakes and other species – and have responsibilities toward them all. *Kaitiakitanga* in an intergenerational obligation of respect that flows directly form *whanaungatanga* because of the web of kin relationships. (133)

In Australia, Descola argues, '[n]owhere else do we find such a vast gathering of peoples that has so systematically, explicitly, and uniformly developed the idea that there exists a moral and physical continuity between groups of humans and groups of nonhumans' (2013, 165–6). The terms *totam* and *totamism* appear for the first time in the memoirs of a fur trader, John Long, operating at the end of the eighteenth century among the Ojibwa Indians north of the Great Lakes (Long, 1901), and 'Algonquins customarily established an individual personal relationship with benevolent and protective entities that Hallowell calls *pagwagának*. These would manifest themselves above all in dreams, although even in a waking state one could sometimes encounter them in an animal form' (Descola, 2013, 167). The term totemic is often extended to explain the nature of Australian relationships with the nonhuman world, whereby each individual 'belongs to a group of persons, each of whom bears the name of, and is especially associated with some natural object' (Spencer & Gillen, 1899, 112). Descola writes that '[t]he most original feature of Australian totemism is certainly the fact that it is rooted in a remarkable cosmological and etiological system that it has become customary to call Dreamtime or "Dreaming in English' (2013, 146).

> "Dreaming" is not just an Aboriginal way of referring to the mythical times that many peoples trace back to a fabled genesis of beings and things. For at the time of that "World-Dawn", as Radcliffe-Brown put it, a movement of continuous generation took off, the effects of which can still be felt. The potential left by the beings of Dreamtime in various sites and routes is constantly realized by successive embodiments of their spirits in entities of various kinds and thanks to the rites, the naming procedures, and the repeated journeys by means of which the Aboriginals make the hidden presence of these entities tangible and alive. For they are the entities that, by modelling beings and things, gave meaning and order to the world. Dreamtime is this neither a remembered past nor a retroactive present. Rather, it is an expression of the eternity that is confirmed in space, an invisible framework for the cosmos that guarantees the permanence of its ontological subdivision. As for the beings of Dreamtime, they cannot be likened to classic mythical heroes, since their organizing impetus, partly given solid material form by various features in the landscape, has continued without interruption even since they abandoned the earth's surface. Nor are they ancestors, in the strict sense, since every existing being, whether human or nonhuman, is linked to the entity that determines it in a direct relationship of duplication, actualization, or formation rather than through an affiliation that unfolds from one generation to the next ... in Australia, totemic organization, that is to say, this association between nonhuman entities and phenomena and groups of human persons, stems from a process that both is originating and also continues ceaselessly to stabilize essences and forms of life that are already differentiated into classes and types, within which social and physical components are inextricably intermingled. (147)

As Spencer and Gillen write, 'the identity of the human individual is often sunk in that of the animal or plant from which he is supposed to have originated' (1899, 119). Deborah Bird Rose observed that Aboriginal peoples 'believe that human life exists within the broader context of a living and conscious cosmos. Humans' responsibility lies in actions that nurture and enhance human life, the life of other species (plants and animals) and the relationships among humans and between humans and others. Other animal species are believed to be acting responsibly. People, other animals, and other categories of beings are moral agents. The whole cosmos is maintained through the conscious and responsible actions of different forms of life' (1988, 379). Paul Elkin wrote that Australian Aboriginal peoples 'bring nature into [their] social and ritual life [and] adopt an attitude of respect toward it' (1964, 141). The Australian Aboriginal perspective presented thus far seems to combine Schweitzer's 'reverence for life' with Leopold 'land ethic', while at the same time answering the question of Nature's normativity (not only passively, but in a very active sense) unquestioningly in the affirmative, all in a cohesive way that none of these distinct perspective has (or perhaps ever could) achieve.

The sense of interconnectedness between ontological perspectives and axiological expectations lead to what Wade Davis calls a 'sacred geography' (2009, 116). Thus, for example, 'for the people living today in the forests of the Piraparanà, the entire natural world is saturated with meaning and cosmological significance. Every rock and waterfall embodies a story. Plants and animals are but distinct manifestations of the same essential spiritual essence' (108). Bruce Pascoe (2014) writes that 'Baiame, the creator Spirit Emu, left the earth after its creation to reside as a dark shape in the Milky Way. The emu is inextricably linked with the wide grasslands of Australia, the landscape managed by Aboriginals. The fate of the emu, people, and grain are locked in step because, for Aboriginal people, the economy and the spirit are inseparable. Europeans stare at the stars, but Aboriginal people also see the spaces in between where the Spirit Emu resides'. Similarly, David Suzuki and Peter Knudtson report that for the Mnong Gar (or Phii Brêe, 'Men of the Forests' for their neighbours) people of Vietnam, time is measured in accordance with the forests that have been eaten in a particular period. To them, 'time is cyclical, local and inextricably a part of the recurrent natural processes of growth and decline, of life and death, of the forest' (1993, 192). As a result, each village will give a different name to each solar year, depending on what section of the forest they have been using for sustenance.[4] The phrase used 'Hii saa brii' ('we ate the forest of…') recognizes that the forest that sustains human beings must be partially consumed, and this ensures the responsibility of doing so in a cyclical fashion. The second part of the phrase thus refers to a particular geographical territory, thus identifying with the same term different years often separated by one or two decades.

Wade Davis (2009) notes that cosmological and metaphysical ideas have very real ecological consequences, not only dictating the way people live but also the collective impact they have on their surrounding environment. Indigenous people are

[4] For example, the village of Sar Luk defined 1949 as 'the year that we ate the forest of the Stone Spirit Gôo'.

remarkably aware of this, and their interest in the environment is now increasingly described as 'native science' (or, more aptly, given the cultural and natural pluralities discussed here, as native sciences—in the plural). As Leroy Little Bear points out, "[i]f science is a search for reality and if science is a search for knowledge at the leading edges of the humanly knowable, then there are 'sciences' other than the Western science of measurement" (2000, x). Gregory Cajete defines 'native science'—which, he adds, 'is most akin to what Western science calls environmental science or ecology' (2000, 4)—as 'a metaphor for a wide range of tribal processes of perceiving, thinking, acting and "coming to know" that have evolved through human experience with the natural world. Native science is born of a lived and storied participation with the natural landscape. To gain a sense of Native science one must become open to the roles of sensation, perception, imagination, emotion, symbols and spirit as well as that of concept, logic and rational empiricism' (2). He then proceeds to explain in details the philosophical underpinnings of Native science, as much as its axiology and practices. The main referents of native sciences are the land, the idea of renewal and the tools of storytelling (particularly cultural emergence stories, commonly known as cosmogonies). Individual creativity plays a particular role, at times potentially greater or more central than the pursuit of universal objectivity. This is what Cajete calls the 'metaphoric mind' (28).

Elders Oren Lyons and Henrietta Mann assert that "reality is more than just facts and figures collected so that humankind might wisely use resources. Rather, to know 'it'—reality—requires respect for the relationships and relatives that constitute the complex web of life' (Wildcat, 2009, 9). As a result, ethical positioning, ontology and epistemology are intertwined in a single cohesive whole. To 'know' is to 'act ethically'. They further summarize the key tenets of this intertwining of science and ethics as follows.

- Being humble, developing the humility to understand that humans, are not (and cannot be) in control.
- Reintroducing a sacred dimension—and related reverence—to the way in which the cosmos is viewed. "According to some Indian herbalists, plants are referred to as the 'hair of the Earth Mother'" (Cajete, 2000, 111).
- An appreciation of experiential, situated and contextual knowledge, as well as the understanding that knowledge is transmitted through experiential modes of pedagogy and communication.
- An acknowledgment of the inherent linguistic and metaphysical plurality of languages and metaphysics that are connected to specific places.
- The understanding that knowledge is inherently relational and not objective and abstract: 'we can only know ourselves through our relationships with relatives in the natural world' (Wildcat, 2009, 69).
- Embracing the idea that relationality leads to seeing the world as comprised of all relatives: in the Lakota expression quoted above, *Mitákuye Oyásin* 'we are all related' (Wildcat, 2009, 69).
- Realizing collaboration ought to be favoured over competition.

- Paying attention to the 'seven generations' principle, the idea to take into consideration the effects that a particular decision taken now will have upon people seven generations removed into the future. A particular version of the seven generations principle is reported by Wildcat: 'Each one of us is the seventh generation—at the centre of life, preceded by three generations and followed by three generations. Our decisions … would take into account the knowledge of our ancestors—an intellectual and spiritual inheritance—and the responsibilities we have for our children and future generations, a sort of intellectual and spiritual trusteeship' (Wildcat, 2009, 91).

Native science (intended as the inextricable interplay of ontology, epistemology and axiology) and Indigenous jurisprudence are, therefore, deeply intertwined, far more than their colonial counterparts. Yugumbeh scholar Christine Black notes how, 'by telling a cosmological story from [her] ancestors' country', she demonstrates that she is 'legally patterned into the web of Law stories that have weaved [her] ancestors into reality' (2011, 4). She then proceeds to articulate how the Law is deeply rooted in the Land through a definition of jurisprudence, *talngai-gawarima*, 'that allows Indigenous peoples to be their voice of authority when expressing the jurisprudence of their ancient laws. This legal ordering is an act of naming—a naming of the Law that is rooted in the Land' (12). The interplay between law, myth and experiential practices had been captured, particularly in relation to sub-saharian Africa, by Norbert Rouland in his classic *Legal Anthropology* (1994). In New Zealand, the *marae* are Māori meeting places of formality and protocol, and are made up of a sacred courtyard and a collection of buildings, including a meeting house. To enter into a *marae* is to enter into a distinct cosmological space. 'Carved walls and woven flax inlays surround the interior of the meeting house, a space empty of furniture and footwear, a place where the spoken word holds power and pledges become law', writes Christine Black. 'This is a law that is not enforced, but rather reinforced through song, oratory and ritual into the very character of each participants; it is a law that calls each individual to be a voice of authority on that in which they have participated and to which they have agreed. The *marae* is a place where the Māori individual is patterned into a cosmology and *whakapapa* (genealogy)' (2011, 90).

Traditional ecological wisdom is conceived of in normative terms that see nature and law as inseparably intertwined. Such inseparability, however, is not necessarily couched within a discourse that emphasizes reason and logic as the epistemological architraves of this ecological normativity and legality. On the contrary, at the core of the ecological normativity and legality of many Indigenous peoples today is the awareness that 'we live in a world of mysterious relationships'. 'Unlike the colonial system imposed upon us, it was not imposed, but rather lived', writes Irene Watson, and 'knowledge of law came through living, singing and storytelling. Law is lived, sung, danced, painted, eaten … Law inheres in all things and is alive in all things' (2015, 12). 'The ancestors—human, animal and plants—are our relations and connect us to law' (14). As a result,

> [f]or First Nations Peoples, ownership of the land is an alien idea. In capitalist thought ruwe [Country, or land] becomes "property", a commodity, which can be traded or sold. The

> Nunga relationship to ruwe is more complex. We live as a part of the natural world; we are in the natural world. The natural world is us ... we nurture it as we do ourselves. ... Colonialists consider the land as belonging to them. This is a different idea from that of belonging to land and having a kinship or ngaitji relationship to it. (16)

The patterns evinced from empirical observation alone, in other words, are inscribed in a 'world [that] seems alive with relationships we cannot see, except as they make their presence felt in other relationships which we *can* see' (Kane, 1998, 40). Law is thus often presented in the form of narratives, stories and poems, which Christine Black calls 'oratories', in order to 'emphasize their spoken and public quality. Unlike Western poetry, which is often individualized, [Indigenous] poems are collective—designed to enable us to "feel", as a group that the Land is celebrated as the Law' (2011, 25). Furthermore, storytelling is connected to a particular geography and a particular period, season, or time. 'A human being', Morris writes, 'is a vehicle for the telling of a story. However, the story cannot be told without the land if the audience is to have complete comprehension. To talk of the great emu and the eggs it lays means nothing unless you can see the piece of topography that depicts this event' (1991, 33). Cosmological narratives contain complex normative and legal elements. Examples of this are the White Buffalo Calf Woman narrative, according to which White Buffalo Calf Woman 'brought the Sacred Pipe to the Lakota, ... through [which] the ceremonies and rituals of the Lakota are empowered' (Gunn Allen, 1992, 344). In this sense 'the source of the land [and the law] is manifested as a recognizable spiritual entity, which instructs the newcomers in the Law and the lawful behaviour' (Black, 2011, 127).

Many of the ideas presented in this section were used by Chief Sealth in his 1853 oration, and books like *Black Elk Speaks* popularized them. Unsurprisingly, US Secretary of the Interior Stewart Udall's history of American conservation characterized Native Americans as the first ecologists (Nash, 1989, 118). The clashes between these worldviews and their colonial counterparts, however, were apparent from the onset of the colonial encounter. As Nash remarks, '[t]raditional tribal cultures professed incredulity at the white tendency to objectify, desacralize and exploit nature. The idea of owning the land was especially unthinkable ... They balked at the notion of exchanging habitat for money. Ownership of nature appeared in their eyes morally wrong, a form of slavery' (1989, 118). However, that notwithstanding, the detrimental impact of colonialism on Indigenous worldviews continues to the present day. In fact, the term often used to refer to Indigenous legality, 'customary law', is a colonial misnomer. As Zulu philosopher Mogobe Ramose notes,

> customary law is not a neutral, value-free scientific classification in the sphere of jurisprudence. On the contrary, customary law is, properly construed, a historical and value-laden experience and concept. As a historical experience, customary law is the manifestation of power relations often privileging the position and ideas of the powerful over the weak. Seen from this perspective ... customary law is the name conferred by the conqueror in the unjust wars of colonization upon the living law of the Indigenous conquered peoples. (2006, 363)

8.3.3 Environmental Colonialism

As mentioned above, the impact of colonialism on Indigenous worldviews has been, and continues to be, deeply pervasive. As Descola writes, "[t]he notion of a 'wilderness', with all its connotations of *terra nullius,* of an original and preserved naturalness, an ecosystem to be protected against the degradations liable to be introduced by human beings, certainly runs contrary to the Aboriginals' own concept of the environment and the multiple relations that they have established with it, and above all it ignores the subtle transformations that they have produced in it' (2013, 35). Yet, such an idea has been used to displace Indigenous peoples from their original territories twice. Firstly, by imagining such a 'wilderness' as a place to be 'civilized' by the colonial project, and then again by imagining such a 'wilderness' as a place to be preserved and protected from human intervention. The dispossession is not a relic of a colonial past, but continues to the present day. Dzil Nchaa Si An, 'Big Sacred Mountain' in Western Apache (also known as 'Mount Graham' in colonial times), is considered one of the four holy mountains by Apache people; yet, multiple organizations have been allowed to set up a series of large telescopes and observatories under a Congressional waiver of US environmental laws for (purportedly universal) scientific reasons. The same sense of impotence toward the desecration of one's sacred geography is certainly experienced, among countless examples, by the Lakota people in relation to the Paha Sapa (or 'Black Hills', where Mount Rashmore has been carved out of one of the most sacred Lakota mountains), or by the Anangu people of the Norther Territory of Australia in relation to Uluru (or 'Ayers Rock'). Tanganekald/Meintangk scholar Irene Watson uses the term 'muldarbi' (loosely translated as 'demon spirit', but more precisely 'an ancestor spirit who failed to uphold the best interests of the collective in relation to the natural world') to describe 'the phenomenon of colonialism and the impact it has had upon Indigenous Peoples' lives, laws and territories, worldwide' (2015, 1). She also adopts the term 'raw law' to describe a natural system of obligations and benefits flowing from an Aboriginal ontology. "The metaphor 'raw' is used to describe Indigenous laws and to draw a connection to pre-invasion identities as naked peoples" (9).

In a profoundly patronizing manner, Article 22 of the League of Nations Covenant had placed, tribal peoples, considered incapable of withstanding the 'strenuous conditions of the modern world', under the direct tutelage of the League of Nations itself as a 'sacred trust of civilization'. The racist implications of such a patronizing attitude (which led—and still leads—to ethnocide, if not always physical genocide) are that

> while we [in the West] have been celebrating and developing technological wizardry, somehow the other peoples of the world have been static and intellectually idle … [Yet] All peoples in all places are always dancing with new possibilities for life. Nor is technology per se a threat to the integrity of culture. The Lakota did not stop being Sioux when they gave up the bow and arrow for the rifle any more than a rancher … ceased being a Canadian when he gave up the horse and buggy in favour of the automobile. It is neither change nor technology that threatens the integrity of culture. It is power, the crude face of domination. (Davis, 2009, 166–7)

The historical imposition of particular worldviews on Indigenous peoples whose physical and political power is less than that of their colonial counterparts is thus also complemented by the risk of essentializing and stereotyping Indigenous peoples by attributing a set of assumed characteristics that crystallize their existence within a static (and often imagined) view of history. The famous and often-quoted speech of Duwamish leader Chief Seeathl, for example (a version of which is reproduced in Appendix six) has often been viewed as 'the quintessential expression of the potential richness of the ecological themes shared by Native and scientific visions of the natural world' (Suzuki & Knudtson, 1992, xx). However, as Suzuki and Knudtson show, the text was mostly apocryphal, and while it is certainly an impressive ecological text in its own rights, it also represents the romanticization of Indigenous peoples, whose views are often reduced to those of quasi-mystical (if not entirely mystical) ecological prophets. Modern versions of this myth (already encountered in Tacitus's *Germania* and Rousseau's romantic version of the noble savage) can be seen in filmic representations of Indigenous peoples (for example the film *Mission*) and of imaginary natives (the *Na'avi* people of the fictional world of Pandora in James Cameron's movie *Avatar* are an apt representation of this). While the ecological knowledge displayed by Indigenous people is outside the realm of doubt, their cultural milieus are far more complex, and do not exist in a historical vacuum, they are outside the 'arcadia in the zoo' imagery to which Nature is often relegated.

The process of dispossession of Indigenous worldviews can thus operate more subtly, under the guise of adopting Indigenous worldviews as (often fabled) primaeval expressions of modern colonial ideas. As a result, it is important to reassert that Indigenous worldviews, even in the fullness of their ecological depth and richness, are *not* 'examples' of any Earth Jurisprudence, Earth Law, or ecological jurisprudence. They are distinct and unique, even though, naturally, many ideas overlap.

Within the realm of law (and particularly ecological jurisprudence), similar subtle processes of dispossession occur. It has been argued with me that, since the concept of rights has a European history, the imposition of a rights of Nature discourse on Indigenous peoples leads to an inevitable imposition of colonial principles upon Indigenous people (Pelizzon, 2014, 186). Such an assertion, however, conceptually deprives Indigenous peoples of their strategic agency, which they have displayed in their involvement in domestic and international rights of Nature initiatives (as discussed above). Moreover, it denies them the cultural adaptation skills deployed by all cultures (and legal orders) around the planet. Additionally, it fails to recognize that legal anthropologists and comparative lawyers (Llewellyn & Hoebel, 1941; Pospisil, 1971; Rouland, 1994; Sacco, 1980) have, over the course of well over a century, devised a highly refined methodology to engage with the question of 'legal equivalents', as I will discuss shortly.

Power differentials thus matter, greatly. Power differentials may entail direct colonial impositions, through the forcible imposition of colonial decisions through the use of force, such as dispossession of traditional lands, forced removal of children, forced relocation of entire communities as well as the more brutal and violent examples that history, sadly, provides. Or they may exert indirect colonial impositions, either via the universalization of novel principles (including ecological ones) that

Indigenous peoples are suddenly bound to uphold, or via the subtle essentializing and stereotyping of Indigenous peoples, such as in the construct of the 'ecological Native' or the determination of what constitutes an acceptable cultural and legal transplant. This is what Cepek (2011) defines as *environmentality*: the risk that environmentalist programmes and movements operate as a form of governmentality (in a Foucauldian sense). Environmental paradigms have been forced upon Indigenous actors in a manner similar to governments with the 'subjects' they create. The result is a host of cultural impositions under the aegis of environmental programmes ostensibly directed toward the care and protection of the environment. In presenting a case study of the Cofan people of Zabalo in the far northeastern Amazonian region of Ecuador, Cepek writes that '[p]erhaps the most important form of alienation involved in Cofan performance of scientific conservation is that the [Indigenous] workers perform the forms of knowledge they produce' (507). Since most Indigenous people currently live in a condition of asymmetry of sovereign power, colonial governments can ultimately exert hegemonic power over traditional cultures, both as a whole and in relation to specific cultural traits. The subtler risks of environmental colonialism are always to be guarded against and one ought to always remember that all interactions among distinct worldviews are always political, not just intercultural.

An even subtler risk of intercultural dispossession, finally may be an unintended consequence of modernity. As Wildcatt recalls, one of the elders who took his sociology course lamented the risk that 'new knowledge' may displace the space occupied by the old songs, which he feared losing. 'I wonder how many good songs, practices and ceremonies about living well in this world humankind may have collectively lost because modern human societies so little value knowledges found beyond the protocols of narrowly defined scientific inquiry' (2009, 14), Wildcat ponders. The problem is that 'as one identifies the construction of knowledge with the logic of experiment … one forgets the knowledge of experience, knowledges gained through attentive living, such as singing and drumming' (15).

In summary, a meaningful dialogical engagement with Indigenous legal orders requires a distinct epistemological approach capable of considering and embracing the distinct ontological and cosmological parameters within which they operate. The constant awareness of the interrelatedness between ontological and epistemological concerns and positive legal issues—or, in other words, between worldviews and law—cannot be overemphasized when dealing with legal traditions as distinct and varied as those of the world's Indigenous peoples. In engaging with such legal traditions, it is not possible to limit the discussion to the boundaries of the 'legal' as construed and perceived—however successfully—in Western legal philosophies. Possibly more importantly, moreover, since Indigenous cultures exist and operate from a position of subordination toward the colonial governments established on their ancestral lands, it is hardly possible to truly, respectfully and fully embrace the cultural diversity contained in their worldviews without acknowledging the continuity of colonial relationships. Westra (2008) writes that 'the interdependence between the basic/survival rights of indigenous peoples, their biological integrity and the ecological integrity of their lands … is constantly under attack through the economic activities of developed countries that view the use of aboriginal lands and peoples as their right, with little or no consideration for the gravity of the consequences that ensue'. Consequently, colonial and post-colonial political issues regarding the status and legal position of Indigenous peoples cannot be separated from an engagement with their distinct environmental philosophies and their articulation of such philosophies in normative terms. As far as ecological jurisprudence is concerned, issues of social justice and environmental sustainability form part of an inseparable continuum.

8.3.4 The Common Ground We Always Seek

It may very well be, as Wildcat suggests, that '[t]he language of the Earth, her mother tongue, is one best understood through he many dialects known by indigenous peoples around the world' (2009, 17). Davis speaks of a greater 'ethnosphere', an 'intellectual and spiritual web that envelops the planet' (2009, 2), comprised of the myriad of the world's human cultures, the variety and diversity of which is as crucial as the maintenance of the biosphere. Most of these cultures have adapted over the millennia to very specific environment, and thus their cultural parameters represent the best localized adaptive knowledge humanity possess. As a result, an 'etnosphere' is 'the sum total of all thoughts and intuitions, myths and beliefs, ideas and inspirations brought into being by the human imagination … It is the product of our dreams, the embodiment of our hopes, the symbol of all we are and all that we, as a wildly inquisitive and astonishingly adaptive species, have created' (Davis, 2009, 2). Davis shows how cultural adaptations to environmental conditions have developed in extremely nuanced and precise ways, from the strategies of the San people of the Kalahari desert during the Season of the Brown Hyena (the worse months of the year) to the 'wayfinders' of Polynesia, the geographically largest human culture sphere, from the 'Peoples of the Anaconda' of the Northwestern Amazonian basin, for whom 'rivers are not just routs of communication, [but rather] the veins of the earth, the link between the living and the dead, the paths along which the ancestors travelled at the beginning of time' (95), to the sense of belonging and connection to the *apus*, the protective mountain spirits who direct the destiny of those born in their shadows, of the Andean Cordillera. All these culture, Andrés Edwards notes, 'possess traditional knowledge that forms part of the cultural DNA of the planet' (2010, 20).

For these many ontological, epistemological, normative and legal 'dialects' to intersect and meaningfully interact (as equals), it is necessary to approach them with a particular comparative awareness. Gerard-René de Groot (2023) introduced the idea of 'legal equivalents', a series of protocols and practices that are seen as functionally equivalent, as the comparative tool to make distinct legal orders mutually commensurable. In this particular instance, the 'function' to be identified as equivalent can be found in the central concern of eco-jurisprudential initiatives: the idea of the 'environment', 'nature' or the ultimate nonhuman other, or in other words, the many *biospheres* (the material spaces with which human groups relate), the many *ethnospheres* (the many ideas within which such biospheres are culturally construed) and the many *nomospheres* (the many ways in which human conduct is constructed in relation to these imagined *bio-ethnospheres*) of the world. This leads to a number of consequences: firstly, to embrace ontological and cosmological differences as part of the legal terrain to be explored by ecological jurisprudence. Secondly, to acknowledge that political and environmental issues are inextricably inseparable, and thus issues of renegotiated sovereignty, political independence and self-determination of Indigenous peoples are fundamental to the project of a truly universal ecological jurisprudence just as much as issues of environmental protection are. Thirdly, it means to draw on disciplines and theoretical perspectives that are effective vehicles for establishing the cognitive bridges required to facilitate an understanding of the cultural and legal milieu of Indigenous (and other) worldviews. Finally, it means to adopt a truly dialogical approach in order to establish meaningful conversations among distinct cultural and legal traditions.[5]

Ecological jurisprudence thus creates a unique opportunity to negotiate the many pluriversal normativities of the many human *nomospheres* by comparatively relating to the nonhuman world. In other words, the reference to a corporeally common nonhuman other allows distinct legal orders to enter into a dialogue with each other, a dialogue focused on the normative and legal quest for the most appropriate way to *be* in the universe. Perhaps for the first time, a tangible term of reference—the nonhuman other—may allow distinct, and often radically opposed, legal traditions to engage in equitable legal comparison and in a pluralistic legal exchange. In a conversation with a local Elder, Cormac Cullinan once asked how a common ground could be found between two separate parties to a case of environmental litigation. Partly bemused, the Elder replied, that it was simple, since 'the common ground we always seek is already here, always beneath our feet'.

References

Abram, D. (1996). *The spell of the sensuous*. Vintage Books.

Anaya, J. (2004). *Indigenous peoples in international law* (2nd ed.). Oxford University Press.

Anker, A. (2020). Ecological jurisprudence and Indigenous relational ontologies. Beyond the "ecological Indian"? In D. Anker, P. D. Burdon, G. Garver, M. Maloney, & C. Sbert (Eds.), *From environmental to ecological law*. Routledge.

Barrow, J. D., & Tipler, F. J. (1988). *The anthropic cosmological principle*. Oxford University Press.

Bellamy Foster, J., Clark, B., & York, R. (2010). *The ecological rift*. Monthly Review Press, New York.

Bennett, J. (2010). *Vibrant matter*. Duke University Press.

Bergson, H. (1998). *Creative evolution* (A. Mitchell, Trans.) Dover.

Berry, T. (2009). *The sacred universe*. Columbia University Press.

Bird Rose, D. (1988). Exploring an aboriginal land ethic. *Meanjin 4*, 378–387.

[5] This, of course, does not mean to accept unquestioningly all cultural traits, arguments and strategies that human traditions have spatially established in bio-specific context over millennia: the political specificity of particular issues does not necessarily entail cultural exceptionalism.

Black, C. F. (2011). *The land is the source of the law. A dialogic encounter with indigenous jurisprudence*. Routledge.

Bogost, I. (2012). *Alien phenomenology*. University of Minnesota Press.

Borrows, J. (1997–8). Frozen rights in Canada: Constitutional interpretation and the trickster. *American Indian Law Review, 22*, 37–64.

Bosselmann, K. (1995). *When two worlds collide: Society and ecology*. RSVP.

Boyd, D. R. (2017). *The rights of nature. A legal revolution that could save the world*. ECW.

Brassier, R. (2007). *Nihil unbound. Enlightenment and extinction*. Palgrave MacMillan.

Bryant, L. R. (2011). *The democracy of objects*. Open Humanities Press.

Burdon, P. D. (2013). The Earth community and ecological Jurisprudence. *Oñati Socio-Legal Series, 3*(5), 815–837.

Burdon, P. (2011). The great jurisprudence. In P. Burdon (Ed.), *Exploring wild law: The philosophy of Earth jurisprudence*. Wakefield Press.

Burdon, P. D. (2015). *Earth jurisprudence. Private property and the environment*. Routledge.

Cajete, G. (2000). *Native science*. Clear Light Publishers.

Capra, F., & Mattei, U. (2015). *The ecology of law: Toward a legal system in tune with nature and community*. Berrett-Koehler.

Capra, F. (1975). *The Tao of physics*. Shambala.

Cepek, M. L. (2011). Foucault in the forest: Questioning environmentality in Amazonia. *American Ethnologist, 38*(3), 501–515.

Chroust, A. H. (1974). The Philosophy of Law of St Thomas Aquinas: His fundamental ideas and some of his historical precursors. *American Journal of Jurisprudence, 19*, 1–38.

Convention on Biological Diversity (Rio de Janeiro) 5 June 1992, in force 29 December 1993, 31 ILM 822 (1992) (1992 Biodiversity Convention).

Cover, R. (1983). Nomos and narrative. *Harvard Law Review, 97*(4–68), 13.

Crowe, J. (2019). *Natural law and the nature of law*. Cambridge University Press.

Cullinan, C. (2011). *Wild law* (2nd ed.). First Published 2002. Chelsea Green Publishing.

Curd, M. (1998). The laws of nature. In M. Curd & J. A. Cover (Eds.), *Philosophy of science: The central issues*. WW Norton and Company.

D'Entrèves, *Natural law* (revised ed., 1970) 16.

Davies, M. (2017). *Asking the law question* (4th ed.). Thomson Reuters.

Davies, M. (2022). *EcoLaw: Legality, life, and the normativity of nature*. Routledge.

Davis, W. (2009). *The wayfinders. Why ancient wisdom matters in the modern world*. House of Anansi Press.

De Groot, G. R. (2023). Legal translation. In J. M. Smits (Ed.), *Elgar Encyclopedia of comparative law* (2nd ed.). Edward Elgar.

De Lucia, V. (2013). Towards an ecological philosophy of law: A comparative discussion. *Journal of Human Rights and the Environment, 4*, 167.

DeLanda, M. (2016). *Assemblage theory*. Edinburgh University Press.

Deleuze, G. (1994). *Difference and repetition* (P. Patton, Trans.) Columbia University Press.

Descola, P. (2013). *Beyond nature and culture* (J. Lloyd, Trans.). First Published in French 2005. University of Chicago Press.

Douzinas, C. (2005). Oubliez critique. *Law and Critique, 16*(1), 47–69.

Edwards, A. R. (2010). *Thriving beyond sustainability. Pathways to a resilient society*. New Society Publishers.

Ehrlich, E. (1936). *Principles of the sociology of law* (W. L. Moll Trans.) Harvard University Press.

Elkin, P. (1964). *Australian aborigines*. Doubleday.

Escobar, A. (2017). *Pluriversal politics*. Duke University Press.

Finnis, J. (1980). *Natural law and natural rights*. Oxford University Press.

Forencich, F. (2021). *Beware false tigers*. Exuberant Animal.

Freeman, M. D. A. (2014). *Lloyd's introduction to jurisprudence* (9th ed.). Sweet & Maxwell.

Fuller, L. L. (1968). *Anatomy of the law*. Praeger.

Galeano, E. (1985). *Memory of fire*. Pantheon Books.

Gare, A. (2017). *The philosophical foundations of ecological civilization. A manifesto for the future.* Routledge.
Gillespie, A. (1997). *International environmental law policy and ethics.* Oxford University Press.
Glenn, H. P. (2010). *Legal traditions of the world* (4th ed.). Oxford University Press.
Glenn, A. (2011). Symbiocene. http://healthearth.blogspot.com.au/2011/05/symbiocene.html
Goldtooth, T. (2008). Protecting the web of life: Indigenous knowledge and Biojustice. In M. K. Nelson (Ed.), *Original instructions. Indigenous teachings for a sustainable future.* Bear & Company.
Goodman, M., & Thornton, J. (2017). *Client Earth.* Scribe.
Grear, A. (2020). Legal imaginaries and the Anthropocene: "Of" and "for." *Law and Critique, 31*, 361–366.
Grosz, E. (2017). *The incorporeal. Ontology, ethics, and the limits of materialism.* Columbia University Press.
Gunn Allen, P. (1992). *The sacred hoop: Recovering the feminine in American Indian traditions.* Beacon Press.
Hallowell, A. I. (1976). Ojibwa ontology, behavior and world view. In A. I. Hallowell (Ed.), *Contributions in anthropology: Selected papers of A. Irving Hallowell.* University of Chicago Press.
Hamilton, C. (2017). *Defiant Earth: The fate of humans in the Anthropocene.* Polity.
Haraway, D. (2016). *Staying with the trouble. Making Kin in the Chthulucene.* Duke University Press.
Harman, G. (2002). *Tool-being: Heidegger and the metaphysics of objects.* Open Court.
Harman, G. (2010). *Towards speculative realism.* Zero Books.
Harman, G. (2016). *Immaterialism.* Polity Press.
Hart, H. L. A. (1963). *The concept of law.* Clarendon.
Harvey, D. (1993). The nature of environment: The dialectics of social and environmental change. In R. Miliband & L. Panitch (Eds.), *Social register 1993: Real problems, false solutions.* Merlin.
Heisenberg, W. (1963). *Physics and philosophy.* Allen & Unwin.
Hudson, W. D. (Ed.). (1969). *The is/ought question.* McMillan.
Hulktrantz, Å. (1987). *Native religions of North America.* Harper and Row.
ILO Convention on Indigenous Tribal Peoples, No 169 of 1989, International Labour Conference (entered into force 5 September 1991).
Jagtenberg, J., & McKie, D. (1997). *Eco-impacts and the greening of postmodernity. New maps for communication studies, cultural studies, and sociology.* Sage Publications.
Jullien, F. (1995). *The propensity of things. Towards a history of efficacy in China* (J. Lloyd, Tran.). Zone.
Kane, S. (1998). *Wisdom of the mythtellers.* Broadview Press.
Kauffman, C. M., & Martin, P. L. (2021). *The politics of rights of nature.* MIT Press.
Kelly, J. M. (1992). *A short history of Western legal theory.* Clarendon Press.
Kim Polistina, K. (2009). Cultural literacy. In A. Stibbe (Ed.), *The handbook of sustainability literacy. Skills for a changing world.* Green Books.
Klein, N. (2019). *On fire. The burning case for a green new deal.* Penguin.
Knudtson, P., & Suzuki, D. (1992). *Wisdom of the elders.* Allen & Unwin.
Koch, A., Brierley, C., Maslin, M. M., & Lewis, S. L. (2019). Earth system impacts of the European arrival and Great Dying in the Americas after 1492. *Quaternary Science Reviews, 207*, 13–36.
Kohn, E. (2013). *How forests think.* University of California Press.
LaDuke, W. (1999). *All our relations.* South End Press.
LaDuke, W. (2008). Protecting the culture and genetics of wild rice. In M. K. Nelson (Ed.), *Original instructions. Indigenous teachings for a sustainable future.* Bear & Company.
Latour, B. (1999). *Pandora's hope.* Harvard University Press.
Latour, P. (2004). *Politics of nature.* Harvard University Press.
Latour, B. (2017). *Facing Gaia. Eight lectures on the new climatic regime* (C. Porter, Trans.) Polity Press, Cambridge.

Little Bear, L. (2000). Foreword. In G. Cajete. *Native science. Natural laws of interdependence.* Clear Light Publishers.

Llewellyn, K., & Hoebel, E. A. (1941). *The Cheyenne way.* University of Oklahoma Press.

Long, J. (1901). *Voyages and travels of an Indian interpreter and trader.* First Published 1791. Arthur Clark.

Luther Standing Bear. (1933). *Land of the spotted eagle.* Houghton Mifflin.

Lyon, P. (2011). Extracting norms from nature: A biogenic approach to ethics. In P. D. Burdon (Ed.), *Exploring wild law: The philosophy of Earth jurisprudence.* Wakefield Press.

Malm, A., & Hronborg, A. (2014). The geology of mankind? A critique of the Anthropocene narrative. *The Anthropocene Review, 1*(1), 62–69.

Marder, M. (2013). *Plant-thinking.* Columbia University Press.

Martinez, D., Salmón, E., & Nelson, M. K. (2008). Restoring indigenous history and culture to nature. In M. K. Nelson (Ed.), *Original instructions. Indigenous teachings for a sustainable future.* Bear & Company.

Mathews, F. (2003). *For love of matter.* State University of New York Press.

Matthews, D. (2021). *Earthbound. The aesthetics of sovereignty in the Anthropocene.* Edinburgh University Press.

McKibben, M. (2010). *Earth. Making life on a tough new planet.* St Martin's Griffin.

Meadows, D. H. (2008). *Thinking in systems.* Chelsea Green.

Meilassoux, Q. (2008). *After finitude: An essay on the necessity of contingency.* Continuum.

Melissaris, E. (2009). *Ubiquitous law. Legal theory and the space for legal pluralism.* Routledge.

Mijieski, K. J., & Beck, S. H. (2011). *Pachakutik and the rise and decline of the Ecuadorian indigenous movement.* University of Ohio Press.

Morris, C. (1991). Oral tradition under threat: An Australian Aboriginal experience. *National Ethnic Association Journal, 14*(2), 33–40.

Morton, T. (2007). *Ecology without nature.* Harvard University Press.

Mylius, B. (2017). *Earth jurisprudence.* Elsevier. https://doi.org/10.1016/B978-0-12-409548-9.10449-X

Nagel, T. (1974). What is it like to be a bat? *The Philosophical Review, 83*(4), 435–450.

Nash, R. (1989). *The rights of nature.* University of Wisconsin Press.

Nelson, M. K. (2008). Lighting the sun of our future—How these teachings can provide illumination. In M. K. Nelson (Ed.), *Original instructions. Indigenous teachings for a sustainable future.* Bear & Company.

Pascoe, B. (2014). *Dark Emu.* Magabala Books.

Passarin d'Entreves, A. (1951). *Natural law: An introduction to legal philosophy.* Hutchinson.

Peat, F. D. (2002). *Blackfoot physics.* WeiserBooks.

Pelizzon, A. (2012). *Laws of the land: Traditional land protocols, native title and legal pluralism in the Illawarra.* Lambert Academic Publishing.

Pelizzon, A. (2014). Earth laws, rights of nature and legal pluralism. In M. Maloney & P. D. Burdon (Eds.), *Wild law—In practice.* Routledge.

Pospisil, L. J. (1971). *Anthropology of law: A comparative theory of law.* Harper & Row.

Putnam, R. A. (2017). Reflections concerning moral objectivity. In G. Marchetti & S. Marchetti (Eds.), *Facts and values: The ethics and metaphysics of normativity.* Routledge.

Rakhyun, K. E., & Bosselmann, K. (2013). International environmental law in the Anthropocene: Towards a purposive system of multilateral environmental agreements. *Transnational Environmental Law, 2*, 285–309.

Ramose, M. (2006). The king as memory and symbol. In M. Hinz (Ed.), *The Shae of leaves.* University of Namibia Press.

Ritchie, D. G. (1894). Natural rights. *Philosophical Review, 4*, 233.

Rouland, N. (1994). *Legal anthropology* (P. G. Planel Trans.). First Published 1988. Athlone Press.

Rowlands, M. (2012). *Can animals be moral?* Oxford University Press.

Sacco, R. (1980). *Introduzione al Diritto Comparato.* Giappichelli.

Schmitt, C. (2006). *The Nomos of the Earth in the international law of the Jus Publicum Europaeum* (G. L. Ulmen Trans.). First Published 1950. Telos Press.
Scruton, R. (1981). *Kant*. Oxford University Press.
Seed, J., Macy, J., Fleming, P., & Naess, A. (2007). *Thinking like a mountain. Towards a council of all beings*. First Published 1988. New Catalyst Books.
Serres, M. (1995). *The natural contract* (E. MacArthur, & W. Paulson, Trans.). First Published 1990. University of Michigan.
Shiva, V. (2005). *Earth democracy. Justice, sustainability, and peace*. South End Press.
Simondon, G. (2017). *On the mode of existence of technical objects* (C. Malaspina & J. Rogove, Trans.). First Published 1958. Univocal Publishing.
Soqluman, N., & Hung, H. (2010). *A Bunun perspective*. Paper presented at the Keeping the Fire Conference, Second Australian Conference on Wild Law and Earth Jurisprudence, Wollongong.
Spencer, W. B., & Gillen, F. J. (1899). *The native tribes of Central Australia*. Macmillan.
Sterlin, J. (2020). The civilicene and its alternatives. In J. Christopher, C. J. Orr, K. Kish, & B. Jennings (Eds.), *Liberty and the ecological crisis: Freedom on a finite planet*. Routledge.
Tallacchini, M. (1996). *Diritto per la Natura. Ecologia e Filosofia del Diritto*. Giappichelli.
Tanasescu, M. (2022). *Understanding the rights of nature*. Transcript Verlag.
Taum, R. (2010). *A Hawaiian indigenous voice*. Paper presented at the Keeping the Fire Conference, Second Australian Conference on Wild Law and Earth Jurisprudence, Wollongong.
Terkildsen, A. (2019). *A path to protect our ancestors. Indigenous communities and Earth jurisprudence*. Thesis, Dartmouth College.
Tuoori, K. (2002). *Critical legal positivism*. Ashgate.
United Nations Declaration on the Rights of Indigenous Peoples.
Vargas Rocancio, I. D. (2017a). Plants and the law: Vegetal ontologies and the rights of nature. A perspective from Latin America. *Australian Feminist Law Journal, 43*(1), 67–87.
Vargas Rocancio, I. D. (2017b). Nomadic ecologies: Plants, embodied knowledge, and temporality in the Colombian Amazon. *Boletín de Antropologia, 32*(53), 255–276.
Vargas Rocancio, I. D. (2020). Towards a relational theory of legal agency for transitions into the Ecozoic. In J. Christopher, C. J. Orr, K. Kish, & B. Jennings (Eds.), *Liberty and the ecological crisis: Freedom on a finite planet*. Routledge.
Watson, I. (2015). *Aboriginal peoples, colonialism and international law. Raw law*. Routledge.
Westra, L. (2008). *Environmental justice and the rights of indigenous peoples. International and domestic perspectives*. Earthscan.
Wildcat, D. R. (2009). *Red alert. Saving the planet with indigenous knowledge*. Fulcrum.
Zelle, A. R., Wilson. G., Adam, R., & Greene, H. F. (Eds.). (2021). *Earth law. Emerging ecocentric law—A guide for practitioners*. Wolters Kluver.
Žižek, S. (1993). *Tarrying with the negative: Kant, Hegel, and the critique of ideology*. Duke University Press.
Žižek, S. (2002). *For they know not what they do: Enjoyment as a political factor*. Verso.
Žižek, S. (2006). *The parallax view*. MIT Press.

Chapter 9
Conclusion

This book has hopefully shown the uncontroversial emergence of an ecological jurisprudence over the past century or so. Inasmuch as ecology has permeated the whole of Western and dominant disciplines, an ecological awareness has entered the realm of legal theory and an ecological jurisprudence has thus followed. Importantly, the emergence of an ecological jurisprudence has occurred (and continues to occur) along an onto-axiological spectrum, ranging from a slightly enlightened anthropocentrism to far more radical ecocentrism. The many eco-jurisprudential initiatives that have occurred are also located within the same spectrum. Overall, the emergence of an ecological jurisprudence offers a novel and radical reconceptualization of law itself and almost inadvertent new 'grand narrative' of law. At the same time, it also represents an intercultural and internormative platform for legal orders traditionally operating within radical asymmetries of power to enter into a meaningful and equitable dialogue about the fate of humanity's interaction with the great nonhuman *other*. Moreover, the emergence of an ecological jurisprudence represents the possibility of extending the 'pluriversal' beyond the limits of the human and thus includes Nature not only as a strategic subject within the theatre of human legal relationships, but also as an active subject within a normative dialogue that transcends the confine of traditional legal (and philosophical) epistemology.

Crucial to the emergence of an ecological jurisprudence is a deep ecological (and, I would argue, intercultural) awareness. E O Wilson writes that '[s]ome believe that humanity should accept the ecological chaos we have created as just collateral damage to a brilliant destiny' (2017, 47). To them, at least 'in imagination, we may attain the status of what the astronomer Nikolai Kardashev called Type I civilization, a society in control of all the available energy on Earth' (48).[1] Against such a fantastic aspiration, however, Wilson contends, in truth, 'we stumble forward in hopeful chaos, trusting that the light on the horizon is the dawn and not the twilight … [and meanwhile] we are changing the atmosphere and climate away from conditions

[1] Furthermore, 'we could conceivably press on to Type II civilization, in control of available power in the Solar System, and even Type III civilization, taking control of all energy in the galaxy'.

A. Pelizzon, *Ecological Jurisprudence*, Contemporary Environmental Law and Policy,
https://doi.org/10.1007/978-981-96-0173-8_9

best for our bodies and minds, making things a lot more difficult for our descendants. And while at it, we are unnecessarily destroying a large part of the rest of life' (49).

Importantly, Wilson continues, '[t]he human impact is largely due to the excess of the many quotidian activities we perform just to get on with our personal lives'. Yet, he continues, '[t]hose activities have made us the most destructive species in the history of life … before the coming of humanity about two hundred thousand years ago, the rate of origin of new species per extinction of existing species was roughly one species per million species per year. As a consequence of human activity, it is believed that the current rate of extinction is between one hundred and one thousand times higher than it was originally, and all due to human activity' (54). Such human activities lead to an accelerated extinction rate that is the result of a combination of habitat destruction (including via climate change), invasive species, pollution (as a result of the chemically destructive effluents of human activities that damage the rest of life), population growth (and related increases in per capita consumption) and overhunting. Moreover, environmental resistances (species and phenomena that keep other species in check) are necessary for the balance of life, but humanity have dispensed with such resistances and are now operating unchecked. As David Suzuki and others remarked, we humans have become a 'superspecies' (not only one of the—by far—most numerous mammalian species on the planet, but also one whose ecological impact has been explosively amplified by technology) because '[i]n … a world of interconnectedness, every action has consequences… [As a result] since we [are] part of that world, we ha[ve] a responsibility to act properly to keep the world in order' (2007, 10). The capacity of humanity to alter the planet appears to have no boundaries other than itself and the deeper forces of ecology its own *hubris* may unleash. It follows that the checks and balances otherwise provided by an external environment must be internalized if humanity is to regulate its own presence in the world. In other words, these checks and balances must become normative and ethical, rather than ecological. Michel Serres writes that, '[t]hrough our mastery, we have become so much and so little masters of the Earth that it once again threatens to master us in turn. … Why must we now seek to master our mastery? Because, unregulated, exceeding its purpose, counterproductive, pure mastery is turning back on itself' (1995, 33–4).

Frank Forencich argues that we live in what he calls a 'mismatch', also defined as the 'evolutionary discordance hypothesis', which suggests that humans are not physiologically, psychologically and socially adapted to the materialities, social numbers and practices of the modern industrial world, leading to a chronic state of historical, circadian, autonomic, physical, microbial, social, bioregional, cultural and cosmological confusion. The modern 'psycho-physical angst', Forencich argues, 'is … the result of trying to live outside our normal ecological range' (2020, 30–4). Moreover, this book has argued that the mismatch could also be normative and legal. Indeed, many of us live as strangers in our natural homes, which act as veritable 'strange lands' to as, since '[h]igh speed travel gives us the ability to parachute into any bioregion with no real knowledge of the plants and animals on the ground. Most of the time we live as aliens' in the bioregion we inhabit (105).

Certainly, since Çatalhöyük and Göbekli Tepe, the two oldest remains of cities found in Turkey, we have progressively and increasingly become an urban species, physically disconnected from the rhythms and cycles of the rest of the beings and phenomena from which we depend for our own very existence and from the fates of all other species that are kept out of our urban lives. And we have exported the same mindset to the countryside, with monocultures that increasingly rely on the annihilation of most of the nonhuman world for their success. The shift to an ecological jurisprudence thus requires more than a shift of the mind, and it requires a shift of practice, where we can *see* on a daily basis, and be constantly reminded of, the world we share, the bounty of lives and cycles that surround us. Furthermore '[t]he modern supermarket holds the collective bounty of a thousand square miles of land, condensed and refined by the labor of thousands of people, powered by thousands of gallons fossil fuels and nitrogen fertilizers' (Forencich, 2020, 151). 'The modern world', Forencich continues, 'has become a twenty-four-hour distraction machine, a conspiracy against focused attention' (156). Importantly, such a 'mismatch' could be even subtler.

> Even when civilization provides us with sensible, healthy living conditions, it also tends to eclipse our primal attention to the living world. In the world of economics, we'd say that civilization has a displacement cost. That is, for all the time we spend paying attention to modern human innovations, commerce and culture, that's time that we *don't* spend paying attention to the very things that would normally sustain our lives and our sanity: the world of plants, animals, habitat and weather. For every hour that we're indoors, that's an hour that we're not outdoors. For every hour we spend shopping or doing work on the computer, that's an hour that we're *not* looking at the living world. And the contrast is stark. ... today, many of us go months, years, even entire lifetimes without substantive contact with the living habitat. (Forencich, 2021, 72-3)

This attentional shift is reflected in popular culture, and 'references to nature have been decreasing steadily in fiction books, song lyrics, and film storylines, whereas references to the human-made environment have not'. Freya Matthews notes that

> a culture deprived of any symbolic representation of the universe and of its own relation to it will be a culture of non-plussed, unmotivated individuals, set down inescapably in a world which makes no sense to them, and which accordingly baffles their agency. What are they to do in this world to which they do not belong? No natural directives appoint themselves. Self-interest is the only rational motive. Any other values smack of arbitrariness. Vocationless, such individuals must sink into apathy and alienation, or into the mindless and joyless pursuit of material ends. With no cosmological foundation for their identity, they invent precarious individual self-pictures, self-stories, ego-images, but their sense of who they are is tenuous. Metaphysically adrift, these individuals experience insecurity. (1991, 13)

If, as Aldo Leopold famously said, '[o]ne of the penalties of an ecological education is that one lives alone in a world of wounds', then the development (or re-development) of a deep ecological awareness appears to be the central demand of a healthier human relationship with the cosmos. That is, the understanding, as Matthew Fox writes, that 'our true home is the universe itself' (Fox 1994, 141). This understanding is at the core of an ecological jurisprudence. The concept of 'living well' central to many Andean eco-jurisprudential initiatives, in the Kichwa language of the

Indigenous people of Ecuador, is called *sumak kawsay*; in Spanish, it is *buen vivir*. The Buryat people of the Lake Baikal region, Osprey Orielle Lake (2013) notes, 'express it this way: "To live a life of honor is to live with *tegsh*," meaning to live in appreciation and balance with all of life'.

Such is the project of an ecological jurisprudence, then. Not to 'constrain' but to 'restrain' human activities. Not to 'limit' but to 'regulate' humanity's interaction with the cosmos. To see self-restraint not as a limit, but as an act of generous and respectful citizenry as active members of the cosmos. The project may very well be inspired by Gandhi's words that 'the earth provides enough resources for everyone's need, but not for some people's greed' (in Shiva, 2000, 131). This project, importantly, is not one of *submission*, as Daniel Matthews (2021) suggested in relation to Earth Jurisprudence (unless, by 'submission', one intends the acceptance of ecological forces greater than the human desire to control and reshape them), but rather one of normative *abundance*, where the number of normative subjects is expanded to include all entities.

The issue, moreover, is not one of harmonies with 'Nature' in the abstract sense, but rather with the specific, contextual and temporally situated natural environs in which we individually live. However, at the same time, rather than being geographically bounded, such a harmony is also understood in relation to the broader planet (and, indeed, cosmos) we inhabit, within the spectrum of biological and geological extremes that allow our existence, and within which our creativity can unfold. Moreover, as Cormac Cullinan once pointed out to me, the issue is not merely to live in harmony *with* Nature, but in harmony *within* Nature. The emergence of an ecological jurisprudence, therefore, does not represent a desire to maintain an imagined pristine Nature against human behaviour, but rather to regulate (and, as a result, constantly interrogate) human behaviour, individually and, more importantly, collectively.

The emergence of an ecological jurisprudence has proposed a number of solutions to the environmental predicament humanity is currently faced with. Theoretically speaking, a holistic approach marked by a hyper-precautionary principle seems to be the common denominator of all existing proposals. That is, the idea of considering the world as worthy of respect (either strategically or metaphysically) in itself, and, consequently, the ethical mandate not to interfere with the operation of the nonhuman world unless one cannot avoid it, and one cannot avoid it only for very specific needs (such needs may entail complex cultural activities, but a constant reflection on the impact of such activities—and an ongoing measurement of their ecological cost—is required). Certainly, consumerism is to be abandoned. Moreover, ecological jurisprudence challenges the existing boundaries of the normative and the legal, inviting a radical and unprecedented theoretical openness. Moreover, the theoretical standpoint discussed above leads to a clear prioritizing of proximate and ultimate goals to be pursued: ultimately, to both safeguard the continuity of human civilisation in its present (or more ecologically amended) form without any profound disruption and suffering, *and* to maintain (or to contribute to the maintenance of) 'nature' (the totality of present ecosystems) in their present form (i.e. to maintain homeostasis, and, or, to adapt to any required changes in a progressive manner). More immediately, the pursuit of such a goal may entail, among other things, a radical reduction of material consumptions—by valuing things more, by using and reusing them rather than disposing of them after one use, by reflecting upon (and reducing) individual needs (and by rejecting the illusion of competitive individualism and its related plague of monetary inequality, 'status', and 'fame')—and, likely, by reconsidering the overall population growth in relation to a world of finite resources.

The individual solutions that follow include a host of initiatives, such as downshifting and voluntary simplicity. The collective solutions that have been proposed thus far, however, entail a range of techniques, from direct and indirect incentives and disincentives in the form of taxation regimes to direct and indirect regulatory structures such as the attribution of rights to Nature and the imposition of criminal responsibilities in the form of crimes of Ecocide (and environmental destruction more in general). Herman Daly (1996, 88–83) suggests to stop counting the consumption of natural capital as income, to tax labour income less, and tax resource throughput more, and to maximize the productivity of natural capital in the short run, and invest in increasing its supply in the long run option, having recourse to international trade only when clearly much more efficient. Others suggest to enlarge the use of the precautionary principle. Overall, after environmental law provisions, rights of Nature provisions are the most numerous among the initiatives that have been *actually* occurred. Among them, bottom-up initiatives (such as local rights of Nature ordnances in the USA) seem to be immediately (in a pragmatic sense) less effective (even though the symbolic power they entail far outweighs, many of their advocate argue, their immediate efficacy). Top-down constitutional and, or, legislative initiatives seem to be more effective, particularly if led by official authorities and, or, the courts themselves (less so if driven by civil society initiatives). Court activism, in this regard, has mixed results. Clearly, a lot more work is yet required to more clearly establish the parameters of rights of/for Nature and human responsibilities toward it. My intuition is that the list of actual rights of Nature will be categorized in a simple form (as already somewhat suggested by the Ecuadorian Constitution) but that both the jurisprudence of the courts and the articulation of the legislative will clarify the issue of conflict of rights of Nature and other human rights. More work is also required to more clearly establish the parameters of an 'environmental person'. My intuition is that an emerging category of an 'environmental person' will apply to geographically identifiable keystone natural features (rivers, forests, et cetera) and species. Individual animal (and possibly, other nonhuman) rights will continue to develop separately. While more work is also needed, it seems to me that the examples from New Zealand already present the best exemplars of how to articulate the issue of stewardship/guardianship/representation. My intuition is that this will develop in line with the identification of the environmental person above, with general Guardians or Ombudspersons for the Global Commons (Oceans, the Climate, etc.), and specific ones for individuated features. In regards to responsibilities, I believe that the work of ecocide and ecocrimes activists will progressively yield increased results (simply by extending the existing scope of the criminal system, without necessarily having to alter it) by forcing individual and collective human behaviour to change. Underpinning these advances, I believe more nuanced judicial training will be seen as increasingly necessary for the effective interpretation and application of the above provisions. And judicial 'training' in reality means a shift in perspective, in *jurisprudence* as legal theory.

The radical shift in perspective required, and the expansion of an ecological awareness that it entails, cannot occur within the realm of jurisprudence alone, and require a host of multidisciplinary pursuits. 'In a bright green future, everyone is ecologically literate', David Boyd suggests (2015, 199), noting that '[a] vital element of environmental literacy is simply spending time outside in natural settings. Research proves that this has physical and psychological benefits' (200). Similarly, Brian Swimme suggests that '[w]hat we need is just the simple recognition that as we deprive ourselves and our children of direct contact with the numinous powers that fill the universe, we are choosing a diminished existence' (1996, 46). The transition to a more ecologically aware jurisprudential world, Arran Stibbe and Heather Luna propose, requires skills in '*ecological intelligence*, to understand the impact of actions on the ecosystems which support life, *systems thinking*, to gain a holistic picture of inputs, outputs and waste to maximise reuse and recycling, *appropriate technology* and *appropriate design* to minimize the adverse impacts of the technologies employed, *cultural literacy* to adapt solutions to specific cultures' (2009, 12). Daniel Goleman, pioneering author of *Emotional Intelligence* and *Social Intelligence*, in his 2009 book *Ecological Intelligence* introduced a third kind of intelligence in addition (and related to) the ability to understand one's emotional state and the intelligence that comes into play in relationship with others. 'While social and emotional intelligence extend [our] abilities to see from another's perspective, empathize, and show concern, ecological intelligence applies these capacities to an understanding of natural systems and melds cognitive skills with empathy for all life' (Goleman et al., 2012, 6). Such ecoliteracy involves the ability to understand how nature sustains life, the capacity to 'make the invisible visible' in relation to ecological connections, the ability to anticipate and adapt to unintended consequences, a developed empathy toward all forms of life and the awareness that the project of sustainability is not an individual one, but rather the result of a community practice.

Moreover, as Stephen Harding suggests, '[w]e cannot change the outer world without also changing our inner world' (in Swimme & Berry, 1994, 250). Thomas Berry equally suggests that

> [o]nly a change that profound in human consciousness can remedy the deep cultural pathology manifest in [our collective] destructive behavior. Such a change is not possible, however, so long as we fail to appreciate the planet that provides us with a world abundant in the volume and variety of food for our nourishment, a world exquisite in supplying beauty of form, sweetness of taste, delicate fragrances for our enjoyment, and exciting challenges for us to overcome with skill and action (2009, 48).

This change may lead toward what Joanna Macy and Molly Brown (1998, 17) have called the 'Great Turning', the successful (albeit still hopeful) transition from the Industrial Growth Society to a Life-sustaining Society. To effect such a change, science, rationality and abstract knowledge alone are not sufficient 'While we have more scientific knowledge of the universe than any people ever had,' Berry wrote, 'it is not the type of knowledge that leads to an intimate presence within a meaningful universe' (1999, 15). Of course, this is not a suggestion to abandon science as a knowledge-creating tool. After all, it *is* the degree of scientific knowledge achieved over the last two centuries that has prompted the alarm bells as to the current predicament humanity is now facing. However, science is now revealing that it (science) is not enough. Something else is needed *in addition* to it. Among the many disciplines that have developed in parallel with the emergence of ecology, and that are essential to its development, are disciplines such as ecophilosophy, ecospirituality, environmental ethics, ecopsychology, ecological anthropology, social ecology and cultural ecology, ecological economics, as well as a host of distinct ecoliterary and artistic fields. Moreover, the many worldviews of peoples who have *not* been guided by an extremely anthropocentric view of the cosmos are equally (if not, indeed, more) informative.

Stibbe and Luna suggests that '[t]he deepest level of sustainability literacy is the psychological level, since problems which manifest themselves outwardly in injustice or destruction of the environment arise from social and cultural systems which are, in turn, located in individual psychology and social cognition … [in] *ecological alienation* … the feeling that human being exist independently and separately from an external "environment"' (2009, 15). Theodore Roszak (2001) was among the first to introduce the idea of 'ecopsychology' as the study of the interplay between ecology, cultural cosmology and individual psychology. Certainly, as child psychologist Richard Louv reported in *Last Child in the Woods* (2008), direct exposure to nature (intended as biologically diverse and ecologically integrated, as opposed to artificial, heavily processed human-made urban environments) is essential for a child's healthy physical and emotional development, linking the lack of nature's exposure in children lives with a rise in obesity, attention disorders and depression, with a particular disorder called 'nature-deficit disorder'. In defining humanity as a 'poetic species', Edward O. Wilson reminds us that '[w]e are in the fullest sense a biological species and will find little ultimate meaning apart from the reminder of life' (1984, 81). We are intertwined with the rest of life on earth, and we thus possess an innate sense of 'biophilia', a sense of connection that is psychological as well as physical, and necessary for our well-being. The disappearance of species and of natural connections does affect us deeply—it may even be the cause of mental disorders, as Louv says. Not only our bodies, but our minds require that natural connection to function fully: 'we are human in good part because of the particular way we affiliate with other organisms. They are the matrix in which the human mind originated and is permanently rooted' (Wilson, 1984, 139). Wilson's words evoke an enlarged sense of the Xhosa expression *umntu ngumntu nagbanye*: 'a person is a person because of other persons' (in Cullinan, 2011 ed, 101).

There is more to ecopsychology, however, than the rediscovered intuition of humanity's relationship with the rest of the natural world. Equally important is the notion of treating the cosmos not only with an inquiring and symbolic mind, but also from a place of the most basic human emotions, cantered around love and a sense of sacredness in relation to all. Stephan Harding notes that '[i]t was C G Jung who pointed out that we gain reliable knowledge by means of the four modalities of thinking, feeling, sensing and intuition' (2009, 92). Such is also the insight David Suzuki (2007) has achieved after decades of environmental advocacy, and his reflections echo the teachings of the Dalai Lama as well as the recovered ideas of St Francis of Assisi on the part of Pope Francis's encyclical *Laudato Sí*. As Wade Davis suggests, '[a] child raised to believe that a mountain is the abode of a protective spirit will be a profoundly different human being from a youth brought up to believe that a mountain is an inert mass of rock ready to be mined' (2009, 123). This insight leads to an extended sense of self. As Chief Seeathl said, 'we are the earth and whatever we do to the earth we do to ourselves' (in Suzuki et al., 2007, 10). To shift our gaze in such a way, Brian Swimme (1996, 45) invites us not to 'look up' at the stars, but rather to imagine that we are 'looking down on the Milky Way', gently tethered to the Earth by immense gravitational forces that hold us in a tight embrace, preventing us from falling into the night sky. Moreover, we can reimagine the universe as marked by 'omnicentrictiy': not to think that we are not the centre of the universe, but rather that we are, and that at the same time every other point in the universe also is. This is, after all, one of the great revelations of modern cosmology: '[t]he large-scale structure of the universe is qualitatively more complex either than the geocentric picture of medieval cultures or the fixed Newtonian space of modern culture. For we have discovered an omnicentric evolutionary universe, a developing reality which from the beginning is centered upon itself at each place of its existence' (Swimme, 1996, 85). Such an awareness may even engender a sense of awe toward what Brian Swimme calls the 'nonvisible':

> I say nonvisible rather than invisible, for many things are "invisible" to us and yet capable of being seen ... The *nonvisible*, on the other hand, is that which can never be seen, because it is neither a material thing nor an energy constellation. In addition, the nonvisible world's nature differs so radically from the material world that it cannot even be *pictured*. It is both nonvisible and *nonvisualizable*. (97)

This novel perspective, drawn from the world of cosmological physics, is deeply akin to the classical, Platonic and pre-socratic idea of the 'spirit', the Lakota concept of *Watanka,* or the primordial creative Chaos of Hesiod. 'I use "all-nourisghin abyss"', Swimme writes, 'as a way of pointing to this mystery at the base of being' (1996, 100). Thomas Berry poetically sums such an insight by asserting that '[w]e are each the cosmic person, the *Mahapurusha*, the Great Person of Hindu India, expressed in the universe itself' (1999, 175). Such is the insight of Sufism, and, if we are to go by an ecosophical interpretation of the Aryan Baptistery in Ravenna, of at least part of early Christianity.

The preter-rational and experiential awareness of interconnectedness, moreover, is not mystical or remote, but rather mundane and quotidian. The relatively recent movie *Avatar* depicts an idea of interconnectedness that is inherently mystical and remote, cast in an alien world unfamiliar to the viewer. The immediate (although surely unintended) implication is that what is in front of us, the quotidian and mundane, would not be sufficient to evoke the same degree of interconnectedness. Nothing could be further from the truth, since we are always inherently and inescapably interconnected. To reawaken a sense of interconnectedness, we need to 'decolonize thought', Eduardo Viveiros de Castro (2014) suggests, in order to see that 'thinking is not necessarily circumscribed by language, the symbolic or the human'. Eduardo

Kohn writes that '[h]ow other kinds of beings see us matter ... encounters with other kinds of beings force us to recognize the fact that seeing, representing, and perhaps knowing, even thinking, are not exclusively human affairs' (2013, 1). Kohn writes that 'an anthropology beyond the human is perforce an ontological one. That is, taking nonhumans seriously makes it impossible to confine our anthropological inquires to an epistemological concern for how it is that humans, at some particular time or in some particular place, go about making sense of them' (10). Kohn challenges human exceptionalism within anthropology by arguing that the process of semiosis (or meaning-making) is intrinsic to life and not exclusively human. As his examples of dogs and forests show, what makes a 'self' is their capacity to interpret the world around them, and humans are not the only ones who interpret the world. Viveiros de Castro suggests that

> [a]nimals perceive in the same way as us but perceive different things than we do, because their bodies are different than ours. I do not mean by this physiological differences ... but the affects, or strengths and weakness, that render each species of the body singular: what it eats, its way of moving or communicating, where it lives, whether it is gregarious or solitary, timid or fierce and so on. Corporeal morphology is a powerful sign of these differences, although it can be quite deceiving; the human figure, for instance, can conceal a jaguar-affection. (2014, 72)

The question then arises as to whether these nonhuman interpretive selves can communicate with humans, and, if so, how. Kohn intimates that communication (not merely linguistic, of course) is not limited to interspecies communication, by referring to it as 'trans-species pidgins' (2013, 131). Other authors argue this further. Monica Gagliano's personal account of her interactions with plants is a guide of the novel enlarged communication with plants. A rigorous scientist focused on the study of plant consciousness, Gagliano recollected her own engagement and encounters with plant 'intelligences' in a

> phytobiography – a collection of stories, each written together with and on behalf of a plant person. These stories are told through the narrative voice of both the human and the plant person, through the language *of* plants and my language *for* them... There is no attempt at, or need for, ventriloquizing by assigning a voice to plants or speaking for them to render these stories intelligible to our human mind. Here, the human is not an interpreter who translates a mental representation in her head as if it were plant-speak and then put it into words we can comprehend or scribbles it on a page we know how to read. Rather, the human is a listener who filters out personal noise to hear plant speak, who engages in active dialog with these non-human intelligences, which are far more real than our current scientific constructs allow us to contend with. (2018, 6)

Similarly, Anishinabeckwe scientist Robin Wall Kimmerer's *Braiding Sweetgrass* (2013) is an example of an attempt to bridge Indigenous ways of communicating with Nature and scientific descriptions of it. In all these instances, a degree of antropomorphism is seen as beneficial rather than detrimental. As Jane Bennet notes, '[a] touch of anthropomorphism can catalyze a sensibility that finds a world filled not with ontologically distinct categories of beings (subjects and objects) but with variously composed materialities that form confederations' (2010, 99). 'Non-anthropocentric anthropomorphism', therefore, can be used as a heuristic device to engage more equally and equitably with Nature. If that is the case, then the representation of Nature as a collection of gods cast ancient mythologies under a different light. In a personal conversation with a Hawaiian knowledge holder, I was told that the Hawiian god Kanaloa is not merely the 'god of fresh water', the anthropomorphised entity that exerts control over it, but rather *is* fresh water itself, as much as Kane, the 'god of salt water', *is* the ocean. Equally, the identity of Pontus, Tartarus, Gaia and Ouranos with the primordial partitions of the cosmos is embedded in ancient Greek 'mythology'. Each of them *is* the element they also control. These mythical representations of the landscape are, therefore, tools for understanding the individual connection to place mediated by culture, what Gregory Cajete calls 'the mythical body of the landscape' (2000, 206). Bennet writes that '[i]f a green materialism requires of us a more refined sensitivity to the outside-that-is-inside-too, then maybe a bit of anthropomorphizing will prove valuable. Maybe it is worth running the risks associated with anthropomorphizing (superstition, the divinization of nature, romanticism) because it, oddly enough, work against anthropocentrism: a chord is struck between person and thing, and I am no longer above or outside a nonhuman "environment"' (2010, 120). Anthropomorphism can thus be used as a strategic tool in order to recognize the inherent and irreducible alienness of the nonhuman other (for example of a fungus, or a planet). Anthropomorphism is thus cast as a necessary tool *for humans* to interpret and interface with the nonhuman other, as a way to meaningfully engage with it in a way that can be understood. In a personal interview, Mario Melo said that 'when we manage to see with the eyes of Nature, we see a *someone* and stop our exploitation of it'.

The application of this anthropomorphism is exemplified by the work of scientists such as Monica Gagliano and others in their studies on plant consciousness. Peter Wohlleben has captured many of such insights in *The Hidden Life of Trees* (2016), where he convincingly articulates the 'language' of trees, their 'feelings' for, and 'friendships' with, each other. 'In the symbiotic community of the forest', he says, 'not only trees but also shrubs and grasses—and possibly all plant species—exchange information' (2016, 11). Science now knows this to be true of fungi as well. The application of a small dose of antropomorphism allows us, in this instance, to break down the arbitrary boundary of sentience that, since Peter Singer, has shifted away from the Cartesian exclusion of the natural world from the world of consciousness. Another example of such an epistemological stance is that adopted by Theodor Schwenck in *Sensitive Chaos* (1962). In his gaze at the movements of water as archetypical, and his quest for the unifying forces that underlie all living things, it is hard not to find an echo of Thales's assertion of water as the underlying principle of all reality.

In this strategic adoption of anthropomorphism as an epistemological tool to enlarge our individual ecological consciousness, myths occupy a special place. For Joseph Campbell, a myth has four functions: first, the 'mystical' function,

> to awaken and maintain in the individual a sense of awe and gratitude in relation to the mystery dimension of the universe, not so that he lives in fear of it, but so that he recognizes that he participate in it ... second ... to offer an image of the universe that will be in accord with the knowledge of the time ... third ... to validate, support, and imprint the norms of a

> given specific moral order ... and fourth ... to guide him, stage by stage, in health, strength and harmony of spirit, through the whole foreseeable course of a usual life. (1972, 214-5)

Freya Mathews notes that '[o]n this account, myth closely resembles what [goes] under the name of "worldview". The difference is that "myth" is endowed with a positive connotation by Campbell which I have not extended to "worldview". I have allowed the possibility that a worldview may undermine, as well as uplift, the morale of a community' (1991, 44). Campbell, of course, proposes a very different idea of *myth* from the one offered by Barthes. Thomas Berry wrote that

> we have lost the interpretative patterns of our existence, patterns generally designated as "myths". Myths are narratives that indicate the meaning of the human mode of being as well as the meaning of the universe itself. Our critical failures, committed to the analytical processes of the rational mind, have destroyed the naiveté of ancient beliefs in favor of critical reflection and pragmatic realism. As the excitement of the realism has diminished, we find ourselves encompassed by a world without meaning. There are only facts. (2009, 54)

Jung believed in the universality of nature myths, whereas anthropologist of religion Mircea Eliade believed them to have continued into modern, as well as traditional, cultures. The concern for the loss of connection with nature is a common thread throughout Jung's entire *oeuvre*. Throughout his work, Jung often speaks for the natural mind as the ultimate source of the collective evolutionary experience and accumulated wisdom of humanity. 'There are no longer any gods whom we can invoke to help us. The great religions of the world suffer from increasing anemia, because the helpful numina have fled from the woods, rivers, mountains, and animals, and the God-men have disappeared underground into the unconscious' (Sabini, 2002, 122).

For some, then, it may be a matter of establishing new patterns of understanding the cosmos, new myths. That may entail moving from merely the 'rights' of Nature, to maybe (once again) the 'rites' of Nature. Freya Mathews describes the many attempts to 'resacralize the taken-for-granted ground beneath our feet' (2003, 5): deep ecology workshops, Gaian foundations, pagan festivals and shamanic courses, Councils of All Beings and earth-honouring rituals that now proliferate on the fringes of consumerist society. 'Love of earth, if not the world, is enjoined from many in alternative pulpits' (Mathews, 2003, 5). Such new myths can come in the form of new syncretic metaphysical attempts, such as Starhawk's (1989) novel re-establishment of a worship of the 'Goddess'—not necessarily *Tellus Mater*, but deeply connected to it. Berry, too, notes that 'Earth is the maternal principle out of which we are born and from which we derive all that we are and all that we have. We come into being in and through the Earth. Simply put, we are Earthlings. ... The human and the Earth are totally implicated, each in the other. If there is no spirituality in the Earth, then there is no spirituality in ourselves' (2009, 69). Berry also adds that 'in the doctrine of the Madonna or Divine Mother enunciated in later Christian history, there are many passages indicating that Mary was thought of as the Earth in which the True Vine is planted and which has been made fruitful by the Holy Spirit. Unfortunately, this identity of Mary with the Earth was never adequately developed in association with the doctrine of the Incarnation' (76).

David Abrams write that 'the emphasis, among … new practitioners of popular shamanism, is on personal insight and curing. These are noble aims, to be sure, yet they are secondary to, and derivative from, the primary role of the indigenous shaman, a role that cannot be fulfilled without long and sustained exposure to wild nature, to its patterns and vicissitudes' (1996, 21). Indeed, he adds, '[t]he traditional or tribal shaman … acts as an intermediary between the human community and the larger ecological field, ensuring that there is an appropriate flow of nourishment, not just from the landscape to the human inhabitants, but from the human community back to the local earth' (7). Berry, too, acknowledged that 'the spirituality we need already exists and is being communicated to us by the larger human tradition. Indeed, the human tradition in all its multiform expression is the primary bearer and teacher of the spirituality we seek. This spirituality cannot be created anew. Human history cannot be set aside. The ancient symbols cannot be ignored. We must simply become conscious of the deeper and more universal forces at work in our development' (2009, 60). Sean Kane writes that 'we are discovering the respect for nature demonstrated by archaic humanity. We are now realizing that early humanity negotiated a dialogue with nature that has gone on variously for the better part of 100,000 years … By all accounts, this dialogue was, and still is—an affectionate counterpoint to the earth's voices, with no ambition to direct them to give up their meaning' (1998, 14). He gives this dialogue the name of 'mythtelling', stating that '[t]he proper subject of myth is the ideas and emotions of the Earth'.

Viveiros de Castro clarifies the role of myth in Indigenous worldviews: 'the narrativization of the indigenous plane of immanence articulates in a privileged way the causes and consequences of speciation—the assumption of a specific corporeality—by the personae or actants therein, all of whom are conceived as sharing a general unstable condition in which the aspects of humans and nonhumans are inextricably enmeshed' (2014, 65). 'Amerindian perspectivism', he continues,

> finds in myth a geometrical locus where the difference between points of view is at once annulled and exacerbated. In this absolute discourse, each kind of being appears to other beings as it appears to itself – as human – even as it already acts by manifesting its distinct and definitive animal, plant, or spirit nature. Myth, the universal point of flight of perspectivism, speaks of a state of being where bodies and names, souls and actions, egos and others are interpenetrated, immersed in one and the same presubjective and preobjective milieu. The aim of mythology is precisely to recount the "end" of this "milieu"; in other words, to describe the passage from "Nature to Culture". (68)

This novel understanding of myths as ecological and normative indicators allows us to read ancient texts of mythology, often interpreted as, at best, allegorical fables, in a different way. This has implications for an ecological jurisprudence, since, for example, the relationship between *Themis* and *Dike* may be reimagined as a mythical, symbolic and ultimately metaphorical reference to the relationship between the understanding of natural cycles and the operation of human normativity, with the awareness that the latter cannot operate in contradiction with the former over time. Equally, the Norse goddess Jörd can be interpreted as another articulation of Lovelock's Gaia principle, recasting the entirety of the Prose Edda as a legal and normative ecological text. The comparative gaze cast upon parallel legal traditions of the world encoded in myth may suggest that pre-Christian European mythology provides a fertile avenue to appraise a holistic symbolic understanding of nature, normativity and law as an inseparable whole.

Against the accusation of an unrealistic construction of Nature's 'harmony', ancient myths also act as powerful reminders that '[t]he monsters of myth, such as Medusa, were not nursery tales for innocent children. They were confrontations with wild destructive forces of preternatural might' (Berry, 2009, 57). Such are, indeed, the ecological forces we now visibly face. Equally, it is worth remembering that in the idea of Gaia lies the primordial power to be feared as much as to be respected, '[f]or Gaia, Ge, Earth, is not a goddess properly speaking, but a force from the time before the gods'. Marcel Detienne writes that '[i]n Hesiod's theogony Earth is a great power of beginnings' (2009, 165). 'Prolific, dangerous, savvy,' Latour suggests, 'the ancient Gaia emerges in great outpourings of blood, steam, and terror, in the company of Chaos and Eros' (2017, 81). The same feeling of primal, mystical and mythical respect for Nature had already been uttered by Thoreau, who agonized that the 'animal in us, which awakens in proportion as our higher nature slumbers. It is reptile and sensual, and perhaps cannot be wholly expelled' (1973, 219).

Finally, if myths are the narrative representation in anthropomorphised forms of an expanded ecological awareness that connects individual humans to the cosmos they culturally inhabit, it is important to remember that myths are encoded in language and that there exists a connection, forgotten in most modern languages, between language and landscape. I became aware of the depth of such a connection, which far exceed the occasional onomatopoeia, while in conversation with Bundjulung Elder Uncle Charles Moran, who taught me that the learning of traditional Bundjulung words entailed their precise repetition until the sound was perfectly pitched and reproduced. That sound, he suggested, was one that Country could understand, one that (euhemerising the explanation in biophysical terms) could resonate with the frequencies, pitch and rythms of the entire surrounding landscape. I was surprised to find the same insight reflected in Abram's work: 'If we listen, first, to the sounds of an oral language—to the rhythms, tones, and inflections that play through the speech of an oral culture—we will likely find that these elements are attuned, in multiple and subtle ways, to the contour and scale of the local landscape, to the depth of its valleys or the open stretch of its distances, to the visual rhythms of the local topography' (1996, 140). Such is what he calls '[t]he intertwining of human speech with the calls and cries of local earth' (145).

Human communities, therefore, are and have always been 'woven into the fabric of the landscape' (Davis, 2009, 143).

> Every place we went, we became that place. That is the brilliant power provided by symbolic consciousness. With their cultural inventions, humans could adapt to new environments much more quickly than would be the case if they had to rely solely upon genetic changes. That's why the humans who decided to follow the reindeer rapidly became the reindeer people. They walked the same pathways as the reindeer. They ate some of the same foods. At night, in their feasts and their dancing, they celebrated the thrill of being the reindeer people. Other humans aligned themselves with the whales and became the whale people. Some identified with the birds and began wearing feather and greeting each dawn with song – their highest fulfillment became the act of joining with the birds' celebration. The early humans did not

> just journey through Earth's worlds. The spirit of each world captivated their imaginations as they revisioned their lives in terms of that place. They absorbed every color and sound into their life and soul. (Swimme & Tucker, 2011, 93-4)

It may be time for humanity to reshape itself according to these traditional principles at a planetary scale, without losing sight of the many bioregional connections we inevitably inhabit. It may be time for humanity as a whole not only to reacquaint itself with the places it inhabits (and that many of us have forgotten), but also to embrace our global nature as veritable *children of the winds and seas.* This project, even more than the profoundly transformative possibilities it entails at a legal and jurisprudential level, is the ultimate horizon of possibilities encoded within the emergence of an ecological jurisprudence. While at an individual level it may engender, once again, values of simplicity, restrain and self-worth not measured against ephemeral material possessions, as well as a renewed respect, awe and gratitude toward the rest of the cosmos, it can also lead to empathy, sympathy and even compassion for all that exists. It may entail moving from the mere realm of intellectual *knowledge* to a space of more holistic *wisdom.* And in the process of doing so, the current journey toward an eco-*logical* jurisprudence may even turn toward a veritable eco-*sophical* one.

References

Abram, D. (1996). *The spell of the sensuous*. Vintage Books.
Bennett, J. (2010). *Vibrant matter*. Duke University Press, Durham.
Berry, T. (1999). *The great work*. Three Rivers Press.
Berry, T. (2009). *The sacred universe*. Columbia University Press.
Boyd, D. R. (2015). *The optimistic environmentalist: Progressing towards a greener future*. ECW Press.
Cajete, G. (2000). *Native science*. Clear Light Publishers.
Campbell, J. (1972). *Myths to live by*. Viking Press.
Cullinan, C. (2011). *Wild law* (2nd ed.). First Published 2002. Chelsea Green Publishing.
Daly, H. (1996). *Beyond growth*. Beacon Press.
Davis, W. (2009). *The wayfinders. Why ancient wisdom matters in the modern world*. House of Anansi Press.
Detienne, M. (2009). *Apollon, the couteau à la main*. Gallimard.
Forencich, F. (2020). *The sapience curriculum. Exuberant animal.*
Forencich, F. (2021). *Beware false tigers. Exuberant animal.*
Fox, M. (1994). *The reinvention of work: A new vision for livelihood in our time*. Harper Collins.
Gagliano, M. (2018). *Thus spoke the plant. A remarkable journey of groundbreaking scientific discoveries and personal encounters with plants*. North Atlantic Books.
Goleman, D., Lisa Bennet, L., & Barlow, Z. (2012). *Eco literate. How educators are cultivating emotional, social and ecological intelligence*. Jossey-Bass.
Harding, S. (2009). Gaia awareness. In A. Stibbe (Ed.), *The handbook of sustainability literacy. skills for a changing world*. Green Books.
Hesiod. (1966, ed) *Theogony* (M. L. West, Trans.). Oxford University Press.
Kane, S. (1998). *Wisdom of the mythtellers* (2nd ed.). Broadview Press.
Kimmerer, R. W. (2013). *Braiding sweetgrass: Indigenous wisdom, scientific knowledge and the teachings of plants*. Penguin.
Kohn, E. (2013). *How forests think*. University of California Press, Berkeley.

Latour, B. (2017). *Facing Gaia*. John Wiley & Sons.
Louv, R. (2008). *Last child in the woods. Saving our children from nature-deficit disorder*. Algonquin Books.
Lovelock, J. (1979). *Gaia: A new look at life on Earth*. Oxford University Press.
Macy, J., & Brown, M. Y. (1998). *Coming back to life*. New Society Publishers.
Maloof, J. (2016). *Nature's temples*. Timber Press.
Mathews, F. (1991). *The ecological self*. Routledge.
Mathews, F. (2003). *For love of matter*. State University of New York Press.
Matthews, D. (2021). *Earthbound. The aesthetics of sovereignty in the Anthropocene*. Edinburgh University Press.
Roszak, T. (2001). *The voice of the Earth. An exploration of ecopsychology* (2nd ed.). First Published 1992. Phane Press.
Sabini, M. (ed.), (2002). *Carl Gustav Jung, The Earth has a soul: C. G. Jung on nature, technology and modern life*. North Atlantic Books.
Schwenck, T. (1996). *Sensitive Chaos. The creation. Of flowing forms in water and air* (2nd ed.). First Published 1962. Rudolf Steiner Press.
Serres, M. (1995). *The natural contract* (E. MacArthur & W. Paulson, Trans.). First Published 1990. University of Michigan.
Shiva, V. (2000). *Tomorrow's biodiversity*. Thames & Hudson.
Starhawk, *The spiral dance. A rebirth of the ancient religion of the great goddess*. HarperCollins.
Arran Stibbe, A., & Luna, H. (2009). Introduction. In A. Stibbe (ed.), *The handbook of sustainability literacy. Skills for a changing world*. Green Books.
Suzuki, D., McConnell, A., & Mason, A. (2007). *The sacred balance. Rediscovering our place in nature—Updated and expanded*. Greystone Books.
Swimme, B. (1996). *The hidden heart of the cosmos*. Orbis Books.
Brian Swimme, B., & Berry, T. (1994). *The universe story. From the Primordial Flaring Forth to the ecozoic era*. HarperCollins.
Swimme, B., & Tucker, M. E. (2011). *Journey of the universe*. Yale University Press.
Thoreau, H. D. (1854). *Walden*. Ticknor and Fields.
Viveiros de Castro, E. (2014). *Cannibal metaphysics* (P. Skafish Trans.). First Published 2009. Univocal.
Wilson, E. O. (1984). *Biophilia. The human bond with other species*. Harvard University Press.
Wilson, E. O. (2016). *Half-Earth. Our planet's fight for life*. Liveright Publishing Corporation.
Wohlleben, P. (2015). *The hidden life of trees. What they feel, how they communicate*. Black Inc.

Appendix A
World Charter for Nature

Reaffirming the fundamental purposes of the United Nations, in particular the maintenance of international peace and security, the development of friendly relations among nations and the achievement of international co-operation in solving international problems of an economic, social, cultural, technical, intellectual or humanitarian character.

Aware that:

(a) Mankind is a part of nature and life depends on the uninterrupted functioning of natural systems which ensure the supply of energy and nutrients,
(b) Civilization is rooted in nature, which has shaped human culture and influenced all artistic and scientific achievement, and living in harmony with nature gives man the best opportunities for the development of his creativity, and for rest and recreation.

Convinced that:

(a) Every form of life is unique, warranting respect regardless of its worth to man, and, to accord other organisms such recognition, man must be guided by a moral code of action,
(b) Man can alter nature and exhaust natural resources by his action or its consequences and, therefore, must fully recognize the urgency of maintaining the stability and quality of nature and of conserving natural resources.

Persuaded that:

(a) Lasting benefits from nature depend upon the maintenance of essential ecological processes and life support systems, and upon the diversity of lifeforms, which are jeopardized through excessive exploitation and habitat destruction by man,
(b) The degradation of natural systems owing to excessive consumption and misuse of natural resources, as well as to failure to establish an appropriate economic order among peoples and among States, leads to the breakdown of the economic, social and political framework of civilization,

A. Pelizzon, *Ecological Jurisprudence*, Contemporary Environmental Law and Policy,
https://doi.org/10.1007/978-981-96-0173-8

(c) Competition for scarce resources creates conflicts, whereas the conservation of nature and natural resources contributes to justice and the maintenance of peace and cannot be achieved until mankind learns to live in peace and to forsake war and armaments.

Reaffirming that man must acquire the knowledge to maintain and enhance his ability to use natural resources in a manner which ensures the preservation of the species and ecosystems for the benefit of present and future generations,

Firmly convinced of the need for appropriate measures, at the national and international, individual and collective, and private and public levels, to protect nature and promote international co-operation in this field,

Adopts, to these ends, the present World Charter for Nature, which proclaims the following principles of conservation by which all human conduct affecting nature is to be guided and judged.

I. General Principles

1. Nature shall be respected and its essential processes shall not be impaired.
2. The genetic viability on the earth shall not be compromised; the population levels of all lifeforms, wild and domesticated, must be at least sufficient for their survival, and to this end necessary habitats shall be safeguarded.
3. All areas of the earth, both land and sea, shall be subject to these principles of conservation; special protection shall be given to unique areas, to representative samples of all the different types of ecosystems and to the habitats of rare or endangered species.
4. Ecosystems and organisms, as well as the land, marine and atmospheric resources that are utilized by man, shall be managed to achieve and maintain optimum sustainable productivity, but not in such a way as to endanger the integrity of those other ecosystems or species with which they coexist.
5. Nature shall be secured against degradation caused by warfare or other hostile activities.

II. Functions

6. In the decision-making process it shall be recognized that man's needs can be met only by ensuring the proper functioning of natural systems and by respecting the principles set forth in the present Charter.
7. In the planning and implementation of social and economic development activities, due account shall be taken of the fact that the conservation of nature is an integral part of those activities.
8. In formulating long-term plans for economic development, population growth and the improvement of standards of living, due account shall be taken of the long-term capacity of natural systems to ensure the subsistence and settlement of the populations concerned, recognizing that this capacity may be enhanced through science and technology.
9. The allocation of areas of the earth to various uses shall be planned, and due account shall be taken of the physical constraints, the biological productivity and diversity and the natural beauty of the areas concerned.

10. Natural resources shall not be wasted, but used with a restraint appropriate to the principles set forth in the present Charter, in accordance with the following rules:

    (a) Living resources shall not be utilized in excess of their natural capacity for regeneration;
    (b) The productivity of soils shall be maintained or enhanced through measures which safeguard their long-term fertility and the process of organic decomposition, and prevent erosion and all other forms of degradation;
    (c) Resources, including water, which are not consumed as they are used shall be reused or recycled;
    (d) Non-renewable resources which are consumed as they are used shall be exploited with restraint, taking into account their abundance, the rational possibilities of converting them for consumption and the compatibility of their exploitation with the functioning of natural systems.

11. Activities which might have an impact on nature shall be controlled, and the best available technologies that minimize significant risks to nature or other adverse effects shall be used; in particular:

    (a) Activities which are likely to cause irreversible damage to nature shall be avoided;
    (b) Activities which are likely to pose a significant risk to nature shall be preceded by an exhaustive examination; their proponents shall demonstrate that expected benefits outweigh potential damage to nature, and where potential adverse effects are not fully understood, the activities should not proceed;
    (c) Activities which may disturb nature shall be preceded by assessment of their consequences, and environmental impact studies of development projects shall be conducted sufficiently in advance, and if they are to be undertaken, such activities shall be planned and carried out so as to minimize potential adverse effects;
    (d) Agriculture, grazing, forestry and fisheries practices shall be adapted to the natural characteristics and constraints of given areas;
    (e) Areas degraded by human activities shall be rehabilitated for purposes in accord with their natural potential and compatible with the well-being of affected populations.

12. Discharge of pollutants into natural systems shall be avoided and:

    (a) Where this is not feasible, such pollutants shall be treated at the source, using the best practicable means available;
    (b) Special precautions shall be taken to prevent discharge of radioactive or toxic wastes.

13. Measures intended to prevent, control or limit natural disasters, infestations and diseases shall be specifically directed to the causes of these scourges and shall avoid adverse side-effects on nature.

III. Implementation

14. The principles set forth in the present Charter shall be reflected in the law and practice of each State, as well as at the international level.
15. Knowledge of nature shall be broadly disseminated by all possible means, particularly by ecological education as an integral part of general education.
16. All planning shall include, among its essential elements, the formulation of strategies for the conservation of nature, the establishment of inventories of ecosystems and assessments of the effects on nature of proposed policies and activities; all of these elements shall be disclosed to the public by appropriate means in time to permit effective consultation and participation.
17. Funds, programmes and administrative structures necessary to achieve the objective of the conservation of nature shall be provided.
18. Constant efforts shall be made to increase knowledge of nature by scientific research and to disseminate such knowledge unimpeded by restrictions of any kind.
19. The status of natural processes, ecosystems and species shall be closely monitored to enable early detection of degradation or threat, ensure timely intervention and facilitate the evaluation of conservation policies and methods.
20. Military activities damaging to nature shall be avoided.
21. States and, to the extent they are able, other public authorities, international organizations, individuals, groups and corporations shall:

    (a) Co-operate in the task of conserving nature through common activities and other relevant actions, including information exchange and consultations;
    (b) Establish standards for products and manufacturing processes that may have adverse effects on nature, as well as agreed methodologies for assessing these effects;
    (c) Implement the applicable international legal provisions for the conservation of nature and the protection of the environment;
    (d) Ensure that activities within their jurisdictions or control do not cause damage to the natural systems located within other States or in the areas beyond the limits of national jurisdiction;
    (e) Safeguard and conserve nature in areas beyond national jurisdiction.

22. Taking fully into account the sovereignty of States over their natural resources, each State shall give effect to the provisions of the present Charter through its competent organs and in co-operation with other States.
23. All persons, in accordance with their national legislation, shall have the opportunity to participate, individually or with others, in the formulation of decisions of direct concern to their environment, and shall have access to means of redress when their environment has suffered damage or degradation.
24. Each person has a duty to act in accordance with the provisions of the present Charter; acting individually, in association with others or through participation in the political process, each person shall strive to ensure that the objectives and requirements of the present Charter are met.

Appendix B
The Earth Charter

Preamble

We stand at a critical moment in Earth's history, a time when humanity must choose its future. As the world becomes increasingly interdependent and fragile, the future at once holds great peril and great promise. To move forward we must recognize that in the midst of a magnificent diversity of cultures and lifeforms we are one human family and one Earth community with a common destiny. We must join together to bring forth a sustainable global society founded on respect for nature, universal human rights, economic justice and a culture of peace. Toward this end, it is imperative that we, the peoples of Earth, declare our responsibility to one another, to the greater community of life and to future generations.

Earth, Our Home

Humanity is part of a vast evolving universe. Earth, our home, is alive with a unique community of life. The forces of nature make existence a demanding and uncertain adventure, but Earth has provided the conditions essential to life's evolution. The resilience of the community of life and the well-being of humanity depend upon preserving a healthy biosphere with all its ecological systems, a rich variety of plants and animals, fertile soils, pure waters and clean air. The global environment with its finite resources is a common concern of all peoples. The protection of Earth's vitality, diversity and beauty is a sacred trust.

The Global Situation

The dominant patterns of production and consumption are causing environmental devastation, the depletion of resources and a massive extinction of species. Communities are being undermined. The benefits of development are not shared equitably and the gap between rich and poor is widening. Injustice, poverty, ignorance and violent conflict are widespread and the cause of great suffering. An unprecedented rise in human population has overburdened ecological and social systems. The foundations of global security are threatened. These trends are perilous—but not inevitable.

A. Pelizzon, *Ecological Jurisprudence*, Contemporary Environmental Law and Policy,
https://doi.org/10.1007/978-981-96-0173-8

The Challenges Ahead

The choice is ours: form a global partnership to care for Earth and one another or risk the destruction of ourselves and the diversity of life. Fundamental changes are needed in our values, institutions and ways of living. We must realize that when basic needs have been met, human development is primarily about being more, not having more. We have the knowledge and technology to provide for all and to reduce our impacts on the environment. The emergence of a global civil society is creating new opportunities to build a democratic and humane world. Our environmental, economic, political, social and spiritual challenges are interconnected, and together we can forge inclusive solutions.

Universal Responsibility

To realize these aspirations, we must decide to live with a sense of universal responsibility, identifying ourselves with the whole Earth community as well as our local communities. We are at once citizens of different nations and of one world in which the local and global are linked. Everyone shares responsibility for the present and future well-being of the human family and the larger living world. The spirit of human solidarity and kinship with all life is strengthened when we live with reverence for the mystery of being, gratitude for the gift of life and humility regarding the human place in nature.

We urgently need a shared vision of basic values to provide an ethical foundation for the emerging world community. Therefore, together in hope we affirm the following interdependent principles for a sustainable way of life as a common standard by which the conduct of all individuals, organizations, businesses, governments and transnational institutions is to be guided and assessed.

Principles

I. **Respect and Care for the Community of Life**

1. Respect Earth and life in all its diversity.
    a. Recognize that all beings are interdependent and every form of life has value regardless of its worth to human beings.
    b. Affirm faith in the inherent dignity of all human beings and in the intellectual, artistic, ethical and spiritual potential of humanity.
2. Care for the community of life with understanding, compassion and love.
    a. Accept that with the right to own, manage and use natural resources comes the duty to prevent environmental harm and to protect the rights of people.
    b. Affirm that with increased freedom, knowledge and power comes increased responsibility to promote the common good.
3. Build democratic societies that are just, participatory, sustainable and peaceful.

a. Ensure that communities at all levels guarantee human rights and fundamental freedoms and provide everyone an opportunity to realize his or her full potential.
b. Promote social and economic justice, enabling all to achieve a secure and meaningful livelihood that is ecologically responsible.

4. Secure Earth's bounty and beauty for present and future generations.

a. Recognize that the freedom of action of each generation is qualified by the needs of future generations.
b. Transmit to future generations' values, traditions and institutions that support the long-term flourishing of Earth's human and ecological communities. In order to fulfil these four broad commitments, it is necessary to:

II. **Ecological Integrity**

5. Protect and restore the integrity of Earth's ecological systems, with special concern for biological diversity and the natural processes that sustain life.

a. Adopt at all levels sustainable development plans and regulations that make environmental conservation and rehabilitation integral to all development initiatives.
b. Establish and safeguard viable nature and biosphere reserves, including wild lands and marine areas, to protect Earth's life support systems, maintain biodiversity and preserve our natural heritage.
c. Promote the recovery of endangered species and ecosystems.
d. Control and eradicate non-native or genetically modified organisms harmful to native species and the environment, and prevent introduction of such harmful organisms.
e. Manage the use of renewable resources such as water, soil, forest products and marine life in ways that do not exceed rates of regeneration and that protect the health of ecosystems.
f. Manage the extraction and use of non-renewable resources such as minerals and fossil fuels in ways that minimize depletion and cause no serious environmental damage.

6. Prevent harm as the best method of environmental protection and, when knowledge is limited, apply a precautionary approach.

a. Take action to avoid the possibility of serious or irreversible environmental harm even when scientific knowledge is incomplete or inconclusive.
b. Place the burden of proof on those who argue that a proposed activity will not cause significant harm, and make the responsible parties liable for environmental harm.
c. Ensure that decision-making addresses the cumulative, long-term, indirect, long distance and global consequences of human activities.
d. Prevent pollution of any part of the environment and allow no build-up of radioactive, toxic, or other hazardous substances.

e. Avoid military activities damaging to the environment.

7. Adopt patterns of production, consumption and reproduction that safeguard Earth's regenerative capacities, human rights and community well-being.

   a. Reduce, reuse and recycle the materials used in production and consumption systems, and ensure that residual waste can be assimilated by ecological systems.
   b. Act with restraint and efficiency when using energy, and rely increasingly on renewable energy sources such as solar and wind.
   c. Promote the development, adoption and equitable transfer of environmentally sound technologies.
   d. Internalize the full environmental and social costs of goods and services in the selling price, and enable consumers to identify products that meet the highest social and environmental standards.
   e. Ensure universal access to health care that fosters reproductive health and responsible reproduction.
   f. Adopt lifestyles that emphasize the quality of life and material sufficiency in a finite world.

8. Advance the study of ecological sustainability and promote the open exchange and wide application of the knowledge acquired.

   a. Support international scientific and technical cooperation on sustainability, with special attention to the needs of developing nations.
   b. Recognize and preserve the traditional knowledge and spiritual wisdom in all cultures that contribute to environmental protection and human well-being.
   c. Ensure that information of vital importance to human health and environmental protection, including genetic information, remains available in the public domain.

III. **Social and Economic Justice**

9. Eradicate poverty as an ethical, social and environmental imperative.

   a. Guarantee the right to potable water, clean air, food security, uncontaminated soil, shelter and safe sanitation, allocating the national and international resources required.
   b. Empower every human being with the education and resources to secure a sustainable livelihood, and provide social security and safety nets for those who are unable to support themselves.
   c. Recognize the ignored, protect the vulnerable, serve those who suffer and enable them to develop their capacities and to pursue their aspirations.

10. Ensure that economic activities and institutions at all levels promote human development in an equitable and sustainable manner.

   a. Promote the equitable distribution of wealth within nations and among nations.

b. Enhance the intellectual, financial, technical and social resources of developing nations, and relieve them of onerous international debt.
c. Ensure that all trade supports sustainable resource use, environmental protection and progressive labour standards.
d. Require multinational corporations and international financial organizations to act transparently in the public good, and hold them accountable for the consequences of their activities.

11. Affirm gender equality and equity as prerequisites to sustainable development and ensure universal access to education, health care and economic opportunity.

a. Secure the human rights of women and girls and end all violence against them.
b. Promote the active participation of women in all aspects of economic, political, civil, social and cultural life as full and equal partners, decision-makers, leaders and beneficiaries.
c. Strengthen families and ensure the safety and loving nurture of all family members.

12. Uphold the right of all, without discrimination, to a natural and social environment supportive of human dignity, bodily health and spiritual well-being, with special attention to the rights of indigenous peoples and minorities.

a. Eliminate discrimination in all its forms, such as that based on race, colour, sex, sexual orientation, religion, language, and national, ethnic or social origin.
b. Affirm the right of indigenous peoples to their spirituality, knowledge, lands and resources and to their related practice of sustainable livelihoods.
c. Honour and support the young people of our communities, enabling them to fulfil their essential role in creating sustainable societies.
d. Protect and restore outstanding places of cultural and spiritual significance.

IV. **Democracy, Non-violence and Peace**

13. Strengthen democratic institutions at all levels, and provide transparency and accountability in governance, inclusive participation in decision-making, and access to justice.

a. Uphold the right of everyone to receive clear and timely information on environmental matters and all development plans and activities which are likely to affect them or in which they have an interest.
b. Support local, regional and global civil society, and promote the meaningful participation of all interested individuals and organizations in decision-making.
c. Protect the rights to freedom of opinion, expression, peaceful assembly, association and dissent.
d. Institute effective and efficient access to administrative and independent judicial procedures, including remedies and redress for environmental harm and the threat of such harm.

e. Eliminate corruption in all public and private institutions.
f. Strengthen local communities, enabling them to care for their environments, and assign environmental responsibilities to the levels of government where they can be carried out most effectively.

14. Integrate into formal education and lifelong learning the knowledge, values and skills needed for a sustainable way of life.

a. Provide all, especially children and youth, with educational opportunities that empower them to contribute actively to sustainable development.
b. Promote the contribution of the arts and humanities as well as the sciences in sustainability education.
c. Enhance the role of the mass media in raising awareness of ecological and social challenges.
d. Recognize the importance of moral and spiritual education for sustainable living.

15. Treat all living beings with respect and consideration.

a. Prevent cruelty to animals kept in human societies and protect them from suffering.
b. Protect wild animals from methods of hunting, trapping and fishing that cause extreme, prolonged or avoidable suffering.
c. Avoid or eliminate to the full extent possible the taking or destruction of non-targeted species.

16. Promote a culture of tolerance, non-violence and peace.

a. Encourage and support mutual understanding, solidarity and cooperation among all peoples and within and among nations.
b. Implement comprehensive strategies to prevent violent conflict and use collaborative problem solving to manage and resolve environmental conflicts and other disputes.
c. Demilitarize national security systems to the level of a non-provocative defence posture, and convert military resources to peaceful purposes, including ecological restoration.
d. Eliminate nuclear, biological and toxic weapons and other weapons of mass destruction.
e. Ensure that the use of orbital and outer space supports environmental protection and peace.
f. Recognize that peace is the wholeness created by right relationships with oneself, other persons, other cultures, other life, Earth and the larger whole of which all are a part.

The Way Forward

As never before in history, common destiny beckons us to seek a new beginning. Such renewal is the promise of these Earth Charter principles. To fulfil this promise, we must commit ourselves to adopt and promote the values and objectives of the Charter.

This requires a change of mind and heart. It requires a new sense of global interdependence and universal responsibility. We must imaginatively develop and apply the vision of a sustainable way of life locally, nationally, regionally and globally. Our cultural diversity is a precious heritage and different cultures will find their own distinctive ways to realize the vision. We must deepen and expand the global dialogue that generated the Earth Charter, for we have much to learn from the ongoing collaborative search for truth and wisdom.

Life often involves tensions between important values. This can mean difficult choices. However, we must find ways to harmonize diversity with unity, the exercise of freedom with the common good, short-term objectives with long-term goals. Every individual, family, organization and community has a vital role to play. The arts, sciences, religions, educational institutions, media, businesses, non-governmental organizations and governments are all called to offer creative leadership. The partnership of government, civil society and business is essential for effective governance.

In order to build a sustainable global community, the nations of the world must renew their commitment to the United Nations, fulfil their obligations under existing international agreements and support the implementation of Earth Charter principles with an international legally binding instrument on environment and development.

Let ours be a time remembered for the awakening of a new reverence for life, the firm resolve to achieve sustainability, the quickening of the struggle for justice and peace, and the joyful celebration of life.

Origin of the Earth Charter

The Earth Charter was created by the independent Earth Charter Commission, which was convened as a follow-up to the 1992 Earth Summit in order to produce a global consensus statement of values and principles for a sustainable future. The document was developed over nearly a decade through an extensive process of international consultation, to which over five thousand people contributed. The Charter has been formally endorsed by thousands of organizations, including UNESCO and the IUCN (World Conservation Union). For more information, please visit www.EarthCharter.org.

Appendix C
Universal Declaration on the Rights of Mother Earth

Preamble

We, the peoples and nations of Earth:

considering that we are all part of Mother Earth, an indivisible, living community of interrelated and interdependent beings with a common destiny;
gratefully acknowledging that Mother Earth is the source of life, nourishment and learning and provides everything we need to live well;
recognizing that the capitalist system and all forms of depredation, exploitation, abuse and contamination have caused great destruction, degradation and disruption of Mother Earth, putting life as we know it today at risk through phenomena such as climate change;
convinced that in an interdependent living community it is not possible to recognize the rights of only human beings without causing an imbalance within Mother Earth;
affirming that to guarantee human rights it is necessary to recognize and defend the rights of Mother Earth and all beings in her and that there are existing cultures, practices and laws that do so;
conscious of the urgency of taking decisive, collective action to transform structures and systems that cause climate change and other threats to Mother Earth;
proclaim this Universal Declaration of the Rights of Mother Earth, and call on the General Assembly of the United Nation to adopt it, as a common standard of achievement for all peoples and all nations of the world, and to the end that every individual and institution takes responsibility for promoting through teaching, education and consciousness raising, respect for the rights recognized in this Declaration and ensure through prompt and progressive measures and mechanisms, national and international, their universal and effective recognition and observance among all peoples and States in the world.

A. Pelizzon, *Ecological Jurisprudence*, Contemporary Environmental Law and Policy,
https://doi.org/10.1007/978-981-96-0173-8

Article 1. Mother Earth

(1) Mother Earth is a living being.
(2) Mother Earth is a unique, indivisible, self-regulating community of interrelated beings that sustains, contains and reproduces all beings.
(3) Each being is defined by its relationships as an integral part of Mother Earth.
(4) The inherent rights of Mother Earth are inalienable in that they arise from the same source as existence.
(5) Mother Earth and all beings are entitled to all the inherent rights recognized in this Declaration without distinction of any kind, such as may be made between organic and inorganic beings, species, origin, use to human beings, or any other status.
(6) Just as human beings have human rights, all other beings also have rights which are specific to their species or kind and appropriate for their role and function within the communities within which they exist.
(7) The rights of each being are limited by the rights of other beings and any conflict between their rights must be resolved in a way that maintains the integrity, balance and health of Mother Earth.

Article 2. Inherent Rights of Mother Earth

(1) Mother Earth and all beings of which she is composed have the following inherent rights:

    (a) the right to life and to exist;
    (b) the right to be respected;
    (c) the right to regenerate its biocapacity and to continue its vital cycles and processes free from human disruptions;
    (d) the right to maintain its identity and integrity as a distinct, self-regulating and interrelated being;
    (e) the right to water as a source of life;
    (f) the right to clean air;
    (g) the right to integral health;
    (h) the right to be free from contamination, pollution and toxic or radioactive waste;
    (i) the right to not have its genetic structure modified or disrupted in a manner that threatens its integrity or vital and healthy functioning;
    (j) the right to full and prompt restoration for violation of the rights recognized in this Declaration caused by human activities;

(2) Each being has the right to a place and to play its role in Mother Earth for her harmonious functioning.
(3) Every being has the right to well-being and to live free from torture or cruel treatment by human beings.

Article 3. Obligations of human beings to Mother Earth

(1) Every human being is responsible for respecting and living in harmony with Mother Earth.

(2) Human beings, all States and all public and private institutions must:

   (a) act in accordance with the rights and obligations recognized in this Declaration;
   (b) recognize and promote the full implementation and enforcement of the rights and obligations recognized in this Declaration;
   (c) promote and participate in learning, analysis, interpretation and communication about how to live in harmony with Mother Earth in accordance with this Declaration;
   (d) ensure that the pursuit of human well-being contributes to the well-being of Mother Earth, now and in the future;
   (e) establish and apply effective norms and laws for the defence, protection and conservation of the rights of Mother Earth;
   (f) respect, protect, conserve and where necessary, restore the integrity, of the vital ecological cycles, processes and balances of Mother Earth;
   (g) guarantee that the damages caused by human violations of the inherent rights recognized in this Declaration are rectified and that those responsible are held accountable for restoring the integrity and health of Mother Earth;
   (h) empower human beings and institutions to defend the rights of Mother Earth and of all beings;
   (i) establish precautionary and restrictive measures to prevent human activities from causing species extinction, the destruction of ecosystems or the disruption of ecological cycles;
   (j) guarantee peace and eliminate nuclear, chemical and biological weapons;
   (k) promote and support practices of respect for Mother Earth and all beings, in accordance with their own cultures, traditions and customs;
   (l) promote economic systems that are in harmony with Mother Earth and in accordance with the rights recognized in this Declaration.

Article 4. Definitions

(1) The term 'being' includes ecosystems, natural communities, species and all other natural entities which exist as part of Mother Earth.
(2) Nothing in this Declaration restricts the recognition of other inherent rights of all beings or specified beings.

Appendix D
The Hague Principles for a Universal Declaration on Responsibilities for Human Rights and Earth Trusteeship

1. **Background**

On 10 December 2018, the world celebrates the 70th anniversary of the Universal Declaration of Human Rights adopted by the United Nations. The Universal Declaration and subsequent human rights covenants are treasured as precious manifestations of the human spirit. The recognition of equal and unalienable rights of all human beings is an indispensable prerequisite for achieving just and sustainable societies. Our globalized world, however, brings new challenges to this prospect. We all belong to the community of life, the Earth community, which determines what rights and responsibilities we must recognize and honour for each other, for future generations, for all living beings and the Earth, our home.

The Earth community is in grave danger. Over the last 70 years the human population has tripled and disparities in economic wealth have greatly increased. Moreover, overall consumption of Earth's natural resources by humans has grown at such a rate that the entire Earth system with its interconnected components—the geosphere, the hydrosphere, the atmosphere and the biosphere—are all now at risk. In this way, humanity is threatening the very living conditions that make the enjoyment of civil, political, cultural and economic rights possible in the first place. Human rights must therefore include responsibilities for the Earth community and the entire Earth system. These imply obligations and new opportunities for all human beings to act as Earth trustees.

In the course of the last 70 years, people and organizations in many countries and cultures have called for the recognition of human responsibilities. There are numerous declarations of duties, obligations and responsibilities that are acknowledged and celebrated, including those listed in the Annex hereto. Drawing on these declarations and aware of the challenges that humanity and Earth as a whole are now facing, it is urgently necessary to supplement these instruments with new ones that formally recognize the human responsibilities that exist toward the Earth community and the Earth system.

Human beings must therefore act as Earth trustees individually and collectively through new arrangements of Earth Trusteeship at all levels. We, members of global

A. Pelizzon, *Ecological Jurisprudence*, Contemporary Environmental Law and Policy,
https://doi.org/10.1007/978-981-96-0173-8

civil society and representatives of organizations involved with the creation of the documents listed in the Annex, have come together in The Hague, on the occasion of the 70th Anniversary of the Universal Declaration of Human Rights, to reaffirm our common course and declare our responsibilities as trustees for Earth. We celebrate and embrace the Universal Declaration of Human Rights and, at the same time, call upon all peoples, the United Nations, and the international community of states, not only to reaffirm their responsibilities for human rights, but also to recognize their responsibilities to the Earth community and the Earth system and to adopt Earth Trusteeship as an active and all-encompassing way forward.

2. Principles for a Universal Declaration on Responsibilities for Human Rights and Earth Trusteeship

We, citizens of nation-states, actors in the world economy and members of global civil society, Acknowledging that well-being of human beings, our lives and our survival as a species and as individuals depend on the health and well-being of other beings and ecosystems, Noting that consumerist society and competitive nationalism repeatedly inflicts unbearable injuries to Nature, leading to catastrophic climate change, unprecedented biodiversity loss, and eventual disintegration of the Earth system, Recognizing that disintegration and collapse of ecological systems force numerous people to leave their homelands, creating political and economic instability that may lead to conflict and upheaval in many parts of the world, Considering that the totality of beings and ecosystems on Earth forms a community of life (the 'Earth community'), Realizing that just as human beings have rights that suit their needs, other beings have the right to exist and flourish according to their specific needs, and that these rights have their source in being part of the Earth community, Understanding that a new, more mindful and appropriate relationship with Earth and Nature is necessary for the flourishing of all beings, Confident that inspired common effort and dedicated collaboration between political, economic and cultural transformation movements can ultimately result in adequate responses to the challenges of the twenty-first century, HEREBY DECLARE that we have agreed on the following principles as a guide for drawing up a Universal Declaration on Responsibilities for Human Rights and Earth Trusteeship:

Principle 1 Responsibilities for Earth

1.1 All human beings, individually and collectively, share responsibility to protect Nature, of which we are an integral part, the integrity of Earth's ecological systems and Earth as a whole, home of all living beings.

1.2 Each state individually, and the international community of states collectively, acknowledge that they have and share, responsibilities for Nature, in cooperation and in alliance with their citizens as equal trustees of Earth and the integrity of Earth's ecological systems.

Principle 2 Responsibilities within the Community of Life

2.1. Human rights are grounded in our membership within the community of life, the Earth community, which qualifies what rights we are called on to honour and what responsibilities we have for each other and for Nature.
2.2. Responsibilities for Nature, the Earth community and rights of Nature are grounded in the intrinsic values of nature and of all living beings.

Principle 3 Responsibilities for Human Rights

3.1. All human beings are responsible for the protection of human rights and for affirming human rights in their ways of thinking and acting.
3.2. Each state has a prime responsibility for the protection of human rights as a trustee of its citizens and all human beings.

WE CALL UPON the United Nations to initiate a process of consultation, negotiation and eventual adoption of a Universal Declaration on Responsibilities for Human Rights and Earth Trusteeship based on these principles.

Appendix E
Oslo Manifesto

From Environmental Law to Ecological Law: A Call for Re-Framing Law and Governance

1. Environmental law is at a crossroads. As a legal discipline, environmental law has always aimed at protecting the natural environment and ecological systems. Yet, in fifty years of its history environmental law has failed to halt ecological degradation and continues to fall short of its objectives. The Earth's ecological systems deteriorate at an accelerating rate with no signs of regaining their integrity and sustainability.
2. There are many reasons for the growing ecological crisis. Among them are the dynamics of economic growth, population development and overconsumption, aptly described as the 'Great Acceleration'. However, there are also reasons peculiar to the philosophy, ontology and methodology underpinning environmental law.
3. Environmental law is rooted in modern Western law with its origins in religious anthropocentrism, Cartesian dualism, philosophical individualism and ethical utilitarianism. In our ecological age, this worldview is out-dated and counterproductive, yet it continues to dominate the way environmental laws are conceived and interpreted. Most notably, nature is perceived as 'the other' overlooking ecological interdependencies and human-nature interrelations.
4. Among the flaws of environmental law are its anthropocentric, fragmented and reductionist characteristics. It is not only blind to ecological interdependencies, but also politically weak as it competes with other, more powerful areas of law such as individualized property and corporate rights. As a consequence, the legal system has become imbalanced and unable to secure the physical and biological conditions, upon which all human and other life depends.
5. To overcome the flaws of environmental law, mere reform is not enough. We do not need more laws, but different laws from which no area of the legal system is exempted. The ecological approach to law is based on ecocentrism, holism and intra-/intergenerational and interspecies justice. From this perspective, or worldview, the law will recognize ecological interdependencies and no longer

A. Pelizzon, *Ecological Jurisprudence*, Contemporary Environmental Law and Policy,
https://doi.org/10.1007/978-981-96-0173-8

favour humans over nature and individual rights over collective responsibilities. Essentially, ecological law internalizes the natural living conditions of human existence and makes them the basis of all law, including constitutions, human rights, property rights, corporate rights and state sovereignty.

6. The difference between environmental law and ecological law is not merely a matter of degree, but fundamental. The former allows human activities and aspirations to determine whether or not the integrity of ecological systems should be protected. The latter requires human activities and aspirations to be determined by the need to protect the integrity of ecological systems. Ecological integrity becomes a precondition for human aspirations and a fundamental principle of law. In other words, ecological law reverses the principle of human dominance over nature, which the current iteration of environmental law tends to reinforce, to a principle of human responsibility for nature. This reversed logic is arguably the key challenge of the Anthropocene.
7. The transformation from environmental law to ecological law will not occur without people committed to the change. For environmental law scholars such commitment includes critical self-reflection, imagination, courage and a willingness to become truly ecoliterate. In this way environmental lawyers transform themselves into 'ecolawyers'.
8. The approach of ecological law is, however, not new. Its foundational values and principles have guided ancient cultures and indigenous peoples in all parts of the world and are also part of the pre-industrial history of Western civilisation. After all, if previous generations were not so successful in maintaining, at least, a degree of sustainability, the present generation would not be here. It is important, therefore, to recognize history and continuity of ecological values and principles. They have also informed modern environmental law, albeit in a more rudimentary form and hidden behind the dominant values of modernity (anthropocentrism, dualism, utilitarianism etc.).
9. The values and principles of ecological law are expressed in ecocentric jurisprudence (e.g. rights of nature, 'Mother Earth' rights, Earth jurisprudence, ecofeminism, ecological legal theory, 'environmental law methodology') and are also present in constitutional and international theory (e.g. ecological human rights, 'ecoconstitutional state', 'Pachamama' constitutions, ecological sustainability and integrity, ecocide campaign, commons movement, global commons theory, ecoconstitutionalism, global environmental constitutionalism). While different in their approaches and emphasis, they share a common ground and can be perceived as complimentary and mutually reinforcing.
10. This makes it possible to identify ecological approaches to law with a view to create a unifying framework for promoting effective law and governance. As we face disintegrating ecological and socio-economic systems and in the light of greater, but still incomplete understanding of how ecosystems function and maintain their resilience, now is the time for creating an alternative.
11. To this effect, a roadmap for the establishment of an Ecological Law and Governance Alliance (ELGA) is proposed. It should be conceived as a unifying and inclusive platform for existing ecological approaches to law and should promote

coordinated efforts to formulate the ecological alternative to business-as-usual law and governance.

12. The first steps of the roadmap include the establishment of a working group, the creation of a website, the start of a brainstorming activity for the development of new research and higher education projects, the launch of an international conference (on moving from environmental law to ecological law) and the general promotion of ELGA (through individual and institutional membership).

Appendix F
Chief Seattle 1854 Oration–Ver. 3

The Great Chief in Washington sends word that he wishes to buy our land. The Great Chief also sends us words of friendship and goodwill. This is kind of him, since we know he has little need of our friendship in return. But we will consider your offer, for we know if we do not so the white man may come with guns and take our land. What Chief Seattle says you can count on as truly as our white brothers can count on the return of the seasons. My words are like the stars–they do not set.

How can you buy or sell the sky—the warmth of the land? The idea is strange to us. Yet we do not own the freshness of the air or the sparkle of the water. How can you buy them from us? We will decide in our time. Every part of this earth is sacred to my people. Every shining pine needle, every sandy shore, every mist in the dark woods, every clearing and every humming insect is holy in the memory and experience of my people. The sap that runs through the trees carries the memories of the red-skinned man.

The dead among the white man forget their birthplace when they leave to walk among the stars. Our dead never forget this beautiful earth because she is the redman's mother. We are part of the earth and she is part of us. The scented flowers are our sisters: the horned beasts, the horse and the majestic eagle are our brothers. The fields, the warm body of the foal and man, all belong to the same family. Thus when the Great Chief in Washington sends word that he wishes to buy our lands, he is asking for a great deal. The Great Chief sends word that he will reserve a space for us to live comfortably with each other. He will be our father and we will be his children. Because of this, we will consider his offer to buy our lands. But this will not be easy, because these lands are a sacred to us. The sparkling water that runs in the rivers and streams is not only water; it is the blood of our ancestors. If we sell you these lands, you must remember that they are sacred and teach your children that they are, and that every ghostly reflection in the clear waters of the lakes speaks of the lives and memories of the life of my people. The murmur of the stream is the voice of my father's father.

The rivers are our sisters and calm our thirst. The rivers carry our canoes and feed our children. If we sell you our lands, you must remember and teach your children

A. Pelizzon, *Ecological Jurisprudence*, Contemporary Environmental Law and Policy,
https://doi.org/10.1007/978-981-96-0173-8

that the rivers are our kin and your kin; you must henceforth treat the rivers as kindly as you would your brothers and sisters.

We know that the white man does not understand our ways. One portion of land is the same to him as the next, for he is a stranger who comes in the night and takes from the land whatever he needs. The earth is not his brother, but his enemy, and when he has conquered it, he moves on. He leaves his father's graves and his children's birthright is forgotten. He strips the earth from his children and cares not. He forgets his father's tomb and the rights of his children. He treats his mother, the earth, and his brother the heavens, as if they were things that could be bought, plundered and sold, as though they were lambs and glass beads. His insatiable hunger will devour the earth and leave behind a desert.

I do not understand. Our ways are different to yours. The sight of your cities pains the eyes of the redman. But perhaps it is because the redman is a savage and does not understand. There is no quiet place in the white man's cities. No place to listen to the leaves of spring or the rustle of insect wings. But perhaps because I am a savage and do not understand –the clatter only seems to insult the ears. And what is there to life if a man cannot hear the lovely cry of the whippoorwill or the arguments of the frogs around a pond at night? I am a redman and I do not understand.

The Indian prefers the soft sound of the wind itself cleansed by a mid-day rain, or scented by a pinõn pine.

The air is precious to the redman. For all things share the same breath—the beasts, the trees and the man. The white man does not seem to notice the air he breathes. Like a man dying for many days, he is numb to the stench. If we sell you our lands, you must remember that the air is precious to us, that the air shares its spirit with all the life it sustains. And, if we sell you our lands, you must set them aside and keep them sacred as a place that even the white man may go to taste the wind sweetened by the flowers in the grasslands.

If I decide to accept your offer, I will make one condition. The white man must treat the beasts of this land as his brothers. I am a savage and I do not understand any other way. I have seen thousands of rotting buffaloes on the prairie left by the white man who shot them from a passing train. I am a savage and do not understand how the smoking iron horse can be more important than the buffalo that we kill only to stay alive. What is man without the beasts? If all the beasts were gone, men would die from great loneliness of spirit, for whatever happens to the beast also happens to the man. All things are connected. Whatever befalls the earth befalls the sons of the earth.

You must teach your children that the ground beneath their feet is the ashes of their grandparents. In order that they may respect the earth, teach them that the earth is full of the life of our ancestors. You must teach your children what we have taught ours: that the earth is our mother. Everything that affects the earth affects the sons of the earth. When men spit on the ground they spit on themselves.

We know this: the earth does not belong to man. Man belongs to the earth. Man has not woven the net of life: he is just a thread in it. Everything he does to this net he does to himself. What befalls the earth will befall the sons of the earth. We know this. All things are bound up in each other like the blood that binds the family.

Even the white man, whose God walks with him and speaks with him, cannot be excluded from a common destiny. We may even be brothers in the end. We will see. One thing we know that the white man may one day discover. Our God is the same God. You may think that you own him as you wish to own our land, but you cannot. He is the Body of man, and his compassion is equal for the redman and the white. This earth is precious to him, and to harm the earth is to heap contempt on its Creator. The whites, too, shall pass—perhaps sooner than other tribes. Continue to contaminate your bed, and you will one night suffocate in your own waste. But even in your last hours you will feel illuminated by the idea that God brought you to these lands and gave you a special purpose, and ownership over them and over the redman. When the buffalo are all slaughtered, the wild horses all tamed, the secret corners of the forest heavy with the scent of many men, and the view of the ripe hills blotted by the talking wires, where is the thicket? Gone. Where is the eagle? Gone. And what is it to say goodbye to the swift and the hunt? The end of living and the beginning of survival.

Appendix G
A Bill of Rights for the Planet Earth

By Thomas Berry

1. Rights originate where existence originates. That which determines existence determines rights.
2. Since it has no further context of existence in the phenomenal order, the universe is self-referent in its being and self-normative in its activities. It is also the primary referent in the being and activities of all derivative modes of being.
3. The universe is a communion of subjects, not a collection of objects. As subjects, the component members of the universe are capable of having rights.
4. The natural world on the planet Earth gets its rights from the same source that humans get their rights, from the universe that brought them into being.
5. Every component of the Earth community has three rights. The right to be, the right to habitat and the right to fulfil its role in the ever-renewing process of the Earth community.
6. All rights are species specific and limited. Rivers have river rights. Birds have bird rights. Insects have insect rights. Humans have human rights. Difference of rights is qualitative not quantitative. The rights of an insect would be of no use to a tree or fish.
7. Human rights do not cancel out the rights of other modes of being to exist in their natural state. Human property rights are not absolute. Property rights are simply a special relationship between a particular human 'owner' and a particular piece of 'property' *for the benefit of both.*
8. Species exist in the form of individuals and groupings—flock, herds, schools of fish and so forth. Rights refer to individuals and groupings, not simply in a general way to species.
9. These rights as presented here establish the relationships that the various components of the Earth have toward each other. The planet earth is a single community bound together with interdependent relationships. Every component of the Earth community is immediately or mediately dependent on every other member of the Community for the nourishment and assistance it needs for its own survival. This mutual nourishment, which includes predator-prey relationship, is integral

A. Pelizzon, *Ecological Jurisprudence*, Contemporary Environmental Law and Policy,
https://doi.org/10.1007/978-981-96-0173-8

with the role that each component of the Earth has within the comprehensive community of existence.

10. In a special manner humans have not only a need for but a right of access to the natural world, not only to supply their physical needs but also to provide the wonder needed by human intelligence, the beauty needed by human imagination and the intimacy needed by the human emotions.

The manufacturer's authorised representative in the EU is Springer Nature Customer Service Centre GmbH, Europaplatz 3, 69115 Heidelberg, Germany. If you have any concerns regarding our products, please contact ProductSafety@springernature.com

Printed and bound by CPI Group (UK) Ltd, Croydon, CR0 4YY
08/10/2026
02229819-0002